TimeOut

Istanbul

timeout.com/istanbul

Penguin Books

PENGUIN BOOKS

Published by the Penguin Group
Penguin Books Ltd, 80 Strand, London WC2R ORL, England
Penguin Books USA Inc., 375 Hudson Street, New York, New York 10014, USA
Penguin Books Australia Ltd, 250 Camberwell Road, Camberwell, Victoria 3124, Australia
Penguin Books Canada Ltd, 10 Alcorn Avenue, Toronto, Ontario, Canada M4V 3B2
Penguin Books (NZ) Ltd, cnr Rosedale and Airborne Roads, Albany, Auckland, New Zealand

Penguin Books Ltd, Registered Offices: Harmondsworth, Middlesex, England

First published 2001

Second edition 2004
10 9 8 7 6 5 4 3 2 1

Copyright © Time Out Group Ltd 2001, 2004
All rights reserved

Colour reprographics by Icon, Crowne House, 56-58 Southwark Street, London SE1 1UN
Printed and bound by Cayfosa-Quebecor, Ctra. de Caldes, Km 3 08 130 Sta, Perpètua de Mogoda, Barcelona, Spain

Edited and designed by
Time Out Guides Limited
Universal House
251 Tottenham Court Road
London W1T 7AB
Tel + 44 (0)20 7813 3000
Fax + 44 (0)20 7813 6001
Email guides@timeout.com
www.timeout.com

Editorial
Editor Andrew Humphreys
Deputy Editor Hugh Graham
Listings Editor Yeşim Erdem Holland
Proofreader Julian Richards
Indexer Jonathan Cox

Editorial/Managing Director Peter Fiennes
Series Editor Ruth Jarvis
Deputy Series Editor Lesley McCave
Guides Co-ordinator Anna Norman
Accountant Sarah Bostock

Design
Art Director Mandy Martin
Acting Art Director Scott Moore
Acting Art Editor Tracey Ridgewell
Senior Designer Averil Sinnott
Designers Astrid Kogler, Sam Lands
Digital Imaging Dan Conway
Ad Make-up Charlotte Blythe

Picture Desk
Picture Editor Jael Marschner
Deputy Picture Editor Kit Burnet
Picture Researcher Alex Ortiz

Advertising
Sales Director Mark Phillips
International Sales Manager Ross Canadé
International Sales Executive James Tuson
Advertising Sales (Istanbul) Ajans Medya
Advertising Assistant Sabrina Ancilleri

Marketing
Marketing Manager Mandy Martinez
US Publicity & Marketing Associate Rosella Albanese

Production
Guides Production Director Mark Lamond
Production Controller Samantha Furniss

Time Out Group
Chairman Tony Elliott
Managing Director Mike Hardwick
Group Financial Director Richard Waterlow
Group Commercial Director Lesley Gill
Group Marketing Director Christine Cort
Group General Manager Nichola Coulthard
Group Art Director John Oakey
Online Managing Director David Pepper

Contributors
Introduction Andrew Humphreys. **History** Andrew Humphreys, Gareth Jenkins, David O'Byrne (*Swords of misrule, Atta Turk!* David O'Byrne; *Istanbul not Constantinople* Andrew Humphreys; *The drop of a hat* Jeremy Seal). **Istanbul Today** Ken Dakan. **Istanbul vs Islam** Ken Dakan. **Architecture** Andrew Humphreys. **Where to Stay** Andrew Humphreys. **Sightseeing: Introduction** Andrew Humphreys. **Sultanahmet** Jon Gorvett (*Harem-scarem* Andrew Humphreys). **The Bazaar Quarter** Jon Gorvett (*Shopping the bazaar* Ken Dakan). **Eminönü & the Golden Horn** Jon Gorvett (*The extravagant express* Andrew Humphreys). **The Western Districts** David O'Byrne. **Beyoğlu** David O'Byrne (*Ikmen's Istanbul* Andrew Humphreys; *Right round, baby, right round* Hugh Graham). **The Bosphorus Villages** David O'Byrne, Dominic Whiting (*King Mustafa and the golden bowl* Lucy Wood). **The Asian Shore** David O'Byrne. **Museums** Jon Gorvett. **Restaurants** Ken Dakan, Andrew Humphreys (*All boxes* Ken Dakan). **Bars & Cafés** Andrew Humphreys. *Additional reviews* Ken Dakan, Andy Footner, Jon Gorvett (*Hava nargile* Andrew Humphreys; *Cheap girls, pricey drinks* Andy Footner). **Shops & Services** Lucy Wood (*All boxes* Ken Dakan). **Festivals & Events** Jon Gorvett. **Children** Yeşim Erdem Holland. **Film** Lucy Wood (*This sure ain't Kansas, Toto* Andrew Humphreys). **Galleries** Sandra Harrison. **Gay & Lesbian** Ken Dakan. **Hamams** Andrew Humphreys. **Music: Pop, Rock, World & Jazz** Andy Footner. **Music: Turkish** Andy Footner (*The belly fling thing* Ken Dakan). **Nightlife** Andy Footner. **Performing Arts** Nicolas Monceau. **Sport & Fitness** Jon Gorvett (*Welcome to Hell?* Ben Holland). **The Upper Bosphorus** Jon Gorvett. **The Princes' Islands** Jon Gorvett. **The Marmara Islands** Jon Gorvett. **Directory** Lucy Wood (*Sightseeing buses, Mosque etiquette* Andrew Humphreys; *Waiting for the big one, Istanbul for women* Lucy Wood; *Bored, or just getting it regularly?* Ben Holland).

Maps JS Graphics (john@jsgraphics.co.uk).

Photography Jon Perugia, except: pages 7, 13, 15, 17, 19 Bridgeman Art Library; page 11 Heritage-images.com; page 100 Getty Images. The following images were provided by the featured establishments/artists: pages 182, 183, 187, 188, 193, 211, 213, 214, 215, 226, 227, 228, 229, 231, 238.

The Editor would like to thank Etienne Gilfillan, and Deniz Huysal, Berna Karamercan and the staff at *Time Out Istanbul*.

Contents

Eminönü & the Golden Horn	85
The Western Districts	89
Map: City Walls	92
Beyoğlu	95
The Bosphorus Villages	101
The Asian Shore	107
Museums	111

Eat, Drink, Shop

Restaurants	118
Bars & Cafés	141
Shops & Services	157

Arts & Entertainment

Festivals & Events	182
Children	189
Film	192
Galleries	197
Gay & Lesbian	201
Hamams	206
Music: Pop, Rock, World & Jazz	210
Music: Turkish	216
Nightlife	222
Performing Arts	227
Sport & Fitness	232

Trips Out of Town

The Upper Bosphorus	240
Map: Upper Bosphorus	241
The Princes' Islands	248
The Marmara Islands	252

Directory

Getting Around	256
Resources A-Z	261
Vocabulary	273
Further Reference	275

Maps

Istanbul Overview	286
Sultanahmet	288
The Western Districts	290
Beyoğlu	292
Istiklal Caddesi	294
Üsküdar	296
Kadıköy	297
Street Index	298

Introduction	2

In Context

History	6
Istanbul Today	30
Istanbul vs Islam	34
Architecture	38

Where to Stay

Where to Stay	45

Sightseeing

Introduction	66
Sultanahmet	69
Map: Topkapı Palace	71
The Bazaar Quarter	78
Map: Grand Bazaar	81

Introduction

Istanbul has never lacked style. From as far back as the purple robes of the Byzantines, the hallucinatory pattern-makers of the Ottomans (coming back into fashion with young Turkish designers) and that gorgeous republican sickle-moon-and-star red flag, this city has always known how to cut a dash. Over the past two millennia it has retained a vibrancy and flair that, despite the odd ups and downs of politics and the economy, has never been anything less than vital.

The Istanbul of today manages the trick of combining age-old glories (she's been around a bit has Istanbul née Constantinople née Byzantium) with modern worldwide cultural trends, courtesy of a new youthful generation of Turks who have been educated abroad and brought the best of what they saw there back home. Some examples of what we mean? Make a reservation at the restaurant Lokanta for superb fusion cuisine cooked by a Finno-Turkish chef who trained in Sweden, all served up in fashionably stripped-down surrounds. Windowshop the high streets of Nişantaşı for ceramics and glassware by Defne Koz, a leading light in local design, and sometime resident of Milan. Check the 'what's on' listings in the local press for exhibitions by Barcelona-based Istanbul boy made good, Kutluğ Ataman, who in spring 2003 was wowing London with a retrospective at the Serpentine Gallery. We could go on.

All of these people – and many more besides – are helping to transform Istanbul into something much more than all those old clichés of the orient.

Of course, if clichés of the orient are what you're after then, please, step this way. The gulls still swirl over the minarets of the indecently curvaceous Blue Mosque. Wizened old men still drink scalding glasses of dark tea in the shady recesses of the glittering Grand Bazaar. And every ordinary, grimy street still leads to a tomb or a fountain or a kiosk that is breathtaking in its proportions and decoration.

Best of all is that, as well as forging forward, the Turks are ever more aware of the riches of the past that surround them. It's no longer the case that somewhere like the Topkapı Palace is seen as a good thing solely on the basis of all the tourists that it pulls in. The locals have a new found and immense interest in their own history (check out all the lavish Turkish-language coffee-table volumes devoted to old Istanbul in the city's book-shops). This translates to increasingly large amounts of money being spent on clean ups and restoration, with the restored buildings then being put to imaginative use rather than simply being pickled for visitors' consumption. Visit the Galata House (a restaurant in an old prison) or Kethuda (a bar in a 16th-century hamam) or the Four Seasons (a luxury hotel in another former prison) or the Çırağan (a luxury hotel in a former imperial palace).

All these are perfect examples of what makes this city so great: a fusion of tradition and internationalism, served up with panache. At just 1,800 years old, Istanbul is more alive and animated than ever.

ABOUT TIME OUT GUIDES

This is the second edition of the *Time Out Istanbul Guide*, one of an expanding series of *Time Out* guides produced by the people behind London and New York's successful listings magazine. Our team of writers and researchers, residents of Istanbul and experts in their fields, have plumbed the deepest cellar bars and peered from the highest minaret tops to compile this guide, certainly the most comprehensive collection of listings, reviews and informed comment yet to be published on the city. It provides all the most up-to-date information you'll need to explore Istanbul or read up on its background, whether you're a local or a first-time visitor.

THE LOWDOWN ON THE LISTINGS

Above all, we've tried to make this book as useful as possible. Addresses, telephone numbers, websites, transport information, opening times, admission prices and credit card details are all included in our listings, where relevant. All were checked and correct as we went to press. However, owners and managers can change their arrangements at any time. Before you go out of your way, we'd advise you to telephone and check opening times, ticket prices and other particulars.

While every effort has been made to ensure the accuracy of the information contained in this guide, the publishers cannot accept responsibility for any errors it may contain.

PRICES AND PAYMENT

The prices we've supplied should be treated as guidelines, not gospel. Fluctuating exchange rates as well as rampant inflation can cause charges, particularly in shops and restaurants, to change rapidly. Inflation is also the reason that we quote prices in US dollars throughout this book and not in Turkish Lira.

We have noted whether venues such as shops, hotels and restaurants accept credit cards or not, but have only listed the major cards – American Express (**AmEx**), Diners Club (**DC**), MasterCard (**MC**) and Visa (**V**). Some businesses may accept other cards, a few may even take travellers' cheques.

For restaurants we have given the price range for starters and main courses, as well as set menus where relevant. Accommodation prices are summer rates; expect to pay less in winter.

If prices vary wildly from those we've quoted, ask whether there's a good reason. If not, go elsewhere. We aim to give the best and most up-to-date advice, so we always want to know if you've been badly treated or overcharged.

THE LIE OF THE LAND

Istanbul is nightmarish when it comes to finding your way around. Streets can have two or more names but quite often nobody seems to know what any of them are anyway. Postal codes are not used outside of the newer northern suburbs and even building numbers are frequently missing. Turkish addresses tend to be things like 'Across from the green mosque beside the old bridge'. But in almost all cases we have managed to provide a street name and number, and the name of the district. We have used the names of the main central districts (Sultanahmet, the Bazaar Quarter, Eminönü, Beyoğlu, the Asian shore) as the divisions in our Sightseeing section and in chapters that are organised by area. Map references indicate the page and square on the street maps at the back of the book.

TELEPHONE NUMBERS

To phone Istanbul from outside Turkey, first dial the international code 00, then 90 (the code for Turkey) then either 212 (the city code for

Istanbul's European shore) or 216 (the city code for Istanbul's Asian shore), and finally the local seven-digit number. Within Istanbul, if you are on the European side, only dial the city code if you are phoning the Asian side, and vice versa.

ESSENTIAL INFORMATION

For practical information, including visa and customs information, emergency telephone numbers and local transport, turn to the **Directory** chapter. It starts on page 256. For further information on getting around, see the Sightseeing Introduction on page 66.

MAPS

The map section at the back of this book includes useful orientation and overview maps of the city (starting on page 286). The street index begins on page 298.

LET US KNOW WHAT YOU THINK

We hope you enjoy the *Time Out Istanbul Guide*, and we'd like to know what you think of it. We welcome tips for places that you consider we should include in future editions, and take note of your criticism of our choices. There's a reader's reply card at the back of this book for your feedback – or you can email us on guides@timeout.com.

There is an online version of this guide, and guides to over 35 international cities, at **www.timeout.com**.

www.tween.com.tr

BAHREIN
BULGARIA
GERMANY
HUNGARY
JORDAN
LATVIA
LEBANON
NETHERLANDS
NORTHERN CYPRUS
TURKISH REPUBLIC
ROMANIA
RUSSIA
SOUTH AFRICA
SPAIN
SULTANATE OF OMAN
SYRIA
TURKMENISTAN
U.A.E
UKRAINE
USA

tween

In Context

History	6
Istanbul Today	30
Istanbul vs Islam	34
Architecture	38

Features

Swords of misrule	16
Istanbul (not Constantinople)	19
The drop of a hat	20
Atta Turk!	25
Key events	29
Mr Erdoğan goes to Brussels	33
Istanbul idols	37
Keeping up with the domes's	40

History

First Byzantium, then Constantinople, now Istanbul;
here history is writ large.

Few cities have occupied the imagination as
Istanbul has. Fought over throughout its
history by armies from western Europe, the
Middle East and Central Asia, in succession
capital and centre of two of the greatest empires
the world has seen, intriguing, perplexing and
often frustrating, it still has the power to
captivate as few other cities can.

Most books will tell you that Istanbul's
importance stems from being the only city in
the world to bestride two continents, Europe
and Asia. But in fact it's the other way round
– the history of the area defined what we today
know as the continents. The unique geography
of the 35-kilometre (22-mile) Bosphorus Strait,
with its steeply sloping shores running almost
due north-south, must have suggested to early
seafarers that this indeed was where two
worlds met.

The 'meeting of two worlds' idea was
already well established by the fifth century
BC, when Herodotus was able to devote much
of his *Histories* to the conflict between Greece
and Persia, East and West. His writings came
to define the 'them and us' attitude that still
dominates relations between inhabitants of
the two continents and leads every writer to
suppose that Istanbul must be a bridge
between the two.

BLIND BEGINNINGS

Despite its geographical advantages,
prehistoric finds around Istanbul have been
scarce, likely due to the sheer intensity of
occupation that followed. Those that have
been identified suggest that the area has been
occupied since the first humans spread out of
Africa. Neolithic sites from about 7000 BC have
been found close to Kadıköy and Bronze Age
remains dated to 3200 BC have been unearthed
in Sultanahmet, but these early chapters are
still blank pages waiting to be written.

Around 1600 BC, seafaring Greeks had begun
moving out of the Ionian peninsula, founding
colonies around the Aegean and Mediterranean.
By 750 BC they had passed through the
Bosphorus and established settlements on
the Black Sea coast of Anatolia and in the
Caucasus. The 'clashing rocks' episode from the
legend of Jason and the Argonauts was likely
inspired by the voyage up the Bosphorus Strait.
The first Greek settlement in the area of what's
now Istanbul was the colony of Chalcedon,
founded around 675 BC in what's now Kadıköy,
the Asian suburb. According to Herodotus (the
best source of classical soundbite), Chalcedon
was dubbed 'the city of the blind', its founders
having missed the clear geographical
advantages of the opposite European shore.

Within less than 20 years more clear-sighted parties had established themselves across the water on land now enclosed by the walls of Topkapı Palace. Roughly triangular, bounded on two sides by water, it was a natural fortress. To the north, the Golden Horn was a 6.5-kilometre (four-mile) long, half-mile-wide perfect deep-water harbour. The site offered access by sea to the Mediterranean, Africa and the Black Sea, and lay at the crossroads of routes between Europe and Asia. It was destined to be a city of world importance. Its founding was attributed to a sailor by the name of Byzas, hence the name Byzantium.

Once it was established, others were quick to recognise the strategic importance of the new city and it was repeatedly taken by warring regional powers: first the Persians in 550 BC, then the Spartans, then the Athenians. The Byzantines quickly developed a skill for diplomacy and kept their predatory neighbours at bay through a series of shrewd alliances. When that failed, the city buckled down and dug in, successfully weathering a siege from Philip of Macedon in 340 BC.

Good judgement ran out in AD 196 when, after three centuries of independence as part of the Roman province of Asia, the Byzantines backed the wrong side in an imperial power struggle. After a prolonged siege, the stern emperor Septimius Severus had Byzantium's walls torn down, the city put to the torch and a fair chunk of the population put to death. Such a strategic location couldn't lie wasted for too long, and within a few years the emperor had rebuilt the city on a far grander scale with new temples, a colonnaded way and bigger walls. For all its pomp, like earlier Greek Byzantium, nothing of Severus's city has survived.

NEW ROME

By the end of the third century, the Roman Empire had become too unwieldy to govern effectively from Rome and had been subdivided, with part of the power shifted to Byzantium. The result was to create internal rivalries that ultimately could only be settled on the battlefield. In AD 324, Constantine, Emperor of the West, defeated Licinius, Emperor of the East, first in a naval battle on the Sea of Marmara, then on land on the Asian shore at a place called Chrysopolis, today's Üsküdar. With the empire reunited, Constantine set about changing the course of history, first by promoting Christianity as the official religion of the empire, then by shifting the capital from a jaded and cynical Rome to the upstart city on the Bosphorus. On 11 May 330, Constantine inaugurated his new seat of power as 'Nova Roma', a name by which the city has never been known since.

Constantine I, founder of the city of New Rome, more popularly known as Constantinople.

Historical Hotels of Turkey

ÖZBİ
Historical Hoteliers Association

Historical Hotels of Turkey is an association representing the Historical Hotels and Ottoman Mansions of Turkey.
Each hotel represents a unique blend of this contry's rich and diverse history, architecture and reflects the mosaic
of Turkey created by a history of landscape human kind itself, and by geographic location where continent and religions meet.
At these hotels, you will not only experience modern comfort in a historical atmosphere,
but also enjoy traditional Turkish hospitality. The days spent there will surely occupy a very special place in your memories.

Amisos Hotel
Tel: (212) 512 70 50
Web: http://www.amisoshotel.com
İSTANBUL

Anemon Galata Hotel
Tel: (212) 293 23 43
Web: http://www.anemongalata.com
İSTANBUL

Arena Hotel
Tel: (212) 458 03 64
Web: http://www.arenahotel.com
İSTANBUL

Artemis Hotel
Tel: (212) 516 58 65
Web: http://www.artemishotel.com
İSTANBUL

Celal Sultan Hotel
Tel: (212) 520 93 23-24
Web: http://www.celalsultan.com
İSTANBUL

Fehmi Bey Hotel
Tel: (212) 638 90 83/85
Web: http://www.fehmibey.com
İSTANBUL

Galata Residence
Camando Apart Hotel
Tel: (212) 292 48 41 Pbx
Web: http://www.galataresidence.com
İSTANBUL

Kybele Hotel
Tel: (212) 511 77 66 - 511 77 67
Web: http://www.kybelehotel.com
İSTANBUL

Safran Hotel
Tel: (224) 224 72 16 (3 Lines)
Web: http://www.charminghotelsofturkey.org
BURSA

Sarnıç Hotel
Tel: (212) 518 23 23
Web: http://www.sarnichotel.com
İSTANBUL

Triade Residence
Tel: (212) 251 01 01
Web: http://www.triaderesidence.com
İSTANBUL

Turkoman Hotel
Tel: (212) 516 29 56
Web: http://www.turkomanhotel.com
İSTANBUL

Acropol Hotel Best Western
Tel: (212) 638 90 21
Web: http://www.acropolhotel.com
OLDCITY - İSTANBUL

Alp Paşa Hotel
Tel: (242) 247 56 76
Web: http://www.alppasa.com
ANTALYA

Alzer Hotel
Tel: (212) 516 62 62
Web: http://www.alzerhotel.com
İSTANBUL

Amber Hotel Best Western
Tel: (212) 518 48 01 (5 Lines) Pbx
Web: http://www.hotelamber.com
İSTANBUL

Ataman Hotel
Tel: (384) 271 23 10 Pbx
Web: http://www.atamanhotel.com
NEVŞEHİR

Avicenna Hotel
Tel: (212) 517 05 50 (4 Lines)
Web: http://www.avicennahotel.com
İSTANBUL

Ayasofya Hotel
Tel: (212) 517 48 55
Web: http://www.ayasofyahotel.com
İSTANBUL

Blue House
Tel: (212) 638 90 10
Web: http://www.bluehouse.com.tr
İSTANBUL

Orient Express
Tel: (212) 520 71 61 Pbx
Web: http://www.orientexpresshotel.com
İSTANBUL

Pera Palas
Tel: (212) 251 45 60 (12 Lines)
Web: http://www.perapalas.com
İSTANBUL

Poem Hotel
Tel: (212) 638 97 44
Web: http://www.hotelpoem.com
İSTANBUL

Romance Hotel
Tel: (212) 512 86 76 Pbx
Web: http://www.romancehotel.com
İSTANBUL

Uyan Hotel
Tel: (212) 516 48 92 - 518 92 55
Web: http://www.uyanhotel.com
İSTANBUL

Valide Sultan
Tel: (212) 638 06 00
Web: http://www.hotelvalidesultan.com
İSTANBUL

Vardar Palas
Tel: (212) 252 28 88 Pbx
Web: http://www.vardarhotel.com
İSTANBUL

In Nova Roma, more popularly called Constantinople, the new uncontested emperor had a city hitherto uncorrupted by power that he could make over as he saw fit. He embarked on a building programme, plundering the empire to bring in the tallest columns, the finest marble and an abundance of Christian relics, including the True Cross itself. He endowed the church of Haghia Irene (see p72) as the city's first Christian cathedral and commissioned a great palace, built adjacent to an extended hippodrome. To safeguard his capital, Constantine had new walls erected in an arc from close to what is now the Atatürk Bridge over the Golden Horn looping south to present-day Mustafa Paşa, enlarging the area of the city fourfold. Other than a burnt and badly aged column (see p78) little physical evidence of Constantine's work survives, but he laid the foundations for an empire that was to endure for over 1,000 years.

The beginnings were not auspicious. On Constantine's death in 337, achievement and stability ended. His three sons quarrelled over the succession and the empire was divided between Eastern and Western emperors, who sometimes co-operated but more often fought. Fortunately, Constantinople was largely unaffected by the ensuing two centuries of turbulence and was even enlarged by the construction of new city walls during the reign of Theodosius II (408-50), completed just in time to halt Attila's advancing hordes. Rome was not so fortunate and was ripped apart by tribes of Goths and Vandals from the north. With no rival, Constantinople was left to move towards a new era of greatness, reaching its apogee during the era of Justinian (527-65).

CROWD TROUBLE

Justinian's reign was marked by great confidence, which saw the empire extend itself round most of the Mediterranean coast, including the recapture of the lost dominion of Italy from the 'barbarian hordes'. But a great deal of the glory belongs to the emperor's supporting cast. He was fortunate in having at his service a supremely competent general, Belisarius, who takes credit for all military successes. Similarly exceptional was Justinian's wife, Theodora, a former street entertainer and prostitute.

Theodora is credited with saving her husband's skin when a revolt broke out among factions at the hippodrome. Known as the Greens and the Blues, these factions originated in trade guilds and were a cross between political parties and football hooligans. Normally rivals, the Greens (lower-class radicals) and the Blues (upper-class

conservatives) united in 532 to protest against the execution of some of their members. The subsequent uprising, buoyed on by chants of 'Nika, nika' ('Victory, victory') plunged the city into chaos. Justinian, bags packed and in the hall, was all for fleeing but Theodora persuaded him that it was 'better to die as an emperor than live as a fugitive'. In the event Belisarius, still only in his twenties, succeeded in trapping and massacring 30,000 rebels in the hippodrome, thereby restoring civil order.

Left presiding over a city of ruins soaked in its citizens' blood, Justinian needed to restore public faith. His answer was to embark on a grand programme of reconstruction, providing for the city spiritually (he endowed the city with more than 40 churches) and in a more temporal fashion: for example, providing the city with immense water cisterns, one of which still draws appreciative gasps from visitors (**Yerebatan Sarnıcı**; see p74). The crowning glory was a new cathedral, Sancta Sophia. In the eyes of contemporary chronicler Procopius, 'God allowed the mob to commit this sacrilege knowing how great the beauty of this church would be.'

Although the death of Justinian was followed by a prolonged period of decline, largely resulting from internal rivalries, Constantinople remained, as one Byzantine writer put it, 'the city of the world's desire'. There were plenty who acted on those desires. Slavs (581), Avars (617), Persians and Avars (626), Arabs (669-79 and 717-18), Bulgars (813, 913 and 924), Russians (four times between 860 and 1043) and Pechenegs (1087) all marched on the city. Some armies were sufficiently daunted by the walls alone and quit before they'd begun to fight. Others persisted and laid siege. But all failed. Fortified defences were backed by the Byzantines' skilled and well-equipped navy and more unconventional deterrents such as 'Greek Fire', a mysterious liquid fire that was sprayed with devastating effect.

TROUBLE WITH PICTURES

Trouble was also brewing internally on the theological front when the iconoclast Leo III became emperor in 726. Iconoclasts believed literally in the first commandment, which forbids the worshipping of 'graven images'. Their stance was a complete break with the Greek tradition of adorning churches with elaborate frescoes and mosaics, and the veneration of icons and the relics of martyred saints. Thus began a 'dark age' of almost 120 years, during which churches were stripped of their decoration and those who stayed faithful to icons (iconodules) were forced to flee to distant monasteries or to worship in secret at

In Context

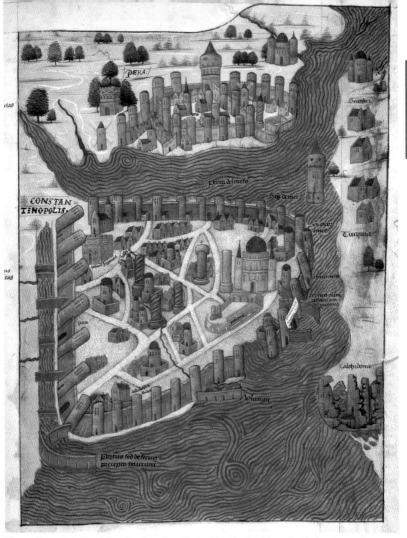

The early walled city of Constantinople with the Haghia Sophia cathedral at its centre.

risk of denunciation and death. The feud over icons burned on until 845 and it wasn't until 867 that the first new mosaic was unveiled in Haghia Sophia – that of the Madonna and child, still *in situ* today.

Religious problems of a different kind surfaced during the iconoclastic period when in 800 the Roman pope crowned the Frankish leader Charlemagne the first Emperor of the West for over 400 years. This was followed by emissaries to Constantinople proposing a marriage between Charlemagne and the then Byzantine empress Eirene. The aim was to re-

unite the two halves of the later Roman Empire but the grandees of the Eastern church created by Constantine felt that they alone had the right to crown emperors. Unwilling to accept as supreme ruler an illiterate tribal leader unable to speak either Latin or Greek, they deposed Eirene shortly after the emissaries' arrival.

A restoration in Byzantine fortunes came during the reign of Basil II (976-1025) who succeeded not just in holding the fort but also expanding the empire into Armenia and Georgia. A conscientious ruler, he was also incredibly harsh: he is best-known for meting

Gül Küçükserim has restored this family mansion with the purpose of offering tastes of the past to both native and foreign guests, with the Turkish hospitality in the comfort of a home.

Arena hotel is an exciting place. It continues its story in a very different image now, which it started as a house at the end of 1800s. Furniture reaming from the past was also used in the interior decoration of the hotel which has given service as a botique hotel since 1998.

Gül Küçükserim meticulously works for the service quality which is continuously increasing ; and attends every detail.

The Hotel has 27 Rooms including 4 suites and has a capacity of 54 beds. Located in City Center and walking distance to the Blue Mosque, St. Sophia, The Underground Cistern, Topkap Palace and The Grand Bazaar. Atatürk Airport is 18 km.

Rates : $60-$90 Single; $80-$110 Double;
$110-$130 Tripple; $120-$150 Suites
Credit : AmEx, Visa, MC, EC
Map : 303 M11
Hotel Services : Heating and Air-Conditioning, Garden Bar, Restaurant, Turkish Bath, Parking, Laundry, Generator.
Room Services : Room Service, Mini-Bar, Telephone, TV: Cable, Safe Box.

Şehit Mehmet Paşa Yokuşu Üçler Hamam Sokak
No: 13-15 Sultanahmet - Istanbul - Turkey
Tel: (90-212) 458 03 64-65-67 Fax: (90-212) 458 03 66
www.arenahotel.com / www.delightrestaurant.com

out one of the most horrific punishments that Europe has ever seen: in 1014 after taking 15,000 Bulgars prisoner, he had 99 out of every 100 blinded. The remainder were left with one eye to lead their fellow soldiers home. When he saw the ruined army that returned to his capital, Bulgarian Tsar Samuel is said to have collapsed and died two days later.

Basil's most significant contribution to history came in 989 when he gave his 25-year-old sister Anna in marriage to Vladimir, Prince of Kiev, in return for the pagan prince's promise to convert to Orthodox Christianity. This Vladimir did, then founded the Russian church and converted his subjects *en masse*, earning himself a sainthood in the process.

FRYING PAN OR FIRE?

The death of Basil marked a turning point in Byzantine fortunes as the city entered a period of terminal decline. This was signalled to all when, in 1071, a combination of incompetence and treachery led to the annihilation of a Byzantine army at Manzikert in Anatolia. The victors were a new menace, the Selçuk Turks, who now flooded west across Asia Minor right up to the shores of the Sea of Marmara.

Meanwhile, to the west, Europe had emerged from its dark ages to become a patchwork of states owing religious allegiance to the Pope in Rome. Both the West and Byzantium were nominally Christian, but theological differences coupled with the Western church's envy of its older and richer neighbour meant any common cause was superficial. In 1054, a dispute between papal officials and the Patriarch of Constantinople had resulted in mutual excommunications. The animosity inaugurated the schism between the Roman and Orthodox churches that still exists today.

In its time of trouble, the empire fell into the hands of the scheming Ducas and Comneni families. They indulged their tastes for luxury, learning, and culture, making Constantinople perhaps the richest city in the world. Also the most decadent, as the dynasties followed their penchant for intermarrying, intriguing, dethroning and murder. Where once Byzantine armies had conquered, the bloated and effete empire now relied on wealth and diplomacy. With the Selçuk Turks as the greater threat, Byzantium was forced to enlist the aid of Latin armies as paid mercenaries. The Latins were crusading to recapture the Holy Lands lost to the Turks and, passing through Constantinople in 1097, they agreed to return to the emperor any formerly imperial territory that they might recapture. This was a promise they failed to keep. Instead, the crusaders set up their own Holy Land states. There followed 50 years of

Justinian I and **Belisarius**. *See p10.*

confused bruising between the Byzantine, Latin and Muslim armies, culminating in the Byzantines cutting crusader supply lines and enabling the Selçuks to retake lost territory.

Two or three relatively able emperors, notably John II (1118-43) and Manuel I (1143-80), applied clever diplomacy and judicious use of force to keep the empire intact and even extend its borders, but the good work was undone in 1185 with the accession of Isaac II. Isaac was totally incompetent and set the gains of the last 70 years in reverse. He was deposed by his brother Alexius III and imprisoned, but Isaac's son escaped and fled west, where he offered enormous sums of money to the armies massing in Venice for the Fourth Crusade in exchange for helping his father and himself regain the imperial throne. With interest in a long and probably futile struggle in the Middle East never deep, the Latins needed little encouragement to accept.

Threatened with the vastly superior force of the crusaders, the Byzantines agreed to restore Isaac II to the throne. But Alexius III fled with the contents of the treasury and the crown jewels, leaving the reinstated emperor with no

World Of Carrefour SA Shopping Centers

featuring; Fashion
Technology
Jewellery
Entertainment
Dining

Home To The Best Stores In Town

The CarrefourSA Shopping Centers:

İstanbul:
İçerenköy Shopping Center Adress: Near of The Hal Building, Old Genoto Area 81120 İçerenköy / İstanbul Tel: 0 216 448 02 9

Ümraniye Shopping Center Adress: Küçüksu St., No:68 Ümraniye / İstanbul Tel: 0 216 525 10 50

Bayrampaşa Shopping Center Adress: Ferhatpaşa Farm, Near Of The Istanbul Bus Terminal Bayrampaşa/İstanbul Tel: 0 212 640 00 99

Haramidere Shopping Center Adress: Old London Highway Haramidere / Istanbul Tel: 0 212 853 01 77

İzmit:
CarrefourSa İzmit Shopping Center Adress: Eskibaş İskele St, Near of The New Bus Terminal Kocaeli / İstanbul Tel: 0 262 335 34 9

Bursa:
CarrefourSa Bursa Shopping Center: Adress: Odunluk District,On The Way Of İzmir Highway No:35 Bursa Tel: 0 224 452 69 00

Ankara:
CarrefourSa Shopping Center 12 Km's to İstanbul Highway, In Front Of The Jandarma Yenimahalle / Ankara Tel: 0 312 278 27 80

İzmir:
CarrefourSa İzmir Shopping Center 6524. St., No.6 Şemikli Karşıyaka / İzmir Tel: 0 232 324 40 64

Adana:
CarrefourSa Adana Shopping Center 100. Yıl District, 100 Evler Area Seyhan / Adana Tel: 0 322 256 54 56

Mersin:
CarrefourSa Mersin Shopping Center Limonluk District, İsmet İnönü Squre, No:33/120 Mersin Tel: 0 324 329 16 17

'Rivers of blood': Palma II Giovane's **The Taking of Constantinople**.

money to pay his mercenary allies. On 13 April 1204, the crusaders stormed Constantinople. They sacked the city, stripping it of its treasures and relics and sending them back west; the four gilded bronze horses that now stand over the doorway of St Mark's cathedral in Venice came from Constantinople's hippodrome. What the crusaders couldn't strip away they destroyed, leaving the city in ruins.

The victorious Latins then appointed one of their own, Baldwin of Flanders, as emperor and divided up the empire into a patchwork of fiefdoms and city states. Haghia Sophia and many Orthodox churches were converted to the Latin rite. The Latin state lasted until 1261 before the Byzantines mustered enough force to reclaim what remained of Constantinople.

OTTOMANS AT THE GATE

That the Byzantine state was able to survive for another 190 ineffectual years was down to the fact that the rival Selçuk empire had splintered into myriad warring *beyliks*, or fiefdoms. It was only a matter of time, though, before one *beylik* won out and by the first years of the 14th century a new power had emerged, the Osmanlı Turks, named after their first leader Osman, and better known to Westerners as the Ottomans. During the reign of their first sultan,

Orhan Gazi (1326-62), the Ottomans conquered most of western Asia Minor and advanced into Europe as far as Bulgaria, establishing a new capital at Adrianople, now Edirne.

Constantinople had become a Byzantine island on an Ottoman sea. Inevitably the severely weakened, ruined and depopulated city was confronted with a Turkish army at its walls. This first occurred in 1394, and again in 1400, 1422 and 1442. Each time the attacks were repelled, but this only forestalled the inevitable. Soon after becoming Ottoman sultan in 1452, Mehmet II constructed the fortress of Rumeli Hisarı on the European shore of the Bosphorus just north of the city. Fitted with cannons, it gave the Ottomans control of the straits and deprived Constantinople of vital grain supplies.

By April 1453, the Ottoman forces surrounding Constantinople numbered some 80,000; facing them were just 5,000 able-bodied men in a city whose population had fallen to less than 50,000. The Ottoman navy was anchored in the Sea of Marmara. However, it could not gain access to the Golden Horn because of a great chain that the Byzantines had stretched across its mouth from Galata castle to modern-day Sirkeci. But one night, several weeks into the siege, in an audacious move, the Ottomans circumvented the boom by hauling 70 ships on rollers up over the ridge above Galata and down to the water on the other side, so that by morning they were in the Golden Horn and up against the city walls.

On 27 May, Mehmet invited the last Byzantine emperor, named Constantine, like the first, to surrender. He refused. The final assault was launched two days later. The defenders on the walls threw back waves of attackers as they had many times before. This time, however, the besiegers forced an opening near the Golden Horn, and poured into the city in their thousands. By dawn it was all over, with an estimated 4,000 defenders lying dead. A contemporary account describes how 'blood flowed through the streets like rainwater after a sudden storm; corpses floated out to sea like melons on a canal'.

With the conquest of Constantinople, Mehmet, still only 21 years old, took the name 'Fatih', or Conqueror. He was apparently shocked at the ruined state of the once-great city. As he walked among the wrecked imperial palace, he is said to have recited lines from an old Persian poem: 'The spider spins the curtains in the palace of the Caesars, and the owl hoots its night call on the towers of Afrasiab.'

A MULTINATIONAL CAPITAL

Mehmet was intoxicated by the notion of Constantinople and its heritage as capital of Eastern and Western empires. It fitted his own imperial ambitions. Justinian's great cathedral, Haghia Sophia, was reconsecrated as a mosque and the sultan attended prayer there the first Friday after the conquest. The Ottomans immediately set about repairing the damage sustained during the siege and the decay of preceding centuries. Defences were strengthened with a great citadel at Yedikule where the land walls met the Sea of Marmara, and a palace was constructed on the site of what is now Istanbul University. Mehmet ordered craftsmen and artisans from Bursa and Edirne to move to his new city. The sultan's *viziers* (ministers) were encouraged to build and endow the new capital with mosques and the beginnings of what would develop into the Grand Bazaar.

Swords of misrule

Created in the early years of the Ottoman dynasty, the Janissaries were the sultan's shock troops, reputedly the first to breach the walls in the conquest of Constantinople. Initially they were entirely of Christian origin, boys who were forcibly converted to Islam and trained up into a crack and fiercely loyal fighting force. In times of peace they served to maintain order in the capital and other main cities, for which they were richly rewarded. But their privileged status meant that in later years they were also frequently the cause of disorder. Well-paid and overly pampered, there was no institution to control the imperial guard. *Quis custodiet ipsos custodes?* as the Romans might ask – 'Who guards the guardians?' In the case of the Janissaries the answer was, very definitely, no one.

When Süleyman the Magnificent died in 1566, at the height of imperial power, the Janissaries were strong enough to bring the capital to a standstill until they'd received the traditional 'accession bonus' paid by every new sultan to ensure his guards' loyalty – a dangerous tradition that meant the Janissaries had a vested in interest in changing sultans frequently. Later, as imperial power declined during the 'rule of women', the soldiers had even less respect for the imperial offices and Istanbul became almost a battleground between the sultan and his guard. In 1622, worried at planned reforms, they deposed and brutally murdered 18-year-old Sultan Osman II, cutting off his ear and presenting it to his mother, while between 1651 and 1783 they staged no fewer than 11 revolts. A favourite tactic was to put the city to fire, looting and raping in the ensuing panic.

Attempts to control them with the regular armed forces backfired. In 1807-8 the Janissaries provoked a full-scale civil war, slaughtering great numbers of the regular army, murdering Sultan Selim III and attempting to murder his successor, Mahmut II.

On gaining the throne Mahmut swore, 'Either the Janissaries will all be massacred or the cats will walk over the ruins of Constantinople.' Their end came in 1826 when yet another revolt was met by Mahmut's new Western-style army aided by a civilian population eager for revenge after decades of abuse. More than 5,000 Janissaries were killed and 6,000 sent into exile in several days of bloodletting that became known thereafter as 'the blessed event'.

Efforts were made to repopulate the half-deserted city. Greeks, who had fled in the preceding years, were offered land and houses and temporary tax exemption. Craftsmen, merchants and those who would enhance the city's wealth were invited regardless of race or religion. At a time when 'heretics' were being burnt alive in western Europe, the Ottoman regime granted all religions freedom of worship and the uncontested right to appoint their own religious leaders. Large numbers of Sephardic Jews expelled from Spain and Portugal took sanctuary in Istanbul, the only multinational, multi-faith capital in Europe.

On the Conqueror's death in 1481 a scuffle for succession was won by his elder son Beyazıt II, succeeded in turn by his son Selim I, known as 'the Grim' for his habit of having his grand viziers executed (inspiring the popular Ottoman curse, 'May you be a vizier of Selim!'). Although Selim's reign lasted only eight years, he presided over significant military victories, adding Syria and Egypt to the imperial portfolio. Further south, he saw off a Portuguese threat to Mecca and was rewarded with the keys to the Holy City, the sacred relics of the Prophet, and the title of Caliph, Champion of Islam. This made Istanbul not only the capital of one of the most powerful empires in the world, but, as it was still the home of the Orthodox Patriarchate, also the centre of two major religions.

While Mehmet II made Istanbul the Ottoman capital, it was during the 46-year reign of Süleyman I (1520-66) that the city became a true imperial centre. Not without reason was Süleyman able to describe himself in his official correspondence as 'Sultan of Sultans, Sovereign of Sovereigns, Distributor of Crowns, the Shadow of God on Earth, Perfecter of the Perfect Number…' These days historians just settle for plain 'Süleyman the Magnificent'. By the time of his death he ruled an empire that covered the spread of North Africa, stretched east to India, and rolled from the Caucasus through Anatolia and the Balkans to Budapest and most of modern-day Hungary. Süleyman's armies reached the walls of Vienna in 1529, where they were finally turned back after an unsuccessful siege.

Key to Süleyman's military successes were the Janissaries, whose name comes from the Turkish *yeni ceri*, or 'new troops'. During the 16th century they were the most disciplined, well-armed and effective of all European armies, universally admired and feared. Later, though, their unchecked appetites for power and their lack of discipline would almost prove the empire's undoing (*see p16* **Swords of misrule**).

Sultan Mehmet II by Gentile Bellini

Under Süleyman, Istanbul became synonymous with grandeur, the source of which was the imperial palace, Topkapı, founded by Mehmet the Conqueror, but gilded by the wealth, tributes and taxes from newly conquered territories. Severe and grave, Süleyman surprised all by falling under the spell of a slave girl, Haseki Hürrem, known universally as Roxelana due to her alleged Russian origins. So besotted was Süleyman that in the early 1530s he married Roxelana and dispensed with the company of all other women. In 1538, as a further expression of devotion, he commissioned a promising young architect, Mimar Sinan, to construct the Haseki Hürrem Mosque complex as a birthday present. This was Sinan's first major commission in Istanbul, launching a glorious career which was to span 50 years. During that time, he, more than any of the sultans or pashas, left his indelible mark on the city and indeed on most major cities of the Ottoman Empire (*see p38* **Keeping up with the domes's**).

THE RULE OF WOMEN

Süleyman should have been succeeded by his first son, Mustafa, an able soldier and administrator, but Roxelana schemed against it. Mustafa was not her son. She succeeded in convincing the sultan that he was traitorous and Süleyman had him strangled. Selim, Roxelana's son, became heir apparent.

Such bloodletting to secure the imperial throne was not uncommon. Although the sultanate always remained in the family – every ruler of the Ottoman Empire until its end was a

The second court at the **Topkapı Palace** in an 1815 engraving. *See p17.*

descendant of Osman – the choice of which son or male relative would inherit the throne was left to 'the will of Allah'. More pragmatically, whichever of the sultan's sons happened to be in Istanbul, or got there first after the ruler's death, got the throne. Succession was a matter of life or death, for Mehmet the Conqueror had declared, 'For the welfare of the state, the one of my sons to whom Allah grants the sultanate may lawfully put his brothers to death.' They were strangled with a silken bowstring, preferably by deaf mutes who would not hear their cries. The beautiful and elaborate tombs built to house the families of butchered children scarcely hid the brutality of the deed. Thus

when Süleyman died on campaign in Hungary, the grand vizier sent a secret messenger to the preferred heir, Selim, then maintained the fiction that the sultan was merely ill. Once Selim was secure in Istanbul the vizier announced the sultan's demise.

Far from being grim, Selim II was known as Selim 'the Sot'. His rampant drunkenness rendered him useless as a ruler. The real power behind the throne was Nurbanu ('Princess of Light'), one of Selim's wives, who used his drunkenness to take control of both the harem and the palace, marking the beginning of an 80-year period referred to as 'the rule of women'. It was an era that saw weak sultans

Istanbul (not Constantinople)

Istanbul was Constantinople but when did the name change? All that's sure is that nobody can agree. According to one well circulated story, early inhabitants did not refer to the city by its actual name but, because of it size, simply as 'Polis' (the City), and when they wanted to say 'to the City', they said 'eiet enpolin' (is-tin-polin), which was the (possible) origin of the name 'Istanbul'. If that sounds a bit too neat, recent research has shown that the name 'Istanbul' was used if not during the Byzantine period, at least during the 11th century and that the Turks knew the city by this name, too. The city went by other names too. During the Turkish period the names 'Dersaadet' (City of Peace) and 'Deraliye' (the Sublime) were also used, though not widely and not for any great period

of time. Some official correspondence and coins also carried the transcription 'Konstantinoupolis' or 'Konstantiniye'.

The name controversy was assumed to be settled when Atatürk officially renamed the city Istanbul in the 1935, banning the use of the imperial Latin moniker Constantinople (*see p24*). It took Westerners a few decades to accept the name, as Constantinople continued to appear on maps well into the 1960s. The Greeks still prefer not to use the Turkish name, and Konstantinopolis continues to be used on maps and road signs in Greece today.

One thing is clear, as songwriters Kennedy and Simon made plain in 1953, 'Why did Constantinople get the works? That's nobody's business but the Turks.'

manipulated by their wives and mothers, the *valide sultana*, between whom there were often struggles for power (*see p73* **Harem-scarem**).

Selim's drunkeness had fatal results: he drowned in his bath and Nurbanu had four of his five sons killed, leaving her own child Murat III to succeed as sultan. When Murat died in 1595, his wife Safiye in turn had 19 brothers of her son, Mehmet III, strangled. With Mehmet's successor, Ahmet I, builder of the Sultanahmet (Blue) Mosque (*see p74*), the killing stopped, possibly out of fear of dynastic extinction. From Ahmet's time, male relatives of the sultan were instead confined to the Kafes, literally 'cage', a closed apartment deep inside the Topkapı Palace. Here they were kept in complete isolation, apart from a few concubines who had been sterilised by the removal of their ovaries. Guards whose eardrums had been pierced and tongues slit served the prisoners.

Although slightly more humane than the earlier fratricidal practices, confinement in the Kafes did little for the captives' mental health. Numerous sultans died prematurely without leaving an heir and their siblings were uniquely unsuited to rule, having spent most of their adult lives incarcerated. In the last years of the empire the problem was to grow more acute as successive sultans had little experience of the outside world, or of government. Some emerged quite simply mad.

THE TURNING POINT

In 1683 the Ottomans failed in a second attempt to take Vienna. This marked the end of Ottoman military successes and expansions and the beginning of a series of reverses. Within three years the imperial armies had lost Buda to the Austrians, and two years after that, Belgrade. More defeats followed. In less than a hundred years, times had changed from

The drop of a hat

Istanbul has seen some moments in her remarkable history but few more compellingly bizarre than those of 25 November 1925, when Mustafa Kemal Atatürk's ban on the fez came into force. The Ottoman national headgear was to give way by decree to modern Western hats that morning. Near the Dolmabahçe Palace, a bemused muezzin appeared on a minaret balcony to give the call to prayer in a bowler. Elsewhere, the city's more theatrical citizens tossed their fezzes into the Bosphorus or left them to be collected by charities and turned into slippers for the destitute. Articles appeared in the press on the right way to wear the new sartorial order – homburgs, panamas and flat caps.

Atatürk's wide-ranging revolution was intended to turn subjects of empire – Eastern, orthodox and Islamic – into citizens of the republic – Western, liberal and secular. But of all the sweeping reforms of the 1920s, the new leader regarded the abolition of the fez as of particular social significance. 'Gentlemen,' Atatürk explained in a 1927 speech, 'it was necessary to abolish the fez, which sat on the heads of our nation as an emblem of ignorance, negligence, fanaticism and hatred of progress and civilisation.'

Far from being a mere prop of music-hall comedians, the fez was the very badge of orthodox Turkish identity. It did not go quietly. Riots marked the abolition of the red hat

whose tassel was said to symbolise the single hair by which devout Muslims were effortlessly raised to Paradise on their death. The unrest ended in executions. Caches of clandestine fezzes were uncovered. Special constables took to the streets and ordered citizens to remove their new hats in case fezzes lurked beneath them.

Nor was it the first time that headgear had been targeted to political ends. A century before, in the 1820s, Sultan Mahmut II had abolished the religious and reactionary turban for the fez; but by the 1920s, its 'modern' replacement looked equally dated and had become a symbol of similar reaction.

Turkey's modernisers have long yearned for that ultimate measure of Westernisation, the bare head. But things go round; the turban is once again a common sight in Istanbul districts such as Fatih, heartland of the Islamic revival. And the battle between Turkey's secular and orthodox wings continues to be fought over the thorny issue of whether women should be allowed to wear headscarves in the universities. The fez, meanwhile, is remembered in a street name deep in the Grand Bazaar – Feşçiler Caddesi, or 'Fez-makers' Street'. These days, the conical hat is sold to tourists, and some Istanbul hotel staff and ice-cream sellers continue to wear it. It has become a banal parody of its former, significant self. Just as Atatürk would have wished it.

the days when Süleyman the Magnificent was treated as a virtual god and all had to lower their eyes in his presence.

Pleasure-loving sultan Mehmet IV was accused of indifference to affairs of state and deposed by his vizier. His brother Süleyman was appointed instead, but, having spent 40 years in the Kafes, he refused to come out, believing that executioners were waiting. He had to be coaxed from hiding like a skittish kitten.

'Mahmut II's addiction to champagne allegedly led to his untimely death.'

The problem lay not just with addled sultans. In the absence of a strong figurehead, the Janissaries, once the sultan's finest troops, were now completely out of hand, threatening the sultan and killing ministers. Plagues were recurrent. In 1603 a fifth of the population was wiped out, in 1778 a third. Such outbreaks had been eliminated in Europe by the early 1700s by the use of quarantines, but the fatalistic Turks accepted the epidemics as God's will.

Of the advances in science and technology that were revolutionising Western societies and economies in the 18th century, the Ottomans were not only ignorant but arrogantly dismissive. One Turkish dignitary visiting a scientific lab in Vienna in 1748 could describe all he had seen as 'toys' and 'Frankish trickery'.

When Selim III took the throne in 1789 his position was perilous: disobedient guards, recurrent plague, economic decline, military defeats, moribund culture and a restless populace heavily taxed and suffering under poor administration. But he was at least sufficiently aware to know that he had to do something to remedy the empire's ills.

He looked to the West for inspiration. He established a consultative council and Western architectural influences started to make themselves felt at the palaces. More crucially, he attempted to reform the army. For this the sultan earned the enmity of the Janissaries, who felt that their privileges were being threatened. They rose up in revolt, deposed Selim and murdered him.

The Janissaries were finally crushed in 1826 by Sultan Mahmut II (1808-39), who had narrowly escaped from the palace with his life the day Selim had been killed. He went on to implement extensive and much-needed reforms, instigating what historian Philip Mansel calls 'revolution from above'. Local government was introduced to Istanbul for the first time, together with the city's first police and fire

services. Quarantine and plague hospitals were established on his orders. He allowed the formation of limited companies and in 1828 brought an Italian conductor to train the imperial band to play Western music.

Mahmut appeared at public functions wearing Western clothes, and, most striking of all, banned the wearing of robes and turbans, except for the clergy, introducing the crimson-wool fez from Morocco. This was soon taken to heart by the city, worn by all as a symbol of modernism. More than just a hat, the fez became, in the words of nationalist writer Falih Rifki Atay, 'part of the Turkish soul'. However Mahmut's addiction to all things Western led to his untimely death – allegedly from cirrhosis caused by a love of champagne.

THE TANZIMAT ERA

Mahmut's successor, Abdül Mecit (1839-61), continued his father's reforming programme, resulting in what was to be a last blossoming of the Ottoman Empire. Again according to Philip Mansel, 19th-century Istanbul 'owed its grandeur to its defiance of nationalism'. As in the city of Mehmet the Conqueror, race and religion were not supposed to be an issue. Greek, Armenian, Kurd, Circassian, Turk, Christian, Muslim and Jew were all to be equal: to this end two great imperial decrees of 1839 and 1856 were issued, forming the basis for what was known as *tanzimat* or 'the reforms'.

'Mark Twain thought the Haghia Sophia "the rustiest old barn in Heathendom".'

The sultan further embraced the new era by moving out of Topkapı and into a new Western-style imperial palace at Dolmabahçe. But the real hub of the city was the bridge built across the Golden Horn in 1845. The first to link the two sides of the water, it became the most popular of places, where a dozen or more races dressed like peacocks spent each evening promenading. Between palace and bridge, the largely non-Muslim, European districts of Galata and Pera (modern-day Beyoğlu), originally founded as Italian traders' enclaves in Byzantine times, were rapidly developing into a new commercial and entertainment district centred on the Grand Rue de Pera, location for an increasing number of theatres, cafés, bars and hotels. Istanbul was shifting its locus from south of the Golden Horn to north.

In the middle of the 19th century the city began to receive its first proper 'tourists', drawn by the oriental mystique of the capital of the Ottoman sultans. Almost immediately the

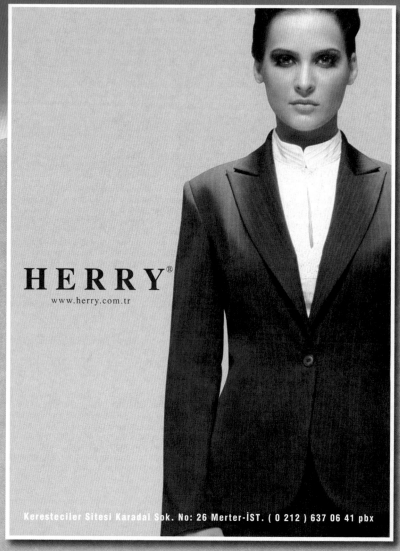

sightseeing circuit experienced by visitors today was set. Mark Twain road-tested it in the late 1860s and wrote of it in *Innocents Abroad*. Tourists dropped anchor in the Golden Horn and were rowed ashore to visit Haghia Sophia ('the rustiest old barn in Heathendom'), the Whirling Dervishes ('about as barbarous an exhibition as we have witnessed'), the Grand Bazaar ('a monstrous hive of little shops') and a hamam ('a malignant swindle'). He was, however, fascinated by the beggars – the three-legged woman, the man with an eye in his cheek, the man with fingers on his elbow. 'Bismillah! The cripples of Europe are a delusion and a fraud. The truly gifted flourish only in the byways of Pera and Stamboul.'

Had Twain been visiting just 15 years later his mood might have been improved by the opportunity to roll into Stamboul on the Orient Express (*see p86* **The extravagant express**), which pulled into Sirkeci station for the first time in October 1883.

> **'Lord Curzon, in the face of clear evidence to the contrary, claimed that the Muslims were in the minority in Istanbul.'**

Political reforms culminated in 1876 in the drafting of a constitution and the establishment the following year of the first Turkish parliament – albeit with very limited powers. But it was short-lived. A year later, despite their defeat by the Turks and allies in the Crimean War just 30 year earlier, the Russians again seized Ottoman lands in the Balkans and Caucasus. Called to account, Sultan Abdül Hamit responded by dissolving parliament and ruling by decree from his new labyrinthine palace at Yıldız. A paranoid ruler, he hid at Yıldız in constant fear of being bumped off and had several close members of his family and many ministers, generals and other court officials killed. British prime minister William Gladstone called him the 'Great Assassin'. Turks called him 'Abdül the Damned'.

Reform had already progressed too far to allow this reversion to complete imperial rule. Small clandestine groups later known as 'Young Turks' kept up the pressure for change. Most were weeded out and crushed, but one, the Committee of Union and Progress, based in Salonika, succeeded in seizing control of the Ottoman army in Macedonia. By 1908 the CUP was powerful enough to send a telegram to the ageing despotic sultan demanding the restoration of the constitution and parliament.

Faced with a rebellious revolutionary army marching on Constantinople, Abdül Hamit acceded to their demands.

Elections to the new parliament saw all but one of the seats won by the CUP, whose elected deputies included Arabs, Greeks, Jews, Armenians and Albanians. It took a pitched battle in Taksim Square to fight off the challenge of Islamic groups, but once that was won reforms were back on the agenda. What should then have been a period of rebirth was instead one of chaos and turmoil as Europe saw the imminent demise of Ottoman rule as a chance to carve up what remained of its empire.

EMPIRE'S END

In 1911 Italy seized Rhodes and blockaded the Dardanelles. The following year the Balkan states launched their own offensive, which saw them take all Ottoman possessions in Europe and Bulgarian troops advance to within 40 kilometres (25 miles) of Istanbul. News that Russia, which had long coveted Istanbul and control of the Bosphorus Strait, had joined an alliance with Britain and France left Turkey with little option but to turn to Germany and the two signed a formal alliance. Despite a historic victory at Gallipoli, in which they stemmed the Allied invasion and forced a withdrawal, the country was on the losing side in World War I. In the aftermath, they could do nothing but watch as the former Ottoman Empire was divided up between European powers. The British and French took over the Arab lands, occupied Istanbul in 1919 and enthroned a puppet sultan there.

A Greek army occupied much of the remaining territory. Many in Greece had long aspired to the 'great idea' of retaking 'Constantinople' and making it the capital of a Greater Greece. This had support in high places, including from British cabinet minister Lord Curzon, who, in the face of clear evidence to the contrary, claimed that Muslims were in the minority in Istanbul. Greece was permitted by the European powers to occupy parts of the Aegean coast and eastern Thrace.

Turkish leaders in Istanbul seemed incapable of countering the threat and groups of disillusioned soldiers began slipping out of the city, banding together under the leadership of Mustafa Kemal, the young Turkish general who had masterminded resistance at Gallipoli. In 1919 Kemal led a revolt from the interior, formally declaring independence and forming a new government in Ankara. 'Henceforth,' he declared, 'Istanbul does not control Anatolia, but Anatolia Istanbul.' In other words: 'Turkey for the Turks.'

After two years of bitter fighting, the Turks succeeded in forcing the Greeks back to Izmir, which was all but destroyed in the final battle. It was a defining moment for the emergent Turkish state, which was now able to negotiate with the Allies on equal terms. In 1922 the sultanate was abolished and the reigning sultan reduced to little more than a ceremonial figurehead. In fear of his life, the last sultan, Vadettin, fled Istanbul for Italy, with his son accepting the throne. In July 1923 the new state was strong enough to win back some of the territory lost through the treaty of Lausanne, paving the way for a complete allied withdrawal from Istanbul three months later.

'Atatürk exiled the last members of the Ottoman dynasty and banned the name Constantinople.'

LET THE GOOD TIMES ROLL

A matter of days after reoccupying Istanbul, on 29 October 1923 Turkey adopted a new secular republican constitution, appointed Mustafa Kemal 'Atatürk' ('father of the Turks') as its president and fixed upon Ankara as its capital. It was a break with almost 1,600 years of tradition, which saw the replacement of one of the world's most fabulous cities by a small windswept hillside town that lacked almost every modern amenity, but which was far enough from the new country's borders to make it secure from invasion. Within six months the 1,300-year-old tradition of the sultanate was completely abolished and the last members of the Ottoman dynasty sent into exile.

Bold, sweeping reforms followed. The European calendar was adopted, then the Swiss civil code and the Italian penal code – abolishing the role of religion in law. The fez – itself a fairly recent replacement for the turban – was banned in favour of Western hats (see p20 The drop of a hat), women were granted equal rights to men, and language reforms replaced Arabic script with the Latin alphabet. Later, in 1935, all Turks were obliged to adopt surnames and lists of suggested ones were posted everywhere. The name Constantinople, still common in official and popular usage, was banned because of its imperial associations. The post office would only accept 'Istanbul' as an address on letters.

On a deeper level, Atatürk precipitated a change in national self-perception. Previously 'Turk' was a term applied to backward provincials; the cultured elite saw themselves as Ottoman. Now the slogan was 'How happy

are they who call themselves Turks'. From being the most international of cities, Istanbul rapidly became the most nationalistic.

Although supplanted by Ankara as the country's political powerhouse, Istanbul continued to prosper as the undisputed cultural and economic capital of the new republic. The Grand Bazaar remained the centre of commerce, while Pera – now renamed Beyoğlu – entered a wild and heady period buoyed by pro-Western reforms that allowed for previously unheard-of levels of freedom. Added to the cocktail were a couple of hundred thousand White Russian refugees fleeing the far more po-faced Soviet revolution, including the odd genuine aristocrat. The Russians were to dominate the cultural life of the district for decades, opening cafés, bars and restaurants, and even introducing Istanbul to the 'jazz age' via a black American, a Mr Thomas, who'd owned a famous bar in Tsarist Russia, but joined the exodus to the city of the Bosphorus where he opened a dance hall.

As a leader Atatürk was the personification of good-time Turkey. A man of immense energy, he drank and gambled all night, napped for a couple of hours then got up to conduct the country's affairs. He may have moved the capital to Ankara, but his heart was in Istanbul.

Atatürk died in 1938. His casket was placed in the throne room of Dolmabahçe Palace, where hundreds of thousands came to view the body. Crowds at the palace grew so disorderly that riot police charged and a dozen people were trampled to death. He was succeeded by Ismet Inönü, who had masterminded the Turkish forces in the war against Greece, but Atatürk has hardly been allowed to die and his image is still to be seen all over Istanbul today (see p25 Atta Turk!).

TURKIFICATION AND TURMOIL

At the renewed outbreak of war in Europe, Turkey opted to remain neutral. Battle did go on in Istanbul, however, as the city became the espionage capital of World War II. No less than 17 different intelligence agencies operated there and half the population seemed to be making a living trading information. Allied and axis spies would regularly dine at the same restaurants, such as Rejans (which still exists, see p134), just off Istiklal Caddesi, where they would glare at each other across the room. Occasionally the rivalry would turn violent. In 1941 a bomb hidden by pro-Axis Bulgarian agents in the luggage of the British ambassador exploded shortly after he had arrived at the Pera Palas Hotel. The ambassador escaped unhurt but six Turks were killed and the hotel lobby seriously damaged. To the chagrin of the British government, it was then sued for compensation

Atta Turk!

He's the centre of a personality cult that makes those of Lenin and Mao Tse Tung seem shy and retiring by comparison. What's more, he's dead and absolutely nobody is being forced to put up his posters, erect statues, parrot his slogans, buy the mug, the clock, the teapot, the T-shirt. But they all still do. More than 60 years after his death, the image of **Mustafa Kemal Atatürk** remains omnipresent, from the paper banknotes with their bewildering number of zeros to profiles carved into hillsides. His name honours airports and stadiums, boulevards and bridges. Back in the 1920s it was seriously proposed that they rename Istanbul Gazi Mustafa Kemal. In 1999 a coordinated internet voting campaign almost boosted Atatürk on to the front cover of *Time* magazine as the readers' choice of 'Man of the Century' until the ploy was scuppered by a Greek and Armenian counter-action.

Many Turks will privately admit that they find the iconography excessive but accept it as a necessary counter to the threat of anti-secular political Islam. Fervent 'Kemalists' (as proponents of Atatürk are known) often give the impression that the only thing standing between Turkey and the plunge into Iranian-style Islamic revolution is the image of the 'Father of the Turks' and a few choice slogans daubed around.

What is beyond debate is Atatürk's status as one of the most influential political figures of the 20th century, not to say a military commander of true genius. His effect on the outcome of the allied landings at Gallipoli in World War I can best be summed up in the official British army history: 'Seldom in history can the exertions of a single divisional commander have exercised so profound an influence not only on the course of a battle but on the destiny of a nation.'

Kitsch and iconography aside, each year Atatürk is commemorated at 9.05am on 10 November – the anniversary of his death. Sirens blare out across the country signalling a minute's silence. People stand motionless, traffic pulls over and drivers get out to stand. It is a moving, not to say eerie experience, and one that speaks far more eloquently than the mini-industry of memorabilia.

by the Turkish authorities. The cracks in the marble on the walls of the lobby can still be seen today. For more on this period so the excellent *Istanbul Intrigues* by Barry Rubin.

Packed with refugees from all over Europe, Istanbul was also something of a safe haven for Jews escaping the Nazis. Purges in Germany had coincided with a reorganisation of Istanbul University and by 1940 the institution employed some 120 Jewish exiles, many of them leaders in their respective fields.

However, Istanbul's indigenous religious minorities, who at the time still accounted for around one-third of the city's total population, were less fortunate. In 1942, on the pretext of combating war profiteering, the Turkish government introduced an 'asset tax', which was levied primarily on Jews, Armenians and Greeks. Fortunes accumulated over generations were wiped out overnight as many were forced

to sell off their assets to Muslims at a fraction of their worth. Thousands of those who were still unable to meet their payments were deported to labour camps in eastern Turkey. Although, under pressure from the British, the tax was repealed in 1944, it dealt the minorities of Istanbul a crippling financial and psychological blow from which they have never recovered. The result was a steady flow of emigrants to Greece, the US and, after 1948, the newly established state of Israel.

Turkey finally entered the war on the Allied side in February 1945 in order to secure a seat at the United Nations when it was founded later that year. During the Cold War Turkey also sided with the West. Under pressure from its new allies, Turkey introduced parliamentary democracy. In 1950, in the first fully free elections, the Democrat Party (DP) led by Adnan Menderes swept to power with a

Tax -Free Shopping in Turkey

As a foreign visitor you are entitled to claim back the tax you pay on your purchases when you take them home. The easy and safe way to reclaim your tax is with Global Refund, the world's leading tax refund company. This service is offered by major Retailers world-wide.Note: All foreign visitors as well as Turkish citizens living abroad are entitled for tax refund.The VAT rate in our country is 18 %. Your total purchases in a store must exceed TRL 100.000.000,- +VAT Your Global Refund Cheque must be stamped by Customs at departure within 3 months. Your refund amount is the VAT less an administration fee.

3 easy steps to claiming your refund

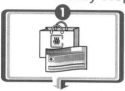

Shop wherever you see the Global Refund TAX FREE SHOPPING sign. Whenever you make a purchase, just ask for the Global Refund Cheque. You'll find more than 210.000 shops around the world offering the Global Refund service.

When leaving Turkey, simply show your purchases, invoices and passport to customs officials and have your Global Refund invoice / cheques stamped.
Customs personnel are well informed of the Global Refund system.

Finnaly, receive your cash refund at our nearby Cash Refund Office on departure or latest in 30 days you can mail your validated cheques and request the crediting of a chosen credit card or even a bank check to be sent to your address.

Cash Refund

İSTANBUL

Atatürk Airport	Cash Refund Office	Open every day - 24 hours
Atatürk Airport	İşbank	Open every day - 24 hours
S. Gökçen Airport	İşbank	Open Monday - Friday 09:00 -12:30 / 13:30 -17:30
Karaköy Harbor	İşbank	Open Monday - Friday 09:00 -12:30 / 13:30 -17:30

ANKARA

Esenboğa Airport	Post Office	Open every day - 24 hours

İZMİR

A.Menderes Airport	Post Office	Open Monday - Saturday 08:00 - 20:00

ANTALYA

Antalya Airport	Cash Refund Office	Open every day - 24 hours
Antalya Airport	Post Office	Open every day - 24 hours

BODRUM

Milas Airport	İşbank	Open Monday - Saturday 09:00 - 12:30 / 13:30 - 17:30
Seaport	Cash Refund Office	Open every day - 08:00 - 20:00

DALAMAN

Dalaman	İşbank	Open Monday - Friday 09:00 -12:30 /13:30 - 17:30

TRABZON

Seaport	Karden Turizm	Open every day - 24 hours

KAPIKULE

Border Crossing	Post Office	Open every day 08:00 / 17:30

İPSALA

Border Crossing	Post Office	Open every day 08:00 / 17:30

DEREKÖY

Border Crossing	Post Office	Open every day 08:00 / 17:30

For more information contact Global Refund Turistik Hizmetler A.Ş.
Ferah Sokak, No:19/A-2 Teşvikiye 34365 İstanbul - Turkey
Tel: +90(0212) 232 11 21 Fax: +90(0212) 241 77 28
E-mail:taxfree@tr.globalrefund.com   Http: www.globalrefund.com

massive majority. With the help of an economic boom assisted by anti-Soviet-inspired US aid, Menderes was able to reshape Istanbul with mass imports of cars and trucks and a programme of road-building implemented to accommodate them. Vast areas of old Istanbul were flattened to make way for the broad concrete strips of Vatan Caddesi, Millet Caddesi and Atatürk Bulvarı.

But the boom proved short-lived. Menderes became increasingly nationalistic and authoritarian. In September 1955, he attempted to exploit tensions over Cyprus by encouraging anti-Greek protests in Istanbul. The protests became a riot and then a pogrom as mobs attacked the Greek population, killing and looting. The police, apparently under orders not to intervene, stood back and watched. The pogrom sounded the death knell for the Greek community. Emigration accelerated. Today there are only 2,500 Greeks left in Turkey, less than the number of expatriate Britons.

In 1960, as Menderes moved to stifle all opposition to his rule, the military staged a coup and, in 1961, hanged Menderes and two of his senior ministers for treason.

Although democracy was restored and a new constitution promulgated, the 1960s were characterised by a rise in political extremism, initially on the far left. Istanbul became the scene of mass demonstrations and terrorist attacks. The extreme right responded in kind. In 1971 the military intervened again, toppling the government and appointing an administration of technocrats.

But within a few years of the restoration of civilian rule, the streets of Istanbul were the battleground for a low-level civil war between left-wing extremists and far-right groups, who often worked in tandem with elements within the security forces. Both groups conducted armed robberies to finance campaigns of assassinations, arrests, demonstrations and bombings. On 1 May 1977 unidentified gunmen opened fire on a leftist May Day rally in Taksim Square, killing 39 demonstrators. The violence escalated. By 1980 the daily death toll in Istanbul rarely fell below 20. A succession of weak coalition governments in Ankara seemed unable or unwilling to tackle the problem, with then-prime minister Suleyman Demirel dismissing the anarchy as mere hooliganism. On 12 September 1980, to the relief of much of the population, the military again seized power.

For the next three years, Istanbul was under martial law. The ruling military junta banned public meetings, outlawed all existing political parties, closed newspapers and magazines, burned books and arrested tens of thousands of real or suspected political activists, many of whom were subjected to torture. The repression took its toll on public sympathy for the military. When, in 1983, the junta restored civilian rule by allowing free elections, Turks rejected the military's preferred party and voted overwhelmingly for the broad-based Motherland Party and its founder Turgut Özal.

A NEW COSMOPOLITANISM

Faced with an economy that still closely resembled those found throughout Eastern Europe, Ozal implemented a series of market-oriented reforms that helped attract investment, but also resulted in widespread corruption and sleaze. As the Turkish saying goes, 'He who holds the honeypot is going to lick his fingers.' He also relaxed controls on religious organisations, allowing the creation of hundreds of religious-instruction schools that within a decade would become breeding grounds for Islamist extremism.

Ozal's economic reforms quickened the pace of urbanisation as millions of Anatolian peasants moved to major cities – particularly Istanbul – in search of a better life. They settled on the city fringes in *gecekondu* – literally 'night settlements', a term used to describe squatter houses put up overnight without permission. These newcomers swelled the population from three million in 1970 to approximately 12 million in 2003, changing the shape of the city. Istanbul has become a collection of villages with names such as 'little Gaziantep' and 'little Sivas', named after the Anatolian towns from which most of the residents originate. In 2003, an estimated 500 peasants were still arriving in Istanbul every day from Anatolia by train and bus.

Cheap labour from the *gecekondu* helped fuel the economic boom of the 1980s, although the spread of unplanned suburbs put an unbearable strain on the city's infrastructure, clogging roads and polluting out-of-town reservoirs, leaving some areas without water for weeks at a time. The new arrivals also brought with them the piety of the Anatolian villages, where many paid only lip-service to Ataturk's secularising reforms. In the local elections of March 1994, the people of Istanbul voted in the 40-year-old Tayyip Erdogan, making him city's first Islamist mayor in republican history. Erdogan used his record as mayor of Istanbul – where even his opponents grudgingly admit he improved services – as a platform to enter national politics. He became prime minister in March 2003.

The city continues to grow, not just outwards but upwards. Over the last 20 years a series of high-rise office blocks and luxury hotels have transformed the city's skyline. Many have been

Modern Istanbul: civic pride and a bridge between Europe and Asia.

built by large corporations that have grown rich on the back of Ozal's free-market reforms. Others have been constructed by Turkey's drug barons, who launder their profits from the lucrative heroin trade by pumping money into real estate. Over 80 per cent of the heroin entering Europe goes through Istanbul, much of it refined in temporary laboratories set up in the *gecekondu*, before being concealed in long-haul trucks ready to be smuggled across the border. In recent years, the smugglers have begun dealing in a new commodity: people. Nobody knows how many illegal immigrants are smuggled through Istanbul each year on their way into Europe, but the estimates range from 150,000 to half a million.

Many of these migrants from Africa and Asia who originally planned to pass through Istanbul on the way to Europe have stayed on to work in the city's vast unregistered economy of factories, sweatshops, construction sites, bars and restaurants. Added to them is the massive influx Eastern Europeans, arriving following the collapse of communism in 1989. Millions flocked to Istanbul to sell cheap consumer goods by day (and often themselves at night), transforming areas such as Laleli to the south of the Golden Horn into vast street markets.

In the meantime, the city has also regained much of its assertiveness and pride, becoming a regular venue for international conferences and sports events and a seemingly permanent feature amongst the cities applying to host the Olympics (*see p232*). Ambition off the field has been accompanied by success on it, particularly in football. In 2000 Galatasaray, one of the top three Istanbul teams, won the UEFA Cup. Meanwhile the Turkish national team, which invariably plays its home matches in Istanbul rather than Ankara, followed up qualification for the quarter-finals of Euro 2000 by finishing third in the 2002 World Cup.

As Turkey edges closer to full membership of the EU, efforts are under way to transform Istanbul into a cosmopolitan European city. After decades of neglect, money is being invested in preserving the city's battered heritage and easing the strain on its creaking infrastructure. A long-awaited metro system, promising relief from the worst of the traffic congestion, has finally opened, and plans are afoot for a tunnel under the Marmara to link the European and Asian rail lines. Although no one doubts that the city, for all its bewitching beauty, still faces major problems, a corner does seem to have been turned.

Key events

Pre-history
7000 BC Neolithic fishing settlements at Kadıköy, Pendık and Yarımburgaz.
3200 BC Bronze Age settlement at Sarayburunu.
750 BC Greek sailors pass through the Bosphorus.

The Greek colony
675 BC Greek colony of Chalcedon founded in what is now Kadıköy.
658 BC Greek colony of Byzantium founded.
546 BC Byzantium falls to Persians.
129 BC Creation of Roman province of Asia Minor; Byzantium keeps independence.
AD 73 Byzantium incorporated into Roman province of Bithynia.
196 Byzantium sacked by Roman Emperor Septimius Severus.
324 Constantine defeats co-emperor, makes the city new capital of Roman empire.

From Eastern Rome to Byzantine Empire
326-330 Constantine christens the city 'New Rome'. Instead it becomes Constantinople.
413 Theodosius II constructs new city walls.
537 Emperor Justinian dedicates new cathedral of Haghia Sophia.
745-7 Plague wipes out one third of the city.
976-1025 Reign of Basil II, longest reigning and most successful Byzantine emperor.
1071 Selçuk Turkish army conquers Anatolia.
1096 First Crusade reaches Constantinople, helps recapture lands lost to Selçuk Turks.
1147 Manuel I makes peace with Selçuks.
1204 Fourth Crusade sacks Constantinople.

Ottomans at the gate
1394-1442 Ottomans besiege Constantinople four times.
1453 Mehmet II conquers the city and declares it capital of the Ottoman empire.
1492 Spain's exiled Jewish population invited by Beyazıt II to settle in Istanbul.
1517 Selim the Grim captures Cairo and appoints himself Caliph of all Islam.
1520-66 Reign of Süleyman the Magnificent – empire reaches its zenith.

Decline of the empire
1566 Beginning of the 'rule of women'.
1622 Janissaries murder Osman II.
1651-1783 Janissaries revolt 11 more times.
1778 Plague wipes out one third of the city.

1807-8 Janissaries wage civil war.
1813 Hundreds of thousands die of plague.
1826 Janissaries destroyed by Mahmut II.

From reform to repression and revolution
1839 Beginning of the 'Tanzminat' era.
1845 Galata bridge spans the Golden Horn.
1853 Dolmabahçe Palace completed.
1854 First Istanbul stock exchange opens.
1854-6 Crimean War and revolts against Ottoman rule in the Balkans.
1877 First Ottoman parliament.
1878 Russians sieze Balkans, Abdül Hamit closes parliament and rules by decree.
1883 Orient Express pulls into Istanbul.
1899 'Young Turk' groups formed in military.
1908 First elections. CUP emerges victorious.
1912 First Balkan war.
1913 Second Balkan war.

The Great War
1914 Ottomans enter war on German side.
1918 Allied forces occupy Istanbul.
1919 Atatürk declares independent Turkey.
1920 Turkish parliament formed in Ankara.
1922 After two years fighting Turks force Greeks out of Iznik. Sultanate abolished.

The republic
1923 Allied occupation of Istanbul ends, Ankara declared capital of new republic.
1938 Atatürk dies.
1935-1941 Turkey provides safe haven for Jews fleeing German Reich.
1950 First democratically elected Turkish government.
1960 Prime Minister Adnan Menderes deposed in coup, hanged the following year.
1971 Instability in government and extremism prompts second army coup.
1980 Warring between left and right groups prompts military coup. Over 100,000 arrested.
1983-present Growth of shanty towns on outskirts of Istanbul as mıgrants move in from rural areas.
17 August 1999 Earthquake devastates parts of Istanbul and north-west Turkey.
June 2002 Turkey come third in the FIFA World Cup.
May 2003 Turkey wins the Eurovision Song Contest.
November 2003 Over 20 die in suicide bomb attacks on synagogues; days later, bombs hit the British consulate and the HSBC bank HQ.

Istanbul Today

'The world's favourite city'? 'The city that keeps on giving'?
Just how do you market Istanbul?

It used to be so effortless. Once upon a time Istanbul – or Constantinople, as it was – was the 'Sublime Port' and the 'City of the World's Desire', appellations concocted by foreign commentators but recognised by the world at large. And the city's residents didn't waste any time wondering what outsiders thought of them.

More recent generations haven't had such peace of mind. Since the giddy promise of the early republic, Istanbul has endured recurrent political turmoil and instability, along with a corresponding decline in wealth and prestige. There's just no avoiding the awful truth: the world's desire for the city has worn thin. The name 'Istanbul' may be just as evocative today as the word 'Constantinople' was a century ago but the vivid images it conjures up aren't necessarily what anyone would call 'sublime'. They was amplified in November 2003, when first synagogues and then the British consulate were bombed in a series of horrific attacks that killed over 40 and left hundreds injured.

From being the wealthy capital of a vast empire, Istanbul is now just the biggest city in a country politely termed by the world as 'developing'. Europe continues to keep Turkey at a distance (*see p33* **Mr Erdoğan goes to Brussels**), while the US sees it as somewhere conveniently close to Iraq to bunk thousands of its troops. Istanbul has gone from empress to an old girlfriend hit hard times, good for an occasional shag when there's nothing else on.

However, at least until the bomb attacks of late 2003, the general feeling among Istanbulus who have the time to think about such weighty matters is that after all the crap of recent times, the city is about to bounce back. It's had a bit of a nip and tuck, cleaned out the wardrobe and applied the slap. There's even a hint of glamour back in the air. Now its citizens are determined to make the world sit up and take notice. But how?

An answer is needed. It's not just a question of prestige, although national pride certainly plays a role. Istanbul is home to about 15 per

-The water's fine. Honest.

cent of the country's population (statisticians project that it will be 'Europe's' biggest city by 2015), and it is the capital in all senses but the political. Showing off Istanbul's finery to the world is good not only for the ego, but for the wallet as well.

So the movers and shakers of the city finally put their heads and considerable assets together. The professionals were called in and assigned the not inconsiderable task of rebranding the city. And so the next question: how do you brand something as complex as a city like Istanbul? Initial attempts in what is a very ill-defined mission to turn the world on to the city's charms are at least intriguing.

The first salvo in an admirably multi-pronged modern marketing campaign is a website (www.istanbul.com). Backed by the municipality, arts associations, tour operators, Turkish Airlines, convention organisers and historical foundations, it's a promotional portal with the stated function of peddling Istanbul as a tourist destination. Interestingly, the home page is presented in Turkish, suggesting that the first phase in selling the city to foreigners is to sell it to its own citizens first.

Click on the English translation and then the main heading to be exhorted to 'Explore and enjoy Istanbul! An almighty city for which wars were made and millions of lives were lost through thousands of years.' Ah, it's a history of the Galatasaray football club, then.

This is a vast improvement over certain other earlier hare-brained schemes. Mehmet Yıldırım, chairman of the Istanbul Chamber of Commerce Chairman read somewhere that the 1953 film *Roman Holiday* supposedly attracted some 11 million cinema-goers to flock out of the auditorium and onto flights bound for the Italian capital. He proposed putting up $50 million towards costs as an enticement to any Hollywood director willing to come and do similar for Istanbul. Nice idea, but what he forgot is that nowadays people just settle for buying the McDonald's tie-in meal. Yıldırım also suggested his own scenario: taking the Audrey Hepburn role, Chelsea Clinton, playing herself, falls in love with a Turkish journalist, visits the sites of Istanbul and goes home. Unsurprisingly, there have been no takers yet.

Equally naff have been the travel ad slogans – 'Meet where the continents meet' and the truly appalling 'Catch the rhythm', which seems more appropriate to a tropical fruit juice than a twice imperial capital. Hurrah then for the efforts of the slick lobbyists whose hand-shaking and PowerPoint presentations have got Istanbul short-listed to host the 2012 Olympics and the European Football Championships, jointly with Greece, that same year. And hurrah for Sertap Erener's belly, which, flung around the stage in Riga in May 2003, helped secure a Turkish victory in the Eurovision Song Contest, rewarded with the dubious honour of playing host to the cheesefest in 2004.

DEAD SHEEP AND PACKED PEWS

Ad campaigns and managed events only go so far in selling a city. The slickest packaging means absolutely nothing if the product fails to live up to expectations. Crucially, for all the websites, slogans and logos, the one thing the marketers have not done is identify exactly what that product is.

On the one hand, Istanbul has inevitably become a museum city as its denizens are capitalising on the historical treasure-trove they live among. This is something that's not just confined to mosques and mosaics: wealthy industrial families like the Koçs and Sabancıs – the Rothschilds and Vanderbilts of Istanbul – have also nailed their nameplates to spectacular collections of cars, boats, planes and 20th-century art. But all of this is to miss what's going on in the city of today, which remains, as it has ever been, a morass of polar opposites and contradictions, a mix of the Middle Eastern and the modern European, and a place in which no generalisation goes unchallenged and exceptions outnumber rules. This is much harder to define and so much harder to brand and package.

For example, a few snapshots from the last 12 months. This March, Anatolian peasants celebrating *Kurban Bayramı* (the Muslim 'Feast of the Sacrifice') defied health-minded authorities and ritually sacrificed sheep in public, in one instance beside an eight-lane motorway where they almost caused pile-ups. Female university students were again turned back from the gates of Istanbul University for wearing Islamic-style headscarves (this is at least an improvement on years past when the teenage girls were met with tear gas, water cannon and rubber bullets). In another religious twist, Christians were turned away from the doors of churches on Christmas Eve, but in this case because the pews were too packed with curious Muslim Turks to allow anybody else in.

It's this mind-boggling diversity that is Istanbul's true selling point. In fact, it's true to say that tolerance and multiculturalism were a way of life in Istanbul long before the West embraced them as their own inventions. There have, of course, been blips – let's not talk about the Armenians, and what happened to the city's Greek communities in the 1950s is still shocking – but historically the track record is a good one, and it's getting better.

Muslim Istanbul remains the capital of the Greek Orthodox world, home to the spiritual leader of an estimated 200 million Orthodox Christians. While the hometown congregation numbers only in the thousands, the Greek presence is still strongly felt. Scratch the

Ethnic Istanbul.

surface of many a Turkish building, custom or dish and you'll find it has Byzantine (that is, Greek) origins. The tiny community is also becoming visible in more tangible ways. Following a 50-year interval, Greek Orthodox youths celebrated their new year in 2003 by diving into the Golden Horn to retrieve a cross blessed by the local Greek Orthodox Patriarch. (Incidentally, diving into the waters around Istanbul is also something that has only recently once again become possible in the wake of a massive cleanup of the city's formerly polluted waterways. Like British minister John Gummer feeding his daughter British beef to prove its safety, the way was led by the Istanbul mayor taking the plunge and swallowing a few lung fuls of Bosphorus).

MINORITY TURKS

However, the largest and most significant minority in Istanbul today is not Greek, Armenian or Jewish but Turkish. These are the Anatolian Turks, who comprise about 36% of the city's population. Okay, so they're Turks, and not really minorities, but many Istanbulus regard them as foreigners. Nearly a million Anatolian Turks immigrated to Istanbul in the period 1985 to 1990 alone – and from places much closer to the Iraqi and Iranian borders than to nearby Greece and Bulgaria. Resourceful types, on arriving in Istanbul many of them simply threw up illegal shanties on state property (known as *gecekondu*), taking advantage of a loophole in the law that states any property built overnight has a right to remain standing. An estimated one-third of Istanbulus now live in such settlements.

Miraculously, the hordes of newcomers have been successfully absorbed. Up until the mid 1990s, it looked as though Istanbul would be overwhelmed and might even end up becoming a sprawling large-scale version of the villages left behind. But massive investments have had stunning results. Cash-strapped Istanbul has somehow managed to cope with an influx that would have sunk far wealthier cities.

That's not to say that old-timers don't sometimes grumble about the recent arrivals. The prime minister – a former mayor of Istanbul has even floated the controversial idea of requiring Anatolians to apply for work and residence permits. In response, current mayor Ali Müfit Gürtuna – himself from

faraway Konya – has launched his own campaign, this one aimed at locals. It features made-it-good Istanbulus born in other parts calling on everyone to act like a 'proper Istanbulu' – whatever that means. Tolerance wins the day, perhaps.

In terms of the Istanbul brand, immigrants – be they from Anatolia, Kurdistan, eastern Europe or Asia – give the city appeal. This is something that other municipalities and tourist boards around the world cottoned on to years ago. Sure, Istanbul's unsurpassable history, its glorious imperial architecture, its fine cuisine and exotic hills-and-waterways topography are all enviable by any standards. But perhaps the real glory of this ancient multicultural metropolis is the quality that might remake it the 'city of the world's desire' for the 21st century: its tolerance.

Mr Erdoğan goes to Brussels

'Its capital is not in Europe; 95% of its population live outside Europe; it is not a European country.' Valery Giscard d'Estaing, the head of Europe's constitutional convention, certainly didn't mince his words just weeks before a December 2002 meeting in Copenhagen at which Turkey hoped to be granted a date to start negotiations to enter the European Union.

The response from Turkish prime minister Recep Tayyip Erdoğan was to quote back the words of another Frenchman, Napoleon Bonaparte, who once said, 'If the world were a single state its capital would be Istanbul.'

What's more, according to straight-talking Mr Erdoğan, a promise is a promise: the EEC Council of Ministers accepted Ankara's application for associate membership way back in September 1959. Forty years later, Turkey was officially designated a candidate for EU membership at the Helsinki summit in December 1999. Now Europe should deliver.

By playing up Turkey's status as a major regional player, with an historic role in Central Asia and the Middle East, as well as in frequently troubled south-eastern Europe, Erdoğan neatly sidestepped the issue of Turkey's European identity.

Instead, the Turkish prime minister boldly questioned the criteria for admission to the European Union: 'Is the EU really nothing more than a wealthy Christian club? Are inclusiveness and tolerance of other cultures and religions not the true measures of Western civilisation?' he queried.

Well might he ask. Unlike previous negotiators – former PM Tansu Çiller and blue-eyed former foreign minister Ismail Cem, both fluent English-speakers and both the sorts you might run into at the opera, or who could be counted on to pick the right wine for dinner – Erdoğan is an unapologetic Islamist. He doesn't touch alcohol and makes no pretence of an interest in the arts. He was raised in Kaşimpaşa, one of Istanbul's roughest districts, but is clearly a product of remote, provincial Anatolia. Not the best man, the critics said, to present an 'us Turks, we're just like you' face to the inquisitors at the EU.

But more than Erdoğan, it was his wife, Emine, who caused a great deal of hand-wringing in the Istanbul press. As the Erdoğans prepared to head off to Davos for an economic summit, a columnist with the daily *Sabah* pleaded with Emine to consider wearing some kind of 'bonnet' instead of that 'dreaded' Islamic headscarf. Another hack offered fashion advice to the PM himself, superimposing his head onto models dressed in carefully coordinated casual sportswear.

In the event, they needn't have worried. Eventually, when the Erdoğans turned up for the crucial talks he wore trendy sunglasses, she a cream-coloured scarf and matching fur collar. The well-dressed couple returned to Ankara triumphant, bearing a pledge from EU leaders that Turkey could begin formal negotiations for accession as early as December 2004. Who says stylists are a waste of time?

Istanbul vs Islam

The oft-quoted cliché about 'East meets West' isn't as simple – or harmonious – as the tourist brochures make out.

Amid concern that post 9-11 the dreaded 'clash of civilisations' was rapidly morphing from an alarmist theory to a frightening reality, Istanbul was chosen to host the first Islamic-European Dialogue Forum in early 2002. Present were foreign ministers from the European Union and the Organisation of Islamic Conferences. Ismail Cem, Turkish foreign minister at the time, took the floor and called for 'respect of the various cultures', to rousing applause.

Istanbul was having its day in the sun, and ready to assume the role it believed itself uniquely qualified to hold; all those old clichés about 'East meets West', 'bridging cultures' and 'uniting continents' seemed to be paying off. No other city could claim to have been the centre of two such major religions; for half a millennia, Istanbul has been both home to the Orthodox Patriarchate (precursor and old rival to Rome) and to the Keeper of the Keys to Mecca. And no other country has been as successful at balancing the pious sensibilities of an overwhelmingly Muslim population with a strictly secular state structure.

Away from the international spotlight, however, it has become clear that the balancing act is far from a done deal. As knicker-twisted media commentators constantly remind their public, Istanbul has its own 'clash of civilisations' brewing, one that perhaps threatens to undermine the city's cherished traditions of tolerance and diversity.

Take the presidential reception thrown in September 2003 to mark the 80th anniversary of the republic. This occasion, meant to celebrate national unity, was boycotted by most deputies from the ruling Islamic Justice and Development Party (AKP). The reason? The invitations delivered to AKP ministers did not extend to spouses, while those given to the opposition Republican People's Party (CHP) did.

An easily remedied oversight, surely? No. Just an example of Turkish secularism at work. It transpired that the reason the AKP wives weren't invited was because of their penchant for wearing headscarves, in line with the Koranic prohibition on women exposing their hair to males other than close family. CHP wives, on the other hand, go bareheaded and, hence, get to go to the ball.

The secularists argue that state spaces should remain scarf-free zones if the relatively recent gains of modern women are not to be rolled back. After all, for hundreds of years Muslim women in this part of the world had no choice but to cover up in public. Emancipation, the secularists argue, necessitates similar but reverse restrictions.

The state plays down all the headscarf brouhaha and stays clear of the secular versus Islam debate, but this under-the-carpet attitude doesn't stop everybody else from talking.

For a case in point, flash back to August 2003 at the Istanbul Convention and Exhibition Centre. The occasion was the XXI World Congress of Philosophy, the first such conference ever organised in a Muslim country and the first held since 9-11. The theme was 'Philosophy facing world problems'. Yet strangely conspicuous by their absence were any leading Islamic philosophers from Turkish universities. They had been excluded by the conference's secularist organisers. One Turkish philosopher was furious: 'You would expect a broad discourse on Islamic thought and philosophy at a philosophy congress in a Muslim country,' said Dr Bekir Karliga from Marmara University. 'Wouldn't people from 83 countries wonder perhaps if there is any philosophy in Turkey? Wouldn't they be curious to know what philosophers in Turkey, a Muslim country, might have to say on the philosophy of Islam?' Apparently not, thought the secularists.

At the same venue, on the same evening, another cultural clash was about to take place as 7,000 guests attended the wedding of the prime minister's son to 17-year-old Reyhan Uzuner in an arranged marriage. Nearly the entire female contingent present were as carefully covered as the bride, whose lacy veil was fitted over a turban. Amid all the Islamic trappings, one guest stood out like a sore thumb: the best man, Italian prime minister Silvio Berlusconi. An odd choice perhaps given that in September 2001 the Italian enraged Muslims worldwide when he suggested Western civilisation was 'superior' to Islam.

Surprisingly, when the inevitable awkward moment occured, the Turkish dailies largely excused Berlusconi's and instead excoriated the bride for her ignorance of 'European manners' when she visibly recoiled at the Italian's attempt to plant a chivalrous kiss on her gloved hand.

THE RISE OF ISLAMIC CHIC

The wedding also provided a perfect example of how the the issue of Islam has infiltrated the world of fashion. The day after the nuptials, numerous journalists commented not only on the abundance of turbans, but the variety of colours, patterns and silky fabrics out of which the headgear was made. Such fancified Muslim dress is part of a new wave of 'Islamic chic' that is sweeping Istanbul.

Bizarrely, the fickle world of fashion is proving to be something of a force for unity. Designers, with their successful melding of traditional and modern influences, could well succeed where politicians fail. A leading exponent of this fashion harmony comes in the highly unlikely figure of Cemil Ipekçi, known as the Turkish Versace. He is about to create a sartorial revolution by dressing the big cheese himself, the new state-appointed head of the religious affairs directorate. A reformist, Ali Bardakoğlu has suggested that it's time for modern Muslims to embrace a new mentality. He intends to start by updating his *cüppe*, a ceremonial robe with full sleeves and long

Islam chic: white is the new black.

Brides flock to **Telli Baba**. *See p37.*

Istanbul idols

Turkey's population might be 99% Islamic, but the country's colourful history has yielded a strand of Islam which is remarkably flexible and multi-hued.

Take the Turkish phenomenon of the Islamic idol. Strictly speaking, Islam does not recognise the existence of saints, or any other intermediaries between the faithful and their God. But try telling that to the thousands of Turks who congregate at any of the city's 173 *türbes* (tombs), the burial places of *evliya*, or saintly persons. These tombs are believed to harbour the remains of *sahabe*, companions of the Prophet Mohammed, or Arab warriors.

With such illustrious figures laid to rest in these tombs, the *türbe* have an obvious appeal to devoted Muslims. But the various rites practiced by the assorted faithful who flock to them have little to do with Islam.

Some of these saintly monuments trace their roots back to Greek mythology, traces of which still remain in Anatolia. They also display evidence of shamanism as practiced by pre-Islamic Turkic tribes. At some *türbe*, a nearby tree is tightly embraced while the supplicant silently repeats his or her wish – it is believed that when the wish is granted the tree will sway. Those who desire a car shake their keys, and wannabe home-owners leave paper models of houses. Other ways of thanking holy benefactors include sacrificing a chicken or a sheep.

The most popular city tomb is that of **Telli Baba** (*see p242*), located on the European shores of the Bosphorus up near Rumeli Kavağı. It is said to house the female half of a pair of young lovers who died of anguish when their parents forbade them to marry. The boy's body, meanwhile, was tossed out to sea. Today, fishermen come here to pray for a good catch, and so do single women: if they take away a piece of golden wire from the tomb, legend has it that they'll snag a husband. Newlyweds also come here and tie a ribbon around a nearby tree for good luck.

But perhaps the best illustration of Istanbul's religious melting pot is rooted in tragedy, rather than legend. In 2001, Uzeyir Gariha, a prominent businessman and member of the Jewish community, was knifed to death by a crazed assailant as he visited the shrine of a Muslim mystic in Eyüp cemetery. One year later, the memorial service was a multicultural mosaic: it was held at former Greek Orthodox church Haghia Irene, featured mystical hymns sung in Hebrew by a Jewish choir and was followed by performances by four Mevlevi dervishes.

---

skirts, and his *sarik*, or turban. To achieve these ends, Bardakoğlu has turned to Ipekçi, a man best known for creating the vivid frock worn by Miss World 2002, as well as for his recent revelation that, yes, he is homosexual.

The prospect of the flamboyant Ipekçi dressing the chief imam is irresistible. The designer declared himself thrilled, both with Bardakoglu's easy acceptance of his sexuality and the chance to have a go at that nasty black, Arab-inspired gear. Ipekçi reckons that his grand designs have a pretty important historical supporter in the person of the Prophet Mohammed: 'The Prophet was big on colours like white, ivory, green and blue,' said Ipekçi.

Joining Ipekçi in the fashion-fusion stakes is Rabia Yalçin, who creates haute *tessetür* – exquisite designer veils. A wealthy 4X4-driving Istanbulu who decided early on that 'covered' didn't have to mean dowdy or invisible, the religiously-observant Yalçin stitched together some outfits for her own use. So impressed were her friends by her sense of style that she was inspired to go into business.

Despite the growing popularity of Islamic chic, fundamentalists fret that these sorts of gussied-up women are part of an insidious plot to undermine true believers and distort the true meaning of Allah-ordained modesty. But the people who count – and right now they include the headscarved wives of the prime minister, Istanbul's mayor, the foreign minister and the speaker of the house – flock to Yalçin's shows.

However, the prime minister is aware that conservative Muslims are getting fed up with the excesses of the new Islamic bourgeoisie. In a bid to quell growing discontent, he recently made news on the first day of Ramazan; he publicly called on members of his party to refrain from indulging in lavish *iftar* (breakfast) meals at five-star hotels and to display the piety appropriate to the holy month. So wary was he of offending Muslim sensibilities, the PM broke his own fast in a humble municipal tent.

In today's fraught religious climate, Istanbul's much-vaunted 'bridging of cultures' still remains undermined by some serious structural instabilities.

Architecture

A thousand years' worth of extraordinary structures.

In Istanbul, architecture is history. Those looking for contemporary cutting-edge building design will have to go elsewhere. High-profile projects, especially those with big names attached, are the preserve of cities with resources to spare. Istanbul hasn't any. It's all the municipality can do to provide basic accommodation for the continued influx of settlers. Added to which, the business of shoring up a failing city infrastructure and the need for quick-fix solutions leaves little opportunity for the promotion of a modern architectural culture.

This hasn't always been the case. Had *Architectural Digest* been around any time during the sixth to the 17th centuries, Istanbul's architects would have been front-cover material issue after issue. As the imperial capital of the Byzantines and then the Ottomans, for more than a millennium Istanbul was endowed with some of the most remarkable architecture the loaded treasury of an empire could buy. At the time they were built, Justinian's Church of St Sophia (now the **Haghia Sophia**, *see p69*) and Sinan's **Süleymaniye Mosque** (*see picture*) were marvels of engineering and milestones in artistic development to rival anything created in Europe. Styles developed here were exported far and wide, south through the Levant to Egypt and west throughout Greece and the Balkans.

When the era of the great empires passed, Istanbul became an assimilator of architectural styles from elsewhere, all reworked with a particular Turkish twist. So while it's certainly no Brussels or Vienna, Istanbul does harbour a little-known legacy of art nouveau twists and fancies. No less interesting is the reaction to this referencing of Europe, which manifested itself in a new, equally eclectic, national architecture movement that briefly flourished following the birth of the Turkish republic. So even if there isn't much to excite in glass and steel, Istanbul's legacy in stone is sufficiently rich and vast to offer more than ample compensation.

ARCHES, VAULTS AND DOMES

When, in AD 330, Constantine began to build his new capital on the Bosphorus, 'Nova Roma' was literally that, a new Rome constructed in the same style as the old one, but a thousand miles to the east. The change in location proved significant, as the proximity to Asia Minor and Syria resulted in an infusion of new ideas and methods. Very quickly the traditional Roman column-and-lintel way of building, inherited from the Greeks, gave way to a more fluid architecture based on arches, vaults and domes. Supplanting stone, the smaller and more malleable unit of the brick became the building material of choice.

Although Constantine's city boasted great secular structures, including fortified walls, forums, a hippodrome and an imperial palace (none of which survive in their original form), it's the churches he built that most came to symbolise the Byzantine style. Originally these took two distinctive forms: longitudinal basilicas, usually with three aisles, and 'centralised' churches, which were circular, square or octagonal. Through a merging of the two a characteristic Byzantine form emerged. Istanbul's oldest surviving church, St John of Studius (the ruins of which stand just east of Yedikule Station: *see p93*), was built in AD 463, a century and a quarter after Constantine's death. It's a basilica in that it has three aisles, but it's also nearly square in plan.

Development continued during the reign of the emperor Justinian (AD 527-565), possibly the greatest builder in the city's history. He was patron to four great churches: SS Sergius and Bacchus, now the **Küçük Haghia Sophia Mosque** (*see p77*); the rebuilt **Haghia Eirene** (*see p72*); the Church of the Holy Apostles, which was quarried for the Fatih Mosque; and the great cathedral of **Haghia Sophia**. What distinguished these structures from all that had come before was the dome. Domes had indeed been built previously, but never on this scale. With Haghia Sophia, Justinian's goal was to enclose the greatest space possible, creating a physical impression of the kingdom of God, one that was tended by the emperor. To achieve this he is said to have eschewed traditional builders and master craftsmen and instead employed the services of two mathematicians. Such was the impression created that the huge dome was described by Byzantine historian Procopius (a contemporary of Justinian) as 'appearing to be suspended from heaven by a golden chain'.

Byzantine innovations elsewhere included the **city walls** (*see pp93-4*) erected early in the fifth century by Theodosius II. These also made use of vaulting to support the floors in the 192 towers that punctuated their length. Vaults and domes underground rather than above ground were employed to create Constantinople's distinctive cisterns, of which there were more than 30 (*see p74*).

Post-Justinian, the Byzantine empire was to continue for close to another 800 years, during which time architectural styles evolved further. No emperor ever tried to match Justinian's audacious cathedral. Instead, later structures tended to be more modest in size and more harmoniously proportioned. Decoration came to play a larger part. For all its spatial grandeur Haghia Sophia is dull, dull, dull on the outside, whereas surviving later churches such as **St Saviour in Chora** (*see p92*) and

the 12th-century Church of the Pantocrator (now the **Zeyrek Mosque**; *see p89*) employ multiple domes, narthexes and apses executed in alternating bands of brick and roughly dressed stone. Glazed pottery set into the external walls forms friezes that echo interior mosaics and tiling, which flourished in the later Byzantine period following the miserable repressions of the Iconoclastic era (*see p10*). These buildings are thoroughly charming and deserve much greater attention than the few visitors they generally receive.

> **'Istanbul was endowed with some of the most remarkable architecture the loaded treasury of an empire could buy.'**

DOMES AND MINARETS

Ottoman architecture is often presented as essentially a continuation of the Byzantine tradition, but that's an oversimplification. Established in the 14th century, it grew out of the development of a great many architectural influences all over Anatolia, most notably the Selçuks. But, like the Byzantines, especially those of the early era, the Ottomans shared a predilection for centrally-planned structures topped by big domes. In that respect, the Haghia Sophia was inspirational. More than that, it was a benchmark. A great challenge.

Once the Ottomans had captured the city in 1453 the task of constructing a dome larger than Justinian's was to occupy imperial architects for more than a century. It was eventually achieved by a masterbuilder named Sinan (*see p40* **Keeping up with the domes's**) during the reign of Sultan Süleyman the Magnificent, although the dome in question graced a mosque in Edirne, not the capital.

Islam also defined how Ottoman architecture would develop. An egalitarian religion with no hierarchical orders, no saints in need of side chapels, no use for obfuscating trappings like naves and apses, its mosques required nothing more than a single, large, open space with as little clutter as possible. A domed central chamber proved to be the best way of achieving this. Ottoman architects were perpetually questing to minimise the number of columns and supports needed. That's what all the half domes are about, extending the internal space while spreading the structural load. It's almost incidental that the external effect is so beautiful – a cascade of gracefully descending curves. Slender, pencil-pointed minarets, originally

Keeping up with the domes's

If there was a poll to name the person who's made the single biggest contribution to Istanbul, in whatever way, odds are that name would be Mimar Sinan. He was chief of imperial architects under Süleyman I 'the Magnificent' and two successive sultans, and it's quite likely Süleyman would never have been considered quite so magnificent if wasn't for the legacy of Sinan.

Born around 1490 into a Christian family in central Turkey, Sinan was taken into the sultan's service as part of an annual levy of Christian boys. Trained as a military engineer, he served in seven of Süleyman's campaigns before being appointed chief imperial architect in 1538. He constructed his first mosque in Aleppo, Syria, that same year, and by the time he died exactly 50 years later he'd racked up an incredible 477 buildings, of which more than 100 were mosques. Pretty much single-handedly, Sinan wrote the stylebook for Ottoman architecture, in particular developing the typology of the great imperial mosque as a single main domed square surrounded by half domes and domed side aisles. This he exhibited to near perfection in his **Süleymaniye Mosque** (pictured p38), which set the pattern for mosque-building for almost the next 200 years and continues to dominate the Istanbul skyline until today.

As with earlier mosques, the plan follows that of Hagia Sophia, with a huge dome flanked by two semi-domes. Sinan's genius was to support the whole structure on four piers, avoiding the need for additional columns or arcading, creating one immense unified enclosed space. From the outside the profile is the most beautiful on the skyline, a confection of rippling semi-domes. The buildings of the surrounding complex are also beautifully proportioned.

Sinan's genius wasn't confined to huge imperial buildings. The **Sokollu Mehmet Paşa Mosque** (see p77) demonstrates his ability to work in difficult, confined spaces, the sloping site proving no obstacle to designing one of the most beautiful of the city's smaller mosques.

However, according to his own writings, Sinan considered the Süleymaniye merely 'good workmanship', withholding his pride instead for his Selimiye Mosque in Edirne: 'Architects of any importance in Christian countries consider themselves far superior to Muslims, because until now the latter haven't accomplished anything comparable to the dome of Haghia Sophia. Thanks to the All Powerful and the favour of the sultan, I have succeeded in building a dome for Sultan Selim's mosque that surpasses that of Haghia Sophia.'

Over 200 buildings credited to Sinan still stand, most in either Istanbul or Edirne. Apart from Süleymaniye and Sokollu Mehmet Paşa Mosque, the most prominent in Istanbul are the **Rüstem Paşa Mosque** (see p86) and **Şehzade Mosque** (see p89).

intended as platforms for the five daily calls to prayer, frame the composition, while surrounding courts keep the secular city at bay.

Mosques also served as a focal point for related institutions, such as a theological school (*medrese*), hospital (*daruşşifa*), library (*kitaplık*), mausoleums (*türbe*), public kitchen (*imaret*) and even public baths (*hamam*). Such complexes were known as *külliyes*.

Istanbul's Ottoman architectural glory is the city's most photogenic asset, with a series of great mosques and *külliyes* dominating the skyline. Tragically, although the empire survived for almost half a millennium, in terms of building achievements it peaked as early as the 16th century. Even the much-admired **Sultanahmet Mosque** (see p74), built across from the Haghia Sophia in the 17th century, is no more than a reprise of what Sinan had achieved a century earlier.

FRILLS AND LACE

As the Ottoman empire declined so European influence made itself felt. This was most definitely not a good thing. From the early 17th century to the mid 18th century much of Europe had undergone a flirtation with baroque (originally a term of abuse deriving from the Italian word *barocco*, meaning a contorted idea) and rococo (from the French *rocaille*, used to describe a certain type of shell-and-pebble decoration in the 16th century and with definite derogatory overtones). So to the Ottoman simplicity and clarity of function was wedded the decorative excesses and indulgences of these decadent and redundant imported stylings. Their bastard offspring goes by the name of 'Turkish Baroque'. One of the earliest and most accessible examples is the **Nuruosmaniye Mosque** (see p83) beside the Grand Bazaar, completed in 1755. Its large

dome rests on four huge semicircular arches
filled with long vertical windows that brighten
the interior, but the absence of semi-domes
makes the profile appear stumpy

By the 19th century, European styles were
almost completely dominant, with the 'Turkish'
dropping out of 'Turkish Baroque' altogether.
Rather than mosques or religious institutions,
the defining structures of the time are palaces.
Dolmabahçe (*see p102*), for example, is a good
illustration of the changes taking place in
Istanbul architecture at the time. It was the
work of the Armenian Balyan family, who for
almost a century were the most important and
influential architects in the empire. The elders
of the family got their knowledge of Western
building styles from drawings and etchings
brought by travellers and diplomats; younger
sons were sent to study at the École des Beaux-
Arts in Paris. As a result Dolmabahçe is a
showy mix of baroque and neoclassicism, with
interiors designed by Sechan, who had also
done the interiors of Garnier's grand Paris
Opera House. Further palaces at **Çırağan**
(*see p103*) and **Beylerbeyi** (*see p110*) are also
the work of the Balyans. A younger Balyan is
responsible for the dynasty's most appealing
work, Ortaköy's **Mecidiye Mosque** (*see
p103*), built 1853-5. It's still a muddle of
competing influences but benefits from a
superb waterside site, strangely improved
by the backdrop of the high-tech Atatürk
suspension bridge.

STAMBOUL NOUVEAU

It wasn't just foreign architectural influences
making their way to Istanbul, but foreign
architects too. Sir Charles Barry, who designed
the Houses of Parliament in London, knocked
up a neo-renaissance **British embassy**
building (1845), now the consulate: *see p99*.
A German named Jachmund designed **Sirkeci
Station** (*see p85*), terminus of the Orient
Express. The prolific Swiss-born Fossati
brothers, for a time official architects to Czar
Nicholas I, designed a handsome embassy
(now consulate) for the Russians (1837) and
another for the Dutch (1855), both on lower
Istiklal Caddesi. They also undertook a major
restoration of the Haghia Sophia in 1847-9.
And an Italian, Raimondo D'Aronco, introduced
Istanbul to art nouveau.

The existence of Istanbul's art nouveau
heritage generally comes as a surprise but at
the turn of the 19th century, suburbs such as
Galata and Pera (now Beyoğlu) were as wealthy,
influential and style-conscious as any in Europe
and it was only natural that they should import
international architectural fashions. D'Aronco
lived in the city between 1893 and 1909, serving

Şeyh Zafir Complex.
See p42.

Floral and cherubic: the **Botter House** by Raimondo D'Aronco.

ten years as chief of the imperial architects. Foremost among his existing buildings is the **Botter House** at Istiklal Caddesi 475-7. A seven-storey residence built for a Dutch couturier to the imperial court, it has a narrow frontage 'overgrown' with cast-iron flora. It would be a national treasure in any European capital, but here its interior was ripped out in the 1960s as part of a conversion to a bank and it now lies semi-derelict and decaying. D'Aronco's nearby and equally excellent **Laleli Fountain** (Laleli Çeşmesi) at the corner of Laleli Çeşme Sokak and Şair Ziya Paşa Caddesi beside the Galata Tower is happily in a better state of repair. Also worth a look are the same architect's **Şeyh Zafir Complex** (see p103) on Yıldız Caddesi in Beşiktaş and the **Egyptian consulate** (see p105) in the Bosphorus suburb of Bebek.

BRUTAL BUT TURKISH

European style went out of fashion overnight in 1923 when the Turkish National Assembly declared the founding of the republic. In keeping with the spirit of the times, there was a new popular building style, the First National Architectural Movement (FNAM), pioneered by Vedat Tek and Kemalettin Bey, a former student of Jachmund. FNAM was all about reinterpreting Turkey's classical Ottoman heritage using contemporary Western building technology. Notable examples include Bey's **Hotel Merit Antique** (see p49) in Laleli, with its typically wavy Ottoman roofs and Islamic-styled arches executed in reinforced concrete, and an office building known as **4 Vakıf Hanı** at Hamidiye Caddesi 64-8 in Eminönü, with gratuitous frilly domes plonked at the corners of an otherwise dour block.

Flirtations with modernism occurred in the 1930s, but that always seemed more suited to Ankara, the country's recently created 'modern' capital. In Istanbul, architects generally continued to prefer to reference the city's centuries of architectural heritage. Sedad Eldem may be Turkey's best-known 20th-century architect, responsible for more than 100 buildings over a 50-year career. His work often straddled the line between slavish historicism and clever re-rendering. His **Taşlık Coffee House** (now the Şark restaurant in the Swissôtel complex, Maçka), is a 17th-century Bosphorus mansion (yalı) slightly adapted and rebuilt with modern materials. Sadly the hotel has done some revisionism of its own and made disfiguring changes to Eldem's original design.

For the past 50 years, overriding all style issues have been two factors: low cost and maximum return. The architectural result is a lot of badly poured concrete and anonymous off-the-peg designs allowing for little creative input. The cause of good architecture has also not been helped any by the lack of regulated urban planning, seen to most hideous effect in the mirrors-and-Meccano **Gökkafes** ('Skyscraper'), the ugly pink-capped block that towers over central Istanbul – and is now occupied by the Ritz-Carlton hotel.

The one showpiece project of recent times has been the new 82,000-seater **Olympic Stadium** (completed 1991), designed by French architects Macary and Zublena, who also designed the Stade de France in Paris. Located in the Ikitelli district out near the airport, it's currently appreciated by fans of the football club Galatasaray, who play their home games out here.

yes

please clean my room

bentleyhotel

Where to Stay

Where to Stay   **45**

Features

The best Hotels   45
The chain gang   46
Bed, board and legends   52

Where to Stay

Breakfast surrounded by Sultanahmet minarets or stay within crawling distance of Beyoğlu's bars and clubs.

Curiously, Istanbul's hotel scene has developed little in recent years. A few more big boys have arrived, notably the **Ritz-Carlton** (*see p46*), and there's the new, sleek-lined **Bentley** (*see p60*) with the city's first 'boutique' beds, but otherwise, it's all rumours. Several landmark sites have apparently been earmarked by the city treasurer for development, including part of Haydarpaşa station and the grand post office in Sirkeci, but the builders have yet to begin. Philippe Starck came and sniffed around in 2001 but in the end did nothing.

Still, as a long-standing tourist mecca that has been accommodating curious Westerners since the middle of the 19th century, Istanbul is thick with hotels. At the same time, as a long-standing tourist mecca, a lot of the city's hotels are a bit on the well-worn side of things. Even some of the high-end, five-star places have been around since the 1950s and are seriously showing their age. In some cases, age has been used to good effect. Istanbul does have a nice semi-hip line in 'Ottoman' boutique hotels. These are Ottoman-era houses imaginatively converted into some unique accommodation. In many cases it goes a lot further than mere conversion, as in some instances the original building has been demolished and then reconstructed entirely from scratch in concrete, with set-dressing applied on top. So guests get nostalgia and all modern amenities in one go.

The first of these Ottoman boutique places was **Ayasofya Pansiyonları** (*see p51*), founded by the Turkish Touring and Automobile Association, which funded the project with revenues accrued from issuing import documents to cars. Committed to the promotion of Turkish culture, the TTAA went on to open several similar hotels, with the pick of the bunch being perhaps **Yeşil Ev** (*see p51*). In the late 1990s, policy changes deprived the TTAA of import licence revenues and the organisation's money dried up, but other businesses and individuals have picked up the baton, such as American Ann Nevans at the **Empress Zoe** (*see p52*).

LOCATION, LOCATION AND LOCATION

There are basically two choices: south of the Golden Horn or north of the Golden Horn. Whichever you choose, expect to spend plenty of time in taxis, as most visitors split their time about equally between the two areas. South of the Golden Horn means mosques, the Grand Bazaars and all the tourist sights of Sultanahmet. This has traditionally been the centre for the city's budget and mid-range accommodation. Almost all the cheapest options are on and around Akbıyık Caddesi and Utangaç Sokak, two parallel streets east of the Haghia Sophia. But despite its reputation for budget places, increasingly the area is moving upmarket and now has one of the best deluxe options in the **Four Seasons** (*see p47*). This is also the area in which you'll find all the Ottoman boutique places. Most Sultanahmet hotels have rooftop breakfast terraces and it's hard to beat morning coffee and croissants nestled between the domes of the Haghia Sophia and Blue Mosque – a classic cleavage if ever there was one.

The best Hotels

When money is no object
For the epitome of luxurious living, check in to the **Four Seasons**, regularly voted one of the world's best hotels. See p47.

For high style on a low budget
Small but perfectly formed, the **Empress Zoe** is sheer (affordable) class. See p52.

For wilfully wacky decor
Gypsy colours and circus-stylings make the **Kybele Hotel** about as fun as board and lodgings get. See p55.

For murderous passions
Agatha Christie found inspiration at the **Pera Palas** and a British ambassador survived a bomb. See p52.

For Hemingway fans
He didn't much care for 'old Constan' but probably appreciated the fine little bar at the **Büyük Londra Hotel**. See p63.

For breakfast with a view
Minarets, domes and seascapes come as part of the package with near enough every hotel in Sultanahmet. See pp47-59.

North of the Golden Horn is the business and entertainment district of Beyoğlu. There are plenty of backstreet mid-range places that put you right among the shopping, restaurants, bars and clubs. They lack the views or romance of the Sultanahmet hotels, but are just a short stagger home to bed at night. Most of the city's high-rise, high-end options are clustered around Harbiye, an area of green parkland just north of Taksim Square.

As well as being close to Beyoğlu, Harbiye is conveniently situated for shopping trips to the fashionable areas of Nişantaşı and Teşvikiye. All the culture of old Istanbul is a ten-minute taxi ride away ($4 to $5), downhill and across the Galata or Atatürk bridges, although at the wrong time of day – morning and evening rush hours, for example – that can stretch to up to half an hour or more.

RESERVATIONS

In line with the basic economic principles of supply and demand, hotels don't come cheap in Istanbul. Competitively priced places book up quickly, particularly during the summer when they're choked with large tour groups, conventions and conferences. May to September, Christmas, New Year and national holidays (*see p271*) are the busiest times. Beware also of major cultural events like the various major international film, theatre and music festivals (*see chapter* **Festivals & Events**). At such times you definitely need to book your room well in advance.

Plenty of hotels now take bookings by email and there are also a few useful internet sites for bookings, notably **www.istanbulhotels.com**, which brings together about 80 of the city's hotels and offers discounts for online booking. Alternatively, **www.istanbul.hotelguide.net** provides links to local hotel websites.

If you arrive without a reservation there are several booking agents at Atatürk Airport in the international arrivals hall (at the opposite end to the tourist information desk). They have an extensive list of mainly three and four-star hotels and don't take any commission from the customer.

In all but a few of the high-end hotels, room rates include tax (18 per cent) and breakfast. Prices quoted in this book are high-season rates, which normally apply from the end of May to the beginning of September, at Christmas and New Year, as well as during national holidays. Outside these times you can expect a discount of up to 30 per cent. Rates are particularly open to bargaining in the mid-range and budget categories, especially if you can pay cash in foreign currency. Conversely, payments by credit card often incur a five per cent surcharge to cover the cost of processing. Most places happily accept dollars or sterling.

The chain gang

A growing number of global chains have branches in Istanbul (including the **Four Seasons**, see p47; and **Kempinski**, see p59), with more on the way. Other than the aforementioned two places, don't, as a rule, expect a great deal of individual character, but do rest assured that you'll get the same standard of service and level of comfort that you last found at the same chain's outlet in Dallas, Kuala Lumpur, Zurich... wherever, really.

● The **Hilton Istanbul** (Cumhuriyet Caddesi, Harbiye, 0212 315 6000, www.hilton.com) was first of the modern high-rise blocks to brutalise the skyline. Given the price bracket, it's far from exceptional in terms of rooms, decor and facilities, although the parkland setting is a bonus. It's a ten-minute walk north of central Taksim Square.

● The **Hyatt Regency Istanbul** (0212 225 7000, Taşkışla Caddesi, www.istanbul.hyatt. com.tr) is to be commended for keeping its building low. It scores high on business facilities, with an information library and private offices for rent and a luxury apart-hotel with its own separate check-in and elevators. It's a ten-minute walk north-east of Taksim Square.

● The **Ritz-Carlton** (0212 334 4444, Asker Ocaği Caddesi, www.ritzcarlton.com) occupies the appalling blue-glass block that dominates the city skyline. The interior is merely bland. Facilities are good and house restaurant Margaux (see p133) is excellent. You'll need a taxi to get anywhere.

● The **Swissôtel Istanbul The Bosphorus** (0212 326 1100, Bayıldım Caddesi 2, Maçka, www.swissotel.com) sits on the hillside above the Dolmabahçe Palace. Rooms are a exceptionally comfortable and packed with all the gimmickry a modern hotel can offer. Sports facilities are particularly good and the hotel has two fine restaurants in La Corne d'Or and Taşlık.

From prison to palace – the **Four Seasons**.

Listings in this guide are divided into the following categories: **Deluxe** (upwards of $250 a night for a double); **High-end** ($150-$250); **Mid-range** ($70-$150); **Budget** ($30-$70); and **Rock-bottom** (under $30).

South of the Golden Horn

Deluxe

Four Seasons

Tevkifhane Sokak 1, Sultanahmet (0212 638 8200/ fax 638 8210/www.fourseasons.com). Tram Sultanahmet. **Rates** $290-$520 single; $320-$550 double; $700-$2,500 suite (excluding tax). **Credit** AmEx, DC, MC, V. **Map** p289 N10.
Always a fairly elite sort of place, for 66 years this building served as the infamous Sultanahmet Prison, whose inmates included some celebrated political prisoners. In 1986 it was renovated and now sits at the very top of the city's hotel hierarchy. Underneath all the glamour, the building's original function remains evident in wall-top watchtowers and a central court which, if stripped of its flowers and shrubbery, takes little imagination to see as a prison yard. Cells have given way to 54 beautiful high-ceilinged rooms, a modest number that ensures intimacy and top-class service. There's an excellent gazebo restaurant (Seasons Restaurant, *see p125*) and if you can't afford a room here it's at least worth stretching the plastic for lunch.
Hotel services *Air-conditioning. Babysitting. Bar. Business services. Gym. Parking. Restaurant.*
Room services *CD player. Minibar. Room service. Safe box. Telephone: 2 lines. TV: cable; VCR. Voicemail.*

passionately in love!

cafe les bones

executive suit

if restaurant & bar

First Class

RICHMOND
HOTELS
ISTANBUL

İstiklal Caddesi No: 445 Tünel Beyoğlu 80670 İstanbul-Türkiye Tel: +90 212 252 54 60 Fax: +90 212 252 97 07
info@richmondhotels.com.tr www.richmondhotels.com.tr

• İstanbul • Ephesus Resort •Pamukkale Thermal • Pamukkale Savanna • Pamukkale SPA

Yeşil Ev. *See p51.*

High-end

Armada

Ahırkapı Sokak 24, Cankurtaran, Sultanahmet (0212 638 1370/fax 518 5060/www.armada hotel.com.tr). **Rates** $130 single; $150 double; $225 suite. **Credit** AmEx, MC, V. **Map** p289 O11.
Sandwiched between waterside Kennedy Caddesi and the suburban railway line in a middle-of-nowhere-seeming sort of area, the Armada scores low on location, although it is only a ten-minute walk up the hill to sight-studded Sultanahmet. However, most rooms have fantastic uninterrupted Bosphorus views and the building itself has been modelled on a row of 16th-century houses that formerly stood on the site. The lobby area is attractive with a terrapin pond and café, while the rooms (110 of them), if not exceptional, are certainly comfortable. If the budget doesn't stretch to the Four Seasons and the Yeşil Ev is packed, then of the few high-end options south of the Bosphorus, this is definitely one of the best.
Hotel services *Air-conditioning. Bar. Business services. Garden. Parking. Restaurant. Wheelchair access.* **Room services** *Minibar. Room service. Telephone. TV.*

Merit Antique

226 Ordu Caddesi, Laleli (0212 513 9300/fax 512 6390/www.merithotels.com). Tram Laleli. **Rates** $160 single; $200 double; $240 suite. **Credit** AmEx, DC, MC, V. **Map** p288 H10.
Head and shoulders above everything else in this district of mostly mediocre, mid-range places, the architecturally significant Merit Antique (*see p42*)

is frequented by a curious blend of holidaying Europeans and seriously besuited businessmen. Transformed in a 1986 facelift, the four original buildings are linked by an airy atrium in which several restaurants, including the only kosher venue in town, compete for space with an aviary of chattering birds and a glitzy water feature. Ostentation rather than style marks the decor but the comfortable rooms are more restrained. Despite the double glazing you'd be wise to think twice about a room overlooking the ceaseless traffic of Ordu Caddesi.
Hotel services *Air-conditioning. Bar. Business facilities. Gym. Parking. Restaurant. Swimming pool.* **Room services** *Minibar. Room service. Telephone. TV: cable.*

Polat Renaissance Istanbul Hotel

Sahil Caddesi, Yeşilyurt (0212 414 1800/fax 414 1970/www.renaissancehotels.com). **Rates** $110-$143 single; $120-$145 double; $250 suite. **Credit** AmEx, DC, MC, V.
Our airport hotel of choice, the Polat Renaissance (part of the Marriott group) is just a five-minute taxi ride from the international terminal in the coastal suburb of Yeşilköy (although that does mean that it's 18 kilometres, or 12 miles from the city centre). A striking blue-glass, 27-storey skyscraper by the sea, it's ultra-modern and stylish with a soaring central atrium overlooked by balconies. At least half of the 390 rooms have views over the Marmara. The full range of facilities includes a heated outdoor pool.
Hotel services *Air-conditioning. Bar. Business services. Childcare. Gym. Handicapped-equipped rooms. Restaurant. Swimming pool.* **Room services** *Minibar. Room service. Telephone. TV: cable.*

A hotel that thinks it's a street – **Ayasofya Pansiyonları**.

Yeşil Ev

Kabasakal Caddesi 5, Sultanahmet (0212 517 6785/ fax 517 6780/yesilevhotel@superonline.com). Tram Sultanahmet. **Rates** $120 single; $160 double; $250 Pasha's room. **Credit** AmEx, MC, V. **Map** p289 N10.

Flagship of the TTAA's fleet of restored Ottoman properties, this place, the 'Green House', enjoys an unrivalled location on a leafy cobbled street midway between the Haghia Sophia and Sultanahmet Mosque. A stately wooden mansion painted green (of course) and white, it's like some grand country house. To step over the threshold is to enter the set of a 19th-century costume drama, with every room decked out with repro furniture, wood-panelled ceilings, creaky parquet flooring and artfully positioned antique rugs. If yours is an Ottoman fantasy, then go for room 31, the 'Pasha's Room', which boasts its own hamam. Best of all is the well-kept shady garden, in summer the venue for a fine café (*see p143*) and a restaurant. This place is popular and with only 19 rooms advance booking is essential.

Hotel services *Cafe. Restaurant. Room service.* **Room services** *Minibar. Telephone.*

Mid-range

Hotel Ararat

Torun Sokak 3, Sultanahmet (0212 516 0411/ fax 518 5241/www.ararathotel.com). Tram Sultanahmet. **Rates** $50 single; $55 double; $65 room with view; $70 triple. **Credit** MC, V. **Map** p289 N11.

Noting the success of the Empress Zoe, the young Turkish owners of the Ararat called in its architect Nicos Papadakis to have a go at their place. It opened early in 2000 and if the results aren't quite as inspired as the Zoe, the Ararat still breaks the mould with marbled walls and an effective orange-tinged colour scheme that works well with the dark stained-wood floors. Rooms vary greatly in terms of size and comfort: some are windowless boxes while others have wooden four-posters for guests to loll in while getting an eyeful of the Sultanahmet Mosque over the road, which looms at the window threatening to muscle its way in. Breakfast area on the roof.

Hotel services *Bar.* **Room services** *Telephone.*

Ayasofya Pansiyonları

Soğukçeşme Sokak, Sultanahmet (0212 513 3660/ fax 513 3669/www.ayasofyapensions.com). Tram Gülhane. **Rates** $90 single; $120 double; $200 suite. **Credit** AmEx, MC, V. **Map** p289 N10.

This is the scheme that kicked off the whole Ottoman boutique hotel phenomenon. Constructed in the 1980s by the Turkish Touring and Automobile Association as pristine clones of buildings that once stood on the site, Ayasofya Pansiyonları is a row of pastel-painted clapboard-clad houses simply furnished in period style. Between them they provide 57 single and double rooms and four three-bedroom suites. The setting is fantastic, a narrow sloping cobbled lane squeezed between the high walls of Topkapı Palace and the back of Haghia Sophia. Breakfast is served in the garden or gazebo of the Konut Evi, a four-storey annexe of the hotel at the end of the street. At night the whole thing is lamp-lit. Walt Disney couldn't create more magic. **Hotel services** Bar. Parking. Restaurant. **Room services** Telephone.

Citadel

Kennedy Caddesi 32, Ahırkapı (0212 516 2313/ fax 516 1384/www.citadelhotel.com). **Rates** $70 single; $80 double; $125 suite. **Credit** MC, V. **Map** p389 O11.

Occupying a renovated and strikingly pink three-storey mansion, this Best Western affiliate has 25 rooms and six suites decked out in Barbie colours and the only thing between you and the Sea of Marmara is – alas – six lanes of speeding traffic. It's not far from the fish restaurants of Kumkapı, though, and the conservatory bar and decent restaurant lessen the feeling of isolation. The hotel does free airport pick-ups.
Hotel services Air-conditioning. Bar. Garden. Restaurants (3). **Room services** Minibar. Telephone. TV: satellite.

Dersaadet

Kuçuk Ayasofya Caddesi 5, Sultanahmet (0212 458 0760/www.dersaadethotel.com). **Rates** $90 single; $125 double. **Credit** MC, V. **Map** p289 M11.

Though less than five years old, the Dersaadet (one of the many former names for Istanbul) appears far more venerable thanks to some very attractive external wood cladding. Inside is all shiny and new but with a strong Ottoman influence in the decor (antique-style furniture, painted ceilings, brass chandeliers). There are 17 rooms on four floors, all very comfortable, though with no real views to speak of. Nicest of the lot is the 'Sultan's suite' ($165) with a lovely low wooden ceiling, big windows and a jacuzzi. There's a rooftop breakfast terrace and a pleasant, large seated reception on the ground floor. The place is owned and run by a family that has been in the hotel business for three generations; manager Deniz trained in New York.
Hotel services Air-conditioning. Safe. **Room services** Minibar. Telephone. TV: satellite.

Empress Zoe

Adliye Sokak 10, off Akbıyık Caddesi, Sultanahmet (0212 518 2504/fax 518 5699/www.emzoe.com). Tram Sultanahmet. **Rates** $65 single; $70-$100 double; $105-$150 suite. 10% discount for cash. **Credit** MC, V. **Map** p289 O11.

Named after a racy Byzantine regent (see p70), the Zoe is one of the best and quirkiest of the city's small hotels. Its sunken reception area incorporates parts of a 15th-century hamam. Guests should be nimble,

Bed, board and legends

Built in 1892 as the last stop on the Orient Express, the **Pera Palas** is the most fadedly aristocratic of hotels. It was built by the same company that ran the famed Paris-to-Istanbul trains and in the early days its pampered guests were carried on cushioned sedans from Sirkeci station to waiting hotel transport. Today, superseded in comfort and facilities by the modern sleek and efficient five-stars, the Palas is the preserve of a less exalted crowd than the statesmen, stars and spies that used to cross its still well-polished and buffed lobby, site of one successful and one failed assassination attempt.

Up a short flight of steps, the hotel lift is at the centre of a sweeping staircase and has large ornate gates, a velvet bench and a bellboy in brocaded livery. Rooms are off long corridors and a great many of the 145 have brass plaques with the names of famous past guests: Sarah Bernhardt, Greta Garbo, Mata Hari, Alfred Hitchcock and Jackie Onassis. One just says 'Petroleum Billionaire' while another belongs to Yakup Kadri Karaosmanoğlu, apparently a 'Well Known Writer'. Slightly better-known writer Agatha Christie wrote part of Murder on the Orient Express while staying here. The whole of the fourth floor is named in her honour (however, the rooms on this floor are the worst in the hotel and if you are offered Agatha's lodgings we recommend you decline). A bigger draw, attracting bus-loads of local schoolkids, is room 101, Atatürk's room, complete with original furniture, photos and such excellent presidential memorabilia as the Great Turk's driving goggles and Panama hat.

Rooms are not particularly luxurious but compensate in charm and idiosyncracies, including hardwood floors, brass beds and vast chrome-filled bathrooms. The Pera Patisserie is a fine little Viennese-style coffee shop, while the bar is the place to muse upon the decline of servile porters, silk-stocking glamour and lobby shoot-outs, rarities in the hotel industry of today.

Pera Palas

Meşrutiyet Caddesi 98, Tepebaşı, Beyoğlu (0212 251 4560/fax 251 4089/ www.perapalas.com). **Rates** $140 single; $220 double; $380 suite. **Credit** AmEx, DC, MC, V. **Map** p294 M4.
Hotel services Bar. Parking. Restaurant. **Room services** Minibar. Room service. Telephone. TV.

Less of the Ottoman at the
Ibrahim Paşa Hotel. *See p55.*

a time between us

things are more fun when shared with others,
but pampering yourself is so fulfilling.
you will enjoy the perfect harmony here.

this is bentley hotel istanbul.

Comfort in **simplicity**

bentleyhotel

Halaskargazi Cad. No.75 Harbiye, 80220 İstanbul Turkey
Tel: +90 212 291 77 30 (pbx) Fax: +90 212 291 77 40 www.bentley-hotel.com e-mail: istanbul@bentley-hotel.com

as rooms are reached up a tight wrought-iron spiral staircase (although there is an alternative side entrance). In contrast to the gilt and frills of most other 'period' hotels, the Zoe's 19 small rooms are tastefully decorated in dark wood and richly coloured textiles, enlivened by personal touches chosen by friendly proprietress and former San Franciscan Ann Nevans. A new wing of suites has recently been added and the gorgeous 'archaeological garden' has been expanded. Add a fine rooftop bar for a nightcap with a view and this place is sheer class from top to bottom.

Hotel services *Bar.* **Room services** *Telephone.*

Ibrahim Paşa Hotel

Terzihane Sokak 5, Sultanahmet (0212 518 0394/ fax 518 4457/www.ibrahimpasha.com). Tram Sultanahmet. **Rates** $75 single; $90 double; $140 deluxe. **Credit** AmEx, DC, MC, V. **Map** p289 M11.

Benefiting from a recent spruce-up, the Ibrahim Paşa is an absolute peach of a place. It's a cream-painted three-storey stone townhouse tucked round the corner from the Museum of Turkish and Islamic Art. It doesn't overplay the old Ottoman card and instead is stylishly modern, smart and bright, with just enough judiciously placed rugs and such to remind you that this is Istanbul. Of the 19 rooms, the nicest of the bunch are those on the front with large windows, even though the view is only a blank wall. There are plenty of minarets and domes on show from the rooftop terrace. It helps if guests like lolloping big sandy labradors.

Hotel services *Bar. Book exchange. Parking.* **Room services** *Air-conditioning. Minibar. Room services. Safe. Telephone. TV.*

Kariye Hotel

Kariye Camii Sokak 18, Edirnekapı (0212 534 8414/ fax 521 6631/www.kariyeotel.com). **Rates** $80 single; $110 double; $160 suite. **Credit** AmEx, MC, V. **Map** p290 D4.

Another 19th-century Ottoman residence stripped down and dressed up by the Turkish Touring and Automobile Association and pressed into service as a hotel. There are 26 rooms, all done out in an early 1900s fashion. Downstairs, the house restaurant, Asıtane (*see p127*), is renowned for its fine Ottoman cuisine. Next door is the Church of St Saviour in Chora (*see p92*), one of Istanbul's most essential sights. But the big snag is the location, right out by the old city walls and the best part of a half-hour's bus ride from Sultanahmet, or around $6 in a taxi. We can't think of a single plus to being out in this part of town, but if you had a reason to be around here, then this would be the place to stay.

Hotel services *Bar. Parking. Restaurant.* **Room services** *Minibar. Telephone.*

Kybele Hotel

Yerebatan Caddesi 33-5, Sultanahmet (0212 511 7766/fax 513 4393/www.kybelehotel.com). Tram Sultanahmet. **Rates** $60 single; $90 double; $110 treble or suite. 10% discount for cash. **Credit** MC, V. **Map** p289 N10.

Owners the Akbayrak brothers have a thing about vintage glass lamps, that much is obvious, as the interior is hung with 2,000 of them (so they say, we didn't count). The eccentricities continue, as every room is crammed with kilims, candlestands, empty bottles and other knick-knacks. Garish pink and green paint schemes heighten the sense of fun. It all makes sense when you learn that one of the brothers was formerly an antique dealer, while another spent three years with an Australian circus. The 16 bedrooms are smallish, particularly the singles, but they are comfortable enough and have beautiful en suite marble bathrooms. Breakfast is served in a courtyard as colourful as a Gypsy caravan.

Hotel services *Bar. Cafe. Library.* **Room services** *Air-conditioning. Minibar. Telephone.*

Hotel St Sophia

Alemdar Caddesi 2, Sultanahmet (0212 528 0973/ fax 511 5491/www.saintsophiahotel.com). Tram Gülhane. **Rates** $100 single; $160 double; $180 suite. **Credit** AmEx, DC, MC, V. **Map** p289 N10.

Right in the shadow of the Haghia Sophia and across the road from the Yerebatan Sarnıcı, this hotel is another conversion job on a 19th-century Ottoman house. Extensive renovations have perhaps left it a bit over-polished and low on atmosphere, but it can't be faulted in the comfort stakes. Of the 27 rooms, all

Empress Zoe. *See p52.*

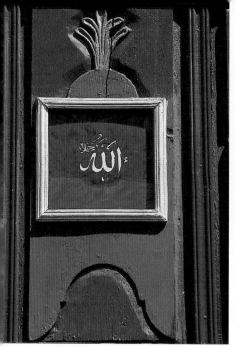

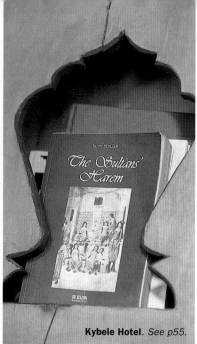

Kybele Hotel. *See p55.*

of them tastefully furnished and decorated in warm yellow tones, the suites on the top two floors have jacuzzis and balconies that overlook Justinian's great cathedral. In the warmer months, breakfast is served in a small and pleasant courtyard. A Best Western affiliate.

Hotel services *Air-conditioning. Babysitting. Bar. Parking.* **Room services** *Minibar. Room service. Telephone. TV: cable.*

Sarniç

Kuçuk Ayasofya Caddesi 26, Sultanahmet (0212 518 2323/www.sarnichotel.com). **Rates** $70 single; $85 double; $100 suite. **Credit** MC, V. **Map** p289 M11.
Owned and managed since 2001 by a feisty Dutch lady, Eveline Zoutendijk (who previously worked for the prestigious Four Seasons chain), the Sarniç is a tightly run little place with ambitions far above its modest appearance. The 16 rooms are immaculate (some are notably bigger than others) with new carpets, furnishings and bedding, en suite bathrooms filled with fluffy white towels and toiletries, and a complimentary copy of the monthly *Time Out Istanbul* on the bedside table. We like, we like. There is a top-floor dining terrace used for breakfast and for four-course evening meals of regional Turkish cuisine. The basement kitchens are also used for occasional cookery courses (Zoutendijk is a former cordon bleu chef, hence the focus on food) – contact the hotel for further details. Other than from the terrace, there are no views, but the hotel is only a few minutes' walk from the Hippodrome.

Hotel services *Air-conditioning. Internet access (free). Restaurant. Safe.* **Room services** *Minibar. Telephone. TV: satellite.*

Hotel Turkoman

Asmalıçeşme Sokak 2, off the Hippodrome, Sultanahmet (0212 516 2956/fax 516 2957/ www.turkomanhotel.com). Tram Sultanahmet. **Rates** $70 single; $110 triple. **Credit** AmEx, MC, V. **Map** p289 M11.
Set just slightly off the Hippodrome and about opposite the Egyptian obelisk, the Turkoman's rooftop terrace affords perhaps the best views of the Sultanahmet Mosque – or, as the hotel itself more lyrically puts it, 'You will catch the exciting and amazing Blue Mosque almost with your hands.' The bright, unfussy and very yellow rooms with brass bedsteads and parquet flooring also benefit from large windows, although in the summer months the mosque is hidden from the lower floors by foliage.

Hotel services *Cafe. Bar.* **Room services** *Minibar. Telephone.*

Budget

Berk Guesthouse

Kutlugün Sokak 27, Sultanahmet (0212 517 6561/fax 517 7715/www.berkguesthouse.com). Tram Sultanahmet. **Rates** $30-$60 single; $40-$80 double. **No credit cards. Map** p289 N11.
A family-run guesthouse in a quiet street next to the Four Seasons Hotel. The original house was owned by Grandma Yeşim, but that was torn down and rebuilt in the mid 1980s as a hotel that is now run by her grandchildren. In truth, for a place with such basic facilities, the hotel is on the pricey side, and extra charge for the deluxe is outrageous but lots of people appreciate the family atmosphere and there's

the the Four Seasons. It has ten freshly painted prim-rose-yellow rooms, which all have new en suites with hairdryers and heated towel rails. Couples with kids might appreciate the family rooms which come with a double and two twins and the best Marmara views in the hotel. There are more views from the roof terrace, which is slightly higher than those surrounding, so sightlines are unobstructed.
Room services *Air-conditioning. Safe. Telephone.*

Side Hotel & Pension

Utangaç Sokak 20, Sultanahmet (0212 517 2282/fax 517 6590/www.sidehotel.com). Tram Sultanahmet. **Rates** $15-$40 single; $25-$50 double. **Credit** V. **Map** p289 N11.

Clean and well looked-after by a genuinely friendly management who seem to get a kick out of having all these nice people come to stay with them. Most rooms, certainly those on the hotel side, have en suite bathrooms with modern plumbing, even shower cubicles in some cases – the Istanbul norm is just a showerhead flooding the bathroom. Rooms vary greatly, so take a look at a few before deciding. Pension rooms are slightly more basic, the cheapest with shared bathroom. As is standard with Sultanahmet hotels, there's a rooftop terrace where breakfast is served. Free tea in the foyer and a small book-exchange shelf. Recommended.
Hotel services *Left luggage.* **Room services** *(hotel rooms only) Refrigerator. Telephone. TV.*

Hotel Uyan

Utangaç Sokak 25, Sultanahmet (0212 516 4892/fax 517 1582/www.uyanhotel.com). Tram Sultanahmet. **Rates** $30-$60 single; $60-$80 double. **Credit** MC, V. **Map** p289 N11.

A large attractive corner-sited hotel housed in a 75-year-old wooden building that until fairly recently was a family residence. Rooms (26 of them) are simply furnished and airy, and a small bathroom has been added in the corner of each. Main selling point – with so many similar places all competing for business, every hotel has to have its unique feature – is that the Uyan has the highest roof terrace in the immediate neighbourhood, so guests can watch the nightly sound and light show at Sultanahmet Mosque without moving farther than a few feet from their rooms. During the day, the terrace deck is private enough for sunbathing. The hotel offers free airport pick-ups.
Hotel services *Bar. Internet access.* **Room services** *Air-conditioning. Telephone. TV: cable.*

a whole bunch of regulars who check in year after year. There's a tiny walled garden where breakfast is served, as well as a lounge area and the standard roof terrace with minaret and Marmara views.
Hotel services *Safe.* **Room services** *Air-conditioning (extra). Refrigerator (some rooms). Telephone.*

Nomade Hotel

15 Ticarethane Sokak, Sultanahmet (0212 511 1296/fax 513 2404/www.hotelnomade.com). Tram Sultanahmet. **Rates** $50 single; $60 double; $75 treble. **Credit** MC, V. **Map** p289 N10.

The comfortable kilim-hung reception is perfect for watching the bustling pedestrian traffic outside, while the cushion-strewn rooftop terrace is one of the most scenic in Istanbul. In between lie 16 elegantly homely rooms (although some are notably better than others), with minimal mustard-hued decor, walnut furniture and ethnic bedspreads. French-educated twin sister proprietors Esra and Hamra ensure that standards remain high, and though there's no restaurant in the hotel, they also run the Rumeli Café (*see p121*) just across the road.
Room services *Telephone.*

Hotel Hanedan

Adliye Sokak 3, off Akbıyık Caddesi, Sultanahmet (0212 516 4869/fax 458 2248/www.hanedan hotel.com). Tram Sultanahmet. **Rates** $35 single; $55 double; $75 family room. 10% discount for cash. **Credit** AmEx, MC, V. **Map** p289 O11.

Recently upgraded and under new management, the Hanedan is now the smartest of a handful of independent hotels on this small cul-de-sac just south of

Rock-bottom

Orient Hostel

Akbıyık Caddesi 13, Sultanahmet (0212 517 9493/ fax 518 3894/www.orienthostel.com). Tram Sultanahmet. **Rates** $7 dorm bed; $17 single; $19 double. **Credit** AmEx, MC, V. **Map** p289 N11.

For years now, the Orient has been the mainstay of Istanbul's backpacker scene, base camp for a constant stream of the great unwashed and footloose

We are aware of your expectations...

Fast facts

108 rooms, 2 suites, 207 beds.
Room details: All rooms are equipped with direct dial telephone, shower & toilet, bathroom, TV, air conditioning, minibar, safe deposit and hair-dryer. Rooms are heated by central heating.

General facilities

This hotel also has air conditioning and central heating in public areas, Turkish bath, sauna, gym, steam bath and business room.

Wining & dining

There is a restaurant with 100 pax indoor capacity. The breakfast lounge can serve up to 100 pax. The lobby bar and pool bar will be serving for your leisure time.

Meeting facilities

There is 2 meeting hall with various equipment which includes overhead projector, slide projector, video player, TV, whiteboard, flipchart and sound equipment. The equipped meeting hall has a total capacity of 90 + 40 pax.

Sports & recreation

The indoor swimming pool is at your disposal for your swimming leisure.

Location

The distance from Atatürk Airport is 20 km.

THE MADISON HOTEL
★ ★ ★ ★

Recep Paşa Cd. No: 23   34437 Taksim / İSTANBUL
Phone: +90 212 238 54 60 (pbx)   Fax : +90 212 238 51 51
e-mail : themadisonhotel@superonline.com   internet : www.themadisonhotel.com.tr

tramping their way across Asia or down through the Middle East. Despite a clientele whose idea of adapting to local customs is to dispense with soap and other fascistic implements of personal hygiene, the place is kept commendably clean – even the much-abused shower cubicles and toilets are serviceable. As well as a whole gamut of backpackerish services, including cheap internet access and discounted airline tickets, the Orient has a lively social scene, including barbecues, belly-dancing (*see p218*) and film nights. There is also a women-only dormitory. **Hotel services** *Bar. Internet access, Left luggage. Restaurant. Safe. Telephone & fax. Travel agency.*

Sultan Tourist Hostel

Terbıyık Sokak 3, off Akbıyık Caddesi, Sultanahmet (0212 516 9260/www.sultanhostel.com). Tram Sultanahmet. **Rates** $7 dorm bed; $15 single; $20 double. **Credit** MC, V. **Map** p289 N11.
Another backpacker staple, virtually next door to the Orient, the Sultan has bright and airy singles, doubles and mixed-sex dormitories, although having only a single shower/toilet on each floor is a major drawback. There's a restaurant on top, as well as a bar, pub, disco, a games room with table tennis and darts, and a computer centre.
Hotel services *Bar. Book exchange. Internet access. Laundry. Left luggage. Restaurant. Safe. Telephone & fax. Travel agency.*

Yücelt Interyouth Hostel

Caferiye Sokak 6/1, Sultanahmet (0212 513 6150/ fax 512 7628/www.yucelthostel.com). Tram Gülhane or Sultanahmet. **Rates** $8 dorm bed; $14 single; $19 double. **Credit** AmEx, MC, V. **Map** p289 N10.
Before the Orient (*see p57*), there was the Yücelt, the overlanders' Istanbul hangout en route to the maharishis in the 1960s and '70s. Billy Hayes of *Midnight Express* fame stayed here prior to being busted and incarcerated, as did a young Billy Clinton (who of, course, never inhaled). The location is incredible, on the cobbled lane that runs right by the side of Haghia Sophia, and must have added a fair bit of magic to many a stoned evening. Today it's more like a school camp, with 320 beds for eager travel virgins, bunked up in six-bed dorms. Some very basic singles and doubles are also available. Huge range of facilities of a youth-club nature.
Hotel services *Bar. Internet access. Laundry. Left luggage. Restaurant. TV: satellite.*

North of the Golden Horn

Deluxe

Ceylan Inter-Continental

Asker Ocağı Caddesi 1, Taksim (0212 231 2121/fax 231 2180/www.interconti.com.tr). **Rates** $325-$443 standard room; $826-$4,425 suite. **Credit** AmEx, DC, MC, V. **Map** p293 P1.
Formerly the Sheraton, the Inter-Continental is an 18-floor Goliath and was, until recently, the highest hotel on the city skyline. The style is brash, the tone

set by a horrendous golden staircase spiralling its way up from the lobby area. Aversions to the decor aside, the hotel is plenty comfortable, with full facilities that even run to a golf simulator to keep your swing in. The pick of the dining offerings is the Safran on the very top floor, which combines excellent Ottoman cuisine with unsurpassable views. Vertigo sufferers should stay well back from the windows in the City Lights Bar next door. The hotel is a ten-minute walk from central Taksim Square.
Hotel services *Air-conditioning. Bar. Business services. Gym. Hamam. Handicapped suites. Health club. Parking. Restaurant. Swimming pool.* **Room services** *Minibar. Room service. Telephone. TV: cable.*

Çırağan Palace Hotel Kempinski

Çırağan Caddesi 32, Beşiktaş (0212 258 3377/ fax 259 6687/www.ciraganpalace.com). **Rates** $300-$790 standard room (excluding tax). **Credit** AmEx, DC, MC, V. **Map** p287.
A modern annexe to a 19th-century palace on the Bosphorus that was originally built in 1874 for Sultan Abdülaziz, an ill-fated ruler who disposed of himself with a pair of scissors in one of its chambers. In 1908 it became the seat of parliament but burnt down two years later. In the following decades, the ruins were used as a football stadium and outdoor swimming pool. In 1986, following ambitious rebuilding and restoration, parts of the original complex, together with additional new buildings, became an extraordinarily luxurious 310-room hotel under the management of the German Kempinski chain. In fact, only 12 suites are in the palace itself, along with the restaurants (including the splendid Laledan and Tuğra) and public rooms – the latter worth a look for the bizarre decor, described by one journalist as 'post-Orientalist psychotropic'. All other rooms are in the annexe. If you're paying out this much cash, then make sure to get rooms on the waterfront, not the park side, and hope that the weather's fine enough to make use of the stunning outdoor pool, which appears to flow into the Bosphorus (*see p236*). Armchair travellers should check out the excellent website.
Hotel services *Air-conditioning. Bars. Business services. Data ports. Disabled access. Gym. Hamam. Parking. Restaurant. Swimming pool.* **Room services** *Minibar. Room service. Telephone. TV: cable.*

The Marmara Istanbul

Taksim Square, Taksim (0212 251 4696/fax 244 0509/www.themarmara.com.tr). **Rates** $230-$315 single; $260-$345 double; $380-$1,000 suite. **Credit** AmEx, DC, MC, V. **Map** p295 P2.
Situated at ground zero on Taksim Square, this is definitely the place if you've a preference for city accommodation that places you right at the heart of the action. It's Turkish-owned (with a sister establishment in Manhattan) and maybe isn't quite as polished as some of the more recent international competition, but it definitely has the best buzz of any

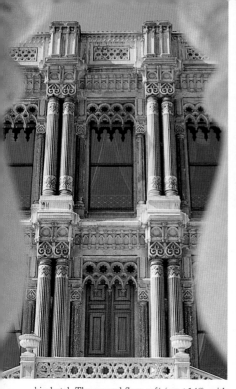

Çırağan Palace Hotel Kempinski.
See p59.

big hotel. The ground-floor café (*see p148*), with large picture windows overlooking the square, is an established meeting-place for the city's chic set, and the first-floor Aqua Lounge, across from reception, is always packed with conspicuously busy suited types socialising between conferences. Most of its 410 rooms have decent views but the best are from the top-floor Tepe Lounge.

Hotel services *Air-conditioning. Bar. Beauty salon. Business services. Dry cleaning. Gym. Hamam. Laundry. Parking. Restaurant. Swimming pool.* **Room services** *Data port. Minibar. Room service. Telephone. TV: cable.*

High-end

Bebek Hotel
Cevdet Paşa Caddesi 34, Bebek (0212 358 2000/ www.hotelbebek.com). **Rates** $135 street view; $235 water view. **Credit** AmEx, MC, V. **Map** p241.
Because of its distance from the centre and all the city's sights, this is primarily a business hotel but, God, it's gorgeous. It's just four storeys high and has only 21 suites, so it's intimate. The look is modern classic and the quality of finishing is exquisite – lots of polished dark wood, brown leather, flesh-coloured marble and rattan furniture. It looks like the place was kitted out at Harrods. But the real wow is the view. Half the rooms have balconies over the Bosphorus, boasting what is without doubt the most

perfect Istanbul panorama. Is it worth the extra $100? We'd have to say yes. However, if somebody screwed up and booked you into a room overlooking the street, never mind, you can always enjoy the same view from the bar downstairs (*see p151*).
Hotel services *Air-conditioning. Bar.* **Room services** *Internet ports. Minibar. Safe. Telephone. TV: satellite.*

Bentley Hotel
Halaskargazi Caddesi 75, Harbiye (0212 291 7730/ fax 291 7740/www.bentley-hotel.com). **Rates** $150 single; $200-$250 double; $300-$400 suite. **Credit** AmEx, MC, V. **Map** p287.
Istanbul's first (self-proclaimed) 'hip' hotel, the Bentley is a purpose-built, clean-lined affair with a minimalist chocolate-and-cream lobby that looks like the reception to an upmarket ad agency. Rooms are similarly smart and understated; the best are the corner rooms with curving glass walls (just a pity that there's no view to speak of). There are two penthouse suites with wine minibars, plasma screen TVs and espresso machines. One comes with a free adjacent single room suitable for a nanny or bodyguard. There's a basement fitness room, a first-floor restaurant (open to the public) and a lobby bar. Our only quibble is the rather duff location, miles north of Taksim and near nowhere in particular – although the high-class shopping districts of Nişantaşı and Teşvikiye aren't far away.

Hotel services *Air-conditioning. Bar. Business services. Fitness centre. Jacuzzi. Parking. Restaurant.* **Room services** *Internet ports. Minibar. Room service. Safe box. Telephone: 2 lines. TV: satellite.*

Divan Hotel

Cumhuriyet Caddesi 2, Elmadağ (0212 231 4100/fax 248 8527/www.divanoteli.com.tr). **Rates** $175 single; $210 double; $330 suite. **Credit** AmEx, DC, MC, V. **Map** p293 P1.

A quiet, Turkish-owned 169-room hotel which benefits from a decent location just north of Taksim Square. It's slightly old-school in appearance – very 1970s (which in Istanbul generally means that it actually dates from the mid 1980s) – but well-looked after. Rooms are large, but avoid those overlooking the main road, Cumhuriyet Caddesi, which is far too noisy to be silenced by mere double glazing.

Hotel services *Air-conditioning. Bar. Beauty salon. Business services. Gym. Parking. Restaurant.* **Room services** *Minibar. Room service. Telephone. TV: cable.*

Taksim Suites. *See p63.*

The Madison Hotel

Recep Paşa Caddesi 23, Taksim (0212 238 5460/ fax 238 5151/www.themadisonhotel.com.tr). **Rates** $60 single; $80 double; $250 suite. **Credit** AmEx, MC, V. **Map** p293 P1.

North-west of Taksim Square, between Tarlabaşı Bulvarı and Cumhuriyet Caddesi, are a series of parallel streets, quiet and almost residential in character, that are home to a handful of good mid-range hotels, including this one. The Madison is a modern, four-star hotel with decent-sized rooms. Apart from an insipid colour scheme, there's little cause for complaint. Bathrooms are small but elegant, decked out in marble, and some thoughtful person has even put an extra telephone next to the toilet. The indoor poolside bar is most pleasant.

Hotel services *Air-conditioning. Bar. Gym. Parking. Restaurant. Swimming pool.* **Room services** *Hamam. Minibar. Room service. Telephone. TV.*

Princess Hotel Ortaköy

Dereboyu Caddesi 10, Ortaköy (0212 227 6010/ fax 260 2148/www.ortakoyprincess.com). **Rates** $153 single; $200 double; $318-$466 suite. **Credit** AmEx, DC, MC, V.

This hotel is far from the sights, and few people other than those doing business up in nearby Levent and Maslak choose to stay in Ortaköy, but if scurrying around all the mosques isn't on your agenda, then this is an option well worth considering. It's a modern hotel with 82 generously sized rooms and a full complement of facilities. Most appealing is its proximity to the waterfront and its craft shops, bars, cafés and fish restaurants. From here you have the option of avoiding the traffic that clogs Istanbul's roads by catching a Bosphorus ferry all the way down to the sightseeing district of Sultanahmet.

Hotel services *Air-conditioning. Bar. Business services. Gym. Hamam. Parking. Restaurant. Swimming pool.* **Room services** *Minibar. Room service. Telephone. TV: cable.*

Ottoman Living Style

Richmond Hotel

Istiklal Caddesi 445, Beyoğlu (0212 252 5460/fax 252 9707/www.richmondhotels.com.tr). **Rates** $165 single; $195 double; $270 suite. **Credit** AmEx, MC, V. **Map** p294 M4.

Amazingly, the Richmond is the only hotel on the whole mile-and-a-half length of Istiklal Caddesi. Why this should be so is baffling, as the street is perfect for hotels; scenically cobbled, lined with shops, cafés and bars, traffic-free and with plenty of grand old apartment blocks ripe for conversion. What the Richmond has done is rip out the guts of an old building while retaining the façade and then dropped a brand-spanking-new structure in behind. If the interior isn't quite so clever, the hotel does have a good, relaxed atmosphere and a friendly staff. There are just 28 modern rooms, a lovely big seated reception, plus the obligatory rooftop restaurant and a decent bar.

Hotel services *Air-conditioning. Bar. Business services. Restaurant.* **Room services** *Internet ports. Minibar. Room service. Telephone. TV: cable.*

Taksim Square Hotel

Sıraselviler Caddesi 15, Taksim Square (0212 292 6440/fax 292 6449/www.taksimsquarehotel.com). **Rates** $60-$70 single; $80-$90 double. **Credit** AmEx, DC, MC, V. **Map** p295 P2.

Smart, modern – only around six years old – and bang in the centre of town, but one can only presume that the recent drop in visitor numbers to Istanbul has seriously hurt this place because room rates seem to have halved since we published the first edition of this guide (a double used to be $180). Of the 87 rooms, 32 of them have a view across rooftops to the Bosphorus; in the rest, guests have to be content with overlooking the street life down on busy Sıraselviler and the diners on the rooftop terrace of the Burger King opposite.

Hotel services *Air-conditioning. Bar. Business services. Restaurant.* **Room services** *Minibar. Room service. Telephone. TV.*

Taksim Suites

Cumhuriyet Caddesi 49, Taksim (0212 254 7777/ www.taximsuites.com). **Rates** $165 suite; $416 penthouse. **Credit** AmEx, MC, V. **Map** p293 P1.

A home away from home for business people who've seen one too many standard hotel rooms. Operated by the Divan hotel chain (*see p61*), the whole thing is beautifully done – the rooms are understated, done out in muted tones (oatmeal, beige and white, in a kind of Japan-meets-Sweden style) and offering, as the brochure puts it, 'Zen-like simplicity'. Except here, simplicity stretches to mean soaking in your own jacuzzi in a 109-square-metre, two-storey penthouse with a view of the Bosphorus. For those who can afford it, the suites offer a gorgeous environment in which to 'live' and work, and they have an excellent location just minutes from Taksim Square.

Hotel services *Air-conditioning. Business services. Gym. Sauna.* **Room services** *CD player. Internet portal. Telephone. TV: cable. Voice mail.*

Büyük Londra Hotel.

Mid-range

Büyük Londra Hotel

Meşrutiyet Caddesi 117, Tepebaşı (0212 245 0670/ fax 249 1025). **Rates** $60 single; $80 double; $100- $150 'super' rooms. **Credit** AmEx, MC, V. **Map** p294 M3.

It was built in 1892, so it's roughly the same age as the nearby Pera Palas (*see p52* **Bed, board and legends**). But whereas the Pera Palas is like some grand old sleep-in museum, the Londra is homely and eccentric. Caged parrots peer dolefully out of their cages on the windowsills in the lounge-bar (*see p144*). Portable coal burners, wind-up gramophones, valve radios and other ancient junk clutters the corridors. Hemingway stayed here in 1922, sent by the *Toronto Daily Star* to cover the Turkish war of independence, and the place is still favoured by artists, writers and film crews, many of whom are returning customers. Some of the rooms are a little down-at-heel but they are clean. The management is in the process of upgrading the place and the upper floors now have 'super' rooms with double glazing, plush carpets and even jacuzzis.

Hotel services *Bar.* **Room services** *Refrigerator. Telephone.*

Galata Residence

Selek Sokak 27, off Bankalar Caddesi, Karaköy (0212 2924841/fax 244 2323/www.galata residence.com). **Rates** $60 for an apartment for two; $100 for an apartment for four (excluding tax). **Credit** MC, V. **Map** p292 M6.

An apartment hotel with history. The building formerly belonged to an important Levantine banking family, the Kamondos, who gave their name to the arty public staircase (see p97) that leads up to the residence from Voyvoda Caddesi, the old banking street of 19th-century Pera. It later served as a Jewish school. In recent times, the solid brick building has been split into 16 comfortably furnished apartments, each of which sleeps four. Every unit is furnished in a homely sort of way, maybe a bit maiden-auntish, but certainly not objectionable, and each has its own fully equipped kitchen. There's a restaurant on the roof and a bare-brick vaulted cellar café. The location is a big plus, close enough to walk over the bridge to Eminönü and the bazaar area and just down the hill from the Galata Tower and Beyoğlu. Discounted rates are available for extended stays. **Hotel services** Air-conditioning. Parking. Restaurant. **Room services** Kitchenette. Room service. Safe. Telephone. TV: cable.

Hotel Residence

Sadri Alışık Sokak 19, off Istiklal Caddesi, Beyoğlu (0212 252 7685/fax 243 0084/www.cantur.com.tr). **Rates** $30 single; $54 double; $80 suite. **Credit** AmEx, DC, MC, V. **Map** 309 O3.

A bit difficult to find, tucked away up a narrow side street, but worth the effort of searching. The rooms, though small, are bright and very well-equipped. The location is great too, right among the bars and nightlife of Beyoğlu. Unlike many other places in the area, the Residence doesn't accept short-stay customers, so you won't be woken by things going bump, bump, bump in the night. Note that the prices we were quoted in person (given above) are far below those that were listed on the official rate card hung at reception – in other words, rates fluctuate hugely depending on business.
Hotel services Air-conditioning. Bar. Restaurant. **Room services** Minibar. Room service. Telephone. TV.

Villa Zurich

Akarsu Yokuşu Caddesi 44-6, Cihangir (0212 293 0604/fax 249 0232/www.hotelvillazurich.com). **Rates** $40 single; $60 double. **Credit** AmEx, MC, V. **Map** p295 O4.

Ten minutes' walk down Sıraselviler Caddesi from Taksim Square in the *yabancı* (foreigner) neighbourhood of Cihangir, the Villa Zurich is conveniently close to the centre but also pleasantly removed from all the fuss. Cihangir has a good local feel with small grocers, butchers and other essential businesses mixed in with the odd Western-style café or continental-style charcuterie catering for the area's high density of expats. The hotel is vaguely European in character, with restrained decor and 43 comfortable, well-equipped guestrooms. Breakfast is taken on the rooftop restaurant and there's a superb fish restaurant in the Doğa Balık (see p131). **Hotel services** Air-conditioning. Bar. Restaurant. Parking. **Room services** Minibar. Room service. Telephone. TV.

Budget

Hotel Avrupa

Topçu Caddesi 30, Talimhane, Taksim (0212 250 9420/fax 250 7399). **Rates** $25-$30 single; $30-$39 double. **Credit** MC, V. **Map** p293 O1.

In business since 1966, which makes it a relative old-timer round here, the Avrupa has recently been spruced up with a new paint job and some refurnishing. Brightly painted, unfussy rooms with small en suite bathrooms are good value. There's a breakfast room, but no restaurant or bar – not really a problem so close to Taksim Square. **Room services** Telephone.

Hotel Monopol

Meşrutiyet Caddesi 223, Tepebaşı, Beyoğlu (0212 251 7326/fax 251 7333). **Rates** $24 single; $34 double; $60 suite. **Credit** MC, V. **Map** p294 M4.

The Monopol is the best of a row of otherwise samey mid-range hotels. Despite the early-1980s look of the decor, the hotel has been open for less than ten years. The 75 rooms with en suites are a good size and well equipped. Management needs to tighten up though: *Time Out*'s photographer was checked into a room with an unemptied ashtray and filthy towels. Still, the desk staff are friendly and speak good English. **Hotel services** Air-conditioning. Safe. **Room services** Minibar. Telephone. TV.

Vardar Palace Hotel

Sıraselviler Caddesi 54, Taksim (0212 252 2888/ fax 252 1527/www.vardarhotel.com.tr). **Rates** $50 single; $60 double. **Credit** AmEx, DC, MC, V. **Map** p295 O3.

Two minutes from Taksim Square, the Vardar occupies a drab-looking 19th-century building on Istanbul's sleaziest strip, where Sıraselviler narrows to canyon-like proportions and fills up at night with the backwash from metal bars and pimp joints. Inside, however, the hotel is bright and pleasant and a typical middling three-star. Rooms have good high ceilings, although any feeling of airiness is sabotaged by a too-dark colour scheme. Front-facing rooms can get noisy when the clubs kick out. **Hotel services** Air-conditioning. Bar. Laundry. Restaurant. **Room services** Minibar. Safe. Telephone. TV.

Camping

Ataköy Tatil Köyü

Rauf Orbay Caddesi, off Ataköy Tatil Köyü, Bakırköy (0212 559 6014/fax 560 0426). **Rates** $10 per tent (two-man); $6 per caravan; $2.50 extra for car. **Credit** DC, MC, V.

On the Marmara coast about 15km (10 miles) from the centre, this campsite is conveniently situated near Ataköy train station, from where there are regular trains into Sirkeci. The site is clean and has good facilities, including a tennis court, pool (summer only) and bar, although make sure you don't get a pitch too close to the noisy road.

Sightseeing

Introduction	66
Sultanahmet	69
The Bazaar Quarter	78
Eminönü & the	
Golden Horn	85
The Western Districts	89
Beyoğlu	95
The Bosphorus Villages	101
The Asian Shore	107
Museums	111

Features

The best Sightseeing	66
Crossing the Golden Horn	67
Harem-scarem	73
Shopping the bazaar	80
The extravagant express	86
Ikmen's Istanbul	96
Right round, baby, right round	100
King Mustafa and the	
golden bowl	105

Introduction

Read this first.

Map p286 & p287
Istanbul is sightseeing heaven. You want
churches? It's got 'em. Mosques? Istanbul has
gorgeous mosques, maybe the world's finest.
Palaces? In abundance. Bazaars? The biggest.
And then there are the fortresses, city walls,
underground cisterns, public baths, museums,
parks, islands... It wouldn't be an exaggeration

The best Sightseeing

For a course in city history
From Byzantium to Istanbul, learn how the
city got the way it is at the **Archaeology
Museum**. *See p112.*

For further enlightenment
Centrepiece of two empires, the **Haghia
Sophia** is the historical heart and soul of
Istanbul. *See p69.*

For imperial excesses
The harem quarters at the **Topkapı Palace**
are the ultimate in despotic indulgence.
See p70.

For imperial elegance
The **Süleymaniye Mosque** gets our vote as
perhaps the most beautiful thing ever built.
See p84.

For the oriental experience
Part pantomime, part mall, the **Grand
Bazaar** is everything most people imagine
the 'exotic East' to be. *See p79.*

For a real rare find
Scandalously overlooked by locals and
visitors alike, the **Rahmi M Koç Museum**
would be a top-draw attraction in any
European capital. *See p116.*

For getting hot & bothered
Without a good sweat, scrape and pummel,
no Istanbul experience is complete. Get it
all at the **Cağaloğlu Hamam**. *See p208.*

For cooling off
Get on the water. Either a ferry over to the
Asian shore (*see p107*) or a boat up the
Bosphorus (*see p240*).

to say that in its sheer volume of things to see,
Istanbul gives London, Paris and even Rome a
run for their money.

But there's little logic to how it's all laid out.
The topography is confusing, involving three
land masses, two on the European side of the
Bosphorus – divided by the Golden Horn – and
one on the Asian shore. There's no uptown or
downtown, inner circle or any other convenient
way to read the city. Its street patterns are
irregular, with generations of city planners
seemingly almost phobic when it comes to
straight lines and right angles. Buildings crowd
sightlines, every now and again opening up to
expose a view that takes you completely by
surprise. In such a set-up there's no such thing
as a wrong turn, only alternative routes.

THE HISTORIC HEART
Most of the sights that could properly be
described as unmissable – either because you
really ought to see them or simply because you
couldn't avoid them if you tried – are in and
around **Sultanahmet** and the **Bazaar
Quarter**, which together constitute the city's
historic centre. This is the ancient walled
capital of the Byzantines and the Ottomans. If
this is your first time in Istanbul, then here's
where you are going to be spending the greater
part of your waking hours (and your sleeping
hours too, because the majority of hotels are
also around here). The area occupies the highest
part of a fat thumb of land that's wrapped by
the Sea of Marmara and the Golden Horn. Its
spine is **Divan Yolu**, along which a tram runs.
With stops beside the main mosques and
bazaars, the tram is the best way to get around
this side of town.

South of Divan Yolu there's little of interest,
but to the north the streets slope precipitously
down to the waterside district of **Eminönü**
beside the **Golden Horn**. Here the tram
terminates, over the road from a wharfside
busy with ferries departing for destinations
up the Bosphorus and over to the Asian shore.

Beyond the Bazaar Quarter are the **Western
Districts**, old and highly conservative
neighbourhoods such as **Fatih**, **Fener**, **Balat**
and, further afield, **Eyüp**. Few visitors make
it out here but there are several worthwhile
monuments, notably the **Byzantine Church
of St Saviour in Chora** *(see p92)* and the
city walls *(see p93)*.

The Topkapı Palace viewed across the Golden Horn.

Crossing the Golden Horn

Sultanahmet (south of the Golden Horn) is great for filling the days but Beyoğlu (north of the Golden Horn) is the place to be by night. Annoyingly, the city lacks a transport system sufficiently integrated to link the two – although it is coming, with plans to extend the tram line north across the Galata Bridge and up to Beşiktaş where it will link with a funicular up to Taksim Square. Until then, there is a bus (T4) from Sultanahmet Square to Taksim but it only goes every half hour. The alternative is to walk down the hill and across the Galata Bridge and then take the funicular up to the bottom end of Istiklal Caddesi, all of which takes a good 30-40 minutes. Or from Eminönü catch a bus going to Taksim (*see p257*), but this again takes about 30 minutes. The simplest and fastest option is to flag a cab, which will take about ten minutes from Sultanahmet Square to Taksim Square and cost the equivalent of $3-$4.

PLACES TO PLAY

The Golden Horn bisects European Istanbul, but the two parts are linked by a number of bridges including, most prominently, the Galata and, further west, the Atatürk. North of the Golden Horn is the 'modern' city, developed largely in the 19th century. Ground zero is **Beyoğlu**, which is the place to play once sightseeing is done. Beyoğlu subdivides into several smaller neighbourhoods (including, from south to north, **Galata**, **Tünel**, **Asmalımescit** and **Galatasaray**), all linked by the main spine of **Istiklal Caddesi**, a broad pedestrianised European-style boulevard sprouting a tangle of narrow side-streets filled with shops, cafés, bars, restaurants and clubs.

At its north end, Istiklal Caddesi empties into Taksim Square – large and charmless, recommended only as a place to pick up a taxi. North of Taksim are the newer districts of **Harbiye**, **Şişli**, **Nişantaşı** and **Teşvikiye**, of little interest to most visitors but where middle-class Istanbulus shop, eat and socialise. Further north still (reachable by metro), **Etiler** and **Levent** are out where the real money's at; dine or club up here and your bank manager is going to know about it.

All these areas line up along the spine of one of the city's many hills; down beside the water are a string of small neighbourhoods, sometimes referred to as the 'Bosphorus villages'. Places like **Ortaköy**, **Arnavutköy** and **Bebek** are picturesque clusters of attractive wooden villas, folksy shops and markets and open-air cafés and restaurants. There's not much in the way of major sights, but these neighbourhoods are definitely worth a wander. They are linked by bus services or, better still, you can travel up here by ferry (*see p101*).

Ferry is also the way to go to get over to the **Asian shore** and its two main neighbourhoods, **Kadıköy** and **Üsküdar**. Visitors expecting some significant change in character to mark a hop of continents are going to be disappointed. Knives and forks aren't suddenly exchanged for chopsticks midway across the Bosphorus. Instead, the Asian shore is a vast dormitory for Istanbulus who commute to jobs on the west side of the water. Real estate is cheaper here and it's less crowded than densely urban European Istanbul. The character of the Asian shore is heavily shaped by large numbers of immigrants from the Turkish provinces.

▶ For more on **getting around** Istanbul, see pp256-61.
▶ For **boat trips** to the upper Bosphorus, see p240.

Sightseeing

Sultanahmet

Mosques and palaces, museums and minarets: Istanbul's oldest district basks in the splendour of two empires.

Map p288 & p289

Sultanahmet is the Istanbul of postcards. The 'orient' of the Turkish Delight ad. It's a thumbnail of land surrounded by sea on three sides with a panoramic profile of spiky minarets and cascading domes. Surrounding the mosques are palaces, museums and assorted historical oddments, testament to a heritage that encompasses the birth, youthful exuberance, mature middle age and drooling dotage of not one but two great empires: the Byzantine empire and the Ottoman empire.

Focal point for disgorging tour buses and feeding ground for taxis, **Sultanahmet**

Square (Ayasofya Meydanı) is the obvious place to begin exploring. Most of the city's major monuments are just a few minutes' walk from here, including the Topkapı Palace (*see p70*), the underground cistern Yerebatan Sarnıcı (*see p74*), the Blue Mosque (visible across the park; *see p74*) and the Museum of Turkish & Islamic Art (*see p114*). Most notably the square also acts as a forecourt to what for close to a thousand years was the greatest church in Eastern Christendom, the Haghia Sophia (Ayasofya in Turkish). After the Turkish conquest it served for five centuries as the chief mosque of the Ottoman empire and is now open to all as a museum.

Haghia Sophia (Ayasofya)

Third on the site to bear the name, the existing Haghia Sophia ('Divine Wisdom') was dedicated on 26 December AD 537 by Emperor Justinian. He had come to power less than a century after the fall of Rome and was eager to prove his capital a worthy successor to imperial glory. Approached by a grand colonnaded avenue beginning at the city gates, Justinian's cathedral towered over all else and was topped

Haghia Sophia Felix.

by the largest dome ever constructed – a record it held until the Romans reclaimed their pride just over a thousand years later with Michelangelo's dome for St Peter's (1590). In the meantime, Justinian's dome took on almost fabled status. It was of such thin material, wrote the chroniclers of old, that the hundreds of candles hung high within would cause it to glow at night like a great golden beacon, visible to ships far out on the Marmara Sea.

Adding to the wonder, the church served as a vast reliquary housing a pilgrim's delight of biblical treasures, including fragments of the True Cross, the Virgin's veils, the lance that pierced Jesus' side, St Thomas's doubting finger and a large assortment of other saintly limbs, skulls and clippings.

All of this was lost in 1204 when adventurers and freebooters on Western Christendom's Fourth Crusade, raised to liberate Jerusalem and the Holy Lands, decided they would be equally content with a treasure-grabbing raid on the luxurious capital of their Eastern brethren. At Haghia Sophia they ripped the place apart, carrying off everything they could, and added insult to thievery by infamously placing a prostitute on the imperial throne.

Further destruction was narrowly avoided in 1453, when the Ottoman Turk armies, led by Mehmet II, breached the walls of Constantinople and put its Byzantine defenders to flight. Those taking refuge in the church were slaughtered, but the conquering sultan was supposed to have rounded on a looting soldier he found hacking at the marble floors, telling him: 'The gold is thine, the building mine.' Haghia Sophia was spared but it was lost to Christianity. The following Friday after the conquest it resounded to the chant, 'There is no god but Allah and Mohammed is his Prophet,' as the church became a mosque.

To the basilica were added four minarets from which to deliver the Muslim call to prayer. The construction of these was staggered and only two are matching. In 1317 a series of unsightly buttresses was deemed necessary when the church seemed in danger of collapse. These aside, what you see today is essentially the church as it was in Justinian's time.

At the death of the Ottoman Empire, with plans afoot to partition Istanbul along national lines, both the Greeks (on behalf of the Eastern Church) and the Italians (on behalf of the Western Church) lobbied for Haghia Sophia to be handed over to them, and in Britain a St Sophia Redemption Committee was formed. The Ottoman government posted soldiers in the mosque with machine guns to thwart any attempt at a Christian coup. An expedient solution was effected by the leaders of the new Turkish republic in 1934, who deconsecrated the building and declared it a museum. It's an action that still evokes controversy, with Islamists periodically calling for its restoration as a mosque. Comparing the pristine state of neighbouring historical mosques with the shabby peeling state of Haghia Sophia, you have to wonder if they don't have a point.

MASSES OF MOSAICS

At least the cathedral's interior remains impressive, particularly the main chamber, roofed by its still fabulous dome, 30m (98ft) in diameter. The other great feature is the mosaics. Plastered over by the Muslims, they were only rediscovered during renovations in the mid 19th century. Some of the best decorate the outer and inner narthexes, which are the long, vaulted chambers inside the present main entrance. The non-figurative geometrical and floral designs are the earliest and date from the reign of Justinian. Further mosaics adorn the galleries, which are reached by a stone ramp at the northern end of the inner narthex.

At the east end of the south gallery, just to the right of the apse, is a glimmering representation of Christ flanked by the famous 11th-century empress, Zoe, and her third husband, Constantine IX. One of the few women to rule Byzantium, Zoe married late and was a virgin until the age of 50. She must have developed a taste for what she discovered, going through a succession of husbands and lovers in the years left to her. On the mosaic in question, the heads and inscriptions show signs of being altered, possibly in an attempt to keep up with her active love life. En route to see Zoe is a slab marking the burial place of Enrico Dandolo, doge of Venice, a leader of the Fourth Crusade, and the man held responsible for persuading the Latins to attack Constantinople. Following the Ottoman conquest of the city, it's said that his tomb was smashed open and his bones thrown to the dogs.

Haghia Sophia

Ayasofya Camii Müzesi

Sultanahmet Square (0212 522 1750). Tram Sultanahmet. **Open** 9am-7.30pm Tue-Sun. Galleries close 1hr earlier. **Admission** $11. **No credit cards**. **Map** p289 N10.

Topkapı Palace

Directly north of (ie behind) Haghia Sophia are the walls shielding the imperial enclave of Topkapı Palace. Part command centre for a massive military empire, part archetypal Eastern pleasure dome, the palace was the hub of Ottoman power for more than three centuries, until it was superseded by the

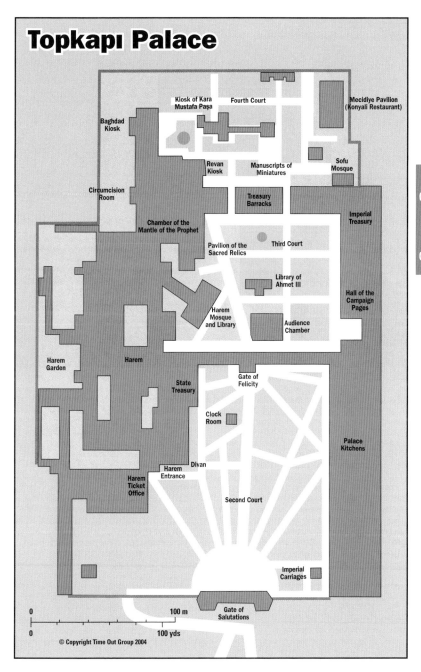

Topkapı Palace

Baghdad Kiosk

Kiosk of Kara Mustafa Paşa

Fourth Court

Mecidiye Pavilion (Konyali Restaurant)

Circumcision Room

Revan Kiosk

Manuscripts of Miniatures

Sofu Mosque

Chamber of the Mantle of the Prophet

Treasury Barracks

Imperial Treasury

Pavilion of the Sacred Relics

Third Court

Library of Ahmet III

Hall of the Campaign Pages

Harem Mosque and Library

Audience Chamber

Harem Garden

Harem

State Treasury

Gate of Felicity

Clock Room

Palace Kitchens

Harem Entrance

Divan

Harem Ticket Office

Second Court

Imperial Carriages

Gate of Salutations

0   100 m

0   100 yds

© Copyright Time Out Group 2004

Excessive Ottomania on display
at the **Topkapı Palace**.

Dolmabahçe Palace in 1853. In terms of lavish
decor and exquisite siting, it rivals Granada's
Alhambra and beats hands down almost
anything else in Europe. At least half a day
is needed to explore the place fully, although
given the high admissions you might want
to take a full day over it to get your money's
worth. If pushed for time, the must-see elements
are the Harem, Imperial Treasury and the views
from the fourth and innermost courtyard.

Entrance is via the **Imperial Gate** (Bab-ı
Hümayûn), erected by the Sultan Fatih in 1478
and decorated with niches that during Ottoman
times were used to display the severed heads of
rebels and criminals. The gate leads into the
first of a series of four courts that become more
private the deeper into the complex you
penetrate. The **First Court** was public and not
considered part of the palace proper. It housed a
hospital and dormitories for the palace guards,
hence the popular name, Court of the
Janissaries. Off to the left is the church of
Haghia Irene (Aya Irini Kilisesi), built by
Justinian and thus a contemporary of Haghia
Sophia. It has the distinction of being the only
pre-Ottoman-conquest church in the city that

was never turned into a mosque. Closed most of
the time, the church serves as a concert venue
during the International Istanbul Music
Festival (*see p185*).

Still in the First Court, down the hill to the
left, is the superb **Archaeological Museum**
(*see p112*), but the palace proper is entered
through the Disneyesque gate ahead. Tickets
can be bought on the right, just before you
reach the gate, beside the **Executioner's
Fountain**, where the chief axeman washed his
blade after carrying out his grisly work. The
heads of his victims were also displayed on top
of the truncated columns that stand on either
side of the fountain.

A semi-public space, the enormous **Second
Court** is where the business of running the
empire was carried out. This is where the
viziers of the imperial council sat in session in
the *divan*, overlooking gardens landscaped with
cypresses, plane trees and rose bushes. Where
once there would have been crowds of
petitioners awaiting their turn for an audience,
nowadays there are queues lined up waiting to
get in to the **Harem** (*see p73* **Harem-scarem**),
an introverted complex of around 300 brilliantly

tiled chambers on several levels, connected by arcaded courts and fountain gardens. Unfortunately, access is severely limited: you must wait to join a group that leaves every half-hour and is led through no more than a dozen chambers by an official guide. It's not the ideal way to see the place – locked in a crowd and herded around – but it's the only way. Tickets are sold separately, from a window located beside the Harem entrance.

Around from the Harem ticket window, a low brick building topped by shallow domes is the former **State Treasury**, present home of an exhibition of arms and armour, interesting for the contrast between cumbersome, bludgeonly European swords and the lighter, more deadly-looking Ottoman model. Across the gardens, a long row of ventilation chimneys punctuates the roof line of the enormous **kitchens**, which catered for up to 5,000 inhabitants of the palace.

They now contain a collection of ceramics, glass and silverware, much of it originating from China and Japan and imported via Central Asia along the legendary Silk Route. The earliest pieces are Chinese celadon, particularly valued by the sultans because it was supposed to change colour when brought into contact with poison.

All paths in the Second Court converge on the **Gate of Felicity** (Bab-üs Saadet), which serves as the backdrop every year for a performance of Mozart's *Abduction From the Seraglio* – again, part of the International Istanbul Music Festival. The gate also gives access to the **Third Court**.

The Third Court was the holy of holies, the sultan's private domain. Confronting all who enter is the **Audience Chamber** (*Arz Odası*), which is where, until it was supplanted in the role by the Sublime Porte (*see p85*), foreign

Harem-scarem

From its inception in around 1540 until its dissolution in the early 20th century, the Topkapı harem was home, prison and entire world to almost four centuries of palace women. The word means 'forbidden', a ruling that applied to all men except the sultan, the princes and the eunuch guards. Women had no problem getting in, but once admitted they were in for life. Most entered as slave girls presented to the sultan as gifts: it was forbidden to make slaves of Muslims so they were all Christians or Jews. Circassian girls who came from what is now Georgia and Armenia were favoured because of their fair skin, although even the fairest was still only valued at a fifth of the price of a good horse. The girls were converted to Islam and 'palace-trained', which means they were taught to sing, dance, play instruments and to give pleasure of a more tactile kind.

But notions of the harem as a sensual hothouse are misplaced. It was a highly competitive and cut-throat environment in which each girl sought to catch the eye of the sultan or a prince and so secure a better station. At any one time a dozen or so girls would be chosen as imperial handmaids and bedmates. Giving birth to the sultan's child ensured exalted status. If it was a boy there was even the chance he might one day become sultan and his mother *valide sultana*, 'mother of the sultan' and, as such, the most powerful woman in the land. With such high stakes, along with the sex came violence as

the women manoeuvred, plotted, poisoned and knifed their way up the harem hierarchy. A mother with the sultan's child was particularly vulnerable – Murat III (1574-95), for example, fathered 103 children, only one of which was ever going to make the throne.

All the while, harem girls also had to court the favour of the present *valide sultana*, responsible for selecting girls for the sultan, while avoiding the displeasure of the *kizlar ağasi*, the chief black eunuch. These latter characters were the go-betweens for the sultan and his mother and so privy to all palace secrets. At the same time, physically and psychologically mutilated as they were, the chief black eunuchs tended to be a dangerous combination of corrupt, scheming and vindictive. Some of them got their kicks stuffing girls in sacks, loading them into a boat and dumping them overboard into the Bosphorus, usually on the instructions of the *valide sultana* (although Sultans Ibrahim and Murat II are both alleged to have ordered their entire harems drowned, one out of boredom, the other through paranoia).

Alev Lytle Croutier sums it all up very nicely in her fine book *Harem: The World Behind the Veil*, describing it as a world of 'frightened women plotting with men who were not men against absolute rulers who kept their relatives immured for decades'. Far from being a palace of sensual delights, the Topkapı harem must have been more of a nerve-shredding chamber of horrors.

ambassadors would present their credentials. Although the sultan would be present on such occasions, he would never deign to speak with a non-Turk and all conversation was conducted via the grand vizier.

Off to the right is the **Hall of the Campaign Pages** (Seferli Koğuşu), whose task it was to look after the royal wardrobe. They did an excellent job: there's a perfectly preserved 550-year-old, red-and-gold silk kaftan worn by Mehmet II, conqueror of Constantinople.

Things get even more glittery next door in the **Imperial Treasury** (Hazine). Many of the items here were made specifically for the palace by a team of court artisans, which at its height numbered over 600. A lot of what's displayed here has never left the confines of the inner courts. Not that too many people outside the sultan's circle would have had much use for a diamond-encrusted set of chain mail or a Koran bound in jade. Items like the Topkapı Dagger, its handle set with three eyeball-sized emeralds (one of which conceals a watch face), are breathtaking in their excessiveness, vulgarity and sheer bloody uselessness.

From the ridiculous to the sublime: the final and **Fourth Court** is a garden with terraces stepping down towards Seraglio Point, the protrudance of land that watches over the entrance to the Golden Horn. Buildings are limited to a bunch of reasonably restrained pavilions, while the views over the Bosphorus are wonderful, as are the sea breezes on a sun-beaten summer's day. The very last building to be constructed within the palace, the **Mecidiye Pavilion** (Mecidiye Köşkü), built in 1840, houses a restaurant and café, notable for its covetable terrace seating.

Topkapı Palace

Topkapı Sarayı
Bab-ı Hümayün Caddesi, Gülhane (0212 512 0480). Tram Gülhane or Sultanahmet. **Open** 9am-5pm Mon, Wed-Sun. *Harem* 10am-noon, 1-4pm Mon, Wed-Sun; closed Tue. **Admission** $9; Harem $7; Treasury $7. **Credit** MC, V. **Map** p289 O9.

The Cisterns

Running downhill from Topkapı's Imperial Gate, **Soğukçeşme Sokak** is a wool-over-the-eyes bit of urban set design. Formerly a row of dilapidated old wooden buildings, in the 1980s the original street was demolished and recreated in concrete disguised under pastel-painted weatherboard panelling. Intended to evoke the atmosphere of Ottoman Istanbul, the 'old houses' are one long straggly boutiquey hotel, apart from one which contains the **Istanbul Library** (*see p264*).

Following the tram tracks back uphill leads to a right turn and a lone, single-storey building that sits over the entrance to the **Yerebatan Sarnıcı** (Basilica Cistern), the grandest of several underground reservoirs that riddle the foundations of this part of the city.

Built by the Emperor Justinian at the same time as the Haghia Sophia, it was forgotten for centuries and only rediscovered by a Frenchman, Peter Gyllius, in 1545 when he noticed that people in the neighbourhood got water by lowering buckets through holes in their basements. It's a tremendous engineering feat, with brick vaults supported on 336 columns spaced at 4m (13ft) intervals. Prior to restoration in 1987 the cistern could only be explored by boat (James Bond rowed through in *From Russia With Love*). These days there are concrete walkways. The subdued lighting and subterranean cool are especially welcome on hot days. Look for the two Medusa heads at the far end from the entrance, both recycled from an even more ancient building and casually employed as column bases. There's a café down here and a platform on which occasional concerts of classical Turkish and Western music are performed; check with the ticket office for further details.

A second cistern, the **Binbirdirek Sarnıcı** (the 'Cistern of 1001 Columns', except that there are only 224) has recently opened to the public. It's another Byzantine forest of pillars and brick-vaulted ceilings but sadly the restorers have put in a false floor that halves the original height of the chamber (a well at the centre illustrates the original floor level). No one has yet figured out what to do with the place and it currently unsuccessfully accommodates a couple of cafés, a bar and a restaurant. The admission fee gets you a free drink.

Binbirdirek Sarnıcı

Imran Ökten Sokak 4, Sultanahmet (0212 517 8751/ www.binbirdirek.com.tr). Tram Sultanahmet. **Open** 8am-7pm daily. **Admission** $6. **Credit** MC, V. **Map** p289 M10.

Yerebatan Sarnıcı

Yerebatan Caddesi 13, Sultanahmet (0212 522 1259/ www.yerebatansarnici.com). Tram Sultanahmet. **Open** *May-Oct* 9am-7pm daily. *Nov-Apr* 9am-6pm daily. **Admission** $7. **Credit** MC, V. **Map** p289 N10.

Sultanahmet Mosque

Seductively curvaceous and enhanced by a lovingly attended park in front, Sultanahmet Mosque is Islamic architecture at its sexiest. Commissioned by Sultan Ahmet I (1603-17) and built for him by Mehmet Ağa, a student of the

True blue at the **Sultanahmet Mosque**.

Going underground at the **Yerebatan Sarnıcı**. *See p74.*

great Sinan, this was the last of Istanbul's magnificent imperial mosques, the final flourish before the rot set in. It provoked hostility at the time because of its six minarets – such a display was previously reserved only for the Prophet's mosque at Mecca – but they do make for a beautifully elegant silhouette, particularly gorgeous when floodlit at night.

By contrast, the interior is clumsy, marred by four immense pillars, disproportionately large for the fairly modest dome they support (especially when compared to the vast yet seemingly unsupported dome that caps Haghia Sophia). Most surfaces are covered by a mismatch of Iznik tiles: their colour gives the place its popular name, the Blue Mosque.

A part of the mosque complex, the Imperial Pavilion, now houses the entirely missable **Vakıflar Carpet Museum** (*see p116*). In the north-east corner of the surrounding park is the *türbe* or **Tomb of Sultan Ahmet I**. It also contains the cenotaphs of his wife and three of his sons, two of whom, Osman II and Murat IV, ruled in their turn, Ahmet being the sultan who abandoned the nasty Ottoman practice of strangling other potential heirs on the succession of the favoured son.

Sultanahmet (Blue) Mosque

Sultanahmet Camii
At Meydan Sokak 17, Sultanahmet (0212 518 1319). Tram Sultanahmet. **Open** *May-Oct* 9am-9pm daily. *Nov-Apr* 9am-7pm daily. Sound & light show May-Oct just after dusk daily. **Admission** free. **Map** p289 N11.

The Hippodrome & South

On the north-west side of the Sultanahmet Mosque, a strip of over-touristed tea-houses and souvenir shops fringes the Hippodrome (At Meydanı), formerly the focal point of Byzantine Constantinople. At one time, this ancient arena was used for races, court ceremonies, coronations and parades. Originally laid out by the Roman emperor Septimius Severus during his rebuilding of the city, the arena was later enlarged by Constantine to its present dimensions – the modern road exactly follows the tracks of the old racing lanes. Now an elongated park circled by traffic, the Hippodrome retains an odd assortment of monuments standing on what was the *spina*, the raised area around which chariots would have thundered. Closest to the mosque is an **Egyptian obelisk**, removed from the Temple of Karnak at Thebes (now Luxor). The obelisk was originally carved in around 1500 BC in order to commemorate the great victories of Pharaoh Thutmosis III. The Byzantine emperor Theodosius had it moved to Constantinople in

AD 390 and set upon a marble pedestal sculpted with scenes of himself and family enjoying a day at the races.

Next to the obelisk is the bronze **Serpentine Column** (also known as the Spiral Column), carried off from the Temple of Apollo at Delphi, where it had been set to commemorate Greek victory over the Persians in 480 BC. When it was brought to the Byzantine capital by Constantine its three entwined serpents had heads, but each was decapitated over the years. One detached head survives and is displayed in the **Archaeology Museum** (*see p112*). A third monument, known as the **Column of Constantine**, is a pockmarked and crumbling affair, once sheathed in gold-plated bronze, but stripped by the looting Fourth Crusaders.

Overlooking the Hippodrome is the grand **Museum of Turkish & Islamic Art** (*see p114*), while downhill from its south-west corner is the **Sokollu Mehmet Paşa Mosque**, another tour de force by Sinan. It's one of his later buildings (constructed 1571-2), praised by architectural historians for the way it copes with an uneven, sloping site. If you can get inside (hang around and somebody will usually turn up with a key) you'll notice the lovely tiling and painted calligraphic inscriptions, set among vivid floral motifs.

The streets round here twist and jog between creaky wooden buildings and are a delight to explore. Head south, downhill toward the sea, for the **Küçük Haghia Sophia Mosque**, or 'Little Haghia Sophia', so called because of its resemblance to Justinian's great cathedral. Like its larger namesake, it was originally a church, in this case dedicated to Sergius and Bacchus, the patron saints of the Christianised Roman army. Also like its namesake, it's not much to look at from the outside but possesses a fine interior, including a frieze honouring Justinian and his wife, Theodora. There's also a pleasant garden with an attached café.

Following Küçük Ayasofya Caddesi back uphill leads past the very worthwhile **Mosaic Museum** (*see p114*) and the Ottoman-era shopping centre, the **Arasta Bazaar**, beyond which is a sunken terrace café where you can smoke nargile (*see p152*).

Küçük Haghia Sophia Mosque

Küçük Ayasofya Camii
Küçük Ayasofya Caddesi, Sultanahmet. Tram Sultanahmet. **Open** prayer times only, daily. **Admission** free. **Map** p289 M12.

Sokollu Mehmet Paşa Mosque

Sokollu Mehmet Paşa Camii
Şehit Mehmet Paşa Sokak 20, Sultanahmet. Tram Sultanahmet. **Open** 7am-dusk daily. **Admission** free. **Map** p289 M11.

Sightseeing

The Bazaar Quarter

Beauty, bargains and bedlam: welcome to the world's oldest shopping centre.

Map p272 & p273

Forget the mall, the Grand Bazaar is shopping at its rawest: a vast disordered sprawl of a million and one goods. The aisles here quite literally go on for miles. In place of 'don't mind if you do' sales assistants are some of the most charming and ruthless traders in the Near East. You want a discount, a cut-price offer, then you're going to have to bargain for it. That goes for Turks as much as tourists, because what seems like an oriental wonderland to visitors is Saturday's shopping venue for the locals. Buying and selling aside, the area around the bazaar is packed with historical monuments and other sightseeing interludes.

To get to the Grand Bazaar from the Sultanahmet Square area, follow the tramlines west up Divan Yolu.

Divan Yolu

Narrow, sloping, partially cobbled and given over to purring trams, the street known as Divan Yolu is modestly attractive but low-key. There's little indication that this was formerly the ancient Mese, or Middle Way, the main thoroughfare of Byzantine Constantinople and later Ottoman Stamboul. It ran from the vicinity of the imperial centre (today's Sultanahmet) due west over the city's seven hills to exit by the Topkapı Gate. From Byzantium, the Mese continued all the way to Durres (Durazzo) on the Albanian coast. A large marble sliver at the bottom of Divan Yolu, in the small park behind the Yerebatan Sarnıçı (*see p74*), is all that remains of a Byzantine triumphal arch, known as the **Milion**, which originally marked the point from which all distances along the route were measured.

Modern Divan Yolu is defined by postcard shops, cheap eateries, money exchange bureaux and bucket-shop travel agencies, but reflecting its historic status, there's also a variety of antiquity. On the corner with Babıali Caddesi (head up here for the **Cağaloğlu Hamam**; *see p208*) is a small, well-tended cemetery with the **Tomb of Mahmut II** (1808-39), the sultan who crushed the Janissaries (*see p116* **Swords of misrule**). He had 15 sons and 12 daughters, many now crammed into the domed tomb chamber with him. Over the road, and down a side street beside the Pierre Loti Café is the **Theodosius Cistern**, an unrestored Byzantine reservoir. It's what the more famous Yerebatan Sarnıçı would have looked like before it was cleaned up for tourists. It sits under the big blue 'Eminönü Belediye Başkanlığı' building.

Back on Divan Yolu is the **Basın Müzesi (Press Museum)**, which is really dull but has a popular café on the ground floor. Next door, the big, bulbous, yellow-faced dome belongs to the **Çemberlitaş Hamam** (*see p208*).

The buildings fall back at this point to create a small, untidy and pigeon-infested plaza, marked by the equally scruffy **Burnt Column** (or Hooped Column). This is, in fact, one of the city's oldest and key monuments, erected by Constantine to celebrate the city's dedication as new imperial capital in AD 330. The column was topped by a statue of the emperor until this was destroyed in an 1106 hurricane. Its present sorry, blackened state results from one of the city's periodic fires. The iron hoops are structural reinforcements originally added in the fifth century and replaced in the 1970s.

By now Divan Yolu has become **Yeniçeriler Caddesi**, lined with a string of various small mosques, tombs and medreses (theological schools), a couple of which have small court-yards that double as **nargile cafés** (*see p152*).

From here the Grand Bazaar is immediately to the north.

Theodosius Cistern

Şerefiye Sarnıçı
Piyer Loti Caddesi, Sultanahmet. Tram Sultanahmet.
Open 9am-5pm Mon-Fri. **Admission** free.
Map p289 M10.

Tomb of Mahmut II

82 Divan Yolu, Sultanahmet. Tram Sultanahmet.
Open 9.30am-7.30pm daily. **Admission** free.
Map p289 M10.

Five centuries of haggling at the **Grand Bazaar**.

Grand Bazaar

The Grand Bazaar (in Turkish *Kapalı Çarşı*, or 'Covered Market') is truly a world apart. Made up of a maze of interconnecting vaulted passages, the bazaar has its own banks, baths, mosques, cafés and restaurants, a police station and post office, not to mention the thousands of shops, all glittery and fairy-lit in the absence of natural light. Since the rise of the mall it's no longer the biggest shopping centre in the world, but it can still claim to be the oldest.

Part of the building dates back to the ninth century, when it was used as something akin to a Byzantine ministry of finance. Trading proper started in 1461, a mere eight years after the Turkish conquest of Constantinople. The Ottomans ushered in a new economic era, with the city at the centre of an empire that stretched from the Arabian deserts almost to the European Alps. Mehmet the Conqueror ordered the construction of a *bedesten*, a great secure building with thick stone walls, massive iron gates and space for several dozen shops. This survives in modified form as the **Old Bedesten** (*İç Bedesten*), at the very heart of the bazaar. It remains a place where the most precious items are sold, including the finest old silver and antiques. The **Sandal Bedesten** was added later, named after a fine Bursan silk and filled with textile traders. It now hosts a carpet auction at 1pm every Wednesday, which is a real crowd-pleasing spectacle.

A network of covered streets grew up around the two bedestens, sealed at night behind 18 great gates. Whenever the economy was booming, the market would physically expand, only to be cut back by fires. Then, as the

Shopping the bazaar

Most visitors enter Istanbul's Grand Bazaar prepared to admire its historical and architectural details but disinclined to peruse the billions of articles stocked by the 5,480 shops arrayed along 65 alleys that together make up the underlying reason for its continued existence.

Shopkeepers, for their part, cajole and entreat in a dozen languages and are determined not to permit visitors to indulge in such a non-commercial activity as sightseeing. Remember, you are not dealing with sales clerks paid by the hour but most likely the owners themselves, or at least a trusted brother or nephew. Their rents have to be paid in gold – a stunning seven kilos per year for shops on the main avenue.

Fortunately, the perception that hard-core hustling is bad for long-term trade has been taken on board. Visitors will find the Grand Bazaar a kindler, gentler place than it was even five years ago.

Practical tips

Serious shoppers should have on hand a notepad, a calculator and plenty of time – three hours is about the minimum needed for a purchasing expedition here. The notepad is useful because when you find something you like we recommend jotting down the price and the location of the seller. Then find the item elsewhere and get more quotes – adding up eight and nine digit figures can be confusing, hence the calculator. Continue for as long as you have the patience

Don't assume that wildly varying prices for the same item represents a rip-off. Shopkeepers price according to their needs. Someone may require ready cash to pay overheads or buy new stock and will be happy to settle for a quick cheap sale. Also, it's not true that large, sleek shops in busy central locations always charge more. Even though they pay higher rents, higher turnover often allows them to sell for less.

Bargaining etiquette

If you begin bargaining, start somewhere well under your ideal price (there are no hard and fast rules as to how much), just as the shopowner will start well above his. The hope is that you can meet in the middle. Remember, though, that it's considered bad form to walk away empty-handed after an elaborate bargaining process.

Where to buy what

There are over a dozen main gates into the Grand Bazaar but at least five of them open onto **Kalpakçılar Caddesi**, an opulent east-west thoroughfare lined with gleaming jewellery shops. On this street, you'll also find **Pako** (at No.87), the place for some of the city's best handbags and purses.

South of Kalpakçılar is the **Kürkcüler Çarşısı**, filled with leather jackets and coats. It's also where you'll find **Yörük** (*see p167* **The rug trade**), a highly recommended little carpet shop, located at the base of some steps leading up and out of the bazaar.

For more carpets visit the **Rabia Hanı** at the eastern end of Kürkcüler Çarşısı. **Tradition** (*see p166* **The rug trade**) at No.11 is well stocked and hassle-free.

Running north from Kalpakçılar Caddesi, **Kolonçılar Sokak** is lined with shops peddling a typical mix of souvenirs, ceramics, tea sets, silks, water pipes, chess sets and carved wood. It crosses **Keseciler Caddesi** (location of the quality rural crafts shop **Derviş**; *see p175*) before making a beeline for the ancient heart of the bazaar, the **Old Bedesten**. In here the atmosphere is hushed, almost scholarly – a suitable setting for dealers in Ottoman-era prayer beads, icons, chess sets, firearms, pocket watches, painted miniatures, snuff boxes and Soviet memorabilia. The museum quality is enhanced by the display of a brass diver's suit, art nouveau jewellery and a meerschaum pipe that took an artisan one whole year to carve – proudly displayed below a photograph of an admiring Hillary Clinton.

For validation of the oldness of the 'Old' Bedesten, check out the ancient Byzantine eagle, carved into the stone on the outside face of its eastern entrance.

On the north side of the Bedesten is **Halıcılar Caddesi**, no longer, as its name professes, 'the Street of the Carpet Sellers', but the front line of gentrification, with **Café Fes** and **Café Sultan** offering Illy coffee and fresh flowers, plus **Abdulla** (*see p175*), one of a new breed of Grand Bazaar boutiques that employ chic presentation to shift traditional product.

West along Halıcılar are further alternatives to carpets, notably at **Galeri Apollo** (No.22-6), a shop stocked with silky soft goat-hair rugs and calf-skin hides, hand-stitched into patchwork designs.

Halıcılar connects to **Yağlıkçılar Sokağı**, a long, wide, north-south-running street and the place for belly-dance costumes, incredible fabrics, lamps, knitwear and, of course, more unnecessary souvenirs. Off Yağlıkçılar is the tranquil **Cebeci Hanı** and, beyond, the **Iç Cebeci**, where a large open court is ringed by a second floor, lined with antique and metalwork shops, plus a few places selling Central Asian fabrics and garments.

To visit the most beautiful *han* in the bazaar, head east from Yağlıkçılar along **Perdahçılar Sokağı**; at the end follow the signs for **Zincirli Hanı**, which is also the lair of the bazaar's most famous carpet dealer, **Sisko Osman** (*see p166*).

One last word of guidance: shopping the Grand Bazaar is not a rational exercise but all about emotions.

Time out

Outside the southern entrance to the Old Bedesten are **Julia's Kitchen** (Keseciler Caddesi 92), a great breakfast stop, and **Köşk** (Keseciler Caddesi 98-100), which serves traditional *sulu yemek* (home cooking) from bain-maries. The **Şark Kahvesi** (at the corner of Yağlıkçılar and Fesciler Caddesi) is a utilitarian old-style coffee-house, where the walls are dotted with some rather wonderful pictures of old fellows on flying carpets. The courtyard of the **Iç Cebeci Hanı** has an excellent kebab shop and a tea-house where off-duty merchants get serious over games of cards. **Havuzlu Lokantasi** (Gani Çelebi Sokak 3) is a good, basic old fashioned place doing kebabs and such. All cafés and restaurants in the bazaar are shut by 6.30pm at the latest.

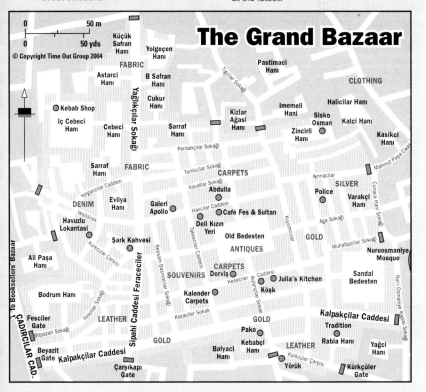

The Grand Bazaar

Journey to the past

The first major museum in Turkey dedicated to the history of industry, transport and communications, with thousands upon thousands of items from gramophone needles to a full-size submarine... A magnificent collection beautifully housed in more than 11,000 square metres of historic buildings on the shore of Golden Horn... Awaiting you in a city as old as history itself.

Opening Times:
Tuesday-Friday 10.00-17.00,
Saturday and Sunday 10.00-19.00

Group rates for parties more than 10

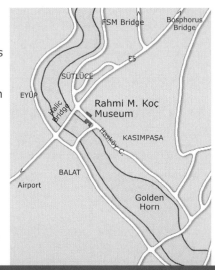

RAHMİ M. KOÇ
M Ü Z E S İ
M U S E U M

Hasköy Cad. No. 27, Hasköy 34445 ISTANBUL - TURKEY
Tel: +90 212 297 66 39 - 40 • Fax: +90 212 297 66 37
web: www.rmk-museum.org.tr • e-mail: rmkmuseum@koc.com.tr

Ottoman Empire declined after 300 years of wealth, so did the legendary splendour of the bazaar. In 1894 a devastating earthquake hit the traders particularly hard. It wasn't until the 1950s that the bazaar began to revive, as the republic found its economic footing. These days it's taking tentative steps into the 21st century with chic boutiques flogging Conranesque product, hip cafés and even a web presence (www.grand-bazaar.com).

Much of the current prosperity comes from gold, of which nearly 100 tonnes is sold in the bazaar each year. Then there are the 'black bag' shoppers from the former Soviet Union, so called because of their habit of filling bin sacks with cheap clothing. Among the sea of inessential goods, mantelpiece trinkets, nasty leather jackets, no-label jeans and hippie-wear, there are attractive quality goods to be had (*see p80* **Shopping the bazaar**).

AROUND THE BAZAAR

If you can find your way out of the east side of the bazaar, you emerge into daylight beside the **Nuruosmaniye Mosque**, the first in the city executed in the style known as Turkish Baroque. Istanbul historian John Freely describes the architecture as possessing a 'certain perverse genius'. Certainly the plane-tree courtyard is lovely.

To the north the bazaar extends much further than the limits of the covered area, spilling over into a crazed warren of narrow streets that zag and zig all the way to the districts of Tahtakale and Eminönü (*see p85*) beside the Golden Horn. A rule of thumb is that if you're lost, just keep heading downhill. On the way, you'll see the contemporary bazaar at its most frenetic. From the Nuruosmaniye Mosque follow **Mahmut Paşa Yokuşu** north. This principal market street is given over to the rag-trade: it's lined with wholesalers knocking out 'Lacoste' T-shirts and 'Levi's' jeans in basement workshops. The street's great stone-arch gateways lead into numerous *hans*, medieval merchant hostels with storage rooms and accommodation around a central courtyard.

Exit the Grand Bazaar on the west side for **Çadırcılar Caddesi**. At No.27 is a large derelict courtyard graced with a mosaic of Yunus Emre (a 13th-century Sufi poet: 'God is our professor and love is our academy', quoth he); ascend the staircase to be greeted by wholesaler Ahmet and his stock of Central Asian kaftans, Pakistani fabrics, shamanistic artifacts and jewellery at prices you won't find anywhere else in the bazaar.

West of Çadırcılar is the **Booksellers' Bazaar**, a lane and courtyard where the written word has been traded since early

Istanbulsheet.

Ottoman times. Initially, printed books were considered a corrupting European influence, so only hand-lettered manuscripts were sold until 1729, the year the first book in Turkish was published. Much of the trade now is in student textbooks (the university is nearby), as well as plentiful coffeetable volumes and framed calligraphy for the tourists. Sadly, the booksellers are under threat from merchants pushing everything from Byzantine coins to used mobile phones.

Booksellers' Bazaar

Sahaflar Çarşısı
Sahaflar Çarşısı Sokak, Beyazıt. Tram Beyazıt.
Open 8am-8pm daily. **Map** p288 K10.

Grand Bazaar

Kapalı Çarşı
Beyazıt (www.grand-bazaar.com). Tram Beyazıt or Çemberlitaş. **Open** 8.30am-7pm Mon-Sat.
Map p288 L9.

Nuruosmaniye Mosque

Nuruosmaniye Camii
Vezirhanı Caddesi, Beyazıt. Tram Beyazıt or Çemberlitaş. **Open** 9am-dusk. **Admission** free.
Map p288 L9.

To be taken with a pinch of salt.

To the left of the gate is a small *medrese*, originally part of the Beyazıt Mosque complex but now the **Calligraphy Museum** (*see p113*).

Follow either of the roads that hug the university walls to reach the architectural perfection of the Süleymaniye Mosque.

Beyazıt Mosque
Beyazıt Camii
Beyazıt Square, Yeniçeriler Caddesi (0212 519 3644). Tram Beyazıt. **Open** 10am-final prayer call daily. **Admission** free. **Map** p288 K9.

Süleymaniye Mosque

Completed in 1557, the Süleymaniye represents both the empire at its height under Süleyman the Magnificent and arguably the crowning achievement of architect Mimar Sinan.

It's built on Istanbul's highest hill, exploiting the topography to impress. The approach is along Prof Sıddık Sami Onar Caddesi, formerly known as 'Addicts Alley' because its cafés sold hashish. No longer, although the area's tea houses are still popular student hangouts. The low-rise multi-domed buildings surrounding the mosque are part of its *külliye* and include a hospital, asylum, hamam and soup kitchen.

The mosque itself is entered via gardens, then an arcaded courtyard, the columns of which are said to have come from the Byzantine royal box at the Hippodrome. Its interior is remarkable for the lightness of its soaring central prayer space, enhanced by some 200 windows. Decoration is minimal but effective, including stained glass added by Ibrahim the Mad and sparing use of Iznik tiles (which Sinan would later go a bundle on at the Rüstem Pasha Mosque, just down the hill; *see p86*).

Behind the mosque are several *türbes* (tombs) including that of Süleyman, recently beautifully restored. Adjacent is the tomb of Haseki Hürrem, the sultan's influential wife, better known as Roxelana. Outside the compound wall, just to the north in a walled triangular garden at the apex of two streets, is the modest **Tomb of Sinan**.

The mosque's former kitchens are back at work, employed by the **Darüzziyafe** (*see p125*), which is a good place for lunch. Also worth a look is the neighbouring **Lalezar** tea-house, which occupies a sunken courtyard with a marble fountain, cushioned seats along the walls, low wooden tables and nargile.

Süleymaniye Mosque
Süleymaniye Camii
Tiryakiler Çarşısı, off Prof Sıddık Sami Onar Caddesi, Süleymaniye (0212 514 0139). Tram Beyazıt or Eminönü. **Open** 9am-7pm daily. **Admission** free. **Map** p288 K8.

Beyazıt Square

A large, irregularly shaped plaza west of the bazaar, **Beyazıt Square** was the site of the forum in Roman times. It regained importance when the early Ottomans built a palace here, which served as the pre-Topkapı seat of power. It burnt down in 1541. Other significant Ottoman structures still stand, notably the **Beyazıt Mosque**, built in 1501-6, and only the second great mosque complex to be founded in the city. The first, the Fatih Mosque (*see p90*), was destroyed, which makes Beyazıt the oldest imperial mosque in town. In effect, it's the architectural link between the Byzantine Haghia Sophia – the obvious inspiration – and the later great Ottoman mosques such as the nearby Süleymaniye (*see below*). It's still in use and full of market traders at prayer times.

Facing the mosque is the monumental gate to **Istanbul University**, previously the Ottoman Ministry of War. In the 1960s and '70s, the campus was a favourite battleground for both left and right, and is still a centre for political protest, with bullets occasionally whizzing across the square. As a result, the university grounds and **Beyazıt Tower**, built in 1828 as a fire lookout and a prominent city landmark, are off limits to all but accredited students.

Eminönü & the Golden Horn

The former gateway to Istanbul, now a crossroads for traders and commuters – and a byword for bedlam.

Map p288 & p289

A former maritime gateway to the city, the waterfront district of Eminönü remains a place of constant exchange – from the commuters who use its ferry terminals to the commerce that fills the backstreets. To get here from central Sultanahmet, ride the tram north to its terminus, or follow the tramlines on foot (it's a ten-minute walk from Sultanahmet Square).

En route, the way curves sharply around the walls enclosing **Gülhane Park**. Formerly part of the lower grounds of the Topkapı Palace, the park's now a fairly sad place with more concrete than grass. It contains a dire little zoo and, for connoisseurs of lost causes, the **Tanzimat Museum**, which commemorates the 1839 liberalising reforms proclaimed from this spot by Sultan Abdel Mecid and then roundly ignored by all (*see p21*). The exhibits amount to little more than a wall of portraits, a waxwork bust and some yellowing imperial decrees, all housed in a small wooden hut that's easily mistaken for a public toilet.

Back on the tram tracks, just west of the Gülhane stop, is an ornate monumental gateway with floppy rococo roof: this is the historic **Sublime Porte** (Bab-ı Ali). At one time it was the entrance to the palace of the grand vizier, the true administrator of the empire in the dotage of the sultans. Foreign ambassadors were accredited to the 'Sublime Porte', and the term became a synonym for the Ottoman government. The current gate dates from 1843 and is now the entrance to the city governorate.

Opposite, on a corner of the Gülhane Park wall is the **Alay Köşkü**, an elaborate treehouse-like platform from which the sultans would observe parades or, in the case of Ibrahim the Mad, take potshots with a crossbow at passing pedestrians.

END OF THE LINE

Following Gülhane the tram stops next in sight of the Golden Horn at Sirkeci for **Sirkeci Station** (Sirkeci Istasyonu), the last train stop in Europe. On its completion in 1881, this was the eastern terminus for trains from Europe, including the legendary Orient Express (*see p86* **The extravagant express**). Its street facade has been disfigured by modern additions but the waterfront side still retains an element of grandeur. Despite the station's relegation to the status of suburban shuttle shed (the only international trains are to Thessalonika and Bucharest), the old Orient Express restaurant remains largely intact beside platform one (*see p126*). Sadly, it's far too fancy for the commuter crowd and nobody seems to use the place.

Over the road from the station, more than holding its own against the neighbouring McDonald's, **Konyalı** is a Turkish takeaway institution. It specialises in pastries, both savoury *börek*, stuffed with minced meat or cheese, and sweet stuff, filled with crushed nuts and doused in syrup.

Just past Konyalı the tram tracks swing left, terminating 200 metres further on at Eminönü, grandly signposted by the imposing **New Mosque**. Construction on the mosque began in 1598, but suffered a setback when the architect was executed for heresy, and it wasn't until 1663 that the building was finally completed. The fact that it is so obviously a working mosque tends to keep visitors at bay, but nobody objects to non-Muslims entering. Though it was built after the classical period of Ottoman architecture had passed, it is nonetheless a regal structure, and particularly uplifting seen floodlit from a taxi, barrelling by after a night on the town.

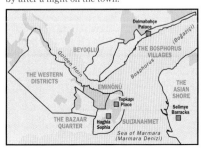

Konyalı

Mimar Kemalettin Caddesi 5, Sirkeci (0212 513 9610). Tram Sirkeci. **Open** 7am-9.30pm daily. **No credit cards.** Map p289 M8.

New Mosque

Yeni Camii
Eminönü Meydanı, Eminönü (0212 527 8505). Tram Eminönü. **Open** 9am-dusk daily. **Admission** free. Map p289 M8.

Tanzimat Museum

Tanzimat Müzesi
Gülhane Park (0212 512 6384). Tram Gülhane. **Open** 9am-4.30pm Mon-Fri. **Admission** free. Map p289 O9.

The Egyptian Bazaar

In front of the New Mosque is a pigeon-plagued plaza busy with itinerant sales-people and dominated on its south side by the high brick arch leading into the Egyptian Bazaar, also known as the Spice Bazaar. The market was constructed as part of the mosque's complex and its revenues helped support a series of philanthropic institutions. The name comes from its ages-past association with the arrival of the annual 'Cairo caravan', a flotilla of ships bearing rice, coffee and incense from Egypt.

While the bazaar's L-shaped vaulted hall is undeniably pretty, at first glance its 90 shops seem to be hustling nothing more than a motley assortment of oily perfumes, cheap gold and sachets of something called 'Turkish Viagra'. It's a tourist trap, sure, but to dismiss it out of hand is to miss out on one of the world's finest delis: check out **Erzincanlilar** (shop No.14) for delicious honeycomb and the mature hard Turkish cheese known as *eski kaşar*; **Güzel Istanbul Şekercisi** (No.39) for excellent *lokum* (Turkish delight); **Papağan** (No.65) for pistachios, nuts, honey-covered mulberries and dried figs stuffed with walnuts; and **Güllüoğlu Baklavacısı** (No.88) for pastries.

One other reason to pay a visit to the market is to lunch at **Pandeli's** (*see p126*), a famed Greek-run restaurant reached up a steep flight of stone steps just inside the main entrance.

Running west from the market, **Hasırcılar Caddesi** is one of the city's most vibrant and aromatic streets thanks to a clutch of delis (*see p171* **Namlı Pastırmacı**), spice merchants and coffee sellers, including **Kurukahveci Mehmet Efendi** (*see p170*), where caffeine addicts queue at the serving hatch to purchase the little brown, own-logoed bags of beans.

Further along the same street look out for the arched stone doorways through which flights of stairs lead up to the **Rüstem Paşa Mosque**, built in 1561 for a grand vizier of Süleyman the Great. Raised above the shops, (which pay for its upkeep courtesy of their rents), the mosque is invisible from the street. It's a bit of a city secret, despite being one of the most beautiful of the smaller mosques of the renowned Sinan.

The extravagant express

A byword for glamour, the Orient Express existed in several versions on various routes, most famously Paris-Vienna-Budapest-Istanbul. Its maiden departure was 4 October 1883 from Gare de l'Est, Paris. Between the Western 'city of light' and the shimmering Eastern exoticism of its ultimate destination, the train passed through a patchwork of mercurial Balkan kingdoms, always tinged with the promise of war or revolution. A couple of notorious incidents added to the legend: in 1891, bandits held up the train and took its passengers hostage; in 1929, it was stranded in a snowdrift for six days.

Such episodes could be endured in the comfort of carpeted cabins, decked out with damask drapes and silk sheets for the fold-down beds, or the saloon, which evoked the atmosphere of a London gentlemen's club with its leather armchairs and bookcases. Meals were served in the Wagon Restaurant, beneath gas-lit brass chandeliers at tables set with Baccarat crystal, starched napery and monogrammed porcelain. The kind of passengers who could afford all this tended to be minor royals, wealthy nobility, diplomats and financiers, not to mention spies, nightclub performers and high-class whores – the perfect cast list for thriller-writers such as Agatha Christie and Graham Greene, both of whom famously used the express as a setting for their novels (*see p275*).

The drawing of the Iron Curtain at the end of World War II signalled the end of this particular line: the final run was in 1961. Sporadic revivals have proved nothing more than sops to moneyed nostalgia buffs. In the age of EasyJet and Ryanair, spending three days, nine hours and 40 minutes – for the price of a second mortgage on the house – just to get from Paris to Istanbul seems just a bit extravagant. But then, it always was.

Sirkeci Station, once the transit point for royalty, diplomats and spies, now the gateway to suburbia. *See p85.*

It's notably smaller in scale than most of his other works and noted for its overwhelming use of coloured tiles. The first-floor forecourt, with its colonnaded canopy, well-tended potted plants and slight remove from the chaos down below is, in our opinion, one of the Istanbul's loveliest spots.

TAHTAKALE

The view from the Rüstem Paşa's forecourt is dominated by a large dome, which belongs to the nearby **Tahtakale Hamam Çarşısı**, a 500-year-old bathhouse in the process of being converted into a 21st-century shopping centre. At the time of going to press most of the shop units had yet to be let but there was a pleasant café occupying the main dome chamber.

This area north of Hasırcılar Caddesi is known as Tahtekale. Its streets heave with locals out to snap up bargain clothing, underwear and household accessories. Women shop here to top up their dowries, picking up linens, bedwear, lingerie and towels. This is the place to buy the traditional circumcision outfits that consist of a crown, a white satin cape and a golden staff. Local traders also do a brisk business in wood and wicker ware, knives and tools (garden and otherwise). If you're in the market for handmade wooden spoons and coat-hangers, look no further. **Tahtakale Caddesi** is renowned for its 'portable stalls' manned by nervous, shifty-eyed gents peddling pirated CDs, VCDs, DVDs, computer software, smuggled electronics and cigars. At the first whisper of police in the area, stalls are snapped shut and the owners leg it.

Egyptian Bazaar

Mısır Çarşısı
Yeni Camii Meydanı, Eminönü (0212 513 6597).
Tram Eminönü. **Open** 8am-7pm Mon-Sat.
Map p289 L8.

Booze, bar snacks and boat-watching under the **Galata Bridge**.

Rüstem Paşa Mosque

Rüstem Paşa Camii
*Hasırcılar Caddesi 90 (0212 526 7350). Tram
Eminönü.* **Open** 9am-dusk daily. **Admission** free.
Map p288 L7.

The Golden Horn

Eminönü is the departure point for ferries up
the Bosphorus (*see p240*), across to the Asian
shore (*see p107*) and out to the Princes' and
Marmara Islands (*see pp248-53*). There are also
a few services heading west up the Golden
Horn, which is a scimitar-shaped inlet of the
Marmara some 7.5 kilometres (five miles) long.
It takes its name from the ancient Greek,
Chrysokeras, the linguistic derivation of which
is obscure. The boat traffic is frantic as hulking
vessels skirmish with tiny motor launches for

berthing positions. With busy local bus stations
either side of the road, pedestrian traffic is
similarly intense – watch your bags and wallets.

Mingling with the smell of diesel is the whiff
of deep-frying fish. This comes from the small
boats moored at the dockside, cooking up their
day's catch of small fry for sale in sandwiches.

The best place to observe the hustle and
bustle is from the **Galata Bridge**, the vital link
between the two sides of European Istanbul.
The current ugly structure replaces a much-
loved earlier bridge; this one, a concrete ramp
with four steel towers at its centre (they're
supposed to raise the bridge but don't work)
was built in the 1980s to accommodate the
growing traffic. Its saving grace is the lower
deck of restaurants, bars and tea-houses that
provide ring-side, waterfront seating for a
cheap beer and a session of boat-watching.

The Western Districts

The most conservative Islamic neighbourhoods feature a strong Christian and Jewish heritage.

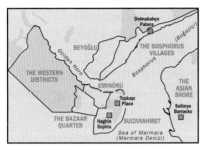

Map p290 & p291

West of Sultanahmet and the Bazaar Quarter are some of the most religiously conservative neighbourhoods in Istanbul. In areas such as **Fatih**, **Fener** and **Balat**, headscarves, chadors and the baggy *şalvar* trousers worn by devout men are much in evidence. But although now Islamic strongholds, these areas also provide a reminder that until as recently as the early 20th century, Christians and Jews made up some 40 per cent of Istanbul's population: the districts are sprinkled with churches, synagogues and Greek Orthodox schools. Also out this way is the **Church of St Saviour in Chora**, one of the city's most dazzling Byzantine monuments. Beyond the ancient city walls, the mosque at **Eyüp** offers a glimpse of a working pilgrimage site, with stunning views from the top of the hill behind. Visitors should dress modestly.

Fatih

Fatih is the neighbourhood immediately west of the Bazaar Quarter. The easiest way to visit is to take the tram from Sultanahmet and hop off at the Üniversite or Laleli stop. Walk north, past rows of leather and suede shops with window-posted signs in Cyrillic reading TREYESTA DEVUSHKA NA RABOTY ('Russian spoken here'), to the **Şehzade Mosque**, the first great complex by Sinan, completed in 1548 and regarded by him as 'apprentice work'.

Cross the mosque's gardens to reach the mighty **Aqueduct of Valens**. Constructed by Roman emperor Valens in the fourth century AD, the aqueduct channeled water from the lakes north of the city to Istanbul's cisterns and continued to do so until the late 19th century.

For a city often under siege, a reliable water supply was of supreme importance. These days, the aqueduct forms a dramatic entrance to the city as modern Atatürk Bulvarı passes beneath its two-tiered arches.

Huddled in the shadow of the the the aqueduct is the attractive little Medrese of Gazanfer Ağa, now the **Cartoon Museum** (*see p109*). A short walk further north is what's now known as the **Zeyrek Mosque** (Zeyrek Camii) but before the Muslim conquest was the Byzantine Church of the Pantocrator. Built in the 12th century for the wife of Emperor John II Comnenus (1118-43), the church became the imperial residence during the Latin occupation and a mosque after the conquest. Although in a deplorable state of repair, it retains some fine internal decoration, including exquisitely carved door frames and marble mosaic paving which, if you're lucky, one of the caretakers will reveal by drawing back the carpets. The church was once the centre of a huge monastery complex, bits of

The old Jewish district of **Balat**. See p90.

which litter the surrounding streets. Archaeological oddments are displayed on a terrace that overlooks the Golden Horn, and which also serves as the swish Zeyrekhane restaurant.

Ten minutes' walk due west from the church is one of the most significant historical sites in the city, albeit one that's frequently overlooked by visitors: the Fatih Mosque.

FATIH MOSQUE

The current vast and unlovely 18th-century baroque structure replaced an earlier mosque, which, in turn, occupied the site of the Church of the Holy Apostles, burial place of most of the Byzantine emperors, Constantine included. However, the church was already in ruins by the time Mehmet II conquered Constantinople, and he used it as a quarry for his own mosque, built in 1470 to celebrate his victory (*fatih* means 'conqueror'). His building was in turn destroyed by a 1766 earthquake. Now all that remains of Mehmet's original structure is the courtyard and parts of the main entrance. The tomb of the Conqueror stands behind the prayer hall. To this day, Fatih Mosque remains a popular place for the pious, many of whom bring picnics and make a day of their visit.

Each Wednesday the streets around the mosque are filled with a vast **street market** (*see p174* **Market trading**).

From the Fatih Mosque follow Darüşşafaka Caddesi north; turn right onto Yavuz Selim Caddesi to pass the fifth-century **Cistern of Aspar** (which now houses a sports complex) and the **Selim I Mosque** (Yavuz Selim Camii), built to commemorate sultan Selim the Grim, so nicknamed for his habit of executing senior officials on a whim. Notwithstanding the barbaric reputation of its founder, the mosque is one of the most beautiful in the city. Little visited, it has a beautiful garden courtyard, while the views from the terrace, which overlooks the Golden Horn, are breathtaking.

Fatih Mosque

Fatih Camii
Fevzi Paşa Caddesi, Fatih. **Open** *9am-dusk daily.* **Admission** free. **Map** p291 G7.

Selim I Mosque

Yavuz Selim Camii
Yavuz Selim Caddesi, Fatih. **Bus** 90, 99A. **Open** 9am-dusk daily. **Admission** free. **Map** p291 G5.

Şehzade Mosque

Şehzade Camii
Şehzadebaşı Caddesi. Tram Üniversite or Laleli. **Open** 9am-dusk daily. **Admission** free. **Map** p288 H8.

Zeyrek Mosque

Zeyrek Camii
İbadethane Sokak, Küçükpazar. **Open** 9am-dusk daily. **Admission** free. **Map** p288 H7.

Fener & Balat

Until the early part of the last century, Fener was primarily Greek, while Balat was mainly Jewish. Although lacking major monuments, these are fascinating areas in which to wander. The most picturesque approach to the two districts is on foot from the Selim I Mosque (*see above*), which is a ten-minute taxi ride from central Sultanahmet.

From the mosque head downhill past the red-brick Fener Greek School for Boys. A little below and to the left is the only Byzantine church still in Greek hands, the **Church of Panaghia Mouchliotissa**. It was built in the 13th century to honour Princess Maria, daughter of Emperor Michael VIII, who was sent as a bride to the khan of the Mongols – hence the alternative name, St Mary of the Mongols. Its immunity from conversion was reputedly at the request of one of Mehmet II's architects, a Greek, and a decree issued by the Conqueror to this effect is the church's proudest possession.

Immediately to the north of the church is the stretch of Byzantine sea wall breached by the Crusaders in 1204. East along İncebal Sokak is the **Greek Orthodox Patriarchate**, an unprepossessing walled compound that has been the world centre of the Greek Orthodox faith for the past 400 years. Entrance is through a three-sided gate. The central section is welded permanently closed in memory of Patriarch Gregory V, who was hanged from it in 1821 as punishment for the outbreak of the Greek War of Independence. The main Church of St George dates from only 1720 and is unremarkable save for three unusual free-standing mosaic icons.

Back west along Yıldırım Street are some of the city's finest old Greek residences, including the Fener Mansions, which date from the 17th and 18th centuries. Most are in a terrible state of repair. Only one is presently occupied, housing a dedicated womens' library (Kadın Kütüphanesi), the first of its type in Turkey.

Equally unique is the church of **St Stephen of the Bulgars**, which is one of Turkey's only examples of a neo-Gothic building. Erected in 1871, it's also exceptional for being constructed entirely from prefabricated cast-iron sections, cast in Vienna and brought to Istanbul by barge down the Danube. It was built for Istanbul's Bulgarian community and is still used today by Macedonian Christians.

THE JEWISH QUARTER

Inland from St Stephen, the streets take on a grid pattern in what used to be Istanbul's main Jewish district. The area boasts the city's oldest synagogue, the **Ahrida Synagogue**, founded in the 15th century before the Ottoman

Home delivery
Western district style.

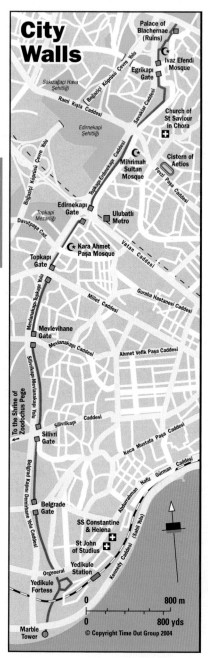

City Walls

Palace of Blachernae (Ruins)

Ivaz Efendi Mosque

Egrikapı Gate

Sakızağaçı Hava Şehitliği

Bağaçı Köprüsü Çevre Yolu

Savaklar Caddesi

Church of St Saviour in Chora

Rami Kışla Caddesi

Edirnekapı Şehitliği

Cistern of Aetios

Mihrimah Sultan Mosque

Topkapı-Edirnekapı Caddesi

Fevzi Paşa Caddesi

Bağaçı Köprüsü Çevre Yolu

Topkapı Mezarlığı

Edirnekapı Gate

Ulubatlı Metro

Davutpaşa Cad.

Kara Ahmet Paşa Mosque

Vatan Caddesi

Topkapı Gate

Mevlanakapı-Topkapı Yolu

Mevlevihane Gate

Guraba Hastanesi Caddesi

Mevlanakapı Caddesi

Millet Caddesi

Ahmet Vefik Paşa Caddesi

Silivrikapı-Mevlanakapı Yolu

To the Shrine of Zoodochus Pege

Silivrikapı

Caddesi

Silivri Gate

Koca Mustafa Paşa Caddesi

Belgrad Kapısı Demirhane Yolu Caddesi

Belgrade Gate

SS Constantine & Helena

Nafiz Gürman Caddesi

Abdurrahman

Kennedy Caddesi (Sahil Yolu)

St John of Studius

Yedikule Station

Orgeneral

Yedikule Fortress

0   800 m

0   800 yds

© Copyright Time Out Group 2004

Marble Tower

conquest. Although it was founded by Macedonians from the town of Ohrid (of which 'Ahrida' is a corruption), its congregation was later formed from the Sephardic community that was booted out of Spain during the inquisitions. The wooden dome, restored in 17th-century baroque style, remains exquisitely beautiful. The place is still in use by the Sephardic community, many of whom speak the medieval Spanish dialect Ladino.

Just around the corner is one of the most interesting churches in the city: the Armenian Orthodox **Church of Surp Hireşdagabet** (Holy Archangels). Originally a Byzantine church, tentatively dated to the 13th century, it was taken over by the Armenians in the early 17th century. Although much of the building dates only from 1835, the side chapel and the *ayazma* (sacred spring) below it are original Byzantine features. The regular congregation is composed almost exclusively of headscarved Muslim women – many devout Muslims take both Christian and Jewish rituals very seriously as 'precursors' of Islam. Even more curiously, every 16 September a miracle cure is reputedly bestowed on one member of the congregation, and on this day Muslims from all over Turkey, many with birth defects or incurable illnesses, crowd the church hoping to be the lucky one.

Ahrida Synagogue
Ahrida Sinagogu
Kürkçüçeşme Sokak 9, Balat. **Map** p291 F3.
Entrance is only by appointment with the Chief Rabbinate (0212 243 5166).

Church of Panghia Mouchliotissa
Kanlı Kilise
Tevkii Caddesi, Fener. **Open** 10am-5pm daily.
Admission free. **Map** p291 G4.

Church of St Stephen of the Bulgars
Mürsel Paşa Caddesi 85-7, Fener (0212 521 1121).
Open 9am-6pm daily. **Admission** free. **Map** p291 G3.

Church of Surp Hireşdagabet
Kamış Sokak, Balat. **Open** Thur morning services only. **Admission** free. **Map** p291 F3.

Greek Patriarchate
Sadrazam Ali Paşa Caddesi, Fener. **Open** 9am-5pm daily. **Map** p291 G4.

Church of St Saviour in Chora

It is often overlooked because it's so far off the beaten track, but in terms of Byzantine splendour, the Church of St Saviour in Chora (also known as the Kariye Mosque or Museum) is second perhaps only to the Haghia Sophia. It was built in the late 11th century but the mosaics and frescos at the root of its fame were added when the church was remodelled in the 14th century. These are arguably the most important surviving examples of Byzantine art anywhere in the world, unparalleled both in execution and state of preservation.

The mosaics in the narthexes depict the genealogy and life of Christ, and the life of the Virgin Mary. Elsewhere are scenes of the Day of Judgement, Heaven and Hell, and the Second Coming. Most spectacular of all is the Resurrection, which has Christ breaking the gates of Hell beneath his feet and wrenching Adam and Eve from their tombs.

Ironically, this Christian art owes its state of preservation to the church's conversion to Islam in the early 16th century, when the frescos and mosaics were covered over. They stayed concealed until their rediscovery in 1860.

At the end of the street leading to the church is the Kariye Hotel which has an excellent restaurant, the **Asitane** (*see p127*).

To get to the church, from Eminönü take any bus for Edirnekapı (37E, 38E, 91O) and get off at the stop beside the Vefa Stadium, which is sunk down below road level off to the right. Alternatively, a taxi from Sultanahmet will cost around $4 to $5.

Church of St Saviour in Chora

Kariye Müzesi
*Kariye Camii Sokak 26, Edirnekapı (0212 631 9241).
Bus 37E, 38E, 91O.* **Open** 9am-4.30pm Mon, Tue, Thur-Sun. **Admission** $7. **Map** p290 D4.

Pigeon trading by the **city walls**.

City walls

Constructed during the reign of Theodosius II (408-450), the walls of Constantinople are the largest remaining Byzantine structure in modern-day Istanbul. Up to the Ottoman conquest in 1453, they stood for over 1,000 years against invading armies, resisting siege on more than 20 occasions.

From the Golden Horn in the north the walls encompass the old city in a great arc, stretching some 6.5 kilometres (four miles) to the Sea of Marmara in the south. Coupled with the sea walls that also ringed Constantinople, they constituted Europe's most extensive set of medieval fortifications.

A triumph of engineering, the land walls comprise inner and outer ramparts with a terrace in between. The outer wall is two metres (seven feet) thick and around 8.5 metres (30 feet) high with 96 towers overlooking the 20-metre (70-feet) moat below. The five-metre (16-feet) thick inner wall looms above at a height of around 12 metres (40 feet), and sports a further 96 fortified towers.

Large stretches have been rebuilt in recent years, drawing criticism from scholars for inappropriate use of modern materials, but the restored sections are undeniably impressive.

WALL WALKING

There are several ways to get to the walls depending on which bit you want to visit. It's possible to walk the whole length, along both the inside and outside and occasionally on top, although care should be taken as some sections are deserted save for vagrants.

The best place to begin is on the Marmara coast at **Yedikule**. Take a bus from Eminönü (80) or Taksim (80T) or, for a more scenic ride, a suburban train from Sirkeci station to the small commuter station at Yedikule. The line passes under the ramparts of Topkapı Palace and winds in and out of what remains of the southern stretch of sea walls.

The walls begin down on the Marmara shore with the imposing **Marble Tower** on a promontory by the sea. It served as an imperial summer pavilion and also as a prison. A chute is still visible through which the corpses of the executed were dumped into the sea.

Back over the coast road is the near-pristine **Gate of Christ**, the first of 11 fortified gates in the walls, and north beyond that, over the other side of the railway line, **Yedikule Fortress**. Impressively restored, the originally Byzantine 'castle of the seven towers' was remodelled by the Ottomans. Its western face incorporates the Golden Gate (now bricked up), a late Roman triumphal arch erected by Theodosius I around AD 390, predating the city walls. Entrance is through a door in the north-east wall; the vertiginous battlements offer wonderful views.

FLYING FRYING FISH

From Yedikule to the **Belgrade Gate** (Belgrad Kapısı), formerly the main Byzantine military gate, and onwards to the **Silivri Gate** (Silivri Kapısı) it is possible to walk on top of the walls or on the terrace below.

In the vicinity of the latter, just outside the walls, is the **Shrine of Zoodochus Pege** ('life-giving spring'). Originally an ancient sanctuary of Artemis, the first church was built over the spring in the early Byzantine era. Destroyed and rebuilt many times since, the present structure dates only from 1833. The shrine itself is a pool containing 'sacred' fish, said to have leapt into the spring from a monk's frying pan on hearing him say that a Turkish invasion of Constantinople was as likely as fish coming back to life.

The next gate along, the **Mevlevihane Gate**, bears several inscriptions including one in Latin boasting how Constantine erected the final phase of the walls in 'less than two months'. Further north beyond Millet Caddesi stands **Topkapı Gate**, or Cannon Gate.

North of Topkapı the walls descend into the Lycus river valley, now a channel for the six lanes of Vatan Caddesi. Lower than the surrounding land, this stretch was particularly difficult to defend. It was here in 1453 that the besieging Ottomans finally broke through. More than 500 years later, the battlements in this section remain in the worst state of repair.

A little to the north, Mehmet the Conqueror made his triumphal entry into the city on the afternoon of the conquest through **Edirnekapı** (Edirne Gate). A plaque on the south side of the gate commemorates the event.

As the city walls approach the Golden Horn, they terminate at the Byzantine **Blachernae Palace**. First constructed around AD 500, the palace was extended in the 11th and 12th centuries, by which time it had become the favoured imperial residence. It's now mostly in ruins. The best-preserved sections are the brick-and-marble three-storey façade known as the Palace of the Porphyrogenitus and the five floors of tunnels and galleries below the Ahmet tea garden, which were cleared of rubble in 1999 for a film shoot and are rather awesome in their medieval splendour.

Blachernae Palace

Anemas Zindanları
Ivaz Ağa Caddesi, Ayvansaray. Bus 5T, 99A. **Open** 9am-7pm daily. **Admission** $1.50. **Map** p92.

Shrine of Zoodochus Pege

Balıklı Kilise
Seyit Nizam Caddesi 3, Silivrikapı (0212 582 3081). Tram Seyitnizam. **Open** 8.30am-4pm daily. **Admission** free.

Yedikule Fortress

Yedikule Müzesi
Yedikule Meydanı Sokak, Yedikule. Bus 80, 80T/ train from Sirkeci. **Open** 9.30am-4.30pm Mon,Tue, Thur-Sun. **Admission** $2. **Map** p92.

Eyüp

Beyond the city walls, a further mile west along the shore of the Golden Horn, is the village of Eyüp (pronounced 'eh-oop'). City historian John Freely describes its traditional image as a 'peaceful backwater devoted to religion and death'. These days the place is on the verge of being absorbed by suburbia, but for the time being it still retains rural and spiritual qualities. This atmosphere comes courtesy of two large, wooded hills that rise up above the village, their slopes kept free of development by virtue of being devoted to the dead. The area's popularity as a burial spot derives from the **Eyüp Mosque**, the holiest mosque in Istanbul, and the third-most sacred site in Islam after Mecca and Jerusalem. Its holy status comes from being the – reputed – burial place of Ayoub al-Ansari (in Turkish, Eyüp Ensari), companion and standard-bearer of the Prophet Mohammed. His tomb is adjacent to the mosque and boasts a golden-framed footprint of Mohammed, as well as some nice Iznik tiling. A constant trail of pilgrims queues for the chance to supplicate themselves before the gilt-caged, green-draped cenotaph. Non-Muslims may also visit. Headscarves are available for women.

There's a vast *külliye* (complex) surrounding the mosque, with most buildings dating – like the mosque and tomb – to 1458 and the reign of Mehmet the Conqueror.

Running north from the main plaza is an attractive shopping street full of bakeries and interesting food shops. From the top end, flag a taxi and ride up all the way up the hill to the **Pierre Loti Café**, named for the 19th-century French romantic novelist who spent several years living in Eyüp. You'll be dropped at a modern touristic development that boasts fantastic views from its terrace, but for something with a little more charm (and equally good views) follow the path down the hill for a modest little tea shop with rickety tables set out beneath the trees.

GETTING THERE

Take the No.99 from Eminönü bus station (the one beside the water) and get off at the Eyüp stop. It's a 15-minute ride. Alternatively, you can catch a ferry, also from Eminönü, stopping off at Kasımpaşa, Fener and Balat en route. The first ferry departs Eminönü at 7.20am and they run hourly until 8pm.

Beyoğlu

The 'other' Istanbul, Beyoğlu is the heart and soul of the modern secular city.

Galata Tower. *See p97.*

Avrupa Pasajı. *See p99.*

Map p292 & p293

Istanbul's 'downtown', Beyoğlu is where the city comes to work, shop and play. A vast area with boundaries that are hard to define, for the purposes of this guide it's everything up the hill north of the Golden Horn as far as Taksim Square. The focus, however, is unmistakably

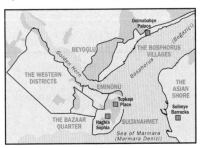

Istiklal Caddesi, the broad pedestrianised spine off which spread countless narrow streets. Since most streets are unsuitable for traffic, the only way to explore the various neighbourhoods that make up Beyoğlu is by foot.

Historically, the district went by two different names: Galata, for the hillside just north of the Golden Horn, and Pera, denoting what's now the lower Istiklal Caddesi area. Foreign-occupied areas since Byzantine times, these were trading colonies across the water from the walls of Constantinople proper, founded by merchants from Italian city-states such as Genoa and Venice.

After the Ottoman conquest in the 15th century, it was to Galata that the European powers sent their first ambassadors. By the 17th century, Galata/Pera was a substantial city in its own right, with a multi-ethnic population known collectively as 'Levantines'. As well as the

Italians, there were many other significant communities, as outlined by a Turkish chronicler of the time: 'The Greeks keep the taverns; most of the Armenians are merchants or money-changers; the Jews are the go-betweens in amorous intrigues and their youths are the worst of all the devotees of debauchery.'

OLD PERA TO NEW PERA

It was during the 19th century that the area acquired its present character. The increased use of iron and brick as building materials instead of the traditional wood made it feasible to construct buildings that could survive the fires that regularly devastated the city.

After the foundation of the republic in the 1930s, the area officially became known as Beyoğlu and blossomed with new restaurants, theatres and concert halls. Older residents still speak wistfully of never daring to go to Istiklal Caddesi without a collar and tie. World War II brought a discriminatory wealth tax that hit the Christians and Jews hard (Muslims were exempt) and many left for Greece, America or Israel. In the '50s and '60s, political tensions caused most of the remaining Greeks to depart. In their place came a flood of poor migrants from Anatolia, and Beyoğlu lost its cachet.

By the late 1980s, Istiklal Caddesi and the area around it was run-down, sleazy and even a little dangerous. That began changing in late 1990 after the simple measure of closing the street to traffic and making it a pedestrian precinct. The subsequent transformation has been swift and continues at pace. December 2003 should see the opening of **Passage Markiz** on lower Istiklal Caddesi, a five-storey complex of shops, bars and restaurants. In contrast to the cut-rate clothing, music and book shops currently associated with Beyoğlu, this will be the place to pick up Cuban cigars, imported wines, Mont Blanc pens and tailored-to-order Ravelli dress shirts. Two narrow lanes behind the Galatasaray Lycée are also set to get a makeover with no less than 24 currently derelict buildings set to be filled with cafés, bars, galleries, restaurants and a boutique hotel, all of which will be marketed under the title **Rue Française**.

Ikmen's Istanbul

If you don't know Çetin Ikmen, he's a fastidious Turkish police inspector, small and thin with a sunken face. He teeters on the edge of alcoholism, chain-smokes and swears like Lily Savage in a whisky-and-cigarettes voice. As it happens, he has a cousin who is a transvestite fortune-teller. Ikmen occasionally seeks his/her help in the frequently convoluted and macabre cases that come his way. A strange and complicated character then, the inspector takes the lead in five novels (with a sixth due in 2004) by London-born author Barbara Nadel.

Even more to the fore than Ikmen in Nadel's books is Istanbul, which is the setting shared by all her stories to date. The city permeates every page. Her descriptions of neighbourhoods, landmarks and locations are as precise and exact as those of a travel writer. Ikmen works out of a police station on Yerebatan Caddesi near the underground cistern in Sultanahmet. He lives nearby on Ticarethane Sokak, just off Divan Yolu. Nadel's first novel, *Belshazzar's Daughter*, begins in the vividly realised backstreets of Balat. In her second, *A Chemical Prison*, a corpse is discovered locked in an attic on Ishak Paşa Caddesi, just down from the gate of the Topkapı Palace. The fourth, *Deep Waters*, begins with a murder victim being dumped on waterfront Reşadiye Caddesi beside the Galata Bridge; the fifth, *Harem*, ends with a shoot-out at the Malta Köşkü in Yıldız Park.

A frequent visitor to Istanbul, Nadel travels armed with a digital camera in order to capture the urban landscapes through which her characters move. It could all be a bit pedantic and trainspotterish but in fact it's handled so skilfully that, taken together, the descriptions and detailing all add up to one great passionate homage to the city. 'It's this place that I love,' says Nadel, 'and I want other people to love it as well.'

Not that she's afraid of showing the spots and blemishes. Her books also deal with AIDS, prostitution, rent boys, family blood feuds and drug use. Not to mention some graphic kinky sex, including in *Belshazzar's Daughter* a woman who gets off on fellating guns (based, claims Nadel, who is a former psychiatric hospital worker, on someone she once met – but socially, not professionally).

To date, three of the books have been translated into Turkish, with the rest to follow. Local press in Istanbul has been good and sales are respectable. Ikmen may not be the perfect Turk but native Istanbulus seem to have taken their fictional compatriot to their hearts, wide flaws and all.

Kamondo Steps: sculpted street furniture.

Galata

Echoing its mercantile origins, Galata remains almost completely commercial. There's even a row of ships, chandlers still trading down along Yüzbaşı Sabahattin Evren Caddesi.

Central to the area's history and easily the most distinctive landmark north of the Golden Horn, the conical-capped **Galata Tower** was originally constructed in 1348. Named the Tower of Christ, it stood at the apex of fortified walls. After the Ottoman conquest it was used to house prisoners of war and was for a time an astronomical observatory. During the 19th century it was a fire-spotting station. In the 1960s it was restored and had a restaurant and nightclub added. Both are completely missable but it is worth paying to ascend to the 360-degree viewing gallery up top, which offers some of the most distinctive views of the city.

Just downhill of the tower on Camekan Sokak, **Beyoğlu hospital** is a large building with a vaguely Gothic tower. It was built in 1904 as the British Seaman's Hospital, designed by Percy Adams, better known as architect of Senate House at London University. The tower afforded clear sightlines to incoming ships, allowing them

to signal ahead news of any disease or illness onboard, an important consideration in the days before ship-to-shore radio.

Around the corner on Galata Kulesi Sokak stands the former British consular prison: the Ottomans allowed favoured nations to imprison their own nationals. The building has been put to imaginative new use as the **Galata House** restaurant (*see p131*).

On the same street is what was formerly the parish church of Galata's Maltese community, the Dominican **Church of St Peter and Paul**. It's a superb neo-classical affair built by the Swiss-born Fossati brothers, dating from 1841 but containing a number of much older relics.

From the 18th century on it was the Galata bankers who kept the declining Ottoman Empire afloat, albeit at ruinous rates of interest. **Voyvoda Caddesi**, at the bottom of Galata Kulesi Sokak, was the banking centre and although the financial institutions have moved out, the street remains lined with imposing pieces of 19th-century grandeur.

Running up from Voyvoda, the **Kamondo Steps** are named after the local Jewish banking family who paid for their construction. They are also one of the city's finest bits of urban design.

Awaiting regentrification.

Mudo Pera. *See p99.*

Part staircase, part sculpture, they were immortalised in the early 1960s in a famous photograph by Henri Cartier Bresson.

ARABS AND JEWS

Galata's historic Jewish presence is celebrated at the western end of Voyvoda Caddesi at the **Jewish Museum** (*see p113*), housed in the beautifully-restored Zülfaris Synagogue.

South of Voyvoda, **Perşembe Pazarı Caddesi** boasts some fine 18th-century merchants' houses, while 100 metres (320 feet) west on Fütühat Sokak stands the only remaining Genoese church, now known as the **Arap Mosque**. Constructed between 1323 and 1337 and dedicated to St Dominic and St Paul, it was the largest of Constantinople's Latin churches. In the early 16th century it was converted to a mosque to serve the needs of Moorish exiles from Spain, which is possibly the source of its current name, 'Arab mosque'. Despite extensive alterations, the design is clearly that of a typical medieval church with apses and belfry.

Just to the north on Yanıkkapı Sokak are more Genoese remains in the shape of the **Burned Gate** (Yanık Kapı), the only remaining gate from the old walls. It still bears a plaque with St George's cross, symbol of Genoa.

Arap Mosque

Arap Camii
Fütühat Sokak, Galata. **Open** 9am to dusk daily. **Admission** free. **Map** p292 L6.

Galata Tower

Galata Kulesi
Galata Square (0212 293 8180). **Open** 9am-8pm daily. **Admission** $3.50. **Map** p292 M5.

Tünel

Opened in 1876, the one-stop **funicular railway** that runs from lower Galata up to Tünel Square on southernmost Istiklal Caddesi is, after London and New York, the third-oldest passenger underground in the world.

Tünel, the area around the upper station, is currently in transition between shabby neglect and arty affluence. Best example of this is the proliferation of chic new businesses such as **KV Café** (*see p148*), occupying a 19th-century Italianate passageway opposite the funicular, and the host of fine new bars and restaurants on Sofyalı Sokak, beyond, such as **Bina** (*see p144*).

Just round the corner from Tünel Square, on Galip Dede Caddesi, is the **Galata Mevlevihanesi**, a working dervish lodge, which also goes by the name of the Museum for Classical Literature. Home of the Whirling Dervishes, it's the only institution of its kind in Istanbul open to the public. A courtyard leads through to the octagonal *tekke* (lodge), a restored version of the 1491 original. The *tekke* can be visited to see exhibits of musical instruments and a number of beautifully illuminated Korans. Also within the complex is the tomb of Galip Dede, the 17th-century Sufi poet after whom the street is named. For more details on the dervishes and their whirlings, *see p100* **Right round, baby, right round**.

Galata Mevlevihanesi

Galip Dede Caddesi 15, Tünel (0212 245 4141).
Open 9.30am-4.30pm Mon, Wed-Sun.
Admission $1.50. **Map** p308 M5.

Istiklal Caddesi

Originally known as Cadde-i Kebir (the high street), and later La Grande Rue De Pera, Istiklal Caddesi gained its present name – 'independence street' – in the wake of the founding of the republic. In character though, it remains completely pre-republican, graced with some wonderfully early 20th-century architecture. The **Botter House** at No.475-7 is an art nouveau masterpiece by Raimondo D'Aronco (*see p41*), built for Jean Botter, Sultan Abdül Hamit's tailor. His daughter offered to leave the building to the city council, but they refused to guarantee its preservation and since her death it has been falling into ever-worsening decay. A few doors up at No.401 the **Mudo Pera** has an art nouveau interior of highly polished wood.

The street's churches are more restrained, often hidden from the street – the result of a restriction forbidding non-Muslim buildings to appear on the city skyline that held sway until the 19th century. Oldest is **St Mary Draperis** at No.429, a fairly humble building dating from 1789 that at one time served as the Austro-Hungarian embassy. This particular stretch of Istiklal is lined with former embassies, some of the buildings still serving as consulates, others converted to new uses.

West of the main street is the small backstreet neighbourhood of **Asmalımescit**, home of the city's low-rent art scene, full of studios and small galleries, and a good locale for casual cafés, cheap eateries and bars. Its western boundary is Meşrutiyet Caddesi, address of the famed **Pera Palas Hotel** (*see p52* **Bed, board & legends**) with its Orient Express associations and celebrity-filled guest book.

Galatasaray & the Flower Passage

Hardly big enough to constitute a district, Galatasaray refers simply to the streets surrounding the old French **Galatasaray Lycée**, founded in 1868. The current building, which dates from 1907, includes the small **Galatasaray Museum** (*see p113*), dedicated to the top Istanbul football team, whose origins lie with the school.

The slight widening of Istiklal in front of the Lycée is known as **Galatasaray Square**. In recent years it's become the venue for regular political demonstrations, most notably by the 'Saturday Mothers', female relatives of the many political activists who have 'disappeared' over the past 20 years. Such demonstrations are illegal and the 'mothers' are usually met by bus-loads of armoured riot police.

Beyoğlu nightlife once revolved around the *meyhanes* (Turkish tavernas) of **Çiçek Pasajı**, formerly the Cité de Pera building (1876), a combination shopping arcade and apartment block. Its heavily restored façade faces the school gates. These days it's the domain of tourists, a beautiful glass-roofed setting for an over priced middling meal (*see p122*). Adjacent is the **Balık Pazarı** (Fish Market), still lined with shops fronted by great wooden trays of piscine still-life on ice. On the east side of the market passage at No.24A, hidden behind big black doors, is the **Armenian Church of the Three Altars** – it's rarely open but worth sticking your head in if you spot the chance.

Just beyond is **Nevizade Sokak** (*see p122*), crammed full of pavement restaurants and the liveliest and loudest dining spot in town. On the west side are two old arcades, the **Avrupa Pasajı** and **Aslıhan Pasajı**: the former is a mini Grand Bazaar, the latter is full of second-hand book and record shops. The *pasajı* lead through to Hamalbaşı Caddesi and the **British Consulate** (1845), designed by Charles Barry, architect of the Houses of Parliament in London, but completed by WS Smith in a neo-renaissance style. The building was bombed in November 2003, in an attack that killed British Consul-General Roger Short and over a dozen others.

TRASH, JUNK AND ANTIQUES

The Çiçek Pasajı is just the most famous of a whole host of covered arcades off Istiklal Caddesi. A few steps south is **Aznavur Pasajı** with three floors of dippy teen-bedroom accessories (incense and candles, *South Park* clocks, comics and clubwear); a few steps north is the **Atlas Pasajı** with more unessential but fun buys from furry lampshades to tribal masks. The Atlas also has two fine bars in the **Eski Kulis** and **Sefahathane** (*see p147*).

The side streets sloping away south of Istiklal Caddesi at this point filter down into the decrepit district of **Çukurcuma**, full of jogging, twisting, narrow alleys that are home to the antique/junk trade (*see p158*). Among the dealers of wedding chests, period furniture and other 'real antiques' are also some dim, dusty cubbyhole stores offering delightful finds like an old London temporary bus stop or cigarette tins painted with scenes of Old Stamboul.

Sightseeing

Taksim

If Çicek Pasajı represents old Beyoğlu, the new Beyoğlu is focused on the stretch of Istiklal Caddesi north of Galatasaray. Arcades, churches and period architecture give way to malls, megastores and multiplexes, plus an ever-proliferating number of bars and cafés.

At its north end, Istiklal Caddesi empties into **Taksim Square**. The name comes from the stone reservoir (*taksim*) on the west side. Built in 1732 on the orders of Mahmut I, the *taksim* was at the end of a series of canals and aqueducts that brought water down from the Belgrad Forest (*see p242*). Despite such picturesque associations, the square is one of the world's uglier public plazas. Big it may be, but it is completely lacking in grandeur – it's little more than a snarled transport hub with a small park attached. It's a place to pass through on the way to somewhere else.

Still, the square is regarded as the heart of modern Istanbul and symbol of the secular republic. So much so that in 1997, when the short-lived Islamist government unveiled plans to build a huge mosque on an adjacent lot, they were forced to backtrack in the face of public disapproval. Instead, the municipality has decided on a $500,000 fountain for the site, complete with sound system and dancing lights.

Right round, baby, right round

When Oscar Hammerstein had Sister Agatha sing of Maria that 'she could throw a whirling dervish out of whirl,' was the *Sound of Music* lyricist aware that he was setting up a clash of religions? Catholic nun versus adherent of an obscure Islamic sect? 'Whirling dervish' is such a familiar phrase, but how many people know just what a dervish is, and, more to the point, why it is that he whirls?

The practice has its origins back in 13th century Anatolia (eastern Turkey), in the city of Konya. There, the Persian-born mystic, Celaleddin Rumi (1207-73), settled after fleeing the destruction of his home city by the Mongol warlord Tamburlaine. Renaming himself the 'Mevlana' (Our Leader), Rumi headed up a very New-Agey school of belief that advocated 'unlimited tolerance, positive reasoning, goodness, charity and awareness through love' (the mission statement is taken from the website of the Celebi family, descendants of the first Mevlana: www.mevlana.net). He preached the hugely subversive notion that all religions are more or less true, and espoused equality for Muslims, Christians and Jews alike.

The whirling was – and still is – a means to attain higher union with God. The spinning is conducted as part of a ceremony known as the *sema* and induces a trance-like state, moving the dancer from the earthly to the spiritual. But this is not something anyone can try at home. In order to whirl properly, the dervishes are forced to undergo a gruelling, three-year training regime. This involves revolving around a brass stud that is kept between the big toe and the second toe. To combat dizziness, the dervishes are taught to keep the eyes fixed on one point – usually the thumb of the left hand.

Most dervishes still reside in Konya but there is a working lodge (*tekke*) in Istanbul, the **Galata Mevlevihanesi** (*see p98*), where dervishes still whirl at 5pm every Sunday from May to September.

If you don't catch the dervishes in action, you can at least listen to the theory. Rumi's writings have been discovered by Hollywood's flakiest celebrities, and his books have shot up the bestseller lists in America. For a truly surreal experience, check out Deepak Chopra's CD *A Gift of Love*, which features the mystic's words recited by the likes of Madonna, Demi Moore and Goldie Hawn.

The Bosphorus Villages

Palaces, parks and waterfront walks.

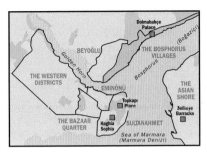

Map p241, p292 & p293

The districts that comprise the heart of modern Istanbul lie high up on the hill above the Bosphorus (*see pp95-100* **Beyoğlu**), but down at water level a chain of small historic neighbourhoods stretches from the Galata Bridge north along the shore of the strait. Exploring them couldn't be simpler, as several buses (including Nos.22, 22R and 25E from Eminönü) run along the coast road. A far more relaxed way of travelling is to take one of the half-hourly ferry services from Eminönü, stopping at Beşiktaş, Ortaköy and Bebek. Unfortunately these are commuter services and so only run in the mornings (around 8am to 10am) and evenings (around 5pm to 8pm).

For an exceedingly pleasant day out, take a bus or boat up to Bebek, explore Rumeli Hisarı and then walk back down to Ortaköy along the waterside promenade.

Karaköy

Karaköy has been a port area since Byzantine times when the north shore of the Golden Horn was a separate settlement – Galata (*see p95*) – distinct from Constantinople. Much of the maritime traffic has since moved out and Karaköy is currently being cleaned up, but the area still boasts a number of monuments reflecting its grittier past. One street inland is the district's oldest building, the **Yeraltı Mosque**. Buried beneath a 19th-century wooden mansion, its interior boasts a forest of squat columns supporting low vaults, and was clearly never designed as a mosque. In fact, this is the remains of the Byzantine castle of Galata that once guarded the entrance to the Golden Horn. It was from here that a great chain was

stretched across the waterway, blocking access to enemy ships in times of siege. The upper part of the castle was demolished following the Ottoman conquest and the remaining lower floor was converted into a mosque in 1757.

Further inland are a couple of curious churches. The Russian Orthodox **Church of St Andrea** on Balyoz Sokak is located on the top floor of what appears to be a 19th-century apartment building but was actually built as a monastery. The monks have long gone but the church has experienced a resurgence over the past decade thanks to the multitudes of Russian tourists who have been visiting the city since the collapse of the Soviet Union. Around the corner is the **Church of St Panagia** belonging to the tiny Turkish Orthodox sect, which broke away from the Greek church in the 1920s and whose mass is delivered in the Karamanli Turkish dialect.

GUNS AND SMOKE

North along Kemeraltı Caddesi, the road passes in the shadow of the looming and slightly sinister **Tophane**, a former Ottoman cannon foundry. There's been a foundry here since the days of Mehmet the Conqueror, although the current building, with its distinctive row of ventilation towers, dates from 1803. Recently renovated, it's now used as an occasional arts and exhibition centre.

Opposite the Tophane are two mosques. The southernmost is the **Kılıç Ali Paşa Mosque**, named for a famed admiral who was born in Calabria of Italian parents, captured by pirates in his youth and then, after gaining his freedom, entered Süleyman's navy and rose to become the commander of the entire Ottoman fleet. It was built by the famed architect Sinan, who was by this time (1580) in his 90s. The northern is the **Nusretiye Mosque**, built in the late 1820s in a baroque style by Kikor Balyan, an Armenian architect whose sons would later design the nearby Dolmabahçe Palace. Behind the mosque is the city's current 24-hour hotspot, a row of cafés specialising in nargiles (*see p152* **Hava nargile**).

From here the main road continues past the modern port, more mosques and, just uphill, the **İnönü Stadium**, home of Beşiktaş football club (*see p233*). Towering over the stadium is the monstrous high-rise development currently leased out to the Ritz-Carlton hotel chain. The

Architectural indigestion guaranteed at the **Dolmabahçe Palace**.

hotel may not be a pretty sight, but high-rollers appreciate it: they often book suites overlooking the stadium when there's a big game on.

Dolmabahçe

A celebration of just about everything that was awful about 19th-century European design, the **Dolmabahçe Palace** is irrefutable evidence of an empire on its last legs. It was built for Abdül Mecit by Karabet Balyan and his son Nikoğos, and completed in 1855, whereupon the sultan and his household moved in, abandoning the Topkapı Palace, which had been the imperial residence for four centuries. The outside is overwrought enough – though the seaside façade of white marble is striking when viewed from the water – but it's trumped by the interior, the work of the French decorator Sechan, who designed the Paris Opera. 'Highlights' are the 36-metre-high throne room with its four-ton, crystal chandelier (a gift from Queen Victoria), the alabaster baths and a 'crystal staircase' that wouldn't look out of place in Las Vegas. It was in Dolmabahçe in 1938 that Atatürk died, although his apartment is not on the tour itinerary (visitors are only allowed round the palace in guided groups). The palace is still occasionally used for gala state functions.

Passing the palace, the road is flanked by impressive colonnades of plane trees. These were planted last century when the palace was constructed and though it almost certainly wasn't a consideration at the time, the choice of the plane was a good one, given the tree's high tolerance to air pollution.

As the plane trees end, the road enters **Beşiktaş**, an unsightly concrete shopping and transport hub with a silvery statue of

Atatürk for a centrepiece. It wasn't always this way: the area was once a quiet suburb of dignified terraced houses and plush mansions. The last remaining terrace is on Spor Caddesi, built to house the staff of Dolmabahçe Palace.

Despite having no real harbour, Beşiktaş can boast strong nautical connections. Down on the waterfront is the **Naval Museum** (*see p115*) and nearby the tomb and statue of Hayrettin Paşa, the Ottoman admiral known in the West as Barbarossa.

Dolmabahçe Palace

Dolmabahçe Sarayı
Dolmabahçe Caddesi, Beşiktaş (0212 236 9000).
Open 9am-4pm Tue, Wed, Fri-Sun. Closes one hour earlier Nov-Apr. **Admission** $10. **Map** p293 R2.

Yıldız

To the north-west of Beşiktaş are the extensive grounds of **Yıldız Palace**, a sprawling complex of buildings of which only a small part is open. Most of the palace's buildings date from the late 19th century when the paranoid Sultan Abül Hamit II ('Abdül the Damned') abandoned waterfront Dolmabahçe for fear of attack by foreign warships. The sultan was so fearful for his safety that labourers on this new palace were reputedly not permitted to communicate with workers on other shifts and no architect was allowed to see the complete plans. Only the sultan knew the overall layout and the location of the rumoured secret passages. He never slept in the same suite two nights running and placed large objects in the palatial passageways to obstruct the escape of any would-be assassins. Rooms open to visitors contain porcelain and furniture from the palace and some of Abdül Hamit's possessions, most

poignantly the carpentry set with which he passed his time after being deposed in 1908.

Back on Yıldız Caddesi is one of the most striking monuments in the city, the **Şeyh Zafir Complex**. Comprising a tomb, library and fountain, it commemorates an Islamic sheikh but is designed in art nouveau style by Raimondo D'Aronco (*see p41*).

YILDIZ PARK

A little further along, a side road leads off Yıldız Caddesi to the left into Yıldız Park, formerly the palace grounds, now a pleasantly overgrown hillside forest. Sadly, the small tea house built for Abdül Hamit, of which he was the sole patron, is long gone but there are several former imperial pavilions including the Şale Pavilion, a D'Aronco-designed building set in private gardens at the top of the park, open to the public as the **Yıldız Chalet Museum**. Inside, the long, creaking wooden corridors have a dark and musty quality, the 60 rooms furnished with the original ornate furniture of the period. The obligatory tour takes you to the Grand Salon, a massive court chamber, empty except for a line of chairs around the edge that point up the empty grandeur of the place.

Also in the park is the **Imperial Porcelain Factory**, which mass-produces rather weedy china but does so in another splendid building designed by D'Aronco, and the **Malta Köşkü**, an 1870 pavilion in which Abül Hamit had his brother Murad imprisoned. It now makes an attractive café-restaurant; the terrace offers an excellent view of the Bosphorus and makes for a great lunch venue.

Across from the park entrance, between Yıldız Caddesi and the Bosphorus, is what's left of the **Çırağan Palace**, the last of the Ottoman imperial palaces, built for Abdül Aziz who died there – probably murdered – in 1876, two years after it was completed. In 1908, it was restored to house the Ottoman parliament but it burnt down in 1910 and remained a shell until it was rebuilt as a hotel by the Kempinski chain. The tawdriness of the restoration has attracted criticism but the view from the waterside terrace is undeniably spectacular.

Imperial Porcelain Factory

Yıldız Parkı ici (0212 260 2370). **Open** 9am-noon; 1-5pm Mon-Fri. **Admission** $1. **No credit cards**.

Malta Köşkü

Yıldız Park, Beşiktaş (0212 258 9453). **Open** 9am-midnight daily. **Starters** $4-$6. **Main courses** $5-$12. **Credit** MC, V.

Yıldız Chalet Museum

Yıldız Şale Müzesi
Palanga Caddesi 23, Yıldız Park, Beşiktaş (0212 259 4570). **Open** 9am-5pm Tue, Wed, Fri-Sun. **Admission** $1.50. **No credit cards**.

Yıldız Palace

Yıldız Sarayı
Yıldız Caddesi, Beşiktaş (0212 258 3080). **Open** 9.30am-4.30pm Tue-Sun. **Admission** $1. **No credit cards**.

Ortaköy

Ortaköy has long been a thriving social and commercial centre for anyone wanting to escape the crush of the inner city. In the 17th century, Ottoman chronicler Evliya Çelebi noted with a hint of disdain, 'The place is full of infidels and Jews; there are 200 shops, of which a great number are taverns.'

It continues to hold great appeal, with narrow cobblestone streets closed to traffic, tiny two- and three-storey houses painted in pastels and a pretty waterfront plaza overlooked by the **Mecidiye Mosque**. Set dramatically on a promontory jutting into the strait, the mosque was built for Sultan Abdül Mecit in 1854 by Nikoğos Balyan, the architect responsible for the excesses of the Dolmabahçe. Happily, it avoids the vulgarity of the palace, standing instead as one of the most attractive baroque buildings in the city.

Just to the south of the mosque, beside the ferry landing stage, the waterfront piazza **Ortaköy Square** (Iskele Meydanı) is fringed with open-air cafés and restaurants (*see p139* **Çinar Restaurant**; *p155* **Sedir**).

The tight nexus of streets inland from the square has been brutally gentrified in recent years, scrubbed up and filled with unnecessary shops; at weekends it's the venue for a popular **craft market** (*see p174* **Market trading**).

Nearby and besieged by traffic crawling around the one-way system are the twin domes of a 16th-century hamam, yet another work by Mimar Sinan. Recently restored, it is now open as bar-restaurant **Kethuda** (*see p152*).

North of Ortaköy, the road passes under the Golden Gate-like, kilometre-long **Atatürk Bridge**, finished just in time for the Turkish republic's 50th birthday celebrations in 1973. Beyond is a fairly dull stretch, notable only for a string of exclusive nightspots where Istanbul high-society go to shake its stuff (*see p224* **Bosphorus Babylon**).

Arnavutköy

Arnavutköy, the 'Albanian Village', is far more low-key than Ortaköy and has yet to be spoilt by an influx of venture capital. To the water, it presents an attractive face, with its picturesque terrace of 19th-century wooden *yalıs* (Bosphorus mansions), although the traffic sweeping past them does detract from the effect.

In Ottoman times, the local population was not Albanian, as the name would imply, but predominantly Greek and Armenian. It's overwhelmingly Turkish today but a small community of Greeks still lives around here and celebrates mass at the Orthodox **Church of Taxiarchs** in the backstreets. Next to the church is a small chapel containing a sacred spring, or *ayazma*, which is reached down a set of polished marble stairs.

More than a few of the local businesses occupy great old wooden houses with lace-like trim, pulpit balconies and ridiculous amounts of ornamentation. The number of such buildings undergoing restoration increases almost weekly and Arnavutköy is rapidly taking on an almost fairytale appearance.

Soaking up the sun at **Ortaköy**. *See p103.*

Supposedly enjoying official protection, this architectural heritage has ironically long been under threat from the government itself – plans for a third Bosphorus bridge threatened literally to rip apart the neighbourhood with great concrete supports. However, opposition from local residents has swayed officials towards a less contentious tunnel project.

Bebek

Just north of Arnavutköy, a small white light-house marks **Akıntı Burnu**, a promontory jutting out into the straits, named after the strong current that swirls and eddies past the shore. It's a favourite spot for local fishermen who cast out from the shore, but also trawl from rickety wooden boats, battling all the while against a flow so brisk that in days gone by sailing ships often had to be towed around the point by porters.

From Akıntı Burnu it's a ten-minute stroll along a broad promenade set low beside the water to the next 'village', Bebek. Ranged around an arching bay backed by wooded hills, it occupies a hugely attractive spot and has been developed into an affluent suburb with the air of a Hampstead on the Bosphorus.

At the southern edge of Bebek, on the fringe of a small waterfront park, is a handsome white, wooden, art-nouveau mansion, commissioned by the ruler of Egypt and still in service as the **Egyptian consulate**. It was designed by the prolific Italian architect, Raimondo D'Aronco, who would be aggrieved at the clusters of satellite dishes that mar its profile and its general state of dilapidation.

At the top end of the park is Bebek's tiny ferry station and an equally diminutive brown stone mosque dating from 1912. Next door, the **Bebek Café** is as basic as they come, but it's a pleasant, unaffected place for a coffee. Round the corner, the high street is a bit of a let-down, lined with modern buildings, including an overly prominent McDonald's, and choked by traffic. But take any of the streets heading uphill, away from the water, and almost immediately you're surrounded by greenery and wooden terraces. Head up Hamam Sokak opposite the park and after a few minutes' walk there's another good place to take a break and get something to eat in the **Café de Pera**.

Back on the high street, among the shops selling silk ties and antiques is **Meşhur Bebek Badem Ezmesi**, specialising in marzipan, which is beautifully displayed in glass-fronted hardwood display cabinets.

From Bebek, the promenade winds north towards the fortress of Rumeli Hisarı, about a ten- to 15-minute walk. Before reaching the castle, a sign points up a steep road beside the Kayalar Mezarlışı, one of Istanbul's oldest Muslim cemeteries, to the **Aşıyan Museum** housed in the eyrie of celebrated poet Tevfik Fikret (1867-1915). It's an attractive wooden mansion and although the exhibits don't amount to much, the views from the upper-storey balconies are wonderful.

Aşıyan Museum

Aşıyan Müzesi
Aşıyan Yolu, Rumeli Hisarı (0212 263 6986). Bus 25E, 40. **Open** 9am-4.30pm Tue, Wed, Fri, Sat. **Admission** $2.

Rumeli Hisarı

Rounding the point to the north of Bebek brings you face-to-face with the imposing fortress of Rumeli Hisarı and below it, the village suburb of the same name. Just before the small central square is a real oddity, **Edwards of Hisar**, an upper-crust tailor more suited to Savile Row than the middle Bosphorus. The scene is given

King Mustafa and the golden bowl

Beşiktaş may be short on sights (just the Naval Museum, really) but when it comes to facilities it can't be beat: it's a major transport hub for buses, *dolmuş* and ferries, it has a good produce market and in the 'Altun Tuvalet' – the Golden Toilet – it has the city's model public convenience.

A few steps from the post office (PTT) the entrance is advertised with a sea of coloured lights, plastic roses and busts of Atatürk. Mount the shallow step (gents to the left, ladies to the right) to a world of white-tiled hygiene to render a health inspector speechless with awe. The toilets themselves are so spotless that it seems somehow sacrilegious to actually pee in them. As you wash your hands afterwards you'll find all manner of other aspects of personal grooming are also catered for. Broken a nail? Manicure sets are provided. Popped a button? Get to work with the sewing kit. Need a shave? Help yourself to a razor and foam. If that's not enough, there are even shower facilities and hair dryers.

The Istanbul municipality can claim no credit for any of this; instead, it's all the doing of one man, the self-proclaimed 'King

Mustafa', monarch of the Golden Bowl. His real name is Mustafa Soydan. His obsession with toilets dates back almost 30 years when, as a taxi driver, Mustafa constantly encountered tourists who were horrified at the state of Istanbul's dirty public loos. Later, working as a truck driver in continental Europe, he came into contact with the clean bowls of Germany and Belgium and an obsession was born.

He's now been operating the Altun Tuvalet for close to 20 years. It doubles as his home and a platform for his philosophies on public hygiene, which are spelt out on notices: 'When a cat's a cat, it covers over its shit'. King Mustafa feels that most of those using his facilities fall short of the feline ideal. Every now and again, though, someone walks in who passes his cleanliness test and they are rewarded with a souvenir of their visit in the form of an inscribed plaque and a golden Atatürk paperweight.

Altun Tuvalet

Büyük Beşiktaş Çarşısı 16, Beşiktaş (0212 227 3562). **Open** 7am-9pm daily. **Charges** $0.70 WC; $1.75 shave; $3.50 shower.

Bosphorus throat-cutter **Rumeli Hisarı**.

added incongruity by the presence of the **Fatih Mehmet Bridge**, which at a span of 1,096 metres (3,634 feet), is among the longest suspension bridges in the world. Designed, like the Atatürk Bridge, by a British engineer, it was completed in 1988 but has a historic precedent: it spans the straits at the point where King Darius of Persia crossed via a pontoon bridge with his army in 512 BC.

THE FORTRESS

Consisting of three huge towers joined by crenellated defensive walls, the fortress was raised in a hurry as part of Mehmet II's master plan to capture Constantinople. Facing the 14th-century castle of Anadolu Hisarı (already in Ottoman hands) across the Bosphorus' narrowest stretch, Rumeli Hisarı was designed to cut Byzantine maritime supply lines and isolate Constantinople from its allies. For this, it earned itself the nickname Boğazkesen, the 'Throat-Cutter'. Designed by the sultan himself, work was completed in August 1452, just four months after commencing. Garrisoned by a troop of Janissaries and bristling with cannon, several of which can be seen lying below the walls, Rumeli Hisarı proved its effectiveness instantly, sinking a Venetian merchant vessel that attempted to run the blockade. Having helped secure the Ottoman conquest of Constantinople, the castle lost its military importance and was downgraded to a prison.

The castle was restored by the government in 1953 and contemporary visitors can clamber around the walls, playing out childhood fantasies. An open-air theatre within the courtyard hosts musical events almost nightly through the summer (*see p181*).

Two bus stops north of Rumeli Hisarı is **Emirgan**, famed for its tulip gardens (best visited late April or early May), and also the location for the excellent **Sakıp Sabancı Museum** (*see p116*), dedicated to calligraphy and 19th-century fine art.

Rumeli Hisarı

Rumeli Hisarı Müzesi
Yahya Kemal Caddesi, Rumeli Hisarı. Bus 25E, 40.
Open 9am-4.30pm Tue-Sun. **Admission** $2.
Map p241.

Sightseeing

The Asian Shore

Istanbul's other continent is less hectic, more rural and lures Europe over to shop.

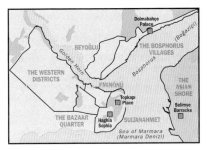

Map p296 & p297

Seen on the map, Istanbul may appear to be split into two cities, one in Europe and one in Asia, but this has never been the reality. Historically 'the city' was always the area within the Byzantine walls, south of the Golden Horn, with even nearby districts such as Galata regarded as separate entities. As late as the early 1980s, the Asian shore was little more than a bunch of disconnected villages. Today these have coalesced into a sprawl of dormitory suburbs which make up Asian Istanbul.

Though lacking the European city's richness, the Asian shore does offer a pleasantly less hectic experience. The two main centres of Üsküdar and Kadıköy offer shopping with a regional slant and a sprinkling of historic sights. North of Üsküdar, the settlements along the Asian Bosphorus still resemble the quiet fishing villages they so recently were.

Although two great suspension bridges now span the straits, the best way to get here is by boat. Between 6am and midnight, ferries depart every 15 minutes from Eminönü (just west of Sirkeci station), Karaköy and Beşiktaş for both Üsküdar and Kadıköy. The crossing takes around 20 minutes.

AN EARLY START

While most of what's interesting dates from the past 100 years or so, the area's history predates that of the European shore. The oldest settlement in the Istanbul metropolitan area, Chalcedon, was discovered near Kadıköy and dates from neolithic times, much earlier than anything on the European side. The first Greek city was also founded at Kadıköy in 675 BC – 17 years before the founding of Byzantium.

But, separated by water from their more powerful European neighbour, the Asian settlements suffered badly over subsequent millennia; the work of various invading armies explains the lack of substantial early remains.

Before the 19th century, only Üsküdar saw any significant development. That changed in 1852 when a steam ferry company, Şirket-i Hayriye (literally 'the good deeds company'), started plying its trade across the straits. Rich Levantines from Beyoğlu began constructing elaborate summer mansions along the shore to the south and east of Kadıköy.

For the first 50 years of the service, the ferries were all products of British shipyards. In fact, trade between the Ottoman and British empires was at such a level that by the end of the 19th century the Kadıköy suburb of Moda was more or less an English colony.

Under the republic, most of the mansions were demolished and replaced by apartment blocks. These retained the mansion garden settings, though, something which gives the Asian shore, especially between Kadıköy and Bostancı, a more spacious feel than the European side.

Kadıköy

No trace remains of the Greek or Byzantine settlements of Chalcedon, but modern Kadıköy does retain many hints of its 19th-century incarnation as an area largely settled by Greeks and Armenians. Arriving by ferry, this isn't immediately apparent as the two most visible buildings, Kadıköy Municipality and the local theatre, are in an unlovely modernist style.

Bear right for the main Söğütlüçeşme Caddesi and cut into the alleys to the south of it beside the **Mustafa Iskele Mosque**. This is the old bazaar, an area of narrow streets lined with tiny two- and three-storey buildings, many dating from the 19th century. Some of the best food shopping in Istanbul is to be had here. At the top end of **Yasa Sokak** are delis stocking a huge range of regional Turkish produce. A few steps south on Mühürdar Caddesi, opposite a small Armenian church, **Esmer Ekmek** bakes on the premises in a wood-fired oven.

Other than the bakery, Mühürdar is almost completely given over to booksellers, most specialising in academic textbooks. Narrow,

Kadıköy Market.

Beyoğlu, and has something of a student quarter feel. It's worth aiming to be here on a Tuesday or Sunday for the street market (*see p174* **Market trading**), which fills the streets north of the bull statue, a local landmark on Söğütlüçeşme Caddesi, the main street.

South of the bull statue, on Bahariye Caddesi, is the **Sürreya Cinema** (*see p195*), the oldest picture house in town. Originally built by an Ottoman paşa as an opera house, its over-the-top neo-classical façade is a reminder that this area was once distinctly well-to-do.

Beyond the cinema, Kadıköy gives way to the posher suburb of **Moda**. A few minutes' walk south is the waterfront, a popular promenade with a tiny ferry terminal designed in late-Ottoman revival style by Vedat Tek (*see p42*).

SOCCER AND SHOPPING

East of Kadıköy is **Rüştü Saraçoğlu Stadium**, home of Fenerbahçe football club. Although currently eclipsed by Galatasaray, Fener has traditionally been one of Turkey's top three teams, its support drawn from the lower middle classes. Such is the fanaticism of supporters round here that the area is often referred to as the 'Republic of Fenerbahçe'.

Behind the stadium is **Bağdat Caddesi**, one of the city's best-known streets. For much of its immense length it's an unremarkable swathe of asphalt, but passing through the plush suburb of Suadiye it metamorphoses into fashion-victim heaven. Lined with upmarket clothing and design stores, beauty clinics, pavement cafés and restaurants, it's the cruising strip of choice for *nouveau-riche* Istanbul.

Haydarpaşa

Across the bay from Kadıköy stands the imposing edifice of **Haydarpaşa station**, looking like nothing so much as a Rhineland castle – not surprising, given that it was a gift from Kaiser Wilhelm of Germany and was designed by German architects. It's the terminus of the Anatolian railway system, the end of the line for trains from as far east as Tehran (serviced by the weekly TransAsya Express). On the waterfront piazza fronting the station is a small but perfectly formed **ferry terminal**, another Vedat Tek design.

The area north of Haydarpaşa is thinly developed, largely because it belongs to the military and to Marmara University. Each owns one of the two imposing buildings that truly dominate the area.

The **Selimiye Barracks** were originally constructed in 1799 during the reign of Selim III as part of his plan to create a 'new army' to challenge the hegemony of the Janissaries. He

sloping **Dumlupınar Sokak** boasts more bookshops, including, at No.17, **Greenhouse Books**, run by an American lady, Charlotte McPherson, who offers tea and coffee as well as a large English-language stock.

Güneşlibahçe Sokak has more great delis and food shops, including one devoted to just honey, another to olive oil, and some fantastic fishmongers. One block east, **Dellalzade Sokak** is lined with shops selling antiques.

The whole area has a lively café and bar scene (centred on **Kadife Sokak**) – it's the Asian shore's rather downmarket answer to was murdered for his efforts and his barracks burnt down. Thirty years later Mahmut II was more successful, defeating the Janissaries and raising the present building. During the Crimean War (1853-6) the barracks served as a hospital run by Florence Nightingale; the north-west corner is preserved as the **Florence Nightingale Museum** (*see p113*).

The other grand building is the former **Haydarpaşa High School**, now Marmara University medical faculty. It's the largest of the many commissions completed by Raimondo D'Aronco (*see p41*).

Close by the High School, just off Burhan Felek Caddesi, is the **British Crimean War Cemetery**, containing the graves of Crimean War and World War I dead. As far-flung corners of foreign fields go, it's rather pleasant, with neatly manicured lawns tended by the Commonwealth War Graves Commission. Access is through the gate lodge, which is usually manned.

Largest of the area's cemeteries is the **Karaca Ahmet cemetery**, named after a warrior companion of the second Ottoman sultan, Orhan. The cemetery is thought to have been founded as early as the mid 14th century and estimates put the number of interments at over a million, making it easily the largest boneyard in Turkey.

To get to the barracks and cemeteries take any Üsküdar-bound *dolmuş* ($0.60) from the ranks just south of Haydarpaşa Station.

Üsküdar

Stepping ashore from the ferry, the newly arrived are pitched into a nightmare of buses, *dolmuş* and taxis tearing round the central square. All this activity is a bit misleading because in contrast to lively Kadıköy, Üsküdar is highly conservative, populated largely by transplants from rural Anatolia. During the Muslim holy month of Ramazan, Üsküdar is the site of one of the city's largest *iftar* (literally 'break-fast') tents, with masses of food donated by local businesses. The main point of interest for shoppers are the antique shops on **Büyük Hamam Sokak**, which is one block south of the **Mimar Sinan Çarşısı**, a 16th-century hamam converted into a small market.

Otherwise, the district's attractions are its mosques. Üsküdar was a favourite place to build these because the Asian side lies closer to Mecca. The **Iskele Mosque** (1548) opposite the ferry terminal, and the **Şemsi Ahmet Paşa Mosque** (1580), down on the shore, are both the work of Sinan. The Şemsi is particularly attractive; get there by walking south along the waterfront promenade past a string of floating fish restaurants. Inland on Şemsi Paşa Caddesi stands the earliest of Üsküdar's mosques, the **Rumi Mehmet Paşa Mosque**, built in 1471 for the then grand vizier. He was of Greek origin, which may explain the strong Byzantine influence in a design which incorporates a cylindrical drum under the dome.

Sightseeing

Journey's end/journey's beginning: **Haydarpaşa station**.

The **Yeni Valide Mosque** back on Uncular Caddesi also has a Greek connection. It was constructed for Sultan Ahmet III, whose mother was born Greek, captured at the age of three, and grew up in the harem where she graduated from mistress to wife to mother of the sultan (*valide sultana*). The building is a late example of classical Ottoman style, with an attractive façade but a disappointing interior.

LEANDER'S TOWER

On a small island off the southern shore of Üsküdar is a stubby white tower, diminutive but for some reason one of the city's best-loved landmarks, endlessly recycled in graphics and logos. Although the island was occupied by a fortress in Byzantine times, the tower dates only from the last century. It has been used as a quarantine centre, a lighthouse, a customs control point and a hideout for the villainous Elektra (Sophie Marceau) in 1999's James Bond picture, *The World is Not Enough*.

In Turkish it's known as Kız Kulesi, or **Maiden's Tower** – supposedly because a princess was once confined here after a prophet foretold that she would die from a snakebite. The fatal bite was duly delivered by a serpent that arrived in a basket of fruit. The same story is associated with numerous other castles around the coast. In English it's known as Leander's Tower, the name deriving from the Greek myth of Leander, who swam the Hellespont – again, absolutely nothing to do with this island.

The tower is open to the public as a café-restaurant. To get here, walk the shoreline promenade to Salacak (about a 15-minute walk from central Üsküdar), where boats leave every 15 minutes from noon to 1am. The return trip costs $3. Lunch (frankfurters, fish in a basket, salads) is $5 to $10 in the ground floor restaurant, which is done out as an Ottoman banquet hall. Dinner is a pricey reservations-only affair and not really worth the bother.

Maiden's Tower

Kız Kulesi
(0216 342 4747). **Open** *Tower* noon-7pm.
Restaurant 8.30pm-1am Mon-Sat. **Set menu** $35.
Credit AmEx, MC, V. **Map** p296 U3.

The Asian Bosphorus

Just beyond the first Bosphorus Bridge stands **Beylerbeyi Palace**, last of the great ugly Ottoman palaces. Facing north-west, it gets little direct sunlight – the place was intended as a summer annexe to the main palace at Dolmabahçe. Beylerbeyi didn't even have its own kitchen: food was brought over from the European shore by boat. After being deposed in

The legendary **Maiden's Tower**.

1908, Sultan Abdül Hamit II spent the last years of his life here. Tours take 15 to 20 minutes and, apart from the main palace with its sumptuous furnishings, immense crystal chandeliers and over-the-top decoration, also take in some of the five adjoining pavilions.

The village of **Beylerbeyi** boasts a pretty harbour with tea houses and a few pleasant restaurants. The nearby **Hamidievvel Mosque** is unusual in having a rose garden. At weekends, the area by the ferry jetty gets taken over by craft stalls.

North from here the landscape gets a whole lot greener. The 1990s saw property prices soar as rich refugees from the European shore began to move in. The most expensive properties are the *yalıs*, the wooden shoreside mansions which hug the strip between the road and the sea. As they're mostly invisible behind high security walls, you'll need to take a Bosphorus cruise (*see p240*) to see them.

Çengelköy, the next town up, was a village until it featured in a long-running TV soap, *Süper Baba*, precipitating an influx of money and car showrooms. The harbour is still pleasant, though, and there are a couple of waterside fish restaurants offering good views.

The wide valley to the north of Kandilli is split by two narrow rivers, Küçüksu and Göksu Deresi, together once known as the 'Sweet Waters of Asia'. In Ottoman times, the water meadows between the two were a popular picnic ground for the rich. Even Sultan Abdül Mecit got in on the act, erecting the modest **Küçüksu Palace** on the shore.

Beylerbeyi Palace

Beylerbeyi Sarayı
Abdullah Ağa Caddesi 12 (0216 321 9320). Bus 15 from Üsküdar. **Open** 9.30am-5pm Tue, Wed, Fri-Sun (closes 1hr earlier Nov-Mar). **Admission** $4.

Küçüksu Palace

Küçüksu Sarayı
Küçüksu Caddesi, Beykoz (0216 332 3303). Bus 15 from Üsküdar/101 from Beşiktaş. **Open** 9.30am-4pm Tue, Wed, Fri-Sun. **Admission** $2.

Museums

The wealth of seven millennia exhibited, from Alexander's sarcophagus to Atatürk's underwear and alien autopsies.

Given the city's epic empire-building history, it's little surprise that Istanbul's museums are so richly and variedly stocked. Energetic museophiles can flit from hulking fourth-century BC sarcophagi to alien autopsies to Atatürk's monogrammed underwear in the space of a single afternoon. However, with sweeping budget cutbacks and bureaucracies that can make glaciers seem fast moving, many of these institutions are in an advanced state of decay. Lack of funds also means large sections of centrepiece museums are closed, while other parts are being indefinitely 'redecorated'.

Antiquities also continue to be half-inched in bulk occasionally to resurface in the auction houses of London, New York and Amsterdam. (Although the latest fashion is to jimmy the tiles off the city's many medieval mosques.)

Principal among the museums are the old imperial palaces of **Topkapı** (*see p70*) and **Dolmabahçe** (*see p102*), after which the most

important and extensive collections are held at the **Archaeology Museum** and the **Museum of Turkish & Islamic Art**. The new **Sakıp Sabancı Museum** shows what money can buy, while the superb **Rahmi M Koç Museum** breaks the Turkish mould with well-lit, informative and even interactive displays. The **UFO Museum** represents a welcome diversion into the twilight zone.

Elsewhere, be prepared for exhibits labelled – if at all – in Turkish only. Inquiries about English-speaking tour guides are likely to bring hopeless, embarrassed shrugs from the museum attendants. Check around the entrance for printed foreign-language guides, which, as well as offering a pointer on what's inside, are often also great exercises in syntactic meltdown. A few of the major museums have book and souvenir shops (the one at the Archaeology Museum is good), but film shows and cultural programmes are well off the radar.

Big boys and little girls all love the **Rahmi M Koç Museum**. See p116.

Vast bodies of history at the **Archaeology Museum**.

ber of items it has to house. Even so, the bulk of the collection remains in storage due to lack of display space and funds.

Greeting visitors is a grinning statue of Bes, a demonic Cypriot demigod of inexhaustible power and strength, qualities required by anyone hoping to get through even a fraction of the 20 galleries within. Starting with the pre-Classical world, they cover 5,000 years of history, with artefacts gathered from all over Turkey and the Near East and grouped thematically. Highlights include a collection of sixth to fourth-century BC sarcophagi from a royal necropolis at Sidon, in modern Lebanon, of which the finest is known as the Alexander Sarcophagus because of the scenes of the Macedonian general's victory at Issus (333 BC) adorning its side panels.

Up on the first floor, 'Istanbul Through the Ages' is the city's history presented through a few key pieces, including a serpent's head lopped off the column in the Hippodrome (*see p77*) and a section of the iron chain that stretched across the Bosphorus to bar the way of invaders. One great innovation is a small children's area, complete with low cabinets and a Wooden Horse.

The **Tiled Pavilion** (Çinili Köşk), which is out in the museum courtyard, dates back to 1472 and the reign of Sultan Mehmet II, Ottoman conqueror of Constantinople. Built in a Persian style it was an imperial viewing stand that overlooked a large gaming field, now occupied by the main museum building. Unfortunately, it's currently closed to the public. To the south, beside the entrance to the complex, is the **Museum of the Ancient Orient**, containing antiquities from the Mesopotamian, Egyptian and Hittite cultures, including some wonderful monumental glazed-brick friezes from the main Ishtar Gate of sixth-century Babylon. There is also the world's first peace treaty (1283 BC), a clay tablet signed by the Hittite king Hattushilish III and Egyptian pharaoh Rameses II that ended a lengthy conflict between these two ancient rival empires.

Atatürk Museum

Atatürk Müzesi
Halaskargazi Caddesi 250, Şişli (0212 233 4723).
Bus 46H. **Open** 9am-4pm Tue-Sat. **Admission** free.
Map p287.
In northern Şişli, a short bus ride from Taksim Square, the iconic candy-pink Atatürk Museum is an old Ottoman house in which Mustafa Kemal once stayed. It now contains three floors of memorabilia of the great man, from his astrakhan hat to his silk underwear, via a wine-stained tablecloth on which he bashed out the new Turkish alphabet over a picnic lunch in 1928. The top floor also has a collection of propaganda paintings from the liberation war, depicting scenes of Greek brutality with, in a couple of instances, the flag of the perfidious British fluttering in the background. Marvel at how Greek soldiers of the period could ever have been taken seriously advancing into battle with those fluffy pom-poms on their shoes.

Opening hours vary but, by and large, Monday is the day they all close. Tickets are sold on the door only and students generally get half-price admission on presentation of an ISIC card. Photography is almost always permitted, provided you don't use a flash, although there is often an extra charge.

Archaeology Museum

Arkeoloji Müzesi
Osman Hamdi Bey Yokuşu, Topkapı Sarayı, Gülhane (0212 520 7740). Tram Gülhane. **Open** 9.30am-5pm Tue-Sun. **Admission** $3.75 inc Museum of the Ancient Orient. **Credit** MC, V. **Map** p289 O9.
The collection of classical antiquities displayed here is world class and – rarely for Istanbul – everything is well lit and comprehensively labelled. Sitting within the grounds of the Topkapı Palace (*see p70*), the museum was founded in the mid-19th century in an attempt to staunch the flow of antiquities then being spirited out of the country by foreigners to fill the museums of Europe. The exhibits were originally housed in the Tiled Pavilion (*see below*) until the commissioning of a new building, since extended on three occasions to keep up with the burgeoning num-

Calligraphy Museum

Vakıf Hat Sanatları Müzesi
*Beyazıt Square, Beyazıt (0212 527 5851). Tram
Beyazıt.* **Open** 9am-4pm Tue-Sat. **Admission** $1.50.
No credit cards. Map p288 K10.

A sad reminder of the perishable nature of human
endeavour, this limited celebration of what was one
of the principal arts of the Ottoman Empire now
reeks of rotting manuscripts. Occupying an historic
former *medrese* (theological college) beside the monumental university gate, the museum has what was
once an impressive display of calligraphic work, now
gone to seed. Forbidden to portray living beings by
their religion (although this wasn't always strictly
adhered to), Islamic artists developed alternative
forms of virtuosity. Calligraphy was regarded as a
particularly noble art because it was a way of beau-
tifying the text of the Koran. But the sanctity of the
text placed restrictions on the flourishes that could
be added. Not so with the sultan's *tuğra*, or mono-
gram, which incorporated his name, titles and
patronymics in one highly stylised and elaborate
motif – the forerunner of the modern logo. Despite
the museum's dearth of labelling, there's a lot here
that's worth seeing. The tile art is excellent and there
are a number of brilliantly illuminated Korans from
the 13th to 16th centuries. The museum also has a
pleasant courtyard that features examples of stone-
carved calligraphy.

Cartoon Museum

Karikatür ve Mizah Müzesi
*Kavacılar Sokak 12, off Atatürk Bulvarı, Fatih
(0212 521 1264).* **Open** 10am-6pm Tue-Sat.
Admission free. **Map** p288 H8.

Sheltering beneath the Aqueduct of Valens (*see p89*)
and set in a beautiful 17th-century *medrese*, this is
one of the city's more unusual, not to say attractive
and educational, museums. Where instructors once
lectured students in Islamic theory, they now give
sketching lessons and host workshops on engraving and screen-printing. The permanent collection,
which includes pieces dating back to the 1870s, illustrates the long-standing popularity of caricature and
satire in Turkey, and the recurrence of certain
themes, particularly the insidious impact of the
West. In 2003 only the permanent exhibition area
was open to the public, but once some extensive
redecoration is completed a temporary exhibition
area is also due to come back on stream. There's also
a humour library and an archive open to the public:
ask at the box office to be let in.

Florence Nightingale Museum

Florence Nightingale Müzesi
*Birinci Ordu Komutanlığı, Selimiye Kışlası, Üsküdar
(0216 343 7310/fax 0216 553 1009).* **Open** By
appointment only 9am-5pm Sat. **Admission** free.
Map p287.

The least known of the city's museums is secreted
away on the Asian shore, buried deep inside the
heavily guarded Selimye Barracks, HQ of the
Turkish 1st Army. A visit requires some planning:

it's a restricted military zone, so just turning up and
knocking on doors risks a major international incident. To gain access, fax your passport details,
expected time of arrival and a contact phone number. The army will call back to issue the permission.
Take your passport along when you go. Visitors
then progress through a series of guard posts at
which the military ranking and level of English
improves progressively. On the way glance along
the enormous corridors of the quadrangular building; back in 1854-6, during the Crimean War, these
would have been packed with wounded and dying
British, French and Turkish soldiers, brought in by
boat from the battlefields of Balaclava and
Sebastopol. The overcrowded and unsanitary conditions actually increased the likelihood of death, not
recovery, and many former patients are buried up
the hill in nearby Haydarpaşa Cemetery. It was
among this carnage that Florence Nightingale and
her team of nurses hit on the idea that a hospital
should make people better, not worse, and that
attending to hygiene might be one way of achieving
this. Modern hospital and nursing practice was in
many ways born in this building.

The museum is housed in a north-west corner
tower. The lower floor displays a collection of life-
sized statues of Turkish soldiers from the Crimean
War to the War of Independence. Behind a Krupps
field gun, on the left, is a small room containing the
first of the Florence Nightingale exhibits – a waxwork of her with a wounded patient. On the period
table is the famous lamp. Up a winding wooden stair
is the room where Nightingale stayed. Look out for
a letter written by Florence to a British MP, asking
him to investigate the disappearance of a war
widow's pension.

To get to the barracks take a ferry from Eminönü
to either Kadıköy or Üsküdar – Selimiye is roughly
half way between – and jump in a taxi and ask for
the Birinci Ordu Komutanlığı. With luck, you'll end
up at the main gate of the gigantic headquarters
building. Alternatively, take a Kadıköy-Üsküdar
dolmuş and look out for the roadside sign for the
Florence Nightingale Museum (it's in English).

Galatasaray Museum

*Galatasaray Lisesi, Istiklal Caddesi 263, Beyoğlu
(0212 249 1100).* **Open** 1.30-4pm Wed.
Admission free. **Map** p294 N3.

This is the official museum of the Galatasaray
School sports club, now more famous for its football
team (*see p234*). Barely more than a trophy room,
the exhibits include photographs, memorabilia and
numerous cases crammed with medals and trophies.
Microscopic opening hours surely make it one of the
world's most difficult museums to visit.

Jewish Museum

Türk Musevileri Müzesi
*Karaköy Meydanı, Perçemli Sokak, Karaköy (0212
292 6333/www.muze500.com).* **Open** 10am-4pm
Mon-Thur; 10am-2pm Fri, Sun. **Admission** $2.20.
No credit cards. Map p292 M6.

Housed in the immaculately restored Zülfaris Synagogue (in existence since 1671 but dating in its present form to the early 19th century) a collection of well-presented objects, documents, photographs and storyboards (in English) tells the story of more than 500 years of Jewish presence in Turkey. The Jews first arrived in the Ottoman Empire fleeing the pogroms of Christian Europe and seem to have been made welcome ever since. They have been significant contributors to Istanbul life, particularly in the financial sector. Tellingly, of all Muslim Middle Eastern countries, Turkey is the only one to have close ties to Israel. An ethnography section presents costumes and accessories related to circumsion ceremonies, dowries and weddings.

Military Museum

Askeri Müze ve Kültür Sitesi
Vali Konağı Caddesi, Harbiye (0212 233 2720).
Bus 46H, 46KY, 69YM/metro Osmanbey. **Open**
9am-5pm Wed-Sun. **Admission** $1.20. **No credit cards. Map** p287.

The sheer size and wealth of this place says as much about the military's current clout in Turkey as it does about its history. For many years this was one of the few national museums to have any money spent on it, so the collection is nothing if not comprehensive. However, all but the most hardened of military enthusiasts is likely to suffer serious battle fatigue well before the interminable procession of rooms and corridors comes to an end. Definitely worth seeing are the campaign pavilions of the Ottoman sultans: gloriously colourful silk and cotton affairs with embroidered decoration. Upstairs in the 20th-century section there's a decent display dealing with the 1915 Gallipoli campaign, plus a bizarre set of furniture constructed out of bayonets and gun parts. For sheer morbidity, nothing beats the car in which Grand Vizier Mahmut Şevket Paşa was assassinated while travelling along Divan Yolu back in 1913. The number of bullet holes shows the gunmen left little to chance.

The museum is also the venue for performances by the Mehter Band, a modern-day incarnation of the marching band that traditionally accompanied the sultan into battle. Their bombastic music, with accompanying lyrics of heroism, actually had an impact on Europe, giving rise to the Spanish *à la turca* style and inspiring both Mozart (*Marcia Turca*) and Beethoven (*Opus 13*). The band performs every day that the museum is open; the music kicks off at 3pm, lasts 45 minutes and is preceded by a 15-minute audio-visual presentation in English in the museum theatre.

Mimar Sinan University Museum of Fine Arts

Mimar Sinan Üniversitesi Istanbul Resim ve Heykel Müzesi
Barbaros Hayrettin Paşa Iskelesi Sokak, off Beşiktaş Caddesi, Beşiktaş (0212 261 4299). Bus 25E, 28, 40, 56. **Open** 9.30am-4.30pm Mon, Wed-Sun. **Admission** free. **Map** p287.

The decrepit state of the once-fine waterside mansion in which the museum is housed and the lack of signposting suggest that few visitors ever find their way here. Shame, because the collection of Turkish art exhibited in the high-ceilinged halls includes some fine pieces. It all dates from the mid-19th to mid-20th century and much of the work is in Orientalist style but there's plenty to admire, notably several works by Osman Hamdi Bey, archaeologist and one-time director of the Archaeology Museum. To find the place, walk down the side-street south of the Naval Museum, pass through the gateway with the armed guard, cross the waterfront plaza and turn right at the end; it's the building on the left.

Mosaic Museum

Büyüksaray Mozaik Müzesi
Arasta Çarşısı, Torun Sokak 103, Sultanahmet (0212 518 1205). Tram Sultanahmet. **Open** 9am-4.30pm Tue-Sun. **Admission** $3. **No credit cards. Map** p289 N11.

Behind the Sultanahmet Mosque and slightly downhill towards the Marmara is a small 17th-century shopping street, built to provide rental revenue to provide for the upkeep of the mosque. It's been converted into a tourist bazaar (the Arasta Bazaar), off which is a prefab hut sheltering a fantastic archaeological find. Uncovered in the mid-1950s, it's an ornamental pavement belonging to the Byzantine Great Palace (Büyüksaray), which stood where the mosque is now, and probably dates from the era of Justinian. The surviving segments depict mythological and hunting scenes, with pastoral idylls disturbingly skewed by bloody depictions of animal combat: elephant vs lion, snake vs gazelle, stags and lizards being eaten by winged unicorns. It's also worth a visit for the informative wall panels and particularly the pictorial reconstructions of what the Byzantine palace quarter would have looked like.

Museum of Turkish & Islamic Art

Türk ve Islam Eserleri Müzesi
At Meydan 46, Sultanahmet (0212 518 1805). Tram Sultanahmet. **Open** 9am-5pm Tue-Sun. **Admission** $3. **Credit** MC, V. **Map** p289 M10.

Overlooking the Hippodrome, the museum occupies the restored 16th-century palace of Ibrahim Paşa. A Greek convert to Islam, Ibrahim was the confidant of Süleyman I and in 1523 was appointed Grand Vizier. When his palace was completed the following year it was the grandest private residence in the Ottoman Empire, rivalling any building of the Topkapı Palace. When Süleyman fell under the influence of the scheming Roxelana (*see p17*), he was persuaded that Ibrahim had to go and the vizier was strangled in his sleep. The palace was seized by the state and has variously been used as a school, a dormitory, a court, a barracks and a prison, before being restored as a museum. The well-planned collections, all housed in cool rooms around a central courtyard, include carpets, manuscripts, miniatures, woodwork, metalwork and glasswork. Items range from the earliest period of Islam through to modern

The truth is
really far out
there at the
UFO Museum.
See p116.

times, all presented chronologically and geographically, with full explanations provided. On the ground floor, a gallery showcases modern Turkish and foreign artists. There's an interesting ethnographic section, including a recreation of a *kara cadır* or 'black tent', the residence of choice for many of the nomadic Anatolian tribes who developed the art of the *kilim*. Upstairs, the Great Hall contains what's reckoned to be one of the finest collections of carpets in the world. There's also an excellent café in a shaded courtyard with an adjacent covered terrace overlooking the Hippodrome.

Naval Museum

Deniz Müzesi
Barbaros Hayrettin Paşa Iskelesi Sokak, off Beşiktaş Caddesi, Beşiktaş (0212 327 4345). Bus 25E, 28, 40, 56. **Open** 9am-12.30pm, 1.30-5pm Wed-Sun. **Admission** $1.20. **No credit cards. Map** p287.

Announced by a roadside garden full of blue-grey big guns, the museum is housed in two buildings on the Bosphorus east of Dolmabahçe Palace and right next to the ferry terminal at Beşiktaş. The larger of the two buildings holds an extensive collection of model ships, ship figureheads and oil paintings, along with plenty of captured standards from various British and French warships sunk during the abortive Dardanelles campaign of World War I. Upstairs is a room of commemorative plaques to Turkish sailors killed on duty from 1319 to the Cyprus war of 1974 and the battle flag of Barbarossa, the 16th-century Ottoman pirate hero. Downstairs, meanwhile, you'll find just about everything that wasn't nailed down on Atatürk's yacht, the *Savarona*, including a set of silver toothpicks. In the smaller building is a collection of Ottoman *caiques*. Elegant, bird-like barges of light wood that

Time Out Istanbul **115**

were built for speed, at one time these vessels were as symbolic of the city as the gondola is of Venice. Back then, boats rivalled horse and carriage as the common mode of transport (a lesson lost on the present municipality). The sultans' *caiques*, displayed here, were rowed by Bostancı, an imperial naval unit that doubled as palace gardeners. The largest, a 1648 model, required some 144 Bostancı to power it along. They were apparently required to bark like dogs as they rowed so they wouldn't overhear the sultan's conversations. An enterprising Black Sea firm has made modern replicas that convey tourists to some of the city's smarter hotels although, regrettably, the banks of oarsmen have now been replaced by an outboard motor.

Rahmi M Koç Museum

Rahmi M Koç Müzesi

Hasköy Caddesi 27, Hasköy (0212 256 7153/ www.rmk-museum.org.tr). Buses 47E, 54HT. **Open** 10am-5pm Tue-Fri; 10am-7pm Sat, Sun. **Admission** $3.75, submarine $1.50. **No credit cards. Map** p286.

Although situated way out of the city centre, this museum is definitely worth travelling for. Founded by the head of the Koç industrial group, one of Turkey's major players, it fills an 18th-century waterfront foundry with the technologies and tomorrow's worlds of times past. The collection includes Ottoman astrolabes, giant clunky German telex machines, plus halls and halls of trains and boats and planes, old Istanbul trams and even a submarine moored in the Golden Horn. Plenty of the exhibits have moving parts that can be manually activated by buttons or levers, and there's a walk-on ship's bridge with a wheel, sonar machines and alarm bells. Great fun. Try to visit on a Saturday, when all the working models are in action. Across the road from the main complex, an old domed workshop makes a beautiful setting for more industrial curios including the forward section of a US airforce bomber, *Hadley's Harem*, shot down in 1943 and recovered from the seabed off Turkey's Med coast some 50 years later. Everything is fully labelled in English. Plus – will wonders never cease – the museum has two top-rank restaurants in the Frenchified Café du Levant and Halat (*see p128*), with open-air wharf-side seating. If you don't fancy the bus, a taxi from Eminönü or Taksim Square takes 15 minutes and costs about the equivalent of $4. Note that the splendidly eccentric Miniaturk (*see p190*) is only another couple of miles from here.

Sakıp Sabancı Museum

Istiniye Caddesi 22, Emirgan, (0212 277 2200/ www.muze.sabanciuniv.edu). Bus 22, 22RV, 25E. **Open** 10am-6pm Tue-Fri; 11am-5pm Sat, Sun. **Admission** $3. **No credit cards. Map** p241.

Mr Sabancı is one of Turkey's wealthiest businessmen. Just how wealthy can be garnered from a visit to his recently opened museum, housed in a fabulous Bosphorus shore villa that was originally built for Egyptian royalty back in the 1920s. Approach up steeply sloped lawns, set with stone treasures on loan from the Archaeology Museum, to view two floors of ceramics and calligraphy, from the grand (vast gilded pronouncements of imperial greatness) to the delicate (intricate notebooks crammed with roses formed out of bouquets of poetry). It's all exceptionally fine stuff, beautifully displayed with informative text in English. A modern two-storey extension in glass, steel and marble holds a collection of 19th and 20th-century Turkish art that unfortunately fails to do justice to its coolly elegant surrounds: the paintings play second fiddle to the panoramic views. To get here, ride the bus until it passes under the second great Bosphorus bridge and then shortly after Rumeli Hisarı alight at the stop beside the pencil-sharp minaret of the Hamidiye Mosque: the villa is 100m further on.

UFO Museum

UFO Müzesi

Büyükparmakkapı Sokak 14, off Istiklal Caddesi, Beyoğlu (0212 252 8646/www.siriusufo.org). **Open** 11am-8pm Mon-Sat; noon-7pm Sun. **Admission** $3. **No credit cards. Map** p295 O3.

There's a giant frog dressed in bin bags who hangs out on Istiklal Caddesi frightening the kids: he's supposed to be an alien and he's there to drum up trade for this, Turkey's first museum of the paranormal. Up one flight of suitably darkened stairs in a crumbly old building are a series of small, dimly illuminated rooms filled with hundreds of photos and press clippings of UFO sightings from around the world (everything's in English as well as Turkish). There are saucer identification charts and a small-scale diorama of the famous Roswell crash, complete with Action Man figurines, plus whole families of wizened grey creatures secure behind glass. In one spooky display, shifty scientist types perform a gory autopsy on a recovered alien. Across the room the bug-eyed critters get their own back by cutting up a shop-window dummy. Great stuff. Upstairs is a library and research centre, reserved for serious ufologists only, who get the chance to sit in furniture straight off the set of *Star Trek*.

Vakıflar Carpet Museum

Vakıflar Halı Müzesi

Sultanahmet Mosque, Sultanahmet (0212 518 1330). Tram Sultanahmet. **Open** 9am-noon, 1-4pm Tue-Sat. **Admission** $1.50. **No credit cards. Map** p273 N11.

What was once the Imperial Pavilion in the outer courtyard of Sultanahmet Mosque (*see p74*), used by the sultan whenever he visited for prayers, is now a display space for an extensive collection of carpets from all over Turkey. The setting is appropriate, considering that until quite recently most of these carpets and rugs lay inside working mosques, but presentation is sparse, lighting is poor and the whole enterprise is handicapped by meagre funding. This is all done much better at the Museum of Turkish & Islamic Art (*see p114*) making the Vakıflar one for committed rug enthusiasts only.

Eat, Drink, Shop

Restaurants	**118**
Bars & Cafés	**141**
Shops & Services	**157**

Features

The best Restaurants	118
Çiçek Pasajı & Nevizade Sokak	122
Kebab cuisine	127
Kumkapı	132
What's on the menu	136
The best Bars & cafés	141
Hava Nargile	152
Cheap girls, pricey drinks	156
Shopping by area	158
The rug trade	166
Mall contents	173
Market trading	174

Restaurants

Meat and fish prevail but young Turks favour fusion.

Engage any local gourmand on the subject and they'll proudly inform you that Turkish is one of the world's three major cuisines, up there with French and Chinese. A preposterous claim? Well, maybe not.

As the Ottomans once controlled the entire eastern Mediterranean basin, imperial chefs were able to raid the ingredients and cuisines of Greece, the Balkans, the Caucasus and the Levant for inspiration. A continual quest for imperial approval inspired ever more creative dishes and their often enigmatic names such as 'the imam fainted' (*imambayıldı*: an aubergine dish), 'lady's lips' (*dilberdudağı*: pastry in thick syrup), 'slit stomach' (*karnıyarık*: aubergine stuffed with minced meat) and 'ladies' thighs' (*kadınbudu köfte*: battered, fried meatballs).

The indigenous cuisine encountered in Istanbul today is simplified palace food that long ago made its way outside the imperial quarters and into common kitchens.

DINING OUT

Not too long ago, dining out in Istanbul was largely limited to boozy, all-male affairs at the local *meyhane* – folksy taverna-type places featuring tapas-like plates of meze (hors d'oeuvre), washed down with copious amounts of *rakı*, the anise-flavoured national spirit. Either that or the *lokanta*, a canteen-style restaurant where tradesmen eat *hazır yemek* (ready food) served out of a bain-marie. Fine dining? A rarity, limited largely to top-end hotels and their well-heeled clientele. Needless to say, conservatism ruled in the kitchen.

What a difference a decade makes. Rising incomes, more working women, single dwellers, smaller families and greater curiosity about how the rest of the world eats have opened up the Istanbul restaurant scene. Running a restaurant is no longer viewed on a par with bar or brothel work. Young Turks are signing up at cooking colleges overseas and returning home to infuse home cuisine with exotic new twists. In the process they're rediscovering the rich regional cuisines of Turkey. Exciting new venues like **Lokanta** (owned by talented young Turko-Finnish chef Mehmet Gürs) can offer the likes of Black Sea corn bread baked with anchovies, fiery south-eastern kebabs or delicately flavoured Aegean greens, alongside a globe-trot of international fusions.

WHERE TO EAT

The quintessential Istanbul eating experience remains the *meyhane*. These places are cheap, frequently boisterous and filling the table with myriad small meze dishes means everyone can be kept happy, even vegetarians. *Meyhanes* are found city-wide but with a heavy concentration around **Nevizade Sokak** (*see p122*) in Beyoğlu. Other recommendations include **Kallavi 20** (*see p219*), **Refik**, **Sofyalı 9** and **Yakup 2** (for all *see p134*).

Fish is the other big local speciality. Most visitors are directed to **Kumkapı** (*see p132*), which has the greatest concentration of seafood

The best Restaurants

For going native
Buhara (*see p121*). Karaköy Balıkçısı (*see p125*). Musa Ustam Ocakbaşı (*see p134*). Refik (*see p134*).

For old Istanbul
Galata House (*see p131*). Orient Express Restaurant (*see p126*). Pandeli (*see p126*). Rejans (*see p134*).

For the in thing
Changa (*see p131*). Loft (*see p139*). Lokal (*see p132*). Lokanta (*see p133*). Vogue (*see p140*).

For haute cuisine
Changa (*see p131*). Seasons Restaurant (*see p125*). Sunset Grill and Bar (*see p140*). Ulus 29 (*see p140*).

For city views
Besinci Kat (*see p131*). Hamdi Et Lokantası (*see p125*). Ulus 29 (*see p140*). Vogue (*see p140*).

On the waterfront
Çinar Restaurant (*see p139*). Feriye (*see p139*). Halat (*see p128*). Körfez (*see p140*). Poseidon (*see p139*).

For vegetarians
Nature and Peace (*see p134*). Zencefil (*see p135*).

Eat, Drink, Shop

Interesting things on plates at the **Rumeli Cafe**. *See p121.*

restaurants, plus it's close to the hotel district of Sultanahmet. There are better options. We really rate **Doğa Balık** (*see p131*), which is just downhill from Taksim, and the humble **Karaköy Balıkçısı** (*see p125*). For more refined dining on the day's catch, head up the Bosphorus to **Poseidon** (*see p139*) in Bebek, **Rumeli Iskele** (*see p139*) up at Rumeli Hisarı or **Körfez** (*see p140*) over on the Asian Shore.

Find out what a real kebab is at a *kebapçı* or *ocakbaşı*, places that specialise in charred flesh. There are more varieties than you can shake a skewer at (*see p127* **Kebab cuisine**) and you may come to appreciate that a döner is to a properly prepared kebab what a hamburger is to a choice T-bone steak.

For the kind of food that used to pleasure the palates of sultans, visit one of the restaurants serving traditional 'Ottoman' cuisine. The cooking in such places has its ancestry back in the Topkapı kitchens. Expect elaborate dishes mixing rice, fruit and vegetables with meat and fish; venues include **Rami** (*see p121*), **Asitane** (*see p127*) and **Feriye** (*see p139*).

TIPPING AND RESERVATIONS

Tipping is expected. Ten per cent is sufficient. It is rarely figured into the bill except in high-end places – but then tipping is expected *in addition* to the added service charge. Reservations are normally a must on Friday and Saturday evenings but are not usually necessary during the week.

Sultanahmet

Big on sights it may be, but Sultanahmet is woefully underserved by restaurants. It'd be unfair say that all the eateries here are tourist traps, but it wouldn't be far off the mark either. With the few exceptions noted below, most of the places on and just off **Divan Yolu** should be avoided, and even though new restaurants and cafés seem to open daily among the hotels on **Akbıyık Caddesi**, standards remain resolutely mediocre.

Amedros

Hoca Rüstem Sokak 7, off Divan Yolu (0212 522 8356). Tram Sultanahmet. **Open** 10am-midnight daily. **Starters** $3-$4. **Main courses** $7-$10. **Credit** DC, MC, V. **Map** p289 M10.

Although the streets off main Divan Yolu are stuffed full of cafés and restaurants, there are very few of them that we can wholeheartedly recommend. Amedros is an exception. It's a European-style bistro that also does some interesting Ottoman dishes. House special, *testi kebapı*, is lamb roasted with vegetables, served in a sealed clay pot which is cracked open tableside. In summer, candle-lit tables are lined up in the narrow cobbled alley out front; in winter the action retreats inside, where diners are warmed by a crackling fire.

> ▶ Most **Bars & cafés** also serve food, much of it excellent: *see pp141-156*.

Balıkcı Sabahatin

Seyit Hasan Kuyu Sokak 50, off Cankurtaran Caddesi (0212 458 1824). **Open** noon-1am daily. **Starters** $3. **Main courses** $21. **Credit** AmEx, MC, V. **Map** p289 N11.

Most visitors staying around Sultanahmet head to Kumkapı for fish, unaware that there's a far better option right on their doorstep. In fact, Balıkcı Sabahatin is one of the very few restaurants that will tempt Istanbulus down from Beyoğlu and over the Golden Horn. It benefits from a gorgeous setting in a street of picturesquely decrepit wooden houses, periodically rattled to their foundations by the commuter trains passing in and out of Sirkeci. There's no menu: instead jacket-and-bow-tie waiters present a tray of various meze and, later, a huge iced platter of seasonal fish and seafood from which choices are made. Entertainment comes in the form of skittering cats with practised doleful looks and pleading meowls. Reservations are essential.

Buhara

Nuruosmaniye Caddesi 7, Cağaloğlu (0212 513 7799). Tram Gülhane or Sultanahmet. **Open** noon-2am Mon-Sat. **Starters** $2-$3. **Main courses** $4-$6. **Credit** MC, V. **Map** p289 M9.

It's only a couple of blocks north of Divan Yolu (just east of the Cağaloğlu Hamam) but that's far enough that this small neighbourhood *ocakbaşı* remains largely unknown to tourists. For a restaurant of its humble type, it's surprisingly well looked after (carpets! tablecloths!) with a prominent bar serving draught Efes, wine and lots of liqueurs of dubious provenance, plus a big-screen TV reserved, according to the notice, for Fenerbahçe and Galatasaray games only. The menu is subtitled in an English of sorts, in which *içli köfte* becomes 'buhara with balls'. Excellent if you want to dine à la Turca without having to traipse over to Beyoğlu.

Develi

Samatya Balık Pazarı, Gümüşyüzük Sokak 7, Mustafa Paşa (0212 529 0833). Train Mustafa Paşa. **Open** noon-midnight daily. **Starters** $1-$6. **Main courses** $7-$10. **Credit** AmEx, DC, MC, V.

The Develi family introduced Istanbul to the piquant flavours of south-eastern cuisine way back in 1912, and locals have been flocking here ever since. The three immaculate floors, done up in bordeaux and cream, are traversed by an army of black-clad waiters bearing trays of meze and over 30 types of kebabs (for some help identifying what's what, *see p127* **Kebab cuisine**). The restaurant is a bit out of the way, west of Sultanahmet along coastal Sahil Yolu (aka Kennedy Caddesi), but it is well worth the $7 fare and ten-minute taxi ride. You can also get there on any of the ancient commuter trains that depart Sirkeci Station; the ride takes in crumbling Byzantine walls and the back of the Topkapı Palace. Get off at Mustafa Paşa (also spelt Kocamustafa-paşa), follow the crowd through the narrow tunnel at the end of the platform and then ask one of the fishmongers for directions.

Dubb Indian Restaurant

Incili Çavuş Sokak 10 (0212 513 7308). Tram Sultanahmet. **Open** noon-10.30pm Tue-Sun. **Starters** $4-$6. **Main courses** $7-$14. **Credit** AmEx, MC, V. **Map** p289 N10.

One of the scant few Indian restaurants in the entire city and a welcome option for those who tire of grilled meats and fish. The menu is also strong on veggie options. Choose from sitting outdoors on bustling Incili Çavuş Sokak or cosy dining on three saffron-hued, pastel-accented floors, housed in a restored wooden Ottoman home. However, the best spot to dig into your biriyani is on the new glass-enclosed rooftop terrace, over which the Haghia Sophia looms to your left and a magnificent Marmara Sea panorama unfolds to your right. Note that the tandoori oven isn't in operation between 3.30pm and 6pm.

Pudding Shop

Divan Yolu 6 (0212 522 2970). Tram Sultanahmet. **Open** 7am-11pm daily. **Starters** $2-$3. **Main courses** $2-$5. **Credit** MC, V. **Map** p289 N10.

A recent revamp has rendered the infamous Pudding Shop of old almost unrecognisable. In the pre-Lonely Planet days of the late '60s and early '70s, the Pudding Shop (founded 1957) was a bottleneck for all the overland traffic passing through on its tie-dyed, spliff-spirited way east to Kathmandu. In addition to the food, the place traditionally served up travel information courtesy of the two brothers that owned the place and a busy bulletin board, plus like-minded company. It crops up in the movie *Midnight Express*. These days, it's been smartened up for the 21st-century tourist – think plate-glass windows, gleaming display cabinets and smart white-shirt-and-blue-tie staff – but the restaurant still doles out basic canteen-style fare, no better or worse than a half-dozen similar restaurants along this strip.

Rami

Utangaç Sokak 6, Cankurtaran (0212 517 6593/ www.ramirestaurant.com). Tram Sultanahmet. **Open** noon-midnight daily. **Starters** $7-$9. **Main courses** $14-$17. **No credit cards**. **Map** p289 N11.

One of the district's classier options, Rami fills three storeys of an old Ottoman house with antiquity and sepia-toned nostalgia. It's slightly fussy but essentially charming, especially the attic-like top floor with starched white-clothed tables and panoramic views of the neighbouring Blue Mosque (book for 8pm when the sound and light show kicks off). The menu also casts glances backwards with old court-inspired cooking, including dishes like the Turkish variant on cottage pie, *elbasan tava*: oven-baked diced lamb and veg under a fluffy, potatoey top.

Rumeli Cafe

Ticarethane Sokak 8, off Divan Yolu (0212 512 0008). Tram Sultanahmet. **Open** 9am-midnight daily. **Starters** $4-$8. **Main courses** $6-$10. **Credit** AmEx, DC, MC, V. **Map** p289 N10.

Çiçek Pasajı & Nevizade Sokak

Imroz.

Everybody needs a place to let loose. The British down pints in pubs. The French slurp wine in brasseries. The Greeks smash plates in tavernas. And the Turks? They make merry in the *meyhane*, the age-old Istanbul version of a Mediterranean tapas bar. These are places in which locals eat meze, drink *rakı* and are cajoled by house musicians into belting out folk songs.

The city's most famous *meyhane* locale is the **Çiçek Pasajı (Flower Passage)**, an elegant 19th-century arcade just off Istiklal Caddesi, opposite the Galatasaray Lycée. It's a pretty spot with refined neo-Classical façades beneath a barrelled glass roof, cobbled paving, old-fashioned street lamps and an unashamedly romantic atmosphere. The tourists lap it up. However, those who fail

to confirm prices in advance are easy pickings for unscrupulous waiters.

Locals tend to give the place a miss, heading instead down neighbouring Balık Pazarı (Fish Market) and taking a right about half-way along into **Nevizade Sokak**. This is where you find some of the best *meyhanes* in town. It's a narrow alley lined both sides with restaurant after restaurant, maybe 20 of them in 50 metres, all with tables laid outside as if for one giant street party. And one giant street party is what the place resembles most evenings. There's a great buzz with every seat filled by garrulous gossiping groups of diners, waiters dashing around, street musicians and wandering vendors. If you have just one night to spend in Istanbul, spend it on Nevizade Sokak.

The *meyhanes* themselves are much of a muchness in terms of food and prices. In addition to the tables out on the street they have two or three floors of dining inside with perhaps the top floor employed as an open terrace. Everyone has their own favourites: we like **Boncuk**, which specialises in Armenian dishes and features live *fasıl* music. **Imroz** is more Greek in character and is known for particularly fine meze. **Cumhuriyet Meyhanesi**, which is in the neighbouring Balık Pazarı, was once frequented by Atatürk, and is notable for its resident *fasıl* musicians.

When ordering, the more dishes the merrier, since sharing is what it's all about. A waiter will present a heaped tray from which to make your choice. Cold dishes cost about $2, hot ones $2 to $4, and seafood appetizers $6 to $8. For two people, six dishes are usually sufficient. After the meze, you can order main courses, if you have enough room.

Boncuk

Nevizade Sokak 19 (0212 243 1219). **Open** noon-2am daily. **Credit** MC, V. **Map** p294 N3.

Cumhuriyet Meyhanesi

Sahne Sokak 47, Balık Pazarı (0212 293 1977). **Open** 11am-2am daily. **Credit** MC, V. **Map** p294 N3.

Imroz

Nevizade Sokak 19 (0212 249 9073). **Open** noon-11.30pm daily. **Credit** MC, V. **Map** p294 N3.

Another stand-out among the second-rate joints at the bottom of Divan Yolu, the Rumeli is a former printworks with an attractive cave-like interior of unclad brick and stone, and stained floorboards. Tables are put out on cobbled Ticarethane during summer, while in winter there's a crackling open fire burning inside. The food is traditional Turkish with a Mediterranean twist, so besides the ubiquitous çöp şiş and köfte the menu also stretches to some very good salads and accomplished pastas. There's a very decent wine list too.

Seasons Restaurant

Four Seasons Hotel, Tevfikhane Sokak 1 (0212 638 8200). Tram Sultanahmet. **Open** noon-3pm, 7-11pm daily. **Starters** $6-$16. **Main courses** $16-$26. **Credit** AmEx, DC, MC, V. **Map** p289 N10.
For a world-class, if not particularly Turkish, experience, Seasons Restaurant is an oasis of refined tranquillity in the heart of Sultanahmet. Housed in an elegant glass pavilion in the main courtyard of the Four Seasons Hotel (*see pXX*), it's among the finest (and priciest) options in Istanbul for international cuisine. Sicilian master-chef Gian Carlo Gattardo heads the kitchen (and also supervises each step of the production of domestic buffalo milk mozzarella) and makes regular appearances to accept the heartfelt plaudits of delighted local gourmets and international guests. Book for the Sunday brunch buffet extravaganza ($40).

Tarihi Selim Usta Sultanahmet Köftecisi

12 Divan Yolu (0212 513 1438). Tram Sultanahmet. **Open** 11am-11pm daily. **Main courses** $2.50. **No credit cards. Map** p289 N10.
This is the local alternative to McDonald's (which is just up the street), but instead of burgers it solos in *köfte*: spiced ground beef, shaped into balls and prepared over a great open-flame grill. Bread, green salad, *pilav* (rice) and *piyaz* (white-bean salad) are the only accompaniments. It's basic and utilitarian but they must be doing something right judging by the queues of office workers at the door most weekday lunchtimes. This place has been in business for around 80 years and in that time has spawned many imitators, hence the specifics of the name 'Historical Sultan Ahmet Köfte Restaurant'.

The Bazaar Quarter

A few entrepreneurs have realised that even dedicated shoppers need sustenance and eating options are on the increase at the Grand Bazaar, but as yet these are confined to cafés and *lokanta*-style joints; *see pp80-81* **Shopping the bazaar.**

Darüzziyafe

Şifahane Sokak 6, Süleymaniye (0212 511 8414/ www.daruzziyafe.com.tr). Tram Beyazıt, Eminönü or Üniversite. **Open** noon-11pm daily. **Starters** $2-$4. **Main courses** $4-$14. **Credit** AmEx, MC, V. **Map** p288 K8.

The former soup kitchens of the Süleymaniye Mosque complex (*see p84*) now turn out more varied fare. But if the present menu runs to several pages, the food is still canteen cooking, with the usual meze and grilled meats – great for lunch (when it's a big favourite with the tour buses) but too prosaic for dinner. The setting, a large Ottoman courtyard filled with rose bushes and trees (seating is in the surrounding arcades), is potentially lovely but at the moment is rendered institutional by cheap furniture and lack of care. Vegetarians beware: the lentil soup contains submerged mini-meatballs. The restaurant is located to the north of the mosque, separate from the row of small eateries which line the west side. No alcohol.

Eminönü & the Golden Horn

Two blocks south of Sirkeci Station, narrow **Ibni Kemal Caddesi** is a whole street of small eateries serving the local working population. The presence of neighbouring Hoca Paşa Mosque means no alcohol is served but a meal will come in at less than $5 per person. The underslung section of the **Galata Bridge** is also crammed with budget restaurants, with prices clearly marked, menus in English and beer by the flagon for $2.

Hamdi Et Lokantasi

Kalçın Sokak 17, Tahmis Caddesi (0212 528 0390). Tram Eminönü. **Open** 11.30am-midnight daily. **Starters** $1-$2. **Main courses** $4-$8. **Credit** AmEx, MC, V. **Map** p288 L7.
Facing Eminönü bus station, this garish temple to seared meat is fronted by a fatted (stuffed) lamb and an elevator operator to greet the faithful congregation of businessman and devotees of south-eastern cuisine. If the weather's nice, bypass the first floor 'Oriental Saloon', complete with cuckoo clocks and startled nymphs, and head straight for the third-floor open-air terrace, where the stupendous view of the Golden Horn and Galata opposite thankfully overwhelms the concrete grotto in the corner. Ignore the English-language descriptions of 'smashed salads', 'crocked wheat' and 'mincing lambs' and order any combination of starters and kebabs, secure in the knowledge that, unlike the decor, when it comes to food, Hamdi gets it spot on.

Karaköy Balıkçısı

Near Tersane Caddesi 30, Karaköy (0212 251 1371). **Open** 11.30am-4pm daily. **Main courses** $9-$16. **No credit cards. Map** p292 M6.
Just off the north side of the Galata Bridge, this rustic, wooden restaurant has been serving simple lunches of freshly caught fish in its two tiny upstairs dining rooms for the last 75 years. It's a charming package, from the fishy frieze and potted plants on the window-sills to the owner's determination to do just one thing but to do it right. Daily specials typically include sea bass in parchment, piping hot fish

chowder, grilled prawns and bonito kebab. Finding the place is a bit of a treasure hunt: descend the stairs at the Karaköy end of the bridge, then walk west along a narrow (unnamed) alley lined with hardware and paint stalls, which is at the back of the fish market; take the first right, then the first left and you're there. If in doubt, ask a local.

Orient Express Restaurant

Sirkeci Station, Istasyon Caddesi (0212 522 2280). *Tram Sirkeci.* **Open** 10am-midnight daily. **Starters** $2-$3. **Main courses** $5-$7. **Credit** AmEx, MC, V. **Map** p289 N8.

In business since 1890 this is the original restaurant meant for passengers of the famed train service (*see p87* **The extravagant express**). It comprises two vast salons built in the same Oriental Gothic style as the rest of the station, although the grandeur is slightly undermined by a grotto and water feature and a persistent Lionel Ritchie soundtrack. The food is standard Turkish fare of meze and grilled meats but it's considerably better than the acres of perpetually empty tables would suggest. This is also one of the few places in town at which it's worth leaving room for dessert: go for the house special of *chocolat parfait*.

Pandeli

Mısır Çarşısı 1, Eminönü Square (0212 527 3909). *Tram Eminönü.* **Open** noon-4pm Mon-Sat. **Starters** $4-$14. **Main courses** $6-$14. **Credit** MC, V. **Map** p288 L8.

Dining at Pandeli's remains an experience, but not necessarily a happy one. Occupying a wonderful set of domed rooms above the entrance of the Egyptian

Bazaar (*see p86*) this place is very much the essence of genteel old Stamboul. Decorated throughout in blue-and-white tiling, it is worth a visit for the interior, although these days that's about all that there is to recommend. The food is run-of-the-mill Turkish and grossly overpriced, while waiters are brusque and pushier than the worst of bazaar traders. If you do decide to give it a go, ask for a table in the front room with views of the Golden Horn – but don't be surprised if the maître d' sneers and puts you by the toilets. Note that it is open for lunch only.

The Western Districts

These are relatively poor, religiously conservative parts of town that receive few visitors. There's little call for restaurants, then. That may be about to change as Balat is tipped as the hot new neighbourhood in which to invest but, for the time being, if exploring out here be prepared to hop in a taxi to go and look elsewhere for lunch.

Argos

Mürsel Paşa Caddesi 101, Balat (0212 621 8239). *Bus 99.* **Open** 1pm-midnight Mon-Sat. **Fixed-price menu** $24. **No credit cards. Map** p291 G4.

A newly opened *meyhane* run by ex-journalist Canan Konuk, Argos is a cosier and less expensive version of the fish restaurants found further up the Bosphorus. The meze are prepared from the catch of the day and have their origins in Anatolian and Aegean cooking that doesn't normally make it on to Istanbul menus: highlights include *dolma* stuffed

Reach out and touch somebody at the **Hamdi Et Lokantasi**. *See p125.*

Kebab cuisine

Not too long ago, sophisticated Istanbullus turned up their noses at the kebab (the word *kebap* means simply 'roast meat'). They would dismiss it as uncouth provincial grub. Can you blame them? Do cultured Londoners dine out on fish and chips? Do Manhattan socialites serve up burgers?

Kebabs are synonymous with south-eastern Turkey. The stereotypical kebab restaurateur is a mustachioed sort from rural Droolsville. But over the years the foodie snobs have gradually come around. So much so that these days *kebap c'est chic*. A new wave of restaurants – notably **Köşebaşı** (*see p132*) and four-strong Tike – now peddle kebabs to the middle-classes in designer settings with wine on the side.

For all its south-eastern associations, the initial spotting of the gourmet potential of grilled meat took place in western Turkey. Back in 1867, a chef in the city of Bursa (155 miles, or 250 kilometres south of Istanbul) by the name of Iskender Usta hit upon the idea of layering slabs of boneless lamb onto a spit, then revolving the resulting meaty mass in front of glowing coals. He then shaved off thin layers with a long knife. Voila! The birth of the *döner kebab* and Turkey's contribution to worldwide post-booze binging. Not content to stop there, Mr Usta went on to jazz up the *döner* with pide bread, tomato and yoghurt to create his namesake, the *Iskender kebab*. His contribution to kebab cuisine was enshrined in law in 2002 when Usta's descendents were awarded a patent to protect their family delicacy from imitators. Thousands of eateries throughout Turkey were obliged to relabel their 'Iskender kebabs' as 'Bursa kebabs' in order to forestall potential lawsuits.

His name may be protected but Iskender's crown has been lost for good. The current king of kebabs is Beyti Guler. His family opened 'Beyti's' restaurant in the outskirts of

Istanbul in 1945. By the '60s Turcophile diplomat and author Lord Kinross was declaring that it served 'the best meat in Europe'. The plaudits have continued and the celebrity guests keep coming – Richard Nixon, Jimmy Carter and Arthur Miller have all eaten here (although it should be noted that Chelsea Clinton favoured Tike). And, of course, there's a trademark 'Beyti kebab'.

As if Turkey needed another kebab. The Turks have more names for grilled meat than the Eskimos for snow or the English for getting drunk. It makes menus a little bit daunting for visitors, so for a little help in knowing your *begendi* from a *Beyti*, beef up on the following:

Adana kebap minced lamb seasoned with red peppers and grilled on a spit

begendi kebap chunks of beef cooked with onions and tomatoes and served on a bed of puréed aubergine

Beyti kebap chopped lamb flavoured with a hint of garlic and red pepper. Served either wrapped in filo pastry or on cubes of toasted pide bread

çöp şiş tiny bits of slightly fatty lamb grilled on a skewer, then rolled up in paper-thin pide with onions and parsley

döner kebab compressed meat sliced in strips off a vertically rotating spit

fistikli kebab minced low-fat suckling lamb studded with pistachios

Iskender kebab slices of doner drizzled with tomato sauce and melted butter served with a side of yogurt on cubes of toasted pide bread

patlican kebab minced lamb grilled with chunks of aubergine

şiş kebap chunks of marinated lamb, chicken or fish grilled on skewers

testi kebab diced meat, tomatoes, shallots, garlic and green peppers simmered in a clay pot for several hours

with calmari, octopus and shrimp, and raw fish marinated in olive oil. Certain fish mains are served in light cream sauces, something that is unheard of in Turkish restaurants. In nice weather patrons can take advantage of a terrace with lovely views of neighbouring St Stephen of the Bulgars (*see p90*) and the Golden Horn. The fixed-menu includes meze, fish of the day, dessert and unlimited local booze. The restaurant is just a few minutes' ride by bus from Eminönü (the station on the waterfront).

Asitane

Kariye Hotel, Kariye Camii Sokak 18, Edirnekapı (0212 534 8414). Bus 87. **Open** noon-11pm daily. **Starters** $5-$8. **Main courses** $6-$17. **Credit** AmEx, DC, MC, V. **Map** p290 D4.

For a taste of imperial decadence, the Asitane specialises in full-tilt Ottoman, with a menu inspired by descriptions of a feast served at the Edirne Palace in 1539. Expect odd mixes of sweet and sour, flesh and fruit, such as honeydew melon scooped and

Eat, Drink, Shop

House special sea bass in parchment at the **Karaköy Balıkçısı**. *See p125.*

filled with minced meat, rice, raisins, almonds and pistachios. The dishes aren't always wholly successful but you can't fault the ambition. And the setting is lovely: choose between the modish, lemon-yellow dining room or a tree-filled garden courtyard. The only drawback is the location, way out west toward the old city walls (although lunch could be combined with a visit to the Church of St Saviour in Chora, which is right next door). Still, for serious foodies, the trek reaps its rewards.

Beyti

Orman Sokak 8, Florya (0212 663 2990/ www.beyti.com). **Open** 11.30am-11.30pm Tue-Sun. **Starters** $3-$5. **Main courses** $10-$25. **Credit** AmEx, DC, MC, V.

Beyti Güler is a genuine legend on the Turkish dining scene: *see p127* **Kebab cuisine**. His self-monikered restaurant is suitably regal with 11 dining rooms on three floors all done out in a kitschy 1970's twist on Ottoman grandeur. Close to celebrating 60 years in business it remains one of the best, if not the best, *kebapcı* in town. However, it is a real haul from the city centre, being out near the airport. A place for a farewell lunch maybe? Order the house special of Beyti kebab and keep an eye out for the silver-haired 'king of kebabs' himself who table hops, hobnobing with regulars and his frequent famous guests.

Halat

Kumbarhane Caddesi 2, Hasköy (0212 297 6644). Bus 54T. **Open** 10am-midnight Tue-Sun. **Starters** $5-$10. **Main courses** $10-$14. **Credit** AmEx, DC, MC, V. **Map** p286.

In addition to being a world-class museum (don't argue, just go; *see p116*), the Rahmi Koç boasts a couple of excellent restaurants in the **Café du Levant**, an accomplished French bistro, and Halat, which offers quayside dining shaded under canvas awnings. The menu is Turkish/international and highly appealing, ranging from a 'tea-time' menu of sandwiches and tarts ($4-$7) through the likes of breaded crab claws with salad and bluefish pastries to a heavenly dessert list. Black-waistcoated staff and a classical music soundtrack suggest formality, but the vibe is laid-back. And the views – across the Golden Horn to the tumbling orange pantile roofs of Balat – are stunning.

Beyoğlu

Istanbul's 'West End' or 'Downtown', Beyoğlu (*see pp95-100*) is the number one destination for dining in terms of volume and choice. Its narrow backstreets are loaded with traditional restaurants and meze-specialising *meyhanes* (particularly the area around the 'Flower Passage', Çiçek Pasajı, and Nevizade Sokak, *see p122-3*), while the main drag **Istiklal Caddesi** is full of quick-eat canteen-style *lokantas*. The micro-neighbourhoods of **Tünel** and **Asmalımescit** (*see map p286*) are host to some of the most exciting new eateries.

Eat, Drink, Shop

Puttin' on the glitz at **Margaux** at the Ritz (Carlton). *See p133.*

Beşinci Kat: for local colour.

Beşinci Kat (5.Kat)

5th floor, Soğancı Sokak 7, off Sıraselviler Caddesi, Cihangir (0212 293 3774/www.5kat.com). **Open** 10am-2am daily. **Starters** $3.50-$5. **Main courses** $6-$11. **Credit** DC, MC, V. **Map** p295 O3.

Under the watchful eye of its film actress owner, Beşinci Kat has evolved from a funky bar (*see p143*) that does food into a busy restaurant that happens to have a great bar. The menu is a curious mishmash of Turkish (grilled meats), Italian (plenty of pasta), French (fillet in sauces) and Asian (shrimp with coconut, Chinese beef, Thai-style chicken), but it's all beautifully done – the owner and her mother work the kitchen. The range of salads is particularly impressive and there's a good value three-course set menu for $15 per person. Breakfast is also served from 10am to noon weekdays and 10.30am to 2pm on weekends. Spectacular views, a cool dance soundtrack, divinely decadent decor and a creative crowd also all help give the place a happening buzz. There's no better place to catch a cool breeze than over dinner on the rooftop summer terrace.

Changa

Sıraselviler Caddesi 87/1, Taksim (0212 249 1348/www.changa-istanbul.com). **Open** 6pm-1am Mon-Thur; 6pm-2am Fri, Sat. **Starters** $6-$10. **Main courses** $10-$17. **Map** p295 O3.

In Istanbul, the best restaurants often follow the same formula: simple food and great views. Changa shatters the mould. Housed in an art nouveau townhouse, it's all about design and ostentation. Settle into Charles Eames chairs below turn-of-the-century ceilings with an oval window set into the floor for voyeuristic viewing of the goings on in the basement kitchen below. The food is fusion (Changa can be credited with launching the current fusion fad sweeping the city) from a menu prepared by Peter Gordon of London's Sugar Club and finessed by the marketing men: starters, mains, desserts, followed by the autographed cookbook, the house soundtrack CD, the liqueur service set and the logo'd T-shirt. Lifestyle badging aside, what comes out of the

kitchen is undeniably excellent – world class Pacific Rim cuisine at near to bargain prices. And for would-be lounge lizards, the house bar is a gem.

Doğa Balık

Akarsu Yokuşu Caddesi 46, Cihangir (0212 293 9143). **Open** noon-2am daily. **Starters** $2-$5. **Main courses** $5-$21. **Credit** MC, V. **Map** p295 O4.

An absolutely splendid neighbourhood fish restaurant. The entrance is via the dismal lobby of the Villa Zurich Hotel but don't let this put you off. The dining rooms are up on the seventh and eighth floors and include a rooftop terrace with great views across the water to Sultanahmet. The kitchen specialises in lightly cooked fresh greens (up to 18 varieties) and perfectly grilled seasonal fish drizzled with garlicky olive oil. It's Aegean comfort food, with the added bonus of being terribly healthy.

Galata House

Galata Kulesi Sokak 61, Galata (0212 245 1861/www.thegalatahouse.com). **Open** noon-midnight Tue-Sun. **Starters** $3-$6. **Main courses** $7-$12. **Credit** V, MC. **Map** p292 M5.

A highly unusual restaurant that also goes by the name of 'the Old British Jail' (Eski Ingiliz Karakolu), a nod to the building's heritage: from 1904-29 it served as the British Empire's civil prison in Istanbul. It's been lovingly restored by owners Mete and Nadire Göktuğ. Although they've left the peeling paint on the walls, complete with prisoners' graffiti, the atmosphere is more eccentric old aunt's parlour than gaol. The food is an equally unusual mix of Georgian, Russian and Tartar. When Nadire isn't taking orders or supervising in the kitchen, she adds piano accompaniment. Odd but wonderful. The place is very easy to find – it's just downhill from the Galata Tower.

Hacı Abdullah

Sakızağacı Caddesi 17, off Istiklal Caddesi (0212 293 8561). **Open** 11am-10.30pm daily. **Starters** $2.50-$3. **Main courses** $6-$10. **Credit** AmEx, V, MC. **Map** p294 N3.

Kumkapı

Kumkapı, a former bustling fishing port, is like a culinary version of the Grand Bazaar. Situated inside the city walls on the Sea of Marmara coast, it's now a inner-city neighbourhood of narrow cobbled streets packed with seafood restaurants and taverns. Most of these places are fronted by hawkers intent on waylaying passers-by. As at the bazaar, prices are conspicuously absent from menus and it's necessary to agree the bill before sitting down to eat. Most places offer some sort of fixed meal deals, kicking off with meze followed by fish of the day and dessert. Expect to pay around $30 per person with booze (*rakı* or local wine or beer) thrown in.

Food is not the only attraction. As with the Grand Bazaar, a colourful ambience is half the fun. In this case it's supplied by groups of gypsy musicians roaming between the restaurants serenading outdoor diners, plus a truly odd assortment of street vendors flogging everything from almonds presented on trays of ice to Cuban cigars.

In total, are about 50 restaurants, all within a few hundred metres of each other. Of these, there are a few that local Turks rate higher than the rest, including **Akvaryum Fish Restaurant**, which has its own live *fasıl* music, as does **Çapari**, one of the neighbourhood's oldest restaurants. **Kartallar Balıkcı** is famous for its *balık çorbass* (fish chowder)

and *buğulama* (steamed fish) – and boasts a large celeb quotient among its clientele – while **Kör Agop**, in business since 1938, is known to have particularly good fish and fantastic *fasıl*.

To get here, take the tram to Beyazıt and walk due south down to the very bottom of Tıyatro Caddesi, or take the train from from Sirkeci two stops to Kumkapı station and then head north up Ördekli Bakkal Sokak (Grocer With a Duck Street). A taxi from Sultanahmet will cost around $5.

Akvaryum Fish Restaurant
Çapari Sokak 39 (0212 517 2273). Kumkapı station. **Open** noon-1am daily. **Credit** MC, V. **Map** p288 K11.

Çapari
Çapari Sokak 22 (0212 517 7530). Kumkapı station. **Open** noon-2am daily. **Credit** MC, V. **Map** p288 K11.

Kartallar Balıkcı
Ördekli Bakkal Sokak 32 (0212 517 2254). Kumkapı station. **Open** 10am-midnight daily. **Credit** MC, V. **Map** p288 K11.

Kör Agop
Ördekli Bakkal Sokak 32 (0212 517 2334). Kumkapı station. **Open** 8am-2am daily. **Credit** MC, V. **Map** p288 K11.

At almost 115 years old, this restaurant lays claim to being the oldest in Istanbul. That said, the light, airy decor and fresh paintwork lend the place an almost contemporary feel. Of the three rooms, by far the most pleasant is the one at the back, which has a skylight, a glittering chandelier and pinkish tones. There is an English-language menu listing what is possibly the choicest selection of ready-prepared Turkish/Ottoman dishes in town. It's a particularly popular spot for lunch. Hacı Abdullah is also renowned for its preserved pickles and fruits, jars of which make for a colourful display in the front room; somewhat oddly, these are described in the house brochure as 'the symbols of pooped politicians'. Note that there's no alcohol served.

Köşebaşı Pera
Istiklal Caddesi 405 (0212 243 7696). **Open** noon-midnight daily. **Starters** $2-$4. **Main courses** $5-$8. **Credit** MC, V. **Map** p294 M4.
Just as in the UK, Pizza Express took the pizza chain concept and smartened it up for the style-conscious middle classes, so Köşebaşı has done for the kebab. This is the most recent of four branches. Outside,

the buidling has art nouveau stylings but inside it's simplistic and modern with all hard, shiny surfaces. It's divided into fast-food and restaurant sections. The former specialises in take-out chicken or beef wraps known as *dürüms*, while the latter has a menu that covers the whole extensive kebab repertoire (for help in ordering *see p127* **Kebab cuisine**). A limited selection of meze is also available. Unusually for a restaurant of this type, it serves alcohol.

Lokal
Müeyyet Sokak 9, off Istiklal Caddesi, Asmalımescit (0212 245 5744). **Open** noon-midnight Tue-Thur, Sun; noon-1am Fri, Sat. **Starters** $3-$5. **Main courses** $6-$10. **Credit** AmEx, MC, V. **Map** p294 M4.
The slogan is 'think global, act lokal'. And Lokal does global with a vengeance – the food travels on a round-the-world ticket taking in Italian (linguini pesto), Indian (chicken tikka), Thai (phad Thai), Vietnamese (beef pho), Japanese (teriyaki salmon), Cajun (black beef steak) and Deep South (dirty love chicken wings). Ambitious or what? Amazingly, the chefs pull it off: the quality of the dishes is tiptop. The wizardry of the kitchen is open to view, with all

Straight from the fields to **Zencefil**. *See p135.*

Eat, Drink, Shop

the flaming, sizzling and searing going on at one end of the sparse dining space. The minimalism is complemented by knowingly kitsch trimmings (menus are pasted into the gatefold sleeves of classic albums) and a phat beats soundtrack. Coupled with arsey staff and that all-important Asmalımescit address, it adds up to one of the hippest eateries in town.

Lokanta
Meşrutiyet Caddesi 149/1, Tepebaşı (0212 245 6070). **Open** noon-3pm, 7pm-2am daily. **Starters** $7-$14. **Main courses** $10-$20. **Credit** MC, V. **Map** p294 M4.

Arguably the best of Istanbul's international restaurants, Lokanta is the creation of a young, talented Turko-Finnish chef, Mehmet Gürs. His menu is the best read in town – how about 'poor man's lobster', which is described as 'sautéed monkfish served with lemon cream pasta, crazy fresh herbs and a caper butter sauce'? Expect lots of seafood as well as meat and lighter fare such as pizzas, pasta and salads. Presentation is artful and the food itself sublime. The setting is stylishly minimal: one big high-ceilinged room of bare brick, iron columns and exposed ducting. There's a long bar with an alluring underlit display of bottled spirits. The crowd are a gossipy mix of cigar-chomping suits and young professionals. It could be SoHo New York, it could be Soho London. Afterwards, ascend to the rooftop bar **Nu Teras** (*see p149*) for digestifs and a view that could only be Istanbul. Reservations for the restaurant are recommended.

Margaux
Ritz Carlton Hotel, Asker Ocağı Caddesi, Süzer Plaza 15, Elmadağ (0212 292 4252). **Open** noon-2am Mon-Fri, Sun; 6pm-2am Sat. **Starters** $7-$14. **Main courses** $7-$27. **Credit** AmEx, DC, MC, V. **Map** p293 Q1.

Housed on the ground floor of the towering Ritz Carlton, Margaux gives the appearance of having been decorated by a very bored, very rich housewife who was unable to resist any object that glittered expensively. The funny thing is, it works. Kitsch as it is, the place also manages to be chic and intimate. The cuisine is classic French and Italian, and the quality is consistently high. There's also live jazz and plenty of room at the bar, a boon to the crowd of moneyed scenesters, business high-rollers and newly minted footballers and their model girlfriends, who appreciate the restaurant's carefully contrived, moneyed vibe and the late hours.

Musa Ustam Ocakbaşı

Küçükparmakkapı Sokak 14, off Istiklal Caddesi (0212 245 2932). **Open** noon-1am daily. **Starters** $1-$3.50. **Main courses** $4-$7. **Credit** MC, V. **Map** p295 O3.

On the ground floor, this place is the quintessential smoky *ocakbaşı*, with meat displayed prominently in the window cabinets, landscape paintings and lots of mustachioed men locked in on the blaring TVs. The two upper floors, however, offer tables on outdoor terraces and are invariably packed with Beyoğlu bohos, students, expats and the odd adventurous tourist. Our prefered seats are downstairs round the *ocak*, the open coal grill where the restaurant's trademark *çöp şiş* – tiny chunks of lamb on skewers – are grilled. Alcohol is served and, as a consequence, the atmosphere can get a bit boisterous, but for an authentic south-eastern dining experience order a glass of *şalgam* (beet juice).

Nature and Peace

Büyükparmakkapı Sokak, 21-3 (0212 252 8609). **Open** 11.30am-1pm, 7am-midnight daily. **Set menus** $7-$10. **Credit** MC, V. **Map** p295 O3.

This was one of the first restaurants to cater specifically to vegetarians and although still firmly aimed at non-carnivores and the health-conscious, it has diversified and now dabbles with the odd bit of turkey. Set menus include a combination of homemade soups, salads and pastas. For strict vegetarians, the potatoes stuffed with spinach and soy-meat is as good as it gets (note that this is one of the very few places serving meat substitutes such as tofu and seitan). Feeling all self-congratulatory after a meal of pulses, grains and greens, blow it with a piece of the finest cheesecake in Istanbul.

Refik

Sofyalı Sokak 10-12, Asmalımescit (0212 243 2834). **Open** noon-3pm, 6pm-midnight Mon-Fri; 6pm-midnight Sat. **Fixed-price menu** $20. **No credit cards. Map** p294 M4.

Established in 1954, this is a great place to immerse yourself in meze culture and *rakı*. It's a famous leftist haunt with a devoted clientele of journalists and intellectuals presided over by gruff-voiced Refik Arslan, who still meets patrons at the door. Most of the regulars smoke and drink far more than they eat, but the restaurant is also known for its food. Many of the dishes come from the Black Sea region – fishy things – and choices are made from glass-fronted refrigerators. Look and point. There's no music, as it would interfere with the intense conversation.

Rejans

Emir Nevrus Sokak 17, Galatasary (0212 244 1610). **Open** noon-3pm, 7pm-midnight Mon-Sat. **Starters** $3-$21. **Main courses** $8-$21. **Credit** AmEx, MC, V. **Map** p294 N3.

Founded by White Russians who relocated to Istanbul in the wake of the Soviet revolution, Rejans was reputedly one of Atatürk's favourite restaurants. It was also long the haunt of left-wing Turkish intellectuals who would grouch and gripe over borscht and white spirits. However, since the latest Slavic upheaval, in which the red star was spurned in favour of the gold card, Rejans is now frequented by groups of visiting Russkies with deep pockets, who drink themselves silly on flavoured vodkas as they gorge on 'tsar's *zakuski*' (the caviar goes from $17 to $118 for 100 grammes). And if the Slavic-styled food is merely so-so, the place still has bags of charm, with acres of polished wood, high ceilings, a musicians' gallery and an often drunk doorman to hang winter coats on hooks personalised with the names of long-dead customers.

Sofyalı 9

Sofyalı Sokak 9, Tünel (0212 245 0362). **Open** noon-1am Mon-Sat. **Starters** $3-$5. **Main courses** $6-$10. **Credit** MC, V. **Map** p294 M4.

A *meyhane*, but *très* genteel. It feels like someone's front room, albeit someone with money and taste and a fine old house: mustard walls, bits of exposed brick, wooden flooring, big fireplace, pretty chandeliers and hanging lanterns. The ground floor dining space is small but seven doors fold back to allow tables to spill into the alley. Plus there are two more floors upstairs (even so, reservations are a must). The crowd is cultured, verging on intellectual, with a notable gay presence. The food is a cut above. It's the standard meze off a tray and meat and fish from a recited menu but ingredients are fresh and zestful, and there's a lightness of touch in the preparation. Highly recommended.

Yakup 2

Asmalımescit Caddesi 35-7, Tünel (0212 249 2925). **Open** noon-2am daily. Closed Sun May-mid Sept. **Starters** $2-$4. **Main courses** $4-$14. **Credit** AmEx, DC, MC, V. **Map** p294 M4.

Owned by Yakup Arslan, brother of Refik (*see above*), this is a larger, more utilitarian-looking establishment than its sibling restaurant, but it draws a similar clientele. Again, it's very smoky and boozy, but the selection of meze is vast and most are excellent. Forget mains, just take a table here and fill it with small plate after small plate of octopus salad, sautéed carrots in a yoghurt garlic sauce, stuffed clams or Albanian-style liver. It's not a place for intimate dining so come with a crowd. Don't expect to be going home sober.

Zarifi

Çukurluçeşme Sokak 13, Çukurcuma (0212 293 5480). **Open** 8pm-4am daily. **Starters** $2-$7. **Main courses** $9-$13. **Credit** AmEx, MC, V. **Map** p295 O3.

Another fashionable update on the *meyhane*. Zarifi has the meze and all the traditional favourites like grilled meats, but the menu also encompasses foods like sashimi, smoked pork chops in Dijon sauce and panacotta with blackberry sauce. And instead of old-fashioned *fasıl* and Turkish folk music, a DJ spins chill-out and pop. However, at some point most evenings, the true spirit of the *meyhane* wins through – usually when everyone has drunk too much – and spontaneous dancing on the tables breaks out. The formula is duplicated every summer at Zarifi's super supper club up in Maslak, which has a capacity for over a thousand. Let's hope the tables are up to it.

Zencefil

Kurabiye Sokak 8 (0212 244 4082). **Open** 9am-10.30pm Mon-Sat. **Main courses** $4-$7. **No credit cards**. **Map** p295 O2.

As a result of a recent move into spacious new premises (just across the street from the original location) some of the cosiness of old has been lost. On the plus side, patrons now no longer have to stand and queue for the marinated vegetables, home-baked breads, hearty soups and daily, vegetarian-friendly specials. And the new place doesn't look so bad either. Rustic has been replaced by modern, with glass-enclosed walls and deep bold colours, but there's still a bit of that open country kitchen thing going, with shelves lined with jars of dried beans and preservatives. And the main thing is that the food is as good as ever.

Views and fusion at **Vogue**. *See p140.*

Few visitors make it up here, but as well as being the place for high-street shopping, there are a wealth of good eating places, particularly on and just off the two main streets **Abdi Ipekçi Caddesi** and **Teşvikiye Caddesi**. Most offer a credible local take on Western dining, although more interesting are those that attempt to take Turkish upscale, like **Borsa**, **Hünkar** and **Kantin**.

Banyan

Abdi Ipekçi Caddesi 40/3, Nişantaşı (0212 219 6011). **Open** noon-2am Mon-Sat. **Starters** $3-$8. **Main courses** $8-$21. **Credit** AmEx, MC, V.

Boldly striding across national boundaries, South African chef Mike Norman has plundered the whole of South-east Asia in assembling the menu at Banyan. We recommend all comers kick off with the out-standing Thai tom yam soup spiced with kafi lime leaves, ginger, lemon grass, galangal and chilli but, after that, wander at will through the likes of Vietnamese-style sea bass in banana leaves, Singapore seafood noodles, salmon on wasabi mash and the odd weird Turko-Malay crossover like lamb satay. Ceilings are oddly low, so the place feels like it's squeezed into some tiny left-over space between

What's on the menu

Useful phrases

Can I see a menu?
Menüye bakabilir miyim?
Do you have a table for (number) people?
(Number) kişilik masanız var mı?
I want to book a table for (time) o'clock.
Saat (time) için bir masa ayırmak istiyorum.
I'll have (name of food).
Ben (name of food) istiyorum.
I'll have (name of food) without salt.
Ben tuzsuz (name of food) istiyorum.
I'll have (name of food) without oil.
Ben yagsiz (name of food) istiyorum.
I'm a vegetarian.
Et yemiyorum.
Can I have an ashtray?
Kültablası alabilir miyim?
Can I have the bill please?
Hesap, lütfen.

Basics

breakfast **kahvaltı**
lunch **öğle yemeği**
dinner **akşam yemeği**
dessert **tatlı**
menu **menü**
service charge **servis**
glass **bardak**
cup **fincan**
knife **bıçak**
fork **çatal**
spoon **kaşık**
napkin **peçete**
plate **tabak**

To eat

baked **fırında pişmiş**
boiled **kaynamiş**

fried **kizarmiş**
grilled **ızgara**
roast **kavrulmuş**
bread **ekmek**; thin flat bread **pide** or **lavaş**
brown bread **kepekli ekmek**
rice **pilav**
soup **çorba**
pasta **makarna**
hardboiled/softboiled egg **katı yumurta/ rafadan yumurta**
cheese **peynir**
yoghurt **yoğurt**
garlic **sarımsak**
salt **tuz**
red/black/hot pepper **pul/kara/acı biber**

Meat

For a list of kebab types *see p127* **Kebab cuisine.**
beef **dana**
chicken **tavuk**
lamb **kuzu**

Fish

fish **balık**
dil sole
fener monkfish
hamsi anchovy
istakoz lobster
karides shrimp
kılıç swordfish
levrek sea bass
lüfer bluefish
palamut bonito
sardalya sardines
sarıgöz/sinarit sea bream
torik tuna
uskumra mackerel
yengeç crab

floors, as in *Being John Malkovich*, but the columns shaped like tree trunks are fun and bonsai on the tables is a nice touch.

Borsa
Lütfi Kırdar Kongre Merkezi, Darülbedai Caddesi 6, Harbiye (0212 296 3055). **Open** noon-3.30pm, 6.30pm-midnight daily. **Starters** $2.60-$8. **Main courses** $10-$18. **Credit** AmEx, MC, V. **Map** p301.
Borsa, a family-run chain, has been an Istanbul institution for 75 years. All this time later and it's still reckoned to be perhaps the best Turkish restaurant in town. This is a new branch of the original, which first opened in Sirkeci. The location couldn't be more unappealing, lodged at the Istanbul Convention & Exhibition Centre, accessible only by car, but it has

an imposing interior, all gleaming marble and plush banquettes, and a stunning summer terrace. All in, the place seats 500 and it's regularly packed out, making reservations a must. Expect the full gamut of meze, followed by meat and fish dishes, all clearly explained in English on the menu.

Cookbook Café
Güzelbahçe Sokak 5/2, off Valikonağı Caddesi, Nişantaşı (0212 219 1394). **Open** 10am-5.30pm Mon-Sat. **Starters** $5-$6. **Main courses** $5.60-$8. **Credit** AmEx, MC, V.
A cookery book store that doubles as a lunch-only restaurant with a menu of international dishes that changes each week. Diners are seated among the shelves with a view of the large, laboratory-like open

Vegetables

aubergine **patlıcan**
carrots **havuç**
cucumber **salatalık**
lentils **mercimek**
lettuce **marul**
okra **bamya**
onions **soğan**
peas **bezelye**
peppers **biber**
potatoes **patates**
spinach **ıspanak**
tomatoes **domates**
courgette **kabak**

Fruit and nuts

fruit **meyve**
apples **elma**
banana **muz**
cherries **kiraz**
grapes **üzüm**
hazelnuts **fındık**
honeydew melon **kavun**
lemon **limon**
peanuts **fıstık**
pistachio nuts **şam fıstığı**
oranges **portakal**
walnuts **ceviz**
watermelon **karpuz**

Meze

börek flaky savoury pastry with parsley
and/or white cheese, minced meat,
spinach or other vegetables
çerkez tavuğu shredded chicken served cold
in a walnut cream sauce
çoban salata 'shepherd's salad' of tomatoes,
cucumbers, hot peppers and onions with
lemon and olive oil

dolma vegetable such as cabbage, grape
leaves, pepper or squash, served cold and
stuffed with rice, pine nuts, currants and
spices. Served hot, they're usually also
stuffed with minced meat
imambayıldı aubergines cooked with onion
and tomato and olive oil, served cold
karnıyarık baked aubergines stuffed with
minced meat, onion, tomato spices
kısır Turkish tabouleh salad with parsley,
bulgar, lemon, tomato, onion, olive oil,
pomegranate, mint
lahmacun spiced minced meat on a thin crust
pizza-like bread called pide
mücver deep-fried patties made with grated
courgette in a batter of egg and flour
zeytinyağli cold dishes with olive oil

Mains

güveç casserole cooked in a clay pot
karides güveç shrimps cooked with onions in
a peppery tomato sauce
köfte meatballs
pirzola lamb chops

To drink

water **su**
milk **süt**
orange juice **taze portakal suyu**
apple juice **elma suyu**
cherry juice **vişne suyu**
peach juice **şeftali suyu**
red wine **kırmızı şarap**
white wine **beyaz şarap**
beer **bira**
tea **çay**
coffee **kahve**; Turkish coffee **Türk kahvesi**;
without sugar **sade**; a little sugar **az şekerli**;
medium sweet **orta şekerli**; sweet **şekerli**

Eat, Drink, Shop

kitchen (where cookery classes are also held in the evenings). Recurring house specials include crepes with Camembert and mushrooms, swordfish club sandwich, veal with lemon and capers, and pear poached in red wine. Note that the place is easy to miss, being at the rear of a fairly nondescript apartment building.

The House Café

Atiye Sokak 10/1, off Abdi Ipekçi Caddesi, Teşvikiye (0212 259 2377). **Open** 8am-11pm daily. **Starters** $3-$7. **Main courses** $6.50-$11. **Credit** DC, MC, V.
The address is an ordinary apartment building and the layout of the café is of a typical two-bedroom flat. There's a 'living room' up front with a big communal table in the middle, with more private tables in the smaller rooms at the back. It's cosy and unpretentious and we like the friendly staff too. Food is similarly unaffected. Drop by at breakfast for 'House toast' or lunch for 'House burger'. Last visit we enjoyed grilled sea bass with rocket sandwiched in home-made cornbread, followed by delicious fruit cobbler. Avoid the frequently frantic lunch hour if you're hoping to linger over coffee.

Hünkar

Mim Kemal Öke Caddesi 21, Nişantaşı (0212 287 8470). **Open** noon-midnight daily. **Starters** $3-$5. **Main courses** $7-$10. **Credit** AmEx, MC, V.
The original Hünkar (from *hünkar beşendi*, 'the sultan enjoyed it', an old court dish of lamb on aubergine purée) opened in 1950 in the old western

A TASTE OF FRESH BEER IN A LIVELY ENVIRONMENT

TAPS Brewery & Restaurant, located in the trendy Nişantaşı district combines two floors of restaurants with a lively bar. Taps brews 4 different kinds of fresh beer every week ranging from Kölsch to Red Ale while the restaurant features fresh pasta, pizza and international meat dishes where the fresh beer is used for marinating and sauces. Taps also has a beatiful garden for those who want to enjoy the summer breeze of the city.

Taps is open 7 days a week from 11.30 A.M.
(Sundays 2.00 P.M.)
Advance reservation is advised for dinners and weekends.
Valet service is provided.
All credit cards are accepted.

For more information visit www.tapsistanbul.com

district of Fatih. As part of a trend for trad restaurants to reinvent themselves as upscale eateries, it has recently opened branches here in Nişantaşı and even further upmarket in Etiler. Chanel-daubed power suits and deal-brokering jackets can now chow down on sheep's trotter soup, stuffed cabbage or *pilaf* with anchovies. Shelves of jarred preserves and antique copper artefacts maintain one foot in the past, street-side terrace seating allows punters to keep one eye on the present.

Kantin
Akkavak Sokak 16/2, Nişantaşı (0212 219 3114). **Open** 11.30am-7pm Mon-Sat. **Starters** $3-$6. **Main courses** $4-$7. **Credit** MC, V.
Under the stewardship of ace cook Semsa Denizsel, Kantin's *raison d'etre* is to provide a lunchtime business crowd with healthy versions of Turkish fast-food faves. Every day a blackboard lists three unchanging entrées – pizza, a Kantin burger and chicken schnitzel – supplemented by three hot daily specials: last visit we had ground chicken-breast meatballs with fresh artichokes and herbed vermicelli and bulgur. There are also summer salads dressed with cold-press Ayvalık olive oil, winter soups, fresh fruit juices, desserts and frothy cappuccinos served with a chunk of candied green fig.

Loft
Lütfi Kırdar Kongre Merkezi, Darülbedai Caddesi 6, Harbiye (0212 219 6384). **Open** noon-2am Mon-Sat; 5pm-2am Sun. **Starters** $5-$10. **Main courses** $8-$20. **Credit** AmEx, DC, MC, V. **Map** p301.
There is nothing remotely loft-like about this stylish update of a Manhattan supper club. In fact, it occupies space in the distinctly unglamorous Istanbul Convention & Exhibition Centre building. The interior, though, is gorgeous – geometric groupings of leather banquettes, low-hanging Japanese lanterns and a long marble bar provide a drop-dead setting for ambitous international fare concocted by French-trained chef Ümit Ozkanca (heir to the Borsa empire, headquartered upstairs; *see p136*). Expect the likes of Moroccan spicy shrimp salad or grilled quail, simple T-bone steak or Peking duck with porcini mushrooms and bok choy. The drinks list runs from the domestic (Cankaya at $29 a bottle) to the downright decadent (Dom Perignon at $525).

The Bosphorus Villages

By which we mean the string of small waterfront settlements downhill of Beyoğlu and Taksim, beginning with **Beşiktaş** and running north through **Ortaköy**, **Arnavutköy** and **Bebek**, up to the fortress of **Rumeli Hisarı**. Unsurprisingly, it's all about fish.

Çınar Restaurant
İskele Meydanı, Ortaköy (0212 261 5818). Bus 22, 22R, 25E, 30D, 40, 42T. **Open** noon-2am daily. **Starters** $3-$5. **Main courses** $6-$11. **Credit** AmEx, DC, MC, V.

A handful of almost identical restaurants line up on the west side of the waterfront square at Ortaköy. They are all fine places to pass an evening, with banquette seating, sociable atmospheres and views of moonlight on the Bosphorus. There's no menu: meze with a seafood slant are presented on a tray for selection and if you're still hungry after that, another tray comes out with an artful presentation of different fish. Alcohol is served and entertainment comes in the form of fortune-telling gypsies and street vendors peddling the most unbelievable tat.

Feriye
Feriye Sarayı, Çırağan Caddesi 124, Ortaköy (0212 227 2216). Bus 22, 22R, 25E, 30D, 40, 42T. **Open** noon-3pm, 7-midnight daily. **Main courses** $8-$26. **Credit** AmEx, DC, MC, V.
Good views are ten a penny along the Bosphorus shore but, still, the watery panorama as seen from Feriye is really something special. The restaurant is housed in what used to be the Ottoman sultans' palatial grounds (next to the swanky Çırağan Palace) and, though it's only a short walk from central Ortaköy, it's tranquillity personified. Vedat Başaran, co-owner and celebrity chef, has taken an obsession with Ottoman cooking to new heights, even going as far as to learn Arabic so he could read old recipes in their original form. The results are stunning. At its best in summer with outdoor dining besides the straits, Feriye is also lovely in winter, when the elegant interior is cheered by a piano player.

Poseidon
Küçük Bebek, Cevdat Paşa Caddesi 58, Bebek (0212 263 3823). Bus 22, 22R, 25E, 30D, 40, 42T. **Open** noon-2am daily. **Starters** $3-$10. **Main courses** $10-$20. **Credit** AmEx, MC, V.
Bebek is a long way to go for dinner, but Poseidon repays the effort. It's a supremely stylish affair, pitched right up at the top end of the fish-eating experience. Specialities include stuffed calamari, marinated sea bass and fish croquettes. Your dining companions will be well bred, well manicured and free-spending. There is an outdoor terrace virtually overhanging the water with seating for 120, but if the weather's not up to it, the view from indoors is equally fine. Afterwards we recommend continuing the evening at the bar of the Bebek Hotel (*see p151*).

Rumeli Iskele
Yahya Kemal Caddesi 1, Rumeli Hisarı (0212 263 2997). Bus 22, 22R, 25E, 30D, 40, 42T. **Open** noon-2am daily. **Starters** $2-$7. **Main courses** $5-$30. **Credit** AmEx, MC, V.
The waterfront deck here faces across the straits to the hilltop castle of Anadolu Hisarı. And it's not that bad inside either: traditional in style but elegant. The menu holds few surprises – meze and Mediterranean fish – but the food is consistently good. Service is unobtrusive and efficient. They must be doing something right because despite the ever-increasing competition from newly arrived, more upscale seafood restaurants this place is always packed.

Eat, Drink, Shop

Vogue

Spor Caddesi 92, BJK Plaza A Blok 13, Akaretler, Beşiktaş (0212 227 2545). Bus 22, 22R, 25E, 30D, 40, 42T. **Open** 10.30am-3pm, 7pm-midnight daily. **Starters** $3-$10. **Main courses** $8-$26. **Credit** AmEx, MC, V.

The view alone is reason enough to visit Vogue but for those already sated on panoramic Istanbul there are plenty of other draws: a superb sushi bar, deftly prepared Californian fusion cuisine (with a few Turkish touches), chic white and chrome decor, a lounge patio with throw cushions and a bar staffed by people who actually know how to mix a cocktail. The place was named Best Restaurant 2002 by *Time Out Istanbul* magazine, in recognition of the fact that style and substance are not always mutually exclusive. Reservations are essential – but make them in plenty of time if you hope to turn up for the Thursday night bar parties or Sunday brunch.

The Asian Shore

Çiya

Güneşlibahçe Sokak 43 & 44, Kadıköy (0216 418 5115). **Open** 11am-10pm daily. **Starters** $2-$3. **Main courses** $3.50-$6. **Credit** AmEx, MC, V. **Map** p297 W7.

Small eateries are chock-a-block on Güneşlibahçe and often indistinguishable from each other. But this place is so good, and so successful, it's expanding into multiple properties. Currently, on one side of the street is Çiya Sofrası (rural specialities), while opposite is Çiya Kebapçı. Both are two floors of smart and clean efficiency, with tiled white floors and pine kitchen furniture, uniformed staff and sepia photos of peasantry on the walls. The ground floor of the *kebapçı* is dominated by a big open kitchen with white-hatted chefs pounding dough and twirling skewered meats. The sheer variety of kebabs is mind-boggling; for help *see p127* **Kebab cuisine**.

Kanaat

Selmanipak Caddesi 25, Üsküdar (0216 333 3791) **Open** 6am-11pm daily. **Starters** $1-$3. **Main courses** $2-$4. **No credit cards. Map** p296 W2.

Founded in 1933, Kanaat is a fine example of a historical *lokanta*. It serves traditional, hard-to-find Turkish food on simple wooden tables, and is a cheap and popular option for lunch and dinner. The service is good too. Even without the extensive range of meat and vegetable dishes, desserts such as the poached quince with clotted cream and delicate puddings are reason enough to visit. A short walk from the ferry landing in Üsküdar, a trip to Kanaat can be combined with a seaside stroll towards the Maiden's Tower.

Körfez

Körfez Caddesi 78, Kanlıca (0216 413 4314/ www.korfez.com). **Open** noon-4pm, 7pm-midnight daily. **Starters** $3-$8. **Main courses** $20-$54. **Credit** MC, V.

It's midway up the Asian Shore of the Bosphorus, a boat ride away from the city centre, but gourmands from all over regularly make the pilgrimage to Kanlıca (*see p240*) for what many swear is the finest fish in Istanbul. As is the case with nearly all of Istanbul's seafood restaurants, the emphasis here is on whatever is freshest but the signature dish is *tuzda balık* – literally 'fish in salt'. To get here, take a bus to Rumeli Hisarı, from where there's a special shuttle laid on across the Bosphorus, departing from opposite Edwards of Hisar. Alternatively, take an ordinary ferry from Eminönü or Beşiktaş across to Üsküdar and there jump in a taxi for the 15-minute ride. Reservations are essential.

Levent & Etiler

Two upmarket districts of blue-glass skyscrapers, monolithic malls, terraced Starbucks, cigar shops and kerb-to-kerb SUVs. But there are also a handful of fine restaurants. To get up here take the metro from Taksim Square and hop off at Levent (not 4 Levent). It's a 15-minute ride and costs less than a dollar. A taxi over the same journey is around $15.

Sunset Grill & Bar

Yol Sokak 1, off Adnan Saygun Caddesi, Ulus Parkı, Ulus (0212 287 0357). **Metro** Levent. **Open** noon-3pm, 7pm-2am daily. **Starters** $6-$18. **Main courses** $10-$19. **Credit** AmEx, DC, MC, V.

A gorgeous venue serving up modern Californian fusion cuisine in a soft-hued venue high on a hillside above the Bosphorus, commanding fantastic views. As well as imaginative meat and fish dishes, there's a highly regarded sushi bar. Make the most of it by going in warm weather on a clear night to sit in the verdant garden. To get here take a taxi from the Levent metro station: it's a five- to ten-minute ($2) ride.

Ulus 29

Kireçhane Sokak 1, Adnan Saygun Caddesi, Ulus Parkı, Ulus (0212 265 6181/www.club29.com). **Metro** Levent. **Open** noon-4pm, 7pm-midnight daily. **Starters** $11-$20. **Main courses** $13-$30. **Credit** AmEx, MC, V.

Someone to impress? Something to celebrate? Or just feel like living out a Sinatra song? For all forms of high-living excess, Ulus 29 fits the bill. Thanks to a setting way up the hillside above the Bosphorus (just above the Sunset Grill & Bar; *see above*), the views from its semicircular terrace are simply magnificent – among the best commanded by any venue in the city. The restaurant itself is no eyesore either, beautifully crafted by Istanbul nightlife impresario Metin Fadıllıoğlu and his interior designer wife Zeynap (the couple also own the highly rated Chintamani restaurant in London). The food is Ottoman cuisine in the broadest sense, with dishes drawn from all around the eastern Mediterranean. Be careful who you come with – the place is so seductive you just might fall in love.

Bars & Cafés

Historically abstemious, Istanbul is making up for lost time.

Istanbul was never beery or steeped in viti-culture, and dabbling with booze was never a part of the local social scene. Later Ottoman sultans were frequently off their heads on alcohol, or worse (Murat III probably barely noticed his three months on the throne in 1876, such was his addiction to morphine), and Atatürk liked a drop, but for the common people coffee was as strong as it got. Mind you, that's pretty strong. A proper Turkish *kahve* has the bitter kick of a double espresso. That is all changing. Not only has the consumption of alcohol now moved out of its traditional ghetto of grizzly old men's tavernas, but the likes of Starbucks have arrived, adding milk and froth to the local 'black mud'.

Since the mid 1990s the bar and café business has boomed. Initially the style was Parisian Left Bank meets student squat – bare brick, wooden floorboards and flea-market furnishings – but somebody's got a sub-scription to *Wallpaper** because recent interiors have suddenly developed a heavy wow factor. Modern bar design has come to Istanbul and, jeez, does it look good, especially when combined with the killer locations that plenty of venues boast, either down beside the Bosphorus or up high on rooftop terraces. Inevitably, prices have risen accordingly and although the standard price for a beer (*bira*) is around $2 (for a bottle or 33cl glass of lagery local Efes), anywhere that looks like the paint scheme and furniture might match is probably going to charge $4 or more.

WHERE TO DRINK

The age-old local coffee-house (or tea-house), known as a *kıraathane*, has been in decline but recent years have seen a bit of an upswing thanks to the sudden fashionability of the *nargile* (waterpipe): *see p152* **Hava nargile**. There's no alcohol at such places, though. Otherwise, there is no real template: there are out-and-out bars and there are cafés, but most places blur the line between the two. They typically serve coffee and food throughout the day, getting increasingly smoky and boozy as the evening wears on.

Beyoğlu is party central, with a density of drinking venues that would do a German city proud. There's little of value on main Istiklal Caddesi itself but the surrounding streets are a barfly's delight. An evening around Ortaköy or Arnavutköy is pleasant but quality options are limited; similarly, Nişantaşı and Teşvikye. A night on Kadife Sokak over in Kadıköy on the Asian shore has the potential to turn into something enjoyably regrettable, although getting home is potentially troublesome.

WHAT TO DRINK

There are maybe just three places at which you could order a cocktail with confidence (**Beşinci Kat**, **Bina** and **Nu Teras**) and one for a dry martini (**Vogue**, *see p140*). The rest of the time, it's beer or, increasingly, wine (*şarap*). Thanks to media hype, wine is catching on and local producers are pulling out all the stops to match rising consumer expectations. The result is a

Eat, Drink, Shop

The best Bars & cafés

Bebek Bar
In a city where even the Burger King boasts brilliant Bosphorus views, this is the best. *See p152.*

Beşinci Kat
A bar so snug-fittingly comfortable you want to wrap it up and take it home. *See p144.*

Dulcinea
Art on the walls, dancing on the tables at a fine multi-purpose venue. *See p147.*

Nu Teras
Seventh (floor) heaven and the perfect venue for a long cool drink on a hot summer's night. *See p149.*

Soho Teras
And more views – but how much better the city looks with a drink in your hand. *See p151.*

Tophane nargile cafés
Istanbul's 24-hour all-smoking zone. *See p152* **Hava nargile**.

greater variety of labels on the shelves and steadily improving quality. Prices, however, are not cheap, which is a bit cheeky given that although the local stuff *is* drinkable it's hardly chateau standard.

Rakı, the local aniseed spirit (similar to the Greek *ouzo* or French *pastis*), is sold in twice the quantity of all other alcoholic drinks combined. It was national role-model Atatürk's favourite tipple and, more to the point, it's cheap. However, it is rarely drunk away from the dinner table and goes down best in company.

Sultanahmet

Other than a row of overpriced tourist cafés on the east side of the Hippodrome, the odd rowdy backpacker joint on Akbıyık Caddesi and one or two somnolent hotel bars, there's next to no alternative to a restaurant as a place to pass an evening around Sultanahmet. Extend your options by walking down the hill to Eminönü where there's the **Orient Express bar** on platform 1 of Sirkeci station and countless beer-serving places underslung beneath the **Galata**

Bridge. Or consider forgoing the booze and giving your lungs a workout at one of the local nargile cafés (*see p152* **Hava nargile**).

Cheers
Akbıyık Caddesi 20 (no phone). Tram Sultanahmet. **Open** 10am-2am daily. **Licensed. No credit cards**. **Map** p289 N11.
Akbıyık Caddesi is backpacker boulevard, busy with cut-rate travel agencies, hostels and last-ditch dining options. Bars are as transient as the clientele they serve but Cheers has been around longer than most. It's small and cramped, and crowded most

Bina: the name means 'building'. *See p144.*

nights with an international throng delighted to find themselves in each other's company. On the right night, it feels like a student house party; on the wrong night you may find yourself trading tales of bad bowels with a Lonely Planet-wielding round-the-worlder from Denmark.

Sultan Pub
Divan Yolu 2 (0212 528 1719). Tram Sultanahmet. **Open** 8am-2am daily. **Licensed**. **Credit** AmEx, MC, V. **Map** p289 N10.
About the only streets in Sultanahmet offering any signs of nightlife are tiny Seftalı Sokak, at the bottom end of Divan Yolu, and Ticarethane Sokak, one block back. On Seftalı two or three small bar/restaurants have tables on the street. One of them is a crowded little cellar dive with loud music, another is the Sultan, which proudly boasts to have been around since 1975 – no big shakes given that the neighbouring underground cistern dates back 1,500 years. If you can snag a pavement seat with a view across the Hippodrome to Sultanahmet Mosque, then there are worse places to nurse a beer.

Yeşil Ev Beer Garden
Kabasakal Caddesi 5 (0212 517 6785). Tram Sultanahmet. **Open** 10.30am-11pm daily. **Licensed**. **Credit** AmEx, MC, V. **Map** p289 N10.
This pretty garden, filled with towering laurel, linden and horse chestnut trees, belongs to the Yeşil Ev guesthouse (*see p51*). It's a beautiful setting, almost unique for Istanbul, and easily the finest place for an early-evening drink anywhere this side of the Golden Horn. In winter, guests are sheltered in a large glasshouse-type structure amid luxurious hanging gardens. Pricey but worth it.

Beyoğlu

Beyoğlu is bar and café bliss. Almost every little side-street off the mile-and-a-half length of **Istiklal Caddesi** is packed with 'em. Greatest concentration is up at the Taksim end, with venues that meet the needs of every tribe: Africans, Anatolians, goths, bikers, students, intellectuals, queens and trannies. The more discerning drink south around **Galatasaray**, while the scene setters have settled on the tightly wound backstreets of **Asmalımescit** and **Tünel**, which is where a lot of the new good stuff is happening.

Badehane
General Yazgan Sokak 5, Tünel (0212 249 0550). **Open** 9am-2am daily. **Licensed. No credit cards**. **Map** p294 M4.
A modest single-room venue just off Tünel Square, Badehane began life as a semi-vegetarian eaterie but quickly degenerated into one of the best little bars in town. In summer it's stripped bare as all the tables and seating are hauled out into the alley; in winter everything moves back inside again. The décor is what in the West would be called spit 'n' sawdust,

except the Turks are too well-mannered to gob on the floor. The diminutive but feisty madam Bade still runs the show and continues to provide decent, well-priced food. Watch your footing on the way down to the toilets.

Beşinci Kat (5.Kat)

5th floor, Soğancı Sokak 7, off Sıraselviler Caddesi, Cihangir (0212 293 3774/www.5kat.com). **Open** 10am-2am daily. **Licensed. Credit** MC, V. **Map** p295 O3.

Presided over by the fabulously flame-haired Yasemin Alkaya, Beşinci Kat (Fifth Floor) is the natural home of resting film types, off-duty club promoters, sultry vamps and committed barflys. It has a fine long bar to prop up; alternatively, you can artfully drape yourself over leopard-skin sofas against a backdrop of blood-red heavy drapes. The bar staff are trained to cope with cocktails, and the view from the full-length windows is a killer. Fine food too: *see p131*. It's a great 'last of the night' stop-off, when, long past the pumpkin hour, there's just you and a few like-minded individuals gazing out at the city, laid out below like a carpet of smouldering embers, served by a barman who's never in too much of a hurry to call time.

Beşinci Peron

Şehbender Sokak 5A, Asmalımescit (0212 292 7015). **Open** noon-2am daily. **Licensed. No credit cards. Map** p294 M4.

There's a station clock outside, a steam train on the business cards and the name means 'platform 5', but the only real rail connection is that most nights this little basement bar is as ram-packed as a commuter carriage at the height of rush hour. It's a young, studenty crowd, pushed up against the walls to leave a puddle of space in the middle for girls in singlets to dance to the 'DJ' and his CD collection. But it's with the arrival (10pm-ish) of the musicians – clarinet, *saz* and *qanun* – that the place really takes off, erupting into wholesale whooping, stamping, clapping, dancing and, of course, mass singalongs. Be warned, it's only a matter of time before someone insists that you join in.

Beyoğlu Pub

Halep Pasajı, Istiklal Caddesi 140 (0212 252 3842). **Open** noon-2am daily. **Licensed. Credit** AmEx, MC, V. **Map** p294 N3.

Well hidden away, the BP is (badly signposted) up on the first floor of the shabby Halep Pasajı, above all the hippy-shit shops and the Beyoğlu cinema. It's a surprisingly polished affair (terracotta-tiled floor, lots of stained wood, a long gleaming bar counter) with an almost country-club air. Best of all is the large open-air terrace, filled with potted greenery, although the only views are of the backsides of the surrounding buildings. It's one of the oldest bars around and retains a loyal following, heavy on politicos and people from the entertainment biz. Most come to eat (schnitzel, filet mignon, that sort of thing) and booze on bottles of the distilled, peaty stuff.

Bina

Sofyalı Sokak 11, Tünel (0212 244 0241). **Open** 11am-midnight Mon-Fri; 11am-4am Sat, Sun. **Licensed. Credit** MC, V. **Map** p294 M4.

New on the block as we prepare this guide, it's still too early to tell exactly what Bina might be. Is it a bar that does quality food, or a restaurant with a stylish bar attached? Whichever, it very elegantly fills three floors of a fine old building that has been stripped back to bare bricks and given new life by judicious use of glass and steel. The ground floor hosts the bar area, with a sleek high counter, well stocked with the necessary ingredients for the dozen or so cocktails listed on the menu ($7 each). Upstairs is for dining: the menu is meaty and includes pork chops ('pig chops' in Turkish) – a real rarity in Muslim Istanbul. Upstairs is also the owner's drum kit but he promises to stay off it if you're nice.

Büyük Londra

Meşrutiyet Caddesi 117, Tepebaşı (0212 245 0670). **Open** 24 hrs daily. **Licensed. Credit** MC, V. **Map** p294 M3.

Fans of old colonial watering holes tend to head for the lovely though overly expensive bar at the Pera Palas Hotel, but that's because they don't know about the Büyük Londra. Its bar is about the same vintage (late 19th century) and what it lacks in grandeur it more than makes up for with eccentricity. A serving counter no bigger than a kiosk is tucked into the corner of the rear of two connected large saloons, both plushly carpeted and bedecked with titanic chandeliers. The barman occasionally sallies forth to change the 78 on the wind-up gramophone, otherwise the soundtrack is the chattering songbirds caged on the windowsills. Smoking jackets are optional but it'd be nice if you made the effort.

Café Marmara

Marmara Hotel, Taksim Square (0212 251 4696). **Open** 7.30am-1.30pm daily. **Licensed. Credit** AmEx, DC, MC, V. **Map** p295 P2.

An Istanbul institution, the Marmara has bit of a démodé 1970s feel redolent of a department store cafeteria. The constant chatter and symphony of clattering crockery creates a buzz, and even though it's nearly always full to capacity, it rarely feels crowded thanks to high ceilings and great glass windows overlooking the square – not that there's much of a view. The bakery is one of the best for takeaway chocolate, cakes and pastries, and in a city short on breakfast venues the Marmara is your best bet for everything from a kick-start coffee through muesli and omelettes to pancakes and maple syrup.

Çiçek Bar

Billurcu Sokak 25, off Sıraselviler Caddesi (0212 244 2619). **Open** 5.30pm-2am daily. **Licensed. Credit** MC, V. **Map** p295 O3.

This is possibly as close as Istanbul gets to a media members-only haunt like London or New York's Soho House, except that the Turks are so laissez-faire that anyone who looks as though they've man-

Bazaar break at **Café Fes**. *See p80*.

The cultured patrons of **Kafe Ara**. *See p148.*

aged to tie their own shoelaces will generally get in. It's a lovely place too, with a little courtyard garden fronting a well-padded lounge, with well-padded seats, occupied by well-padded success stories from the film world. The club is owned by one-time producer Arif Keskiner (known as 'Çiçek Arif' – 'Arif the Flower' – for the floral arrangements in his buttonhole); the premises used to be his office but so many people would regularly drop by for drinkies that he began charging.

Dulcinea

Meşelik Sokak 20, off Istiklal Caddesi (0212 245 1071/www.dulcinea.org). **Open** 10am-2am daily Mon-Thur, Sun; 10am-4am Fri, Sat. **Licensed**. **Credit** MC, V. **Map** p295 O2.

This is such a great venue. It's one long, long room with a long, long bar, mirror backed and racked with spirits. You could probably get a whole football team sat up at the counter, subs and all, with stools left over – except they couldn't come wearing colours; they'd have to be wearing Cargo and Campers and Diesel and that sort of stuff, like everyone else here. They'd have to order cocktails or wine and discourse intelligently on the artworks on the walls. Then they could wander back and take seats on the mezzanine and order surprisingly reasonably priced dinners. And maybe later take a look downstairs to see what's going on in the basement club-performance space (*see p224*). Heavens, what cultured and sophisticated footballers they would be.

Eski Kulis

Atlas Pasajı, Istiklal Caddesi 209 (0212 293 1423). **Open** noon-2am daily. **Licensed**. **No credit cards**. **Map** p295 N3.

It's the size and shape of a railway carriage, but far more convivial. Passengers here are booked onto a smoke-wreathed journey to *rakı*-fuelled loquacity, ushered there by a maroon-waistcoated gent of sober countenance who commands the leather-padded bar counter. The crowd's an older set – many of them from the theatre biz – and one senses that this is a voyage that they make regularly. There's another similar venue, the **Sefahathane**, across the passage, which is a bit larger and very much younger in character: two equally appealing takes on nighthawks at the diner, Istanbul style.

Gizli Bahçe

Nevizade Sokak 27 (0212 249 2192). **Open** noon-2am daily. **Licensed**. **Credit** MC, V. **Map** p294 N3.

The name means 'Secret Garden', which is appropriate given that you haven't a hope of finding this place unless you know exactly where to look. It's a scabby door into a vacant-looking hallway, easily missed between the hurl-and-burl of surrounding *meyhanes*. Go up two flights of stairs to discover one of the earliest arrivals on the Istanbul's 'lounge' scene. It's a chill-out area of old sofas, easy chairs and coffee tables leading through to an American bar – standing-room only – with DJs spinning funk, trance and techno.

James Joyce

*Zambak Sokak 6, off Istiklal Caddesi (0212 244
0241/www.jamesjoyceirishpub.com). Open* 3pm-2am
Mon-Thur, Sun; 3pm-4am Fri, Sat. **Licensed. No
credit cards. Map** p295 O2.

The first and, surprisingly, only Irish pub in
Istanbul. There's the usual clichéd tat on the walls
but what matters is that punters – a mix of worldly
Turks, expats and foreign visitors – are kept happy
with a decent range of beers (Guinness included, of
course), Irish breakfast served all day, televised
sport and live music almost every night. It gets loud
and crowded downstairs when the bands are on but
there's a slightly quieter mezzanine level with more
elbow room. Note that in autumn 2003 the pub was
due to move to new premises on nearby Balo Sokak;
check the website for the latest and, while there, visit
the noticeboard for some engaging postings ('i pay
you 15.000 us dolor for formality marriage').

Kafe Ara

*Tosbağa Sokak 8/A, off Yeniçarşı Caddesi,
Galatasaray (0212 245 4105). Open* 11am-
midnight. **Not licensed. Credit** AmEx, MC,V.
Map p294 N3.

A continental-styled street café, which, weather per-
mitting, fills a narrow alley beside the Galatasaray
Lycée. In colder months the action shifts inside, into
a smart split-level space hung with regularly changing exhibitions of photo art and scattered with style
mags. Patrons are a cultured bunch: portfolios
tucked under arms, scribbling in notebooks,
engaged in furrowed-brow conversation. No alcohol
is served, but there's a good food menu (with English
subtitling) featuring hot sandwiches, pastas, cakes
and desserts, and they do excellent milkshakes.

Kaffeehaus

Tünel Square 4, Tünel (0212 245 4028). Open
9am-9pm daily. **Not licensed. No credit cards.**
Map p294 M4.

The tiny frontage onto Tünel Square is deceptive:
step inside and it opens out into a high-ceilinged airy
interior of Wedgwood blue walls. The modernist
decor's perhaps a little severe but the waitresses are
just the sweetest. A reading rack of newspapers and
magazines and a noticeboard busy with posters and
fliers also add warmth. Snacks and hot meals are
served but most are here for coffee, juice and cake.
Prime seats are those beside the plate-glass frontage
for unrivalled people-watching opportunities – try
upstairs if those on the ground floor are taken.

Kaktüs

*Imam Adnan Sokak 4, off Istiklal Caddesi (0212
249 5979). Open* 9am-2am Mon-Sat; 11am-2am Sun.
Licensed. Credit MC, V. **Map** p295 O2.

Opened in the early 1990s, Kaktüs was the first of a
new wave of café-bars to hit Istanbul; it has since
spawned countless imitators. The dark-wood interior, elegant tables and chairs owe a great deal to the
classic French café. Certainly its patrons do their
best to enhance the atmosphere by chain-smoking

like troopers, sipping blonde beers and black coffee
and generally looking as though they were audi-
tioning for a role in a Godard movie. Food is served
throughout the day from a constantly changing
short-order menu. Staff are cool but efficient and
exhibit good taste in music.

Kino

*Sofyalı Sokak 4, Asmalımescit (0212 245 0010).
Open* noon-midnight Mon-Sat. **Licensed. Credit**
MC, V. **Map** p294 M4.

It has the appearance of some sort of private club or
gallery: a discreet entrance leading to a clinically
white corridor guarded by a a small reception desk,
or is it a DJ booth? In fact, it turns out to be the bar.
Very minimalist. Very Philippe Starck, especially
the shifting hues of soft lighting. There's no hanging on the counter here: instead all the action goes
on in a couple of chilled rooms at the rear and, in
summer, in the rather pleasant back garden. In addition to the booze and beverages, there's a good menu
of largely vegetarian dishes, of which nothing is
more than about $3.

KV Café

Tünel Geçidi 10, Tünel (0212 251 4338). Open
8am-1.30am daily. **Licensed. Credit** MC, V. **Map**
p294 M4.

Opposite the upper station of the Tünel funicular,
an iron gate opens to a short Italianate 19th-century
passage, overfilled with potted trees and bushes. It
looks like a jungle scene by Henri Rousseau but
instead of wild animals amid the shaggy greenery,
diners sip afternoon tea on wrought-iron furniture.
Inside, the café occupies three beautiful bare-brick
rooms with flagged floors and big arched windows.
As well as teas and coffees, KV has a short menu of
sandwiches, salads, hot entrées and classic desserts.
Pleasant during the day, the place is particularly
enchanting in the evening, when the passage is lit
by candles and Victorian lamps.

Leb-i Derya

*Kumbaracı İş Hanı 115/7, Kumbaracı Yokuşu,
Tünel (0212 293 4989). Open Nov-Apr* 11am-2am
daily. *May-Oct* 5pm-1am daily. **Licensed. Credit**
AmEx, MC, V. **Map** p294 N4.

This smart, covered rooftop terrace is a recent hit
addition to the Asmalımescit-Tünel scene. It owes
its popularity to some fantastic views: Sultanahmet
and the Golden Horn on one side, the Bosphorus on
another. Unlike most terraces which are forced to
close in winter, Leb-i Derya stays open, its customers
protected from the elements by glass panes
(removed in summer). Other pluses include efficient
service and a cool, loungey soundtrack. The civilised
and sophisticated atmosphere is particularly appreciated by women, who make up a high proportion
of the clientele. The downside are the high prices.

Limonlu Bahçe

*Yeniçarşı Caddesi 98, Galatasaray (0212 252 1094).
Open Nov-Mar* noon-11pm daily. *Apr-Oct* 9.30am-
1am daily. **Licensed. Credit** MC, V. **Map** p294 N3.

Part-way down the precipitous slope of Yeniçarşı, Limonlu Bahçe is a café set in a big, bucolic back garden. It's a pretty setting and one that draws a predominantly youthful crowd to loll on throw cushions, flop in hammocks or gather at chunky wooden tables, picking at portions of hot food and locking eyes over cold drinks. There are lots of tight T-shirts, cute little tattoos and bare midriffs on display – and that's just the boys. It's like one big Gap ad. And if there are too few staff for the number of tables, nobody seems in too much of a hurry anyway.

Madrid

İpek Sokak 16 (no phone). **Open** 2pm-2am daily. **Licensed. No credit cards. Map** p295 O2.
A serious good-time drinking den spreading joy over its four levels. There's a loose Spanish theme going on, with the odd bit of Andalusian tiling, some Goya prints and a signed poster of Almodóvar's *All About My Mother* in the basement, but otherwise the real attraction is cheap beer and a lively mix of people knocking it back. The place is notably popular with the city's English-language-teaching crowd. Beware the tight iron staircases, which are lethal if you've had a few too many (and you will).

North Shield

AFM Fitaş Building, Istiklal Caddesi 24-6 (0212 251 2020/www.thenorthshield.com). **Open** 11am-1.30am daily. **Licensed. Credit** MC, V. **Map** p295 O2.
While the adjacent screens of the AFM Fitaş multiplex (*see p193*) peddle cinematic fantasies of all kinds, the North Shield transports its punters to suburban middle England sometime circa the mid 1970s. Props include tartan carpet, Famous Grouse mirrors, etched-glass screens, bench seating and a long, polished dark-wood bar counter with stools. We even got Abba, Elton John and Santana on the sound system. It's a setting for homesick Brit teachers to chat up clueless students; however, with beer (Efes) at $4 a pop they've got to work fast. If you like this, there's five more of them scattered round town.

Nu Teras

Meşrutiyet Caddesi 145-7, Tepebaşı (0212 245 6070). **Open** 6.30pm-2am Mon-Thu, Sun; 6.30pm-4am Fri, Sat. Closed Oct-May. **Licensed. Credit** MC, V. **Map** p294 M4.
Tough luck on winter visitors to Istanbul: the city's most drop-dead stylish bar is open summer only. The reason? It's a seventh-floor, open-air rooftop

The face of new Istanbul, **Nu Teras**.

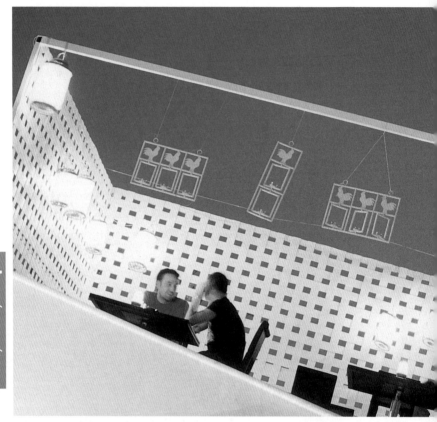

affair, gloriously exposed to the elements. Much of the space is given over to long tables of diners (the same kitchen and similar menu to **Lokanta**, which is down on the ground floor; *see p133*) but the star of the show is the bar. Constructed of smoked glass, it fringes the building like a parapet; customers seated on the high bar stools have an unobstructed and dizzying view of the city below. It's the venue par excellence for sunset cocktails.

Palyaço

Imam Adnan Sokak 30, off Istiklal Caddesi (0212 293 5761). **Open** 9am-2am daily. **Licensed. Credit** MC, V. **Map** p295 O2.

A small, narrow café-bar with theatrical overtones – maroon velvet drapes, recycled cinema seats and a flickering gallery of clowns along one wall. It's one of the area's long players and has a steady regular crown of alt-cultural types and students nosing for a big night out on a small budget. Food is served (winter only) from a menu drawing from minority cuisines such as Jewish and Armenian. The same

people also run **Cambaz**, across the street, which sparsely occupies four floors of a massive old building with a variety of hollow and echoing bars and lounges. It's worth checking out just for the space-age toilets on the first floor.

Pano

Hamalbaşı Caddesi 26, Galatasaray (0212 292 6664). **Open** 9am-2am daily. **Licensed. No credit cards. Map** p294 N3.

Is it our imagination or does the Efes taste better here than at other places? Maybe it's just that it comes in two-handed, half-litre flagons for only $2. In this modern take on a traditional Greek taverna, patrons prop themselves up at long, thin counters that ensure lots of body contact with strangers. Wine is just as popular as beer, sold by the glass and bottle. The place is packed and rowdy most nights, so if you're after a relaxed meal, it's better to visit in the afternoon, when the atmosphere is less boisterous. The lunch menu is great too, full of snacky foods, including an excellent cheese platter.

Rooftop carousing at **Soho Teras**.

Papirüs Cave

Ayhan Işik Sokak, off Istiklal Caddesi (0212 244 5736). **Open** 2pm-2am daily. **Licensed. Credit** MC, V. **Map** p295 O3.

A small basement wine bar-cum-restaurant that ticks all the right boxes. It's cosy and candle-lit, with a low-ceilinged cellar-like ambience. Off the main room are a couple of intimate little dens, perfect for rendezvousing with someone you shouldn't. A walk-in wine lock-up has floor-to-ceiling foreign New and Old World vintages ranging in price from $12 to $88 a bottle. There's also a wide selection of reasonably-priced domestic product.

Pia

Bekar Sokak 6, off Istiklal Caddesi (0212 252 7100). **Open** 10am-2am daily. **Licensed. Credit** MC, V. **Map** p295 O2.

A classic uncluttered look and a gallery-style upper floor give a sense of space where there isn't much at all. Ornate mirrors and a single George Grosz print set the tone. This is a favoured hang-out for writers, filmmakers and other low-key creative types. It's also very female-friendly (some of the most beautiful women seem to drop by Pia, so run a brush through your hair and sort your face out before turning up). Competent staff take orders from an extensive food menu served all day with dishes inspired by the wanderings of the café's owners. The daily specials are worth a gamble.

Smyrna

Akarsu Caddesi 29, Cihangir. **Open** 10am-midnight daily. **Licensed. Credit** MC, V. **Map** p295 O4.

Cihangir's favourite hangout has traditionally been the teahouses beside the mosque, where for the price of a cuppa local loafers can spend the whole day and/or evening at one of the street-side tables, which are shaded beneath the boughs of several age-old plane trees. Nearby Smyrna requires a little more financial outlay, and it's where some of that same crowd of teahouse irregulars come when they've received a pay cheque. It's a bar-café, convivial and laid-back enough for daytime lounging and lunching (the food is excellent and very good value) but capable of shifting up a few gears in the evening. Though just a year old, it already feels comfortably lived in and the retro decor is nicely understated.

Soho Teras

Istiklal Caddesi 365 (0212 244 0241). **Open** 10pm-2am daily. Closed Oct-June. **Licensed. Credit** MC, V. **Map** p294 N4.

This is the summer-only venue for Soho (*see p226*) the bar/club up on Meşelik Sokak near Taksim Square. It's a fabulous site, on a rooftop terrace seven storeys above Istiklal Caddesi. Çukurcuma slopes away at the back down to the shores of the Bosphorus, ensuring the views are uninterrupted. Merry-making punters can look right over the Beyoğlu rooftops to the Sea of Marmara and the spiky silhouettes of Sultanahmet beyond. Meanwhile, the music is both trancy and dancy, and your fellow revellers youthful and good-looking. There's even a gay crèche (**G-Launch**, *see p202*). What have you done to deserve this? To find the place, look for the tatty Beyoğlu İş Merkezi shopping centre and take the lift up to the top.

The Bosphorus Villages

Picturesque little Ortaköy, Arnavutköy and Bebek are custom-made for indolent afternoons measured out in coffee-spoons and evenings in dry gin. Most of the best venues have water front settings, so why settle for anything less?

Aşşk Cafe

Muallim Naci Caddesi 64/B, Kuruçeşme (0212 265 4734). **Bus** 22, 22R, 25E, 30D, 40, 42T. **Open** *Nov-Mar* 9am-7.30pm Tue-Sun. *Apr-Oct* 9am-1am daily. **Licensed. Credit** AmEx, MC, V.

Once you can get past that name – the Turkish word for 'love' drawn out into a lisping 'aşşk' – this place has a lot to recommend it. The setting is gorgeous:

Hava nargile

A nargile is a waterpipe. A hookah.
A 'hubbly-bubbly', if you must. It's been
smoked in Turkey since the beginning of the
17th century, despite religious authorities
periodically denouncing the practice and
calling for it to be banned. The tyrannical
Murat IV (1623-40) went as far as passing
the death sentence on anyone caught having
so much as a quick puff.

In the late 19th and early 20th century,
nargile smoking was the fashionable high-
society thing to do, particularly among
women. That fad passed and in republican
Istanbul the nargile was relegated to a
pastime of the peasantry.

Why now in the 21st century it should
suddenly be making a comeback is anybody's
guess. But in the last couple of years a whole
slew of cafés devoted to the waterpipe have
opened, with more likely to follow. A few of
these are aimed squarely at tourists but
otherwise most custom comes from students.

Nargile tobacco is typically soaked in
molasses or apple juice, giving it a slightly
sweetened flavour, but you can get it straight
and strong by asking for '*tömbeki*'.

Nargile cafés serve tea and coffee but no
alcohol. Prices are around $2 to $3 a pipe,
and a smoke lasts a good hour or more.
Contrary to popular misconception, hashish
is not an option. Also no longer on the menu
is the old Ottoman blend of opium, perfume
and crushed pearls. Shame, but there you go.

The best place to sample a nargile is on
the nameless pedestrian strip off **Tophane
Iskelesi** behind the Nusretiye Mosque (map

p295 O5). Until recently there was nothing
but a row of small shops down here, but now
it's lined with nothing but nargile cafés. At
any given moment, day or night, there might
be upwards of 300-400 people here, an
extraordinary mix of students and couples
and families, all belching forth great clouds of
grey smoke. Certain cafés at the north end of
the strip have recently drawn fire in the press
for providing cushion-strewn banquettes
which, it's claimed, encourage *al fresco*
canoodling and, reputedly, worse. Even
without the bodily contact, this is a fine place
to wind down after a night out in Beyoğlu.
Otherwise, you might try one of the following:

Enjoyer Café

*Incili Çavus Sokak 25, Sultanahmet
(0212 512 8759). Tram Sultanahmet.*
Open *summer* 9am-2am daily; *winter* 9am-
midnight daily. **Not licensed. No credit cards**.
Map p289 N10.
Most touristed of the nargile cafés, lying on
the pedestrianised street just north of Divan
Yolu. Avoid the fruity tobaccos.

Erenler Çay Bahçesi

*Çorlulu Ali Paşa Medresesi, Yeniçeriler
Caddesi 36/28, Beyazıt (0212 528 3785).
Tram Beyazıt.* **Open** *summer* 7am-3am daily;
winter 7am-midnight daily. **Not licensed.**
No credit cards. Map p288 L10.
Occupying the courtyard of an old Ottoman
seminary, Erenler comprises a collection of
low tables and benches under ivy-hung
trellises. Beautiful. Despite signs advertising
'Magic Waterpipe Garden' few tourists

a clubhouse-like venue beside the Bosphorus with a
summer garden attached. The place is renowned for
its lavish breakfasts and organic salads, as well as
the stream of pop stars and celebs dropping by after
a workout at the appallingly trendy Planet Gym next
door. Best to visit weekdays, as you're unlikely to
find a table come evening or at the weekend.

Bebek Bar

*Bebek Hotel, Cevdetpaşa Caddesi 34, Bebek
(0212 358 2000/www.bebekhotel.com.tr). Bus 22,
22R, 25E, 30D, 40, 42T.* **Open** 8am-1am daily.
Licensed. Credit AmEx, DC, MC, V.
The bar at the Bebek Hotel gets our vote for 'bar
with the most fabulous site'. It sits at the back of the
hotel and thus benefits from a waterfront setting.
This is played to maximum advantage with a gorgeous decked veranda that juts out over the water.

Add cool long drinks, rattan seating and a flotilla of
bobbing white yachts moored an arm's-stretch away
for a perfect 'Istanbul Riviera' experience.

Ece Bar

*Tramvay Caddesi 11, Kuruçeşme (0212 265 9600).
Bus 22, 22R, 25E, 30D, 40, 42T.* **Open** 8pm-2am
Mon-Sat. **Licensed. Credit** DC, MC, V.
A bar above a boisterous *meyhane* (the Ece Aynalı)
that also gets pretty lively itself thanks a nightly diet
of live music. Performances can be anything from
folk to pop; the queen herself, Sezen Aksu (*see p212*
The unsung queen of Turkish song), has even
appeared on occasion, being a buddy of the owner.
Otherwise, it's a pleasant glass-enclosed top-floor
space lush with potted plants and with the *de rigeur*
views of the Bosphorus. Expect fellow boozers to be
upscale media, advertising and creative sorts.

actually visit and instead it's filled with students from nearby Beyazıt University.

Meşale
Arasta Bazaar 45, Sultanahmet (0212 518 9562). **Open** 24 hours daily. **Not licensed.** **No credit cards.** **Map** p288 N11.

A sunken café beside an arcade of tourist shops but quite pleasant late on when the shutters have come down and locals replace the visitors. There are nightly performances of Turksih classical music and Dervish dancing shows on Friday, Saturday and Sunday nights between 7pm and 10pm.

Eylülist
1 Cadde 64, Arnavutköy (0212 257 1109). Bus 22, 22R, 25E, 30D, 40, 42T. **Open** 5pm-4am Mon-Sat. **Licensed. Credit** DC, MC, V.

A modest little two-storey building on the Arnavutköy shore road, this is a neighbourhood haunt for some, a night on the town for others. The tiny ground floor functions as a café-bar, while upstairs is a slightly larger but still intimate space of bare stone walls and wooden tables. It's given over each evening to live music that might be anything from jazz to a nostalgic Turkish ballad croonfest. Total pot luck. Note those late, late hours.

Kethuda
Muallim Naci Caddesi 39, Ortaköy (0212 327 4153/ www.kethuda.com). Bus 22, 22R, 25E, 30D, 40, 42T. **Open** noon-4am daily. **Licensed. Credit** MC, V.

Not just a great new bar/restaurant, Kethuda is also a stunning bit of Ottoman architecture, being a converted old hamam. Doorways are framed with heavy velvet drapes, crystal chandeliers hang above white marble floors and the former private wash areas are now chambers for two with flickering candles in the old marble basins. Barflys should wend their way through the chambers to the well-stocked main bar for the rare chance to down a vodka Martini beneath a 16th-century stone dome. Absolut Istanbul.

Pupa
Bebek Arnavutköy Caddesi 66, Arnavutköy (0212 265 6533). Bus 22, 22R, 25E, 30D, 40, 42T. **Open** 2pm-2am daily. **Licensed. No credit cards.**

Istanbul's first reggae bar opened a decade ago. Back then, Pupa was all the rage for cultivating an 'alternative lifestyle' and hoping to meet and mingle

Choose your Hilton

with real-life Africans. The novelty has long gone, but if you arrive early in the evening and score an outside table – separated from the water only by a busy road – you might find that Bob Marley and the Bosphorus isn't such an odd combination after all.

Sedir

Mecidiye Köprüsü Sokak 26, (across from Ortaköy Camii), Ortaköy (0212 327 9870). Bus 22, 22R, 25E, 30D, 40, 42T. **Open** 9am-midnight daily.
Unlicensed. Credit MC, V.

Sedir is a cut above most neighbouring Ortaköy venues. It exudes an air of Mediterranean-styled superior taste, with terracotta floors, a smattering of antiquey furnishings, an open fire for winter and outdoor, candle-lit tables for summer. It's set beside the Mecidiye Mosque, with a decent enough view of the action on Ortaköy Square but at enough of a remove to avoid to impart a feeling of exclusivity. There's an extensive menu of international and Turkish dishes and, again, unlike most of the competition, prices are displayed.

Nişantaşı & Teşvikiye

Nobody who is visiting Istanbul for just a couple of days is going to head up to these two middle-class, north-of-the-centre neighbourhoods for a night on the town; however, for anyone looking for an alternative to Efes and a bowl of peanuts in Beyoğlu, the options do widen a little up around here.

Buz

Abdi Ipekci Caddesi 42/2, Teşvikiye (0212 291 0065). **Open** noon-11pm Mon-Sat. **Licensed. Credit** MC, V.

The decor at Buz, a favourite haunt of Istanbul's chic bohemians (at least that's how they see themselves), is nothing if not eccentric: there's as much furniture and glassware stuck to the ceiling as on the floor and tables. The decadent-dive schtick is augmented by a selection of punchy cocktails (a bit pricey at $12). Lunch and dinner, mostly international dishes, costs about $20 a head, although there are cheaper bar snacks – the house shrimp cocktail is excellent. As with other bars in this neck of the woods, Buz is a place where fabulous PR people do lunch.

Cafein

Abdi Ipekci Caddesi 17/1, Nişantaşı (0212 241 0936). **Open** noon-2am Mon-Sat. **Licensed. Credit** AmEx, MC, V.

Cafein truly comes into its own in summer, when it expands from its cosy basement room up onto the pavement, via a cluster of outside tables. If you eat inside, you'll find a smartly decorated, if not quite fashionable, local. It's a particularly lively lunch spot, and a favourite with businessmen, who pay around $10 for pasta, salad and steak courses. Things are quieter in the early evening, but the pace picks up after 10pm, when a local crowd descends to quaffs credit-card-sapping cocktails ($10-$15).

Taps

Atiye Sokak 5, off Teşvikiye Caddesi, Teşvikiye (0212 296 2020/www.tapsistanbul.com). **Open** 11.30am-1am Mon-Thur, Sun; 11.30am-2am Fri, Sat. **Licensed. Credit** DC, MC, V.

A milestone in Turkish drinking, Taps arrived onto the scene in 2002 as the country's first ever microbrewery. As such, it's the only bar in Istanbul that serves a decent pint. In fact, you wouldn't know you were in Turkey: with its exposed silvery ducting, ferociously-chilly air-conditioning and burble of Beyonce, Britney and Christina, courtesy of multiscreen MTV, it's a bar that could be located in any North American city. The prices are positively Western too: pints of own-brewed beer cost about $4.50, while pizzas go for around $10. Nevertheless, the place is hugely popular, particularly with young, loud-tied professionals. Sadly, although the owners initially claimed they wanted to serve 40 different beers, 18 months on there's still just the three.

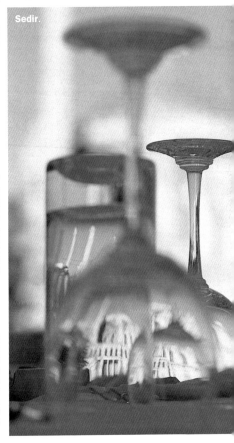

Sedir.

Cheap girls, pricey drinks

'Saatınız var mı, abi?' 'Saatınız var mı, abi?' It's a phrase you hear all the time walking around Taksim in the evening, especially if you are a single male and an obvious foreigner. It means, 'What time is it?'. Pretty soon you get to wondering about the vast numbers of loitering Turkish men who don't have a watch of their own.

It's a clumsy conversational gambit but obviously there are enough gullible tourists around that eventually somebody does stop. The conversation then moves through all the usual pleasantries (Where are you from? What are you doing? Which football team do you support?) and, before too long, to a recommendation of a 'nice place'. Alternative hooks are 'cheap drinks' or even 'cheap girls'. Nothing could be further from the truth.

Just as in London's Soho, the area around Taksim Square is dotted with seedy clip joints – the kind of bars that get few satisfied customers to recommend them and rely on touts to bring in the business. Anyone naive enough to be led into such a place quickly finds themselves making more friends –

particularly of the female kind and possibly Russian-accented – more quickly than they ever imagined possible. It's the usual drill: the hapless visitor has everybody's drinks charged to their bill and when that bill arrives what looked like Coca-Cola is alleged to have contained whisky and is charged at $100 or more. It's a mugging, and if you don't pay up events, as they say, can take a nasty turn for the worse.

Stories of tourists being hit up for hundreds of dollars are far from apocryphal – we at *Time Out* have received letters from misled and mistreated readers, relating their tales of Istanbul nightlife gone wrong. What can we say? Turks are hospitable, generous and often gregarious, but that shouldn't mean that you don't take the same care as you would at home. We're not saying don't talk to strangers, perhaps just don't accompany them to seedy bars, don't entertain over-keen women with too much makeup and don't consent to drinks all round without first knowing the price. Not unless you really want to, of course.

Touchdown

Milli Reasurans Çarşışı 61/11, Abdi Ipekci Caddesi, Teşvikiye (0212 231 3671/www.touchdown.com.tr). **Open** noon-midnight Mon-Thur; noon-2am Fri, Sat. **Licensed. No credit cards.**

Around since 1996, Touchdown successfully recreates the feel of an American corner bar. Although it's a favourite with a youngish media/advertising crowd, it's not flashy; on the contrary, it has a laid-back, almost student-unionish atmosphere. On busy nights, punters spill out of the bar, taking over the stairway of the Reasurans Centre, one of Istanbul's most expensive lumps of real estate. Prices are reasonable then – $3.50 for a beer – given the location.

Asian Shore

Kadıköy's **Kadife Sokak** goes by the alternative name of 'Barlar Sokak' in recognition of the superlative boozing opportunities it offers. In addition to the two places below, there are at least a half dozen other similar bar/cafés, including **Buddha** (*see p213*). Also see the live music venues **Shaft** and **Sondurock** (for both *see p214*).

Karga

Kadife Sokak 16, Kadıköy (0216 449 1725). **Open** 11am-2am daily. **Licensed. Credit** AmEx, DC, MC, V. **Map** p297 W8.

This local legend, situated in the heart of Kadıköy's bar scene, is known for three things: alternative music, cheap beer and fine art (!). The bar's musical policy is eclectic and you can expect themed nights ranging from Belgian pop to Bill Laswell. These take place on the ground floor, which has a pub-like atmosphere, albeit with dimmer lighting and louder music. Upstairs is a more cultured affair: spacious, relatively quiet and a venue for regularly changing exhibitions of fine art (see www.kargart.com).

Isis

Kadife Sokak 26, Kadıköy (0216 349 7381). **Open** 11am-2am daily. **Licensed. Credit** MC, V. **Map** p297 W8.

The Egyptian-themed Isis (wall paintings, statues) fills an old three-storey townhouse with *invino bon-homie* courtesy of a top-floor wine bar that regularly features tasting nights with accompanying live music. It also boasts a large garden – though not so large that it doesn't get rammed on summer nights.

▶ For details of **music bars and other venues**, see **Music: Rock World & Jazz** and **Music: Turkish**, *pp210-221*. For details of **late clubs**, see **Nightlife**, *pp222-226*. For details of **gay bars and clubs**, see **Gay & Lesbian**, *pp201-205*.

Shops & Services

Browsing or seeking, shopping in Istanbul is all about adventure.

Istanbul is shopping paradise. Committed or casual, shoppers will be dazzled. Even phobics may be lured into momentary conversion. The city boasts labyrinthine bazaars and teeming street markets, hippy-chic arcades and designer districts, as well as the ubiquitous one-stop US-style malls. Prize finds include oriental antiques, exotic jewellery, knock-off designer copies, outlandish fabrics, traditional ceramics and, but of course, carpets.

Prices are not as cheap as they once were (what is?), but locally made goods and handicrafts still represent good value. For anything imported you pay over the odds. Services, on the other hand – from shoeshining to knife sharpening – are a steal, provided you can bridge the language gap.

SHOPPING AREAS

Sultanahmet is prime tourist territory, and subsequently well supplied with tacky souvenir stores and pushy carpet sellers. Prices are marked up accordingly. That said, some of the handicraft places and more serious rug stores, particularly off the main drag, can turn up some

interesting stuff – just don't expect bargains. Things get spicier as you head west towards the **Grand Bazaar** area, which may have lost its lustre to locals now attuned to the mall but remains the oriental shopping experience par excellence (*see pp80-1* **Shopping the bazaar**).

By comparison, **Beyoğlu** offers an altogether more Western shopping experience.The main drag, **İstiklal Caddesi**, mixes clothing and department stores with new and second-hand bookshops, Parisian-style passages, music stores and galleries. The Taksim end is mainstream but down around **Galatasaray** and **Tünel** the shops become more interesting and individual.

For committed shoppers in search of the sophisticated, head to **Nişantaşı** and neighbouring **Teşvikiye**, two districts about a mile north of Taksim Square. This is serious label territory. On **Abdi İpekçi Caddesi** are the likes of Armani, Louis Vuitton and Tiffany alongside sophisticated Turkish jewellers, Urart, while one block north on **Teşvikiye Caddesi** are MaxMara rivals Mudo Collection and local designer Yıldırım Mayruk.

Marooned among the shelves at **Robinson Crusoe**. *See p162.*

Shopping by area

TAXES & REFUNDS

VAT (KDV) on goods and services is a standard 18 per cent. Theoretically, non-residents are eligible for refunds on purchases of goods (not services) over $4 from stores displaying the tax-free sticker but it's a tedious process. The retailer fills out a special receipt in quadruple and gives you three copies, which you then present to customs upon departure, as long as it's within three months of the purchase. Once home, you need to send proof of having left the country to the retailer, who then sends you the refund by bank transfer – supposedly within ten days. It can, however, take months.

Antiques

One of the best places for browsing is **Çukurcuma**, a quiet Beyoğlu backwater behind the Galatasaray Lycée. Its roller-coaster streets harbour a plethora of small, cramped shops with a wealth of antiquaria from rural Anatolia – anything from oil lamps and painted trunks to carved doors and ceilings. There's also a fair amount of sophisticated stuff from the city, such as glass and porcelain ware, Ottoman screens and chandeliers, as well as shops specialising in single items such as tin toys. There's also the **Antikacılarçarşısı**

Sultanahmet

Dosim (Handicrafts, *p175*); **Galeri Kayseri** (Books, *p162*); **Istanbul Handicrafts Centre** (Handicrafts, *p175*); **Natural Foreign Book Exchange** (Books, *p163*); **Sırça El Sanatları Merkezi** (Handicrafts, *p175*).

Bazaar Quarter

Abdulla; **Deli Kızın Yeri**; **Derviş** (all Handicrafts, *p175*); **Kalender Carpets**; **Sisko Osman**; **Tradition**; **Yörük** (all The rug trade, *pp166-7*).

Eminönü

Celal Akagün Tuhafiye (Fashion accessories, *p169*); **Kalmaz Baharat** (Health, *p176*); **Kurukahveci Mehmet** (Food & drink, *p170*); **Namlı Pastırmacı** (Food & drink, *p171*); **Özgül Çeyiz** (Household, *p176*); **Ümit Bijuteri** (Fashion accessories, *p169*).

Beyoğlu

Ada Music (Music, *p177*); **Ali Muhiddin Hacı Bekir** (Food & drink, *p171*); **Ambar** (Health, *p175*); **Anadol Antique House** (Antiques, *p159*); **Anadolu Mezat** (Antiques, *p159*); **Antre Gourmet** (Food & drink, *p171*); **Artrium** (Antiques, *p161*); **Asri Turşucu** (Food & drink, *p170*); **Beta** (Shoes, *p179*); **Bilgisayar** (Computer repairs, *p179*); **Hastanesi Bünsa** (Health, *p176*); **Butik Katia** (Fashion accessories, *p176*); **Çam Çiçek Evi** (Florists, *p169*); **Can Shop** (Antiques, *p161*); **Decoded** (Music, *p177*); **Denizler Kitapevi** (Books, *p163*); **DJ Shop** (Music, *p177*); **Emgen Optik** (Fashion accessories, *p176*); **Elma Bilgisayar** (Computer repairs, *p179*); **Eski Fener** (Antiques, *p161*); **Fotis Çiçek Evi** (Florists, *p169*); **Gelgör Antik** (Antiques, *p161*); **Gima** (Supermarkets, *p180*); **Homer Kitapevi** (Books, *p162*); **Hüseyin** (Hair & beauty, *p171*); **Ikinci-el Plak** (Music, *p177*); **La Cave** (Food & drink, *p171*); **Lale Plak** (Music, *p177*); **Leyla** (Antiques, *p161*); **Librairie de Pera** (Books, *p162*); **Mahmut Kundura** (Shoes, *p179*); **Mavi Jeans** (Fashion, *p165*); **Megavizyon** (Music, *p179*); **Makro** (Supermarkets, *p180*); **MMM** (Supermarkets, *p180*); **Mor** (Jewellery, *p176*); **Ottomania** (Books, *p162*); **Oxxo** (Fashion, *p165*); **Pandora** (Books, *p162*); **Paşabahçe** (Household, *p176*); **Raksotck** (Music, *p179*); **Robinson Crusoe** (Books, *p162*); **Roxy By Posus** (Fashion, *p165*); **Saray** (Food & drink, *p171*); **Savoy Pastanesi** (Food & drink, *p171*); **Selim Mumcu Sahaf** (Books, *p163*); **Seyitağaoğulları** (Fashion accessories, *p176*); **Soley Parfümeri** (Cosmetics, *p163*); **Şütte** (Food & drink, *p171*); **Ümit Ünal** (Fashion, *p165*); **Vakko** (Department stores, *p164*) **Yıldız Ceramic** (Handicrafts, *p175*).

Nişantaşı & Teşvikiye

Ayyıldız (Fashion accessories, *p176*); **Aspendos** (Jewellery, *p176*); **Gönül Paksoy** (Fashion, *p165*); **Hakan Yıldırım** (Fashion, *p165*); **Hotiç** (Shoes, *p179*); **MOS** (Hair & beauty, *p171*); **Sema Paksoy** (Jewellery, *p176*); **Sevil Parfümeri** (Cosmetics, *p163*); **Urart** (Jewellery, *p176*); **Yargıcı** (Fashion, *p165*); **Yıldırım Mayruk** (Fashion, *p165*); **YKM** (Department stores, *p164*); **Zeki** (Fashion accessories, *p176*).

Etiler & Levent

Beymen; **Çarşı** (both Department stores, *p163*); **Damat Tween** (Fashion, *p165*); **Derimod** (Leather, *p176*); **Matraş** (Fashion accessories, *p175*); **Mudo City** (Department stores, *p163*); **Remzi Kitabi** (Books, *p163*).

(Horhor Antiques Market) in Aksaray, just south-west of the Aqueduct of Valens (*see p89*).

Items over a century old must be cleared by the Museums Directorate before being taken overseas. Dealers should know the procedure.

Anadol Antique House

Turnacıbaşı Sokak 65, Çukurcuma, Beyoğlu (0212 251 5228). **Open** 9am-7pm Mon-Sat. **No credit cards. Map** p295 O3.

Ignore the unlovely service – this is a cavern of curios, old and new, large and small, original and restored and fantastic to browse. There's everything from genteel turn-of-the-century stoves and Anatolian trunks, to old Kütahya ceramics, hand-painted screens and teasing combs. Be sure to see the pile of elaborately sculpted ceilings at the back, lifted whole from once well-to-do wooden mansions.

Anadolu Mezat

Faikpaşa Caddesi 6/1, Çukurcuma, Beyoğlu (0212 293 8474). **Open** 9.30am-7pm Mon-Sat; noon-4pm Sun. **No credit cards. Map** p295 O3.

A small family-run business, specialising in rustic Anatolian furniture and effects. You'll find the odd original piece here but most stuff is reconstructed to original designs – though you'd never know the difference. Items can also be commissioned.

Other locations: Çukurcuma Caddesi 67, Çukurcuma (0212 251 4613).

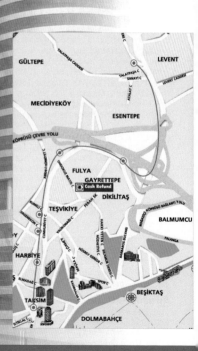

Fine antiques in **Çukurcuma** (nice frame too). *See p158.*

Artrium

Tünel Gecidi İş Hanı, A Blok 7, Tünel, Beyoğlu (0212 251 4302). **Open** 9am-7pm Mon-Sat. **Credit** AmEx, MC, V. **Map** p294 M4.
A shop attracting a more sophisticated breed of antiquarian with three spacious display rooms and a prime location in the passage just across from KV Café (*see p148*). It has a fine selection of miniatures, maps, prints and calligraphy, along with Kütahya ceramics and the odd film and advertising poster.

Can Shop

Avrupa Pasajı 7, Meşrutiyet Caddesi 16, Galatasaray, Beyoğlu (0212 249 3280). **Open** 10.30am-8pm Mon-Sat. **No credit cards**. **Map** p294 N3.
Tins, pins, coins and toys from big clanky cars to planes and tanks. There's a surprising amount of Turkish stuff, dating mostly from Ottoman and early republic days, including dossiers crammed with old share certificates, some of which hail from the Orient and date back 70 years.

Eski Fener

Ağa Hamam Caddesi 25-7, Çukurcuma, Beyoğlu (0212 251 6278). **Open** 11am-7pm Mon-Sat. **No credit cards**. **Map** p295 O3.
A select assortment of furniture, doors, oil lamps, copperware, mostly picked up in rural Anatolia. You'll find things like low-legged dough-rolling tables, wooden butter churns and storm lamps. All items have been painstakingly restored.

Gelgör Antik

Çukurcuma Caddesi 32, Çukurcuma, Beyoğlu (0212 243 4832). **Open** 9am-8pm daily. **No credit cards**. **Map** p294 N4.
A trove of ethnic Uzbek, Turkmen and Pakistani jewellery and accessories. Kurdish owner Aziz buys fragments by the sackful and crafts them into original pieces. Look out for the talismanic hangings he does with spoons and forks. Downstairs, there's a basement full of psychedelic ethnic headgear.

Leyla

Altıpatlar Sokak 10, Çukurcuma, Beyoğlu (0212 293 7410). **Open** 10am-7pm Mon-Sat. **Credit** AmEx, MC, V. **Map** p295 O3.
A massive selection of antique clothes, costumes, hats, embroidered linens, wall hangings and tapestries collected by Leyla Seyhanlı, an old hand in the business. Prices, which are dollar-based, are a bit on the high side, but it's all quality stuff.

Books

Ranging from large American-style chains complete with obligatory coffee bar to tiny specialists in pulp fiction, Istanbul's book shops are a bibliophilic delight. In addition to the places below, don't forget the **Booksellers' Bazaar** (*see p83*), an adjunct to the Grand Bazaar, where among the textbooks and Turkish literature, there are new and used English books.

Galeri Kayseri

Divan Yolu 58, Sultanahmet (0212 512 0456).
Tram Sultanahmet. **Open** 9am-1pm daily.
Credit MC, AmEx. **Map** p289 M10.
This shop is devoted exclusively to books about
Istanbul and Turkey. Whatever the genre, you'll find
it here: fiction, non-fiction, guidebooks and coffee-
table volumes. Also the place to get your back-up
copies of the *Time Out Istanbul Guide*.

Homer Kitapevi

Yeniçarşi Caddesi 28A, Galatasaray, Beyoğlu (0212
249 5902). **Open** 10am-7.30pm Mon-Sat. **Credit**
MC, V. **Map** p294 N3.
Situated just opposite the side of the Galatasaray
Lycée, this smart, air-conditioned shop has what is
widely considered to be the best collection of foreign
non-fiction in town. They're particularly strong on
art and academic subjects.

Pandora

Büyükparmakkapı Sokak 3, Beyoğlu (0212 243 3503/
www.pandora.com.tr). **Open** 10am-8pm Mon-Thur;
10am-10pm Fri, Sat; 1pm-8pm Sun. **Credit** AmEx,
MC, V. **Map** p295 O3.
A fine little bookshop squeezed into three tight
floors. The top one is the best: it's filled with a decent
selection of English-language titles, including fiction, poetry, art, local interest and a decent history
section. Flyers and posters downstairs advertise
what's going on around town.

Remzi Kitapevi

Akmerkez Mall, Nispetiye Caddesi, Etiler (0212 282
2575/www.remzi.com.tr). *Metro Levent.* **Open** 10am-
10pm daily. **Credit** AmEx, DC, MC, V.
Probably the biggest bookstore chain in Turkey,
Remzi has all the hallmarks of an American super-
store: specifically, bulk buying power to secure
reduced prices. The best place to buy bestsellers.
Other locations: Mayadrom Shopping Centre,
Yıldırım Göker Caddesi, Akatlar (0212 284 5701);
Rumeli Caddesi 44, Nişantaşı (0212 234 5475).

Robinson Crusoe

Istiklal Caddesi 389, Beyoğlu (0212 293 6968).
Open 9am-9.30pm Mon-Sat; 10am-9.30pm Sun.
Credit AmEx, DC, MC, V. **Map** p294 M4.
A good-looking little place with an especially well-
chosen selection of English-language fiction, international music and art mags and a decent array of
titles on Istanbul and Turkey.

Antiquarian

Denizler Kitapevi

Istiklal Caddesi 395, Beyoğlu (0212 243 3174).
Open 10am-7.30pm Mon-Sat. **Credit** DC, MC, V.
Map p294 M4.
Specialises in books on a maritime theme (*deniz*
means 'sea') but they're also strong on travel, especially as relates to Turkey. The 130-year-old shop
premises once housed the Dutch Consulate.

Librairie de Pera

Galipdede Cadessi 22, Tünel, Beyoğlu (0212 252 3078/
www.librairiedepera.com.tr). **Open** 10.30am-7pm
Mon-Sat. **Credit** AmEx, V. **Map** p294 M5.
Situated just downhill from Tünel Square, the shop
carries old and rare books in numerous languages,
many concerned with travel and Turkey.

Ottomania

Sofyalı Sokak 30-2, Asmalımescit, Beyoğlu (0212
243 2157/eren@turk.net). **Open** 9am-6.30pm Mon-
Sat. **Credit** AmEx, MC, V. **Map** p294 M4.
Old maps, engravings and rare books. This is a
second-generation, family-owned shop that also has
a stall in the Sahaflar Çarşısı. Serious prices for
serious collectors.

Second-hand

There are half a dozen or more shops jam-
packed with second-hand books, many in
English, in the **Aslıhan Pasajı**, just off the

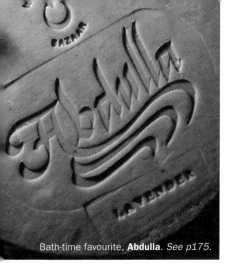

Bath-time favourite, **Abdulla**. See p175.

Balık Pazarı halfway down Istiklal Caddesi. Some shops also deal in vinyl, magazines and old film posters.

Natural Foreign Book Exchange
Akbıyık Caddesi, Sultanahmet (0212 517 0383). Tram Sultanahmet. **Open** 9am-9pm daily May-Sept; 9am-6pm daily Oct-April. **Credit** MC, V. **Map** p289 N11.

Slap in the middle of the backpacker enclave, NFBE predictably has a huge stock of airport fiction and used travel guides. Prices are a bit ridiculous but the stock, shelved in a gloomy basement, is extensive.

Selim Mumcu Sahaf
Yeniçarşu Caddesi 33/C, Galatasaray, Beyoğlu (0212 245 4496). **Open** 10am-9pm Mon-Sat; 1-9pm Sun. **Credit** AmEx, MC, V. **Map** p294 N3.

What the stock lacks in depth it more than makes up for in eclecticism. Added to which there are hundreds of old movie posters, plus old photos and postcards and other assorted memorabilia.

Cosmetics

Toiletries and basic cosmetics are now available in most supermarkets, and some pharmacies also stock imported brands like Vichy and RoC. For more upmarket labels, go to a specialist *parfümeri*, but note that prices are pushed up by stiff import taxes. In other words, stock up at the duty-free before arriving.

Sevil Parfümeri
Valikonağı Caddesi 52/27, Nişantaşı (0212 234 3234/www.sevil.com.tr). **Open** 10am-8pm Mon-Sat. **Credit** AmEx, DC, MC, V.

This shop features beauty from all the big brand names. If you have trouble choosing, there are instore representatives at your elbow to advise. **Other locations**: Akmerkez Mall 321, Nispetiye Caddesi, Etiler (0212 282 0268). Metro City Mall 106, Büykdere Caddesi 171, Levent (0212 344 0377).

Soley Parfümeri
Meşelik Sokak 9-11, off Istiklal Caddesi, Beyoğlu (0212 251 0837/245 1134). **Open** 9am-7.30pm Mon-Sat. **Credit** AmEx, DC, MC, V. **Map** p295 O2.

As Istanbul goes, Soley has a reasonable range of products by leading cosmetic brands, as well as more standard toiletries.

Department stores

Western-style department stores are a rare breed in Turkey. The few that do exist tend to cater to the high end of the market.

Beymen
Akmerkez Mall 107, Nispetiye Caddesi, Etiler (0212 282 0380/www.beymen.com.tr). Metro Levent. **Open** 10am-10pm daily. **Credit** AmEx, MC, V.

Starting life as a men's clothing store, Beymen now commands all-round label status (they had Kate Moss model the 2003 winter collection). The emphasis is on classic men and women's designer clothing and accessories, combining own-brand product with imported names. You'll also find cosmetics, fabrics and home accessories.
Other locations: Bağdat Caddesi 493, Suadiye, Asian Shore (0216 467 1845).

Çarşı
Metro City Mall, Büyükdere Caddesi 171 Levent (0212 344 0575/www.carsi.com.tr). Metro Levent. **Open** 10am-10pm daily. **Credit** DC, MC, V.

Popular mid-range store that uses the tag line 'quality at reasonable prices'. Stocks a comprehensive selection of clothes, shoes, sportswear, cosmetics, fabrics, china, glass and home accessories.

Mudo City
Akmerkez Mall 316, Nispetiye Caddesi, Etiler (0212 282 0473/www.mudo.com.tr). Metro Levent. **Open** 10am-10pm daily. **Credit** DC, MC, V.

A 'tasteful living' concept in the shape of own-label clothing and accessories (Mudo Collection) and some

Eat, Drink, Shop

chic kitchen and bathroom accoutrements (Mudo Concept). Prices are surprisingly reasonable.
Other locations: Mudo Collection, Teşvikiye Caddesi 143, Nişantaşı (0212 225 2941); Mudo Pera, Istiklal Caddesi 401, Beyoğlu (0212 251 8682).

Vakko

Istiklal Caddesi 123-125, Beyoğlu (0212 251 4092/ www.vakko.com.tr). **Open** 10am-7pm Mon-Sat. **Credit** AmEx, DC, MC, V. **Map** p295 O2.
Vakko was once Turkey's authority on fashion and still has huge cachet locally. But aside from eye-catching window displays, the store's designs lack originality. The exceptions are own-label scarves and ties and some lavish Ottoman-design fabrics. There's also a limited selection of china and glass, a bridal floor, textiles, a cosmetics hall and a small fashion museum, located on the seventh floor.
Other locations: Akmerkez Mall 212, Nispetiye Caddesi, Etiler (0212 282 0695).

YKM

Halaskargazi Caddesi 368, Şişli, Nişantaşı (0212 232 7728/www.ykm.com.tr). Metro Şişli. **Open** 10am-9pm Mon-Sat; noon-8pm Sun. **Credit** MC, V.
Turkey's oldest department store started life as a humble shop behind the Spice Bazaar in 1950. These days, it's the closest thing Istanbul has to a true department store. Unlike its more exclusive rivals, it caters to a broad market, selling everything from unisex clothing to sports gear, toys, home accessories and electronics.

Fashion

See also *p177* **Leather**.

Damat Tween

Akmerkez Mall 214, Nispetiye Caddesi, Etiler (0212 282 0112/www.damat.com.tr). Metro Levent. **Open** 10am-10pm daily. **Credit** MC, V.
A local boy made good, Damat has branches in a dozen countries in addition to his mini-empire in Turkey. His stock-in-trade is classic menswear ranging from suits to knitwear. The Tween label features casual collections in bold styles. Clothes here are well ahead of the pack in terms of design and quality.

Gönül Paksoy

Atiye Sokak 6A, Teşvikiye (0212 261 9081). **Open** 1pm-7pm Mon; 10am-7pm Tue-Sat. **Credit** AmEx, MC, V.
Ms Paksoy claims her designs are unique, not just in Turkey, but throughout the world. And she's probably right. Her collections reinterpret Ottoman designs and give them fresh life. Her creations use original fabrics and the finest natural weaves, and are hand-dyed in subtle shades. She also does a great line in Ottoman-style slippers, handbags and shoes.

Mavi Jeans

Istiklal Caddesi 117, Beyoğlu (0212 249 3758/ www.mavijeans.com). **Open** 10am-10pm Mon-Sat; 11am-10pm Sun. **Credit** DC, MC, V. **Map** p295 O3.

Since making it big in the US, Mavi prices have shot skywards but compared to imported brands their jeans are still reasonably priced. Designs are not cutting edge, but there's nothing that will embarrass you. They also do T-shirts, sweatshirts and other casual co-ordinates.
Other locations: Akmerkez Mall 235-238, Nispetiye Caddesi, Etiler (0212 282 0423); Metro City Mall 134-135, Büyükdere Caddesi 171, Levent (0212 344 0070); Yeniçeriler Caddesi 79, Beyazıt (0212 516 2062).

Oxxo

Istiklal Caddesi 146, Beyoğlu (0212 249 4263). **Open** 10am-10.30pm Mon-Sat; 11am-10.30pm Sun. **Credit** AmEx, DC, MC, V. **Map** p295 O3.
Made-in-Turkey casual wear for women, aimed at the younger end of the market. The quality of the clothing is not the best, but that's reflected in some very reasonable prices. It's good for short shelf-life staples like T-shirts.
Other locations: Akmerkez Mall 358, Nispetiye Caddesi, Etiler (0212 282 0425).

Ümit Ünal

Ensiz Sokak 3, Tünel (0212 245 7886/ www.umitunal.com). **Open** 10am-7.30pm Mon-Fri; 10am-noon Sat. **No credit cards.** Map p294 M5.

Jean therapy at **Mavi**.

The rug trade

Pity the poor carpet merchant, the used car dealer of the Orient. Carpet-buying has become so associated with hassle, hustle and hoodwinking that many a tourist makes a deliberate point of *not* buying one. Shame, because with a bit of homework and common sense, you can buy a beautiful carpet at a very attractive price.

Here's the lowdown: if you are interested in hand-made carpets or kilims made of natural fibres, expect to spend upwards of $300. After you've determined your price range – and you must do this before you begin looking – allow dealers to display items that cost twice that amount, and then try to bargain them down.

Don't bother paying a premium for vintage and antique carpets unless you have some expertise in the field. Contemporary carpets made for tourists are often of better quality: they are usually made using natural vegetable dyes, as opposed to chemical dyes, which were used on many carpets a century ago.

Employ the same methods used for any other purchases at the bazaar: arrive armed with lots of patience, time and energy and be prepared to do some comparison shopping.

Keep in mind that the dealers have all the time in the world. They are there to answer your questions, to explain details of origin and design, and to unroll hundreds of kilims, all the while keeping you fortified with strong tea. Ultimately, the final price depends greatly on your rapport with the dealer and your determination to buy a carpet.

It all comes down to one thing: how much do you want it? If you have the slightest hesitations concerning patterns or colours, keep looking. It should be a case of love at first sight. After all, a carpet's not just a souvenir, it's for life.

Nearly all shops, including those listed below, have English-speaking staff, can be trusted to handle overseas posting and allow exchanges of purchases. If you find the Grand Bazaar too bewildering, you can try browsing the shops at the comparatively peaceful Arasta Bazaar; *see p77.*

Kalender Carpets

Tekkeciler Caddesi 24-6, Grand Bazaar (0212 527 5518). Tram Beyazıt or Çemberlitaş. **Open** 8.30am-7.30pm, Mon-Sat. **Credit** AmEx, MC, V. **Map** p81.
Kalender, an economist by trade, stocks a glorious collection of full-size, deep pile Anatolian carpets, some of which go for as little as $1000. This is a good place to start along 'carpet row', in the heart of the bazaar.

Sisko Osman

Zincirli Han 15, Grand Bazaar (0212 528 3548/www.siskoosman.com). Tram Beyazıt or Çemberlitaş. **Open** 8.30am-6.30pm Mon-Sat. **Credit** AmEx, DC, MC, V. **Map** p81.
Sisko 'Fat Man' Osman is acknowledged around the bazaar as the authority on carpets and kilims. His well-stocked shop fills most of the historic Zincirli Han. He has a sizeable international clientele, and an illustrious one too: Osman has sold carpets to the likes of Hillary Clinton. So while you can be sure of quality, don't expect a bargain.

Tradition

Rubiye Han 11-12, Kurkculer Sokak, Grand Bazaar (0212 520 7907). Tram Beyazıt or Çemberlitaş. **Open** 10am-7pm, Mon-Sat. **Credit** AmEx, MC, V. **Map** p81.
It might be called Tradition, but this shop has a very untraditional feature: a female carpet dealer – a rare bazaar sight indeed. Get Sema

---

Ümit Ünal, aged 34, is the best example of an Istanbul-based designer who is plugged into the international fashion scene. His avant-garde shows are performance pieces and his multi-layered, complex creations are art installations as much as mere garments. Ünal's influences are diverse – Celtic banshees, Himalayan mountain life, the tribal life of gypsies – and he combs the globe in search of weird and wonderful fabrics and accessories.

Yargıcı

Valikonğı Caddesi 30, Nişantaşı (0212 225 2912/ www.yargici.com.tr). **Open** 9.30am-7.30pm Mon-Sat; 1pm-6pm Sun. **Credit** AmEx, DC, MC, V.

This popular shop sells middle-of-the-road fashion for men and women. The clothing, while not exactly stylish, is generally of good quality, though sizing can be baffling (you thought you were a 36, here you're a 32). Styles get spicier in the summer and accessories are generally more exciting. There's also a chic range of toiletries.
Other locations: Akmerkez Mall 208, Nispetiye Caddesi, Etiler (0212 282 0500).

Yıldırım Mayruk

Teşvikiye Caddesi 73/4, Teşvikiye (0212 236 1529). **Open** 9am-7pm Mon-Fri, by appointment only. **No credit cards.**

to roll out some of her massive kilims from the Anatolian heartland, woven by mountain nomads. If you're lucky, you might walk away with a gem for under $1000. But only if you can match wits with her.

Yörük

Kürkçüler 16, Grand Bazaar (0212 527 3211). Tram Beyazıt or Çemberlitaş. **Open** 8.30am-7pm, Mon-Sat. **Credit** AmEx, MC, V. **Map** p81.

This shop might be tiny, but it is packed with some of the best treasures to be found in the bazaar. There's the odd kilim but the emphasis is on old ethnic rugs of all sizes, mostly from the Caucasus. One of the best things about the shop is the dashing young owner, Gürsel, who exerts little pressure on customers to buy. If you can't find what you want here, he's happy to lead potential purchasers to other stores in which they might find the rug of their dreams.

This self-deprecating gentleman, a rarity among Turkish designers, produces classic Ottoman-inspired creations. He makes accessories to match his suits, and his stuff is very sophisticated.

Second-hand

Roxy By Posus

Aznavur Pasajı 11, Istiklal Caddesi 212, Galatasaray, Beyoğlu (0212 244 3363). **Open** 10am-9pm daily. **Credit** MC, V. **Map** p294 N3.
Roxy's '60s and '70s clothing is all shipped over from Europe (there's an RBP in the Netherlands); stock includes nylon shirts and skirts, suede and velvet jackets, and Adidas zip-up track-suit tops.

Fashion accessories

See also *p165* **Cosmetics,** *p176* **Jewellery** and *p179* **Shoes.**

Matraş

Akmerkez Mall, Nispetiye Caddesi, Etiler (0212 282 0215/www.matras.com). **Open** 10am-10pm daily. **Credit** AmEx, DC, MC, V.
This shop sells classic designs and high quality from Turkey's leading leather accessories label. As well

as the usual handbags, wallets and belts, products include briefcases, suitcases and a host of smaller items such as cosmetics purses, cardholders, keyrings and eyeglass cases.

Seyitağaoğulları Carpet Kilim Hand Crafts

Avrupa Pasajı 15, Meşrutiyet Caddesi 16, Galatasaray, Beyoğlu (0212 249 2903). **Open** 9.30am-8pm daily. **Credit** MC, V. **Map** p294 N3.
First there were kilims, now there are kilim 'accessories' – belts, bags, purses, slippers, boots and stationery done up in kilim designs and colours, trimmed with genuine leather. Some of this stuff really works, and it's sensibly priced too.
Other locations: Tavukhane Sokak 30, Sultanahmet (0212 518 1295), Arasta Çarşısı, Sultanahmet (0212 516 9351).

Haberdashery

Celal Akagün Tuhafiye

Marpuççular Alacahamam Caddesi 53, Sultanhamam (0212 526 5828). Tram Eminönü. **Open** 8.30am-4pm Mon-Fri; 8.30am-4.30pm Sat. **Credit** MC, V. **Map** p289 M8.
After 58 years in the business, Mr Akagün is the oldest haberdasher around and still working from his original store to boot. His stock, 90 per cent of which is Turkish-made, includes a bewildering array of buttons of all shapes and sizes, lace, embroidered trim, ribbon and elastic.

Ümit Bijuteri

Yarpuz Han 12, Marpuççular Caddesi 15, Eminönü (0212 511 7392). Tram Eminönü. **Open** 8.30am-6pm Mon-Sat. **No credit cards**. **Map** p289 M8.
Attention, arabesque glitter queens. Run to this shop, where you'll find an Aladdin's cave of beads, evil eyes, fake pearls, glitter, sequins, spangles and seashells. It's all imported from the Far East, sold by the kilo and dirt cheap.

Hats

Butik Katia

Danışman Geçidi 37, Galatasaray, Beyoğlu (0212 249 4605). **Open** 11am-6.30pm Mon-Fri; 11am-3pm Sat. **No credit cards**. **Map** p294 N3
Opened by Madam Katia in the 1940s, this was where the society ladies of Pera (now Beyoğlu) once flocked for the latest in Paris hat fashions. Her daughter is now at the helm, selling ready-made own designs and bespoke creations to a well-heeled clientele. Hats can also be hired.

Lingerie and swimwear

Ayyıldız

Atiye Sokak 8, Teşvikiye (0212 261 3164/ www.ayyildiz.com.tr). **Open** 10am-7.30pm, Mon-Sat. **Credit** AmEx, MC, V.

A reputable his-and-hers swimwear brand, offering reasonably exciting styles at sensible prices. It also does a successful line of lingerie, which was a revolutionary concept in Turkey when it started in 1958.
Other locations: Akmerkez Mall 367, Nispetiye Caddesi, Etiler (0212 282 1310).

Zeki

Tunaman Çarşısı, Akkavak Sokak 47/9, Nişantaşı (0212 233 8279/www.zekitriko.com.tr). **Open** 9.30am-7.30pm Mon-Sat. **Credit** AmEx, DC, MC, V.
Not only is Zeki the premiere swimwear label at home but it is also one of Turkey's most successful exports. Prices are high but it's quality stuff. Also check out the own-label lingerie range launched early in 2003.
Other locations: Akmerkez Mall 366, Nispetiye Caddesi, Etiler (0212 282 0591).

Sunglasses

Emgen Optik

Istiklal Caddesi 65, Beyoğlu (0212 292 3577). **Open** 9am-7.30pm Mon-Sat. **Credit** AmEx, DC, MC, V. **Map** p295 O2.
Emgen Optik is one of the many eyeglass stores that does a roaring trade in fashion frames and shades. It has been around since 1925, and carries a huge selection of authentic brand names, including the likes of Ray-Ban, Police, Gucci and Armani. The shop also deals in the more serious business of prescription lenses and repairs.

Florists

Fresh-cut flowers abound at the gypsy stands at the top of Tarlabaşı Caddesi, just off Taksim Square, and by the jetties at Kadıköy, Üsküdar, Karaköy and Beşiktaş. Prices drop as the day wears on but you should still haggle to avoid paying over the odds. For house and outdoor plants, pots, soil and garden accessories, go to the Çiçek Pazarı (Flower Market) beside the Egyptian Bazaar in Eminönü.

Çam Çiçek Evi

Hocazade Sokak 2A, off Sıraselviler Caddesi, Taksim, Beyoğlu (0212 245 2366). **Open** 8.30am-10pm daily. **Credit** MC, V. **Map** p295 O3.
Seasonal, fresh-cut flowers available 365 days a year at this spartan basement shop, situated opposite the German Hospital. Smile sweetly and you'll have a complimentary rose or three thrown in too. Interflora orders accepted.

Fotis Çiçek Evi

Istiklal Caddesi 382, Tünel, Beyoğlu (0212 244 0606). **Open** 8am-8pm daily. **Credit** MC, V. **Map** p294 M4.
This is the only florist to have glided through the glorious days of Old Pera intact. It's situated at the Tünel end of Istiklal Caddesi, where it's been since 1899. The shop is strictly no frills, but the flowers are wonderful. They do Interflora too.

Eat, Drink, Shop

Food & drink

For the freshest, best-quality produce, visit the **Halk Pazarı**, situated opposite the jetty in Beşiktaş, and the more upmarket **Balık Pazarı**, located off Istiklal Caddesi, with delicacies from quails' eggs to fresh clotted cream. For regional specialities, head for the stalls lining the west side of the **Egyptian Bazaar** or the many delicatessens in the backstreets of **Kadıköy** on the Asian shore.

Ali Muhiddin Hacı Bekir

Istiklal Caddesi 129, Beyoğlu (0212 244 2804). **Open** 8am-9pm Mon-Sat; 9am-9pm Sun. **Credit** AmEx, MC, V. **Map** p294 N3.
You can't come to Turkey without trying Turkish delight, and this place – which has been in the confection business since 1777 – is where to try it and buy it. While you're there, you should also suck on some *akide*, a colourful Ottoman boiled sweet which comes in every conceivable flavour. You can also pick up tasty gifts here, such as halva, baklava and marzipan (*badem ezmesi*) which all come in beautiful gift-wrapped boxes.
Other locations: Hamidiye Caddesi 83, Sirkeci (0212 522 0666).

Antre Gourmet Shop

Akarsu Caddesi 52, Cihangir, Beyoğlu (0212 292 8972/www.antregourmet.com). **Open** 9am-9pm Mon-Sat; 9am-8pm Sun. **Credit** AmEx, MC, V. **Map** p295 O4.
Antre stocks some 40 regional cheeses, all bought from local producers and free from additives. There's also a fair selection of cold meats, Austrian wholegrain breads, home-made mezedes and jams, olive oil, honeycomb (in season) and natural yoghurt.

Asri Turşucu

Ağa Hamam Sokak, opposite Firüzağa Mosque off Sıraselviler Caddesi, Cihangir, Beyoğlu (0212 244 4724). **Open** 9am-9pm Mon-Sat; 2pm-6pm Sun. Closed August. **No credit cards. Map** p295 O4.
You name it, this place pickles it, and has been doing so since 1938. Its artistic jar displays are a sight to behold. In addition to good old-fashioned pickles, you can down tankards of *şalgam suyu* (pickle juice) here, as well as *boza* (a fermented millet drink) and *ğıra* (a grape juice drink).

Kurukahveci Mehmet Efendi

Tahmis Sokak 66, Eminönü (0212 511 4262/ www.mehmetefendi.com). Tram Eminönü. **Open** 9am-6pm Mon-Fri; 9am-2pm Sat. **No credit cards. Map** p288 L8.

Departmental fashion at **Vakko**.
See p165.

This was reputed to be the first shop to sell bagged Turkish coffee and it's been doing roaring business since 1871. It's easy to find: situated opposite the west entrance to the Egyptian Market, just follow the smell. Besides the Turkish variety, there's filter and espresso coffee, whole roasted beans, cocoa and *sahlep*, a not-so-eco winter drink made from ground orchid root. Check out the website for an essential guide to coffee-cup fortune telling.

La Cave

Sıraselviler Caddesi 207, Cihangir, Beyoğlu (0212 243 2405/www.lacavesarap.com). **Open** 9am-9pm daily. **Credit** AmEx, DC, MC, V. **Map** p295 O4.
One of the first speciality wine shops and certainly the most serious. Owner Esat Ayhan, a grape connoisseur, keeps a comprehensive cellar filled with wines from all over the country. He also has quality olive oils, pre-packed cheeses (mostly foreign), pork products and cigars.

Namlı Pastırmacı

Hasırcılar Caddesi 14-16, Eminönü (0212 511 6393/ www.namlipastirma.com.tr). Tram Eminönü. **Open** 7am-8pm, Mon-Sat. **Credit** MC, V. **Map** p288 L8.
A hugely popular deli just along from the west end of the Egyptian Market. It specialises in *pastırma* (Turkish pastrami) but is also eye-poppingly well stocked with cold cuts, cheeses, halva, honeycomb, *pekmez* (fruit-based molasses), olives and pickles.

Saray

İstiklal Caddesi 102, Beyoğlu (0212 292 3434). **Open** 6am-2am daily. **Credit** MC, V. **Map** p294 N3.
Take your pick of delectable Turkish desserts, from milk puddings to *aşure*, popularly known as Noah's pudding. Since 1949 it's served as a good refuelling stop during or after a night's session in the bars and cafés of Beyoğlu. There are smoking and non-smoking sections, and a takeaway service too.
Other locations: 105/1 Teşvikiye Caddesi, Teşvikiye (0212 236 1617).

Savoy Pastanesi

Sıraselviler Caddesi 181-3, Beyoğlu (0212 249 1818). **Open** 7am-midnight daily. **Credit** AmEx, MC, V. **Map** p295 O3.
One of Istanbul's best cake shops has been further improved by a recent renovation. The first floor is now a café, providing a welcome alternative to traditional seating on the exhaust filled pavement outside. Savoy Pastanesi is particularly good for breakfast and all-day sinful snacking.

Şütte

Duduodaları Sokak 21, Balık Pazarı, Galatasaray, Beyoğlu (0212 293 9292). **Open** 8.30am-8pm Mon-Sat. **Credit** MC, V. **Map** p294 N3.
This long-running deli, owned by Macedonians, is one of the few places in Istanbul that stocks pork products other than just bacon. It also carries a decent selection of imported cheeses, which are pricey but wonderful, plus local varieties of cheese, mezedes and condiments.

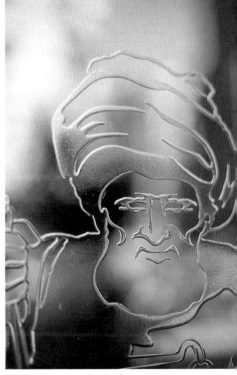

Ali Muhiddin Hacı Bekir. *See p170.*

Hair & beauty salons

Good grooming is next to godliness for Turkish girls and the beauty salon (*güzellik salonu*) is a second home. For the face, it's tweezers and expertly teased thread, for the body it's waxing (*ağda*) and hair removal – facial fluff, armpit, leg and pubic (Turkey's the home of the bikini wax). Alongside this, you have manicures (*manikür*), pedicures (*pedikür*) and all manner of hair treatments. Dyeing (*boya*) is a favourite – there's now a chemical-free, or *organik*, variety – and the blow-dry (*fön*), involving at least two attendants and an army of brushes, essential.

Hüseyin

Sıraselviler Caddesi 184/1, Cihangir, Taksim, Beyoğlu (0212 251 0005/252 0947). **Open** 8am-8pm Mon-Sat. **Credit** MC, V. **Map** p295 O3.
A typical neighbourhood *kuaför* with the full range of beauty services. Armies of bright young things attend to your every whim, and prices are unbelievably reasonable.

MOS

Bronz Sokak 65/7, off Abdi İpekçi Caddesi, Maçka, Teşvikiye (0212 240 1970/246 3222). **Open** 9am-7pm Mon-Sat. **Credit** MC, V.

Enjoy!

There is no drink like the generously foaming, wonderful aroma of Turkish Coffee.

Even when frequently savoured, due to the amount used, Turkish Coffee does not significantly contribute to obesity and the amount of caffeine consumed is measurable.

After drinking a cup of Turkish Coffee, the film left by the coffee grounds in the cup can be interpreted to tell one's fortune. It is believed that the coffee imparts good news concerning the future.

With it wonderful taste Turkish Coffee has been bringing people together throughout history and has over the years had a profound impact on culture and the arts. Countless works of art have been produced about coffee.

Kurukahveci Mehmet Efendi
has been producing coffee in Turkey for 133 years;
coffee that is always fantastic and delicious.

KURUKAHVECİ
MEHMET EFENDİ
MAHDUMLARI

TAHMİS SOKAK 66
EMİNÖNÜ 34116 İSTANBUL TURKEY
TEL: + (90 212) 522 00 80,
511 42 62, 511 42 63
FAX: + (90 212) 511 13 11
www.mehmetefendi.com

Mall contents

Residents of Istanbul only had to wait slightly over 520 years between the opening of the city's first mall and its second. Mehmet the Conqueror launched trading at what was to become the Grand Bazaar around 1461. The Galleria opened its doors in Ataköy in 1988.

But since the arrival of the Galleria, mall mania has taken hold. When Akmerkez opened several years later it had Istanbulus whole-heartedly embracing blue-collar American pastimes such as bowling and hanging out at the food court. But while back in the US this is Homer Simpson territory, the novelty value in Turkey ensures that Akmerkez is of a higher class. Inflated prices, heavy security and its high-rent location conspire to keep out the riffraff. So much so that it's common to spot celebrities on a shopping binge or taking in a movie.

Akmerkez

Nispetiye Caddesi, Etiler (0212 282 0170). Metro Levent. **Open** 10am-10pm daily.
This slick, upmarket mall hoasts 250 shops, a food court, a supermarket, a number of cinemas and one of the city's best Italian restaurants, Paper Moon. The mall is located right by the metro station.

Galleria

Sahil Yolu, Ataköy (0212 559 9560). **Open** 10am-10pm daily.
It once enjoyed a certain cachet as the first mall in town but is now overshadowed by Akmerkez. Still, it has a skating rink, a multiplex cinema and several designer shops including Vakko, Beymen, Paul & Shark, IGS and Pierre Cardin. To get here from Sultanahmet take a taxi along Sahil Yolu; from Taksim catch a Bakirköy dolmuş from opposite the PTT (corner of Şehit Muhtar Bey Caddesi and Aydede Caddesi).

Metro City

Büyükdere Caddesi 171, Levent (212 282 4951). Metro Levent. **Open** 10am-10pm daily.
Opened in May 2003, this four-storey mall houses international brands including Marks & Spencer, Zara, Lacoste and Starbucks. The mall is situated next to the metro station.

Iş Kuleleri Çarşi

Iş Kuleleri, Pembe Gül Sokak, Off Büyükdere Caddesi. **Open** 10am-10pm daily.
Housed in Turkey's largest office block, this mall has 29 shops spread over two floors, plus the Iş Bank Auditorium and Kibele Art Gallery. To get here take the metro to Levent and head for the Gültepe exit; it's then a five- to ten-minute walk, past the Yapı Kredi Plaza.

Mayadrom

Yıldırım Göker Caddesi, Akatlar. Metro Levent. **Open** 10am-10pm daily.
Full of boutiques and particularly strong on gift and gourmet shops. It also boasts a sports centre, home centre and beauty centre, and a luxury cinema. To get here take the metro to Levent and then a taxi (it's a five-minute ride).

Without a doubt, MOS is the biggest name in Istanbul hairdressing, and deservedly so: its staff are absolutely brilliant. As you'd expect, it's a particular favourite with the upper echelons of Istanbul society, who book in for waxings, pluckings and painting. Men needn't miss out either, as MOS offers unisex services. But beauty doesn't come cheap: prices are high by Turkish standards.
Other locations: Akmerkez Mall 122, Nispetiye Caddesi, Etiler (0212 282 0554).

Handicrafts

Besides carpets Turkey offers a wealth of lesser-known – and equally traditional – quality handicrafts. The ceramics trade, for one, dates back to the Selçuk Empire of the 11th century. Original tiles, vases and plates with the traditional tulip motif are now staples of museum exhibits across the world, and the

Market trading

Once a week, a few streets in most neighbourhoods are taken over by the mahalle pazarı, or local market. The awnings go up, wooden stalls jam the streets and stallholders compete at high decibels for custom. These are the places to buy your strawberries, peppers, jumbo olives, village cheese (*köy peyniri*), cheap clothing, pots and pans, tools and household wares at bargain prices. Some of the larger street markets (such as those listed below) have developed such a reputation for variety and bargains that they draw customers from all over the city. As a general rule, markets kick off around 9am and wind down around 5pm (later in summer), when prices are slashed for the small pickings that remain.

Fatih Pazarı
Darüşşafaka Caddesi, Fatih. **Open** Wed. **Map** p291 G7.
This vast open-air market surrounds the Fatih Mosque and fills its rambling courtyard. Join the headscarved crowds to tussle over leopard-print lingerie, surplus clothing and household items. It also has an excellent reputation for its foodstuff: expect to find top village produce, including local cheeses, baskets of fresh rose hips and, in season, cornelian cherries.

Ortaköy Market
Ortaköy Quayside. **Open** Sat, Sun.
Istanbul's answer to London's Camden market. Go for mounds of tacky jewellery and plentiful kitsch imported unnecessarily from India and Africa. But, you might also just find the odd interesting antique, reproduction print or choice bit of trinketry.

Salı Pazarı
Kuşdili Sokak, Kadıköy. **Open** Tue, Sun. **Map** p297 X7.
The best-known, biggest and most popular of the city's street markets, so be prepared to mix it up with middle-class matrons and beetle-browed Anatolian mamas in search of bargain bras and the freshest of figs. On Sunday, the same site metamorphoses into a European-style flea market with stallholders touting antiques, furniture and jewellery.

Ulus Pazarı
Kürkadı Sokak, Etiler. **Open** Thur.
It may be sited in a sophisticated neighbourhood but don't expect a genteel crowd. This is the place for knock-off designer labels and an upmarket range of household ware, fruit, veg and deli items. A free bus service runs between the market and the Akmerkez mall (*see p173* **Mall contents**).

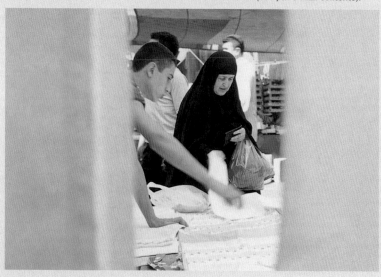

tradition lives on in Kütahya, western Anatolia, where artists hand-craft both reproductions and more contemporary designs. Then there's *ebru*, a Central Asian variation of paper marbling, which took off when calligraphy was in its heyday. Today, it's applied to fabrics and other materials. Other handicrafts include carved meerschaum pipes, prayer beads, backgammon sets, silks and fancy fabrics. Most of this stuff can be found at the **Grand Bazaar** (*see p80* **Shopping the bazaar**).

Abdulla

Halıcılar Caddesi 53, Grand Bazaar (0212 522 9078/ www.abdulla.com). Tram Beyazıt or Çemberlitaş. **Open** 9am-7pm Mon-Sat. **Credit** MC, V. **Map** p81.
Abdulla is part of a new breed of handicraft shops in the Grand Bazaar that take traditional crafts and give them a contemporary twist. The emphasis here is on natural and hand-made items, with a strong line in hamam accessories: towels, *peştemals*, olive oil soaps – in flavours from cinnamon to sesame – and elaborate soap sculptures. Other good buys include tribal mohair, sheepskin throws and silk-and-wool-weave fabrics.

Deli Kızın Yeri

Halıcılar Caddesi 42, Grand Bazaar (0212 511 1914/ www.delikiz.com). Tram Beyazıt or Çemberlitaş. **Open** 8.30am-7pm Mon-Sat. **Credit** AmEx, MC, V. **Map** p81.
Linda Caldwell, a retired American and self-styled crazy lady (*deli kız*), designs and makes most of her product, borrowing traditional Turkish handicrafts, motifs and fabrics to turn out something more off-beat. Stock includes hand-made clothes, tablecloths, placemats, drapes and dolls.

Derviş

Keseciler Caddesi 33-5, Grand Bazaar (0212 514 4525). Tram Beyazıt or Çemberlitaş. **Open** 9am-7pm Mon-Sat. **Credit** AmEx, MC, V. **Map** p81.
A former partner at Abdulla (*see above*), Tayfun Utkan has branched out on his own. There are still the bath products, including hand-made pistachio and nettle soaps, own-label towels and peştemals of unbleached cotton and silk. He's also added trousseau items, from fine embroidered linens and brightly coloured silks to hand-stitched undershirts and jackets. Utkan also commissions exciting work from rural Anatolian craftsmen, who use traditional materials and designs with imaginative twists. Look for the lavender-bag talismans and felt throws.

Dosim

Off Bab-ı Hümayün Caddesi, Sultanahmet (0212 513 3134). Tram Gülhane or Sultanahmet. **Open** 9am-6pm Mon, Wed-Sun. **Credit** MC, V. **Map** p289 O10.
What a location – a former Ottoman canteen right across from the tourist-thronged entrance to the Topkapı Palace. No surprise then that this particular bit of prime retailing is owned and run by the

cultural ministry. But what that also means is that prices are fixed and reasonable. Items include hand-blown glass, copperware, silver and jewellery.

Istanbul Handicrafts Centre

Kabasakal Caddesi 7, Sultanahmet (0212 517 6782). Tram Sultanahmet. **Open** 9am-6.30pm daily. **Credit** AmEx, MC, V. **Map** p289 N10.
A restored *medrese*, located opposite the Baths of Roxelana, which now houses a warren of workshops, each with its own specialisation. Particularly strong are the illuminations, miniatures and calligraphy. Other highlights include cloth-painting, dolls, ceramics, glass and bookbinding. Artists work on site, so you can watch them in full creative flow.

Sırça El Sanatları Merkezi

Akbıyık Caddesi 2, Sultanahmet (0212 638 5184). Tram Sultanahmet. **Open** 8.30am-8pm daily. **Credit** AmEx, MC, V. **Map** p289 N11.
A shop with a huge selection of hand-made ceramics, at prices for every purse. Don't be put off by the tat on the ground floor: quality improves as you climb higher, peaking on the third floor. Most of the product is made at the family-run pottery in Cappadocia, using traditional techniques but new designs and colour combinations.

Yıldız Ceramic

Duduodaları Sokak 6, Balık Pazarı, Galatasaray, Beyoğlu (0212 243 0829). **Open** 10am-10pm Mon-Sat; 1-8pm Sun. **Credit** AmEx, MC, V. **Map** p294 N3.
A tiny store, situated at the British Consulate end of the Balık Pazarı, selling hand-crafted reproductions of original Iznik ceramic designs. There's everything from plates, bowls and coffee cups to tiles, vases and jugs. For lower budgets there's a small number of factory-made items that are ideal for cheap gifts.

Health & herbals

Mainstream consumer brands are catching on to the 'organic' craze, so it's relatively easy to find brown rice, whole-wheat pasta and breads almost anywhere these days. As with Western countries, though, this kind of stuff doesn't come cheap.

Ambar

Kallavi Sokak 12, off Istiklal Caddesi, Beyoğlu (0212 292 9272/www.nuhunambari.com). **Open** 9am-8pm Mon-Sat; noon-8pm Sun. **Credit** AmEx, MC, V. **Map** p294 M3.
One of the few places in Istanbul that sells fresh tofu and pure soya milk. Other items include wholemeal village bread (available fresh on Wednesdays), organic fruit and veg and eco beauty products. At press time, Ambar was about to open an in-store café, sure to be dishing up delectable home-made food at wholesome prices.

Bünsa

Duduodaları Sokak 26, Balık Pazarı, Galatasaray, Beyoğlu (0212 243 6265). **Open** 8.30am-7.30pm daily. **Credit** MC, V. **Map** p294 N3.

Eat, Drink, Shop

Herbal remedies and healing tonics, ranging from medicinal teas to ginseng, karakovan honey to rare varieties of *pekmez* (fruit molasses). Tell 'em your ailment, and they'll prescribe a potion. The most popular panacea is a concoction of honey, royal jelly, nettle and ginseng, guaranteed to fix fatigue.

Kalmaz Baharat

Mısır Çarşısı 41/1, Eminönü (0212 522 6604).
Tram Eminönü. **Open** 8am-7pm Mon-Sat. **No credit cards**. **Map** p289 L8.
One of the oldest stores in the Egyptian Market, this atmospheric place – located just east of the main intersection – still has its original drawers and tea caddies. Specialities include spices, medicinal herbs, healing teas and aromatic oils.

Household

Turkey's particularly strong on textiles, so towels, linens, curtain and upholstery fabrics make excellent buys. For a dazzling choice of furnishing fabrics, go to blocks one and two of the **IMÇ** (Istanbul Manifaturacılar Çarşğsı), located on the west side of Unkapanı between the Golden Horn and the Aqueduct of Valens. Quality towels and linens are best found in Sultanhamam, around the back of the **Egyptian Bazaar** (*see p86*) – look out especially for the Taç label.

Özgül Çeyiz

Mısı Çarşısı 83, Eminönü (0212 522 7068). Tram, bus Eminönü. **Open** 9am-7pm Mon-Sat. **Credit** MC, V. **Map** p289 L8.
The east end of the Egyptian Bazaar was once crammed with stores in the trousseau (*çeyiz*) business. In days of yore, young ladies were wheeled along by the womenfolk in the family to make wholesale purchases that would improve her prospects. Özgül is one of the few survivors from the old times. It's a minimal store packed with fancy embroidered sheets, quilts, towels, robes and the like. Trousseau hunting or not, there's some great stuff here at very reasonable prices – the own-label Begonvill towels in particular.

Paşabahçe

Istiklal Caddesi 314, Beyoğlu (0212 244 0544/ www.pasabahce.com.tr). **Open** 10am-9pm Mon-Fri, Sun; 10am-10pm Sat. **Credit** AmEx, MC, V. **Map** p294 M4.
This stylish shop, a favourite with Istanbul yuppies, is Turkey's answer to Conran and Habitat. Stock ranges from the simple to the elaborate, and is set out on three floors: go to the basement for kitchenware, simple china and glass; the ground floor for barware, vases and ornaments; and head to the first floor for special collections. The latter is impressive for its fancy glasswork, which is often hand-blown using traditional shapes and motifs.
Other locations: Teşvikiye Caddesi 117, Teşvikiye (0212 233 5005).

Jewellery

The **Grand Bazaar** (*see p78*) is first choice for the largest selection of 'classic' jewellery and gold under one roof. For more modern pieces, try **Teşvikye**, specifically **Atiye Sokak** (which runs between the main Abdi Ipekçi Caddesi and Teşvikiye Caddesi), home to several small creative studio showrooms.

Aspendos

Bostan Sokak 111/2, cnr of Teşvikiye Caddesi, Teşvikiye (0212 225 9409). **Open** 9.30am-7pm Mon-Sat. **Credit** MC, V.
This shop specialises in funky costume jewellery with an oriental twist. Expect plenty of big, bright turquoise stones and Eastern motifs. Most items are locally made and carry the Aspendos label.

Mor

Turnacıbaşı Sokak 16/1, Beyoğlu (0212 292 8817/ www.morconcept.com). **Open** 10am-8.30pm Mon-Sat; 2-6pm Sun. **Credit** AmEx, MC, V. **Map** p294 N3.
A stylish, glass-fronted studio just down from the Galatasaray Hamam, selling inspired originals designed by an in-house team. Most pieces are fashioned from silver and bronze, often combining scraps of discarded ethnic jewellery from eastern Turkey, Turkmenistan and Afghanistan.

Sema Paksoy

Atiye Sokak 9, Teşvikiye (0212 219 3941). **Open** 10am-7pm Mon-Sat. **Credit** MC, V.
Simple but stunning original designs from big rings and pins to necklaces and bracelets. Most pieces combine old ethnic bits, big stones (lots of agate, amber, lapis and turquoise) and pure gold or silver settings. It's upmarket stuff. Paksoy's jewellery also does a healthy trade in France and the US.

Urart

Abdi Ipekçi Caddesi 18/1, Nişantaşı (0212 246 7194). **Open** 9am-7pm Mon-Sat. **Credit** AmEx, DC, MC, V.
Sophisticated jewellery with an Anatolian slant. Designs are drawn from the countless civilisations that have peopled Anatolia from Palaeolithic through to Ottoman times and use a combination of silver, gold and semiprecious stones. This stuff is pricey, but beautiful.
Concessions: Topkapı Museum, Swissôtel.

Leather

For the best selection of leather (*deri*) head for the **Grand Bazaar** (*see p78*). Be careful though, because quality can often be poor; 'antelope skin', for example, is unlikely to be genuine antelope. In addition, you'll have to work hard at getting a fair price. If it all seems like too much hassle, there are stores that specialise in quality leather at fixed prices – albeit prices that aren't much cheaper than you'd find at home.

Gönül Paksoy:
Ottoman with a modern twist. *See p165.*

Derimod

*Akmerkez Mall 362, Nispetiye Caddesi, Etiler
(0212 282 0668).* **Open** 10am-10pm daily.
Credit DC, MC, V.
Classic and contemporary designs in top quality
leather for both men and women. There are coat,
jacket and waistcoat collections by the dozen, as well
as an extensive range of leather accessories.
Other locations: Valikonağı Caddesi 103/16,
Nişantaşı (0212 247 7481).

Music

For value for money, confine your shopping list
to local artists on cassette, scratchy vinyl from
decades ago or pirate CDs (sold in the backstreets of Eminönü and at makeshift stalls
along Divan Yolu). International CDs are no
cheaper or more expensive than in Europe.

Ada Music

*Orhan Adli Apaydin Sokak 20, off Istiklal Caddesi,
Tünel, Beyoğlu (0212 251 3878).* **Open** 9am-10pm
Mon-Thur, Sun; 9am-11pm Fri, Sat. **Credit** AmEx,
V. **Map** p294 M4.
Opened by Turkish record company Ada, this is the
first shop to specialise in Turkish rock and protest
music. Given the rabble-rousing genre, the setting
is surprisingly smart, and there's a small café and

Biletix ticket point. The shop also sells a decent
range of foreign CDs, in addition to international
newspapers and magazines.

Decoded

*Atlas Pasaji 16, off Istiklal Caddesi 209, Beyoğlu
(0212 244 2422).* **Open** 12.30-8.30pm Mon-Sat.
Credit MC, V. **Map** p294 N3.
Ground-breaking music shop and a great place to
find out what's hot. A recent change in management
has taken it further towards hip hop, jungle and dub,
but it still boasts the widest selection of independent
music on vinyl and CD, plus demos of new local acts.

DJ Shop

*Bostan Sokak 24, Tünel, Beyoğlu (0212 293 9912/
www.djshoptr.com).* **Open** noon-7pm Mon-Sat.
Credit MC,V. **Map** p294 M4.
Specialist in house, trance and techno, selling new
imported vinyl and technical gear. English-
speaking staff can keep you up to date with what's
going on in the clubs.

Ikinci-el Plak

*Ashhan Sahaflar Çarşısı 18/49, Beyoğlu (0212 252
6877).* **Open** 11am-8pm Mon-Sat. **Credit** AmEx,
MC, V. **Map** p294 N3.
A passageway off the Balık Pazarı, situated opposite Galatasaray Lycée, is crammed with second-
hand book and record shops spread out over two

floors. This tiny shop is the best of the lot. Look for bargain deals on old disco and soundtrack albums, plus rare Turkish releases.

Lale Plak
Galipdede Caddesi 1, Tünel, Beyoğlu (0212 293 7739). **Open** 9am-7pm daily. **Credit** MC, V. **Map** p294 M5.
The city's premier jazz, ethnic and classical music retailer, in business for 45 years. There's also a comprehensive selection of trad Turkish. Staff are knowledgeable – and indeed helpful – and the place has long been hangout of choice for visiting jazzers.

Megavizyon
Istiklal Caddesi 79-81, Beyoğlu (0212 293 0759). **Open** 9am-11pm daily. **Credit** AmEx, MC, V. **Map** p295 O2.
The biggest music store in town, with the widest range of genres. It also sells computer equipment, videos, English-language books, internet packages and a limited selection of magazines.

Raksotek
Istiklal Caddesi 162, Beyoğlu (0212 292 0208). **Open** 9am-11pm Mon-Sat; 10am-11pm Sun. **Credit** MC, V. **Map** p295 O3.
Turkey's answer to the Virgin Megastore, this three-storey shop sells international and Turkish artists, as well as internet packages, CD racks, headsets, speakers and children's toys.

Shoes

Turks tend to have small feet, so Westerners with huge hoofs will be pushed for selection. Not that there's a lot you'd want to buy here anyway. Local shoes may come cheap but they're generally boring and shabby. The malls (*see p173* **Mall contents**) have a handful of shops selling imported brands, mostly Italian, for which you pay through the nose.

Beta
Istiklal Caddesi 69, Taksim, Beyoğlu (0212 292 5786/ www.betashoes.com). **Open** 9am-9pm Mon-Sat; noon-7pm Sun. **Credit** DC, MC, V. **Map** p295 O2.
A colourful, casual specialist in clumpy fashion footwear. Prices are average and there's a limited selection of belts and bags too.

Hotiç
Teşvikiye Caddesi 135/1, Teşvikiye (0212 247 7455). **Open** 9.30am-7.30pm Mon-Sat. **Credit** AmEx, DC, MC, V.
The latest designs, from casual to chic, for both men and women. Most of the product is own-label, with a few Italian imports thrown in. None of it is spectacular, and the quality can be dodgy, so shop carefully. The shop also does a range of handbags.

Mahmut Kundura
Istiklal Caddesi 43, Taksim, Beyoğlu (0212 244 4104). **Open** 8am-7pm Mon-Sat. **No credit cards**. **Map** p295 O2.

Make your feet a part of history: this 77-year-old shop has the distinction of having shod none other than Atatürk himself. And the styles haven't really changed much since – solid, men-only creations designed for conservative feet.

Services

Barbers

Cihangir Erkek Kuaförü
Akarsu Caddesi 49/1, Cihangir (0212 251 1660). **Open** 8am-8.30pm Mon-Sat; noon-6pm Sun. **No credit cards**. **Map** p295 O4.
All the usual services, delivered with a smile and some English. Cihangir's an expat-heavy district, so they're used to trimming foreigners.

Computer repairs

Bilgisayar Hastanesi
Inönü Caddesi 72/3, Gümüşsuyu, Taksim (0212 252 1575/www.bilgisayarhastanesi.com). **Open** 9am-6pm Mon-Fri. **Credit** MC, V. **Map** p293 P2.
This business is an authorised service provider for Compaq, Hewlett Packard and Epson. Here, staff clean, maintain and repair computers and order spare parts. Bilgisayar Hastanesi also operates an emergency service, but you pay a 50% premium for any work done outside office hours. The place also does second-hand trade in laptops.

Elma Bilgisayar
Halep Pasajı 3rd Floor, Istiklal Caddesi 140, Beyoğlu (0212 251 9044/251 9045). **Open** 9am-6pm Mon-Fri; 10am-1pm Sat. **Credit** MC, V.
This Apple (Elma) dealer does repairs and provides back-up services. As the name suggests, Apple computers are the speciality here, both in terms of service and sales. That said, the place also sells a selection of PC hardware.

Keys & locksmiths

Most areas have a locksmith that will do key-cutting, install new locks or break in to broken ones. Look for the large yellow key sign.

Irfan Ülke
Sıraselviler Caddesi 113, Taksim (0212 243 1588; emergencies 0532 553 9414). **Open** 8.30am-7pm Mon-Sat. **Credit** MC, V. **Map** p295 O3.
At the back of the passageway on the ground floor and in the business for 30 years. Civilised service, but minimal English spoken.

Laundry & dry-cleaning

There's no such thing as a coin-operated laundromat in Istanbul. Dry-cleaners, on the other hand, are plentiful and reasonably priced.

Can Laundry

Bakraç Sokak 32/C, off Sıraselviler Caddesi, Cihangir, Beyoğlu (0212 252 9360). **Open** 9am-8pm Mon-Fri; 9am-4pm Sat. **No credit cards. Map** p295 O4.
Prices are charged per load ($6.75) or by item, if you just have one or two ($2, ironed). Ironing for full loads is optional and costs around $1 per item.

Çınar

Sıraselviler Caddesi 152/A, Cihangir, Beyoğlu (0212 251 4204/252 1938). **Open** 8am-7.30pm Mon-Sat. **Credit** MC, V. **Map** p295 O3.
Operates a pick-up and delivery service (including to hotels) within the Taksim area. Dry cleaning: prices are around $3.50 for a skirt, $1.50 trousers, $5 for a jacket. For laundry, washing per load is $7.

Photography

Photographic studios are to be found in almost every high street and many will do portrait and passport-size *(vesikalık)* photos, as well as sell and develop film.

Stüdyo Mor İpek

Selvi Han, Sıraselviler Caddesi 61, Beyoğlu (0212 249 5877/251 9253/www.moripek.com). **Open** 9am-8pm Mon-Sat. **Credit** MC, V. **Map** p295 O3.
Basement studio catering to professionals and amateurs. They also do colour passport photographs.

Yalçınlar

Divan Yolu 22, Sultanahmet (0212 511 9071). **Tram** Sultanahmet. **Open** 8.30am-8pm Mon-Sat. **Credit** AmEx, MC, V. **Map** p289 M10.
One of 30 branches offering developing and printing services for professionals and amateurs. **Other locations:** Cumhuriyet Caddesi 27, Taksim (0212 237 0267).

Shoe repairs

Most neighbourhoods have a resident cobbler, who will re-heel, re-sole or do basic repairs at give-away prices.

Havai Lostra Salonu

Ağa Camii Sokak 27/1, Beyoğlu (0212 245 1652). **Open** 8am-8pm Mon-Sat; 10am-8pm Sun. **No credit cards. Map** p295 O2.
One of Beyoğlu's original shoe-shine salons, complete with customer thrones, the Havai also does repairs and sells a whole array of shoe laces. A standard shoe-shine will set you back around $1.50.

Tailors & mending

Gone are the days when one tailor would an clothe entire neighbourhood, but if the bespoke business is foundering, there's still a living to be made from mending and adjustments. Tailors *(terzi)* are found throughout the city and will do the simplest of mending jobs *(tadilat)* if you can't be bothered yourself.

Acar Terzihane

Yeni Yuva Sokak 34A, Cihangir, Beyoğlu (0212 251 3745/0535 762 7320). **Open** 8.30am-7.30pm Mon-Sat. **No credit cards. Map** p295 O4.
Two brothers competent at all kinds of stitching and mending, and excellent at producing fine, detailed work and custom-made outfits for ladies and gents.

Watch & jewellery repairs

Most gold shops in the **Grand Bazaar** (*see p78*) will repair items made of gold but won't touch silver (and vice versa). For watch repairs (*saat tamiratı*), head to the Grand Bazaar.

Güngenci

Meşelik Sokak 3/1, Beyoğlu (0212 249 3053). **Open** 8.30am-7pm Mon-Sat. **No credit cards. Map** p295 O2.
A spacious, carpeted workshop where they'll fix anything that ticks.

Supermarkets

Ten years ago there were barely any supermarkets in Istanbul. These days they're commonplace, though they haven't yet killed off the local corner store (*bakkal*).

Gima

Sıraselviler Caddesi 180, Cihangir, Taksim, Beyoğlu (0212 293 5158/www.gima.com.tr). **Open** 9am-10pm daily. **Credit** MC, V.
Gima has an excellent in-house bakery franchise. Otherwise standard supermarket fare at average prices. Does home delivery and internet orders, too. **Other locations:** Eski Büyükdere Caddesi 5/7, Şişli (0212 219 6439).

Makro

Abdi İpekçi Caddesi 24-26, Nişantaşı (0212 231 3999/www.tansas.com.tr). **Open** 8.30am-9pm daily. **Credit** AmEx, MC, V.
Caters for the upper end of the market with a wide selection of imported foods and prices to match. Especially good deli, fresh fish and meat counters, plus a wide and fairly priced range of local wines. **Other locations:** Akmerkez Mall 325, Nispetiye Caddesi, Etiler (0212 282 0310); Muallim Naci Caddesi 170, Kuruçeşme (0212 257 1381).

MMM Migros

19 Mayıs Caddesi 1, Şişli, Nişantaşı (0212 246 6480/www.migros.com.tr). **Tram** Şişli, **bus** Şişli Mosque. **Open** 9am-10pm daily. **Credit** MC, V.
This chain has good prices and a bizarre claim to fame: it boasts that it sells enough toilet paper in a year to circle the globe 24 times over. Stores are graded by the 'Ms' preceding them: a single M is basic, the Şişli store with three is hypermarket. **Other locations:** M Migros, Mühürdar Sokak 14-22, Kadıköy (0216 330 5993/330 5994); MMM Migros, Metro City Mall, Büyükdere Caddesi 171, Levent (0212 344 3000).

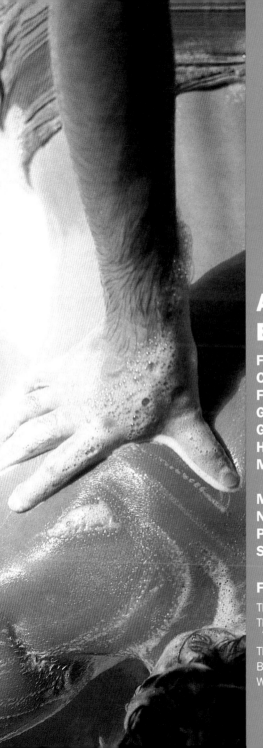

Arts & Entertainment

Festivals & Events	182
Children	189
Film	192
Galleries	197
Gay & Lesbian	201
Hamams	206
Music: Pop, Rock, World & Jazz	210
Music: Turkish	216
Nightlife	222
Performing Arts	227
Sport & Fitness	232

Features

This sure ain't Kansas, Toto	194
The unsung queen of Turkish song	212
The belly fling thing	218
Bosphorus Babylon	224
Welcome to Hell?	233

Festivals & Events

Footie fans celebrate best but culture vultures are no slouches.

When Turkey's footballers won a place in the World Cup semis back in 2002, no one who was around that day could have been in any doubt about the city's dedication to celebration. As the streets packed with singing, dancing and drinking revellers (let's gloss over the fools letting off guns into the air), it was a wondrous reminder that Istanbul once had a glorious and deserved reputation for festivities to outshine any of medieval Europe's more dreary capitals.

Back in the golden days, extravagant-going-on-pottily-decadent celebrations were held on every possible occasion, with the sultan providing most of the excuses. For the circumcision of three of Süleyman's sons in 1530, tents sewn with tulips were erected on gold-plated poles at the Hippodrome, where crowds were entertained by tightrope walkers performing on a cord stretched from the Egyptian Obelisk. The public was fed on roast oxen, out of which fled live foxes as the meat was set down. During the later annual Tulip Festivals, small armies of tortoises were

'Hashirigaki' by Heiner Goebbels at the **International Istanbul Theatre Festival**. *See p183*.

See p183.

released to roam the imperial gardens with candles fixed to their shell tops.

But this kind of behaviour naturally couldn't last. When the republic was founded in 1923, it was just this sort of foppish excess that set the country's new rulers on their move to the austere Anatolian flatlands. Decrees from the new party-pooping capital of Ankara put an end both to imperial traditions and overt religious observance. In their place were inserted a dour bunch of annual excuses for flag-waving, such as Republic Day and Victory Day (*see p272*). Almost as tragic is the recent infiltration, via the marketing powers that be, of a slew of imports, novelties like Sevgililer Günü (Valentine's Day), Mothers' Day and even Christmas, which naturally tends to get confused with New Year's Day, given that more than 95 per cent of the population is Muslim.

Thankfully, in recent years, the proper festive spirit has returned. Nowadays, winter apart, every month sees a festival of some kind, with the city's youthful population giving most of these events a dynamism that more than makes up for any lack of experience. Many of these events are superbly managed and promoted by the Istanbul Foundation for Arts and Cultures (*Istanbul Kültür ve Sanat Vakfı*; www.istfest.org), which is consistently successful in securing the involvement of a roster of international big names. Now all they need to do is get the tortoises back.

Information & tickets

For information about festivals and events, your best bet is to pick up the monthly *Time Out Istanbul*. It has a 40-page English language supplement which lists dates, times and other information. For dance music and clubbing events look out for *Urban Bug* (www.urbanbug.com), the city's self-styled 'alternative urban culture guide', which is available free from several bars and cafés. You can also try the website www.istanbul.com, which lists that particular day's events.

To buy tickets for the various festivals, check out the following outlets:

Atatürk Cultural Centre (AKM)
Taksim Square (0212 251 5600/fax 0212 245 3916). **Open** 10am-6pm daily. **No credit cards**. **Map** p293 P2.

Cecilia Bartoli performs at the **International Istanbul Music Festival**. *See p185.*

This big, ugly 1970s building looms over Taksim Square. Tickets for several of the major festivals are sold inside. Students receive discounts.

Biletix

www.biletix.com (0216 454 1555. **Open** *8.30am-9pm Mon-Fri; 10am-9pm Sat, Sun.* **Credit** DC, MC, V.
Tickets can be booked on the phone or through the website (in English and Turkish), as well as at one of the many desks found in selected outlets of Vakkorama, music retailer Raksotek (*see p179*) and supermarket Migros. There's a booking charge of $1.80 per transaction (irrespective of the number of tickets purchased), while an extra $0.75 will buy delivery to your home address.

Spring

Phonem/Electronic Music Plateau

Various venues (information 0212 334 0772/ www.istfest.org). **Date** 2nd half of March. **Tickets** venues, Biletix. **Admission** varies.
An international platform for exploring electronic music, including discussions, technology exhibitions and performances. Expect a string of parties featuring local and international DJs, plus concerts, video art, film and video screenings, and workshops.

Orthodox Easter

Patrikhane (Orthodox Patriarchate Building), *Sadrazam Ali Paşa Caddesi 35, Fener (0212 531 9674).* **Date** April/May. **Admission** free. **Map** p291 G4.

Celebratory Easter Sunday mass is held in the venerable Patriarchate building in Fener (*see p90*) on the Golden Horn. In a church illuminated by hundreds of candles, the aura of ancient ritual is powerful enough to shake the scepticism of even the most ardent of atheists. In 2004 the date is 11 April.

International Istanbul Film Festival

Various venues (information 0212 334 0723/ www.istfest.org). **Date** April. **Tickets** venues, Biletix. **Admission** $4-$6.
One of the biggest cultural events, eagerly anticipated for the glamour all the visiting celebs. But be warned: this is the city's most popular cultural jamboree, and tickets sell out in advance. For more information on this and other film festivals, *see p196.*

International Istanbul Theatre Festival

Various venues (information 0212 334 0740/ www.istfest.org). **Date** May (even years only). **Tickets** venues, AKM, Biletix. **Admission** varies.
This festival provides one of the few opportunities to see international theatre in Istanbul. In the past, big draws have included famous names such as Robert Wilson, Pina Bausch, the Berliner Ensemble, the Piccolo Teatro di Milano and Britain's RSC. The programme also features a selection of the year's best Turkish plays. Most performances are held at city theatres including the Atatürk Cultural Centre, the Kenter Theatre and the Aksanat Cultural Centre (for venues, *see p228*); however, a few take place at more unusual venues, such as the Rumeli Hisarı fortress on the Bosphorus.

International Istanbul Puppet Festival

Akkarga Sokak 22, Elmadağ (information 0212 232 0224). **Date** 2nd wk of May. **Tickets** venues, Biletix. **Admission** $5-$6. **Credit** MC, V.

Puppet, marionette and shadow theatre was big in Ottoman times but, sadly, it is rarely performed today. The festival provides an opportunity to witness this almost forgotten art, with around a dozen shows by Turkish and international companies at the Kenter Theatre (*see p230*) and various other venues. One of the guests of the 2003 festival was the internationally acclaimed Vietnamese Water Puppet Group. Most of the plays are silent and suitable for both children and adults.

Conquest Week Celebrations

Various venues (information 0212 449 4000/ www.ibb.gov.tr). **Date** late May. **Admission** free.

A municipality-sponsored celebration of the Turkish conquest of Constantinople (29 May 1453). There are usually exhibitions of traditional Turkish arts, concerts of popular songs and parades by the 'Ottoman' Mehter band (*see p114*), plus conferences, lectures, screenings of worthy films, a few fireworks and some rabble-rousing by the nationalist and Islamist parties. The 600th anniversary celebrations in 2003 also merited performances from Anwar Braham and Natacha Atlas – a welcome change from three years earlier when a fancy-dress procession carrying cardboard 'boats' led to gridlock and punch-ups.

Summer

H2000 Music Festival

Ömerli Dam (information 0212 219 6193). **Date** May/June. **Tickets** AKM, Vakkorama. **Admission** 3-day pass $25-$45. **Credit** AmEx, DC, MC, V.

A stab at a Glastonbury-style event, with three days of music at a large open-air site. Venues change year to year, but in recent times it's been Ömerli Dam and Marmaracık Cove, both of which are about 40km (25 miles) from the city centre. Swimming and sunbathing have combined in past years with the likes of Suede, Starsailor and Fun Lovin' Criminals. The festival regularly draws upwards of 25,000, with provision for on-site camping and free shuttle transport back to town for those who prefer their own beds. Tickets go on sale in early May or can be bought at the site for a slightly higher fee.

Fête de la Musique

Various venues (information 0212 334 8740/ www.infist.org). **Date** 21 June. **Admission** free.

Launched in France in 1982, the Fête has since spread across Europe, reaching Istanbul in 1998. Here it takes the form of a couple of days of live performances by local amateur bands and bottom-of-the-barrel foreign solo artists at various open-air locations, mostly on or just off Istiklal Caddesi. Venues include the garden of the French Cultural Centre and Taksim Square.

International Istanbul Music Festival

Various venues (information 0212 334 0736/ www.istfest.org). **Date** June-July. **Tickets** AKM, Biletix. **Admission** $3.50-$150.

Inaugurated in 1973 on the occasion of the 50th anniversary of the republic, the IMF is the most prestigious event on the city's cultural calendar. It comprises about 30 performances of orchestra and chamber music, dance and ballet. Big hitters present at past festivals have included Kiri Te Kanawa, Phillip Glass, the Michael Nyman Ensemble, Cecilia Bartoli and the Kronos Quartet. In addition to the excellent program, it's worth attending just for the venues: the festival is one of the rare occasions on which the public gets inside Haghia Irene (*see p72*).

International Istanbul Jazz Festival

Various venues (information 0212 334 0772/ www.istfest.org). **Date** July. **Tickets** venues, Biletix. **Admission** $15-$30.

Past years have witnessed the likes of Keith Jarrett, Wynton Marsalis and Dizzy Gillespie performing in the 4,000-seat Harbiye open-air theatre, along with those other well-known jazzers Björk, Nick Cave, Lou Reed and Patti Smith. But then, this two-week festival often goes far beyond the bounds of jazz, which might upset purists, but keeps the rest of the city happy with what remains consistently the best programme of any Turkish music festival.

Traditional Istanbul Açıkhava (Open-Air) Concerts

Harbiye (information 0212 257 6200/ www.mostproduction.com). **Date** mid July/early Aug. **Tickets** Açıkhava Tiyatrosu (box office 0212 296 36 0910), Biletix. **Admission** $7-$32.

Ongoing since the mid-1980s, this season of open-air concerts in Harbiye is worth checking out. It combines mainstream names from Turkish pop, rock and folk with a variety of alternative genres. It's a good opportunity to see the more innovative end of the local popular music scene. Concerts in the 2003 season included the Mercan Dede Fusion Project, with its blend of Turkish folk, trance and whirling Dervishes, alongside Balkan stars such as Goran Bregovic and Vassilis Saleas.

Rumeli Hisarı 'Starry Nights'

Rumeli Hisarı (information 0212 335 9335). **Date** July-Aug. **Tickets** Rumeli Hisarı, Biletix. **Admission** $12-$40. **Credit** MC, V.

The appeal here is the venue – open green spaces within the walls of an Ottoman fortress (*see p106*) complete with stunning views of the Bosphorus. Against this backdrop, concerts run throughout the summer with something happening almost every night. The varied programme mixes rock and pop and the odd international name but the focus is largely on Arabesque and other forms of Turkish music. Regardless of who's playing, it's worth attending at least once – it's one of the best ways to pass a balmy summer evening in Istanbul.

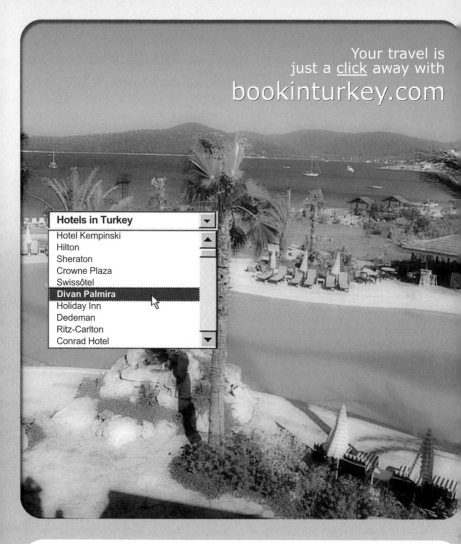

Your travel is just a <u>click</u> away with
bookinturkey.com

Hotels in Turkey

- Hotel Kempinski
- Hilton
- Sheraton
- Crowne Plaza
- Swissôtel
- **Divan Palmira**
- Holiday Inn
- Dedeman
- Ritz-Carlton
- Conrad Hotel

For all your travels to Turkey, **bookinturkey.com** offers you a wide range of hotel alternatives suitable for your budget. Just decide which city you want to go. You can also make your reservations, bookings and all the arrangements at **bookinturkey.com**, that you need for your journey.

Koç

INFO LINE: +90.216.454 00 00

BOOKINTURKEY.COM
Turkey's tourism web site

Lying down on the job – 'Bodies' by Sasha Waltz at the
International Istanbul Theatre Festival. *See p183.*

Bughole Festival

*Solar Beach Kilyos (information 0212 292 3656/
www.urbanbug.com).* **Date** Aug. **Tickets** venue,
Biletix. **Admission** $30. **Credit** MC, V.
In 2003, the second Bughole Festival was headlined
by the Chemical Brothers (2002's big hitters included the Orb), bringing gonzo drum-machine action
and tribal drum rolls to the Black Sea coast. A crowd
of around 13,000 hit the beach for a heavyweight roster of name DJs, bungee jumping, jet skiing and a
mini cult film festival, all squeezed into just 22 hours
(9am till sunrise next day). Shuttle services linked
the venue with Taksim Square. Fingers crossed that
every year is this good.

Autumn

Creamfields Istanbul Festival

*Park Orman (information 0212 257 9455/
www.hippro.com).* **Date** mid Sept. **Tickets** venue,
Biletix. **Admission** $30. **Credit** MC, V.
A replacement for the defunct J&B Techno & Dance
Festival, this 24-hour event features a wide spread
of international acts and DJs playing hip hop, trip
hop, techno, trance, drum 'n' bass, Asian underground, ambient and UK garage. 2003 headliners
included Placebo, Timo Maas and Way Out West.
It's an an open-air event taking place in the wooded
Park Orman out beyond the Maslak suburbs.

International Istanbul Biennale

*Various venues (information 0212 334 0763/
www.istfest.org).* **Date** Sept-Nov odd years only.
Tickets venues. **Admission** $7. **Credit** MC, V.
Alternating with the Istanbul Theatre Festival (*see
p183*), every other year more than 80 artists from,
at last count, 42 different countries exhibit around a
general theme set by a guest curator. In 2003 the
theme was 'poetic justice', and the show's curator
Dan Cameron of New York's New Museum of
Contemporary Art. You can expect to see conventional hangings, installations, video screenings,
walkabouts, films, panel discussions, lectures and
daily guided tours (in English). The next biennale
will be held in 2005.

Intercontinental Istanbul Eurasia Marathon

*Information 0212 234 4200/
www.istanbulmarathon.org.* **Date** 3rd Sun in Oct.
Beginning on the Asian Shore, this marathon route
passes over the Bosphorus Bridge to the European
side, loops through the city centre and across the
Atatürk Bridge, under the Valens Aqueduct then
back along the Sea of Marmara shore, over the
Galata Bridge and up the Bosphorus to finish 42km
(26 miles) later at İnönü Stadium, home ground of
Beşiktaş football club. One of the most scenic
marathons in the world, the event regularly pulls in
around 2,000 runners, half of them foreigners; if the

Michael Lin's installation in the Haghia Irene at the **International Istanbul Biennale** in 2001. *See p187.*

marathon sounds too tiring, you can always join the 200,000-odd runners who participate in the same day's 10km (6-mile) fun run.

Akbank Jazz Festival

Various venues (information 0212 252 5167/ www.pozitif-ist.com). **Date** Oct. **Tickets** venues, Biletix. **Admission** $2-$30.

Unlike July's international jamboree, this festival is less about big names and more about jazz. Some ten bands perform every day over the two weeks, with jam sessions at venues including Babylon (*see p211*) and Nardis (*see p213*). In addition to the music, there are a number of film screenings and workshops. Names such as Max Roach, the Art Ensemble of Chicago, Archie Shepp and Cecil Taylor have all participated in recent years.

Istanbul Arts Fair

Tüyap Centre, E5 Hwy, Gürpınar Jcn, Beylikdüzü (information 0212 886 6843/www.tuyapfair.com.tr). **Date** Oct/Nov. **Tickets** at the door. **Admission** $2, students free. **No credit cards.**

Recently relocated from its traditional city centre home for the far less handy Tüyap Centre, out near the airport, this remains a vast week-long sales fair with mass popular appeal. Some 50 Istanbul galleries take stands, as well as a handful of international companies, all aiming to offload paintings, sculpture and ceramics on an increasingly receptive local market. Don't let the remote location put you off: there are free shuttle services that depart from AKM on Taksim Square, Atatürk airport, the Bakırköy ferry stop and the Esenler bus terminal.

Anniversary of Atatürk's Death

Date 10 Nov.

Every 10 November at 9.05am, the death of Mustafa Kemal Atatürk is commemorated with a minute's silence. Sirens howl mournfully for the duration while people in the streets stop whatever they're doing and stand motionless. Buses and cars halt, while the Bosphorus ferries sound their foghorns.

The whole thing is extremely moving and eerie, a testament to the great leader's continued grip on the Turkish public's imagination.

IFSAK Istanbul Photograph Days

Various venues (information 0212 292 4201/ www.ifsak.org). **Date** Nov. **Admission** free.

A month devoted exclusively to photographic events, including slide shows, seminars and exhibitions by both domestic and foreign photographers. Amateur snappers can take part in a 'photomarathon': participants are given three themes and 48 hours to shoot. Prizes are awarded and all entries are exhibited.

Istanbul Book Fair

Tüyap Centre, E5 Hwy, Gürpınar Jcn, Beylikdüzü (information 0212 886 6843/www.tuyapfair.com.tr). **Date** Nov. **Tickets** at the door. **Admission** $2, students free. **No credit cards.**

Almost all of Turkey's publishing houses – more than 200 – as well as a number from abroad gather for ten days to trade their wares. Attendees get discounts on new publications and non-stop conferences and round-table discussions are held with the participation of leading writers, academics and intellectuals. Free shuttle services run from from AKM on Taksim Square, Atatürk airport, the Bakırköy ferry stop and Esenler bus terminal.

Winter

Efes Pilsen Blues Festival

Lütfü Kırdar Convention Centre, Harbiye (information 0212 252 5167/www.pozitif-ist.com). **Date** Nov/Dec. **Tickets** Biletix. **Admission** $15. **No credit cards.**

This extremely popular festival has been running since 1990. It serves up three bands a night, and the focus is on showcasing new talent. However, this doesn't stop the odd star performer (such as Bobby Rush or Long John Hunter) from showing up.

Children

Turks smother their kids with affection but don't do much to keep them amused.

Turks love children. Having said that, they don't much like entertaining them. Most of all they love displays of physical affection, which may vary from gentle kissing or cuddling to vigorous pinches and even bites on the cheeks or thighs. But don't worry, foreign kids will probably be spared the harassment: most Turks know this is not what Westerners do.

Childhood is quite a different experience here. Kids enjoy being a part of almost all aspects of adult life but there's a shortage of special entertainments aimed only at them. Kids simply hang out in the adult world, accompanying their parents from smoky restaurants to gossip sessions with the neighbours. The good news here is that your child will be welcome almost everywhere in Istanbul.

On the negative side, be prepared to change nappies in the pram while sightseeing, as public toilets lack both facilities and hygiene. And pushing a pram through Istanbul traffic is a battle involving encounters with steep hills, high kerbs and narrow passes – which is why most Turks transport their kids in their arms.

Learn to negotiate these difficulties and sightseeing can be fun. Many children enjoy the colourful tiles of mosques, bizarre objects in museums, and the eastern allure of the markets. They enjoy the freedom to run around, without being hushed, and simply bask in the attention.

As well as the parks and activity venues listed here, other good places to go include the fortresses of **Rumeli Hisarı** (*see p104*) and **Yedikule** (*see p89*), or anything that involves mucking about on boats, such as a **Bosphorus cruise** (*see p240*). For babies under two, try the two excellent – and free – mother-and-baby groups at the **British International School** (Fulyalı Sokak 24, Levent, 0212 270 7801) and **Papatya International School** (Güllü Sokak 20, Levent, 0212 280 0250). For the latter you have to show ID at the door.

Activities

Just north of the city centre, **Yıldız Park** is beautiful and leafy and a fine place to let kids run free off the leash (*see p100*). The summer-only small fairground **Maçka Luna Park** is in a park north of Taksim. **Bebek Park** is small, but great for younger kids – it's got safe toys and sand unpolluted by cats' mess. A little further north of Bebek, is the large **Emirgan Park**, located just beside the Bosphorus, with an ornamental lake, playground and some of the nicest landscaping to be found in Istanbul; take bus Nos.25E or 40 to get here.

Park Orman (parkorman.com.tr) is a lovely woodland area in Maslak, north of the city, with sports facilities for families and kids, including

Miniaturk. *See p190.*

a swimming pool, picnic areas, playground and fast-food outlets. It also hosts organised parties and activities for children.

Although there's no museum devoted especially to kids, several make special provision. The **Archaeology Museum** (*see p112*) has a small area set aside for children, with displays at youngsters' eye level. The **Military Museum** (*see p113*) has tanks and soldiers' uniforms. Another good one is the **Fire Engine Museum** (Itfaiye Caddesi, Fatih, 0212 635 7174) located next to the Aqueduct of Valens (*see p89*), which displays old fire-engine tools, uniforms, and relics from historic fires. Best of the lot is the **Rahmi M Koç Industrial Museum** (*see p115*), which has a heaps of interactive displays and working models, and a submarine to clamber around.

Bosphorus Zoo

Boğaziçi Hayvanat Bahçesi
Tuzla Caddesi 15, Bayramoğlu, Izmit (0262 653 8315). **Open** *May-Oct* 8.30am-8pm daily. *Nov-Apr* 8.30am-5pm daily. **Admission** $7; free under-6s. **Credit** MC, V.
Located way out in Darıca, 45km (30 miles) from the city centre, but worth the trip for its wide range of exotic birds and animals, gardens and playground.

Dance Akademik

Dans Akademik
Tepecik Yolu, Cevher Sokak 6, Etiler (0212 257 0154/www.dansakademik.com). **Open** 10am-8pm Mon-Fri; 10am-2pm Sat. **Credit** MC, V.
Among all the styles of dance on offer here, ballet and jazz classes are available for children. Course prices start at $70 (not including VAT).

Enka Sports Centre

Sadi Gülçelik Spor Sitesi, Istinye (0212 276 5084). **Open** 7am-10pm daily. **Credit** MC, V.
Facilities for swimming, tennis, basketball, football, volleyball and athletics, with regular classes for children. Day passes for fitness cost $21; the pool (you should be accompanied by a member) will set you back $7 on weekdays, $17 on weekends.

In the Kitchen with the Kids

Çocuğumla Mutfaktayız
Tepecik Yolu 28/2, Etiler (0212 358 1825/ www.furla.com.tr). **Open** 9am-6pm Mon-Fri; weekend hrs vary according to course times. **Credit** AmEx, MC, V.
Organises cooking courses for parents and their children. The courses take four weeks, with two to three-hour sessions once a week, and cost $150.

Miniaturk

Imrahor Caddesi, Sütlüce (0212 222 2882/ www.miniaturk.com). **Open** 10am-6pm daily. **Admission** $3. **Credit** MC, V. **Map** p286.
An absolutely magical attraction, which recreates 76 of Turkey's most famous sights in miniature. The models range from a palm-sized Leander's Tower to

a Sultanahmet Mosque the size of a small car and an Atatürk airport complete with taxiing jumbos. The level of detail is incredible; adults will appreciate the chance to see the monuments from all sides. Card-operated speakers deliver commentary in English and Turkish. It's one of our favourite things in Istanbul. To get here (it's just past the Rahmi M Koç Museum; *see p116*) take the 47E or 54H bus.

Play Barn

Kirazlıbağ Sokak 4, Yeniköy (0212 299 4803). **Open** 10am-6pm daily. **Admission** $13/hr; $180 for 30hrs. **Credit** DC, MC, V.
This indoor playground comes with three different rooms – all supervised – and a great outdoor playground, featuring mazes and tube slides. There's a baby crèche, plus a couple of child-friendly cafés.

Science Centre

Deneme Bilim Merkezi
Taşkışla Caddesi, ITU Mimarlık Fakültesi, Taşkışla, Taksim (0212 292 0892/www.bilimmerkezi.org.tr). **Open** 9am-6pm daily. **Admission** $3; $10 family.
Hidden in the gardens of the beautiful Istanbul Technical University building (opposite the Hyatt Regency), this gem of an attraction is dedicated to making science entertaining for children. Weigh yourself on the moon, measure your IQ by playing puzzles, inspect a cricket's stomach or experience a simulated earthquake. The centre also holds regular exhibitions and weekend workshops for kids.

Tatilya

Beylikdüzü Mevkii, Avcılar (0212 852 0505). **Open** *Nov-Apr* 10am-6pm Tue-Fri; 11am-10pm Sat, Sun. *May-Oct* noon-10pm Tue-Fri; 11am-10pm Sat, Sun. **Admission** $4; $15 for all-inclusive package. **Credit** AmEx, MC, V.
A large, covered entertainment complex with fairground rides, restaurants and shops. It also has a small theatre with hourly shows at weekends.

Restaurants

Although most Istanbul restaurants welcome children, few offer amenities such as highchairs or children's menus. If asked, many places will serve children's portions and cook special requests. In fact, having a child often ensures that you receive better service.

Hippopotamus

Park Plaza 22, Eski Büyükdere Caddesi, Maslak (0212 345 0830). **Open** noon-midnight daily. **Children's menu** $8. **Credit** AmEx, MC, V.
This well-known French chain features a set children's menu (including starter, main, dessert and drink). Kids get crayons with their meals.

Mezzaluna

Abdi İpekçi Caddesi 38/1, Nişantaşı (0212 231 3142). **Open** noon-3pm; 7pm-midnight Mon-Fri; noon-midnight Sat; 1-10pm Sun. **Main courses** $7-$17. **Credit** AmEx, DC, MC, V.

In the swim at the **Çırağan Palace Hotel Kempinski**. *See p237.*

This famous Italian chain has a very child-friendly policy, which is why it's always crammed with kids. There's food to please all ages, staff are down-to-earth and the atmosphere's casual. It's noisy, but kids love it. The restaurant also offers highchairs.

Secret Garden

Kalender Üstü, Atadan Sokak, Yeniköy (0212 299 0077). **Open** 10am-1am daily. **Main courses** $5-$10. **Credit** MC, V.

In summer, tables are laid out in this big hilly garden overlooking the Bosphorus. There's a play area for kids with swings, slides and a big lawn. The restaurant also serves decent food: pancakes and sausages, barbecued meatballs and lamb chops.

TGI Fridays

Nişpetiye Caddesi 19, Etiler (0212 257 7078). **Open** 11am-1.30am daily. **Main courses** $7-$20. **Credit** AmEx, MC, V.

A child-friendly place that serves up burgers, hot dogs and fancy ice-cream desserts. It also has a dedicated kids' menu.

Practicalities

Shopping

Kids' clothing and toy stores are at all the large shopping centres (*see p173* **Mall contents**). For young readers, **Remzi Kitapevi** (*see p162*) has a good variety of English-language books for kids. Pharmacists (*eczane*) are found in most neighbourhoods; most carry a range of healthcare products for children. Almost all supermarkets sell a good selection of Milupa baby food and Turkish brands like Ülker. Nappies and wipes can be found at most grocery stores, including **Migros** and **Makro**. For information on supermarkets, *see p180*.

Gelar

Nişpetiye Caddesi, Petrol Sitesi 1. Blok 4, Levent (0212 351 9515). Metro 1 Levent. **Open** 9am-6pm Mon-Fri. **Credit** MC, V.

Imported educational tools, wooden toys and playground equipment of excellent quality. Prices are high but the range is unique in Turkey.

Toys 'R' Us

Migros Building Ground Floor, Büyükdere Caddesi, Maslak (0212 286 0016/www.toyrus.com). **Open** 10am-10pm daily. **Credit** AmEx, DC, MC, V.

The ubiquitous chain has made it to Istanbul, and carries the largest selection of toys in the city. It also has kids' clothing, shoes, baby food and nappies.

Malls

Akmerkez

Nişpetiye Caddesi, Etiler (0212 282 0170). Metro Levent. **Open** 10am-10pm daily.

Shops that sell kids' clothes include Benetton, Chicco and Oilily. There are a few bookshops, several fast-food outlets and Kiddieland, a play area with rides.

Carousel

Halit Ziya Uşaklıgil Caddesi 1, Bakırköy (0212 570 8131). **Open** 10am-10pm daily.

Carousel has clothing stores (Benetton, Chicco), a well-stocked MotherCare and a Toys 'R' Us. There's also a huge kiddies' roundabout in the atrium.

Babysitting

Deluxe hotels provide babysitting services for guests. Smaller hotels will usually make every effort to find someone. Beyond that, you could try **Anglo Nannies London** (0212 287 6898/www.anglonannies.com), which provides live-in nannies from England.

Film

Buoyed by international acclaim and discriminating domestic audiences, Turkish cinema is back on track.

Like much else in Turkey, homegrown contemporary cinema is a miracle. Consider a fragmented sector with no infrastructure to speak of, scant and arbitrary state funding that lands only in well-greased palms, a private sector that runs from investment, continual economic angst, wrangles with the censors, theatrical distributors who sold out to Hollywood long ago, audiences that are shamefully unpatriotic towards local film fare and there you have it: film-making is insanity. But *mashallah* for the insane. Not only do film-makers carry on undaunted but the stuff they produce is also improving in quality, as well as in quantity. Compared with a low-point in the mid 1990s, when only a dozen local films were being made annually at most, there are currently a good 30 or more projects in various stages of production.

As the world over, Turkish cinema divides roughly into commercial and art-house. For commercial, read comedy, which leans heavily on a celeb cast from the world of TV, pop and catwalks. Sometimes it works, sometimes it doesn't. Most recently, Mustafa Altıklar's star-studded *Şimdi Askerde* (*In the Army Now*) did. A sentimental and comic ode to military service, it beat *Matrix Reloaded* at the box office by an easy margin. Not so Erdal Murat Aktaş's *Mumya Firarda* (*Runaway Mummy*), an action-packed romp between Istanbul and Egypt starring rock idol Teoman. The result was spectacularly awful and, despite immense hype, was suitably rewarded when mass audiences gave it a wide berth.

Taking a cue from a recent Hollywood trend, Turkish commercial cinema has also been boosting successful television series up to the big screen. The prime example of this was Osman Sınav's *Deli Yürek* (*Wildheart: Boomerang*), in which an ex-model hunk single-handedly takes on the police, Mafia and Kurdish separatists in south-east Turkey. Leaving aside its objectionably feel-good nationalist stance, this was a slick production that achieved technical standards as yet unseen in Turkey. *Boomerang* also generated

solid admissions, not just in Turkey but also in Germany, where it even managed to scoop a box-office award.

For all its success at home, commercial cinema generally loses something in the translation. Bar the hungry, homesick *gastarbeiter* audiences in Germany, it doesn't travel. This is less true of lower-budget art-house productions, which have sparked growing interest in Turkish cinema abroad. This year, Nuri Bilge Ceylan walked away from Cannes with the Grand Prix and Best Actor award for his latest film, *Uzak* (*Distant*), a simple but subtle reflection on the human condition, reinforced by beautifully bleak photography. In August 2003, *Çamur* (*Mud*), the latest feature by Turkish Cypriot Derviş Zaim, competed in the Contracorrente at Venice where it scooped the UNESCO award. Before this was Yeşim Ustaoğlu's festival hit, *Güneşe Yolculuk* (*Journey to the Sun*), the story of a young guy from the provinces arrested and brutalised in Istanbul because he looks like a Kurd. Sure to ignite more political dynamite, Ustaoğlu's forthcoming feature on the Armenian issue, *Bulutları Beklerken* (*Waiting for Clouds*), is much anticipated overseas but not necessarily in Turkey where the contentious subject-matter necessitates a seriously low profile. At the end of the day, if you want to catch films like this, you're better off at international festivals than in Istanbul.

Cinemas

Istanbul's movie-goers are well served with close to 200 screens, an annual world-class festival and several smaller-scale international film events. Between them they offer a balanced and substantial cinematic diet, ranging from Hollywood blockbuster junk food to a global bean-feast plus plenty of local flavouring. US product predominates but a good handful of theatres specialise in independent movies and Turkish film. There's also a string of cultural institutes that screen regular retrospectives.

All films, except animations and major blockbusters, are shown in the original language with Turkish subtitles. There is talk in the market of dubbing the lot, but for now it's just rumour. Despite the present Islamic

> ▶ For other **films with an Istanbul** connection *see pp275-6.*

Arts & Entertainment

government, censorship is not an issue for foreign films. Gaspar Noe's *Irreversible* was a box-office sensation, shown intact in its full penetrative horror, but it will be interesting to see how Atom Egoyan's *Ararat* fares – it's been snapped up by a bold independent distributor but release is still pending. The censors, however, are not so easy on local product. Most recently Handan Ipekçi's *Hejar* (Kurdish orphan girl meets retired patriotic judge) was banned on the grounds of its title, the Kurdish name of the central character.

Movie-going is not as cheap as it once was now that the lira has strengthened. Tickets cost around $4-$6, except up in Etiler, where everything is more expensive. Most cinemas do a 'People's Day' once or twice a week, usually Monday and/or Wednesday, when all ticket prices are reduced. Matinee screenings generally come cheaper and students/OAPs usually qualify for a discount at all times with proof of identity.

Phone and online reservations are accepted at some cinemas, and an increasing number now take credit cards. Seating is assigned and ushers generally expect a tip; the going rate is about $0.25. Screenings have an intermission so that everyone can nip out for a quick fag.

For cinema listings pick up the *Turkish Daily News*. The monthly *Time Out Istanbul* also says what's on where; however, it doesn't include any screening times.

Sultanahmet

Şafak
Darüşşafaka Sitesi Pasajı, Yeniçeriler Caddesi, Çemberlitaş (0212 516 2660). Tram Çemberlitaş. **Tickets** $6. **Credit** MC, V. **Map** p288 L10.
Get past the grim entrance (the makeover's coming soon), through the cheap clothing arcade and down the stairs to a granite-floored, seven-screen multiplex as expansive as it is spotless. Likewise the WCs. All screens come with Dolby Digital and offer a good choice of current US releases, European and local cinema. This is Sultanahmet's only cinema and couldn't be better positioned, right by a tram stop.

Beyoğlu

AFM Fitaş
Fitaş Pasajı, Istiklal Caddesi 24-6 (0212 292 1111/ www.afm.com.tr). **Tickets** $6; $5 Wed. **Credit** MC, V. **Map** p295 O2.
A sleek US-style multiplex at the back of an arcade selling CDs and books, just down from Taksim Square. The 11 screens offer a fair mix of Hollywood hits, independents and Turkish films and none of the ushers take tips. New to the complex is the IF Festival (*see p196*) in January and an August film

event recycling faves from the last season. Above the arcade is the North Shield pub (*see p149*), plus 35mm, a decent, cinematically themed café.

Alkazar
Istiklal Caddesi 179 (0212 293 2466). **Tickets** $6; Wed $4.50. **No credit cards. Map** p294 N3.
Situated behind an impossibly narrow facade, the Alkazar was a porn theatre until its 1994 restoration. Now it is a wholly respectable establishment, and the only bare breasts belong to the art nouveau caryatids in the foyer. Once a die-hard independent, the cash-conscious owner recently sold out to Hollywood, although at least one of the three screens will be showing art-house fare. While here, check out the soaring interior of the ground-floor café.

Uzak. *See p192.*

This sure ain't Kansas, Toto

With all the kudos heaped on recent fare like *Distant*, Turkish cinema now has international art-house respectability. But how little does the average movie-goer abroad know of Turkey's gloriously sleazy cinematic past?

During the 1960s the stock-in-trade of Istanbul studios was fantasy, violence and sex, all catering to a huge rural hinterland audience eager for cosmopolitan thrills. Inspired by American serials like *Zorro* and the *Lone Ranger*, jobbing directors turned out literally thousands of trashy entertainments full of masked heroes, inflatable monsters, cardboard killer robots and juicy go-go dancing babes.

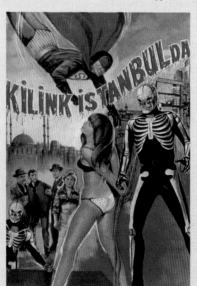

Faced with the threat of television in the '70s, the ante was upped to include lashings of sex and sadism – floggings, decapitations, nude horseback riding, floggings and Satanic nuns. Made for the cost of a kebab, these are films that make Ed Wood look like Tarkovsky.

Pin-up man for all this mondo macabre was karate-chopping Cüneyt Arkın. A cross between Alain Delon and Jackie Chan, Arkın performed all his own stunts, severing his hand on one occasion while riding a horse through a plate-glass window. He picked it up and rode to hospital (so he claims).

When the home market became threatened by output from Hollywood in the late '70s, Turkish directors reacted by playing the Americans at their own game; they made their own versions of *Star Trek*, *Superman*, *The Exorcist* and *The Wizard of Oz*. The latter went by the title of *Ayşecik ve Sihirli Cüceler Rüyalar Ulkesinde* – Ayşecik and the Magic Dwarves In Dreamland – and whisked Dorothy over the rainbow into a world of oriental surrealism peopled by an effeminate scarecrow and a cowardly lion with a particularly hairy groin. But unequalled for cut-rate, ripped-off weirdness is *Dünyayı Kurtaran Adam* (The Man Who Saved The World) aka the Turkish *Star Wars*. It stars the inimitable Arkın who bounds around the movie with two great rocks tied to his legs. Mixed in with grainy pirated footage from the original are blue robots with ambulance lights, knights in flowing red capes and mummies. 'Luke' tears the heads off his opponents, all of which look like fluorescent orange versions of *Sesame Street*'s Cookie Monster. True to the source, in the end the baddies are vanquished and our golden boy glides back to his Turcophone galaxy. As the Turks would say, 'Yok yok' – it has everything.

Atlas

Atlas Pasajı, Istiklal Caddesi 209 (0212 252 8576). **Tickets** $6; $4.50 Mon, Wed. **No credit cards**. **Map** p294 N3.

A recently refurbished cinema with a quaint 1940s-meets-21st-century foyer above a muddled arcade selling anything from costume jewellery, antiques and second-hand clothes to kitsch accessories. The largest of the three screens boasts the city's most steeply raked auditorium. The programming gets bums on seats with a mix of all sorts.

Beyoğlu

Halep Pasajı, Istiklal Caddesi 140 (0212 251 3240/ www.beyoglusinemasi.com.tr). **Tickets** $6; $4.50 Wed. **No credit cards**. **Map** p294 N3.

Directly across from the Atlas Pasajı, the Beyoğlu boasts the authentic feel of an art-house cinema. Programming focuses on European and Turkish independents, with the odd Hollywood hit to boost box-office takings. From July to September it runs a daily programme of local film critics' picks of the past year, but this soon slides into pretty much anything from the past decade. Just across the rambling foyer/café is the small-screen Pera, run by the same people with a similar screening philosophy.

Emek
Yeşilçam Sokak 5, off Istiklal Caddesi (0212 293 8439). **Tickets** $6; $4.50 Mon, Wed. **No credit cards. Map** p294 N3.
During Turkish cinema's golden age, Yeşilçam Sokak was Turkey's answer to Hollywood, or at least Pinewood (no coincidence, perhaps, that yeşilçam translates as 'pine tree'). No more. The Emek remains as a relic of former glories, one of Istanbul's oldest working cinemas, built in the 1920s with an impressive 875-seat hall beneath an ornate ceiling – sadly disfigured since a recent lino/strip-light renovation. Still, if a film is worth watching, try to catch it here.

Sinepop
Yeşilçam Sokak 22, off Istiklal Caddesi (0212 251 1176/www.ozenfilm.com.tr). **Tickets** $6; $4.50 Mon, Wed. **Credit** MC, V. **Map** p294 N3.
Hard to imagine that this sleek new theatre was used as a club by the Germans during World War I, before being converted into a cinema by the French. Owned by the same people as Sultanahmet's Şafak, with similar squeaky-clean decor, it was carved into two in 2002 in the hope of upping box-office takings. Happily, this has also brought variety to a programme that was previously almost exclusively Hollywood pap.

Yeşilçam
Imam Adnan Sokak 10, off Istiklal Caddesi (0212 293 6800). **Tickets** $3.60. **No credit cards. Map** p295 O2.
A small basement art-house cinema run by one of Turkey's new-generation directors. The programming leans towards Turkish films, old and new, including features and documentaries from international festivals, plus the odd world classic. The small foyer is nostalgia itself, crammed with old projection machines and fading posters.

Etiler & Levent

AFM Akmerkez
Akmerkez Mall, Nispetiye Caddesi (0212 282 0505/ www.afm.com.tr). *Metro Levent.* **Tickets** $7.40; $9 after 6pm. **Credit** MC, V.
This anonymous four-screen multiplex is housed in Istanbul's largest mall (*see p173*), which is just fine for shoppers but a hassle for others: it's a bit of a trek out the city centre. It's run by the AFM people, so it shares the same kind of billing as Beyoğlu's Fitaş, as well as the summer rerun programme in August. While the sound and screen quality are good, you pay for it in the ticket price.

Levent Kültür Merkezi Sinema
Çalıkuşu Sokak 2, Levent (0212 325 4331). *Metro Levent.* **Tickets** $4.40. **Credit** MC, V.

About the only out-and-out art-house venue in town is owned by TÜRSAK (the Turkish Foundation of Cinema and Audiovisual Culture). It shows exclusively independent films and runs themed weeks (comedy, Cuban cinema, films from Iran etc) on a regular basis. There's a roomy café, with seats spilling outside in summer. To get here, take the metro and it's just a short walk from the station.

Ortaköy

Feriye
Çırağan Caddesi 124 (0212 236 2864/ www.feriye.com). *Bus 22, 25E, 40.* **Tickets** $5.80; $4.40 Mon, Thur. **Credit** MC, V.
A dressage ground for Feriye police station in a previous life, the cinema's now part of a smart cultural complex on lawns beside the Bosphorus. There's one big screen and two cinematheques, plus the Living Room Café, which is a really pleasant place for hanging out before or after shows. The programming includes some independent content along with the usual Hollywood hits. It's only a short walk from the bars and cafés of waterfront Ortaköy.

Asian Shore

Rexx
Sakız Gülü Sokak 20-22, off Bahariye Caddesi, Kadıköy (0216 336 0112/www.rexx-online.com). **Tickets** $5.80; $4.40 Wed. **No credit cards. Map** p297 W8.
The Rexx may still claim to have Turkey's biggest screen, but it's been overtaken by a multiplex in Adana. The main screen and two smaller ones all dish up standard Hollywood fare, leavened with some European product. This is also a venue for the International Istanbul Film Festival.

Süreyya
Bahariye Caddesi 29, Kadıköy (0216 336 0682/ www.sureyya.com). **Tickets** $5.80; $4.40 Mon, Wed. **Credit** MC, V. **Map** p297 X8.
Built in the mid 1920s on the site of the former Apollon Theatre, this is Istanbul's oldest surviving cinema. What distinguishes it from other veteran theatres is the care taken to preserve its original features including frescoes and wall paintings. Sad then, that the films shown on its twin screens are lowest common-denominator Hollywood fare.

Other venues

Bilgi Cinema Centre
Bilgi'de Sinema
İnönü Caddesi 28, Kuştepe, Şişli (0212 216 2315/ www.bilgi.edu.tr/sinema). **Tickets** $3. **No credit cards.**
A cine club run by Bilgi University but open to all, with an eclectic programme of retrospectives, classics, historical oddities, world cinema – a real grabbag but with plenty of interest. All films have

Arts & Entertainment

English subtitles, except local product. Get here by taxi or take the free minibus that departs one hour before screenings from in front of the university building off Taksim Square. As it's university-run, the programme halts for summer.

Festivals

IF AFM Independent Film Festival

IF AFM Bağımsız Filmler Festivali
AFM Fitaş, Fitaş Pasajı, Istiklal Caddesi 24-6 (0212 292 1111/www.ifistanbul.com). **Date** mid Jan.
Launched in 2002, this well-organised, massively popular event marked a new departure for AFM, its cinema-chain organisers, who till then were steeped in Hollywood and nothing but. It's a move-with-the-times festival: segments in the past have included digital and political cinema, heavy sex/violence and gay/lesbian. Book tickets in advance if possible, either online or at the AFM Fitaş cinema, where screenings are held.

International Istanbul Film Festival

Uluslararası Istanbul Film Festivali
Various venues (0212 334 0723/ www.istfest.org). **Date** April. **Tickets** venues, Biletix. **Admission** $4-$6.
A highlight of the Turkish cultural calendar, the festival brings a buzz to Beyoğlu, cramming a good 150 films from around the world, plus the latest Turkish product, into a hectic two-week programme. Themed segments run alongside the international and national competitions and include tributes to big directors, documentaries, animation, literary adaptations and rising stars of world cinema. Parallel events can be quite classy (there are often orchestral accompaniments to film classics staged at some exceptional venue). Festival time is also a chance to stargaze, with an international contingent of heavy-hitting directors and actors attending most years. To secure tickets make pre-paid reservations as soon as the programme is announced. By the time the festival begins most movies have already sold out.

International 1001 Documentary Film Festival

Uluslararası 1001 Belgesel Film Festivali
Various venues (0212 327 4145/www.bsb-adf.org). **Date** early March.
A one-week fiesta run by the Association of Documentary Film Makers (BSB), which is now in its seventh year. Refreshingly, the festival is bound to no particular theme (the '1001' in its title refers to the multiplicity of themes covered). Last year 80 films were shown from 25 countries. Screenings are mostly in Beyoğlu, with one alternative venue in Kadıköy on the Asian Shore. Admission is free.

International Cinema-History Film Festival

Uluslararası Sinema ve Tarih Buluşması Film Festivali
Various venues (0212 244 5251). **Date** mid Dec.

AFM Fitaş: home-grown fare and Hollywood hits. *See p193.*

This is a serious festival with a serious guest list – Costa Gavras turned up last year with his latest film *Amen*. It's a showcase for some 100 features and documentaries from around the world, usually with a political or human rights dimension. Venues are generally in Beyoğlu plus TÜRSAK's cinema in Levent. Admission costs are nominal.

Istanbul International Short Film Days

Istanbul Uluslararası Kısa Film Günleri
Various venues (0212 292 4201/www.kisafilm.com). **Date** early April.
A long-running event organised by the Istanbul Amateurs of Photography and Cinema Association (IFSAK) and a good chance to binge on otherwise elusive shorts. The week-long festival has two Beyoğlu venues and programmes four screening sessions a day, all free. Billing includes a mix of fiction, experimental and animation from all over the world. All films come with English subtitles.

Galleries

Istanbul might be as pretty as a picture, but its art scene has never made an impression – until now.

Istanbul has never been a name on the international art map, but that's more to do with history than with any lack of raw talent.

Although as early as the 15th century Sultan Mehmet II commissioned a portrait from the Italian artist Gentile Bellini (*see p17*), painting was never really an Ottoman thing. It remained a minor court art, subsidiary to more decorative pursuits such as calligraphy, ceramics, metal, woodwork and textiles, which are favoured by Islam – the faith has traditionally tended to consider representations of human or animal forms idolatrous.

It wasn't until the latter part of the 19th century that the *paşas* (nobles) first took any notice of what had been going on in Europe

since the Renaissance and pursued their new-found interests in art with studies abroad.

A lot of catching up has been done since then and, despite fits and starts over the last few decades, the scene is currently enjoying sustained growth. It has been buoyed by a slew of private collectors who grew rich on the proceeds of government privatisation policies in the mid-1980s.

In a society showy by nature, many wealthy Istanbulus now consider a piece of suitably expensive art a required acquisition to go with the Merc, the Rolex and the Cartier. Visiting the annual **Istanbul Arts Fair** (*see p188*) is a real eye-opener, with vacuous Sunday-school works going for inflated sums of money.

Borusan Culture & Art Centre. See p199.

That's not to say there isn't any fine work around. There is. Just to browse in a handful of the 100-plus galleries around town is to see the diversity of the local scene and understand how aware Turkish artists are of what's going on elsewhere. A recent stroll along Istiklal Caddesi could have taken in a group show at the Garanti Centre involving a small raised dance-floor with a pair of untenanted headphones suspended above hissing music; a huge wall plaque composed of names carved in relief at the Borusan; and a video work of nomadic-shamanistic dances performed by giddy Anatolians in modern dress at the Vakif Bank gallery. Like we said, diverse.

Increasing numbers of Turkish artists are spending time living, studying and working abroad, where some succeed in making names for themselves. Before he died, **Erol Akyavaş** established a following in the United States for his colourful abstracts incorporating 'Ottoman' elements such as tents and calligraphy. In Paris, **Ömer Kaleşi** has achieved notice for his oversize figures, which seem to have a direct link to a Byzantine heritage of icon painting, while in New York **Serdar Arat** has done for air vents, wash-basins and toilets what Francis Bacon did for the human form. In an encouraging sign of the times, after 40 years in America, where his abstract paintings and photography of graffiti and urban decay from cities around the world have been displayed in the MoMA and the Guggenheim, **Burhan Doğançay** has recently returned to the Balkan Big Apple to open a gallery (see p199).

Coverage of exhibitions has also increased in the daily newspapers in recent years and art is no longer an item reserved for Sunday supplements and specialist magazines. Galleries have also been quick to see the benefits of the internet in a city increasingly web-savvy.

WHERE THE ART'S AT

Most of the leading, upmarket commercial galleries are in the moneyed shopping districts of **Maçka**, **Teşvikiye** and **Nişantaşı**, north of Taksim Square. Also, south of the square, on **Istiklal Caddesi** are a good many elegant modern galleries financed by banks or corporate offices: following government privatisation policies in the 1980s, businessmen became the new patrons of the arts, just as Ottoman pashas had been a century earlier. You can see the artistic fruits of their wealth in institutions such as the Garanti Bank and the Yapı Kredi, which stage regular retrospectives of Turkish artists, living and dead.

Less slick and possibly more exciting is what's going on in the small neighbourhood of **Asmalımescit**, just off Istiklal Caddesi in

Beyoğlu. Since the late 1990s the area has been developing into a bustling quarter of artists' studios, galleries and cafés, particularly along Sofyalı Sokak.

In addition to the galleries listed below, the **Istanbul Büyük Şehir Sanat Galerisi**, just north of Taksim on Cumhuriyet Caddesi, is one of several city-council-run exhibition spaces (known as 'Belediye Sanat Galerisi'), funded by the local authorities. Artists and members of the public apply for exhibition slots and shows range from the downright appalling to the… well, admission is free anyway.

Also of note is the biggest event in the Istanbul art calendar, the **International Istanbul Biennale** (see p187), which attracts leading international artists every second autumn, alongside the Turkish contingent. As a barometer of where the art scene is at, the private viewing that precedes the public opening has become a major society event.

Note that most galleries close during July and August.

Beyoğlu

Aksanat Arts Centre

Istiklal Caddesi 16-18, Beyoğlu (0212 252 3500/ www.akbank.com.tr/sanat). **Open** 9.30am-7.30pm Tue-Sat. **No credit cards**. **Map** p295 O2.

This recently renovated gallery is situated in the Aksanat Culture Centre run by Akbank and located at the top end of Istiklal Caddesi close to Taksim Square. The bank, which possesses a large art collection and annually takes a stand at the Istanbul Arts Fair, also has other galleries around Istanbul, but this is the main show space. Past exhibitors have included big Turkish names such as Adnan Çoker, Utku Varlık, Tanju Demirci and the enchanting figurative painter Turan Erol.

Atatürk Cultural Centre

Atatürk Kültür Merkezi
Taksim Square (0212 251 5600 ext 287/325). **Open** 10am-6pm Tue-Sat. **Admission** free. **Map** p293 P2.

This imposing building on Taksim Square is notorious for its 1970s brutalist architecture (which was actually lauded in Western architectural journals of the time) but the offerings inside are more aesthetically pleasing. The centre's large, airy exhibition space regularly hosts prestigious exhibitions, both of local artists and high-profile work from abroad.

Asmalımescit Art Gallery

Asmalçmescit Sanat Galerisi
Sofyalı Sokak 5, Tünel (0212 249 6979/ www.asmalimescit.com). **Open** 10am-8pm daily. **No credit cards**. **Map** p294 M4.

Sometimes art makes far more sense after a few stiff drinks, and this stylish indie gallery has a fab bar at street level. After a couple of liveners, climb the

Yapı Kredi Kazım Tashkent Art Gallery.
See p200.

Arts & Entertainment

winding staircase to the gallery above. Here, owner Ugur Bekdemir has amassed a sizeable collection of canvases, from shimmering pointillist landscapes to abstract expressionist works. Artists represented include Chicago-based Marianne Angersbach and German abstractionist Herbert Enz Enzer.

Borusan Culture & Art Centre

Borusan Kültür ve Sanat Merkezi
Istiklal Caddesi 421 (0212 292 0655). **Open**
10.30am-7pm Tue-Sat. **Admission** free.
Map p294 M4.
A prime example of the alliance between the art world and corporate world, this gallery is sponsored by the largest car manufacturer in Turkey. Expect to see the country's brightest young stars working in a wide range of media, with an emphasis on conceptual art. Recent times have also seen a pretty impressive line-up of international talent hung here too, including Beuys, Man Ray and Warhol.

Burhan Doğançay Gallery & Photo Archive

Cnr of Balo Sokak & Tarlabaşı Bulvarı (0212 247 7770). **Open** by appointment only. **Map** p294 N2.
Doğançay is arguably Turkey's best-known living artist, with work hanging in the Guggenheim and MoMA. His signature project is something called 'Walls of the World', a collection of more than 20,000 photographs taken in 104 countries of walls and doors complete with graffiti, torn posters and other markers of urban decay; some of those images are exhibited here. However, at press time, the artist was still searching for a sponsor and the gallery wasn't officially open to the public, so call to make an appointment before setting out.

> ▶ For art museums and permanent collections, *see pp111-116* **Museums**.

Galeri Apel

Hayriye Caddesi 7, off Yeniçarşı Caddesi,
Galatasaray (0212 292 7236). **Open** 11.30am-6pm
Tue-Sat. **No credit cards. Map** p294 N3.
Generally regarded as one of the most innovative
galleries in Istanbul, Apel hosts exhibitions in a
variety of media. You won't find clichéd colonial pas-
tiches in this space: expect weird and wonderful
works from Turkey's avant-garde, not to mention
surreal paintings by international artists. It's on the
street immediately behind the Galtasaray Lycée.

Karşi Sanat

Elhamra Han, Istiklal Caddesi 258 (0212 245 1508).
Open 11am-7.30pm Mon-Sat. **No credit cards.**
A well-hidden location adds to the exclusive air of
this rather chichi gallery, which specialises in
achingly avant-garde work. Recent shows have
included works by London-based Turkish artist
Kutlug Ataman, who does film and video work on
the marginalised – transsexuals, prostitutes and
political prisoners – and cutting-edge paintworks by
Austrian Michael Hedwig. To find the gallery go up
to the third floor of the Elhamra Han and press the
bell by the door on the left of the landing.

Platform Garanti
Contemporary Art Center

Istiklal Caddesi 276 (0212 293 2361). **Open** 1-8pm
Tue-Thur; 1-10pm Fri, Sat. **Map** p294 M4.
It's neither a showcase for dealers nor a stiflingly
chic venue for art snobs, but be prepared for lots of
intellectual conceptual art, both domestic and
international, with an emphasis on technology and
interactive exhibits. Past exhibitions have included
surreal Turkish photography, weird video art and
baffling, politically themed performance art.

Timurlenk Glass

Sofyalı Sokak 2, Tünel (0212 249 1727). **Open**
8.30am-7.30pm Mon-Sat. **Credit** AmEx, DC, MC, V.
Map p294 M4.
A shop-cum-gallery that specialises in beautiful oils
and watercolours of Istanbul, covering the last
century of Turkish painting. Unlike conventional
galleries, there's no pretentious owner talking up the
price of the art, which means you may come away
with a bargain. Paintings cost in the range of $100
to $1,000 – a fraction of what you might pay for sim-
ilar works in a traditional gallery.

Yapı Kredi Kazım Tashkent
Art Gallery

Yapı Kredi Kazım Taşkent Sanat Galerisi
Istiklal Caddesi 285, Galatasaray (0212 252 4700).
Open 10am-7pm Mon-Fri; 10am-6pm Sat; 1-6pm
Sun. **No credit cards. Map** p294 M4.
This spacious gallery is situated on the first floor of
the Yapı Kredi Bank (just south of the Galatasaray
Lycée). It specialises in retrospectives of important
Turkish artists, living or dead, with styles encom-
passing figurative, abstract and installation art and
exhibitions on Anatolian culture.

As well as high-end shops and upscale
restaurants, these neighbouring districts to the
north of Taksim are home to some of the city's
most cutting-edge commercial galleries. Artists
represented here flit between Istanbul, Paris,
Berlin and New York. Besides those reviewed
below, other worthwhile galleries include
Maçka Sanat (Eytam Caddesi 31/A, Maçka,
0212 240 8023), **Gallery Nev** (Maçka Caddesi
33, Maçka, 0212 231 3733), **Proje4L** (Harmancı
Sokak, Harmancı Giz Plaza, Levent, 0212 281
5150) and the **Teşvikiye Art Gallery** (Abdi
Ipekçi Caddesi 48/3, Teşvikiye, 0212 241 0458).

Tem Art Gallery

Prof Dr Orhan Ersek Sokak 44/2, off Valikonağı
Caddesi, Nişantaşı (0212 247 0899/
www.temartgallery.com). **Open** 11am-7pm Mon-Sat.
Credit MC, V.
Around since the mid-1980s, this is the city's leading
gallery for contemporary figurative art. Owner Besi
Cecan's policy is to exhibit work of quality, regardless of commercial considerations. Her spacious
gallery covers four floors; two for exhibitions, two
for storage. The lower floor is reserved primarily for
sculpture – if Salih Coşkun's wonderful wooden
angels are still there, go and see them. Other Tem
artists include Paris-based painter Ömer Kaleşi,
Kemal Önsoy and Abidin Dino.

Urart Art Gallery

Abdi Ipekçi Caddesi 18/1, Nişantaşi (0212 241
2183). **Open** 9am-7pm Mon-Sat. **Credit** AmEx,
DC, MC, V.
Located above the sumptuous jewellers of the same
name (*see p176*), this art gallery features a collection
of abstract and figurative works incorporating
Hittite, Mesopotamian, Hellenistic and Byzantine
influences. A popular spot with young Turkish
artists and intellectuals.

Gallery Baraz

Kurtuluş Caddesi 191, Kurtuluş (0212 225 4702/
www.galeribaraz.com). **Open** 9am-7pm
Mon-Sat. **Credit** AmEx, DC, MC, V.
More than any other figure, owner Yaşi Baraz is the
dealer responsible for putting Istanbul on the international art map – he's considered the Turkish Leo
Castelli. When he opened his gallery in 1975, the
market for Turkish art was poor: he started off by
selling works for $100. His intrepid spirit yielded
results: he now represents some 80 artists, including Güngör Taner, Adem Genç and Adnan Çoker.
At the moment, there aren't too many exhibitions
held here – Baraz expends most of his energy organising big shows for the Atatürk Cultural Centre –
but there's a permanent display of works from his
stable of artists.

Gay & Lesbian

A history of Ottoman buggery, a transgender tradition and oodles of steamy hamam action.

Gay travellers tend to subscribe to one of two wildly contrasting visions of Istanbul. On the one hand are those who nurture a 19th-century fantasy of the city as some sort of Oriental den of vice and decadence. They're drawn to Turkey by the prospect of mustachioed men in flowing garb lolling about on cushions awaiting the arrival of some lily-skinned visitor to sweep him up and into a vapour-fogged bathhouse for a little steamy interracial exchange.

And it's true that hand-in-sweaty-hand with all that puff-chested machismo, the traditional notion that only the passive partner is homo persists. As a result, many 'straight' Turks are willing to indulge the fantasies of the modern-day Victorian sex voyager.

In stark contrast, the other viewpoint fixates on the country's 'oppressive' Islamic character, its much-maligned human rights record and a location beyond the borders of even Eastern Europe, somewhere in the wastelands where the hard-won fruits of Western civilisation wither and die. They arrive in Istanbul ready to rail at injustices and braced for the self-improvement that comes from wilful exposure to down-trodden alien (sub) cultures. Certainly gay visitors had their eyes rudely opened in 2000: in September of that year, in an incident widely covered by the international press, security officials in the Aegean city of Kuşadası halted buses headed from a cruise liner to Ephesus when they realised the passengers were all queers. All of the tourists were forced to go back to the ship. In fact, the incident was the work of one brain-storming individual. The next day the city's mayor went on board the ship to apologise and in Istanbul, the next port of call, the gay cruisers got the red-carpet deal with young girls in trad dress at the gangplank bearing baskets of complimentary sweets and fruit. But the damage was done.

So which is it? Mustachioed midnight delight or *Midnight Express*? Typically, the real story is somewhere in between. Unlike in many states, there are no laws specifically banning consensual adult sex of any gender combination. Turkey is a candidate for EU membership and Ankara is aware that its legal codes most conform to European cultural norms. As for Islam, Turkey's secular nature means that railing by religious figures on moral issues is muted. When it comes to gay culture, Turkey is neither permissive nor repressive and the long, slow march to full acceptance will be won the same way it will (eventually) be won in the West: a family member, a friend, a colleague, a neighbour at a time. In the meantime, agitation and momentum continue in the form of a gay presence at the annual 1 May parade, positive publicity for the G&L section of the International Istanbul Film Festival, a sprinkling of celebrities daring to speak out, access to international websites, the airing on Turkish cable of gay-themed series such as *Will & Grace*, not to mention the unstoppable determination of a swelling crowd of queers, dykes and trannies to meet, party, have sex and settle down, whether society likes it or not.

Advice & information

KAOS GL
kaosgl@geocities.com.
Although the mainstream Turkish press runs gay-related stories almost daily, and no weekly glossy or evening broadcast news is complete without a dose of same-sex titillation, KAOS GL is Turkey's first and only gay and lesbian magazine. It appears every two months and can be bought at the Mephisto Bookstore at Istiklal Caddesi 173, but it's in Turkish only.

LAMBDA Istanbul
PO Box ACL 222, Istanbul 80800 (0212 233 4966/ lambda@lambdaistanbul.org).
This umbrella group has links to international organisations, including the International Gay and Lesbian Association. LAMBDA is involved in a wide range of legal, social, cultural, health and political issues of concern to the gay community. As part of gay pride celebrations in 2003, the group organised Turkey's first gay issues press conference.

Websites

Begin at **www.geocities.com/GLBTsiteler**, a comprehensive portal in Turkish and English. Although littered with ads, the site has useful links to all things gay in Istanbul and Turkey. A one-man, amateurish labour of love, **www.istanbulgay.com** is a less-polished portal with travel information in Turkish and English, as well as numerous links to Turkish

Arts & Entertainment

gay organisations. The site master also peddles his services as a tour guide and provides links to erotic Turkish pay sites. Smooth 'n' slick, **www.absolutesultans.com** peddles Istanbul as a sophisticated and cultured gay travel destination and offers exclusive package deals. It also provides ungrudging free information via internet or phone. The oldest gay website, **www.eshcinsel.net**, has been in business since 1998. Reviews in Turkish of Madonna's latest album are unlikely to appeal to an international crowd, but visit the busy chat room to strike up pre-travel friendships.

Venues

Considering that it's only been about 14 years since Istanbul's first gay bar opened for business, the current scene is surprisingly diverse. No longer relegated to backstreets and basements, recently opened gay venues boast panoramic views, open-air carousing and central locations at the heart of Beyoğlu. While there's obviously enough pink liras out there to keep some 20 businesses afloat, most clubs and bars are virtually empty except on Wednesdays and at weekends. Don't bother turning up before midnight though, unless you're particularly enamoured of your own company.

Bars and clubs can be roughly separated into one of three categories: Western, as in the kind of places found in any European big city; à la Turca, offering a particularly Istanbul slant on the homo hostelry, and transgender. The scene hasn't yet evolved to cater to niche crowds, while lesbians are faced with the same nightlife choices gay men had 15 years ago: none.

For up-to-date info on current hotspots, openings and events see the Gay & Lesbian page in the monthly *Time Out Istanbul*.

Western

Not places in which chaps with chaps and cowboy hats hang out, by Western we mean the sort of bar where monied, liberated and largely moustache-free gay Turks tend to congregate. While still distinctly local in flavour, they're the kind of places that straights and women – lesbian or otherwise – will feel comfortable. After all, loud music, pretentious airs and sardine-like crowds are standard worldwide.

Academy 14

Meşrutiyet Caddesi 186, Tepebaşı, Beyoğlu (0212 245 7821). **Open** midnight-4am daily. **Admission** free Mon, Tue, Thur, Sun; $14 Wed, Fri, Sat. **Credit** MC, V. **Map** p294 M4.
How times have changed. Across the street from the genteel façade of the once-glorious Pera Palas hotel, a rainbow banner flags the entrance to Academy 14

– and marks the transformation of old Istanbul. This is the cutting edge of 'new Pera', replete with staff in white berets and muscleman aprons, pulsating Western pop, understated white décor and gay goings-on (think a Jean Paul Gaultier aftershave ad). The appeal also stretches to straight scensters – management have helpfully labelled the toilet doors 'gay' and 'hetro'.

Bar Bahçe

1st floor, Soğancı Sokak 7, off Sıraselviler Caddesi, Cihangir (0212 245 1718). **Open** 9pm-2am daily. **Admission** free Mon-Thur; $7 Fri, Sat. **Credit** MC, V. **Map** p295 O3.
Morphing through a variety of incarnations in its decade-long history, BB now boasts a 'chill-out' room illuminated by an enormous aquarium and a tiny darkroom where risqué activity is limited to scrutiny of the tiny black-and-white penises lining the walls. Gorgeous staff, do-your-own-thing attitude, house tunes and a makeshift dance floor draw a mixed crowd of neighbourhood locals and eager young clubbers of both sexes.

Douche Club

Sepetçiler Kasrı, Kennedy Caddesi 3, Sarayburnu, Eminönü (0212 511 6386). **Open** 1am-5am Wed, Fri, Sat. **Admission** $7. **No credit cards.** **Map** p289 O8.
That's the French for 'shower', not a reference to unsavoury fetishes. Traditionally this has been the open-air, summer-only sibling to the winter bolthole of Douche Pera in Beyoglu. However, as of autumn 2003 the DC becomes an all-year venue. It's a fantastic place right on the edge of the Golden Horn below the former grounds of Topkapı Palace. It regularly plays host to the sort of high-energy debauchery last seen during the Tulip Age.

G-Launch

Soho Teras, Beyoğlu İş Merkezi bldg, Istiklal Caddesi 361-5, Beyoğlu (0212 245 0152). **Open** 10pm-2am daily. **Credit** MC, V. **Map** p294 N4.
The surest sign yet that Istanbul is nearly ready for mixed bars is that the creators of Soho Teras (*see p151*) have thoughtfully created a 'gay corner'. Push your way through the beaded curtains to the relative calm and company of kindred spirits sipping cocktails high above Beyoğlu. Then ask yourself why the straights not only have a better view but seem to be having a better time.

Love Point

Cumhuriyet Caddesi 349/1, Harbiye (0212 296 3357). **Open** midnight-4am Wed, Fri, Sat. **Admission** free Wed; $7 Fri; $10 Sat. **Map** p293 P1.
At the stroke of 2am, patrons of Neo (*see p203*) decamp en masse to this, the only winter venue with a full-size dance floor. Encouragement is offered in the form of membership cards, half-price admission (for those transferring from Neo) and the prospect of some elbow room. The late hours and decent music also ensure that Love Point spreads its appeal to straight clubbers too.

The shadowy world of gay Istanbul at **Bar Bahçe**. See p202.

Neo

Lamartin Caddesi 40, Taksim (0212 254 4526).
Open 9pm-2am Tue-Sun. **Admission** free Tue-
Thur, Sun; $7 Fri, Sat. **Credit** MC, V. **Map** p293 O1.
In contrast to the downtown feel of Bar Bahçe (*see
p202*) and other newer venues, long-established Neo
appeals to a largely suburban crowd of young professionals with its high-profile security, hi-energy
tunes, a backroom dance space and relentlessly
cheerful colour scheme. Slick does not necessarily
translate into fun, though: the clientele are too self-
conscious and snooty to really loosen up – at least,
not until they've downed a few drinks and moved
on to Love Point (*see p202*).

Privé

Tarlabaşı Bulvarı 28A, Taksim (0212 235 7999).
Open 11.30pm-4am daily. **Admission** free Mon-
Thur, Sun; $7 Fri, Sat. **Credit** MC, V. **Map** p293 O2.
An after-hours club that mixes the slightly sordid
with the upscale. Minor celebrities and socialites
come here to slum in safety; wet-behind-the-ears hus-
tlers help them to do it. Middle-class queers out for
a late-night drink and last-minute pick-up provide
cover as merchandise is appraised and service fees
agreed upon.

A la Turca

Dingy decor, trashy Turkish pop and downmarket, dog-end crowds – à la Turca bars offer
a full frontal of working-class gay Turks in a
setting unlike anything back home. To put it
bluntly, if you like a bit of rough, drag your
party pants over in this direction. Be warned
though, such places are minefields for anyone
not sufficiently attuned to the local social
dynamics. That tall dark number cruising you
from his dim corner could well be more of a
homophobe than the most redneck straight.
Our list includes only the safer venues but, even
so, brace yourself for the unexpected.

Club 99

*Meşrutiyet Caddesi 81A, Galatasaray (0212 251
4830).* **Open** 11pm-4am daily. **Admission** free
Mon-Thur, Sun; $5 Fri, Sat. **No credit cards**. **Map**
p292 M4.
A note to prospective Istanbul bar owners: forget the
decor (which here is gloomy) and the sound system
(here, vintage), because cheap beer and a more-the-
merrier door policy are sufficient to lure the dregs

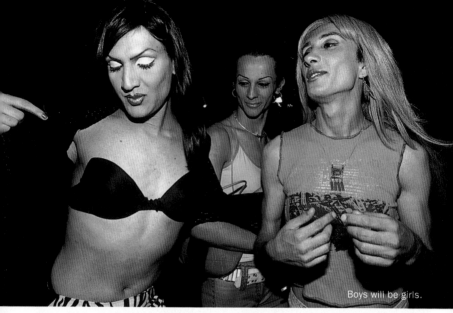
Boys will be girls.

of the nightclub scene and their admirers into your dank basement. For foreign visitors, CC offers a picaresque walk on the wild side but go with friends – the bigger the better.

Değirmen
Guraba Hüseyinağa Mahallesi Şekerci Sokak 20, Aksaray (0212 524 6662). Tram Aksaray. **Open** noon-2am daily. **Admission** free. **Credit** MC, V.
Ever wondered where that rugged taxi driver who winked at you hangs out? Değirmen appeals to mostly married but swinging men who wouldn't be caught dead in a gay venue. Here, far away from the spotlight of Beyoğlu, they nurse beers, exchange furtive glances, twirl their moustaches and swing their prayer beads in time to the overwrought performances of a male chanteuse at whom they fling golden oldie requests scrawled on paper napkins. It's a place for a good ol' gay night out among cologne-doused roustabouts who believe women are for babies but men are for fun.

Déjà Vu
Sadri Alışık Sokak 26/1, Beyoğlu (0212 252 6131). **Open** 10pm-4am daily. **Admission** $3 Mon-Thur, Sun; $5 Fri, Sat. **Map** p295 O3.
The largest and most unintimidating of the à la Turca venues is inconspicuously tucked into a side street across from a gay health club-cum-bordello (and, handily for uniform queens, it's just around the corner from the local police station). Most of the ground floor is taken up by a dance floor filled with 18-year-olds who look as though they've pilfered their mothers' purses for the admission money. Head downstairs for the 'chat room' and relief from the thumping Eurotrash music.

Queen
Zambak Sokak 23/A, Beyoğlu (0212 249 2397). **Open** 11pm-4am daily. **Admission** free. **Credit** MC, V. **Map** p295 O2.
Don't let the name fool you: not all queens are fabulous. Pokey and drab, this one only perks up after 2am thanks to the influx of the downwardly mobile shanty boys looking for a cheaper late-night alternative to Privé or Love Point (*see p202*). Escape the cramped floor space by fighting for a perch on the narrow platform that runs the length of one wall – but, beware, the price paid for the extra elbow room is that you become part of the entertainment.

Tek Yön
Meşrutiyet Caddesi 54/1, Galatsaray (0212 249 7036). **Open** 11pm-4am daily. **Admission** free. **No credit cards. Map** p294 M3.
A refuge for those who don't fit the usual gay stereotype, Tek Yön's the place for whiskers and big bellies. Descend to a rank cellar stifling with testosterone and stale air, whipped up each weekend into an odorous maelstrom of whirling arms and flashing armpits as a cave-load of bears stomps around to Turkish pop. It may not be pretty but as Istanbul gay bars go, this is as diverse as it gets.

Transgender

There are an estimated 3,000 transsexuals in Istanbul, nearly all of whom survive through prostitution. It's a tradition that dates back to Ottoman times when, off on campaigns, the reigning sultan would take along a large contingent of pretty boys for his own personal

Arts & Entertainment

'use'. These days the carousing grounds are the backstreets of Taksim where the 'girls' flock in the safety of numbers, Big boobed, long legged, barely clad in brief bits of anything glam and trashy, they're considered flashy upstarts by the gay community, so tranny admirers are drawn from the ranks of the straight. The bars and clubs they frequent make for a twisted take on the pick-up scene. Go take a look if you dare but don't come crying to us afterwards.

Hengame

Sahne Sokak 6/1, Balık Pazarı, Beyoğlu (0212 249 1178). **Open** midnight-4am daily. **Admission** free Mon-Thur, Sun; $5 Fri, Sat. **No credit cards.** **Map** p294 N3.

Most nights here are like Cinderella's ball well after midnight but everyone's too drunk to notice that the girls have sprouted stubble and the champagne's actually cheap sparkling wine. Football players and minor celebrities are among the Prince Charmings who regularly climb the marble staircase to Hengame's three divinely decadent rooms to there cavort among the ugly sisters.

Sahra

Sadri Alışık Sokak 42/A, off Istiklal Caddesi, Beyoğlu (0212 244 3306). **Open** 10pm-4am daily. **Admission** $2. **No credit cards.** **Map** p295 O3.

Chamber of horrors or fun house? Sahra is three floors of get-it-here trannies basking in the tongue-lolling attention of young greasers, drooling hicks and aged toughs. Meanwhile, the gay boys dance, preen and lock eyes with each other, studiedly ignoring the riot of superheated hetero pheromones threatening to send the place into meltdown. Behind the bar are a mournful middle-aged mom and pop who can only be there to serve out some sort of penance for a past transgression.

Restaurants & cafés

Mor

Lemartin Caddesi 11/4, Taksim (0212 237 4326). **Open** 9am-2am daily. **Credit** MC, V. **Map** p293 01.

Mor has decided to hedge its bets by not billing itself as an exclusively gay restaurant. Come midnight though, a stylish space serving Mediterranean cuisine is suddenly transformed into a club complete with house music and same-sex dancing. Note that it really only gets going on weekends.

Sugar Café

Sakasalim Çıkmazı, off Istiklal Caddesi, Galatasaray, Beyoğlu (0212 244 1275). **Open** 11am-midnight daily. **No credit cards.** **Map** p294 N3.

A reasonably priced menu, smart décor and a handy location just off Istiklal Caddesi: all reason enough to visit. But for the gay traveller, the Sugar Café also provides a rare glimpse of a rainbow flag displayed behind the service bar, plus the chance to socialise with a gay crowd without having to wait until the post-midnight bar scene gets going.

Hamams & saunas

None of Istanbul's hamams and saunas are officially gay but the ones listed below cater almost exclusively to men unabashedly seeking a bit more than a good exfoliation. Hamam owners and staff are usually straight and tolerance of sexual activity is neither consistent nor wholehearted. Pointing out that a couple in the next room were moments ago having sex won't necessarily save you from rapid ejection if you're spotted doing the same. Money, however, is the greatest of lubricants and even straight attendants may well try to inflate their tip by a little groped inflation of yours.

Ağa Hamam

Turnacıbaşı Sokak 66, Çukurcuma, Beyoğlu (0212 249 5027). **Open** *men* 5pm-9am daily; *women* 9am-5pm daily. **Admission** $7; $10 with massage. **No credit cards.** **Map** p295 O3.

A beautifully restored historical hamam. at which management do their best to prevent any unseemly behaviour but when your business is located at the bottom of a street of tranny bars and the place is full of drunken men clad in skimpy wraps, all congregated in a steamy communal space in the early hours of the morning, well, what can you expect?

Çeşme Hamam

Yeni Çeşme Sokak 9, off Perşembe Pazarı Caddesi, Karaköy (0212 252 3441). **Open** 8am-8pm daily. **Admission** $5. **No credit cards.** **Map** p 292 L6.

A makeover of a few years back did little to improve the forbidding appearance of this hard-to-find hamam, hidden among backstreet hardware stores. Staff are apathetic enough to take a relaxed approach to the sight of great tubby things flirting and more in the dungeon-like steam room.

Çukurcuma Hamam

Çukurcuma Caddesi 57, Beyoğlu (no phone). **Open** 9am-9pm daily. **Admission** $14; $28 with massage. **No credit cards.** **Map** p292 N4.

So gay that the main hot room often goes unheated: it just provides a stage for amorous males to parade in skimpy towels. The sauna functions as a back room. The place must be listed in gay travel guides because half the clientele are non-Turks. A lounge and exercise equipment are all part of the package. This is also the only hamam with a bar.

Yeşildirek Hamam

Tersane Caddesi 74, Azapkapı (0212 297 7223). **Open** 5am-midnight daily. **Admission** $7; $10 with massage. **No credit cards.** **Map** p292 L5.

A neighbourhood hamam across from the Azapkapı Mosque at the base of the Atatürk Bridge. It remains as shabby as ever, despite a valiant attempt at a spruce-up in 2002. Whether the lack of lighting in the large new sauna is simply an oversight or a canny management decision, either way it's highly encouraging to furtive fumbling.

Arts & Entertainment

Hamams

Soak in some history and take a good pounding – bath night will never be the same again.

Taking a long, slow steam bath, laid flat out on a marble slab beneath a star-studded dome, is one of Istanbul's hedonistic highlights. As British novelist Maggie O'Farrell put it when she visited the city in 2003: 'If heaven exists, I hope it's a hamam.' And where else might you go to pay a burly, near-naked stranger to scrape, knead and pummel your quivering flesh until you feel that you've just gone 12 rounds with Mike Tyson? Having gone through that ordeal, you emerge feeling so clean it borders on the virginal.

Which is as it should be. Hamams were intended to purify. Part of Islamic tradition is that its followers adhered to a strict set of rules for ablutions, washing hands, arms, face and feet with running water before praying. This wasn't necessarily carried out in a hamam, but the link between mosque and hamam was always close and the precincts of all major mosques incorporated a public bathhouse.

In the earliest times, the hamam was for men only but the privilege was later extended to women. No mixing, of course: either the hamam would have two sections, one for each sex, or it would admit men and women at separate times of day. This is still the case. In male-dominated Ottoman times, women particularly valued their visits as a rare freedom: far more than just somewhere to get clean, the hamam was a rare opportunity to be away from the home unchaperoned. Hamams were the favoured places for arranging marriages, somewhere a mother could get a good eyeful of any prospective daughter-in-law. When the wedding came along, the equivalent of an Ottoman stag or hen night was spent getting steamed, lathered, hennaed and depilated. For a husband to deny his wife access to the hamam was grounds for divorce.

Newborn babies would be taken out of the family home for the first time 40 days after birth for a visit to a hamam, an event that also marked the end of housebound confinement for the mother. And after a lifetime of hamam-going came to its inevitable end, a person's body would be carried in one last time to be washed before being laid out at the mosque. This tradition has expired and these days there's no chance that you might have to share your bath with a corpse.

In fact, hamam-going itself has long been on the verge of extinction, ever since the advent of affordable internal plumbing. Whereas 80 years ago there were more than 2,500 bathhouses in Istanbul, now there are reckoned to be only about a hundred. Many of these struggle to survive. The few that flourish do so largely by courting the tourist dollar – hence some exorbitant admission prices.

BARE ESSENTIALS

For the uninitiated, entering a hamam for the first time can be a daunting experience. Lengthy menus offer such treats as massage, depilation and pedicures (also soap and shampoo, though you may prefer to bring your own – and don't forget a hairbrush or comb). Outside tourist-frequented hamams such as **Çemberlitaş**, **Cağaloğlu** and **Galatasaray**, this will all be in Turkish. What it all boils down to is whether you just want to enter and look after yourself, or whether you want the services of a masseur (who'll also give you a good soaping and scrub).

Once you've paid, you enter the *camekan*, a kind of reception area. Some of these are splendid affairs with several storeys of wooden cubicles, like boxes at an opera house, and a gurgling central fountain. This is where you get changed. You will be given a colourful checked cloth, known as a *peştemal*, to be tied around the waist for modesty. Keep this on at all times – it's bad form to flash. Women are less concerned and often ditch the peştemal in the steam room, though many keep on their knickers. Both sexes also get *takunya*, wooden clogs that can be absolutely lethal on wet marble floors.

A door from the camekan leads through to the *soğukluk*, which is for cooling off and has showers and toilets; another gives into the *hararet*, or steam room. These can be plain or ornate, but are nearly always covered in marble and feature a great dome inset with star-shaped coloured glass admitting a soft, diffuse light. Billowing clouds of steam fog the air.

There are no pools, as Muslims traditionally considered still water to be unclean. Instead, the hararet is dominated by a great marble slab known as the *göbektaşı* or 'navel stone'. Here, customers lie and sizzle like eggs on a skillet.

Çemberlitaş Hamam – setting for centuries of naked indolence. *See p208*.

The massage is delivered on the navel stone. It starts with a rubdown with a *kese*, a cloth usually made of camel hair, which feels like a Brillo pad. After a soaping and a rinse comes the rough stuff. Joints are manipulated in directions that you never thought they could move. Resist the urge to fight back, and relax.

Afterwards, retire to one of the small semi-private rooms off the main chamber, in which you'll find water-filled basins and scoops for sluicing yourself down. There's no limit on the amount of time you can spend inside. When you're done you'll be given a towel and you return to the *camekan*, where soft drinks, tea and coffee are served. Some *camekans* have benches or beds for anyone who's too shagged out to move. Drink lots of water to rehydrate.

The hamams

Anyone interested in the unique architecture of the hamams but who doesn't fancy the heat can visit a few old places that have been restored and converted to other uses. Chief of these are the **Baths of Roxelana** (Haseki Hürrem Hamamı) on Sultanahmet Square across from the Haghia Sophia. Built in the mid 16th century by Sinan and named in honour of the wife of Süleyman the Magnificent, the building is now a state-owned exhibition centre and carpet sales space.

Be warned that, due to a lack of custom and investment, there are a lot of hamams that are badly run-down, not to mention outright filthy. For instance, the highly-visible **Park Hamam**

Peddling bathhouse history at the **Cağaloğlu Hamam**.

Arts & Entertainment

in Sultanahmet, which is just off the main tourist drag Divan Yolu, is somewhere that should be avoided. We recommend sticking to the places reviewed below.

For gay-friendly hamams *see p205*.

Büyük Hamam

Potinciler Sokak 22, Kasımpaşa, Beyoğlu. (men 0212 238 9800/women 0212 256 9835). **Open** *men* 5.30am-10.30pm daily; *women* 8.30am-6pm. **Admission** $5; $7 with massage. **No credit cards. Map** p292 L3.

It's a little out of the way, perhaps a ten-minute walk from central Beyoğlu, but if you want to experience a no-frills locals' hamam, this is it. The name means 'the big bathhouse' and they're not kidding – this is Istanbul's largest. The *hararet* is so huge that it includes no fewer than 60 wash stations, compared to the usual dozen or so. Despite the scale, it's an attractive place with lots of gorgeous detailing courtesy of the architect Sinan (who is also responsible for the mosque next door). In recent years a decent-sized open-air swimming pool has been added to the men's section. To get here, cross six-lane Tarlabaşı Bulvarı beside the Pera Palas hotel and head west along Tepebaşı Caddesi, keeping an eye out for the minaret of the Kasımpaşa Mosque.

Cağaloğlu Hamam

Prof Kazım Ismail Gürkan Caddesi 34, Cağaloğlu, Sultanahmet (0212 522 2424/www.cagaloglu hamami.com.tr). Tram Gülhane or Sultanahmet. **Open** *men* 7am-10pm daily; *women* 8am-8pm daily. **Admission** $10; $20 with massage. **No credit cards. Map** p289 M9.

More or less unchanged since it was built on the orders of Sultan Mahmut I in 1741 (to provide maintenance funds for the Haghia Sophia), Cağaloğlu – pronounced 'jaah-lo-loo' – is the most famous of the city's hamams. It's beloved of TV producers, who consider it an essential backdrop for flogging soap products and shooting videos: Eurovision Song Contest winner Sertab Erener shot her video here. The camekan is a two-storey affair with a baroque central fountain, while the vast *hararet* seems to have drawn its inspiration from the grand domed chamber of an imperial mosque. Bathers past have supposedly included Franz Liszt, Florence Nightingale and Tony Curtis. Unfortunately, the place is starting to rest on its laurels: on a recent visit the steam room was so under-heated we shivered instead of sweating.

Çemberlitaş Hamam

Vezirhan Caddesi 8, Çemberlitaş. (0212 522 7974/ www.cemberlitashamami.com.tr). Tram Çemberlitaş. **Open** 6am-midnight daily. **Admission** $11; $18 with massage. **Credit** MC, V. **Map** p289 M10.

Possibly the best maintained, cleanest and most atmospheric of the city's hamams. These baths were built in 1584 by Sinan, commissioned by Nurbanu, wife of Sultan Selim the Sot, as a charitable foundation to raise money for the poor. They've been in continual use ever since. There are sections for both sexes, which were originally identical until part of the ladies' bit was torn down in the 19th century to accommodate some road widening. Women now have to change in a corridor-like space rather than a proper *camekan*, although the main *hararet* area

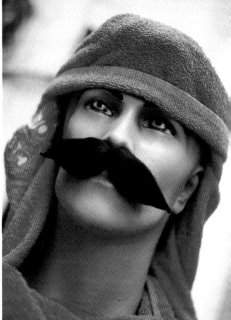

is lovely. Being so close to the heavily touristed Grand Bazaar area, the hamam sees a lot of foreigners and consequently the masseurs are shockingly perfunctory and more interested in hassling for tips. On the plus side, there's usually someone at reception who speaks English. If you have never experienced a hamam before, then this is perhaps a good place to begin. Discounts are offered for ISIC card holders.

Galatasaray Hamam

Turnacıbaşı Sokak 24, Galatasaray, Beyoğlu (men 0212 252 4242/women 0212 249 4342). **Open** *men* 6am-10pm daily; *women* 8am-8pm daily. **Admission** $22; $27 with massage. **Credit** MC, V. **Map** p294 N3.

Built in 1481 during the reign of Sultan Beyazıt II, for almost 500 years this hamam was men-only. That finally changed in 1963 with the addition of a small women's section. Little else has been altered. The *camekan* here is particularly fine, decked out with furniture to make an antiquarian froth. There's also some beautiful tilework at the entrance to the men's steam room. Unlike other hamams, the Galatasaray has marble slabs in the *soğukluk* where bathers can have massages in semi-privacy. Because it's used largely by locals the steam room is kept hot, hot, hot – so much so that towels have to be laid on the *göbektaşı* before anyone can lie on it. Staff here are notorious for having their hands out for tips but at least the massage is good and you'll leave afterwards with a drunkard's stagger. To find the hamam, take the side-street off Istiklal Caddesi immediately north of the Galatasaray Lycée.

Gedikpaşa Hamam

Hamam Caddesi 65-7, off Gedikpaşa Caddesi, Beyazıt (0212 517 8956). Tram Beyazıt. **Open** *men* 5am-11pm daily; *women* 9am-11pm daily. **Admission** $11; $15 with massage. **No credit cards.** **Map** p288 L10.

One of Istanbul's oldest hamams, Gedikpaşa was built in 1457 by one of Mehmet the Conqueror's viziers, next door to the mosque that also bears his name. Although not in the same league architecturally as marble palaces such as the Çemberlitaş or Cağaloğlu, it has suffered little in the way of renovations, a big plus for the connoisseur. It's split into men's and women's sections, both of which are a little run-down but clean. The men's area also includes a small pool and sauna. Low prices mean it attracts a regular local clientele. The women's section occasionally closes early if business is slow.

Köşk Hamam

Alay Köşkü Caddesi 17, Cağaloğlu, Sultanahmet (0212 512 7397). Tram Gülhane. **Open** 8am-8pm daily. **Admission** $5; $11 with massage. **No credit cards.** **Map** p289 N9.

Just up the hill from Gülhane Park, the Köşk, which dates from the mid 15th century, is less grand than most other hamams because it was originally built as a private bath for the grand vizier. However, it is well looked after and has an extremely friendly staff. The clientele are predominantly foreigners, guests from nearby hotels. The Köşk is also worth noting because, although it's a men-only establishment, you can arrange for it to stay open after hours for families or parties, at a price to be negotiated.

Arts & Entertainment

Music: Pop, Rock, World & Jazz

Euro cheese and cut-rate cover bands predominate but there's plenty of interest on the fusionist fringe.

These are heady times for Turkish pop. It may have been sung by Holly Valance but 2002's massive European hit 'Kiss Kiss' originates with Turkish pop idol **Tarkan** (*see p212*). One year later and Turkey scores again with a surprise victory in the Eurovision Song Contest. Add to this a burgeoning domestic industry that churns out stars on demand to a population of 70 million, of whom a third are under 16 years of age, and you've got a pop scene that's big bucks and buoyant.

Strange then, that opportunities to catch Turkish pop performers live are so few. The rare gig from less synthetic pop stars occurs at **Babylon** (*see p211*), and **Sezen Aksu** (*see p212*) will occasionally take to the city's more expensive stages to promote new albums, but the rest of the pop firmament is oddly reticent when it comes to taking the stage. This might be about to change. Industry studies suggest that this part of the world gives the best returns for touring bands in terms of increased sales of product. Plenty of international acts have taken note and now schedule Istanbul into their European tours. Local audiences are developing a taste for gig-going that can only have a beneficial effect on the city's live music scene.

BEYOND THE COVERS

Meanwhile, in an alternate universe where the Eagles still soar and Pink Floyd never faltered, Turkish rock music is alive and well – if not particularly charismatic. Beer-swilling audiences all over central Istanbul may lap up live rock, metal, blues and punk, but too often it's a set of covers performed by a cut-rate local version of a Western band. Sometimes there's an interesting Turkish twist, although that's usually nothing more than mangled pronunciation. Still a top act after 30 years of soft-rocking together are **MFÖ** (featuring sometime David Bowie collaborator Erdal Kızılçay), but keep an eye out for attitudiness female rockers **Şebnem Ferah** and **Özlem Tekin**, veterans of numerous cover outfits but now doing their own thing, and newcomers **Duman**, a power trio with a penchant for catchy choruses. At the punkier end of things are **Rashit**, who sound like the Clash might have done if Joe Strummer had never left Ankara. Look out too for **Athena**, more cover-scene graduates who took a detour into ska and emerged with a refreshing – and very successful – crossover sound.

Fusion finds its home on Doublemoon, a label run by the Pozitif organisation, the good people behind key venue Babylon. Their current stable includes master percussionist **Burhan Öçal**, whose newly formed **Trakya All-Stars** are booting age-old tunes and instrumentation into the 21st century; Montreal-based **Mercan Dede** who electronically massages Sufi rhythms to trippy effect; and **Baba Zula**, madcap experimentalists who use traditional instruments to untraditional ends. **Laço Tayfa** are the equivalent of Motown's Funk Brothers, a group of session musicians who between them have starred on almost every local album of worth. Most recently they've enjoyed a fruitful collaboration with American acid jazzsters the **Brooklyn Funk Essentials**, which has resulted in a bunch of albums and regular gigs.

TICKETS AND INFORMATION

The best way to find out what's going on is incredibly simple: just walk down Istiklal Caddesi and scan the flyposters. The monthly *Time Out Istanbul* carries listings and previews, as does the fortnightly *Zip* (free in bars and cafés round Beyoğlu, but it's in Turkish). On the internet, try individual promoters' websites:

www.pozitif-ist.com
www.istfest.org
www.kodmuzik.com,
www.istanbulpro.com
www.hippro.com

Information on concerts can also be obtained from the online ticket sales organisation **Biletix** (*see p183*). For in-person sales points, you can try music shops such as **Ad** and **Decoded** (for both, *see p179*).

Rockin', funkin', jazzin', dancin',
it all goes on at **Babylon**.

Rock & world music

A few notable exceptions aside, visitors may
be taken aback by the cramped conditions and
poor ventilation of Istanbul's venues, which
are significantly less spacious than their
Western European counterparts. Due to the
disproportionate number of males frequenting
the venues, men may have trouble entering if
not accompanied by women, although
foreigners usually get the nod – one of the few
perks of being an outsider. Another benefit:
you'll find that most places include a drink
in the price of admission.

Beyoğlu

Babylon

*Şehbender Sokak 3, Asmalımescit (0212 292 7368/
www.babylon-ist.com).* **Open** *Mid Sept-mid July*
9.30pm-2am Tue-Thur; 10pm-3am Fri, Sat. Closed
mid July-mid Sept. **Admission** $10-$15. **Credit** MC,
V. **Map** p294 M4.
Istanbul's runaway finest venue is a modestly sized
brick vault with mezzanine, situated in the backstreets near Tünel. Management revel in a laudable
you-name-it-we-book-it policy, mixing the established with the up-and-coming, and local acts with
imports. Past acts have included everything from

the Armenian Navy Band to the Fall, Stereolab and the Gotan Project. Annual refreshing of the sound system and decor (the building currently sports a green- and red-striped facade) ensures that things never get stale. Drop by to pick up a monthly programme or look out for them in the bars and cafés in and around Beyoğlu.

Dersaadet

Erol Dernek Sokak 11/A, Beyoğlu (0212 244 8037/ www.dersaadet.net). **Open** 10.30am-2am daily. **Admission** free. **Credit** MC, V. **Map** p294 N3.
One block south of Istiklal Caddesi in a narrow street lined with tea houses and booze holes, Erol is a haven for politically dissenting drinkers. Most weekend evenings the management lays on protest music and other acoustic flavours, amplified to volumes that are louder than necessary. Despite the racket, by the time everybody's on their third or fourth Efes it all gets a bit cosy and emotional.

Hayal Kahvesi

Büyükparmakkapı Sokak 19, off Istiklal Caddesi (0212 243 6823/www.hayalkahvesi.com). **Open** noon-2am daily. **Admission** free Mon-Thur, Sun; $9 Fri; $7 Sat. **No credit cards. Map** p295 O3.
Pre-Hayal, the Istanbul bar scene consisted of lots of old men slamming dominoes. The Hayal was just about the first bar to specifically cater to youth. Its stripped-back, bare-brick walls, live music and cheap-beer formula was revolutionary; for months, queues of eager scenesters jammed the narrow street outside wanting in. Now the area is filled with copycats but Hayal remains the original and one of the best. It continues to attract good musicians, albeit with typically little more to offer than a conservative repertoire of MOR classics. Soul Stuff on Saturday nights are the current big draw. The music kicks off at 11pm.

Kemancı

Sıraselviler Caddesi 69/1, Taksim (0212 251 2723/ www.kemancirockbar.com). **Open** 9pm-4am daily. **Admission** $4 Mon-Thur, Sun; $9-$11 Fri, Sat. **No credit cards. Map** p295 O3.
A long-standing favourite with the alt rock, goth and metal crowds who come here to commune with the spirits of the dead (Hendrix, Morrison) and those merely in a permanent stupor (Depeche Mode). It's three venues in one: the street-level floor is the most popular, with its cheap, odd-tasting beer and three-chord cover bands. On the two levels below things get darker, faster, louder, flowers wither, canaries keel over and anti-perspirant just don't work.

Mojo

Büyükparmakkapi Sokak 26, off Istiklal Caddesi (0212 243 2927/www.mojomusic.org). **Open** 10pm-4am daily. **Admission** $3.50 Mon-Thur, Sun; $7 Fri, Sat. **No credit cards. Map** p295 O3.
A basement space, decorated with huge posters of the rock 'n' roll pantheon, which hosts conservative trad rock groups performing the back catalogues of the Doobies, Supertramp, the Eagles and worse.

The unsung queen

Prior to 2003, the conjunction of the words 'Turkish' and 'pop' triggered no associations to a whole music-loving world west of Thrace. How lucky we were. But then came 'Every Way That I Can', the victorious Turkish entry in the Eurovision Song Contest, performed by belly-dancing, classically trained soprano **Sertab Erener**. Now Erener, who caused controversy in Turkey for singing her song in English, is recording an English-language album for release in Europe, and others are queuing up to follow. Should we be alarmed?

The Turkish pop scene, as seen on local MTV-knock-off Kral TV, is a bewildering mix of barely dressed Lolitas, mustachioed godfathers in shiny suits, techno-folk song dance productions and dewy-eyed toy boys.

Bright twinklings in the current star-filled firmament include **Candan Erçetin**, who recently blew a reputation for intelligent pop with an album of French cover versions; **Mustafa Sandal**, who plays his boyish good-looks and catchy choruses for far more than they're worth; and leather-clad, half-Essex girl **Nez**, whose gyrating shapely backside has earned her the tag the 'Turkish Shakira'.

But talent sometimes wins through. Prime example is **Tarkan**, perhaps

Better are the regular blues acts and also keep a look out for the excellently monikered Spitney Beers. The live music starts at midnight.

Riddim

Balo Sokak 14/1, off Istiklal Caddesi (0212 244 1183). **Open** 6pm-2am daily. **Admission** free. **No credit cards. Map** p294 N3.
Long-term Istanbul resident Osman Osman has been involved in the running of several Afro-Caribbean music bars around the city over the years. This, his latest venture, is another reggae joint, although the music strays into dub and jungle. Meanwhile, the old Riddim (Büyükparmakkapı Sokak 8/1, off Istiklal Caddesi, 0212 249 8333), to which Osman Osman has no connection save an ongoing lawsuit over the name, continues to keep its crowd of African immigrants and EFL teachers happy with cheap beer, R&B and world music.

Roxy

Arslan Yatağı Sokak 3, off Sıraselviler Caddesi, Taksim (0212 245 6539/www.roxy.com.tr). **Open** 9pm-3am Wed, Thur; 9pm-5am Fri, Sat. Closed July-Sept. **Admission** free Wed, Thur; $15 Fri, Sat. **Credit** MC, V. **Map** p295 O3.

# of Turkish song

Turkey's sole successful pop export to date. His song 'Simarik' was a huge chart success in Belgium, France and Germany, before topping the charts in the UK in the guise of 'Kiss Kiss', recorded by Australian starlet Holly Valance. He's the Turkish Ricky Martin, a preening Bollywood-style hunk whose brooding good looks and slangy come-ons were perfectly suited to the '90s attitude of 'Turks just wanna have fun'. He not only has a good voice and can pick a good tune, but is

blessed with an extraordinary vibrating belly that makes both the girls and the gay community swoon.

Tarkan had more help than just his fantastic abdomen, however. He also enjoyed the patronage of the grand diva of Turkish pop, **Sezen Aksu**. Before Sezen there was only long-haired 'Anatolian rock' (nationalist folky prog from the provinces) or glamour-pusses like Ajda Pekan crooning mid-Med ballads, although she shook it up a little with a hit cover of 'I Will Survive'. Sezen arrived in the late '70s as a sort of Turkish Carly Simon and she's ruled the roost ever since, the acknowledged 'Queen of Pop'. Not that Simon ever came up with anything quite like the suggestive come-on that is 'Is It All Yours?', written for Tarkan and his first mega-selling hit. Sezen also penned 'Simarik'/'Kiss Kiss' and she gave Eurovision winner Sertap Erener her first big stage break as a backing singer.

Now that belly-baring Erener may be about to go global, Tarkan has conquered with a Kiss and everyone from Britney Spears to Atomic Kitten seems to incorporate a bit of hip-swivelling into their choreographed dance numbers, it's somehow ironic that Sezen Aksu isn't better known abroad. Then again, she's only the mind and soul of Turkish pop and these days it's all about the body.

What used to be one of the city's major live venues is a little under-used these days. It tends to only host bands as part of festivals. Last year's scant handful of gigs included funk from DJ Logic and electronica from Four Tet. It does, though, regularly open its basement doors to host club nights (*see p226*) and theatre happenings. These are all well publicised in the monthly house bulletin *Gazette*, which is available around the cafés of Beyoğlu.

Shaman
Kazancı Yokuşu 49, off Sıraselviler Caddesi, Taksim (0212 249 9606/www.shamanwmc.com).
Open 9pm-5.30am Tue-Sat. Closed June-mid Sept.
Admission free Tue-Thur; $11 Fri, Sat.
Credit MC, V. **Map** p295 O3.
Tucked beneath the Dilson Hotel, Shaman bills itself as a 'world music club' but bugger the ethno beats because for many the main attraction of this place is the 6am closing time. After other clubs finish, a hard-core group of regulars finds their way down here to continue boozing and, maybe as an after-thought, indulge in a little grooving to the live sounds banged out by the resident African, Cuban and Eastern European acts.

Yaga
Sıraselviler Caddesi 67/1, Taksim (0212 292 2829/ www.yagabar.com). **Open** 1pm-3am daily.
Admission free Mon, Tue, Thur, Sun; $16 Wed; $7 Fri, Sat. **Credit** MC, V. **Map** p295 O3.
One of Beyoğlu's original rock bars, now located in a large basement on the same street as Kemancı (*see p212*), Yaga attracts lots of balding, beardy old stars ('60s folk rocker Cem Karaca currently plays each Wednesday) as well as cover bands. A rocking atmosphere and good service make it one of the better live venues: the place is always packed.

Asian Shore

Buddha
Kadife Sokak 14/1, Kadıköy (0216 349 7022).
Open 9pm-2am daily. **Admission** free Mon, Thur, Sun; $3.50 Fri, Sat. **No credit cards. Map** p297 W8.
A popular student hangout on two floors, supplemented with a pleasant garden in the summer. It gets busy early with crowds turning up for passable Britpop (check out Suitcase) and standard rock cover bands. The beer's cheap, the atmosphere relaxed.

Arts & Entertainment

Stripped-down sounds at **Hayal Kahvesi**. *See p212.*

anyone over from Beyoğlu but it is one of the few late-night options on this side of the water. But be warned: the last dolmuş back to Taksim leaves the bus station at about 2am.

Sondurock

Kırtasiyeci Sokak 32, Kadıköy (0216 414 7508). **Open** 6pm-4am daily. **Admission** free Mon-Thur, Sun; $3.50 Fri, Sat. **No credit cards. Map** p297 W7.
Not exactly a mould breaker, Kadıköy's latest rock bar (which has already undergone a name change: it opened as Karate) is very much in the traditional Kemancı/Mojo line. What sets it apart is that those places are all in Beyoğlu whereas this one is located on the Asian Shore. It draws from the same roster of cover bands but instead of Asianistas being forced to travel for the music, now the music comes to them. Late hours add to the appeal – this is one of the few places that keeps going after the bars of Kadife Sokak have closed.

Jazz

The fortunes of jazz in Istanbul have been rising and falling like harmolodic scales. That it should have flourished at all among the myriad musical genres of Istanbul is quite remarkable. Much of the credit must go to the International Jazz Festival (*see p185*) and the Akbank Jazz Festival (*see p188*), both of which assemble a mixture of largely famous and hugely talented performers. So while Tünel's venerable **Gramofon** (*Tünel Square 3*) seems on the verge of expiring, the city now has new arrival **Nardis** to take up the slack.

Traditionally the lack of any sort of scene has meant that Istanbul's jazzmen have first found recognition abroad: **Maffy Falay** (discovered by Dizzy Gillespie), percussionist **Okay Temiz** and guitarist **Önder Focan** all relocated to Scandinavia; percussionist **Burhan Öçal** moved to Switzerland, drummer **Selahattin Can Kozlu** went off to Africa and tenor saxophonist **Ilhan Erşahin** emigrated to New York where he has a bar, a record label and high-profile friends like Norah Jones.

Now many are returning, encouraged, perhaps, by the fresh group of musicians making a name for themselves here in Istanbul. Names to look out for are pianists **Kerem Görsev** and **Aydın Esen** – the latter has worked with the likes of Pat Metheny – and trumpeter **Imer Demirer**. Of the old school, Öçal now records for Pozitif's Doublemoon label, Erşahin makes regular visits to support his frequent and excellent releases (also on Doublemoon) in between running his Nu-Blu jazz café in New York, while Temiz has moved back and runs a 'Rhythm School' in Galata where he teaches percussion (for more info visit www.okaytemiz.com).

Shaft

Osmancık Sokak 13, off Serasker Caddesi, Kadıköy (0216 349 9956/www.shaftclub.com). **Open** noon-4am Mon-Thur, Sun; 2pm-4am Fri, Sat. **Admission** free Mon-Thur, Sun; $3-$5 Fri, Sat. **Credit** MC, V. **Map** p297 W7.
The Asian Shore's longest-established live music venue, Shaft offers a varied programme of rock, blues and jazz featuring original artists, cover bands and an open stage on Mondays. As with Sondurock (*see below*), there's really not very much to attract

Jazz Café

Hasnun Galip Sokak 20, off Büyükparmakkapi Sokak, Beyoğlu (0212 245 0516). **Open** 8pm-4am Mon-Sat. Closed July-mid Sept. **Credit** MC, V. **Map** p297 O3.

A dimly lit and comfortable little venue spread out over two floors. Downstairs is a standard bar; upstairs is where the musicians perform to generally respectful silence. Jazz is obliged to share stage space with occasional blues and even pop but, even then, commendably this is one of the few Istanbul venues at which bands offer more than just endless cover versions. Veteran guitarist Bülent Ortaçgil is one of the regular performers.

KV

Tünel Geçidi 10, off Tunel Square, Beyoğlu. (0212 251 4338) **Open** 8am-2am daily. **Admission** free. **Credit** MC, V. **Map** p297 M4.

This pleasant café, situated in a beautiful old building in a passage off Tünel Square, is most notable for its plentiful shrubbery (*see p148*) but it also hosts jazz each evening in the winter, including visits from former Mingus sideman and Istanbul resident, tenor player Ricky Ford.

Nardis Jazz Club

Galata Kulesi Sokak 14, Galata (0212 244 6327/ www.nardisjazz.com). **Open** 7pm-1.30am Mon-Sat. **Admission** $7 for live music. **Credit** MC, V. **Map** p292 M5.

A real blessing, Nardis is a dedicated jazz venue, just a few steps down the hill from the Galata Tower. It's small and sparsely decorated – bare boards, bare brick walls – but it benefits from an intimate atmosphere and its patrons certainly know their jazz. The place is run by guitarist and regular performer Önder Focan and his wife, who together also edit *Jazz* magazine. Food is served and reservations are necessary for tables near the stage. The music usually kicks off around 9.30-10pm.

Q Jazz Club

Çırağan Palace Kempinski Hotel, Çırağan Caddesi 84, Beşiktaş (0212 236 121/www.infoqjazzclub.com). **Open** 24hrs daily. **Admission** $20 for live music. **Credit** AmEx, MC, V. **Map** p287.

Insanely expensive, but then this is the Çırağan Palace, Istanbul's most out-of-this-world hotel. And consider the stunning list of past performers: Natalie Cole, Ray Charles, and sometime hotel-guest Whitney Houston, who has apparently performed an impromptu set on more than one occasion. Most of the time the programme is respectable singer-based jazz. Residents include Keisa Brown, Ilham Gencer and Ferhat Göçer, all classy acts, performing in the cellar bar during winter and in the garden in the summer. The cover charge varies depending on who's in town, so call first to check.

Suzan

1. Caddesi 90, opposite the ferry docks, Arnavutköy (0212 257 0469). **Open** 6pm-2am Mon-Sat. **Admission** $7. **No credit cards.**

With an appealing location along the Bosphorus shore, Suzan is the latest addition to the city's limited jazz scene. Ayşe Gencer and her trio play each night in a tiny space on the first floor of this Balkan-flavoured restaurant and *meyhane*; guests drop in when the mood takes. The club only just opened – this place has the potential to become a real hotspot.

Festivals

Istanbul's biggest promoter, Ahmet San, put the city on the musical map for major tours, staging stadium shows from the likes of the Rolling Stones, Michael Jackson and Madonna. These days promoters seem to prefer festivals, which are proliferating bunny-style year on year. A festival may be anything from a line-up of three acts on one night (**Efes Pilsen Blues Festival**; *see p188*), a three-day marathon with camping and dodgy loos (**H2000**; *see p185*) or a month of themed events (**International Istanbul Jazz Festival**; *see p185*). Add to this **Phonem** (*see p183*), an experimental music fest in March, the summer-long **Traditional Istanbul Açıkhava Concerts** (*see p185*) and **Rumeli Hisarı 'Starry Nights'** (*see p185*), August's **Bughole Festival** (*see p187*), September's **Creamfields** and October's **Akbank Jazz Festival** (*see p188*). September 2003 saw the first **Rock'n'Coke** weekend, headlined by Suede and the Pet Shop Boys, although it's too soon to know whether this is going to be a fixture. Look out for posters and fliers on Istiklal Caddesi and check the information sources given on *p182*.

Nardis Jazz Club.

Music: Turkish

Stuff Britney – with folk, fasıl, classical and Sufi, Turkish musical traditions still obstinately survive and even thrive in the face of globalised pop.

Turkish music – blasting from taxis, echoing out of kebab joints, wafting through markets – is one of the more startling sensual surprises for the visitor to Istanbul. This is a culture that was never overwhelmed by pop and rock to the point of losing a taste for its indigenous sound, and Turkey boasts a local scene as diverse and deep as any found in world music centres such as Brazil, Cuba or West Africa.

Much of what you'll hear around is what's known as 'arabesque'. Much maligned by serious commentators, and often with good reason, arabesque is a melancholic collision of Turkish folk with borrowed 'oriental' frills. It's provincial, overblown and dominated by tabloid stars and tabloid behaviour. **Müslüm Gürses**, for example, is famed for hysterical fans who slash themselves with knives at his concerts, while two girlfriends of superstar **Ibrahim Tatlıses** were shot in the leg in separate incidents by rural immigrants intent on protecting their hero's honour.

But in the days before electrified arabesque conquered Istanbul with its incessant dum-shikka-shikka, Turkish was one of the most influential of the world's musics. The Ottoman courts melded their Central Asian tastes to the remnants of Byzantine and Persian court music: the result was a deep and difficult classical tradition. Elsewhere, provincial Arab princedoms copied and adapted the new musical styles of Istanbul. In time, this classical tradition lightened into the popular sound of *fasıl*. In the 19th century, when playing musical instruments wasn't considered a proper profession for good Muslims, ethnic Armenians, Greeks, Gypsies and Jews supplied the musicians. The result was the inter-ethnic east Mediterranean urban contemporary pop of its time, the echoes of which are heard today in genres from Jewish *klezmer* to Greek *bouzouki* to Romanian *lautar* music. And the roots are still here and growing.

SONGS OF OLD STAMBOUL

To get a sense of how this music courses through the blood of the city, spend an evening in a *meyhane*, one of the boozy backstreet restaurants. As you nibble on plates of meze, a quartet of musicians (usually Roma) starts by warming up the crowd with nostalgic songs from old Stamboul. By the time the main courses arrive – several hours and not a few drinks later – the rhythm has been upped and diners are up on their feet.

One striking feature of the music is the wide variety of rhythms. If you can't keep time clapping, that could well be because it's in 9/8 or 10/16 or some other bizarre signature. Turkish scales also often employ notes between the notes, sometimes referred to as quarter-tones – new spice for your ears.

Traditional Turkish music can be divided into four basic styles: **folk**, which generally has a regional or rural flavour; **fasıl**, the frequently boisterous music found most often in *meyhanes*; **Turkish classical** (or Ottoman music), a refined court music; and **Sufi music**, the ethereal stuff often associated with the Whirling Dervishes. Crossover genres abound, as do forays into jazz and pop.

Folk

Halk müziği (folk music) forms an important part of the local music scene. Usually what gets labelled as folk are the slightly modernised *bağlama*-heavy songs that are played in bars. The *bağlama* is a long-necked lute, also called a *saz*, whose rural Anatolian connotations led it to be adopted by Atatürk's reformers as a national folk symbol of Turkey.

It's also the instrument favoured by the Alevi and Bektaşi, sects of Islam that stress intersectarian tolerance and equality between men and women, and are frowned upon by the orthodox majority. Their folk poets, known as *aşıks*, have been wandering the Anatolian plains since at least the tenth century. Their vast repertoire includes ancient and beautiful folk poems, but they are folkies with a conscience: *aşık* music has a tradition of focusing on social injustices, which in the recent history of Turkey has often led to radio censorship, arrests and even outright violence against musicians.

Istanbul also hosts many immigrants from the Black Sea coast, whose characteristic instrument is the *kemençe*. The wonderfully chaotic music of this pear-shaped fiddle accompanies improvised song 'duels' between singers and players.

Bağlama hero: the 'Ace of Spades' played Turkish style.

Folk venues

Bağlama bars, or 'Alevi bars' with signs announcing 'Halk Müziği', are especially thick in the sidestreets off Istiklal Caddesi (try **Büyükparmakkapı Sokak** and **Hasnun Galip Sokak)** and across the water on the Asian shore in Kadıköy. They are typically cosy venues, with seating low to the ground and decorated with folk art and kilims. They exude nostalgic Anatolian homeliness. It's not unusual to see family groups out together late at night and men and women mingling more freely than is the norm for bars in Turkey. Booze is served, tables are shared and in addition to singing along, there's sure to be dancing too. The band gets paid through customers slipping tips into folded napkins on which they scribble requests before passing them to the band.

Eylül

Erol Dernek Sokak 16, off Istiklal Caddesi, Beyoğlu (0212 245 2415). **Open** noon-2am daily. **Credit** MC, V. **Map** p295 O3.

Eylül means September and this low-key bar engenders that kind of balmy, best-years-of-our-lives type nostalgia all year round. It's a long-established venue with reliably good musicians and an all-singing, up-for-it dancing crowd. It's a great place to while away the afternoons (the music kicks off around 3pm) when unpressured service means it's not necessary to eat, only buy a tea or beer to enjoy the day-long live music. Evenings get much busier and tables are at more of a premium.

Havar

Hasnun Galip Sokak 29, off Istiklal Caddesi, Beyoğlu (0212 251 3359). **Open** noon-1.30am daily. **No credit cards**. **Map** p295 O3.

In amongst a cluster of *bağlama* bars running parallel to Istiklal Caddesi, Havar is one of the best. It's a large room, although there's precious little space for dancing: most nights, it's full to brimming with a young mixed crowd that often includes many all-female groups. From the early evening onwards, there's a heady atmosphere, fuelled by the energetic and loud music. Two shows a day, kicking off at 5pm and 11pm, keep the place buzzing.

Şal

Büyükparmakkapı Sokak 18/A, off Istiklal Caddesi, Beyoğlu (0212 243 4196). **Open** noon-1.30am daily. **Credit** V. **Map** p295 O3.

A grand entrance makes Şal easy to find: hence, it's a favourite with tourists. Inside, it's a low-ceilinged room with bank seats around the edges and low coffee tables. Musicians here often play the *zurna*, a kind of reed pipe that inspires *halays*, the Turkish form of line dancing. At such times spectating is not an option. The music starts at 3pm on weekends, 9pm during the week.

Türkü Bar

Imam Adnan Sokak 9, off Istiklal Caddesi, Beyoğlu (0212 292 9281). **Open** noon-2am daily. **Credit** V. **Map** p295 O2.

A boisterous, open-fronted establishment with low stools spilling out onto one of the busiest bar streets in Beyoğlu. The dancers regularly spill onto the street too, dancing around the potted trees on the pavement before snaking their way back inside. The

The belly fling thing

The pelvis plays a prominent role in Turkish life. Belly-dancing shows are a staple of the package-holiday circuit, gyrations are a required movement for Turkish pop stars and hip-swaying *dansöz* are national celebrities.

Funny then, that belly-dancing isn't even a Turkish tradition. Sure, there were dancing girls in the harems way back when, but the belly-dancing familiar to most Western tourists – long-haired female *dansöz* in gauzy sequined garments, undulating rhythmically – is actually an Egyptian import, which only caught on here during the 20th century. The Turks acknowledge the dance's Arab heritage in their name for it: *Oryantal*.

Whatever its origin, the Turks have embraced hip-swivelling with gusto. Ordinary Turks do similar moves to the professionals but they don't call it *Oryantal*: when civilians gyrate it's referred to as *gobek atmak*, which literally means to 'to fling one's belly'.

Belly-flinging wasn't always so acceptable. Once upon a time, the typical *dansöz* was considered a fallen woman, whose spangles and lamé were confined to entertaining gents in seedy nightclubs. That changed in the late 1970s when a *dansöz* appeared on Turkish television for the first time in history. Nesrin Topkapı's five-minute spot on national television transfixed the country: she became an instant celebrity, dragging belly-dancing out of the backroom and onto the front page.

Topkapı ushered in a new breed of belly-dancers: professional 'artists' who appeared on chat shows and *Wheel of Fortune,* and played weddings and circumcision parties.

But belly-dancing still wasn't able to shake off its sleazy connotations entirely. One star, Sibel Göçke, branched out into the phone sex industry. Asena, who eschewed the trad get-up of bangles and beads for skin-tight lycra costumes, had a torrid, well-publicised affair with TV presenter Ibrahim Tatlıse. Zumre was busted for coke possession. Sibel Can, on the other hand, made the leap from seedy belly-dancing clubs to the pop charts. Today, she's one of Turkey's top-selling recording artists and has done much to clean up belly-dancing's erstwhile unsavoury image.

The big bound forward though, came at the 2003 Eurovision Song Contest. On that occasion, winning Turkish act Sertap Erener performed her song backed by dancers in billowing harem pants. As her ditty was beamed into millions of living rooms across the world, Erener and her dancers, gyrated, rippled their navels and generally 'flung their bellies' in typical *Oryantal* style. There, in an echoing auditorium in the Baltic capital of Riga, Turkish belly-dancing's journey from sleazy to sanitised was made complete.

Kazablanka

Kuytu Sokak 4, off Tarlabaşı Bulvarı, Beyoğlu (0212 293 6212). **Show** 9pm-midnight daily. **Cost** Up to $75 per person incl. dinner and two drinks; groups of ten or more $25 per person. **Credit** AmEx, MC, V. **Map** p294 M4.

Kervansaray

Cumhuriyet Caddesi 30, Elmadağ (0212 247 1630). **Open** 7.30pm-midnight daily. **Show** 9-11pm daily. **Cost** $75 per person incl. dinner and drinks. **Credit** AmEx, DC, MC, V.

Orient Hostel

Akbıyık Caddesi 13, Sultanahmet (0212 517 9493/www.orienthostel.com) **Show** 11pm Mon, Wed, Fri. **Cost** $3 including drink. **Map** p289 O11.

too-cool customers at Kaktus, opposite, look on with barely disguised disdain. The music starts at 3pm on weekends, 6pm during the week.

Fasıl

Defining *fasıl* is one for the musicologists. At times it sounds like Gypsy music, then again it's also quite classical, or maybe it's just folk. In truth, it's all three and then some. How about semi-classical urban folk? *Fasıl* is what Edith Piaf or Jacques Brel would have been singing if they'd been brought up in Kadıköy.

The word *fasıl* comes from Ottoman classical music and refers to a suite involving different types of vocal and instrumental works strung together on the basis of their *makam* (mode and melodic shape). Not that this has too much to do with the *fasıl* that you hear today, except for the tendency of musicians to organise their sets of tunes in a *makam*.

The standard modern *fasıl* band can feature any of the following instruments: *darbuka* (hourglass-shaped hand drum), violin, *ud* (fretless short-necked lute), clarinet and *kanun* (plucked zither). The *cümbüş*, a louder, banjo-like cousin of the *ud*, sometimes makes its appearance in street bands.

Unlike folk, which is bar music, *fasıl* is most commonly encountered in *meyhanes*, the traditional meze and *rakı* places. The musicians tend to appear later in the evening, by which time most of the diners are already softened up by a few glasses of spirits.

The vast majority touring the restaurants are Roma, skilled in working their audience into a state of *keyif* – an ecstatic good mood. Not that anyone needs much help in losing their inhibitions: the Turks don't have any to start with. Every song is belted out by all present and tables are likely to be pushed aside to create an impromptu dance floor.

Most of the songs are standards written in the last 50 years and popularised by artists like **Müzeyeyen Senar**, **Münir Nurettin Selçuk** and the cross-dressing **Zeki Müren**, all big names of the 1940s, '50s and '60s. Nostalgia is a big part of *fasıl*, and most *meyhanes* are decorated to evoke the old days of Beyoğlu, with photos and prints and other memorabilia. Singing *fasıl* brings on the same wistful smiles in Turks as a quavery 'La vie en rose' does for a certain generation of Parisians.

Fasıl venues

Most of these places offer fixed menus with drinks and music included, although it is customary to tip the musicians a dollar or two per person at the end of each set. Bring an

appetite and try to go with a group of Turkish friends. And remember, a *fasıl* night is a participatory event.

A word of warning that applies to every venue on this list: if, for some reason, the *meyhane* isn't filling up – ie if it's a slow night with only one or two tables of people – the musicians may not play or the management may send them home early. This is more likely to occur early in the week and during summer.

Andon

Sıraselviler Caddesi 89, Taksim (0212 251 0222/ www.andon.com.tr). **Open** 7pm-1.30am daily. **Credit** MC, V. **Map** p295 O3.
A four-storey multi-function venue close to Taksim at the top of Sıraselviler Caddesi. In addition to a *meyhane*, it's also equipped with a wine bar, terrace restaurant and disco bar, not to mention Bosphorus views, accomplished musicians and smart service. The dimly lit atmosphere is especially flattering to the dressed-up diners. It's a good place to start exploring *fasıl* if you're not quite ready to jump in at the deep end.

Despina

Açıkyol Sokak 9, Kurtuluş (0212 232 6720). **Open** noon-midnight daily. **Credit** V.
Located in the far-from-glamorous district of Kurtuluş, an area once home to a sizeable Greek community, Despina doesn't look promising. Its fluorescent lights and plastic flowers are a long way from the nostalgia-inducing *meyhanes* of Beyoğlu. But some fine musicians frequent the place, drawing an appreciative and demonstrative audience, who submit requests for their favourite *oyun havaları* (dance songs). On the right night this can be the best party in town. Get here by taxi.

Kallavi 20

Kallavi Sokak 20, off Istiklal Caddesi, Galatasaray, Beyoğlu (0212 251 1010). **Open** noon-3pm, 7pm-1am Mon-Sat. **Credit** MC, V. **Map** p294 M3.
Tucked away on its own little street off Istiklal, this classic little *meyhane* has decent food and, on most weekend nights, a rousing atmosphere. It's got one of the best reputations for *fasıl*: the resident Roma musicians are so good, it's not unknown for clientele to abandon food and tables and hit the streets to dance. The fixed-price menu, including drinks, costs $30 per head. Recommended.

Süheyla

Balık Pazarı, Galatasaray, Beyoğlu (0212 251 8347). **Open** 8pm-2am daily. **Credit** MC, V. **Map** p278 N3.
Another prime *fasıl* venue, nestled among the restaurants in the Nevizade Sokak area (*see p122*). It has two good-sized rooms and better-than-average musicians. The set menu includes unlimited rakı for $25 per head (but note, somewhat bizarrely, you can't pay by credit card when ordering the set menu). The place gets packed at weekends, when reservations are recommended.

Encore, encore at **Kallavi 20**. See p219.

Suzan

*1 Cadde 90, opposite the ferry docks, Arnavutköy
(0212 257 0469).* **Open** noon-2am Mon-Sat.
Credit MC, V.

The sophisticated face of *fasıl*, Suzan attracts a
young, smartly dressed crowd to its top-floor bar,
which is called Bekriya, in honour of its former incarnation as a charming Yugoslavian restaurant.
Downstairs is a quieter restaurant and a jazz club
(*see p215*). Despite the upscale feel, prices remain
reasonable (set menu $20 per head) and the atmos-
phere is friendly and fun. Making reservations is
wise during the week and essential on weekends.

Turkish classical

Real Turkish classical music is not something
that most casual visitors to Istanbul will get to
hear. That's because it's rarely performed in
public nowadays. In the new Turkish republic
of the 1920s, Ottoman classical music was
considered elitist and backward and the state
tried to bury it. But in the last 20 years, there
has been a slow revival and now musicians
such as **Göksel Baktagir** and **Ihsan Özgen**
are attempting to reinvigorate the genre by
wedding Ottoman traditions to contemporary
Western instrumentation. Still, many musicians
find their efforts are better appreciated outside
Turkey, where the public has not been numbed
by decades of bland renditions from massive
state choruses and the uninspired output of
duty-bound radio performers. A pity, because
the Ottomans managed to produce a high art

form that rivals the classical traditions of India,
Iran, the Arab world and the West.

Although definitely not easy listening,
Turkish classical (also known as Ottoman,
Osmanlı or Court-Enderun music), is based on
the principle of *makam*. Like the Indian *raga*
system, the *makams* are modal, whereas
Western music is based on chord changes.
Turkish classical is subtle, the rhythms are
gentle, sometimes quite slow, although towards
the end of a programme you'll often hear lively
numbers. The melodic lines are long and highly
ornamented and singers must have great range
and control. Traditional instruments employed
are the *kanun* (plucked zither), *ud* (fretless
short-necked lute), *tambur* (long-necked lute),
ney (reed flute) and *kemençe* (a pear-shaped
fiddle). For percussion there are various frame
drums, such as the *daire* and *bendir*, and the
kudüm (small kettle drums).

Istanbul-based **Bezmara** is the one ensemble
that has tried to revive and play some of the
older forms of the instruments. Other ensembles
and performers of note include **Lalezar** and
Necdet Yaşar.

Turkish classical venues

This introspective and subtle art form is done
no justice in Istanbul today. No single venue
devotes itself exclusively to performances of
Turkish classical, though it does feature in the
programmes of the **International Istanbul
Music Festival** (*see p185*).

continuum. Many Turkish classical composers, such as **Dede Efendi**, wrote both sacred and secular music. Like classical, *tasavvuf müziği* (Sufi music) is based on the *makam* system, and the two genres share similar instrumentation. The major differences lie in forms and rhythms and in the arrangement of instrumentation. Sufi music accords greater prominence to the *ney* flute and percussion – including frame drums of various types and the *kudüm* kettle drums – creating hypnotic, mind-numbing beats.

Sufis are one of a number of dervish sects that use music, dance and *zikr* (a form of rhythmic breathing) as a way of establishing an ecstatic connection with God. It's a practice frowned upon by orthodox Islam, which considers music at prayer improper and a distraction from pure thoughts.

It's something of an irony, then, that, until recently, the form of Turkish music best known abroad was Sufi music, specifically, the music of the Mevlevi order, the 'Whirling Dervishes'. Sadly, as with Turkish classical, Sufi music has suffered from the vicissitudes of Turkey's 20th-century political history. During the turbulent early years of the republic, *tekkes*, the places of Sufi worship, were outlawed. The influence of the Dervish leaders was seen as a threat by Turkey's struggling new leaders, and Sufism was driven underground. Over time the laws relaxed and a few *tekkes* re-emerged. Best known is the **Galata Mevlevihanesi** (*see p98*) in Tünel, which is sanitised as a Museum for Classical Literature (*Divan Edebiyat Müzesi*), thus relegating Sufism to the status of a colourful historical oddity, with monthly performances solely for the pleasure of tourists.

When the real thing can be found, it is not always accessible to the outsider. One such place is in Fatih, where the Cerrahi brotherhood operates the Museum for the Study and Preservation of Tasavvuf Music, actually a fully functional mosque. Visitors are not necessarily welcome, as the place is obliged to keep a low profile. Apart from performances at the Galata Mevlevihanesi, the only other opportunity to hear Sufi music in Istanbul comes during the mystic music festival.

Atatürk Cultural Centre
Atatürk Kültür Merkezi/AKM
Taksim Square (0212 251 5600/251 1023). **Open** 10am-6pm daily. **No credit cards. Map** p293 P2.
This hall on Taksim Square is the most likely place in which to find Turkish classical music. The Türk Müziği chorus performs here most Sundays from autumn until late spring in the lower auditorium.

Cemal Reşit Rey Concert Hall
Cemal Reşit Rey Konser Salonu
Darülbedai Caddesi 1, Harbiye (0212 248 5392/ 240 5012). **Open** 10.30am-7pm daily. **Credit** MC, V. **Map** p287.
When they do host Turkish classical events, this is the best place to hear them. It's a large, comfortable and under-appreciated auditorium with excellent acoustics not too far north of Taksim Square. It also hosts a wealth of other interesting concerts.

Tarık Zafer Tunaya Salonu
Tarık Zafer Tunaya Kültür Merkezi
Şahkulu Bostanı Sokak 8, Tünel, Beyoğlu (0212 293 1270). **Open** 9am-6pm daily. **No credit cards. Map** p294 M5.
Once a wedding parlour, now a cultural centre, this municipally run venue – situated at the Tünel end of Istiklal Caddesi – hosts some Turkish classical concerts in among a varied programme.

Sufi music

To a casual listener, the music of the Muslim mystical Sufi sects and Turkish classical sound very much alike. They do have much in common, being part of the same musical

International Festival of Mystic Music
Uluslararası Mistik Müzik Festivali
Cemal Reşit Rey Concert Hall, Darülbedai Caddesi 1, Harbiye (information 0212 231 5497/0212 232 9830/www.ibb.gov.tr). **Date** Nov-Dec. **Tickets** Biletix, Cemal Reşit Rey Concert Hall.
Celebrating its ninth year in 2004, the festival gathers quality performers from around the world but especially from closer neighbours in the Middle East. Turkish music always features on the programme, available on the website in November.

Nightlife

Istanbul nights are ever young.

Istanbul's clubbers have a bit of catching up to do. Dance music didn't really hit town until the mid '90s and, truth be told, some of the clubs have yet to pull themselves out of an '80s disco timewarp. But there are bonuses. Unlike in Britain, local clubbers are still pumped up on enthusiasm and the scene isn't old enough to have become jaded. Visitors might find Turkish clubbers a bit low-wattage – in this town, mass passion is reserved for the city's football stadiums. But this too can be a welcome change, as not everyone's off their face on drugs and the overall vibe is less aggressive. Despite their calm demeanour, or perhaps because of it, Turks are generally open to meeting new people, and you won't have trouble finding English speakers. Put aside musical snobbery and clubbing in Istanbul can be a blast.

Meanwhile, the scene is developing as increasing numbers of Istanbul clubbers travel abroad. The exchange is two-way with shed-loads of big name international DJs regularly making their way to Istanbul for annual fieldfests such as **Bughole** (*see p187*) and **Creamfields** (*see p187*), as well as for one-off club nights. During the past few years the likes of Paul Oakenfold, Talvin Singh and Roni Size have all taken to the decks here.

There is a downside to this international trafficking. While the music may be getting better, local clubs are also inheriting some of the worst characteristics of venues in London, Paris, Berlin et al – guest lists, self-important doormen, high cover charges and astro-nomically priced drinks. Pleasingly, there's only so much of this the Turks will bear; when Chinawhite arrived on the shores of the Bosphorus in 2001 the abrasive attitude of its owners and their staff ensured that the venture went out of business inside 12 months.

As the Istanbul scene evolves, clubbers have inevitably discovered the joys of ecstasy. The high-rise district of Maslak is the place to buy the cheapest ecstasy in Europe. Apparently. But be warned, police are clamping down. They enter clubs at random, conducting heavy-handed searches and heaven help anyone caught. While it's not quite *Midnight Express*, penalties for possession are harsh. As a result, very few people carry anything on them. Instead there is a proliferation of after-parties at houses once the clubs close.

The scene is incredibly fickle, with many venues changing management every few months or so. There are lots of big opening parties followed by a few weeks of curious interest that rapidly tails off followed by the inevitable closure. However, most of the clubs we list on the following pages have built a solid and loyal following through a track record of good nights. Even here, turn up too early or on the wrong night (no one goes out on Thursday, for instance) and you might find yourself alone with the DJ and a few bored barmen. Generally speaking, clubbing hours are between 1am and 4am Wednesday, Friday and Saturday, with summers off; from July to September, most hardcore clubbers desert town and head for the south coast party resorts. This leaves Istanbul nightlife dominated by by the flash cash and trashy glamour of the Bosphorus scene; *see p224* **Bosphorus Babylon**.

Finding up-to-date, reliable information on what's going on is a challenge. Try the internet: **www.x-ist.com** carries a good *ajanda* page. Bigger events are flyposted or clubs will distribute programmes at bars, cafés and bookshops in Beyoğlu. Also check the monthly *Time Out Istanbul* or the free *Gig* and *Zip Istanbul* magazine (both fortnightly).

Festivals & events

One-off major parties and annual festivals are a growth industry. The usual sites include **The Venue**, located out on the edges of the rapidly growing business district of Maslak and boasting huge indoor and outdoor arenas, and **Park Orman**, a huge bar/restaurant complex with a pool just beyond Maslak. Despite drawbacks like heavy-handed security, a lack of atmosphere and expensive taxi rides home, there are still some great nights to be had. Over summer party venue of choice switches to **Solar Beach** (*see p245*) up on the Black Sea coast in Kilyos.

Such events are widely publicised (*see above*) and tickets are sold online at **Biletix**: *see p183*. Some useful sites to check for news of upcoming big nights include:

www.hippro.com
www.pozitif-ist.com
www.fabrikainternational.com
www.kodmuzik.com

Tech perfection at the very pink **Crystal**. *See p224.*

Venues

Alegria

Akarsu Sokak 2, off Istiklal Caddesi, Galatasaray, Beyoğlu (0212 245 1306/www.alegria-club.com). **Open** 6pm-4am Tue-Sun. Closed mid June-Sept. **Admission** free Tue-Thur; $7 Fri-Sat. **Credit** MC, V. **Map** p294 N3.

Formerly a venue for young techno-heads, these days Alegria is Latin dance and the crowd is positively middle-class. But while the punters may be wealthier, they are no less sweaty as the hard beats have been replaced by high-kicking, arse-swivelling salsa and Mundo Latino American dancing. There are regular shows and dancing workshops hosted by big names in the Latin dance circle: for more info visit www.mundolatinodance.com.

Babylon

Şehbender Sokak 3, Asmalımescit, Beyoğlu (0212 292 7368/www.babylon-ist.com). **Open** 9.30pm-2am Tue-Thur; 10pm-3am Fri, Sat. Closed mid July-mid Sept. **Admission** $10-$15. **Credit** MC, V. **Map** p294 M4.

More often a live music venue (*see p211*) than a club, Babylon – sporting a very fetching green-and-red painted frontage following a summer 2003 spruce up – nevertheless hosts some of the best big nights in town. It's one of the few places that caters to tastes other than techno. Club nights range from drum 'n' bass to funky house to Ally McBeal parties complete with mushy love songs and bad dancing. Check the very excellent website for details or pick up a flyer from bars and cafés around Beyoğlu.

2C Club Inn

Abdülhakhamit Caddesi 75, Belediye Dükkanları, Taksim (0212 235 6197). **Open** *Mid July-mid Sept* 10pm-4am Mon-Thur, Sun; 10pm-5am Fri, Sat. *Mid Sept-mid July* 11pm-4am Wed, Fri, Sat. **Admission** $13 Mon-Thur, Sun; $16 Fri, Sat. **Credit** MC, V. **Map** p292 O1.

The oldest club in Istanbul (it originally opened as Club 20 back in 1994) and still going strong. The hedonistic atmosphere is slightly edgy but totally infectious and the broad church of punters – old, young, gay, straight and trannies – is inspiring. Friday night's Soulpower is a stand-out when regular guest DJs spin uplifting hi-energy house.

Bosphorus Babylon

Summer is dead season for city clubbing. The regular crowds migrate south to the party resorts on the Med coast or take off to Europe. But there's one gaudy exception to this rule: the flashy clubs on the north shore of the Bosphorus, which are the summer playground for the rich and almost-famous. Don't expect club music. Don't expect a club crowd. Don't even expect to get in.

Still, for a certain kind of person, the likes of **Laila** and **Reina** offered the biggest nights out in the summer of 2003. These are essentially superclubs for the super-rich, vast waterfront open-air arenas with a central dance floor fringed by terraced eateries. Instead of decor there are the latest car models spotlit under giant rigs.

What makes people pay $20-$30 admission to groove to hi-energy Euro pap? Fork out $100 a head at restaurants where the thumping music renders conversation impossible? Push through massed Armani and Prada for a $12 beer? Perhaps the inflated prices themselves create an impression of elitism, the massive walls and massed security a feeling of privilege. It probably also has something to do with spectacular Bosphorus views, moonlight on the water and cooling offshore breezes.

The popularity of these venues certainly says something about aspirants to *sosyete*: fiercely upwardly mobile, keen to consume as conspicuously as possible and firm believers in fame by association. Where else can you toy with your sushi in front of an 'exclusive' audience of 5,000, glide directly off your yacht and up to the bar, or be elbowed aside by a television star desperate for a drink?

Above all else, it is undoubtedly the shrewd packaging and promotion that packs them in. Summer venues stage spectacular spring openings, invariably boasting a fresh *konsept*, a new roster of eateries and ample photo opportunities for the pages of *Alem*, the Turkish version of *Hello!* Never mind that the venues are merely last year's hot spots under different names; last year's Pasha is this year's Laila, Havana becomes Reina.

The epitome of bad taste? Maybe. But a night rattling your jewellery beside the Bosphorus offers an other-wordly take on Istanbul that's every bit as valid and enlightening as the mosque-and-museum circuit. And more fun too.

Anjelique.Buz

Serhane Sokak 10, Ortaköy (0212 327 2844). **Open** *June-mid Sept* 6pm-4am daily. **Admission** varies. **Credit** MC, V.
A joint venture between two upmarket bars, the plush Angelique of Tepebaşı and the exclusive Buz (*see p155*) of Nişantaşı. The past couple of summers have seen them team up and take over a venue down beside the water in Ortaköy. Despite overzealous doormen and an almost prohibitive price list the place has been a huge hit. Floor-to-ceiling angled mirrors make the best of the Bosphorus views. The music is a mixture of classic Western pop and singalong Turkish hits. On Sunday things are a bit more chilled with a more relaxed door policy, guest DJs and a laid-back selection of tunes.

Cafein

Muallim Naci Caddesi 77, Kuruçeşme (0212 259 3671). Open *mid-May-mid Sept* 5pm-2am daily. **Admission** free Mon-Thur, Sun; $27 Fri, Sat. **Credit** AmEx, MC, V.
Cafein is the wrong side of the coastal road and can't boast any waterfront but it is at least perched far enough up the hill opposite

Crystal

Muallim Naci Caddesi 65, Ortaköy (0212 261 1988/www.909pro.com). **Open** midnight-5.30am Wed-Sat. **Admission** free Wed, Thur; $23 Fri, Sat. **Credit** MC, V.
Crystal is a rarity among the city's nightlife venues in that it's open year-round, has a fantastic garden and consistently late hours. Besides its collection of resident DJs, Crystal is a regular destination for tech-luminaries from abroad, drawn by its fantastic sound system. Thursday nights are a more relaxed workout with the Together Collective – a group of DJ/producers with fresh progressive house sounds.

Dulcinea

Meşelik Sokak 20, off Istiklal Caddesi, Beyoğlu (0212 245 1071/www.dulcinea.org). **Open** 10am-2am daily. **Admission** free. **Credit** MC, V. **Map** p295 O2.
Upstairs at Dulcinea is a spacious and stylish bar (*see p144*) and restaurant with an artsy vibe and a loungey soundtrack. Downstairs is a performance space that regularly hosts DJ parties. The genre depends on the visitor: favoured guests tend to spin anything that's classy, involves live instrumental accompaniment or hails from France (such as the Parisan nu-jazz stylings featured at weekends).

Cubuklu Hayal Kahvesi

Burun Bahçe, Ağaçlık Mesire Yeri, A+B, Çubuklu, Asian Shore (0216 413 6880/ www.hayal.kahvesi.com.tr). **Open** 7pm-4am daily. **Admission** $13 Fri-Sat. **Credit** MC, V.
This club has a stunning location, right on the waterfront in a leafy Asian suburb. Free boats whisk you across the Bosphorus to the club's own jetty (they leave from the Istinye Motor Iskelesi every 30 mins from 6pm until closing). Entertainment takes the form of a varied programme of live music and DJs.

Laila

Muallim Naci Caddesi 54, Kuruçeşme (0212 236 3000). **Open** *29 May-Sept* 6.30pm-4am daily. Closed Oct-May 28. **Admission** free Mon-Thur, Sun; $20 Fri, Sat. **Credit** MC, V.
The city's most famous seasonal nightspot and a place that has to be seen to be believed – but be warned, you may need a second mortgage for a night out here. Laila is paparazzi heaven: it is to Istanbul's *sosyete* pages what the Met Bar is to London. It's not quite as much fun when you don't recognise the celebs but you can still appreciate all the cash that went on the tans, teeth and tushes.

Reina

Muallim Naci Caddesi 44, Kuruçeşme (0212 259 5919). **Open** *Mid May-mid Oct* 7pm-4am daily. **Admission** free Mon-Thur, Sun; $23 Fri, Sat. **Credit** AmEx, MC, V.
Laila's big rival is an almost identical set-up: a waterfront venue that resembles nothing so much as a giant, highly priced food court with a dance floor in the middle. The music is pure Euro Med trash, and loud, with occasional PAs by one-hit wonders. Like Laila, it's the perfect place to be seen but not heard.

that it does have Bosphorus views – as well as peeking opportunities into Laila, which lies below. Otherwise, the ingredients are the standard expensive dinners and an equally expensive spot in which to dance afterwards. On Sunday nights there's a hipper chill-out music session but the rest of the week offers run-of-the-mill Turkish pop hits.

Godet

Zambak Sokak 15, off Istiklal Caddesi, Beyoğlu (0212 244 3897/www.soap-system.com). **Open** 10.30pm-4am Wed-Sat. Closed July-Sept. **Admission** free Wed-Thur; $10 Fri-Sat. **Credit** MC, V. **Map** p295 O2.
In its seven years at the cutting edge of the Istanbul scene, Godet has tried its hand as a clubwear store, a techno heaven and more recently, with the introduction of the Red Room, a late-night lounge. Resident DJs Emre and Soulsonic are arguably the best in the city. Istanbul clubbers eagerly await the next incarnation.

Home Bass

Sadri Alışık Sokak 15, off Istiklal Caddesi, Beyoğlu (no phone). **Open** 9pm-4am daily. **Admission** free Sun-Thur; $3 Fri-Sat. **No credit cards.** Map p295 O3.
Dancing to the sound of different drums, Home Bass is a mainly African hangout but all comers are welcome – even the police make frequent visits (ahem). It's busy every night but particularly packed on weekends. The music's an infectious good-time mix of hip hop and Afro beats. The crowd's friendly and the beer's cheap, which makes the grumpy management easier to tolerate.

DJ Krush pushing all the buttons at **Babylon**. See p223.

See p223.

Jukebox

Nizamiye Caddesi 14, Talimhane, Taksim (0212 292 3656/www.jukeboxturkey.com). **Open** 11pm-5.30am Fri, Sat. Closed July-Oct. **Admission** $15-$20. **Credit** MC, V. **Map** p293 O1.

This huge venue has undergone a number of changes in management, decor and music policy over the years, but its best asset remains unchanged – its late, late licence. Last season it was taken over by the Urban Bug group, known for its love of super-clubs, sponsorship deals and branded nights. It's now thriving on a diet of progressive house and trance and it also lures in clubbers with the frequent addition of big-name guests.

Nu Club

Meşrutiyet Caddesi 149/1, Tepebaşı, Beyoğlu. (0212 245 6070). **Open** 11pm-4am Fri, Sat. Closed June-Nov. **Admission** free. **Credit** MC, V. **Map** p294 M4.

The Nu Pera complex is best known for good food (**Lokanta**, *see p133*) and great views (**Nu Teras**, *see p149*), but come winter all the action happens downstairs in the basement club. It's a small and intimate space – everyone knows everyone here and anyone who doesn't soon will. Resident DJs Yunus Güvenen (Istanbul's top record producer – check out his great site at www.yunusguvenen.com) and Barış Türker are two of Istanbul's best jocks: they sprinkle their sets with plenty of references to their time in New York. Once or twice a month guest DJs from Paris make an appearance.

Roxy

Arslan Yatağı Sokak 3, off Sıraselviler Caddesi, Taksim (0212 245 6539/www.roxy.com.tr). **Open** 9pm-3am Wed, Thur; 9pm-5am Fri, Sat. Closed July-Sept. **Admission** free Wed-Thur; $13 Fri, Sat. **Credit** MC, V. **Map** p295 O3.

Roxy is an established club featuring sets by live commercial rock and pop bands (*see p212*). The loyal crowd of regulars may be dressed either up or down, and there's a welcome lack of pretension and

a social, easy-going vibe. The owner, Kaan, is also the DJ and keeps it pumping to a soundtrack of chart-friendly hip hop, funk and dance music.

Safran

Rıhtım Caddesi 52/3, Karaköy, (0212 292 3992/ www.safranist.com). **Open** noon-3pm, 7pm-4am Mon-Sat. Closed June-Sept. **Admission** free. **Credit** MC, V. **Map** p292 M6.

Expect some attitude at the door and prepare to be shocked at bar prices that reflect a target audience of smart professionals but, even so, this is still one hell of a venue. Most nights it's overflowing with clubbers mainlining on eclectic retro sounds or slobbing out on th scattered couches and armchairs. There's also a good large restaurant attached, not to mention an absolute wow of a view.

Soho

Meşelik Sokak 14, off Istiklal Caddesi, Taksim (0212 245 0152). **Open** 11pm-4am daily. Closed June-Sept. **Admission** $10 Fri, Sat. **Credit** MC, V. **Map** p295 O2.

Nominally a bar but when Soho's kitchen closes at around midnight, the music gets pumped up and the well-dressed crowd lets their hair down, dancing wherever they can find space. On weekdays this allows a certain amount of self-expression but on the weekends it gets rammed to the point where shaking your head can be a challenge.

Switch

Muammer Karaca Çıkmazı 3, off Istiklal Caddesi, Beyoğlu (0212 292 7458/www.switchclub.net). **Open** 11pm-4am Fri, Sat. Closed July-mid Oct. **Admission** $15; before midnight $12. **Credit** MC, V. **Map** p294 N4.

Run by Hip Productions, an alternative music promoter, Switch is an underground club situated in an old courthouse. It's got a strong roster of DJs spinning a mix of trance, garage, house and techno and a loyal, hedonistic crowd of clubbers. International names figure frequently on the bill and when the place goes off, it's totally gone.

Performing Arts

Maestros and luvvies are rare breeds in Istanbul.

Despite the best efforts of the reformist Turkish state in the early years of the republic, Western performing arts have always failed to find large audiences. Theatre aside, they are still largely seen as alien impositions competing poorly with a rich heritage of indigenous art forms.

Classical Music, Opera & Ballet

European-style classical music is usually associated with a few overplayed selections such as Vivaldi's *Four Seasons*, which tend to be blasted out through speakers in the gardens of imperial Ottoman palaces like Beylerbeyi to lend 'ambience'. Opera and ballet remain the preserve of the upper classes and educated elite. Ordinary Istanbulus would rather listen to traditional folk music or *fasıl*. And why not ?

Turkey has no long tradition of Western performing arts. Rather it had its own imperial court music which, until it was actively suppressed under the new republic, had inspired big-gun European composers, most notably Mozart. Traffic went both ways and Italian composer Gaetano Donizetti introduced opera to Turkey in the early 19th century when he was invited to the imperial court as General Instructor of the Ottoman State Bands.

Sidelining its imperial heritage, republican Turkey instead emphasised nationalism based on a Western model. The first Turkish operas were written by composers such as Cemal Reşit Rey and Adnan Saygun, both members of 'The Five', the first generation of Turkish opera composers. Hungarian composer Béla Bartok was brought in to advise on a new state conservatory founded in Ankara in 1936. Dame Ninette de Valois, founder of Britain's Royal Ballet, chaired its ballet department.

Despite these solid foundations, performance standards for classical music, opera and ballet are typically less than overwhelming, owing to a lack of popular support and funding. Turkey does produce some high-calibre performing artists, such as conductors **Gürer Aykal** and **Cem Mansur**, soprano **Leyla Gencer**,

Riverdance on the Bosphorus: the Turkish smash hit show **Sultans of the Dance**.

Turkish modern dance group **Dance Theatre**.

violinist **Suna Kan**, pianists **Idil Biret** and
Güher & Süher Pekinel and, more recently,
the exciting young pianist **Fazıl Say**, but
without exception they are forced to ply their
trade abroad.

For anyone looking to attend classical
concerts in Istanbul, the fare is limited. In
the absence of any real public funding most
orchestras are sponsored by private banks.
Opera and ballet are represented solely by the
Istanbul State Opera and Ballet company. The
rare sparkle on the scene is supplied by the
International Istanbul Music Festival
(*see p185*), held each summer, or January's
International Istanbul Baroque Days and
April's **International Dance Festival** held
at the Cemal Reşit Rey Concert Hall, which
features performances by local orchestras
supplemented by foreign guests.

Concert halls

Atatürk Cultural Centre (AKM)

Atatürk Kültür Merkezi
*Taksim Square (box office 0212 251 5600, opera &
ballet enquiries 243 2011/251 1023/
www.idobale.com)*. **Box office** 10am-6pm daily.
Performances *Classical music* 7.30pm Fri; 11am
Sat; *Opera and ballet* 8pm Tue-Thur; 7.30pm Fri;
11am & 3.30pm Sat. **Tickets** $3-$7. **No credit
cards. Map** p293 P2.

Istanbul's premier performing arts venue. Despite
the brutalist 1960s design, the AKM is surprisingly
vibrant inside. It has five halls, plus an art gallery
and movie theatre: the grand hall and concert hall
are mainly for classical concerts, opera and ballet;
the smaller chamber hall, Aziz Nesin stage and
Taksim stage are mostly used for theatre. Ticket

prices are kept low through state subsidies; they go
on sale one month before performances but seats can
usually be secured right up until the last minute.

Cemal Reşit Rey Concert Hall

Cemal Reşit Rey Konser Salonu
*Darülbedai Caddesi 1, Harbiye (0212 232 9830/
www.crrks.org)*. **Box office** 10.30am-7.30pm daily.
Performances 7.30pm daily. Closed June-Sept.
Tickets $2-$8. **No credit cards. Map** p287.

Built in 1989, the municipal 860-seater CRR provides
a diverse programme, including concerts of Turkish
religious and traditional music. This is also the home
of the CRR Symphony Orchestra. The hall is a key
venue for several festivals, including October's
International Mystic Music Festival, December's
International CRR Piano Festival, January's
International Istanbul Baroque Days, April's
International Dance Festival and the International
Youth Festival in May. It also hosts music-related
exhibitions and conferences.

Iş Art and Cultural Centre

Iş Sanat Kültür Merkezi
*Iş Towers (Iş Kuleleri), Levent (0212 316 1083/
www.iskultursanat.com.tr)*. **Box office** 9am-6pm
daily. **Performances** 8pm most Sat & twice during
the week. Closed June-Oct. **Tickets** $5-$47. **Credit**
DC, MC, V.

The Iş Centre is an 800-seat concert hall with a prestigious programme and an unconventional location:
it's situated in the basement of the highest skyscraper in Levent. Here, classical music concerts are
performed by Turkish and foreign symphony and
chamber orchestras. Other performances include
recitals, Turkish traditional music, jazz and world
music. The centre also hosts art exhibitions and
plays and boasts a large shopping centre. To get
here, take the metro to Levent and use the Plazalar

Arts & Entertainment

Performance artist Günseli Kato in 'A Love Story'.

exit. Alternatively, a free shuttle leaves from in front of Atatürk Cultural Centre (Taksim) at 6pm and returns there after the concert is finished. Concert tickets can be purchased through Biletix or at the İş Centre. No children allowed!

Ensembles

Akbank Chamber Orchestra
Akbank Oda Orkestrası
Established in 1992 and sponsored by a private bank, this orchestra performs a broad repertoire of classical music from baroque to contemporary. Top soloists, such as pianist İdil Biret, occasionally guest. Permanent conductor Cem Mansur, a former conductor of the Istanbul State Opera, is wont to give detailed explanations of pieces before performances. The Akbank appears one Thursday evening each month from November to April at the Cemal Reşit Rey Concert Hall (*see p228*). They also frequently turn up on the programmes of events such as the International Istanbul Music Festival or December's International Cemal Reşit Rey Piano Festival.

Borusan Istanbul Philharmonic Orchestra
Borusan Istanbul Filarmoni Orkestrası
Borusan Kültür ve Sanat Merkezi, 421 Istiklal Caddesi, Tünel, Beyoğlu (0212 292 0655/ www.borusansanat.com). **Box office** 10am-7pm Mon-Sat. **Map** p294 M4.
Founded in 1993 as a chamber orchestra, the Borusan became Turkey's largest private orchestra when it evolved into a philharmonic in 1999. Under Gürer Aykal, one of Turkey's leading conductors, it performs two concerts each month, on Wednesday and Thursday of the same week at 8pm (October to June only). Venues for the performances include the

Kadıköy Halk Eğitim Merkezi (Bahariye Caddesi 39, Kadıköy, 216 330 1027) and the Lütfi Kirdar Concert Hall in Harbiye (Darülbedai Caddesi 6, Harbiye, 212 296 3061). You can also catch the orchestra at numerous festivals including the International Istanbul Music festival. Tickets and programme information are available from Biletix and the aforementioned venues. Alternatively, you can purchase tickets at the Borusan Cultural and Arts Centre (see contact details above), which also houses a library boasting the richest music archive in Turkey.

Cemal Reşit Rey Symphony Orchestra
Istanbul Büyükşehir Belediyesi Cemal Reşit Rey Senfoni Orchestrası
Active since 1995, this is the only Turkish orchestra funded by a municipality. Its 90 musicians play from a mixed repertoire, which includes works by Turkish composers. The orchestra also regularly performs with guest conductors and artists of international standing, including in the past tenor José Carreras and celebrated pianists İdil Biret and Fazıl Say. It generally performs four times a month at the Cemal Reşit Rey Concert Hall.

Istanbul State Opera & Ballet
Istanbul Devlet Opera ve Balesi
Established in 1960, the Istanbul State Opera and Ballet Company is out on its own, being the only company of its sort. To compensate for the lack of alternatives, it gives an impressive 25 performances a month from October to May. The repertoire is broad – it includes everything from baroque to classical to modern – and standards are world class. European classics from the likes of Mozart, Bizet, Offenbach and Orff are performed alongside Turkish works. All performances are given at the Atatürk Cultural Centre.

Istanbul State Symphony Orchestra

Istanbul Devlet Senfoni Orchestrası
A Turkish institution, the orchestra was founded in 1945 by local composer, pianist and conductor Cemal Reşit Rey. It has played a crucial role in the country's musical life ever since. Its 105 musicians have occasionally been supplemented by renowned soloists such as Yehudi Menuhin, Luciano Pavarotti and Jean-Pierre Rampal. The orchestra has premiered many works by Turkish composers and has also toured overseas on several occasions. It performs twice a week at the Atatürk Cultural Centre.

Theatre

Theatre in Istanbul is far more vital and varied than the classical music, opera or ballet scenes. More than 30 stages are scattered across the city, even in the remotest districts.

The Istanbul State Company offers a broad programme of classic and contemporary productions, including Turkish works, which are performed regularly in four theatres. About 15 to 20 different plays are staged every month, including plays for children and musicals, at the **Atatürk Cultural Centre** (*see p228*).

The city, meanwhile, owns six theatres in Harbiye, Fatih, Gaziosmanpaşa and the Asian districts of Üsküdar and Kadıköy. Plays are often penned by Turkish writers and performed by the Municipality Theatre Company.

A more eclectic programme is offered by the various private or independent theatre companies. For a healthy mix of classic and contemporary productions, check out the **City Players** (Kent Oyuncuları) starring Yıldız Kenter at the Kenter Theatre (*see below*); the **Theatre Studio** (Tiyatro Stüdyosu) directed by Ahmet Levendoğlu; or the **Production Theatre** (Prodüksiyon Tiyatrosu; *see p231*), run in collaboration with director Isil Kasapoplu. These three are considered Istanbul's leading theatre companies.

Traditionally, foreign theatre (and dance) companies have rarely bothered with Istanbul, but this is starting to change. In recent years, the city has been attracting major international names, including the likes of experimental German choreographer Pina Bausch and US avant garde stage director Robert Wilson, both of whom have both staged works at the annual **International Istanbul Theatre Festival** (*see p183*). Bausch's *Istanbul Project* was such a success that it's set to go off on tour and be performed worldwide.

Note that most theatres are closed from June to September. It's also worth noting that, other than during the international festival, all performances are in the Turkish language.

Istanbul Arts Centre

Istanbul Sanat Merkezi
Tarlabaşı Bulvarı 120-2, Beyoğlu (Kumpanya theatre company 0212 235 5457/Tiyatrooyunevi theatre company 0212 251 6060/5. sokak tiyatrosu theatre company 0212 235 7648). **Box office** 8am-8pm Mon-Fri. Closed July-Sept. **Tickets** $3-$8. **No credit cards. Map** p294 N2.
This venue was originally built in 1843 as an Armenian Catholic convent and school. It reopened as an arts centre in 1989. The complex includes two small theatres, several artists' workshops and a top-floor open-air restaurant with a fine view. It's home to three different independent companies, all of which concentrate on experimental contemporary dance or theatre. Most notable of the three is Kumpanya (Troupe), which has gained a reputation for its ambitious mix of absurd theatre, traditional musicals and design research. Tiyatrooyunevi (Theatre Playhouse) performs plays by the likes of Jean Genet, Bernard-Marie Koltès and Kafka.

Kenter Theatre

Kenter Tiyatrosu
35 Halaskargazi Caddesi, Harbiye (0212 246 3589/ www.kentoyunculari.com. **Box office** 11am-6pm daily. **Performances** 8pm Wed-Sat; 3pm Sun. **Tickets** $4-$12. **Credit** MC, V. **Map** p287.
A private 450-seat theatre, founded in 1968 by Yıldız Kenter, one of Turkish theatre's leading actresses. Here, the City Players (Kent Oyuncuları) perform two or three plays a year, usually classics from the likes of Shakespeare and Chekhov, but also some modern and contemporary plays, including works by French playwright Emmanuel Schmitt, Irish writer Martin McDonagh and David 'The Blue Room' Hare. Performances usually star Yıldız Kenter, are staged by her brother Müşfik, and tend towards the old-fashioned and earnest.

Maya Sahnesi

Halep İş Hanı, 140/20 Istiklal Caddesi, Beyoğlu (0212 252 7452/www.mayasanat.com). **Box office** 9am-7pm daily. **Performances** 7pm daily, subject to change, kids' performance Saturday afternoon. **Tickets** $3-$6. **Credit** MC, V. **Map** p294 N3.
This new art-house theatre, opened in October 2001, is a welcome addition to the scene. Situated at the heart of buzzing Beyoğlu, it is a 100-seat venue that hosts several young theatre companies. It also boasts a cosy café with a piano, library and snack bar. Music performances, film screenings and workshops also take place in the same venue.

Muhsin Ertuğrul Stage

Muhsin Ertuğrul Sahnesi
3 Darülbedai Caddesi, Harbiye (0212 240 7720/ www.ibst.gov.tr). **Box office** 11am-6pm Mon; 11am-8.30pm Tue-Sat; 10am-6pm Sun. **Performances** 8.30pm Tue-Sat; 3pm Sun. Closed May-Sept. **Tickets** $2-$4. **Credit** MC,V.
Founded in 1914 as a conservatory, then renamed the Istanbul Municipal Theatre in 1931, this venue had significant influence on the development of

Turkish theatre. Its golden period occurred under the directorship of Muhsin Ertuğrul, who was appointed to the post in 1927, and is regarded as the founder of modern Turkish theatre. He was the first director to stage great Western classics and was known for his encouragement of Turkish playwrights, not to mention his outstanding abilities as a director and teacher. Nowadays, the Muhsin Ertuğrul hosts regular performances by the Istanbul Municipality Company, which is considered less elitist and more accessible than the state theatre. Of the classic and contemporary plays performed here, half are by Turkish writers and include musicals and children's plays. Low ticket prices ensure packed houses. Booking is recommended at weekends.

Ses-1885 Ortaoyuncular Theatre

Ses-1885 Ortaoyuncular Tiyatrosu
Istiklal Caddesi 140/90, Beyoğlu (0212 251 1865/ www.ortaoyuncular.com). **Box office** 11am-8.30pm daily. **Performances** 8pm Thu-Sat; 3pm & 6pm Sun. Closed June-Sept. **Tickets** $8-$15. **Credit** MC, V. **Map** p294 N3.
Istanbul's oldest functioning theatre and one of its most beautiful. The wooden hall, with 554 seats on two floors, plus boxes and a balcony, is dripping in nostalgia. The Ses-1885 usually hosts performances by the Ortaoyuncular Company under Ferhan Şensoy, who trained in France in the famous Magic Circus band of Jérome Savary. All of the plays are comedies – usually written by Şensoy himself – and most are based on improvisation, word play and slang. The company's productions are extremely popular. *Ferhangi Şeyler*, a solo act by Şensoy and the company's biggest hit, has been performed more

than 1,500 times. Around five plays are staged every season. A recent Ortaoyuncular smash, due to be staged again in 2004, is a parody of reality-TV borefest *Big Brother*.

Production Theatre

Prodüksiyon Tiyatrosu
Akbank Arts Centre, Istiklal Caddesi 4-18, Beyoğlu (0212 252 3500/www.akbanksanat.com). **Box office** 9.30am-7.30pm Mon-Fri. **Performances** 8pm Fri; 5pm & 8pm Sat. **Tickets** $3-$5. **No credit cards. Map** p295 O2.
Established in 1995, the Production Theatre (previously known as the Aksanat Production Theatre) is a showcase for director Işıl Kasapoğlu, one of the city's leading theatrical lights. The repertoire consists of classic plays, both foreign and Turkish, ranging from Strindberg to more recent stuff by Turkish scribe Bilge Karasu. The performances may seem like low-budget productions, with only a handful of actors, minimalist decor and lighting, but the productions utilise the facilities masterfully and the narrow stage makes for an intimate atmosphere.

Taksim Stage

Taksim Sahnesi
Sıraselviler Caddesi 39, Taksim (0212 249 6944/ www.istdt.gov.tr). **Box office** 10am-8pm daily. **Performances** 8pm Tue-Fri; 3pm Sat, Sun. **Tickets** $3-$5. **Credit** MC,V. **Map** p295 O3.
Intimate 520-seat hall owned by the Turkish Ministry of Cultural Affairs and home to the Istanbul State Theatre. Around four different plays are put on every month, each for one week. Productions are a bit po-faced.

The **Akbank Chamber Orchestra**. *See p229.*

Sport & Fitness

Footie fans get their kicks in Istanbul, but other sports barely get a look-in.

Beşiktaş fail to delight. See p233.

Historically, Turkey's had few sporting successes at the international level, except in areas in which most of the rest of the world doesn't give a toss, such as Greco-Roman wrestling and weightlifting. But that is slowly changing. During the last few years, Turkish teams have slowly begun making a name for themselves in football and basketball, although not always for the right reasons (see p233 **Welcome to Hell?**).

Recent international successes in track and field events – notably Süreyya Ayhan's 1500m gold at the 2002 European Championships – are also helping to boost the public profile of athletics. As is the campaign to have Istanbul host the 2012 Olympics: three failed attempts – 2000, 2004 and 2008 – have failed to dampen Istanbul's spirits and the city has already spent $240m in the blind belief that one day it will stage the games.

Revenue from state lotteries, horse racing and one per cent of the city budget is already set aside toward the cost of staging the games. So far, the cash has furnished the city with a spectacular new 80,000-capacity Olympic Stadium at Iktelli, out near the airport, created by the designers of the Stade de France in Paris.

As if that weren't enough, the authorities have plans to spend a further $6 billion over the next ten years on further major projects.

Spectator sports

Chances are that the first conversation any visitor will have with a local will be about football. Maybe 90 per cent of all media sports coverage is concerned with the game, even in close season. Running a distant second is basketball, which takes up most of the remaining ten per cent. And very occasionally, when it isn't too busy floating transfer rumours or putting the boot into Galatasaray's manager, the press may spare the odd paragraph for one of the other few national sporting diversions.

Fixtures for all sporting events are listed in the local press and at the online ticketing agency Biletix (see p183).

Football

With Galatasaray winning the UEFA cup in 2000 and the national team making the semi-finals in the 2003 World Cup, the game has come a long way since the days when the only question before international fixtures was by how many goals the Turkish team would lose. Despite this success, Turkish football still suffers from a chronic lack of cash, with whole squads purchased for less than the price of a single Chelsea player.

Istanbul dominates footballing life, hosting its three biggest clubs: the aforementioned Galatasaray, plus Beşiktaş and Fenerbaçhe. The Black Sea side Trabzonspor supposedly completes a 'big four' but has struggled to keep up in recent years. Domestic competition focuses on the league, which runs from August to May and has a lopsided feel, as little clubs line up for a battering from the Istanbul heavyweights. For a really intense atmosphere, try to catch one of the Istanbul derbies.

To satisfy the TV companies, fixtures are staggered over a whole weekend, from Friday evening to Sunday evening. The fixture list is normally organised so that matches involving Istanbul teams don't clash with each other.

Tickets usually go on sale two or three days before a match, although for all but the biggest games it is surprisingly easy to pick them up at the stadium on the same day. For matches involving the big three, tickets can also be bought in advance via the booking agency Biletix (*see p183*).

Beşiktaş

Inönü Stadium, Dolmabahçe Caddesi, Beşiktaş (0212 236 7202/www.besiktasjk.com.tr). **Tickets** *League games* $8.50-$110. **No credit cards**. **Map** p293 R2.

Welcome to Hell?

It's not only the growing strength of Turkish football clubs on the field that makes them an unwanted draw in European competitions (ask Chelsea, the £110 million team that went down to ten-man Beşiktaş in a recent 2003 Champions League tie). Opposing teams also rarely relish a tie in Istanbul because of the intimidating cauldron that home fans brew up for their foreign visitors.

The days when Turks wielding 'Welcome to Hell' banners would turn up at Istanbul airport to pelt the visiting team buses with bottles and bricks (as happened when Manchester United came to town in 1993) are seemingly gone. The habit of serenading visiting teams outside their hotel rooms in an effort to keep them awake all night seems to have come to an end too. But Turkish fans can still create the most incredibly intimidating, not to say hostile, noise. Football stadiums around the world are hardly places of quiet contemplation, but those in Turkey, and in particular Istanbul, are something else. Reporters in town for the crucial England-Turkey Euro 2004 qualifier in October 2003 noted that the noise level at the Fenerbahçe stadium two hours before kick-off was verging on the demonic (arriving at the ground pissed and at the last minute is not a popular option with Turkish fans). At match time, when the England team took the field they were greeted with a carefully coordinated crescendo of boos.

None of this comes about by chance. Turkish teams have officials responsible for tutoring fans in how to make a racket. At Galatasaray there's a bloke called Osman Guneri responsible for training the terraces to

whistle when the opposition have the ball and for conducting the stands in some chant and response. The results can be impressive, as at Beşiktaş when 25,000 versatile linguists roared in unison, 'Fuck you Chelsea'.

Tragically, passions have a habit of spilling over into violence, as in April 2000, when two Leeds supporters were stabbed to death before a UEFA cup tie against Galatasaray. This was far from being a one-off. Most recently, in August 2003 a 22-year-old Turkish university student died from knife wounds sustained in a brawl during a match in the western city of Izmir. He was stabbed by a fan of the same team. One manic Fenerbahçe supporter, whose exploits have earned him the nickname 'Rambo', managed to break into rival Galatasaray's Ali Sami Yen stadium the day before the first match of the 2002-3 season where he hid out for 24 hours beneath the advertising hoardings and then, as the players took the field, sprinted to the centre spot where he planted a large Fener flag and warded off officials with a knife.

So was Sven right then when he recently advised English fans not to travel to Istanbul for that vital Euro qualifier, warning that they'd be putting their lives were at risk? Hardly. After all, the few write-ups from resourceful souls who managed to breach the embargo on visiting supporters were overwhelmingly positive about the reception they received. As a correspondent in *The Guardian* wrote, it's doubtful whether a Turkish supporter who turned up alone at the same fixture in England would have had such a happy experience.

Arts & Entertainment

National league champions in 2002/3, the 'Black Eagles' get the chance to make an impact on the international game in a 2003/4 Champions League draw that pits them against Lazio, Sparta Prague and Chelsea. Hopes rest on their star striker, national heart-throb Ilhan Mansız. Beşiktaş teams tend to play solid, unflamboyant football, though they have been at the forefront of the trend to import foreign coaches, including Gordon Milne, Christoph Daum and the current coach, the professorial Romanian Mirceu Lucescu. The club's Inönü Stadium is the city's most conveniently located, just uphill from the Dolmabahçe Palace.

Fenerbahçe

Şükrü Saraçoğlu Stadium, Kadıköy (0216 330 8997/ www.fenerbahce.org). **Tickets** *League games $6-$25.* **No credit cards. Map** p297 Y8.

Once indisputably the biggest club in Turkey, in recent years Fener fans have had to look on with a pained smile as arch-rivals Galatasaray have grabbed all the European glory. Despite winning a record number of Turkish league championships, Fener's own European record is weak, although in 1996 they did defeat Manchester United at home. Fenerbahçe was Atatürk's team and it has historic links with the Turkish army, despite its most unmilitary nickname, 'the Canaries'. The home stadium is in the wealthy suburb of Fenerbahçe, on the city's Asian side: from the European side take a boat from Eminönü to Kadıköy, and then a bus or taxi.

Galatasaray

Atatürk Olimiyat Stadium, Ikitelli (0212 688 0223/ www.galatasaray.org). **Tickets** *League games $8-$110.* **No credit cards.**

Easily Turkey's most famous – and infamous – club, Galatasaray boast a string of European successes, crowned by victory over Arsenal in the UEFA Cup final in 2000. Known to fans as 'Cim Bom' for reasons no one can explain, Galatasaray have dominated the league since the mid 1990s. With historic links to the old Galata Lycée, where a large chunk of Turkey's ruling class was educated, Galatasaray see themselves as the aristocracy of Turkish football. This superior attitude was rather undermined by the decrepit state of their home stadium, the hell pit that was the Ali Sami Yen, but for the 2003/4 season they've moved out to the new Olympic Stadium in Ikitelli. Shuttles transfer fans from Taksim Square and the Eminönü and Topkapı bus stations.

Basketball

While international soccer success has tended to eclipse Turkey's long-running love affair with basketball, the game still boasts a large fan base. Results are getting better, with both men's and women's teams regularly winning through to the last stages of European competitions. It's only a matter of time before they bring home a major trophy.

The basketball season lasts roughly from October to June, with clubs playing at least twice a week, usually in the afternoon or early evening. Istanbul's three football giants also have basketball teams, but the top performers have been Efes Pilsen and Ülkerspor, run by a brewer and biscuit-maker respectively. All of the clubs have both men's and women's teams.

Tickets for all but the biggest games are easily available on the day but they can also be bought in advance. Information on games and fixtures can be found at the Turkish Basketball Federation website (www.tbf.org.tr).

Beşiktaş

Süleyman Seba Spor Salonu
Çitlembik Durağı Arkası, off Emirhan Caddesi, Dikilitaş (0212 261 6319/www.besiktasjk.com.tr). **Tickets** $4-$8. **No credit cards.**

Lagging far behind their footballing colleagues, Beşiktaş have failed to win the basketball championship since 1975.

Efes Pilsen

Abdi Ipekçi Spor Salonu
Onuncu Yıl Caddesi, Zeytinburnu (0212 665 8647/www.efesbasket.org). **Tickets** $2-$8. **No credit cards.**

Founded in 1976, Efes Pilsen have since won the Turkish title ten times and in 1996 they scored their biggest success yet when they bagged the European Korac Cup. Since 2002, Efes Pilsen have attracted further international attention by hosting their own Istanbul World Cup, attracting teams from minor basketball countries such as Italy, Lithuania and New Zealand to the city for a five-day tournament.

Fenerbahçe

Fenerbahçe Spor Kulübü
Dereağzı Tesisleri, Basketbol Şubesi, Kızıltoprak (0216 347 8438). **Tickets** $2-$5. **No credit cards.**

Galatasaray's deadly rival, Fenerbahçe last won the national championship in 1991. The address above is the training ground but games are played elsewhere, including the Abdi Ipekçi Spor Salonu (*see* Efes Pilsen above).

Galatasaray

Galatasaray Spor Kulübü
Metin Oktay Tesisleri, Basketbol Şubesi, Florya (0212 574 2916/www.galatasaray.org). **Tickets** $2-$3. **No credit cards.**

While both the men's and women's teams have at different times topped their respective Istanbul leagues, success has faded: neither is the team it once was. Games take place at the Abdi Ipekçi Spor Salonu (*see* Efes Pilsen above).

Ülker

Ahmet Cömert Spor Salonu
Kısımsonu Olimpiyat Evi Yanı 4, Ataköy (0212 559 4819/ticket info 0212 612 7942 ext 16/www.ulkerspor.com). **Tickets** from $2-$3. **No credit cards.**

Misspent youth opportunities at **Omayra Billiards**. *See p236.*

One of the more successful teams, Ulker won the Turkish championship in 1997-8, and got to the last eight of the Korac Cup the season before, making them Efes Pilsen's only serious current rival.

Wrestling

The major annual event is the Republic Cup (*Cumhuriyet Kupası*), an international competition which is held toward the end of each September. For information on this and other wrestling events and facilities, contact the following:

Gençlik ve Spor Müdürlüğü

Barbaros Mahllesi, Okul Sokak 20, Burhanfelek, Usküdar (0216 651 6262). **Open** 8.30am-5pm Mon-Fri. **Map** p295 O3.

Active sports

With sparse facilities to choose from and often little in the way of leisure time, few Turks actively participate in any sports other than the odd works football match played on one of the city's many artificial five-a-side pitches. Exercise in Istanbul is otherwise an expensive habit limited to the well heeled.

The Kadıköy and Bakırköy municipalities have established bicycle paths along coastal roads, which are usually filled with joggers. In-line skating and skateboarding are not specifically catered for, but seaside parks and Beşiktaş Square have been taken over by whizzing teens.

Adventure sports

Recent Ministry of Tourism efforts to pitch Turkey as the ideal destination for outdoorsy types have at least succeeded in interesting more locals in sport. University clubs and organisations catering to the recent demand for sport on the wild side have mushroomed.

Adrenalin

Büyük Beşiktaş Çarşısı 19, off Ortabahçe Caddesi, Beşiktaş (0212 260 6002/www.adrenalin.com.tr). **Open** 10am-8pm Mon-Sat. **Credit** MC, V.
Adrenalin offers training in outdoor adventure sports, prefaced by classroom sessions on surviving the experience. Activities run the gamut from weekends camping in the Istanbul suburbs to winter mountain-climbing courses. Trainers and assistants all speak English, which is always nice when you're scaling vertical cliffs.

Adre-X Extreme Organisation

Sahra Cedid Mahallesi, Mengi Sokak 17/3, Kozyatağı (0216 386 3335/www.adre-x.com). **Open** 9am-6pm Mon-Fri. **No credit cards.**
This organisation provides outdoors training and adventure-sport weekends aimed particularly at business professionals who fancy bonding while going wild in the country. Activities offered include low and high-rope systems, navigation and bungee jumping. English is spoken.

DSM Doga

Rüştiye Sokak 27/8, Kızıltoprak (0216 414 2590/ www.dsm.com.tr). **Open** 9am-6pm Mon-Sat. **Credit** MC, V.

A clean pair of legs at the **Çırağan Palace Hotel Kempinski.** *See p237.*

Adventure sports centre organising group activities that include rafting, mountain climbing, caving, camping, trekking and paragliding, all under the guidance of expert trainers. English is spoken.

Gezici YAK

Selçuk Apt, Recep Paşa Caddesi 14/10, off Cumhuriyet Caddesi, Taksim (0212 238 5107/ www.geziciyak.com). **Open** 9am-7pm Mon-Sat. **Credit** MC, V.

Organises daily trekking tours in the local area and river and rafting trips further afield. Also organises scuba diving trips and training, for which a doctor's certificate is required. English spoken.

Billiards

Sleazy snooker saloons, long a staple of the Beyoğlu scene, have recently been joined by smart American-style pool halls. While the former remain smoke-filled, men-only affairs, the latter are popular with a mix of young male and female students.

Ağa Bilardo Salonu

Ağa Hamamı Caddesi 17/2, Cihangir, Beyoğlu (0212 251 7469). **Open** 11am-midnight daily. **Rates** $2/hr pool; $2.25/hr snooker. **No credit cards. Map** p295 O3.

A spacious hall with two full-sized snooker tables, three proper pool tables and another three that are slightly undersized. For a change of pace, there are also three table tennis tables. Children under 18 must be accompanied by a parent.

Omayra Billiards & Internet Café

Aznavur Pasajı, Istiklal Caddesi 212, Galatasaray, Beyoğlu (0212 244 3002). **Open** 11am-midnight daily. **Rates** $3/hour. **Credit** MC, V. **Map** p294 N3.

Up on the third floor above the dippy hippy stalls of the Aznavur Pasaj things get a lot sharper and wilier as wannabe pool sharks circle the six billiard tables. There's also internet access and a café.

Bowling

The city's bowling alleys are modest in size compared to their American and European counterparts but it's a pastime that's rapidly growing in popularity.

Bab Bowling Café

Yeşilçam Sokak 24, off Istiklal Caddesi, Beyoğlu (0212 251 1595). **Open** 10am-midnight Mon-Thur; 10am-2am Sat, Sun. **Rates** $2.50 per person per game Mon-Fri; $3 Sat, Sun. **Credit** MC, V. **Map** p294 N3.

This bowling alley only has six lanes, so be sure to reserve ahead evenings and weekends if you are going as a group. After you've worked up an appetite attempting to score strikes, there is a fast-food bar and café attached.

Galleria Bowling

3rd floor, Galleria Shopping Mall, Bakırköy Sahil Yolu, Ataköy (0212 661 0322). **Open** 10am-1am daily. **Rates** $2 per person per game Mon-Fri; $4 Sat, Sun. **Credit** MC, V.

An 18-lane alley in Istanbul's first big shopping mall (*see p173*), with restaurant and a bar. Reservations recommended on Friday and Saturday nights.

Time Out Bowling Centre

7th floor, Profilo Shopping Mall, Cemal Sahir Sokak 26/28, Mecidiyeköy (0212 217 0992). **Open** 10am-1am Sun-Thur; 10am-2am Fri, Sat. **Rates** $3.20 per person per game Mon-Thur; $4.30 Fri-Sun. **Credit** MC, V.

The city's largest bowling alley has 20 lanes plus billiard tables and a shop selling bowling equipment. The above rates are evening ones; it's cheaper before 6pm weekdays or before 2pm weekends.

Ice Skating

Hot out? How about some ice – a rink full. Skating is more a summer escape from the heat than a sport, and as such is very popular.

Galleria Ice Skating

Galleria Shopping Mall, Bakırköy Sahil Yolu, Ataköy (0212 560 8550/www.galleria-atakoy.com.tr). **Open** 10am-midnight mon-Fri; 1pm-midnight Sat, Sun. **Rates** $6 for 45 mins. **Credit** AmEx, MC, V.

Slap bang in the middle of a mall, the rink provides great entertainment for shoppers – they can watch collisions from the safety of the escalators.

Swimming

The city's few Olympic-size pools are part of university campuses or members-only sports complexes, where guests must be accompanied by a member. But you can get a day pass or membership at a number of hotels (*details below*). Call in advance prior to showing up, as terms change frequently.

Ceylan Inter-Continental

Asker Ocağı Caddesi 1, Taksim (0212 231 2121/www.interconti.com.tr). **Open** 7am-9pm daily. **Rates** *Day pass* $15 Mon-Fri; $25 Sat, Sun; half price under-12s; free under-6s. **Credit** DC, MC, V. **Map** p293 P1.

It's an outdoor pool 20m (66ft) long. Use of the hotel's health club, hamam and sauna for the day costs an additional $25 during the week or $40 at weekends.

Çırağan Palace Hotel Kempinski

Çırağan Caddesi 32, Beşiktaş (0212 258 3377/www.ciraganpalace.com). **Open** 7am-11pm daily. **Rates** *Day pass* $65 Mon-Fri; $85 weekend; 40% discount under-12s; free under-6s. **Credit** AmEx, DC, MC, V.

The Çırağan's 33m-long (108ft) outdoor pool boasts the most stunning setting in Istanbul – it is separated from the Bosphorus by just a thin lip. The indoor pool is about a third of the size. It also has a jacuzzi, sauna, vapour and fitness rooms.

Conrad International

Yıldız Caddesi, off Barbaros Bulvarı, Beşiktaş (0212 227 3000/www.conradhotels.com). **Open** *Indoor pool* 6am-10pm Mon-Fri; 6am-11pm Sat, Sun; *Outdoor pool* 8am-8pm daily. **Rates** *Day pass* $35 Mon-Fri; $45 Sat, Sun; half price under-12s; free under-6s. **Credit** AmEx, DC, MC, V.

While the indoor pool is a fairly standard 15m-long fun pool, the outdoor one is a generous 23.5m (77ft).

Euro Plaza Health Club

Tarlabaşı Bulvarı 292, Tepebaşı (0212 254 5900/www.hoteleuroplaza.com.tr). **Open** *Indoor pool* 10am-10pm daily; *Outdoor pool* 10am-7pm daily. **Rates** *Day pass* $10 Mon-Fri; $12.50 Sat, Sun; half price under-12s; free under-6s. **Credit** MC, V.

What the pool lacks in size (it's only 10m long) it makes up for with great views across the water to Sultanahmet. It's also extremely cheap.

Hilton Istanbul

Cumhuriyet Caddesi, Harbiye (0212 315 6000/www.hilton.com). **Open** *Outdoor pool* 7am-6pm daily. *Indoor pool* 7am-10pm daily. **Rates** *Outdoor pool* $20 Mon-Fri; $28 Sat, Sun; half price under-12s; free under-6s. *Indoor pool* $22 Mon-Fri; $30 Sat, Sun; half price under-12s; free under-6s. **Credit** AmEx, MC, V. **Map** p293 P1.

The outdoor pool is approximately half Olympic sized, while the indoor pool is 18m long. The price includes all health club facilities.

Hyatt Regency

Taşkışla Caddesi, Taksim (0212 368 12 34/www.istanbul.hyatt.com). **Open** 7am-7pm daily. **Rates** *Day pass* $20 Mon-Fri; $40 Sat, Sun; 25% discount under-10s; free under-2s. **Credit** AmEx, DC, MC, V. **Map** p293 Q2.

This hotel has a pool that is 25m (75ft) long. From June to September, the weekend day rate includes a barbecue buffet served noon-5pm.

Hotel Marble

Sıraselviler Caddesi 75, Taksim (0212 252 2448/www.marblehotel.com). **Open** 9am-9pm daily. **Rates** *Day pass* $7 Mon-Fri; $10.75 Sat, Sun. **Credit** AmEx, MC, V.

This hotel's health club has a 10m-long heated indoor pool, located in the basement. It's open to non-residents, who actually comprise the majority of the clientele (it's rarely used by the hotel guests, who are mainly Arabs).

Marmara

Marmara Hotel, Taksim Square (0212 251 4696/www.themarmaraistanbul.com). **Open** 7am-7pm daily. **Rates** *Day pass* $20 Mon-Fri; $28 Sat, Sun; half price under-12s; free under-6s. **Credit** AmEx, MC, V. **Map** p295 P2.

This 20m-long outdoor pool boasts impressive views of Istanbul and certainly makes for a well-positioned, city centre sun trap.

Swissotel Istanbul

Bayıldım Caddesi 2, Maçka (0212 326 1100). **Open** *Indoor pool* 7-11pm daily. *Outdoor pool* 8am-7pm daily. **Rates** *Indoor pool* $30 Mon-Fri; $40 Sat, Sun; half price under-12s; free under-6s. *Outdoor pool* $12 Mon-Fri; $40 Sat, Sun; half price under-12s; free under-6s. **Credit** AmEx, MC, V.

The indoor pool is 17m long and the day pass also gets you use of all health-club facilities. The outdoor pool is 20m by 20m and the day rate includes a barbecue after 3pm, weekdays only.

Beaches

Although Istanbul is surrounded by water and the municipality has sponsored numerous high-profile clean-up campaigns, swimming in within city limits is still a dodgy proposition. The upper Bosphorus, near Sarıyer is cleaner but subject to treacherous currents.

The closest beach to Istanbul with anything approaching clean sand and clear, unpolluted water is on Marmara Island (*see p252*).

Solar Beach & Party

Eski Turban Yolu 4, Kilyos (0212 201 1012/ www.solar-beach.com). **Admission** $8.

In addition to jet skiing, bungee jumping and trampolining during the day, come nightfall Solar Beach hosts rave parties most summer weekends. To get here take the shuttle bus ($3) from Taksim Square departing 10am, noon and 2pm.

Fitness

Weightlifting and bodybuilding are beloved of Turkish men of all ages and income brackets (marvel at the sheer volume of magazines crowding the newsstands devoted to ballooning musculature). Cheaper gyms and fitness centres tend to be dominated by men but women should find the places listed below hassle-free, largely because they're expensive enough to keep out the oglers.

Most of the big hotels also have fitness centres; *see p237*.

Flash Gym

4th floor, Aznavur Pasajı, Istiklal Caddesi 212, Beyoğlu (0212 249 5347). **Open** 9.30am-10pm Mon-Fri; 9.30am-9pm Sat. **Rates** *Day pass* $6; *monthly membership* $40. **No credit cards. Map** p294 N3.

A case of you get what you pay for: this is one of the cheapest gyms in town. It's not exactly pleasantly scented, due to the lack of air conditioning and the sponge-effect carpet that lines the gym. What's more, the equipment is ageing and the changing rooms are hardly the model of hygiene. Still, it's an economical place to get in shape: evening step class-

Sweating in style at the **Marmara Gym**.

es run three times a week and cost just $43 a month or $11 on a one-off basis. Another strong point: some of the staff speak English.

Kuzey Yıldızı Kültür ve Spor Merkezi

Havyar Sokak 30-32 (off Sıraselviler Caddesi), Cihangir, Taksim (0212 252 6716/243 1016/ www.kuzeyyildizi.com.tr). **Open** 8am-10pm Mon-Fri; 9am-7.30pm Sat; 10am-2.30pm Sun. **Rates** *Day pass* $11; *monthly membership* $42-$81, plus one-off $7 registration fee. **Credit** MC, V. **Map** p295 O4.

Friendly neighbourhood sports complex popular with foreigners, who automatically qualify for a discount. Longer memberships of three, six, nine and twelve months also available, as well as classes in yoga, aikido, tai chi, classical and jazz ballet, modern and Latin dance. The gym is currently cramped and could do with an equipment overhaul, but this is likely to change when the place relocates to Çukurcuma in early 2004.

Marmara Gym

Marmara Hotel, Taksim Square (0212 251 4696/ www.themarmaraistanbul.com). **Open** 7am-10pm daily. **Rates** *Day pass* $22 gym only, $33 all facilities; *monthly membership* $205. **Credit** AmEx, MC, V. **Map** p295 O2.

This spacious, spotless gym has hi-tech equipment, English-speaking trainers and panoramic views over Taksim Square – but you pay for it. Changing rooms come with power showers and steam rooms, but use of the hamam, sauna and jacuzzi costs extra. Likewise the outdoor swimming pool, more sunterrace than pool, that's open June to August. Other extras include Latin dance classes, karate, and yoga. Ask about discount memberships.

Trips Out of Town

The Upper Bosphorus   240
The Princes' Islands   248
The Marmara Islands   252

The Upper Bosphorus

A must-do boat cruise with yoghurt, yalıs and lucky wires for brides.

Sometimes, when you're lost in the narrow, crazed streets of Sultanahmet or Beyoğlu, it's easy to forget that this is a maritime city. The reality is that the Bosphorus is Istanbul's true main drag, a wide watery highway through the heart of town. In Ottoman times, this stretch of water saw as much traffic as the roads.

Out on a boat it quickly becomes clear that the city has always presented its best face to the Bosphorus. The twisting shoreline is tightly punctuated by former imperial palaces, diplomatic hideaways and gorgeous old Ottoman *yalıs* (waterfront mansions), all currently ageing beautifully. Which is why a cruise up the Bosphorus is essential, as crucial to any Istanbul experience as a visit to the Haghia Sophia or the ordeal of the bazaar.

The Bosphorus cruise

The standard Bosphorus cruise takes six hours return and costs all of $5. Ferries depart every day all year round from Eminönü's Boğaz Hattı dock, which is 100 metres east of the Galata Bridge. Tickets are bought at the window labelled Eminönü-Kavaklar Boğaziçi Özel Gezi Seferleri (Eminönü-Kavaklar Bosphorus Special Touristic Excursions). Sailings are at 10.30am and 1.30pm with an extra boat at noon from June to September. In summer and at weekends, board the boat at least 30 minutes before departure if you want to get a seat.

After leaving Eminönü the first stop is Beşiktaş near the Dolmabahçe Palace. The ferry then tacks back and forth between the

Ferry on up the Bosphorus.

European and Asian shores, stopping at several Bosphorous villages along the way: notably Kanlıca, Yeniköy, Sarıyer, Rumeli Kavağı and Anadolu Kavağı (all described on the following pages). You can get off wherever you like but, if you do, you've blown the cruise and will then have to make your own way onwards or back to town. Most first-time visitors stay on until the furthest point north, Anadolu Kavağı, where there's enough time for a fish lunch before reboarding the ferry, which then makes a beeline back to Beşiktaş and Eminönü. For information contact 0212 252 2100.

Numerous private operators run shorter boat trips. These typically go only halfway up the Bosphorus, as far as Rumeli Hisari, where passengers are given an hour for lunch before the boat returns to Eminönü. There are no stops en route, because unlike the 'big' Bosphorus cruise, which is actually a ferry used by the locals, these are purely pleasure boats taking just 60 to 100 people. Departures are roughly every half-hour from Eminönü, starting at 10.30am and finishing at 6pm (4pm October to April). Tickets are sold by touts who roam the wharfside and generally cost about $8 but it's worth bargaining.

KANLICA

The first major sights – and, indeed, the last if you opt for the shorter cruise – are the twin guardian fortresses of **Rumeli Hisarı** (*see p106*) and **Anadolu Hisarı**, one either side of the water. Just before passing under the second of the great suspension bridges (the 1,096-metre-long **Fatih Mehmet Bridge**, opened 1988) over on the Asian side is a battered and barn-like, low-rise wooden structure hanging slightly over the water; this is the **Amcazade Hüseyin Paşa Yalısı**, Istanbul's oldest waterside mansion. Built in 1699, its current state of neglect may be scandalous, but this is nothing new: French writer Pierre Loti, visiting in 1910, pleaded, 'Of all the yalıs on the Bosphorus, you must save the Amcazade Yalı'.

First stop on the standard Bosphorus cruise is **Kanlıca** on the Asian Shore. It's a lovely village dotted with picturesque mansions. The hills above, home to the lush Mihribad Forest Preserve, add to its beauty. But Kanlıca's main claim to fame is bacterial: since the 17th century, the place has been celebrated for its rich yoghurt. On the boat trips, crates of the

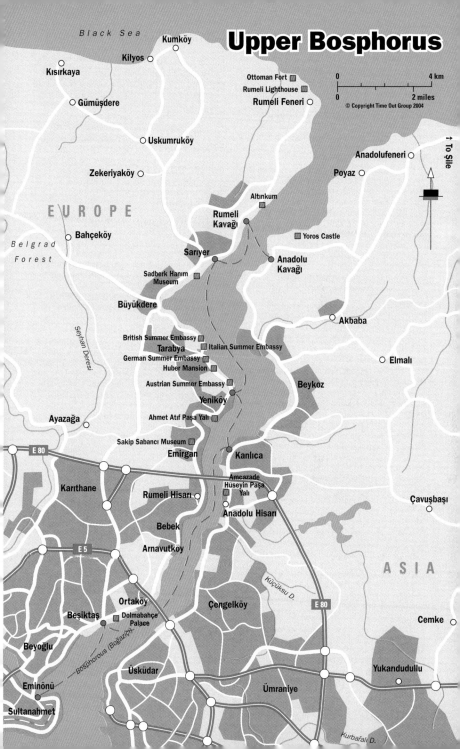

cultured stuff are brought on board for sale. It's worth visiting for the **Khedive's Villa** (Hıdiv Kasrı), a former summer residence of the 19th-century rulers of Egypt. It's a gem of a place, beautifully restored and put into service as a restaurant and tea garden. The views are magnificent. The villa is a 20-minute walk uphill from the landing stage. Kanlıca is also linked by regular ferries to Arnavutköy and Bebek on the European shore.

On departing Kanlıca the ferry noses back toward Europe. Shortly after passing the Istinye Bay inlet is the stunning **Ahmet Atıf Paşa Yalı**, a white neo-baroque fantasy of turrets and Ottoman roofs created by Italian architect Alexandre Villaury for the proprietor of the Pera Palas hotel (*see p52*). It now belongs to Kemal Uzan, the head of one of Turkey's most notorious business families. He's unlikely to be at home any time soon, as he's currently on the run from the Turkish police following a major banking scandal.

YENİKÖY

The ferry then pulls in at **Yeniköy**. As the Ottoman empire deteriorated in the early 19th century, increasingly desperate rulers used lavish gifts of land as a way of securing the support of foreign embassies in Istanbul. Yeniköy was considered choice real estate and the waterfront is lined with the greatest concentration of restored Bosphorus mansions, several of which remain the summer residences of the city's consulates.

Just south of the landing is the boxy, white shuttered **Sait Halim Paşa**, also known as the Pink Lion Mansion because of the two small stone lions on the quay. Sait Halim was grand vizier under Sultan Abdül Hamit in the dying days of the empire. The hapless Halim ended up taking much of the rap for the empire's disastrous decision to fight on Germany's side in World War I. Adding fatal injury to insult, he was then shot dead by an Armenian extremist soon after the end of the fighting. North of the landing is another Bosphorus landmark, the **Twin Yali**, a symmetrical semi-detached whose art nouveau scrollings mark it out as a work by Raimondo D'Aronco (*see p41*).

As the ferry departs Yeniköy it passes a string of old European summer embassies, including a vast, three-storey pinkish building, partially screened by trees, belonging to the Austrians. A mile or so further, spires and pointy gables mark out the fantastic **Huber Mansion**, another D'Aronco design. The Hubers made a vast fortune flogging Mauser rifles to the Ottoman government in the final days of the empire. Their residence was famed for its lavish parties, earning them regular

appearances in the late-19th-century versions of *Hello!* magazine. It is now the official Istanbul residence of the Turkish president. The forested slopes around both of these mansions give an idea of what much of the Bosphorus shoreline looked like not so very long ago.

Several more summer embassies follow in quick succession: the **German Summer Embassy** has a distinctive bell tower and looks not unlike a Black Forest town hall; the dilapidated **Italian Summer Embassy** remains supremely elegant; the **British Summer Embassy** is a small cottage in luxuriant garden.

SARIYER

The shoreline recedes to accommodate Büyükdere Bay and the Bosphorus stretches to its maximum width (3.5 kilometres, or just under two miles). As the ferry approaches land again, there's a curious flat-fronted building distinguished by bold yellow-and-white cross-hatching; this houses the **Sadberk Hanım Museum**, which is stuffed with Ottoman costumes, archaeological and ethnographic artefacts, and examples of old tilework.

The ferry next puts in at **Sarıyer**, beside the fantastical turreted **Naval Officers' Club**: built in 1911, it bears the seal of Sultan Mehmet V Resat on its front and is now a restaurant and social club for naval officers and their families.

Sarıyer is the largest village on the upper Bosphorus and also one of Greater Istanbul's most conservative suburbs. In 1995 a local woman was stoned to death here on suspicion of being a prostitute. For the morally unblemished, it's a lovely place to wander (if you get off the boat here you can catch bus No. 25E back to Eminönü). There's a fine old fish market just north of the ferry landing and several good seafood restaurants.

On Sular Caddesi in Sarıyer *dolmuş* depart for the next waterside village up, Rumeli Kavağı. En route they pass the **burial place of Telli Baba**, a mystic Muslim saint who is revered by local singletons. Wannabe brides come here to pray at the saint's tomb and take away a charmed piece of golden wire, guaranteed to secure them a husband. Newly-weds traditionally return on their wedding day to reattach the wire to the grille of the saint's tomb and pay homage to Telli Baba's magic. Saturday and Sunday afternoons can see major traffic snarl-ups as convoys of husband-seekers pile up along the narrow Bosphorus-side road.

RUMELI AND ANADOLU KAVAĞI

Rumeli Kavağı is a sleepy little place that gets its excitement from the arrival of the ferry. It's no more than a string of houses and restaurants along the shore road that cluster more densely around the ferry landing. From here the road runs north on up the Bosphorus, along the way passing dozens more restaurants set into the cliff face, plus a few small sandy beaches. These are private and usually charge entrance of around $1.50.

The coast road finishes up at the gates of an army base, but just before this is **Altınkum**, the best of the area's beaches, accessed down a narrow path through the trees. There you'll find a restaurant serving meze and cold beer. The water is marked off about 20 metres (65 feet) out by a line of buoys – worth sticking within if you're swimming, as the Bosphorus is swept by some strong currents further out.

Last stop for the ferry is **Anadolu Kavağı** on the Asian Shore, almost opposite Rumeli Kavağı. The boat halts here, giving passengers enough time to have a stroll and eat in one of its many fish restaurants, all of which cater exclusively to passing trade.

Time could also be spent clambering up to the Byzantine **Yoros Castle**, which looms on the headland north of the village offering commanding views of the Black Sea approaches. Originally the site of a temple to Zeus, where early Greek sailors would stop to make a sacrifice to ensure safe passage through the straits, the present fortress was built by the Byzantines, occupied by the Genoese in the mid-

14th century, then by the Turks, who strengthened the battlements. It lay abandoned and out of bounds until the 1980s, when it was opened to the public. Heading back down from the castle, take the steeply descending path across the heath. This gives out into scrub where you'll find a tea house with half a dozen rickety tables and a great view.

From Anadolu Kavağı the ferry sails straight back down to Beşiktaş and Eminönü with no stops on the way.

Khedive's Villa
Hıdiv Kasrı
Çubuklu Yolu 32, Kanlıca (0216 413 9644).
Open 9am-10pm daily. **Admission** free.

Sadberk Hanım Museum
Sadberk Hanım Müzesi
Piyasa Caddesi 27-29, Büyükdere (0212 242 3813).
Open 10.30am-6pm Mon, Tue, Thur-Sun.
Admission $3. **No credit cards**.

Belgrad Forest

Stretching over the hills and valleys north-east of the city, the forest is a popular haunt for summer picnickers and health freaks, cyclists and joggers. Thickly wooded, it is also Istanbul's nearest provider of unpolluted oxygen. It takes its name from the Serbs who historically inhabited the area, entrusted by Süleyman the Magnificent with guarding the

Working folk at Rumeli Kavağı.

Castle ahoy!
The headland at Anadolu Kavağı.

forest reservoirs that served as the city's water supply. With leafy glades and tree-covered hills, populated with oaks, pines, plane trees and beeches, it also has a distinctly Balkan feel. Walking the forest today you'll come across the remains of the reservoirs and aqueducts that supplied Istanbul with most of its fresh water under both Byzantines and Ottomans. The Serbs lived here until the 1890s, when the fruitcake sultan Abdül Hamit II got rid of them: he became suspicious that they might be poisoning the water and had them removed.

The forest was also long popular with wealthy European residents of Istanbul, who would retreat to Belgrad Village come summer to escape the heat and bouts of pestilence. In 1771, Lady Mary Wortley Montagu described the village in her diaries as a kind of Arcadian rural idyll, the inhabitants of which would meet every night 'to sing and dance, the beauty and dress of the women exactly resembling the ancient nymphs'.

Following Mahmut II's purge of the Janissary corps in 1826, those who escaped the massacre fled to the forest, where they took up traditional woodland pursuits such as shooting the sultan's deer and ambushing local traders. The sultan's radical response was to set the forest on fire.

All that's left of the village now are a few bumps in the forest floor, hidden off the road near one of the largest picnic areas at the **Büyük Bend** reservoir. This is one of the oldest parts of the water system, originally Byzantine, though restored by a string of subsequent rulers.

Also worth visiting is the **Long Aqueduct**, on the road to Kısırmandıra, another work by Mimar Sinan (see p40), built for Süleyman the Magnificent in 1563. The stream it crosses is the Kağıthane Suyu, which eventually flows into the Golden Horn.

Getting there

From Eminönü take the 25E bus (from Taksim it's the No 40) to Büyükdere. There switch to a dolmuş for Bahçeköy, which lies on the east side of the forest; it's a one-mile (1.5 kilometre) walk around to Büyük Bend.

The Black Sea coast

North of the twin points of Rumeli Kavağı and Anadolu Kavağı, the mouth of the Bosphorus widens out on both sides to meet the **Black Sea** (Karadeniz). Much of the coast from this point onwards is an off-limits military area, but there are small enclaves of civilian life. On the European side, there's **Rumeli Feneri**, a fishing port that encompasses the 'clashing rocks' of Jason and the Argonauts fame. Further round on the Black Sea shore lies **Kilyos**, one of Istanbul's most popular beach resorts, which is mirrored on the Asian side by the resort town of **Şile**.

RUMELI FENERI

Rumeli Feneri means 'European Lighthouse' in English. The lighthouse in question, perched at the top of steep cliffs with views over the entrance to the Bosphorus, was built by the British during the Crimean War era. But the village is most famous for its rocks: the L-shaped harbour wall extends out to two large humps – in ancient times known as the Symplegades or 'clashing rocks'. In ancient myths, the rocks were depicted as living creatures that would dash out from the shore to crash into passing boats. One such vessel was Jason's *Argo*, which famously managed to make it through the straits into the Black Sea, thanks to a neat trick with a pigeon and a shove from the goddess Athena.

These days, Rumeli Feneri is a working fishing village. The port makes for a laid-back Sunday lunch venue for the few Istanbulus who have discovered it. On the Black Sea side of town lies an **Ottoman fort**, which was once the main customs post in the area. Also of archaeological interest is the white stone altar on the top of the nearest of the Symplegades to shore. This was once used to light fires to warn passing ships – and as an altar for sacrifices to the sea god, Poseidon. The rocks are lumpy enough to climb up, though only if you've got good shoes and a head for heights.

Getting there

First get to Sariyer (see p242) and from there take bus No 150. Departures are hourly, with the last bus returning from Rumeli Feneri at 10.15pm. Alternatively, a taxi between Sariyer and Rumeli Feneri costs about $10.

KILYOS

While Kilyos possesses a couple of extensive sandy beaches (Kilya and Solar), it's also been hung, drawn and quartered by development. These days, it is an ultra-tacky hangout of dodgy bars and disappointed-looking Russian package tourists. Tragically, this formula for development is being repeated up and down the Black Sea coast, which isn't being damaged so much as devoured.

Solar Beach (admission $7) is a bit more exclusive. A middle class hangout, it has lifeguards sponsored by Advantage Card, a beachfront branch of Tommy Hilfiger and a food court with a Köçebaşı Express, an outlet of the chic Levent kebabery. In summer it's also a prime party venue for Istanbul clubbers who hit the sand for 24-hour raves and dance events.

Getting there

Kilyos is ten miles (15 kilometres) north of Sarıyer, from where there are regular dolmuş. These depart from a stop halfway up Sular Caddesi. The journey takes around half an hour and costs $0.50. The last dolmuş back to Sarıyer from Kilyos is around 8pm.

Trips Out of Town

Hillside Beach Club offers countable memories to dream of...

The memories will last if you pick a good choice for your holidays. Hillside Beach Club welcomes you whenever you want to spend a fantastic holiday.

Nature and Fun in Style
Hillside Beach Club is described by its guests as "heaven on earth". Surrounded by pine forests of Fethiye-Kalemya Bay, it has a spectacular nature and a panorama wholly integrated with nature. Hillside Beach Club is a first class holiday village; 350 rooms all with sea view; providing guests with the widest range of top-quality facilities and sports activities so that they may have a lazy, crazy or an active day according to their preference.

Served With Pleasure, Pampered With Care
With its deeply rooted superior service understanding and its commitment to offering high quality, Hillside Beach Club offers warm feelings and enjoyable moments to its guests throughout the summer season that lasts until late October. The care in details, attentive and friendly staff, the excellence in service quality, the unique and innovative approach and the guest-focused policy has been paying off with the national and international awards that Hillside Beach Club receives.

Festival of Food & Beverage All Day Long
Taste joins you in every moment at every point. Hillside Beach Club's main restaurant offers an open buffet feast with a large diversity. On the other hand, Pasha on the Bay serves as an a la carte restaurant. If you wish a little chat with appetizers, you'll have a large selection of delicious snacks and cooling drinks at the bars and corners during the whole day.

Close Your Eyes & Let Yourself To Your Feelings In Hillside Spa
In Hillside Beach Club, two totally seperated places exist for beauty and health, to take good care of yourself and to relax. Hillside Nature Spa offers an atmosphere in the unique nature of Hillside Beach Club and Hillside Day Spa draws a concept appropriate to the modern lifestyle.

In Hillside Beach Club, you will have the time of your life with unforgettable memories in a unique nature!

Hillside Beach Club
Kalemya Koyu
P.O.Box 123
48300 Fethiye - Muğla
TURKEY

T: +90 252 614 8360
F: +90 252 614 1470

W: www.hillside.com.tr
E: hbc@hillside.com.tr

one of

THE GREAT SPA
HOTELS OF THE WORLD

NATURE AND FUN IN STYLE

hillside SU

Hillside Su, located in one of the most breathtaking shores of Antalya, offers its guests a place of purity, where serene, crisp white connects with flashes of fiery red and mysterious black. Hillside Su is an urban hotel, located just 15 minutes away from the Antalya airport and is a member of the Design Hotels Group. Underscored by the ambiance of passion and perfection, Hillside Su is a dynamic and inspirational haven. Glittering disco balls, along with multi-colored lighting turns the heat up at the all-white, 1960s inspired Hillside Su, where the environment encourages exploration and inner freedom. The six enormous disco balls dominate the impressive lobby with a spectacular light show and set the tone for the whole Hillside experience.

Hillside Su meets the alternative expectations of the contemporary individuals with its dynamic lifestyle and its different characteristics. Having a beach of its own, Hillside Su is a holiday hotel with 294 all white rooms, including 39 suites and 2 presidential suites. As recreation, you may find a heated indoor pool, an outdoor pool, a specially decorated SPA including a Turkish bath, treatment and massage rooms where guests can relax and replenish through a specially designed menu. Besides sports options such as squash, tennis, fitness, water sports and beach volleyball, the guests may also enjoy Buffet & A la Carte restaurants that serve Turkish, Asian & Italian cuisines as well as Lounge, pool, beach and Sushi restaurants.

A brand new Hillside is hosting its guests in an infinite setting of white with premium services and exclusive facilities.

Just be yourself. For your dreams, your expectations and much more...

 design hotels™

MANAGED BY
ALARKO
TOURISM GROUP

HILLSIDE SU HOTEL | T.0242 249 0700 | hillside.com.tr
ANTALYA | F.0242 249 0707 |

The Princes' Islands

Gay writers, Trotsky and horse shit – island life Istanbul style.

Dotted out in the Marmara Sea off Istanbul's Asian Shore, the Princes' Islands (also known as the Kızıl Adalar or 'Red Islands') have long been a world apart. For centuries they were a place of exile for the victims of Byzantine and Ottoman court intrigues. Nowadays they are one of the last places where you can catch a glimpse of the old ethnic mix of Istanbul: Greeks, Armenians and Jews still rub shoulders with Turks in the local squares in a way that's no longer the case in the city proper. Churches are more numerous than mosques. The building material of necessity is wood, fretted and sawn into lacy designs to adorn fabulous mansions set in well-tended gardens. The streets are completely car-free and echo with the clip-clop of horse-drawn phaetons. Instead of car fumes, the air is heavy with the smell of horse shit. The overall effect is of a 19th-century time capsule – strongest in winter when the hordes of summer day-trippers are far away.

There are nine islands in total, of which four can be visited. Furthest from European Istanbul (20 kilometres, or 12 miles) is **Büyükada**, which is the largest of the islands and the most popular with visitors. It has traditionally been home to a large Jewish population. **Kınalıada** is Armenian, **Burgazada** is Greek and **Heybeliada** is predominantly Turkish.

Getting there

By ferry

Regular ferries to the islands depart from Eminönü's Adalar iskele, which is the dock nearest Sirkeci railway station. They stop at each of the islands in turn, taking an hour and a half to reach Büyükada (50 minutes to Kınalıada). The fare is $1.50. Departure times from Eminönü change with the season but in summer there are at least a dozen sailings a day from 9.20am onwards. Transport from island to island on the ferries is free so you can hop off at each island and then catch the next ferry on. There is also a less frequent and more expensive fast catamaran service from Eminönü but the time saved is not significant – and anyhow the slow sail is a pleasure in itself.

Kınalıada

Kınalıada is the least green of the islands. Its name (from *kınalı*, Turkish for 'dyed with henna') comes from the reddish tinge of the shoreline cliffs, although the absence of

greenery today is down to the fact that the island is almost completely scabbed over by modern housing. Historically, this was the place of exile of the Byzantine emperor Romanus IV, who suffered defeat by the Selçuks at the Battle of Manzikert in 1071.

The place comes to life during the summer months as the city's Armenian community descends en masse. The island is also a favoured spot for visiting Armenians from the global diaspora. On summer evenings the crowds along the seafront promenade are as dense as those on Istiklal Caddesi but with one significant difference: in Beyoğlu everyone's looking in the shop windows whereas here they're sizing up each other in a search for eligible marriage partners. The older Armenian residents look on from the tables of the **Bahar Patisserie**, one of Istanbul's most famous cafés, which is on the corner of Kınalı Meydanı, the main square by the ferry landing.

Sights include a fine modernist mosque, the **Kınalıada Camii**, erected in 1964 with an angular roof and elegant minaret, and an Armenian church, the **Surp Krikor Lusavoria**, on Narciciyi Sokak, a ten-minute walk inland from the ferry landing. En route pass by the grilled sheep's head vendors on Akasya Caddesi, which is also the place to hire bicycles ($1.25 an hour). Not that there are too many places to go: south of the centre are a number of beaches but they quickly become overcrowded at the first sign of balmy weather.

Where to stay & eat

There is no accommodation on Kınalıada. In addition to the Bahar Patisserie, Kınalı Meydanı also has the **Bahar Pub**; both do cakes and snacks, the latter alcohol too. On **Akasya Caddesi** there are a number of meyhanes with little to choose between them.

Burgazada

Burgazada is best known for its connections with one of Turkey's most famed literary figures, the short-story writer Sait Faik (1906-54), who lived on the island from 1939 until his death. He was a specialist in brief vignettes of the lives of those who lived around him. He was also gay, or at least bisexual, and probably

The only four-wheeled transport permitted on the islands.

found on the island a kind of freedom from the censorious mores of the city. His former home is now the modest **Sait Faik Museum**, which includes a musty collection of his works translated into a dozen languages and the author's death mask. If the place is locked try the shed in the garden, where the museum caretaker lives with his family.

The other thing that everybody knows about Burgazada is that it is strongly Greek in character; hence the dominant local landmark is the Greek Orthodox **Church of St John the Baptist**. The caretaker lives on the grounds and will open the church for interested parties.

On the island's western shore is the **Sait Faik Restaurant**. From here it's possible to look out over a flat Marmara Sea unblemished by land. A shoreline of pine woods and rocky coves adds to the pristine feel. This spot also has one of the scant stretches of coastline clean enough for swimming. The restaurant is about a 20-minute walk from the ferry landing. Alternatively, catch a phaeton from just north of the ferry landing (a tour of the island costs

$12, a trip to the restaurant $6) or rent a bicycle ($1.25 an hour) one street back from the waterfront.

Church of St John the Baptist
Takımağa Meydanı. **Services** 9am Sun.

Sait Faik Museum
15 Burgaz Çayırı Sokak. **Open** 10am-noon, 2-5pm Tue-Fri, Sun. **Admission** free.

Where to stay & eat

There is no accommodation on Burgazada. The area around the ferry landing is laden with fish restaurants, of which the Greek-owned **Barba Meyhane** (6b Yalı Caddesi, 0216 381 2404) is a popular choice. Expect to pay about $15 a head.

Heybeliada

The name means 'saddlebag island', which is a fairly good description of how it looks with a low landmass between between twin summits. These days the place is a big summer favourite

Looking east to Asia from **Büyükada**.

with picnickers. It's also an ongoing source of international tensions since the Turkish authorities closed down the Greek Orthodox school of theology at the hilltop **Haghia Triada Monastery** in the 1970s, depriving Istanbul's Greek community of its priesthood training centre. The justification offered is that all religious instruction, whether Christian, Islamic or Jewish, is 'regulated and supervised by the State' but such hogwash sits badly with Turkey's European Union ambitions and a climb-down may not be too far off.

In an interesting juxtaposition, much of the rest of the island is occupied by the military, which maintains the **Turkish Naval Academy** to the left of the ferry landing. Within the grounds is the grave of Sir Edward Barton, ambassador of Queen Elizabeth I to the Ottoman court, but it's out of bounds to the public unless by special request.

The best way of getting around the island is in a phaeton, picked up on Ayyıldız Caddesi, which runs parallel to the seafront one street back. An island tour takes an hour and costs $13, while a trip up to the monastery will set you back $5 – you can't get in but the views are good. Bicycles are rented at the Trakya Gıda corner store on Işgüzar Sokak, which runs inland from the phaeton stop on Ayyıldız. The going rate is $1.50 an hour.

Where to stay

The budget option is the **Özdemir Pension** (41 Ayyıldız Caddesi, 0216 351 1866, doubles $20-$35), where rooms come with TVs and en suite bathrooms. It's very close to the ferry landing. Across the road from the Özdemir, the **Prenset Pension** (40-2 Ayyıldız Caddesi, 0216 351 0042, doubles $50) has slightly better rooms and also rents out bicycles for $1 an hour. The **Merit Halki Palace** (94 Refah Şehitleri Caddesi, 0216 351 0025, www.merithotels.com, doubles $110) is one of the finest hotels anywhere in Istanbul. Set in a 19th-century Ottoman gingerbread mansion, it was entirely refitted in period style following a disastrous fire in 1991. Its swimming pool is also open to non-guests ($15-$20 a day).

Where to eat

The waterfront is brimming with restaurants. For value for money, hit the **Gökşins Ambrosia** (30B Ayyıldız Caddesi, 0216 351 1388, www.ambrosiada.com), where a basic meal of freshly caught fish, salad and a beer is just $6 all in. At the other end of the scale, the **Merit Halki Palace** (*see above*) restaurant welcomes non-guests; a full meal with wine will weigh in at around $30 a head.

He helps infertile women.

main settlement and ferry landing are on the very northern tip. A few steps south off the boat is the centre of town, Saat Meydanı, an open square with a little conical-capped clock tower. East is the island's motor pool – a corral of horse-drawn phaetons. Drivers offer big ($16) or small ($12) tours of the island, both of which end up at the foot of the hill atop which stands **St George's Monastery**. Climb the steep slope on foot – or hire a donkey for $2 – noting the hundreds of pieces of cloth tied to the branches of the trees: each represents a prayer, tied by the faithful of all religions, mostly by women desperate for a child. The infertile still ascend barefoot.

At the top are fine views and an excellent restaurant. The monastery itself has a chapel that's usually open to visitors with a number of icons depicting the old dragon-slayer himself, plus an assortment of saintly relics.

From up here, the islands of **Yassıada** and **Sivriada** are visible, the former distinguished by a fort-like prison. Neither has a particularly wholesome history. It was in the Yassıada jail that former prime minister Adnan Menderes and two of his ministers were hanged in 1961 following a military coup, while Sivriada gained notoriety in 1911 when Istanbul's stray dogs were rounded up and left to starve on the island. Neither island can be visited.

Getting around

To walk to the monastery, head west from Saat Meydanı past the police station and then continue along main Çankaya Caddesi; it's a walk of around 30 to 40 minutes. Bicycles can be hired from lots of places around Saat Meydanı for about $1.50 an hour.

Where to stay

The **Hotel Princess** (Iskele Caddesi 2, 0216 382 1162, doubles $60-$90) is right by the clock tower square, or there's the **Splendid Palas** (23rd Nisan Caddesi 53, 0216 382 6950, doubles $40-$55), which is just a bit further west of the Princess, along the same street. Both hotels have lovely old wooden façade disguising pleasantly modern rooms. The latter has a pool and a fine restaurant. The Splendid Palas is closed Nov-May.

Where to eat & drink

There are dozens of places all touting for business the minute you step off the ferry. Of them, we happen to like **Ali Baba** (20 Gulistan Caddesi, 0216 382 3733, main courses $10-$15) but there's actually little to choose between.

Büyükada

The biggest of the islands is suitably named: *büyük* means 'big' (*ada* is the word for 'island'). Previously, it was the Greek Prinkipo, as in 'prince', which may well have been a reference to the number of nobles that ended up here, in hiding, in exile or imprisoned – in Byzantine times there were about an equal number of monasteries and gaols on the island. More recently, from 1929 to 1933, Büyükada was the home of Leon Trotsky, who bashed out his *History of the Russian Revolution* in exile at the **Izzet Paşa Köskü**, a recently restored wooden mansion at 55 Çankaya Caddesi. The island was probably the safest place for him, given that at this time the city of Istanbul was also home to some 34,000 White Russians, living in exile after being defeated by Trotsky's Red Army. Trotsky lived in the house surrounded by armed 'secretaries', though, according to Turkish police reports, he did make one trip into Istanbul, to see Charlie Chaplin's *City Lights*. The Izzet Paşa mansion is also where in 1933 his daughter committed suicide.

The island is now a hugely popular but exclusive summer resort – a kind of Turkish take on the Hamptons. For the casual visitor it's just a gorgeous place for a long walk along leafy lanes scented heavily with blossom. The

Trips Out of Town

The Marmara Islands

Sun, sand and shedloads of holidaying Turks.

Not too far away – yet far enough to feel like an escape from the city – this rocky archipelago in the western Sea of Marmara also boasts reliably clean sandy beaches and clear sparkling water.

Not surprisingly then, the islands are a major summer destination for Istanbulus, particularly those without the time or the money to venture further afield. And therein lies the snag, as the islands' settlements have slowly been submerged beneath a wave of unplanned concrete development – particularly the otherwise extraordinarily pretty second island of Avşa. Don't go expecting unspoilt quaint fishing villages. However, for anyone after a couple of unpretentious days on the beach, happy staying in a simple pension, then the Marmara Islands fit the bill.

Marmara and **Avşa** are the two most popular islands, both with regular ferry connections to Istanbul. The former is more laid back and less developed, while the latter gets frantic in the summer months. As for the other five islands in the archipelago, there isn't a lot to do, and hardly anywhere to stay or eat.

Avoid July and August unless you want to satisfy an anthropological interest in the holidaying habits of working-class Turkish families. June and September are the best times to visit. From October to May most guesthouses and restaurants are closed and ferry crossings are frequently affected by bad weather.

Getting there

By ferry

From late June to mid-September there's a ferry at 8.30am each day departing from Eminönü for Marmara and Avşa; it leaves from a pier just east of Sirkeci train station. The journey takes five to six hours. The rest of the year the ferry goes out only on Wednesday and Friday, returning Thursday and Sunday. Tickets are bought from the Turkish Maritime Lines office in Karaköy and cost $5 one way. In August and September there are also ferries at 2pm Friday and Sunday from Tekirdağ on the European shore of the Marmara. During the off season (mid-September to June) another option is to take the regular high-speed ferry from Yenikapı to Bandırma and from there a bus to Erdek. From Erdek there are daily year-round ferries to Marmara Island at 11am (3.15pm Tuesday) and 8pm (10.30pm Friday and Sunday, no service Tuesday). These head back every morning at 6.45am.

By deniz otobüsleri

The *deniz otobüsleri* (sea bus) is a high-speed hydrofoil leaving from Bostancı and Yenikapı every morning at 10am and 10.30am respectively from the end of June to mid-September. This is the fastest option: these sea buses cut the travel time to Marmara to just over two hours. A one-way ticket costs $16. Reservations should be made well in advance. To get to Yenikapı the easiest thing is to jump in a taxi; from Sultanahmet it's about a ten-minute ride and should cost around $6.

Marmara Island

Istanbul Denizotobüsleri

Yenikapı İskele, Yenikapı (information 0212 516 1212/reservations 0212 517 9696/www.ido.com.tr). **Open** 6.30am-9.30pm daily. **Map** p288 H12.

Turkish Maritime Lines

Türkiye Denizcilik İşletmeleri
Rıhtım Caddesi, Karaköy (information 0212 249 1896/reservations 0212 249 922). **Open** 9am-6pm Mon-Fri. **Map** p289 N6.

Marmara

Largest and most mountainous of the seven islands, Marmara is something of a geological club sandwich. It's multi-layered with different rock types. Along the northern coast lies a lengthy band of the most famous local product, marble, from which the island takes its name. Marmara was the source of the celebrated grey-and-blue streaked Proconnesian used in many of Istanbul's great buildings including the Haghia Sophia.

The main settlement, **Marmara town**, is clustered beneath the rugged slopes of Ilyas Dağı on the south side of the island. It wouldn't win any prizes for its native architecture, yet it's pleasant enough, with a small fishing fleet and a row of shore-front cafés where local menfolk sit chatting and playing cards. The short sandy strip of **Kole beach** is five minutes' walk around the point to the west, past a pair of old buildings saved from the bulldozer by a preservation order, but now left somewhat isolated. There are also numerous coves along the coast north from here, some of which can be swum to or accessed via steep staircases along the cliffs. The town also holds the island's only bank, just east of the Kemal restaurant on the main harbourfront road, Sahil Yolu; it has an ATM machine and an exchange office.

In times past Maramara was famed for its wine, as the hundreds of ancient and medieval amphora dotted about its homes and pensions now testify. Many wine-carrying ships came a cropper and the sea hereabouts is littered with ancient wrecks. One of these, a 13th century Byzantine wine carrier, is currently the subject of an underwater archaeological excavation. The finds from this can be inspected by turning up at the warehouse next to the Petrol Ofisi petrol station, which is situated 250 metres east of the ferry landing on Sahil Yolu. Regrettably, the huge volumes of Byzantine wine recovered from the ship turned out, on sampling, to be a little corked.

When you've exhausted the pleasures in town, take a 15-minute dolmuş ride to **Çınarlı** on the west coast. Set in a verdant valley, it must have been an idyllic place before the concrete took over. It still retains some charm

with a long beach backed by small holiday homes and pensions. Shading the village green are the magnificent plane trees (*çınar*) from which the village takes its name. One is said to be more than 1,000 years old. Several local families rent out rooms and there are a clutch of simple eateries on the seafront.

East from Marmara the road soon turns into a dusty track which winds over the scrubby mountains to the north coast. This side of the island has been carved away by centuries of quarrying. Huge piles of slag pour down the mountainsides and everything is covered in a thick layer of dust. Once exposed, the marble is cut into immense blocks that are trucked off to the harbour at **Saraylar**. Populated mainly by migrant quarry workers from the Black Sea coast, the only attraction in Saraylar, apart from cheap marble, is the so-called **Open Air Museum**. Actually it's more of an archaeological dumping ground, a small field filled with Roman and Byzantine stonework discovered in the surrounding area, open to the elements and the public. Nearby, several Roman sarcophagi lie partially buried.

Just over a mile outside Saraylar on the Çınarlı road is a ruined **Genoese castle**, built to protect coastal dwellers from pirate attacks. Access is tricky without your own transport as there are no passing dolmuş and taxis are thin on the ground. Try hitching.

Where to eat

The best the island has to offer is the **Kemal Restaurant** (Sahil Yolu, Imam Meydanı, 0266 885 5257, main courses $5-$10) where meze, grilled meat and fish is served at tables shaded by trees. Also on the front but nearer the ferry station, the simpler **Birsen Restaurant** (Sahil Yolu, main courses $3) does decent soups and stews. Over at Kole beach, try the **Aborda**, which has a limited menu (main courses $3) alongside basic beach/café drinks.

Where to stay

Marmara's guesthouses and pensions open only for the brief holiday season. When summer starts things fill up fast, so booking is essential. Pick of the bunch though is the **Mola Motel** (Osman Ağa Sokak 1, 0266 885 5737, www.molamotel.com, doubles $15), which is just a five-minute walk from the ferry landing. It's decorated with abundant amphoras and fishing nets and has a terrace overlooking Kole beach. The friendly owners are fantastically knowledgable about the island. The **Marmara Hotel** (Kole Plaj Yolu, 0266 885 6140, doubles $15-$20) also to the west of town near Kole

Trips Out of Town

Avşa: summer fun.

beach, has simple, clean rooms with huge expanses of local marble. Rooms at the **Şato Motel** (Kole Mevki, 0266 885 5003, rates $16-$20) are similarly plain but redeemed by sea views from the balconies.

In Çınarlı, head south along the nameless waterfront road for a stretch of pensions and motels, including the **Viking Motel** (0266 895 8087, doubles $30, half board) and, a little further out, the **Motel Kumsal** (0266 895 8001, doubles $40, full board). Given the paucity of dining options in Çınarlı taking up the option of inclusive meals is a good idea.

Avşa

South of Marmara Island, Avşa is gifted and cursed by having the archipelago's best beaches. It draws far more holidaying Istanbulus than its larger neighbour and, as a result, has become something of an aesthetic disaster zone. The main centre, **Türkeli**, is a scrappy affair – a long strip of ramshackle concrete and breeze-block buildings stretching for several kilometres along the west coast. The island's main historic attraction, the Greek **Monastery and Church of Haghia Triada**, is lost amongst the gimcrack shanties to the south of the town. For the best beach, head north out of the centre along the main seafront road and keep going. After a 20-minute walk, past the Çınar Hotel, the concrete sprawl subsides into gentler whitewashed houses and tree-lined streets, finally running out into a fine beach, notable for its clean sand and clear water. At night the focus shifts over to the promenade and the hangar-like cafés by the ferry landing. Here, families sit drinking *çay* and playing cards late into the night.

Across the island, the village of **Yiğitler** has a good stretch of sandy beach, less encroached on by building than those at Türkeli. Nearby **Altinkum** also has a good sandy beach, although it's blighted by some grim bars. For more secluded swimming, head off on foot or by bicycle around the southern coast of the island, where small coves await discovery. Another option is the tractor-pulled 'train' that conveys people north of Türkeli to another stretch of beach and more holiday homes at **Maviköy**.

Where to eat

Yarar (Plaj Yolu, Türkeli, main courses $3-$6) has been serving decent meze, seafood and meat dishes for 30 years. It's on the beach south of the ferry landing, so you can enjoy a meal next to the water. On the other side of the quay, the **Köfteci Tarzan** (Rıhtım Caddesi, main courses $2.50) is also deservedly popular.

Where to stay

Weekend trips to Avşa in season (end of May to end of September) can be difficult, as many pensions and hotels do not let out rooms for only one night. This policy is variable though, so it is best to check out before travelling. In Türkeli, the **Yarar Otel** (0266 896 1134, doubles $40, half board) lies at the northern end of Sahil Yolu, the main waterfront road, on the town's best beach. Guests get free use of recliners and umbrellas. Also north of the ferry landing on Sahil Yolu, but closer in to the centre, is the **Çınar Otel** (0266 896 1014, doubles $55, half board). The architecture may be grim but the hotel has good clean rooms, service is friendly and it's on the beach.

Directory

Getting Around	256
Resources A-Z	261
Vocabulary	273
Further Reference	275

Features

Sightseeing buses	258
Waiting for the big one	262
Mosque etiquette	267
Istanbul for women	269
Bored, or just getting it regularly?	274

Directory

Getting Around

Arriving by air

Istanbul's international air gateway is Atatürk Airport, approximately 25km (15 miles) west of the city centre in Yeşilköy. The airport underwent a major overhaul in 1999/2000 and gained a sparkling new international terminal (Dış Hatlar) with a decent array of shops, restaurants, bars, a massage parlour, post office, 24-hour banking, exchange bureaux, car-hire outlets, a tourist office and a hotel reservation desk. It's also compact and easily navigated. From landing to clearing customs usually takes 20 minutes. Security checks can add time to check-in procedures, so turn up at least 90 minutes before your flight.

A second international airport, Sabiha Gökçen, has also been built in Kurtköy, on the Asian side of the city. Talk was of it handling three million travellers annually, but the finished product sits there forlorn and completely unused. Not an isolated incident, it has to be said: many a president has had airports constructed in extraneous locations near private summer houses.

Atatürk International Airport

Atatürk Hava Limanı Yolu *(24-hr English language flight info 0212 663 6400 ext 4155/ 4157/www.dhmiata.gov.tr).*

Major airlines

In addition to the following, Istanbul is served by many other international carriers, including Air France, Alitalia, Delta, KLM and Lufthansa.

British Airways
Istanbul 0212 234 1300 UK 08708 509850/ www.britishairways.com

Turkish Airlines (THY)
Istanbul 0212 444 0849 UK 020 7766 9300/ www.thy.com

Connections to the city

There are three options for getting from the airport to the city centre: bus, underground or taxi. The choice depends on where you're staying and how much time you've got.

A company called Havaş operates the **express airport bus** service, which leaves for four different destinations from a signposted halt outside the arrivals hall. The only one of use to visitors is the Taksim service – fine if you're staying in Beyoğlu or Taksim – which runs at 5am, 6am and thereafter twice hourly until 11pm, stopping en route at the Bakırköy Sea Bus Terminal, Aksaray and Tepebaşı (just short of Taksim). The fare is around $5 (plus a 25 per cent surcharge between midnight and 6am), which is collected by a conductor on the bus.

The **underground**, or 'light metro' takes you from the international terminal building to Aksaray (currently the end stop) in half an hour and costs just $0.75 – not that you want to be in Aksaray, but you can connect from here by bus to Taksim, or by tram (see p258) to Sultanahmet. Services run 6.15am-midnight Mon-Sat and 6.30am-midnight on Sun.

Otherwise, the simplest option is to take a taxi. There's a large taxi rank right outside the arrivals hall. Fares are metered: journeys to the centre of Sultanahmet, around the Hippodrome and Haghia Sophia, should be around $10-$12 (half as much again at night). The ride takes about 20 minutes but can stretch to 45 minutes if the traffic's bad. To Taksim, it costs around $15 and can take anywhere between 20 and 50 minutes, depending on the time of day.

Arriving by train

The days of the Orient Express are long gone; rail travel from Europe to Istanbul is now the preserve of backpackers and the lower-income end of Turkey's Balkan diaspora. The only direct route to Istanbul from Greece is from Thessalonika, with a daily 7.25am departure taking an average of 15 hours to cover the 850km (510 miles). The one other direct service from Europe is the daily Bosphorus Express, departing Bucharest at 2.05pm and arriving in Istanbul at 8.27am the following morning.

Trains from Europe pull in at **Sirkeci Station** (*gar*), beside the Golden Horn in Eminönü. From here it's a short walk or brief tram ride up the hill to Sultanahmet, or a taxi to Taksim costs $2-$3.

Trains from points south and east terminate at **Haydarpaşa Station** on the Asian shore. International arrivals include the Trans-Asya, which departs from Tehran every Thursday at 8.15pm and limps into Istanbul on Sunday afternoon 69 hours later. From Syria, you could board the Toros Express

Directory

in Damascus at 5.13am on a Tuesday and be in Istanbul at around 6pm the next day.

The two stations, Sirkeci and Haydarpaşa, are connected by ferries, though there's a tunnel link on the drawing board. Info lines serve Sirkeci (0212 5270051) and Haydarpaşa (0216 348 8020 ext 336) between 7am-midnight daily, but in Turkish only. Timetables are posted on the state railways (TCDD) website (www.tcdd.gov.tr). At press time the international services were curiously absent from the English version.

Sirkeci Station

Istasyon Caddesi, Eminönü (0212 520 6575 ext 417/0216 337 8741 7am-7pm daily).

Haydarpaşa Station

Haydarpaşa Istasyon Caddesi, Kadıköy (0216 336 4470 for reservations 7am-7pm daily).

Arriving by coach

Turkish coach companies (such as Ulusoy and Varan) run regular direct services from many European cities. But be prepared for lengthy waits at the border – particularly with Bulgaria, where it can take up to three hours to clear customs. Travellers arriving by coach disembark at the vast main international and inter-city bus terminal (*otogar*) in the western district of Esenler. Although this district is approximately 10 kilometres (six miles) from the city centre, there are courtesy minibuses to Taksim and Sultanahmet. There's also an underground line known as the 'light metro'. This line connects the terminal to Aksaray, where you can trudge to the Taksim bus stop across the road. Alternatively, you can head for a nearby tram stop for Sultanahmet.

Esenler bus terminal

Uluslararası Istanbul Otogarı
Büyük Istanbul Otogan, Bayrampaşa (0212 658 0505). Open 24hrs daily.

Ulusoy

Inönü Caddesi 59, Gümüşsuyu (0212 244 6375/444 1888/ international journeys 0212 658 3006/www.ulusoy.com.tr). **Open** 24hrs daily. **Credit** AmEx, MC, V. Twice-weekly buses to and from Greece (Thessalonika, 12hrs, $50; Athens, 21hrs, $80), Germany (Münich, 48hrs, $115; Frankfurt, 55hrs, $135) and France, via Italy (Milan, 47hrs, Lyon, 54hrs, Paris 60hrs, $150 flat fare). Bookings can be made through the website.

Varan

Inönü Caddesi 29, Gümüşsuyu (0212 251 2739/www.varan.com.tr). **Open** 24hrs daily. **Credit** MC, V. Weekly buses to and from Greece (Thessalonika, 12hrs, $55; Athens, 21hrs, $80) and Austria (Vienna, 33hrs, Salzburg, 37hrs, Innsbruck, 39hrs, $110 flat fare).

Public transport

Public transport is cheap and improving all the time thanks to a municipal campaign to defeat the city's chronic traffic problem. The result is reinforcement to the entire transport infrastructure: extensions to the metro and tram lines, new bypasses and underpasses on the roads, new sea bus routes and funiculars are all under way, and a much-discussed trans-Bosphorus tunnel is in the pipeline. For the time being, though, Istanbul still endures gridlock along major arteries.

Happily, the two main areas in which visitors are likely to spend most time – Sultanahmet and Beyoğlu – are easily, and perhaps better, explored on foot. (For information on getting between the two *see* p67 **Crossing the Golden Horn**). However, there are some journeys that are best undertaken by public transport. Buses are useful for heading up the Bosphorus coast to Ortaköy, Arnavutköy, Bebek and beyond, while trips to the districts of Üsküdar and Kadıköy on the Asian shore are best undertaken by ferry or sea bus. The most convenient way to get to shopping and

business districts in Nişantaşı, Teşvikye, Etiler and Levent is via the modern new metro line that runs north from Taksim.

The website of the IETT, the local transport authority, is informative and has an excellent English version that includes maps, timetables and lost property inquiries.

IETT

Istanbul Elektrik Tramway ve Tünel Işletmeleri Genel Müdüurluğu *Erkan-ı Harp Sokak 4, Tünel (0212 245 0720/free helpline 0800 211 6068/www.iett.gov.tr).*

Akbil

Akbil, the 'smart card', is an electronic travel pass that can be used on all public transport except *dolmuş* and minibuses. Convenient, as well as offering a 10 per cent discount on fares, it's a silver metal stud fixed into a plastic grip. Akbils are available for a small refundable deposit (around $4) from booths at all main bus, sea bus and metro stations. To use, firmly press the circular metal bit into the socket on the orange machine located next to the driver on buses, or to the left of special turnstiles at all metro, light rail, tram and ferry boat stations. Recharge at automatic Akbil machines located at bus, metro and tram stations, sea bus and ferry terminals or at Akbil booths around town.

Particularly useful for visitors is the *mavi* (blue) Akbil, a travel pass that operates on exactly the same principle, but with one-day, one-week or 15-day validity.

Buses

Most city buses (*belediye otobüsü*) are operated by the municipality, but there are also privately run 'public' versions (*halk otobüsü*). Municipal buses are red and white (the old ones) or shades of green, and all have IETT written on

Sightseeing buses

It's taken an amazingly long time for the city's first sightseeing bus company to appear and then, true to form, as soon as one turns up there's another one right behind. So take your pick: the red bus or the yellow bus. Both are open-topped double-deckers, both depart from Sultanahmet Square following similar routes: across the Galata Bridge, along the Bosphorus coastal road to the Dolmabahçe Palace, up to Taksim, back down and over the Atatürk Bridge, west along the Golden Horn to the city walls then back to Sultanahmet via the aqueduct. The full circuit takes about an hour and a half. The red 'City Sightseeing' buses currently set off three times daily (11am, 2pm, 5pm), while the yellow 'Bus Turistik' goes every half hour. The latter is *indi-bindi* – passengers can hop on or hop off at any of the 18 stops. The service runs daily from 10am-8.30pm between 30th March and 25th October and from 10am-5.30pm in winter. Buy a ticket either as you board or from booths at Taksim Square and Sultanahmet. The one-day adult fare is $15 ($17 on weekends and public holidays). Kids aged 5-12 pay $8 ($9 on weekends and public holidays), while under-4s travel free.

the front. Private ones are pale blue and green. Buy tickets (*bilet*) for municipal buses before boarding (they won't take money on the bus). On private buses, pay a conductor seated inside the doorway (they won't take municipal tickets). Tickets for municipal buses are sold from booths at main stops and stations; you can also buy them from newsstands and nearby stalls for a 30 per cent premium.

Most newer buses display electronic signboards with route information. Bus stops also have route maps. Still, the sheer number of routes and the fact that traffic disrupts timetables can make bus travel a nightmare. If you're having problems then scribble your destination on a scrap of paper and someone is bound to be able to point you in the right direction. Bus services run from 6am to 11pm.

The following are some of the more useful routes:

Eminönü–Taksim (via Tepebaşı)
54E, 69E, 74A
Eminönü–Taksim (via Karaköy)
46C, 66, 70FE, 70KE, 74
Eminönü–Eyüp 36CE, 44B, 99, 99A
Eminönü–Edirnekapı 37E, 38E, 91O
Eminönü–Ortaköy-Bebek-Emirgan 22, 22R, 25E, 30D
Eminönü–Hasköy 47E
Taksim–Nişantaşı 43
Taksim–Ortaköy-Bebek-Emirgan 40, 42T
Taksim–Hasköy 54ET
Taksim–Edirnekapı 87

Dolmuş & minibuses

A *dolmuş* (the word means 'full') is basically a shared taxi that sets off once every seat is taken. *Dolmuş* run fixed routes (points of origin and final destination are displayed in the front window) but with no set stops. Passengers flag the driver down to get on (if there's room) and holler out to be let off (*İnecek var!*). For local journeys, there's just one fixed fare. Ask a fellow passenger how much or just watch what everyone else is paying. *Dolmuş* run later than buses, often as late as 2am.

Minibuses are the crowded, less comfortable cousins of the *dolmuş*. They are less common these days, having been banished to the fringes as part of the ongoing municipal drive to clean up the city centre. The advantage of the minibus is that fares are lower, but chances are you'll make your journey standing while being blasted by tinny Turko-pop. Pay and get on/off as you would a *dolmuş*. The main routes are from Beşiktaş to the upper Bosphorus districts.

Metro & trams

New metro and tram systems provide a comfortable, efficient alternative to clogged roads and overcrowded buses. However, coverage remains scant. At present the metro, opened in autumn 2000, runs from Taksim north to the district of 4th Levent, stopping at Osmanbey, Şişli, Gayrettepe and Levent. Given that these are largely business and wealthy residential districts, few of Istanbul's visitors benefit. However, extensions currently under construction and slated for completion in 2008 will eventually take the line south of Taksim to the sea bus jetty at Yenikapı (more useful) and north of 4th Levent to Maslak. There's also the 'light metro', which connects the district of Aksaray (west of the Grand Bazaar) to the Esenler bus terminal beyond and on to the airport.

The city's only modern tramway runs from Zeytinburnu (in the direction of the airport) via Aksaray to Sultanahmet and terminates at Eminönü beside the Galata Bridge. This is a genuinely useful service for visitors, linking tourist spots such as the Grand Bazaar, Haghia

Sophia, Sultanahmet Mosque, Topkapı Palace, the Egyptian Bazaar and Golden Horn area. You can also use the tram to visit the city walls. Where relevant, tram stops are given in the listings throughout this book. Tokens are bought in advance from kiosks at the tram stops, and are fed into automatic barriers to allow you on to the platform. A single trip on the tram costs about $0.70, irrespective of the destination. The service runs daily from around 6am-midnight, depending where you board.

An extension is currently being built between Eminönü and Beşiktaş, crossing the Galata Bridge. There'll be six stops in between including Karaköy and Kabataş, the ferry and sea bus terminal. A yet-to-be-built funicular will then run from Kabataş up to Taksim Square.

Tünel & tram

A 125-year-old funicular, known as the *tünel*, ascends from Karaköy, by the north end of the Galata Bridge, up to Tünel Square at the southern end of Istiklal Caddesi. It's only a very short run, but it saves an extremely tiring climb up steeply sloping streets (or an equally dizzying descent). The service runs 7am-10pm Monday-Saturday and 7.30am-10pm on Sunday and costs around $0.50. It connects at the top with an authentic olde worlde tram, which dates back a century, that shuttles up Istiklal Caddesi to Taksim Square and back. Given that it's a mile-and-a-half-long drag, the idea has merit, but why then give the one tram just a single carriage? Akbil (*see p257*) can be used for either, but regular bus tickets can not. You need to buy a token for the funicular at the entrance, and a ticket for the tram from the Tünel

Square funicular station or from a vendor in Taksim Square. For both tram and funicular, tickets cost $0.50.

Ferries & sea buses

There's a range of boats and ships of all sizes shuttling back and forth between the European and Asian shores, operating to summer and winter timetables. Summer officially runs from mid-June to mid-September and pocket timetables are available from all ferry terminals; departure times are also posted online (*see below*). The main services are between Eminönü, Karaköy and Beşiktaş on the European side and Üsküdar and Kadıköy on the Asian. These are large, once-white ferries (*vapur*) capable of carrying hundreds. Departures are every 15 minutes or so: *see p107*. There are also regular services running up the Golden Horn to Eyüp from Üsküdar via Eminönü. Less frequent are the services that criss-cross the Bosphorus, starting at Eminönü and calling at Haydarpaşa, Ortaköy, Arnavutköy, Bebek, Kandilli and beyond.

Further afield, there are ferries from Eminönü and Kabataş to the Princes' Islands (*see p248*). There's also an extremely popular Bosphorus tour that departs from Eminönü three times daily – a must for visitors (*see p240*).

In addition to the big ferries, there are modern catamarans (called *deniz otobüsleri* or 'sea buses'). These are faster but more expensive and generally restricted to commuter hours. You can pick up timetables from the ferry terminals or check online (*see below*).

Turkish Maritime Organisation

Türkiye Denizcilik İşletmeleri Şehir Hatları İşletmesi AŞ
Rıhtım Caddesi 4, Karaköy (0212 251 5000/www.tdi.com.tr).

Istanbul Fast Ferry

Istanbul Deniz Otobüsleri AŞ
Kennedy Caddesi, Sahil Yolu, Hızlı Feribot İskelesi, Yenikapı (0212 517 9696/516 1212/www.ido.com.tr).

Bikes

One glance at the traffic in Istanbul explains why there are hardly any bicycles on the road. In addition, the city is littered with hills to challenge even the fittest, and streets are often unfriendly, with slippery cobbles, tyre-trapping tram-lines and potholes everywhere. There are a few exceptions, though. The Bosphorus shore road north of Ortaköy is great for biking; it has a wide, well-surfaced road with fine views and sea breezes. The Princes' Islands are also good on two wheels, and in fact, a bike is one of the few options for getting around, as cars are banned. Bicycles can be hired on the islands.

The local motorbike culture, on the other hand, is beginning to burgeon. So if you're planning to travel the length and breadth of the city, are secure on two wheels and prepared to brave the traffic, then it may make sense to hire a motorbike. There's just one place that does this, **Moto Villa** in Levent. They have around 18 bikes and scooters, which range from 101cc to 650cc. All you need is a valid licence and a credit card. Bikes are delivered to your hotel.

Moto Villa

Sülün Sokak 7, Levent (0555 267 0700/0212 2803050/ www.villalevent.com). **Rates** from $30 per day; reduced weekly rates available. **Credit** AmEx, MC, V. Ask for Vasfi or Hakan Bozkurt, both of whom speak English and are available 24 hours a day.

Walking

Walking is absolutely the best way of getting around Istanbul. The main visitors' areas of Sultanahmet, the

Bazaar Quarter and Beyoğlu are all compact and perfect for exploring on foot. Main roads are few, while back-streets are narrow, sloping and better suited to pedestrians than cars.

On a cautionary note, you should pay particular attention when crossing roads, main or otherwise: drivers are not always alert to pedestrians and often jump lights.

Taxis

Taxis are numerous and you won't have a problem finding one whatever the time, day or night. Just stand at the kerb and hail them. Licensed taxis are bright yellow, with a roof-mounted *taksi* sign and plate number stencilled on the door. They're all metered, and relatively cheap by European standards. If the meter isn't running, get out and grab another cab.

During the day the meter displays the word *gündüz* (day rate) and starts off with the equivalent of $0.75 on the clock. From midnight to 6am the *gece* (night) rate kicks in, adding 50 per cent to the cost of the fare. Running rate during the day is about $1 per mile, so a trip between Sultanahmet and Taksim Square costs $3-$4. There's no room for haggling and tips are not required. Cheating is also difficult, but beware drivers who insist you only gave them a TL 1 million note when in fact it was TL 20 million. Also, as in New York, taxi driving is an expedient option for new immigrants, so plenty of Istanbul taxi drivers don't know the streets outside their own neighbourhoods. It's not unusual to have your driver ask you the way, if not other cars and passers-by. If you cross the Bosphorus bridges then the toll (around $2) is added to the fare.

There is no city-wide dispatching system.

Driving

Driving is not recommended in Istanbul, where heavy congestion doesn't stop drivers from flooring the accelerator at every chance. The limit in urban areas is 50kmh (30mph), rising to 120kmh (75mph) on motorways. Turkish road signs conform to international protocol and seat belts are the law, but observance of regulations is laughable.

Street parking is difficult and not always legal, in which case you're liable to get towed. Use car parks, which are plentiful. At open-air car parks you may have to leave the keys so that cars can be shuffled.

Paperwork

If you plan to take your own car to Turkey, prepare to be enmeshed in red tape. Drivers must provide registration documents and a valid international driving licence at the point of entry. Cars, mini-buses, caravans, and motorbikes can be taken into Turkey for up to six months without a *carnet de passage* or *triptyque*. Your vehicle is registered in your passport and you are issued a certificate that should be carried at all times, along with your driving licence and passport. If you stay in Turkey for more than six months, you either have to leave and re-enter the country, or apply to the Turkish Touring & Automobile Association (see *below*) for a *triptyque*. You will not be allowed to visit another country without taking your vehicle unless you first visit the nearest customs office to cancel the registration of the car in your passport. Drivers from Europe also need a Green Card (available from your insurance company).

There is a rarely enforced law requiring cars to be equipped with a fire

extinguisher, first-aid kit and two warning triangles. Accidents should be reported immediately to the traffic police (Trafik Polisi) by dialling Alo Trafik on 154.

Turkish Touring & Automobile Association

Türkiye Turing ve Otomobil Kurumu
1 Sanayi Sitesi Yanı, Seyrantepe, 4 Levent (0212 282 8140/fax 0212 282 8042).
Turkey's equivalent of the AA.

Breakdown services

Gökşenler

Atatürk Oto Sarayi Sitesi 2, Kisim. Gökşenler Plaza 213, Maslak (0212 276 3640). **Open** 8.30am-6.30pm Mon-Fri; 8.30am-3.30pm Sun. **Credit** MC, V.
Provides 24-hour emergency service.

Istanbul Traffic Foundation

0212 282 4232/0212 279 5803
Provides 24-hour towing services.

Car hire

Rental rates generally include third-party liability and unlimited mileage but they're still high compared with Europe. The rates quoted include VAT and insurance.

Avis

Abdülhakhamit Caddesi 84/A, off Cumhuriyet Caddesi, Taksim (0212 297 9610961/www.avis.com.tr). **Open** 9am-7pm daily. **Rates** $70-$130 per day. **Credit** AmEx, DC, MC, V.
Other locations: Atatürk Airport, international arrivals (0212 663 0646/7).

Budget

Cumhuriyet Caddesi 19, Taksim (0212 253 9200/www.budgettr.com). **Open** 8.30am-7pm daily. **Rates** $40-$70 per day. **Credit** AmEx, MC, V.
Other locations: Atatürk Airport, international arrivals (0212 663 0858).

Europcar

Topçu Caddesi 1, off Cumhuriyet Caddesi, Taksim (0212 254 7710/www.europcar.com.tr. **Open** 8.30am-7pm daily. **Rates** $85-$165 per day. **Credit** AmEx, DC, MC, V.
Other locations: Atatürk Airport, international arrivals (0212 663 0746).

Directory

Resources A-Z

Consulates

All foreign embassies are located in Ankara. However, many countries also have a consulate in Istanbul.

Australian Consulate General
Tepecik Yolu 58, Etiler (0212 257 7050). **Open** 8.30am-12.30pm, 1.30pm-5pm Mon-Fri. *Visa section* 8.30am-noon Mon-Thur.

Canadian Honorary Consulate
İstiklal Caddesi 373/5, Beyoğlu (0212 251 9838). **Open** 9.30am-5.30pm, 1.30pm-5.30pm Mon-Thur; 9.30am-1pm Fri. **Map** p294 M4.

Republic of Ireland Honorary Consulate
Acısu Sokak 5/4, Maçka (0212 259 6979). **Open** 11am-5pm Mon-Fri.

New Zealand Honorary Consulate General
İnönü Caddesi 92/3, Gümüşsuyu, Taksim (0212 251 3895). **Open** 9am-7pm Fri.

UK Consulate General
Meşrutiyet Caddesi 34, Tepebaşı, Beyoğlu (0212 334 6400/ www.britishembassy.org.tr). **Open** 8.30am-1pm; 2pm-4.30pm Mon-Fri. *Visas* 8am-noon Mon-Fri. **Map** p294 M3.

US Consulate
İstinye Mahallesi, Kaplıcalar Mevkii Sokak 2, İstinye (0212 335 9000/0212 340 4444 for visa appointments/www.usisist.gov.tr). **Open** 8am-noon, 1pm-4.30pm Mon-Fri.

Courier services

DHL
Customer services (0212 444 0040/444 0041/www.dhl.com.tr). **Sultanahmet office**: *Yerebatan Caddesi 15/2 (0212 512 5452).* **Open** 10am-6pm daily. **Credit** AmEx, MC, V. **Taksim office**: *Cumhuriyet Caddesi 20 (0212 245 5850).* **Open** 10am-6pm Mon-Fri; 10am-5pm Sat. **Credit** AmEx, DC, MC,V.
One of the country's best-known courier companies, DHL offers international service and national deliveries to major cities.

Intercargo
Bıldırcın Sokak 10/A, off Esentepe Caddesi, Mecidiyeköy (0212 275 1544/www.intercargo.com.tr). **Open** 9am-6pm Mon-Fri; 9am-2pm Sat. **No credit cards**
Local and national deliveries.

UPS
Courier bookings (0212 444 0033); customer services (0212 444 0066/ www.ups.com). **Sultanahmet office**: *Aksakal Sokak 14, off Küçükayasofya Caddesi (0212 517 4102).* **Open** 9am-7pm Mon-Fri; 8.30am-4pm Sat. **Credit** AmEx, MC, V. **Taksim office**: *Yedikuyular Caddesi 4/3 (0212 368 8086/87).* **Open** 8.30am-7pm Mon-Fri; 8.30am-6pm Sat. **Credit** AmEx, MC, V.
Domestic and international service.

Yurtiçi Kargo
Eski Büyükdere Caddesi 17-19, Kargo Plaza, Maslak (0212 365 2365/ www.yurticikargo.com.tr). **Open** 8.30am-3.30pm Mon-Fri; 8.30am-1.30pm Sat. **Cağaloğlu office**: *Çatalçeşme Sokak 44/1 (0212 527 0351).* **No credit cards**. **Taksim office**: *Lamartin Caddesi 29A (0212 238 0453).* **No credit cards**.
Local and national deliveries.

Customs

Turkish customs laws allow foreign visitors to import one litre of alcohol, five litres of wine, 200 cigarettes and ten cigars. You may be asked to register electronic equipment to ensure that it leaves Turkey with you. For more details ring the airport information line on 0212 663 6400 ext 3298.

It is illegal to possess antiquities or take them out of the country. You might need proof of purchase when exiting the country with a carpet. For more specific details visit www.gumruk.gov.tr.

Disabled access

Istanbul is tough on anyone with a mobility problem. The city is spread over several hills, roads and pavements are narrow, pitted and often paved with cobblestones, kerbs are high and flights of steps are frequent. Public transport is basically inaccessible – although there are lifts for the disabled on the new metro. Apart from a handful of top hotels, very few buildings make any provision or offer facilities for the handicapped.

Drugs

Turkey is a major transit point for heroin and the use of locally grown marijuana and ecstasy smuggled in from abroad is increasing. Enforcement is uneven but heavy-handed, with police known to conduct random sweeps of bars and nightclubs in the Taksim and Beyoğlu areas. You may be physically searched and have the insides of your forearms checked for needle tracks. Sentencing for drug offences is mild by American standards, but harsh by European ones.

Electricity & gas

Electricity in Turkey runs on 220 volts. Plugs have two round pins. Adaptors for UK appliances are readily available at hardware shops and electricians. Transformers are required for US 110-volt appliances, but these are also easily found. There are frequent, brief power cuts (more often in winter), and it's not a bad idea to have a torch in your baggage.

Estate agents

Agents listed here conduct business in English and generally tend to cater for the top end of the market. For a local realtor it's best to visit the neighbourhood you intend

Waiting for the big one

'Four-fifths [of the city] was demolished and as many as 4,000 people were killed under the ruins. Six mosques collapsed and 600 were killed inside. Aqueducts which bring water to the city collapsed and a 25m-long channel "migrated" ten paces.'

This is how the Ottoman chronicler Silahahdar described the devastation wreaked by an earthquake in Izmit, 50 miles south of Istanbul. The date was 1719. Almost 300 years later, in August 1999, the Izmit region was rocked again by a catastrophic quake, which killed more than 18,500 and left over 100,000 homeless.

Aside from the western district of Avcılar, Istanbul sustained little physical damage in the 1999 disaster. But the psychological impact was devastating. Thousands of residents decamped to the streets and parks for weeks afterwards as rumours abounded of aftershocks and new quakes to come.

The quake was a terrifying reminder of the constant seismological threat to the city. Northern Turkey has a subterranean crack that extends from Erzurum in the east to some indeterminate point in the Aegean to the west. Known as the North Anatolian Fault, this fracture is under constant pressure from the African tectonic plate to the south, which is moving north, and the Asian plate to the north, which is moving south. The result of this friction? Much of Turkey is like a bar of wet soap, being squished out sideways.

History reveals an alarming pattern to all this tectonic activity. Roughly every 250 years, the pressure builds up to a devastating eruption in the Izmit area, then, between ten and 25 years later, the big one goes off right next to Istanbul itself. Many consider the huge regional quake of 1999 to be notice served on the city.

In contrast to its spectacularly slow and largely ineffective response in '99, the state is actively preparing for the quake to come. In 2002, the Istanbul Metropolitan Municipality opened a Disaster Coordination Centre (AKOM), which is charged, among other things, with raising public awareness and drawing up an earthquake master plan. More fatalistically, the municipality is also working to acquire mass supplies of body bags, corpse refrigeration units and land for three vast cemeteries. Urgings to the general public to have their homes surveyed by professionals are, however, largely being ignored. This is hardly a surprise. After the '99 quakes, hordes of fake inspectors did the rounds, extorting large sums from panicked householders.

In fact, the buzz phrase of the moment is 'Earthquakes don't kill; people do.' The '99 quake exposed with tragic potency the corruption lacing the construction business. Many of the buildings that collapsed wouldn't have if contractors hadn't skimped on materials to inflate profits. One such villain in Yalova, on the south shore of the Marmara Sea, was almost lynched by survivors before being detained by the police. Three years later, he was rumoured to be back in business. So much for preparedness.

---

to settle in. Keep your eye out for signs saying *emlakçı*. You can expect to pay a standard commission of ten per cent of annual rent. Landlords generally ask for a month's deposit and two months' advance rent, although you'll find that most landlords are open to bargaining.

The cheaper alternative is to cut out the agent altogether. Wander the streets searching for *kiralık* (for rent) signs. Unfurnished flats are exactly as they say: naked. Light fixtures can be missing and the place might even require

a paint job. Before taking on a place, check that any outstanding utility bills have been paid: you may be lumbered with the debts. Foreigners without residence permits may rent flats, but are unlikely to get a legal contract.

Art
Valikonağı Caddesi 141/4, Nişantaşı (0212 225 6388/ www.artlimited.com.tr). **Open** 9am-6pm Mon-Sat.

Evren
Küçükbebek Caddesi 3/1, Bebek (0212 257 7184/0532 736 1330/ www.evreninternational.com). **Open** 9am-7pm Mon-Fri; 9am-1pm Sat.

Premier
Cevdetpaşa Caddesi 33A, Bebek (0212 287 2797/0533 736 7859/ www.premieremlak.com). **Open** 9am-6.30pm Mon-Fri; 10am-4pm Sat.

Şakayık Sokak
45/7 D3, Nişantaşı (0212 230 1316/ www.premieremlak.com). **Open** 10am-6pm Mon-Sat.

Health

Turkey doesn't have reciprocal health care agreements with any other countries, so taking out medical insurance is advisable. No vaccinations are required for Istanbul, although cases of rabies contracted from stray dogs have been reported as recently as 1999. Some travellers complain of stomach upsets, but this is more often due to the change in diet rather than food poisoning. Play it safe by avoiding tap water; cheap bottled water is available everywhere.

Hospitals & doctors

Turkey's health services suffer the familiar fate of an overstretched, underfunded public sector and an under-stretched, cash-rich private sector. As a result, there is not yet a GP or family doctor system, state hospitals are jammed with queues, and underpaid hospital doctors often have to take on private work. In contrast, private hospitals enjoy state-of-the-art technology, are decked out like five-star hotels and milk their patients royally. If you do need a doctor or medical aid, the simplest solution (especially if you have insurance) is to go straight to a private hospital, where you'll get immediate attention without any red tape and are almost sure to find English speakers.

For emergency dental problems, again head for the dental clinics run by many of the private hospitals (*see below*). Standards are higher than in the state sector, you'll find English speakers and generally be seen to straight away, even if you do pay for it.

American Hospital

Amerikan Hastanesi
Güzelbahçe Sokak 20, Nişantaşı (0212 311 2000/ www.amerikanhastanesi.com.tr).
Credit AmEx, MC, V.
One of the city's best: well equipped, well staffed and under US manage-ment. It also has a dental clinic.

European Florence Nightingale Hospital

Avrupa Florence Nightingale Hastanesi
Fulya Sağlık Tesisleri, Cahit Yalçım Sokak 1, off Mehmetçik Caddesi,

Mecidiyeköy (0212 212 8811/ www.florence.com.tr). **Credit** AmEx, MC, V.
Modern, well equipped and more female-friendly than most. It specialises in treating children.

German Hospital

Sıraselviler Caddesi 119, Cihangir, Taksim (0212 293 2150/ www.almanhastanesi.com.tr).
Credit AmEx, MC, V. **Map** p295 O3.
Part of the Universal Hospitals Group, it incorporates an eye hospital and dental clinic.

International Hospital

Istanbul Caddesi 82, Yeşilköy (0212 663 3000/ www.internationalhospital.com.tr).
Credit AmEx, DC, MC, V.
Way out of the city centre, just five minutes from the airport, but with cutting-edge technology, and eye and dental clinics.

Taksim State Emergency Hospital

Taksim Ilkyardım Hastanesi
Sıralselviler Caddesi 112, Cihangir, Taksim (0212 252 4300). **No credit cards. Map** p295 O3.
A state-run hospital that has recently undergone a much-needed overhaul. It deals with emergencies only and often refers patients to other state hospitals around town.

Pharmacies

Pharmacies (*eczane*) are plentiful and easily found in most neighbourhoods. They also tend to be clustered around hospitals. In addition to dispensing medicine, pharmacists are licensed to measure blood pressure, give injections, clean and bandage minor injuries and suggest medication for minor ailments – in practice, many medicines you'd need a prescription for in Europe are available over the counter in Turkey. Not many pharmacists speak English, but most are conversant in sign language. Opening hours are typically from 9am-7pm Monday-Saturday. Each neighbourhood also has a duty pharmacy (*nöbetçi*) open all night and on Sundays. Any closed pharmacy should have a sign indicating the nearest open pharmacy.

Vets

Animal love is on the rise in Turkey and household pets are no longer the sole preserve of the rich. The residential area of Cihangir, near Taksim, is famous for its street cats, which probably receive more lavish attention than any domestic moggy: the streets are littered with dry biscuits, trays of lovingly cooked food and one street even boasts a feline tent city. Here, and in other areas, pet shops have multiplied. So too have vets, some of them astonishingly sophisticated outfits.

Animalia

Levent Caddesi 41, Levent (0212 280 9277/www.animalia.com.tr). **Open** 24hrs daily. **Credit** MC, V.
Istanbul's first private animal hospital, equipped with three operating theatres, a pharmacy, lab, quarantine area, coiffeur and pet shop. Caters for all animals and also operates an ambulance service.

Cihangir Veterinary Clinic

Cihangir Veteriner Kliniü (0212 293 7993). **Open** 10am-8pm Mon-Sat; 1pm-4pm Sun. **Credit** MC, V.
Small clinic with operating theatre and pet shop out front. One of Cihangir's first.

Turkey is not covered by EU mutual health insurance schemes, which means visitors are advised to get a private insurance policy that covers medical as well as personal loss. Anyone with a a full residence permit is entitled to state health care.

Turkey has embraced e-culture with characteristic alacrity, and Istanbul's internet sector is booming. The number of public terminals has sky-rocketed, although proper cyber cafés – where patrons sip coffee while paying to surf the net – are the exception rather than the rule. More often, and particularly around Sultanahmet, you'll find hybrids such as travel agents that have a couple of online terminals out back. Many hotels now have a computer for guests to access email.

The vast majority of phone sockets take the US-style RJ11 plug, although a few older hotels and apartments use a Turkish model for which there don't seem to be any adaptors.

Internet access kits are sold at most large music/media and computer shops. There is a bewilderingly large range of options. Be sure to bring a Turkish-speaker with you, find a shopkeeper fluent in English or telephone one of the major providers in advance to learn details and the nearest stockist of the internet package you want. The following are reputable providers with English-language technical and back-up services.

Superonline
0212 473 7475.

Turknet
0212 444 0077.

Netone
0212 213 2035.

Internet cafés

Anatolia Internet Café
İncirli Çavuş Sokak 37/2, Sultanahmet (0212 512 0529). Tram Sultanahmet. **Open** 8.30am-midnight daily. **Rates** $1 per hour. **No credit cards. Map** p289 N10.
Eighteen computers in a spacious, second-floor café close to the Yerebatan cistern. Printing and scanning facilities also available. The token 'Anatolian' trimmings combine with a selection of kilim bags on sale to give a 'rustic high-tech' effect. No smoking.

Robin Hood Internet Café
Yeniçarşı Caddesi 24/4, Galatasaray, Beyoğlu (0212 244 8959). **Open** 9am-midnight daily. **Rates** $1 per hour. **No credit cards.**
This pristine fourth-floor café boasts snazzy wooden floors and 30 computers. Smoking and non-

smoking sections. Printing, scanning and other services offered, as well as English-speaking technical support.

Sultan House/ Galeri Ayla
Muhterem Efendi Sokak 6, off Yerebatan Caddesi, Sultanahmet (0212 511 3930/511 9745). Tram Sultanahmet. **Open** 8.30am-9pm daily. **Rates** $2 per hour. **Credit** AmEx, DC, MC, V.
An exquisite carpet store which gives over its first floor to internet users. The two comfortabe, no-smoking rooms house ten computers, printers and scanners, and a second-hand book exchange.

Yağmur Cybercafé
Şehbender Sokak 18/2, Asmalımescit, Beyoğlu (0212 292 3020). **Open** noon-10pm Mon-Sat; 1pm-10pm Sun. **Rates** $1.80 per hour. **Credit** AmEx, DC, MC, V. **Map** p294 M4.
One of the oldest and most civilised internet cafés in town, with ten computers, fax, telephone, printing, scanning and photocopy services. Understated, tasteful decor and all staff speak English. No smoking is permitted in the internet section, but it's allowed in the café.

Libraries

Istanbul lacks the library culture of Western cities. With the exception of the British Council, most libraries are specialist places open to researchers and students only.

British Council Library
Akdoğan Sokak 43, off Barbaros Bulvarı, Beşiktaş (0212 310 1610/ www.britishcouncil.org.tr). **Open** 11.30am-7.30pm Tue, Wed, Thur; 11.30am-5pm Fri-Sat.
The British Council library offers a reasonable selection of fiction and non-fiction. The library also lends books on tape, music tapes and CDs, videos and DVDs, and keeps current issues of British magazines and newspapers. There's a cyber café too. Annual membership, which covers all lending facilities, costs around $50.

Istanbul Library/Çelik Gülersoy Foundation
Ayasofya Pansiyonları, Soğukçeşme Sokak, Sultanahmet (0212 512 5730). **Open** 9am-noon, 1-4.30pm Mon, Fri. **Map** p289 N10.
A collection of antique and modern books on Istanbul in a host of languages, lodged in a restored Ottoman house beside the Topkapı Palace. Used mainly by academics and specialists.

Lost property

To report a crime or loss of belongings, go to the Tourist Police Station (*0212 527 4503*). This is located opposite the Yerebatan Sarnıcı (*see p74*) in Sultanahmet. Most officers here speak English or German. In the event that your passport gets lost or stolen, you must usually fill out a police report before consulates will deal with you.

Media

Until as recently as the mid '80s, print journalism in Turkey was in the doldrums. There were only two TV channels, and just a handful of radio stations – allof which were state owned. Then along came Star TV, beamed in from Germany, flouting regulations on private ownership. The station's owner happened to be the brother of the then Turkish president. Soon after its emergence on the scene, the government loosened up restrictive media laws. The ensuing scramble to get a piece of the pie saw the emergence of several huge and obscenely influential media combines. One mogul, Aydın Doğan, has stakes in three of Turkey's four major newspapers and its biggest magazine group. He also owns a significant number of TV channels, a bank and an internet portal. Monopolies commission? Pah. Doğan almost makes Rupert Murdoch seem benign.

Newspapers

National newspapers fall into two broad categories, secular and pro-Islamic. The secular press is monopolised by two empires – the Doğan and Sabah groups – both of which publish several titles. Between them they account for almost 60 per cent of the market. What remains is split between a handful of smaller media companies and the smaller media interests of a few giants. But baron or otherwise, each newspaper owner vies for what, by European standards, is pitiful circulation. Media warfare is rife, mud-slinging abounds and papers employ every gimmick to boost sales.

At the highbrow end of the spectrum are *Cumhuriyet (Republic)*, a foundering left-of-centre paper that was once the official organ of the republic, and *Radikal*, a Doğan Group title. Competition comes from three big hitters: *Hürriyet*, *Sabah* and *Milliyet*, serious but indistinguishable popular dailies that occupy the political centre ground. Journalistic standards are undermined by low pay and the real news comes from the columnists, of whom there are usually at least one per page.

The main pro-Islamic daily is *Zaman*, distinguished by surprisingly good coverage of international literature and film and the first Turkish newspaper to go online.

Worst by far is the hate-mongering *Akit*, with its habit of insinuating that successful secular business leaders are secretly Jews or Christians.

A few weekly satirical comics also sell well. Popular titles include *Gır Gır*, reckoned to be the third-biggest-selling magazine in Europe in the late 1980s, and *LeMan*, a cross between *Private Eye* and *Viz*. No subject is taboo, and the humour, while crude, is usually on the mark.

Magazines

The magazine scene in Istanbul looks buoyant, but appearances are deceiving: most titles tend to be ephemeral unless they're backed by one of the big media groups. Established leaders of the pack are *Tempo* and *Aktüel*, which mix photo-led

news, fashion and scandal, often with a free cover-mounted CD or VCD. There's a slew of licensed titles ranging from *Cosmopolitan* and *Marie Claire* to *Esquire* and *FHM*, not forgetting *Time Out Istanbul* (*see below*).

English-language media

For such a cosmopolitan city, Istanbul is low on foreign-language publications. The only daily English-language newspaper is the semi-literate *Turkish Daily News*, which offers reasonable coverage of domestic politics, but is plagued by filler, mostly indigestible features and soapbox columnists. The monthly *Turkish Business World* covers exactly what it says, but features read suspiciously like advertorial. The newly launched *Pera Weekly (Beyoğlu Gazetesi)* is sold on the street by vendors but is also available at bookstores and newsstands. It's a tabloid-sized paper of local news with several pages of English summary.

For news, reviews and up-to-date listings pick up the monthly *Time Out Istanbul*. It comes in two separate editions: one in Turkish, one in English. Both include local content and music and film reviews from the London edition. Long-established competitor *Istanbul: The Guide* includes more of the same – hotel, restaurant and club reviews plus sightseeing information – but it is hamstrung by the fact that it only appears every other month.

Foreign press

Foreign newspapers are easy to find, but rarely arrive before late afternoon. On the magazine front, a hunt around will turn up everything from

Sight & Sound to *Wallpaper**. Best places to look are the newsstands in Sultanahmet and around Taksim Square, plus the bookshops along Istiklal Caddesi.

Radio

The airwaves over Istanbul are so crammed with broadcasts that it's practically impossible to pick up any station without overlapping interference from another. Stations generally offer either Turkish music or foreign music, but rarely both. One exception is Açık Radyo (94.9), a more cerebral station than most that balances topical talk shows (often in English) with music from around the universe. Among those offering Western dance and pop music are Kiss FM (90.3), Radio Oxygen (95.9), Metro FM (97.2), Capital Radio (99.5), Power FM (100) and Number One FM (102.5). Radyo Blue (94.5) specialises in Latin and jazz and Energy FM (102) in jazz. For Turkish music try Kral FM (92.0), Best FM (98.4) and Lokum FM (89.0) and for Western classical music ITU Radyosu (103.8). You can pick up the news in English (from the BBC) on NTV Radyo (102.8) daily at 6pm and at 7am and 10.30pm from Monday to Friday. Many of these stations are available online at www.creatonic.com/tronline/.

Television

Amazingly, for a country that had no private TV until 1991, Turkey now has some 20 national channels, and countless more at the regional level. Not surprisingly, production values are low and programme quality is dire. Cable TV is available in many areas, offering improved reception of terrestrial channels, plus BBC Prime, CNN, Discovery, Eurosport and others. For areas without

Directory

cable, satellite TV is cheap and offers further imports. Digital TV is represented by the Digitürk platform, which carries programming from Europe and the US, plus all of the biggest Turkish TV and radio stations.

Money

Currency

Local currency is the Turkish lira, abbreviated TL. The high inflation that has wreaked havoc for more than a decade is now down to a modest 25 per cent (officially), but this still means that any lira-quoted prices in this guide would be out of date in no time. For this reason, prices in this guide are quoted in dollars. Inflation has resulted in ever larger notes. This requires Turks to deal with absurdly long rows of zeros, forking over millions for the smallest of transactions.

Coins come in denominations of 50,000, 100,000 and 250,000 lira, but this kind of small change is so worthless that shopkeepers often give customers chewing gum or sweets in lieu. Banknotes come in denominations of 250,000 (on its way out), 500,000, one million, five million, 10 million and 20 million lira. All feature Atatürk and come in different colours, which helps, but they're still a nightmare for the uninitiated. For years now successive governments have talked of discarding six zeros from the currency once inflation is down to single digits. The latest target for introducing the abbreviated Turkish lira is 2005 – don't hold your breath.

ATMs

Cashpoints are common and easy to find. Most machines will accept UK cards linked into the Cirrus or Plus networks and will supply Turkish lira to order. They'll also give cash advances on major credit cards, provided you know your PIN number.

Banks

Retail banking in Turkey has advanced in leaps and bounds in the past few years. These days most banks provide telephone and internet banking as well as other standard services. In most cases, however, improvement has yet to filter down to the service you actually get at the counter.

Non-residents can open a savings account at a Turkish bank in any currency. Go to any branch with your passport and specify the kind of account you want to open. You'll then be asked to sign a routine account agreement. When you open your account, be sure to choose a branch that is convenient to your place of residence or work. That's because you'll only be able to draw cash from this branch without incurring charges. Cash can be deposited at any branch, though. With a current account you can also apply for an ATM card. When deciding which bank to go for, pick one of the bigger ones that has an extensive ATM network, such as any of those listed below.

Getting a credit card from a Turkish bank is not so easy: you need residency, official employment, proof of income and a Turkish guarantor, as well as patience.

Akbank
www.akbank.com.tr

Citibank
www.citibank.com.tr

Garanti Bank
www.garantibank.com.tr

HSBC
www.hsbc.com.tr

Yapı Kredi Bank
www.yapikredi.com.tr

Money transfer

Most banks will accept transfers sent in the receiver's name even if you don't have an account at that bank. The drawback is that the money doesn't always arrive instantly and the bank blocks the money for up to 20 days once it does arrive. There is a way around this, however: you can withdraw the money in Turkish lira at the bank's discretionary rates or by paying a hefty commission. The quicker and more reliable alternative is to use Western Union Money Transfer. This service is now offered by all branches of Denizbank, Dışbank, Oyak Bank, Finansbank and Ziraat Bankası. Here's how it works: if you're expecting to receive money, just turn up at any branch of the aforementioned banks with your passport and transfer details (time and amount of transfer, plus 'money transfer control number'). You should then be able to draw the money immediately in dollars, euros or lira.

Bureaux de change

Many shops and restaurants accept payment in US dollars, sterling or euros, but there are dozens of exchange bureaux *(döviz bürosu)* in the main tourist and shopping districts. These are easier to deal with than banks, where transactions can take forever and rates are generally lower. Rates don't vary a lot from place to place. Exchange bureaux are open long hours, generally 9am-7.30pm Monday to Saturday.

Çetin Döviz
Istiklal Caddesi 39, Beyoğlu (0212 252 6428). **Open** 9am-7.30pm daily. **Map** p295 O2.

Çözüm Döviz
Istiklal Caddesi 53, Beyoğlu (0212 244 6271). **Open** 9am-8pm Mon-Sat; 11am-7.30pm Sun. **Map** p295 O2.

Klas Döviz

Sıraselviler Caddesi 39, Taksim
(0212 249 3550). **Open** 8.30am-8pm
daily. **Map** p295 O2.

Credit cards

Turkey has been swept by
a credit-card boom in recent
years. On the one hand, banks
have hooked up with the retail
sector to cajole consumers into
spending money they don't
have. On the other, the
government is promoting
plastic in the hope of making
dents in the vast black
economy. The happy result
for visitors is that major credit
cards are widely accepted. All
the same, it's worth carrying
some cash as backup.

American Express

0122 444 2525
www.americanexpress.com.tr
AmEx is represented in Turkey by
Akbank. It's far less widely accepted
than Mastercard or Visa because of
high commission charges.

Diners Club

0216 444 0555
www.dcturkey.com
Represented by Koçbank.

Mastercard

00 800 13 887 0903

Visa International

00 800 13 535 0900

Mosque etiquette

At least half of Istanbul's major sights are mosques. Non-
Muslims are welcome to visit any of them but should steer
clear of busy prayer times, of which noon – and especially
Friday noon – is the main one. Note that prayer times vary
throughout the year, so noon prayers don't take place
exactly on the stroke of midday, but can fall anywhere
between 11.30am and 1.30pm.

Dress modestly: no shorts, short skirts or bare
shoulders. This is especially vital for visits to mosques out
of the tourist loop, such as places in conservative areas
like Fatih, Fener and Balat. Shoes must be removed,
although in some places cloth covers are provided to slip
over your footwear. Women will be given a headscarf to
cover their hair, for which a small tip (a TL 500,000 note)
is expected. Photography is usually allowed, but don't point
your camera at people at prayer.

Travellers' cheques

Travellers' cheques can be
cashed in banks or at post
offices, but not usually at
exchange bureaux. Wherever
you cash them, you will need
to provide a passport.
Individual banks charge
different commission rates,
although some charge none
at all. The post office usually
offers the best deal.

Opening hours

Opening hours are extremely
variable in Istanbul, but here
are some general guidelines:

Banks 9am-12.30pm, 1.30-5pm
Mon-Fri.
Bars 11am or noon-2am daily.
Businesses 9am-6pm Mon-Fri.
Municipal offices 8am-12.30pm,
1.30-5.30pm Mon-Fri.
Museums 8.30am-5.30pm Tue-Sun.
Petrol stations 24 hrs daily.
Post offices see below.
Shops 10am-8pm Mon-Sat, although
in main shopping areas places stay
open as late as 10pm, and also stay
open on Sun. Grocery stores
(bakkals) and supermarkets are
open 9am-10pm daily.

Police & security

Crime against visitors is low
and physical violence (football
supporters aside) is rare. The
main thing to beware of is bag-
snatching, especially around
Sultanahmet, Eminönü and
Beyoğlu. The harassment of
single women (*see p269*) can
be a pain, but it is generally
verbal. That said, women
going home late at night in
the Beyoğlu and Taksim areas
should be accompanied. And
they should steer clear of
Tarlabaşı, one of Istanbul's
seedier districts.

The police have long
suffered bad press, and they've
nobody but themselves to
blame. Accusations run from
ineffectiveness to excessive
use of force and an appetite for
back-handers. Determination
to change this image has
spawned a major PR drive:
check out the new police
website (www.iem.gov.tr) with
its exhaustive catalogue of
services translated into ten
languages. Police departments
now have cutesy names that
evoke 'love, friendship and
trust': for instance, the
policemen on red-and-black
motorbikes, in charge of public
order, are called 'dolphins'
(*yunuslar*) because, as the
website explains, 'dolphins are
the one thing that sharks are
actually afraid of'.

Be aware that it's illegal not
to carry some form of photo
ID, so have your passport or
similar with you at all times.

Tourist police

Yerebatan Caddesi 6, Sultanahmet
(0212 528 5369). Tram Sultanahmet.
Open 24 hrs daily. **Map** p294 N10.
The place to report thefts, losses,
scams and other woes. Most officers
speak English

Post

Post offices can be recognised
by their yellow-and-black PTT
(Posta, Telefon, Telegraf) signs
– even though they no longer
operate the telephone network.

Poste restante mail should
be sent to the central post
office at Sirkeci (*see p268*) and
addressed as follows:

Directory

Recipient's name,
Poste Restante,
Büyük Postane,
Büyük Postane Caddesi,
Sirkeci,
Istanbul

To collect poste restante mail you need your passport. There's a fee of around 50 cents per letter.

Rates

Postcards cost $0.50 to Europe, $0.60 to the US and Australia. Letters up to 50g go to Europe for around $1. Letters of similar weight cost about $1.25 to the US and $1.50 to Australia. Stamps can only be bought at post offices.

For parcels, airmail rates start at $26 to the UK and US, and $31 to Australia for the first kg. Comparable rates for surface mail are $22.50 to the UK, $16 to the US and $19 to Australia.

When sending packages, remember that the contents will be inspected at the post office, so it's a good idea not to seal them completely, and to bring tape with you.

Major post offices

Beyoğlu

Yeniçarşı Caddesi 20, Galatasaray, Beyoğlu (0212 251 5150). **Open** 8.30am-5.30pm Mon-Fri; 8.30am-5pm Sun. **Map** p294 N3.

Sirkeci

Büyük Postane, Büyük Postane Caddesi, Sirkeci (0212 513 5717). **Open** 8.30am-5.30pm daily. **Map** p289 N9.

Taksim

Cumhuriyet Caddesi 2, Taksim (0212 243 0284). **Open** 8.30am-12.30pm, 1.30-5.30pm Mon-Sat. **Map** p295 P2.

Religion

Istanbul might be known as a city of mosques, but it has a multitude of places to worship. After all, Istanbul was once a centre of Christianity, it's still the home of the Greek and Armenian Orthodox Patriarchates, and is also a city with a strong Jewish tradition.

Christian

Christ Church (Anglican)

Serdari Ekrem Sokak 82, Tünel, Beyoğlu (0212 251 5616/ www.anglicanistanbul.beliefnet.com). **Services** 9am, 6pm Mon-Sat; 9am, 10am Sun. **Map** p294 N5.

Union Church of Istanbul (Protestant)

Postacılar Sokak, Beyoğlu (0212 244 5212/www.unionchurchofistanbul.org). **Services** 9.30am, 11am, 1.30pm Sun. **Map** p294 N4.
This church is situated in the garden of the Dutch consulate.

St Anthony's (Catholic)

Istiklal Caddesi 325, Beyoğlu (0212 244 0935). **Open** 8am-noon, 3-7.30pm Mon, Thur-Sat; 7am-6pm Tue; 9am-12.30pm, 3-7.30pm Sun. **Services** English 8am Mon-Sat, 10am Sun. **Map** p294 N3.

Haghia Triada (Greek Orthodox)

Meşelik Sokak 11/1, Taksim (0212 244 1358). **Services** Short 8.30am, 5pm daily, 4pm in winter; Full-length 9am Sun. **Map** p295 O2.

Üç Horon (Gregorian Armenian)

Balık Pazarı, Sahne Sokak 24, Beyoğlu (0212 244 1382). **Open** 9am-5pm daily. **Services** 9am-1pm Tue; 8am-1pm Sun. **Map** p294 N3.

Jewish

Security has long been tight at the city's synagogues, but will surely grow tighter in the wake of the two suicide bombings on the Bet Israel and Neve Shalom synagogues in November 2003. If you want to visit, you must first obtain permission. Call the offices of the Chief Rabbinate (see below) for information. Prayers are usually held daily at 7.30am with Shabbat services at 8am. Friday evening services depend on sundown hours.

Chief Rabbinate

Yeminiçi Sokak 23, Tünel, Beyoğlu (0212 293 8794/5). **Open** 9am-5pm Mon-Thur; 9am-1pm Fri.

Ashkenazi Synagogue

Yüksek Kaldırım Yokuşu, Karaköy. (0212 243 6909/fax 244 2975). **Map** p292 M6.

Bet Israel Synagogue (Sephardic)

Efe Sokak 4, off Rumeli Caddesi, Şişli. Contact the Neve Shalom Foundation (0212 293 6223).

Neve Shalom Synagogue

Büyükhendek Caddesi 67, Şişhane, Karaköy. For more information contact the Neve Shalom Foundation (0212 293 6223).

Removals

The cheapest way to move a few articles of furniture is to hire a truck locally. Ask your local grocer (bakkal) or green-grocer (manav) to help make arrangements. Agree on a price (you shouldn't pay more than $30-$35) taking into account the number of stairs to be climbed and tip a few extra dollars. There are professional movers but they are pricey.

Useful numbers

Police 155
Fire 110
Ambulance 112
Directory Enquiries 118
International Operator 115
International access code 00; **country codes** UK 44; US and Canada 1; Australia 61; Ireland 353; New Zealand 64

Istanbul for women

'Everything we see in the world is the work of women.' The words – who'd have thought? – of Mustafa Kemal Atatürk, architect of the Turkish republic and infamous womaniser. Besotted bedroom cant? No, the Westward-looking leader meant business. By 1934 he'd outlawed polygamy, given women the vote and had 18 of them as MPs. Women had it good. But that was then; what about now?

Take a stroll anywhere in Istanbul, even in the more conservative areas, and you'll find little to back the 'little Iran' myth most Westerners think is Turkey. Instead, anything goes. Witness the girls on the main street, Istiklal Caddesi, with bared midriffs, tattoos and pierced bodies. The flowing black tents known as *chadors* are a real exception, confined largely to the city's few radical outposts such as Fatih, Fener and Balat.

Surface impressions look good; but delve a little deeper and the glow of emancipation loses a little lustre. Consider politics: 24 women sit in parliament today but proportionally that's less than in 1934 and fewer, even, than in Pakistan. Over in the once corporate world, things look brighter. More and more women are elbowing their way into key executive positions, but it's still a hard slog. This will change: statistically, girls do better than boys in education and grab a larger share of university places at undergraduate level.

In terms of women's legal rights, gender equality is on its way, slowly. A new Family Protection Order allows women to seek an expulsion writ against harassing male householders. Legislation has also been passed giving illegitimate children inheritance rights. And pressure groups are now campaigning for reforms to the penal code, specifically legal definitions of rape. But it takes time for theory to translate into practice: women first need to know about their rights, then to have the courage to exercise them.

Family culture is strong, with all its implicit rules and hierarchies. Marriage and motherhood are still the ideal. Women who sashay sexily on the dance floor are often just doing it for show. Indeed, female ignorance of the facts of life can sometimes stun: girls oozing sophistication may worry that oral sex will land them at the abortion clinic. But again, that's changing. Pre-marital sex is on the rise and girls are moving out of the family home for a taste of independence.

Outside the home, public harassment or abuse of women is considered shameful. Recriminations can be fierce: anyone who dares to grope on a crowded bus risks being lynched. This is one reason that Istanbul is an exceptionally safe city for Turkish females.

In the case of foreign women, things are different. Foreigners generally are an object of awe and curiosity. For women, however, this often translates into unsolicited, if usually non-threatening, attention from local males, especially in tourist areas like Sultanahmet. It's not hard to see why: compared with Turkish women, Westerners are easy. The Turkish media has a lot to answer for in this: coverage of the tourism industry is almost guaranteed to feature a photo of a reclining topless blonde. Hence the simmering stares, and sometimes disapproving glares, many foreign women encounter. Perceptions are changing, but not that fast. Dress demurely, avoid eye contact, learn to ignore. At worst, yell for help: you'll get it.

Sumerman International

Menekşe Sokak 1, Tarabya (0212 223 5818/www.sumerman.com). English spoken.

Smoking

Smoking bans are slowly creeping in: first it was public transport, now it's public offices, banks, shops and even private offices. Offenders in public spaces are liable for fines of up to $320 – supposedly. For all that, Istanbul remains firmly in thrall to nicotine. Smokers rule and few restaurants or cafés recognise the concept of a clean-air environment. Foreign cigarette brands cost around $2 for 20, while the best of the domestic product, Tekel 2000, goes for even less. Passive smoking or active, it's your choice, but you've got to inhale some time.

Street names

When writing an address, the house number comes after the street name with a slash separating the flat number. If it's on a side street *(sokak)*, the custom is to include the nearest main street *(cadde)*, usually written first. So in the following case, Mehmet Aksoy lives in flat 7 at 14 Matar Sokak, off Sıraselviler Street, in the district of Cihangir:

Mehmet Aksoy
Sıraselviler Caddesi
Matar Sokak 14/7
Cihangir
Istanbul

Student discounts

Museums, travel agents and
sports centres recognise
International Student Identity
Cards (ISIC), but some cinemas
and theatres offer discounts
only to foreigners studying at
Turkish educational institutes.

Study

Language courses

Turkish at all levels is taught
at a variety of private schools
and colleges, most of which
also offer one-to-one lessons.
You can also find private
tutors via small ads in the
Turkish Daily News.

Bilgi University

*Kurtuluşderesi Caddesi 47,
Dolapadere, Taksim (0212 293
5010/www.bilgi-egitim.com).* **Open**
10am-6pm daily. **Map** p293 Q2.
Courses begin in January, April and
October, taking 40 hours over ten
weeks and costing around $320.

International House

*Aydın Sokak 12, off Korukent Yolu,
Levent (0212 282 9064/282 9065/
www.ihistanbul.com).* **Open** 9am-
10pm Mon-Fri; 9am-6pm Sat, Sun.
Twelve-week Turkish courses at six
different levels, in groups of six to 12.
Each course is 66 hours and costs
$500. Private lessons are $50/hr.

Taksim Dilmer Language Teaching Centre

*Tarık Zafer Tunaya Sokak 18, off
İnönü Caddesi, Taksim (0212 292
9696/www.dilmer.com).* **Open** 9am-
8pm Mon-Fri; 9am-5pm Sat, Sun.
Map p293 Q2.
Courses mornings, afternoons,
evenings or weekends in classes of
no more than 14. Cost of a four-week
course is $280 (80 hours); an eight-
week course is $336 (96 hours).

Telephones

Istanbul's Asian and European
sides have different area codes:
0212 for Europe; 0216 for Asia.

You must use the code
whenever you are calling the
opposite shore. But when
dialling from abroad, be sure
to omit the zero. The country
code for Turkey is 90.

Public phones

Public phones now operate
with pre-paid cards *(telefon
kartı)*, of which there are
two types: the floppy, regular
version, or a rigid 'smart card'.
Some of the newer phones also
take credit cards. Phone cards
can be bought at post offices
or, at a small premium, from
street vendors and kiosks.
They come in units of 30
($1.50), 60 ($3) and 100 ($5).
Metered calls *(kontörlü)* can
also be placed at post offices or
the private phone and fax
offices *(telefon ofisi)* dotted all
over town, but these places
usually charge over the odds.

Standard public phone rates
are around $1 a minute to the
UK and US, $1.50 to Australia.
Reduced rates for international
calls operate from 10pm to
9am Monday to Saturday, and
all day Sunday and holidays.
For local and national calls,
cheap time is 8pm to 8am
weekdays and all weekend.

Mobile phones

There are currently four GSM
networks: Turkcell (the
largest), Telsim, Aria and
Aycell. But with Aycell and
Aria planning to merge and
Telsim on the verge of losing
its licence, the GSM landscape
looks set to change. Not that
this is likely to affect visitors.
Reception is generally
excellent and if you bring your
UK phone, you'll have no
problem logging on to one of
the local operators if you've set
up a roaming facility with your
mobile provider beforehand.

Anyone planning on making
lots of calls should invest in a
local SIM card, known here as
a *hazır kart*. These are offered

by all the GSM operators. To
subscribe, find an authorised
dealer (Turkcell is the most
popular), present a photocopy
of your passport and pay the
subscription fee (between $20-
$25), which includes 100 units,
or roughly 25 minutes of talk-
time within Turkey. Top-up
cards are sold all over the
place (look for the *hazır kart*
sign) and come in units of 100
($7), 250 ($14.50), 500 ($27),
750 ($38.50) and 1000 ($48.50).

Getting a normal mobile
phone line is hard work and
pricey – invoiced bills carry
taxes of 40 per cent. To apply,
you'll need a residence permit
plus a Turkish guarantor
prepared to stump up a
notarised guarantee for $900.
Because the Turkish system
operates on 900 MHz US
mobile phones are useless here.

Time

Turkey is two hours ahead of
Greenwich Mean Time (GMT)
and seven hours ahead of New
York. There is no Turkish
equivalent of am and pm, so the
24-hour clock is used: 1pm is
13.00 and midnight is 24.00.
Daylight-saving runs from the
last Sunday in March to the last
Sunday in October. This creates
a three-hour time difference
between Turkey and the UK for
one month each year, as British
Summer Time doesn't end until
the last Sunday in October.

Tipping

Although not obligatory, the
rule of thumb is to leave about
ten per cent on the bill at cafés
and restaurants. Service is
occasionally factored in, in
which case it'll say *servis dahil*
at the foot of the bill. If in
doubt ask: 'Servis dahil mi?'
With hotel staff, porters and
hairdressers tipping is entirely
discretionary, but $1 or so is
the norm. Hamam attendants
expect more like 25 per cent.
Do not tip taxi drivers.

Toilets

Public toilets are plentiful, especially in tourist areas. They'll be signposted 'WC' (but when asking, use the term *tuvalet*); the gents' is *Bay*; the ladies' is *Bayan*. Public facilities are usually the squat type – a hole in the floor, uncomfortable if you're not used to it, but hygienic. There's often no paper, so get used to carrying around a small pack of tissues *(selpak)*. City plumbing cannot cope with toilet paper so use the wastepaper bin provided.

Hotels, bars and restaurants have Western-style toilets.

Tourist information

There is no central tourist office; instead there are a few small places dotted about the city. Staff speak English.

Atatürk Airport

International Arrivals Hall (0212 663 0793). **Open** 24 hrs daily. Will help book hotel rooms.

Istanbul Hilton

Cumhuriyet Caddesi, Harbiye (0212 233 0592). **Open** 9am-5pm Mon-Sat. **Map** p293 P1.

Karaköy Seaport

Kemankeş Caddesi (0212 249 5776). **Open** 9am-5pm Mon-Sat.

Sirkeci Station

Istasyon Caddesi, Sirkeci (0212 511 5888). Tram Sirkeci. **Open** 9am-5pm daily. **Map** p289 N8.

Sultanahmet Square

Divan Yolu 3 (0212 518 1802). Tram Sultanahmet. **Open** 9am-5pm daily. **Map** p289 N10.

International offices

Australia *Room 17, Level 3, 428 St George St, Sydney, NSW 2000 (02 9223 3055/9223 3204)*. **Canada** *Constitution Square, Suite 801, 360 Albert St, Ottawa, Ontario K1R 7X7 (613 230 8654/230 3683).* **UK** *1st floor, 170-173 Piccadilly, London W1V 9EJ (020-7629 7771/7491 0773/www.turkish tourism.demon.co.uk).*

USA *821 UN Plaza, New York, NY 10017 (212 687 2194/599 7568/www.tourismturkey.org).*

Visas

Visas are required by most nationalities and can be bought at the airport upon arrival. At press time rates were: for citizens of the UK £10; USA and Canada $100; Australia $20; Ireland £5. Visas are good for up to three months. Citizens of New Zealand don't need a visa, just a valid passport. Fees must be paid in foreign currency; no Turkish lira, credit cards or travellers' cheques are accepted. Overstaying your visa, even by a single day, will earn you a fine of around $100 when you leave the country.

When to go

Between December and March Istanbul is cold, grey and blustery. Temperatures average 5°C (42°F). They rarely fall below zero, but humidity and windchill make it feel a lot colder. Sleet and snow showers are not uncommon and the city is usually buried under several feet of the white stuff once each winter – a magical sight, even if it does mean life grinds to a halt. At the other extreme, summers can be oppressive; temperatures average 25-30C (78-88°F) from June to August, occasionally pushing up beyond 35°C (104°F). The heat and humidity can be draining, yet for those who are able to cope, this is a good time to visit. However hot the day, it cools at sundown and the city descends to the Bosphorus to while away languid pink-skied evenings at waterfront cafés.

For the best weather, aim for spring and autumn. Not every day is perfect – *poyraz*, a chill Balkan wind, and *lodos*, hot humid air arriving from the south, can both have a

dramatic effect, resulting in a kind of 'four seasons in a day' syndrome – but generally days are temperate and evenings mild. Both are busy festival seasons, and early autumn is when the bar, club and cultural scenes start to pick up, loaded with energy and enthusiasm after the dormant summer.

Public & religious holidays

Turkey's five secular public holidays occupy a single day each. Banks, offices and post offices close, but many shops stay open and public transport runs as usual.

Religious holidays are different. For a start, they last three or four days; if these happen to fall midweek, then the government commonly extends the holiday to cover the whole working week. With weekends either side, it effectively becomes a nine-day holiday. The city shuts down as Istanbulis flock out to the country. Coaches and flights are jammed, so book ahead if your travel plans coincide.

Observance of **Ramazan**, the Islamic month of fasting, is widespread. Many Turks abstain from food, drink and cigarettes between sunrise and sunset. This has little impact on visitors, as most bars and restaurants remain open, but it's bad form to flaunt your non-participation by smoking or eating in the street, especially in the more religious parts of the city, such as Fatih and Üsküdar. In areas like these, Ramazan nights are some of the busiest of the year. Come sundown, eateries are packed with large groups communally breaking their fast with *iftar* ('breakfast'). There are also festivities in Sultanahmet Square, which turns into an extravaganza of food and music at the twilight hour – a revival of the old Ottoman tradition. The end of

Ramazan is marked by the three-day **Şeker Bayramı**, or 'Sugar Holiday', named after the tradition of giving sweets to friends and family.

The main event in the Islamic calendar, though, is **Kurban Bayramı** (the Feast of the Sacrifice), which marks Abraham's near-sacrifice of Isaac. While Isaac escaped the knife, the local livestock aren't so lucky. The tradition is that families buy a '*kurban*', which could be a sheep, bull, goat or camel, and sacrifice it on the first or second day of the feast. The meat is shared with relatives, neighbours and the poor. There are now stricter regulations on slaughtering sites and techniques, which has reduced the blood-bath effect of yesteryear, but it's still a good idea for the faint-hearted to keep away from mosques around this time.

Islamic religious holidays are based on a lunar calendar, approximately 11 days shorter than the Gregorian (Western) calendar. This means Islamic holidays shift forward by ten or 12 days each year.

New Year's Day (*Yılbaşı Günü*)
1 January
Feast of the Sacrifice
(Kurban Bayramı)
2-7 February (2004); 21-5 January (2005); 10-14 January (2006)
National Sovereignty & Children's Day (*Ulusal Egemenlik ve Çocuk Bayramı*)
23 April
Youth & Sports Day (*Gençlik ve Spor Bayramı*) 19 May
Victory Day (*Zafer Bayramı*)
30 August
Republic Day (*Cumhuriyet Bayramı*) 29 October
Sugar Holiday (*Şeker Bayramı*)
14-16 November (2004); 3-5 November (2005).

Festivals & events

You might want to time your visit to coincide with the **International Film Festival** (*see p196*), one of the most glamorous events on Istanbul's cultural calendar, usually held in late April. The most prestigious event on the calendar, however, is the International Istanbul Music Festival, (*see p185*) held every June/July. It consistently attracts the international elite of classical music and ballet. Other highlights include the **International Istanbul Jazz Festival** (*see p185*), held for two weeks each July, and the **International Istanbul Biennale**, (*see p187*) an international art festival held from September to November in odd years only.

Working in Istanbul

Finding a job is not as easy as the days when tourists would literally be scooped off the streets to teach at language schools. There still is a large market for native-speaker English teachers but most schools and universities now require an internationally recognised qualification, if not an English degree as well. Other foreigners end up working as journalists for local English-language publications, tour guides or managers in bars and clubs. Many work on tourist visas, hopping to North Cyprus or Greece and back every three months to obtain a new visa. Strictly speaking, this is illegal but people get away with it for years.

Work permits

To be legal, you need a work permit, which can only be obtained through a sponsoring employer. In principle, your job should be one that can only be done by a foreigner. The process is long and painfully bureaucratic (don't forget, this is where the term 'byzantine' originated). To begin, the employer submits an application for authorisation with the Treasury in Ankara. This can take a couple of months. Having obtained this, you then submit your own application to the Turkish Consulate General in your country of residence (which shouldn't be Turkey as you are not yet legal) and wait about six weeks for processing. When it's ready, you must show up at the consulate in person with your passport. Once back in Turkey, you'll then need to get a residence permit. Details of the application procedure for British passport holders are available via the internet at www.turkconsulate-london.com.

Residence permits

If you have a work permit, you're automatically entitled to residence for as long as your permit is good. Otherwise, as with work permits, residence applications should be filed with the Turkish Consulate General in your country of residence. You'll need photocopies of your passport, bank statements, proof of income, photographs, a completed application form and covering letter. Applications take around eight weeks to process. You then pick up the visa in person. After arriving in Istanbul, you need to register with the Foreigners' Branch of the Police Department (*Emniyet Müdürlüğü Yabancılar Şubesi*) on Vatan Caddesi (Aksaray) within one month of the visa/work permit being issued. Queues are lengthy and the whole process is tedious. Take a book, patience, a pile of cash and if you can, a local who knows the ropes. Residence permits are valid for one or two years, but you can also apply for a five-year permit. Expect to pay upwards of $150 for the whole process.

Alternatively, you could use the time-honoured tradition of getting a work permit: get hitched to a Turkish national.

Vocabulary

Istanbulus living and working in tourist areas usually have at least some knowledge of English and generally welcome the opportunity to practise it with foreigners. However, a bit of Turkish goes a long way and making the effort to use a few phrases and expressions will be greatly appreciated.

For information on language courses see p270.

Pronunciation

All words are written phonetically and, save for ğ, there are no silent letters; so for example the word for post office, postane, is pronounced 'post-a-neh'. Syllables are articulated clearly and with equal stress. The key to learning basic Turkish is to master the pronunciation of the few letters and vowels that differ from English:

c – like the 'j' in jam, so cami (mosque) is pronounced 'jami'
ç – like the 'ch' in chip, so çiçek (flower) is pronounced 'chi-check'
ğ – silent, but lengthens preceding vowel
ı – an 'uh', like the 'a' in cinema
ö – like the 'ir' in girdle
ş – like the 'sh' in shop, so şiş (as in kebab) is pronounced 'shish'
ü – as in the French 'tu'

Accommodation

air-conditioning klima
bathroom banyo
bed yatak
bed & breakfast pansiyon
breakfast kahvaltı
double bed çift kişilik yatak
excluded hariç
hotel otel
included dahil
invoice fatura
lift asansör
no vacancies yer yok
room oda
shower duş
soap sabun
tax/VAT vergi/KDV
towel havlu
vacancy yer var

Countries & nationalities

America/American
Amerika/Amerikalı
Australia/Australian
Avustralya/Avustralyalı
Britain/British İngiltere/İngiliz
Canada/Canadian
Kanada/Kanadalı
Ireland/Irish İrlanda/İrlandalı
New Zealand/New Zealander
Yeni Zelanda/Yeni Zelandalı
Turkey/Turkish Türkiye/Türk

Days of the week

Monday pazartesi
Tuesday salı
Wednesday çarşamba
Thursday perşembe
Friday cuma
Saturday cumartesi
Sunday pazar

Emergencies

accident kaza
ambulance ambülans
doctor doktor
fire yangın
fire department itfaiye
help! imdat!
hospital hastane
medication ilaç
pharmacy eczane
police polis
sick hasta

Eating out

For food and other Turkish menu terms see p136.

Essentials

a lot/very/too çok
and ve
bad/badly kötü
big büyük
but ama/fakat
good/well iyi
I don't speak Turkish Türkçe bilmiyorum
I don't understand anlayamadım
leave me alone (quite forceful) beni rahat bırak
Mr/Mrs bey/hanım (with first name)
no hayır
OK tamam
or veya
please lütfen
slow(ly) yavaş
small küçük
sorry pardon
thank you teşekkürler/mersi/sağol
yes evet
this/that bu/şu

Getting around

airport havalimanı/havaalanı
aeroplane uçak
bus otobüs
bus/coach station otogar
car park otopark
entrance giriş
exit çıkış
left sol
map harita
maximum speed azami hız
no parking park yapılmaz
petrol benzin
platform peron
right sağ
road yol
station gar
street sokak
toll paralı geçiş
train tren

Greetings

good morning günaydın
good afternoon/goodbye iyi günler
good evening/goodbye iyi akşamlar
good night/goodbye iyi geceler
goodbye güle güle (to the person leaving)
hello merhaba
see you (again) görüşmek üzere

Months & seasons

January Ocak
February Şubat
March Mart
April Nisan
May Mayıs
June Haziran
July Temmuz
August Ağustos
September Eylül
October Ekim
November Kasım
December Aralık
spring ilkbahar

Bored, or just getting it regularly?

Turkish is what's known as an agglutinative language. It works like building blocks do, so you add suffixes to shorter, base words to give them meaning. By adding the appropriate endings, for example, you can turn English (*ingiliz*) into 'I'm English' (*Ingilizim*), and understand (*anla*) into 'I don't understand' (*Anlayamadım*) or 'Do you understand?' (*Anladın mı?*).

Which is all very nice, except as suffixes pile up, words get out of hand. For example, *Çekoslovakyalılaştıramadıklarımızdansınız*, which is more a short story than a single word. Literally translated, it means 'You're one of those guys we were unable to turn into a Czech.' It's not a word that dominates day-to-day conversation, and in fact probably only exists to frighten beginners in Turkish.

But don't let that put you off. There's a lot about Turkish that makes it an easy language to learn. For one, the grammar's completely logical, with no irregular verbs, and it's phonetic, so words are pronounced exactly as written. Anybody with a little French will recognise hundreds of borrowings, from *gar* (station) to *kuaför* (hairdresser) to *mersi* (an essential in courteous Istanbul).

But like other languages, Turkish is littered with traps for the unwary beginner. Just a single vowel sound separates 'Excuse me, waiter' (*bakar mısınızı*) from 'Are you single?'

(*bekar mısınızı*), or 'I'm really bored' (*çok sıkılıyorum*) from the slangy 'I'm getting it regularly' (*çok sikiliyorum*).

Anyone wrestling with beginners' Turkish should spare a thought for the Turks of the 1920s. When Atatürk ditched the Arabic alphabet for the Latin version, it meant the entire nation had to learn the language all over again. At the same time, Atatürk and his nationalist zealots set about purifying the language by purging all foreign influences. This was a somewhat daunting task given the huge influence of Arabic and Persian on Ottoman Turkish and often led to the coining of new words – Atatürk had a blackboard erected in his dining room for the purpose. The result was, however noble the nationalists' reformist ambitions, Atatürk's speeches were often incomprehensible to all but his closest allies.

Fortunately, though, the reformers fell short in their dream of a pure language. Today's Turkish is still packed with Arabic and Persian and has added a new layer of French and English words for a new generation of purists to worry about. They shouldn't worry too much. Turkish is spoken in various dialects by hundreds of millions of people, from the Balkans to western China, and is better placed than most languages to resist the dominance of English.

summer yaz
autumn sonbahar
winter kış

Questions

do you have change? bozuk
  paranız var mı?
do you speak English?
  ingilizce biliyor musunuz?
how? nasıl?
what? ne?
when? ne zaman?
where? nerede?
where to? nereye?
which (one)? hangi(si)?
who? kim?
why? niye/niçin/neden?

Shopping

bank banka
cheap ucuz
credit card kredi kartı

expensive pahalı
how many? kaç tane?
how much (price)? kaç para?
I would like....istiyorum...
is there a/are there any?
  var mı?
post office postane/PTT
price fiyat
stamp pul
till receipt fiş

Sightseeing

castle kale
church kilise
closed kapalı
except Sunday pazar günü hariç
exhibition sergi
free bedava/ücretsiz
open açık
mosque cami
museum müze
palace saray
reduced price indirimli
ticket bilet

Time

at what time? saat kaçta gün
hour saat
minute dakika
month ay
today bugün
tomorrow yarın
week hafta
what time is it? saat kaç?
when? ne zaman?
yesterday dün

Numbers

0 sıfır; 1 bir; 2 iki; 3 üç; 4 dört;
5 beş; 6 altı; 7 yedi; 8 sekiz;
9 dokuz; 10 on; 11 onbir;
12 oniki; 20 yirmi; 21 yirmibir;
22 yirmiiki; 30 otuz; 40 kırk;
50 elli; 60 altmış; 70 yetmiş;
80 seksen; 90 doksan; 100 yüz;
1,000 bin; 1,000,000 milyon;
1,000,000,000 milyar

Directory

Further Reference

Books

Istanbul has a lively literary scene, although that's relative when you actually stop to count the reading public. Little has surfaced in translation, although notable exceptions are Turkey's national poet, **Nazım Hikmet**, and the international award-winning fiction writers **Orhan Pamuk** and **Yaşar Kemal**. Ignoring the present, Western publishers seem fixated on Istanbul's imperial past – admittedly any writer of fiction would find hard to beat. Most titles listed here are available in Istanbul; try the Pandora or Robinson Crusoe bookshops (*see p162*).

Fiction

Ali, Tariq: *The Stone Woman* (2000) Historical novel by the former Trotskyist activist in which the family of an Ottoman noble observes the decay of the empire. The third of his 'Islam Quartet'.
Christie, Agatha: *Murder on the Orient Express* (1934) Christie fans rate it as one of her best, set on the famed train stuck in a snowdrift on the Turkish border (as actually happened) with one of the passengers dead by misdeed.
de Souza, Daniel: *Under A Crescent Moon* (1989) True-life tale of a guy banged up in Istanbul for drug smuggling. Comparisons with *Midnight Express* end there; this is thoughtful, even compassionate, and dedicated 'To the Turks, the most misunderstood people in the world'.
Greene, Graham: *Stamboul Train* (1932) Lesser yarn about a bunch of characters crossing central Europe on the *Orient Express*. Greene's advance wouldn't pay for him to go beyond Cologne, so all the eastern detail was cribbed from a Baedeker.
Kemal, Yashar: *Memed, My Hawk* (1961) The book that established Kemal as Turkey's premier contemporary writer is a gritty insight into Turkish rural life.
Nadel, Barbara *Harem* (2002) Tackling prostitution, sadistic brutality and mafia violence, the latest in the Inspector Ikmen series (*see p96*) wins few friends in the Istanbul tourist office.

Pamuk, Orhan: *My Name Is Red* (2001) A sensation in his native Istanbul and internationally, scooping the IMPAC Dublin Literary Award award. Look out for his latest *Snow*, currently being translated.
Unsworth, Barry: *The Rage of the Vulture* (1982) Booker Prize-winner Unsworth once taught English in Istanbul. His detailed imagery enriches this tale of political intrigue, set as the 'vultures of Europe' circle the dying Ottoman empire.

Non-fiction

Beck, Christa & Fausting, Christiane: *Istanbul: An Architectural Guide* (1997) Excellent little gazetteer of nearly 100 of the city's most significant buildings. Obvious candidates like the works of Justinian and Sinan are in there, but the focus is on more obscure 19th- and 20th-century contributions.
Hellier, Chris & Venturi, Franscesco: *Splendors of Istanbul: Houses and Palaces along the Bosporus* (1993) Glossy photos of the interiors of impossibly lavish waterside mansions, which you'd never get to see any other way.
Hull, Alastair & Luczyc-Wyhowska, Jose: *Kilims: The Complete Guide* (2000) Lavish but practical large format paperback; not the sort of thing to consult at the bazaar, but a definite good read before and after.
Hutchings, Roger & Rugman, Jonathan: *Atatürk's Children: Turkey and the Kurds* (2001) One of the best books on an explosive national issue – the conflict in the country's South-east, a shadowland for a great many of Istanbul's youth.
Kinzer, Stephen: *Crescent and Star* (2002) Opinionated account of contemporary Turkey by the former *New York Times* correspondent for Istanbul. Engaging, largely thanks to its anecdotal content.
Mango, Andrew: *Atatürk* (2002) Latest in a long line of Atatürk bios benefits from earlier works, but adds a strong narrative drive that it reads almost like a novel.
Mansel, Philip: *Constantinople: City of the World's Desire* (1996) Grand discourse on the world of the Ottomans, thematically structured, but enough chronology to provide a good overview of the rise and long decline of the imperial capital.
Norwich, John Julius: *A Short History of Byzantium* (1998) An authoritative tour of the Byzantine Empire's extraordinary 1,123-year history that compresses a trilogy by

the same author into one tome. The pace may sometimes be a little breakneck, but it loses none of the tawdry and riveting detail.
Orga, Irfan: *Portrait of a Turkish Family* (1989) A must-read autobiography that gives a haunting insight into Turkey's uneasy transition from crumbling empire to newborn republic. Orga recalls his wealthy Istanbul family's demise after World War I and packs his pages with captivating detail.
Pope, Hugh & Nicole: *Turkey Unveiled* (2000) The best available primer for a stay in Turkey – a balanced tour of the contemporary political and cultural landscape by two long-term Istanbul journalists.
Procopius: *The Secret History* (1982) The first-century Byzantine historian wrote the official history of Justinian, then wrote what he really thought of the tyrannical emperor and his ex-prostitute wife in these scandalous and salacious diaries.

Travel

Freely, John & Sumner-Boyd, Hilary: *Strolling Through Istanbul* (2003) The first of Freely's many books makes an enlightening companion for wanderings through the city. The emphasis is on history and architecture from Byzantine and Ottoman times, but Istanbul is depicted very much as a living city. Itineraries provided.
Goodwin, Jason: *On Foot to the Golden Horn: A Walk to Istanbul* (2003) Istanbul makes a cameo right at the end of the book, the bulk of which deals with the author's walk from Poland following the path of a Byzantine pilgrim. Fascinating on Ottoman influence in the Balkans.
Kelly, Laurence (ed): *Istanbul: A Traveller's Companion* (1987) A mass of historical writings and travellers' tales (largely 18th and 19th century) covering places, people, court life and social diversions. Lacks context but fun nonetheless.
Montagu, Mary Wortley: *Turkish Embassy Letters* (1763) London socialite Lady Montagu was a diplomatic wife in Istanbul from 1716-8 and an amusing correspondent, equally at home with court politics and harem gossip.

Film

Istanbul has yet to be properly immortalised on celluloid for an international audience as Berlin has been by Wim

Wenders, Rome by Fellini or New York by Woody Allen. Instead, it's been limited to a few brief cameos, employed to add a dash of Oriental spice to some otherwise bland cinematic fare. For Turkish films *see p192.*

Journey Into Fear (*Norman Foster*, 1942) Wonderful murky World War II spy thriller co-written by, produced by and starring Orson Welles who, as intelligence officer Colonel Hakkı, gets to deliver lines in Turkish. The lead is Joseph Cotten, who paired again with Welles seven years later for *The Third Man*. Though not as well known, this is every bit as good.
Istanbul (*Joseph Pevney*, 1957) Suspected diamond smuggler (Errol Flynn) returns to Istanbul to find his old flame, who he thought dead, still alive. Nat King Cole cameos with 'When I Fall in Love'.
From Russia with Love (*Terence Young*, 1962) 'He seems fit enough. Have him report to me in Istanbul in 24 hours.' Lotte Lenya as Rosa Klebb in the best Bond movie of all. 007 casually dispatches Eastern Bloc assailants in a variety of popular tourist spots and gets to shag two wrestling Gypsies.
America, America (*Elia Kazan*, 1963) Autobiographical film (Kazan was born in Istanbul) picturing the working-class neighbourhoods of Istanbul through the eyes of the director's uncle as he journeys from Anatolia to the New World.
Topkapı (*Jules Dassin*, 1964) Caper movie in which a small-time con-man (Peter Ustinov) gets mixed up in a big-time jewellery heist. Good fun, and Istanbul looks stunning. Supposedly the inspiration for *Mission: Impossible.*
Murder on the Orient Express (*Sidney Lumet*, 1974) Albert Finney, Lauren Bacall, Ingrid Bergman, Sean Connery and John Gielgud ham it up something rotten.
Midnight Express (*Alan Parker*, 1978) Still misshaping views of Turkey and the Turkish a quarter century on. A great movie perhaps, but also inexcusably racist.
Pascali's Island (*James Dearden*, 1988) British film based on a novel by Barry Unsworth in which Pascali (Ben Kingsley) is a spy for the Ottoman sultanate. Shot solely in Greece, but has a good feel for the period. Charles Dance and Helen Mirren raise the quality level.
Hamam (*Ferzan Ozpetek*, 1996) Italian man visits Istanbul, repairs bathhouse, falls in love with local boy. A gorgeously photographed, lushly scored ethno-homo romp.

The World Is Not Enough (*Michael Apted*, 1999) Bond is back. In Istanbul. Except he wasn't. Brosnan and co stayed away because of PKK activity. The scenes where he swims in the Bosphorus against distinctive spiky mosque backdrops were all computer-matted.
The Accidental Spy (*Teddy Chen*, 2000) Jackie Chan in Istanbul! And it's a Hong Kong movie rather than Hollywood. Is there any more recommendation required?
In This World (*Michael Winterbottom*, 2002) Grim, documentary-style account of two young Afghans smuggled across countless borders between Pakistan and Britain, featuring dingy sweat-shop scenes in Istanbul. Shot mostly in dizzying, hand-held DV, it scooped the Golden Bear at Berlin in 2003.

Music

Rock and pop releases are on local labels and are not widely available outside of Turkey. Traditional Turkish releases may find their way into the world music sections of larger and specialist stores in major Western cities. One of the best labels with the widest selection of recordings is Kalan Music; its website (www.kalan.com) has RealPlayer downloads. Also good is the roots label Traditional Crossroads (www.rootsworld.com), while Golden Horn, based in California, has a decent catalogue of traditional Turkish music and jazz. Its website (www.goldenhorn.com) acts as a discussion forum as well as selling its CDs.

For background on Turkish music *see p216*; for places to buy CDs and tapes *see p177.*

Fasıl

For such a popular genre, there's surprisingly little out on the market. Two names to ask for are **Müzeyyen Senar** and **Zeki Müren**. Generally, the older the recording, the better. Also look for reissues of recordings by **Hamiyet Yüceses** and **Safiye Ayla**, who epitomise the nostalgic feel many contemporary fasıl

artists strive for. In recent years a young singer, **Muazzez Ersoy**, has built a following doing interpretations of standards and film songs; her CDs are easy to find.

Zeki Müren *1955-63 Recordings* (Kalan) Double CD of gorgeous melodies and Müren's gender-bending alto voice. In these days of watered-down 'world music', this stands out for its urgency, elegance and sheer emotion.

Folk music

Bosphorus *Balkan Dusleri* (Ada Müzik) Turkish classical musicians revive the Istanbul Greek repertoire with funk-influenced bass clarinet.
Ali Ekber Çiçek *Klasikleri* (Mega Müzik) One of the most respected exponents of the *saz*, with a simple but heartfelt sound.
Mehmet Erenler *Mehmet Erenler ve Bozlaklari* (Folk Müzik Center) One of the few non-Alevi *saz* players to make an impact, anything you can find by Erenler is worth picking up; this is his most recent recording.
Neşet Ertaş (Kalan) Now living in Germany, Ertaş is a hugely influential musician and a cult figure on the Turkish folk music scene. The Kalan label has issued an eight-CD series of his stuff.
Fuat Saka *Lazutlar II* (Kalan) Multi-ethnic mix of Black Sea folks (Laz, Turkish, Greek and Georgian) meld hyperkinetic kemançe music into melodious jazz/pop.
Muhabbet *Volumes 1-7* (Kalan) Fantastic *aşık* – Alevi songs of mystical quest – performed by top names such as Arif Sağ, Yavuz Top and Musa Eroğlu.

Ottoman, classical & court music

Erol Deran *Solo Kanun* (Mega) A welcome re-release, this is what Turkish classical music should be: introspective, subtle and virtuosic.
Emirgan Assemble *Klasik Osmanlı Müziği* (Kalan) Ottoman-period instrumental works, some quite lively, featuring *kemençe, ud, kanun, ney* and percussion. A good introduction to the genre.
Kani Karaca *Kani Karaca* (Kalan) He's a *hafız*, someone who can recite the Koran from memory. His voice has the power to cause goosebumps and he's something of a living national treasure.
Münip Utandı *Münip Utandı* (Kalan) This fine singer has a classical sensibility and a repertoire

that straddles both Ottoman and later periods.
Various *Gazeller 1&2* (Kalan) Amazing archival recordings of traditional vocal improvisations, rescued from ancient 78rpm vinyl.
Various *Lalezar* (Istanbul Büyük Belediye) Four-CD set featuring aspects of the Ottoman musical world, including compositions by sultans and a suite of *köçek* – imperial dance music.

Rock & pop

Sezen Aksu *Serçe* (EMI) The former *minik serçe* ('little sparrow'), now turned queen of pop, still puts out an album every 24 months but this, her 1978 debut, is her best.
Baba Zula *Uç Psyche-Belly Dance* (Doublemoon) Studied sampledelia, sophisticated percussion, electric *saz* and wacky lyrics; these guys are the veteran avant savants of Istanbul. A must for fans of Turkish art rock.
Ceza *Med Cezir* (Hammer Müzik) Ceza means 'punishment' but his intense lyrical flurries have been something of a kick-start to the burgeoning Turkish hip-hop scene.
Cem Karaca *Best of* (Yavuz ve Burç Plakçilik) He's been around since the 1960s and still plays almost weekly. This compilation covers the days when he was fab.
Erkin Koray *Şaşkın* (Kalite Ticaret) A great introduction to the legend that is Turkish psychedelia, not to mention a crucial member of the Anatolian rock scene.
Barış Manço *Mançoloği* (Stereo) Former leading proponent of Anatolian rock turned TV celeb whose early death immortalised him as the legend of Turkish rock.
Erkan Oğur *Fuad* (Kalan) An extraordinary and strangely unlauded talent, Erkan brings jazz and blues to Turkish instruments and melodies – or vice versa.
Bulutsuzluk Özlemi *Yol* (Ada Müzik) Not the soundtrack to the famed film of that name but back-to-basics, big-hearted, guitar-driven rock by a well-respected outfit.
Replikas *Dadaruhi* (Ada Müzik) Replikas are patrolling the outer reaches of experimental guitar music in Istanbul – this album makes that sound like a good thing.
Tarkan *Dudu* (Istanbul Plak) Love him or hate him, but you can't escape him. The sultry prince of pop is the sound of Istanbul for a huge percentage of its population. You've probably heard his Euro hit 'Kiss, Kiss', covered by Holly Valance.
Zen *Zenistanbul* (Kodmuzik) Dadaistic sound collages from the original oriental rock experimenters who gave birth to Baba Zula Uç (*see above*). Demanding and outlandish.

Various *East2West* (Doublemoon) A sampler from the Doublemoon label offering a jazz-soaked take on all styles. A useful prelude to a deeper look at their catalogue.

Roma (Gypsy)

Ciguli *Ciguli* (Dost) Accordion-led recording that was hugely popular when released in the late 1990s, catapulting Ahmet Ciguli from street musician to stardom.
Laço Tayfa *Hicaz Dolap* (Doublemoon) Hüsnü Şenlendirici and his bunch of top-quality session musicians gather round to perform Aegean gypsy jams.
Roman Oyun Havaları *Volumeş 1 & 2* (EMI-Kent) Two polished collections of Istanbul's top Roma session musicians thumping out a selection of much-loved dance tunes.
Mustafa Kandıralı *Caz Roman* (World Network) The so-called 'Benny Goodman of Turkey', a wild Gypsy clarinettist who toured the US in the 1960s as a band leader. This album includes some of Turkey's other famous fasıl musicians.
Selim Sesler & Grup Trakya *The Road to Keşan* (Traditional Crossroads) Collection of songs and dances from Keşan, a town on the Turkish-Greek border and centre of a Roma musical community. Excellent sleeve notes.

Sufi religious

Asitane *Simurg* (Istanbul Ajans) Good recording by a young ensemble featuring *tanbur*, *kemençe*, *ney* and *bendir* (frame drum).
Mercan Dede *Secret Tribe Nar* (Doublemoon) Perhaps the most accessible point of entry to Sufi music, Mercan Dede (aka Dj Arkın Allen) layers traditional mystic instruments with electronica without descending into pastiche.
Doğan Ergin *Sufi Music of Turkey Vol 2* (Mega) Improvisations on the *ney* flute. Ephemeral and meditative.
Music of the Whirling Dervishes *Sufi Music of Turkey* (Mega) Music to twirl by. Do try it at home.
Various *Mevlana Dede Efendi* (Kalan) A recording made in 1963 featuring some of the finest performers of the genre, including Kani Karaca.

Websites

Atatürk.com
www.ataturk.com
Evangelistic site aiming both to educate the world about Atatürk and let it know what a bad lot the PKK are, with gruesome photos to prove it.

Compagnie des Wagons-Lits
www.wagons-lits-paris.com
Founders of the original Orient Express. Historic photos, merchandise, notice of special train-related events and a stern warning to others to stop nicking the name.
Daughters of Atatürk
www.dofa.org
Not literally but spiritually. This website is devoted to the great Turk and Turkish women with a strange mixture of ideology and recipes. Sincere and fascinating.
Earthquake News
www.earthquakenews.com
Find out where the earth moves with global news and reviews of all the big shakers. Turkey features heavily.
Galatasaray SK
www.galatasaray.org.tr
Official club site with text in Turkish and English.
Great Buildings Online
www.greatbuildings.com
Download then virtually explore a digital 3D model of the Haghia Sophia or investigate Sinan and his wonderful architectural creations.
HiTiT Turkey
www.hitit.co.uk
Subtitled 'An Alternative Guide'. Destination coverage is thin and text sophomoric but some interesting articles in the background section.
Istanbul Foundation for Culture & Arts
www.istfest.org
Information, programmes and ticket sales for Istanbul's international film, jazz, music and theatre festivals.
Istanbul City Guide
www.istanbulcityguide.com
Closest it gets locally in English to a *Time Out*-style service. Daily updated what's-on listings plus mini-features and news snippets.
Ministry of Foreign Affairs
www.mfa.gov.tr
Get the lowdown on Turkish foreign policy, with special sections on those perennially thorny issues like Cyprus, terrorism, human rights and the EU.
The Turkish Daily News
www.turkishdailynews.com
Livelier than its print counterpart with front-page news, comment, business and sport.
Turkish Music Club
www.turkishmusic.com
This website, which incorporates slick Amazon.com-style presentation, is devoted to selling Turkish music in its many forms. Also the place to purchase your Atatürk CD-ROM.
The World Factbook – Turkey
www.cia.gov/cia/publications/factbook/geos/tu.html
If it's cold hard facts you're after, who better to turn to than the CIA? This website is full of factoids about Turkey, covering everything from geography, people, the economy, the military and politics.

Index

Note: page numbers
in **bold** indicate
section(s) giving key
information on a
topic; *italics* indicate
illustrations.

a

Abdi İpekçi Caddesi 135,
157
Abdül Hamit I **23**, 29
Abdül Hamit II 102-103
Abdül Mecit 21
accommodation **45-64**
    budget 56-57, 64
    chains 46
    deluxe 47, 59-60
    high-end 49-51, 60-63
    mid-range 51-56,
    63-64
    rock-bottom 57-59
adventure sports 235
Ahırkapı, where to stay
in 52
Ahmet Atıf Paşa Yalı
242
Ahmet I 20, 74, 77
Ahrida Synagogue **90**,
92
airlines 256
airport 256
    where to stay near 49
Akbank Chamber
Orchestra 229, 231
Akbank Jazz Festival
188, 215
Akbil 257
Akıntı Burnu 104
AKM *see* Atatürk
Cultural Centre
Aksanat Arts Centre 198
Aksu, Sezen 210, **213**
Akyavaş, Erol 198
Alay Köşkü 85
Alexius III 13
Altınkum 243
    beach 254
Altun Tuvalet 105
Amcazade Hüseyin Paşa
Yalısı 240
Anadolu Hisarı 240
Anadolu Kavağı 243,
244
Anatolian Turks 32-33
Anniversary of
Atatürk's Death 188
antique shops 158-161
Aqueduct of Valens 14
arabesque music 216

Arap Mosque (Genoese
church) 98
Arasta Bazaar 77
Arat, Serdar 198
Archaeology Museum
66, 72, 77, 111, **112**,
112, 189
Arkın, Cüneyt 194
Armenian Church of the
Three Altars 99
Arnavutköy 67, **104**
    bars & cafés 151-155
    restaurants 139-140
art festivals 187, 188
    see also galleries
arts & entertainment
181-238
arts, performing 227-231
Asian Shore 67,
    107-110
    bars & cafés 156
    cinemas 195
    restaurants 140
    rock & world music
    venues 213-214
Aşiyan Museum 105
Aslıhan Pasajı 99
Asmalımescit 67, **99**,
128, 198
    bars & cafés 143
Asmalımescit Art
Gallery 198
Atatürk 20, 23, **25**, *25*,
29, 112, 188
Atatürk Bridge 104
Atatürk Cultural Centre
(AKM) 182, **198**, **221**,
228, 230
Atatürk International
Airport 256
Atatürk Museum 112
ATMs 266
Avrupa Pasajı 95, 99
Avşa 252, **254**, 254
Ayasofya *see* Haghia
Sophia
Aykal, Gürer **227**, 229
Aznavur Pasajı 99

b

Babylon 210, **211**, *211*
babysitting 191
Bağdat Caddesi 108
Baktagir, Göksel 220
Balat 66, 89, 89, **90-92**
Balkan Wars 29
ballet 227-230
Balyan, Karabet &
Nikoğos 102

Balyan, Kikor 101
barbers 179
Bardakoğlu, Ali 34, 35
bars **141-156**
Barton, Sir Edward
250
Basil II **11**, 29
Basın Müzesi (Press
Museum) 78
basketball 234
Baths of Roxelana 207
baths *see* hamams
Bazaar Quarter, the 66,
    78-84
    restaurants 125
    shops & services 157,
    159
    see also Grand Bazaar
beaches 238
    Altınkum beach 254
    Kole beach 253
    Solar beach 245
beauty salons 171-173
Bebek 67, **104-105**
    bars & cafés 151-155
    restaurants 139-140
    where to stay 60
Belgrad Forest 243
Belisarius 10, 13
belly-dancing 218
Berlusconi, Silvio 35
Beşiktaş 102
    restaurants 139-140
    where to stay 59
Beşiktaş football club
101, 232, **233**, 234
Beyazıt II 29
Beyazıt Mosque 84
Beyazıt Square 84
Beyazıt Tower 84
Beylerbeyi 110
Beylerbeyi Palace 41,
    110
Beyoğlu 21, 24, 67,
    95-100
    bars & cafés 143-151
    cinemas 193-195
    galleries 198-199
    hospital 97
    restaurants 128-135
    rock & world music
    venues 211
    shops & services 157,
    159
    where to stay 52, 63,
    64
Beyti kebabs 127
Bezmare 220
bicycles 259
Biletix 183

billiards 236
Binbirdirek Sarnıcı 74
Birit, İdil **228**, 229
Blachernae Palace 94
Black Sea coast 245
Blue Mosque *see*
    Sultanahmet Mosque
books 275
Booksellers' Bazaar 83
bookshops 83, **161-163**
Borusan Culture & Art
Centre 197, 199
Borusan Istanbul
Philharmonic
Orchestra 229
Bosphorus cruises 189,
    240-243
Bosphorus Zoo 189
Bosphorus, Asian 110
Bosphorus, nightlife
scene 224-225
Bosphorus, Upper
240-245
Bosphorus Villages, the
    101-106
    bars & cafés 151-155
    restaurants 139-140
    see also Arnavutköy,
    Bebek, Dolmabahçe,
    Hisarı, Karaköy,
    Ortaköy, Rumeli,
    Yıldız
Botter House 42, *42*,
    99
bowling 236
breakdown services 260
British Consulate 99
British Crimean War
Cemetery 109
British Embassy 41
British Int'l School 189
British Summer
Embassy 242
Bughole Festival **187**,
215, 222
bureaux de change 266
Burgazada 248-249
Burhan Doğançay
Gallery & Photo
Archive 199
Burned Gate 98
Burnt (Hooped) Column
10, **78**
bus services 257-258
Büyük Bend reservoir
245
Büyük Hamam 208
Büyükada 248, 250, **251**
Byzantium **7**, 29
Byzas 7

c

Çadırcılar Caddesi 83
cafés *see* bars & cafés
Cağaloğlu Hamam 66,
    78, 206, **208**, *208*, *209*
Calligraphy Museum 84,
    113
camping 64
carpets & rugs 80-81,
    166-167
cars & car hire 260
Cartoon Museum 89,
    113
Cem, Ismail 33, 34
Cemal Reşit Rey Concert
    Hall **221**, **228**
Cemal Reşit Rey
    Symphony Orchestra
    229
Çemberlitaş Hamam 78,
    206, *207*, **208**
Çengelköy 110
Chalcedon **6**, 29
children **189-191**
churches & monasteries
    268
    Arap Mosque
        (Genoese church) 98
    Armenian Church of
        the Three Altars 99
    Greek Orthodox
        Patriarchate **90**, 92
    Haghia Irene 10, 39,
        72
    Haghia Triada
        Monastery,
        Heybeliada 250
    Haghia Triada, Avşa,
        Monastery and
        Church of 254
    Panaghia
        Mouchliotissa,
        Church of **90**, 92
    St Andrea, Church of
        101
    St George's
        Monastery,
        Büyükada 251
    St John the Baptist,
        Burgazada, Church
        of 249
    St John of Studius 39
    St Mary Draperis 99
    St Panagia, Church of
        101
    St Peter and Paul,
        Church of 97
    St Saviour in Chora,
        Church of 39, 66, 89,
        92-93
    St Stephen of the
        Bulgars **90**, 92
    Surp Hireğdagabet,
        Church of 92

Surp Krikor Lusavoria,
    Kınalıada 248
Taxiarchs, Church of
    104
Çiçek Pasajı 99, **122**, 128
Cihangir, where to stay
    in 64
Çiller, Tansu 33
Çınarlı 253
cinemas 192-196
Çırağan Palace 41, **59**,
    60, **103**, *236*
Cistern of Aspar 90
Cisterns, the 10, **74**, 78,
    90
City Players 230
city walls 39, 66, 92,
    93-94
'clashing rocks' 6, **245**
classical music 227-230
climate 271
clothes shops 165-167
clubs 222-226
coach/bus services
    257-258
coffee, Turkish 141
Column of Constantine
    77
computer repairs 179
concert halls 228-229
Conquest Week
    Celebrations 185
Constantine I **7**, *7*, 29,
    38-39
Constantinople **7**, 19, 29
consulates 261
cosmetics shops 163
courier services 261
Creamfields **187**, 215,
    222
credit cards 267
Crimean War 23, 29, 109
cruises on Bosphorus
    189, **240-243**
Çukurcuma 99
currency 266
customs 261

d

D'Aronco, Raimondo
    41-42, 99, 103, 242
dance, festivals 228
Dance Theatre 228
delis 86, **171**
department stores 163
dervishes, whirling 98,
    100, *100*, *236*
directory **256-277**
disabled access 261
Distant (Uzak) 191, 193
Divan Yolu 66, **78**
doctors 263
Doğabçay, Burhan 198
Dolmabahçe 102

Dolmabahçe Palace 21,
    29, 41, **102**, *102*, *103*,
    111
dolmuş 258
drinking *see* cafés &
    bars
driving 260
drugs 261

e

earthquakes 262
eating *see* restaurants
Edirnekapı 94
    where to stay 55
Efendi, Dede 221
Efes Pilsen Blues
    Festival **188**, 215
Egyptian Bazaar 86-87
Egyptian Consulate 42,
    105
Egyptian obelisk 77
electricity 261
Elmadağ, where to stay
    in 61
emergency phone
    numbers 268
Eminönü & the Golden
    Horn 7, 66, 67, *67*,
    85-88
    restaurants 125-126
    shops & services 159
Emirgan 106
Emirgan Park 189
English-language media
    265
ensembles, music, opera
    & ballet 229-230
entertainment *see* arts &
    entertainment
Erçetin, Candan 212
Erdoğan, Recep Tayyip
    27-28, 33
Erener, Sertab 212
Esenler bus terminal 257
estate agents 261
Etiler *see* Levent &
    Etiler
etiquette, mosque 267
European Union,
    membership of 30, 33
events *see* festivals &
    events
Eyüp 66, 89, **94**
Eyüp Mosque 84

f

Faik, Sait 248-249
    museum 249
fashion accessories
    shops 167-169
fashion shops 165-167
fasıl music 216,
    219-220, 276

Fatih 66, **89-90**
Fatih Mehmet Bridge
    106, 240
Fatih Mosque 90
Fener 66, 89, **90-92**
Fenerbahçe 108, 233,
    234
ferries 259
festivals & events
    182-188, 272
    art 187, 188
    classical music 185,
        228, 229
    dance 228
    film 183, 196
    popular music, dance
        music & jazz 183,
        185, *187*, 188, 222
    sporting 187
    theatre 183, 230
    traditional music 185
Fête de la Musique 185
fez, banning of the **20**,
    21, 24
Fikret, Tevfik 105
Fire Engine Museum 189
film **192-196**, 275-276
    festivals 183
fitness *see* sport &
    fitness
Florence Nightingale
    Museum 113
florists 169
Flower Passage 99
folk music 216, 276
food & drink shops
    170-171
football 232-234
foreign press 265
4 Vakıf Hanı 42
1453 Fall of
    Constantinople **15**, 29
Fourth Crusade & Sack
    of Constantinople 13-14
funicular (tünel) **98**,
    259

g

Galata 21, 67, 95, **97-98**
Galata Bridge 29, **88**,
    88, 125
    bars beneath 142
Galata Mevlevihanesi
    98, 99, 100, 221
Galata Tower **95**, **97**, 98
Galatasaray (district) 67,
    99
    cafés & bars 143
    shops & services 157
Galatasaray football
    team 28, 29, 232, 233,
    234
Galatasaray Hamam
    206, **209**

Galatasaray Lycée 99
Galatasaray Museum 99, **113**
Galatasaray Square 99
Galeri Apel 200
galleries **197-200**
Gallery Baraz 200
Gallipoli 23
gas 261
Gate of Christ 93
gay & lesbian **201-205**
gecekondu 27, 32
Gedikpaşa Hamam 209
Gencer, Leyla 227
Genoese castle, Saraylar 253
German Summer Embassy 242
Gökkafes 42
Golden Horn 7, 88
cleanup of 32
Grand Bazaar 24, 66, **79-83**, 79, 83
Greek Orthodox Patriarchate **90**, 92
Guler, Beyti 127
Gülhane Park 85
Gürses, Müslüm 216
Gürtuna, Ali Müfit 33

h

H2000 Music Festival **185**, 215
haberdashery shops 169
Haghia Irene 10, 39, **72**
Haghia Sophia 10, 16, 29, 38, 39, 66, **69-70**, 69
Haghia Triada Monastery, Heybeliada 250
hairdressers 171-173
Halim, Sait 242
hamams **206-209**
gay-friendly 205
Hamidievvel Mosque 110
handicrafts 173-175
Harbiye 67
where to stay 60
harem, Topkapı Palace 19-20, 72, **73**
Hasırcılar Caddesi 86
hat shops 169
Haydarpaşa 108-109
see also Asian Shore
Haydarpaşa High School 109
Haydarpaşa Station 108, 1*09*, 256, **257**
health & herbals 175-176
health 262-263
Herodotus 6
Heybeliada 248, **249-250**

Hikmet, Nazım 275
Hippodrome 77
history **6-29**
holidays, public & religious 271
hospitals 263
hotels *see* accommodation
household goods shops 176
Huber Mansion 242

i

Ibni Kemal Caddesi 125
ice skating 237
IETT 257
IF AFM Independent Film Festival 196
IFSAK Istanbul Photograph Days 188
Ikmen, Çetin 96
Imperial Porcelain Factory 103
Inönü Stadium 101, **233**
insurance 263
Intercontinental Istanbul Eurasia Marathon 187
International 1001 Documentary Film Festival 196
International Cemal Reşit Rey Piano Festival 229
International Cinema-History Film Festival 196
International Dance Festival 228
International Festival of Mystic Music 221
International İstanbul Baroque Days 228
International İstanbul Biennale **187**, *188*, 198, 272
International İstanbul Film Festival **183**, **196**, 272
International İstanbul Jazz Festival **185**, 215, 272
International İstanbul Music Festival *183*, **185**, 221, 228, 229
International İstanbul Puppet Festival 185
International İstanbul Theatre Festival *182*, **183**, 187, 230
internet 263
internet cafés 264
Ipekçi, Cemil 34, 35
İş Art and Cultural Centre 228

Isaac II 13
Iskele Mosque 109
Iskender kebabs 127
Islam
fashion 35-37
in Istanbul **34-37**
saints 37
Istanbul Arts Centre 230
Istanbul Arts Fair **188**, 197
Istanbul Book Fair 188
Istanbul Büyükşehir Sanat Galerisi 198
Istanbul International Short Film Days 196
Istanbul Library 74, **264**
Istanbul State Opera & Ballet 229
Istanbul State Symphony Orchestra 230
Istanbul University 84
Istiklal Caddesi 67, 95-96, **99**, 128, 143, 157, 198
Izzet Paşa Köskü 251

j

Janissaries **16**, 17, 21, 29, 245
Jason and the Argonauts 6, **245**
jazz 214
festivals 185, 188, **215**
jewellery shops 176
Jewish Museum 98, **113**
John II 13
Justinian **10**, *13*, 29, 39, 69, 74, 76

k

Kadıköy 67, **107-108**
see also Asian Shore
Kadıkoy Market 108, *108*
kahve 141
Kaleşi, Ömer 198
Kamondo Steps 97, *97*
Kan, Suna 228
Kanlıca 240
Karaca Ahmet Cemetery 109
Karaköy 101-102
where to stay 63
Kariye Mosque *see* Church of St Saviour in Chora
Karşi Sanat 200
kebabs 119, **127**
Kemal, Yaşar 275
Kenter Theatre 230
keys & locksmiths 179
Khedive's Villa **242**, 243

Kılıç Ali Paşa Mosque 101
Kilyos 245
Kınalıada Camii 248
Kız Kulesi 110
Kızıl Adalar 248
Kole beach 253
Köşk Hamam 209
Küçük Haghia Sophia Mosque 39, 77
Küçüksu Palace 110
Kumkapı 132
Kunılıada 248
Kurtuluş, galleries in 199

l

Laila 224, **225**
Laleli Fountain 42
Laleli, where to stay in 49
Lalezar 220
language courses 270
laundry & dry-cleaning 179
Leander's Tower 110, *110*
leather shops 176-177
Leo III 10
lesbian *see* gay & lesbian
Levent & Etiler 67
cinemas 195
restaurants 140
shops & services 159
libraries 264
lingerie shops 169
Long Aqueduct 245
lost property 264

m

Maçka 197, 199
Maçka Luna Park 189
magazines 265
Mahmut II **21**, 29, 245
Mahmut Paşa Yokuşu 83
Maiden's Tower 110, *110*
malls, shopping **173**, 191
Malta Köşkü 103
Mansur, Cem **227**, 229
Manuel I **13**, 29
Manzikert, Battle of 248
Marble Tower 93
markets 90, 104, **174**
see also Grand Bazaar
Marmara Island 252, 252, **253-254**
Marmara Islands, the **252-254**
Marmara town 253
Maviköy 254
Maya Sahnesi 230

Mecidiye Mosque 41,
104
media 264
Mehmet Ağa 74
Mehmet II 15, 17, 29
Mehmet IV 21
Menderes, Adnan
25-27, 29, 251
metro 258
Mevlevihane Gate 94
meyhanes 118
Milion 78
Military Museum **114**,
189
Mimar Sinan Çarşısı 109
Mimar Sinan University
Miniatürk 190
minibuses 258
mobile phones 270
Moda 108
Monastery of Haghia
Triada, Avşa 254
money 266
money transfer 266
Mosaic Museum 77, **114**
mosaics 70, 77, 93, 114
mosques
 Arap Mosque 98
 Beyazıt Mosque 84
 etiquette 267
 Eyüp Mosque 84
 Fatih Mosque 90
 Haghia Sophia 10, 16,
 29, 38, 39, 66,
 69-70, *69*
 Hamidievvel Mosque
 110
 Iskele Mosque 109
 Kariye Mosque *see*
 Church of St Saviour
 in Chora
 Kılıç Ali Paşa Mosque
 101
 Kınalıada Camii 248
 Küçük Haghia Sophia
 Mosque 39, **77**
 Mecidiye Mosque 41,
 104
 Mustafa Iskele
 Mosque 107
 New Mosque **85**, 86
 Nuruosmaniye
 Mosque 40, **83**
 Nusretiye Mosque 101
 Rumi Mehmet Paşa
 Mosque 109
 Rüstem Paşa Mosque
 40, **86**, 88
 Şehzade Mosque 40,
 89-90
 Selim I Mosque 90
 Şemsi Ahmet Paşa
 Mosque 109
 Sokollu Mehmet Paşa
 Mosque 40, **77**

Süleymaniye Mosque
38, 38, 40, 66, **84**
Sultanahmet (Blue)
Mosque 20, 40, 69,
74-77, *74*
Yeni Valide Mosque
110
Yeraltı Mosque 101
Zeyrek Mosque 39,
89-90
Motherland Party 27
Mudo Pera *98*, 99
Murat III 20
Müren, Zeki 219
Museum of the Ancient
Orient 112
Museum of Turkish &
Islamic Art 69, 77, 111,
114
museums **111-116**
 Archaeology Museum
 66, 72, 77, 111, **112**,
 112, 189
 Aşıyan Museum 105
 Atatürk Museum 112
 Basın Müzesi (Press
 Museum) 78
 Calligraphy Museum
 84, 113
 Cartoon Museum 89,
 113
 Fire Engine Museum
 189
 Florence Nightingale
 Museum 113
 Galatasaray Museum
 99, **113**
 Jewish Museum 98,
 113
 Military Museum **114**,
 189
 Mimar Sinan
 University Museum
 of Fine Arts 114
 Mosaic Museum 77,
 114
 Museum of the
 Ancient Orient 112
 Museum of Turkish &
 Islamic Art 69, 77,
 111, **114**
 Naval Museum 102,
 115
Open Air Museum,
Saraylar 253
Rahmi M Koç Museum
66, 111, *111*, **116**,
189
Sadberk Hanım
Museum **242**, 243
Sait Faik Museum,
Burgazada 249
Sakıp Sabancı
Museum 106, 111,
116

Tanzimat Museum **85**,
86
UFO Museum 111,
115, **116**
Vakıflar Carpet
Museum 77, **116**
Yıldız Chalet Museum
103
music
 classical 227-230
 festivals 185, 228,
 229
 pop, rock, world &
 jazz **210-215**, 276
 festivals 183, 185,
 187, 188, **215**
 shops 177-179
 traditional Turkish
 276-221
Mustafa Iskele Mosque
107
Mustafa Kemal *see*
Atatürk

Nadel, Barbara 96
nargile cafés 101, 141,
152
Naval Museum 102, **115**
Naval Officers' Club 242
Necdet, Yaşar 220
Nevizade Sokak 99, 118,
122
New Mosque **85**, 86
newspapers 264
Nez 212
Nightingale, Florence
108, **113**
nightlife **222-226**
Nişantaşı *see* Teşvikiye
& Nişantaşı
Nova Roma 7-8
Nurbanu 19
Nuruosmaniye Mosque
40, **83**
Nusretiye Mosque 101

O'Farrell, Maggie 206
Old Bedesten 79
Olympic Stadium 42
Open Air Museum,
Saraylar 253
opera 227-230
Orhan Gazi 15
Orient Express 21, 29,
85, **86**
Ortaköy 67, **103-104**,
104
 bars & cafés 151-155
 restaurants 139-140
 where to stay 61
Orthodox Easter 183

Osman II 29
Ottoman fort, Rumeli
Feneri 245
Özel, Turgut 27
Özgen, Ihsan 220

Pamuk, Orhan 275
Panaghia Mouchliotissa,
Church of **90**, 92
Papatya International
School 189
Park Hamam 207
Park Orman 189
Passage Markiz 96
Patriarch Gregory V 90
Pekinel, Güher & Süher
228
Pera 21, 24, 95, **96**
performing arts
227-231
pharmacies 263
phone numbers, useful
268
Phonem/Electronic Music
Plateau **183**, 215
photography 180
Platform Garanti
Contemporary Art
Center 200
police & security 267
pop music see music
post 267
post offices 268
Princes' Islands, the
248-251, *249*
Production Theatre 230,
231
public phones 270
public & religious
holidays 271
public transport 257-259

radio 265
Rahmi M Koç Museum
66, 111, *111*, **116**, 189
rakı 142
Ramazan 271
'Red Islands' 248
reference, further 276
Reina 224, **225**
religion 268
removals 268
residence permits 272
restaurants **118-140**
 for children 190
Rey, Cemal Reşit 229,
230
rock music see music
Rock'n'Coke 215
Roma (Gypsy) music 277
Roxelana 17

Rue Française 96
'Rule of Women, the' 17
Rumeli Feneri 245
Rumeli Hisarı 15, **105**, *106*, 139, 189, 240
Rumeli Hisarı 'Starry Nights' **185**, 215
Rumeli Kavağı 242, *243*
Rumi Mehmet Paşa Mosque 109
Rüstem Paşa Mosque 40, **86**, 88
Rüştü Saraçoğlu Stadium 108

S

Sabiha Gökçen airport 256
Sadberk Hanım Museum **242**, 243
St Andrea, Church of 101
St George's Monastery, Büyükada 251
St John the Baptist, Burgazada, Church of 249
St John of Studius 39
St Mary Draperis 99
St Mary of the Mongols 90
St Panagia, Church of 101
St Peter and Paul, Church of 97
St Saviour in Chora, Church of *6*, 39, 66, 89, **92-93**
St Stephen of the Bulgars **90**, 92
Sait Faik Museum, Burgazada 249
Sait Halim Paşa 242
Sakıp Sabancı Museum 106, 111, **116**
Sultanahmet 66, **69-77**
    cafés & bars 142-143
    cinemas 193
    restaurants 119-125
    shops & services 157, **159**
    where to stay 47-59
Sandal Bedesten 79
Sandal, Mustafa 212
Saraylar 253
Sarıyer 242
saunas *see* hamams
Say, Fazıl **228**, 229
Science Centre 190
sea buses 259
Şehzade Mosque 40, **89-90**
Selçuk Turks **13**, 29
Selçuk, Münir Nurettin 219

Selim I 'The Grim' **17**, 29
Selim I Mosque 90
Selim II 'The Sot' 18-19
Selim III 21
Selimiye Barracks 108
Şemsi Ahmet Paşa Mosque 109
Senar, Müzeyeyen 219
Septimius Severus **7**, 29, 77
Serpentine Column 77
services *see* shops & services
Ses-1885 Ortaoyuncular Theatre 231
Şeyh Zafir Complex *41*, 42, **103**
shoe repairs 180
shoe shops 179
shops & services **157-180**
    for children 191
    in the Grand Bazaar 80-81
Shrine of Zoodochus Pege 94
sightseeing **65-116**
    buses 258
Silivri Gate 94
Sinan, Mimar 17, **40**, 77, 84, 86, 104, 245
Sirkeci Station 41, 85, *87*, 256, **257**
Şişli 67
Sivriada 251
smoking 269
Soğukçeşme Sokak 74
Sokollu Mehmet Paşa Mosque 40, **77**
Solar Beach 245
Soydan, Mustafa 105
sport & fitness **232-238**
    events 187
street names 269
student discounts 270
study 270
Sublime Porte 85
Sufi music 221
Sufi religious music 277
Süleyman I 'The Magnificent' **17**, 29
Süleymaniye Mosque 38, *38*, 40, 66, **84**
Sultanahmet (Blue) Mosque 20, 40, 69, **74-77**, *74*
Sultanahmet Square 69
Sultans of the Dance *227*
sunglasses shops 169
supermarkets 180
Surp Hireğdagabet, Church of 92
Surp Krikor Lusavoria, Kınalıada 248

swimming 237
swimwear shops 169
Symplegades 245
synagogues 268

T

Tahtakale Caddesi 87
Tahtakale Hamam Çarşısı 87
tailors & mending 180
Taksim 100
    where to stay 59-64
Taksim Square 67, **100**
Taksim Stage 231
'Tanzimat' era 29
Tanzimat Museum **85**, 86
Tarkan 210, **212**
Taşlık Coffee House 42
Tatlıses, İbrahim 216
taxes & refunds 158
Taxiarchs, Church of 104
taxis 260
Tek, Vedat **42**, 108
telephones 270
television 265
Telli Baba, burial place of 35, 37, **242**
Tem Art Gallery 200
Tepebaşı, where to stay 63, 64
Teşvikiye Caddesi 135, 157
Teşvikiye & Nişantaşı 67, 197
    bars & cafés 155-156
    galleries 198, **200**
    restaurants 135-139
    shops & services 157, **159**
theatre 230-231
Theatre Studio 230
theatre, festivals 183, 230
Theodora 10
Theodosius Cistern 78
Theodosius II **10**, 29
tickets 211, 222
time 270
Timerlenk Glass 200
tipping 119, **270**
toilets 105
Tomb of Mahmut II 78
Tomb of Sinan 84
Tomb of Sultan Ahmet I 77
Tophane 101
Topkapı Gate 94
Topkapı Palace 17, *19*, 66, 67, 69, **70-74**, 72, 111
tourist information 270
tourist police 267

Traditional Istanbul Açıkhava (Open-Air) Concerts **185**, 215
trains 256
trams 258-259
transgender bars 204
transport, public 257-259
travellers' cheques 267
Trotsky, Leon 251
Tünel 67, 128
    cafés & bars 143
    shops & services 157
tünel (funicular) **98**, **259**
Turca bars, à la 203
Türkeli 254
'Turkish Baroque' architecture 40-41
Turkish classical music 220-221
Turkish language courses 270
Turkish Naval Academy, Heybeliada 250
Twain, Mark 22
Twin Yali 242

U

UFO Museum 111, *115*, **116**
Upper Bosphorus **240-245**
Urart Art Gallery 200
Üsküdar 67, **109-110**
    see also Asian Shore
Usta, İskender 127
Uzak (Distant) 192, **193**
Uzuner, Reyhan 35

V

Vadettin 24
Vakıflar Carpet Museum 77, **116**
vets 263
Villaury, Alexandre 242
visas 271
vocabulary 273
    menu 136-137
Voyvoda Caddesi 97

W

walking 259
    the city walls 93
watch & jewellery repairs 180
waterpipes 152
weather 271
websites 277
Western Districts, the 66, **89-94**
    gay venues 202-203

restaurants 126-128
women, Istanbul for 269
work permits 272
working in Istanbul 272
World Is Not Enough, The 110
world music *see* music
World War I **23**, 29
World War II 24
wrestling 235

Y

Yalçin, Rabia 37
Yapı Kredi Kazım Taahkent Art Gallery *199*, 200
Yassıada 251
Yedikule **89**, 93, 189
Yedikule Fortress **93**, 94
Yeni Valide Mosque 110
Yeniçeriler Caddesi 78
Yeniköy 242
Yeraltı Mosque 101
Yerebatan Sarnıcı 10, 69, **74**, *76*
Yiğitler 254
Yıldırım, Mehmet 31
Yıldız 102-103
Yıldız Chalet Museum 103
Yıldız Palace 23, **102**, 103
Yıldız Park **100**, 189
Yoros Castle 243
'Young Turks' **23**, 29

Z

Zeyrek Mosque 39, **89-90**

Where to stay

Armada 49
Ataköy Tatil Köyü 64
Ayasofya Pansiyonları 45, **51**, *51*
Bebek Hotel 60
Bentley 45, **60**
Berk Guesthouse 56
Büyük Londra Hotel 45, **63**, *63*
Ceylan Inter-Continental 59
Çırağan Palace Hotel Kempinski 46, **59**, *60*
Citadel 52
Dersaadet 52
Divan Hotel 61
Empress Zoe 45, **52**, *55*
Four Seasons 45, 46, **47**, *47*
Galata Residence 63

Hilton Istanbul 46
Hotel Ararat 51
Hotel Avrupa 64
Hotel Hanedan 57
Hotel Monopol 64
Hotel Residence 64
Hotel St Sophia 55
Hotel Turkoman 56
Hotel Uyan 57
Hyatt Regency Istanbul 46
Ibrahim Paşa Hotel 53, 55
Kariye Hotel 55
Kybele Hotel 45, **55**, *55*, 56
Madison Hotel 61
Marmara Istanbul 59
Merit Antique 42, **49**
Nomade Hotel 57
Orient Hostel 57
Pera Palas 45, **52**, 99
Polat Renaissance Istanbul Hotel 49
Princess Hotel Ortaköy 61
Richmond Hotel 63
Ritz-Carlton 45, **46**
Sarniç 56
Side Hotel & Pension 57
Sultan Tourist Hostel 59
Swissôtel Istanbul The Bosphorus 46
Taksim Square Hotel 63
Taksim Suites 61, 63
Vardar Palace Hotel 64
Villa Zurich 64
Yeşil Ev 45, *49*, **51**
Yücelt Interyouth Hostel 59

Restaurants

Akvaryum Fish Restaurant 132
Amedros 119
Argos 126
Asitane 93, 119, **127**
Balıkcı Sabahatin 121
Banyan 135
Beşincı Kat (5.Kat) 118, **131**, *131*
see also bars & cafés
Beyti 127, **128**
Boncuk 123
Borsa 135, **136**
Buhara 118, **121**
Café du Levant 128
Çapari 132
Changa 118, **131**
Çınar Restaurant 104, 118, **139**
Çiya 140
Cookbook Café 136
Cumhuriyet Meyhanesi 123

Darüzziyafe 84, **125**
Develi 121
Doğa Balık 119, **131**
Dubb Indian Restaurant 121
Feriye 118, 119, **139**
Galata House 97, 118, **131**
Hacı Abdullah 131
Halat 118, **128**
Hamdi Et Lokantasi 118, **125**, *126*
Hippopotamus 190
House Café, the 137
Hünkar 135, **137**
Imroz 123
Kallavi 20 118, **219**
Kanaat 140
Kantin 135, **139**
Karaköy Balıkçısı 118, 119, **125**, *128*
Kartallar Balıkcı 132
Kör Agop 132
Körfez 118, 119, **140**
Köşebaşı Pera 127, **132**
Loft 118, **139**
Lokal 118, **132**
Lokanta 118, **133**
Margaux *129*, 133
Mezzaluna 190
Mor 205
Musa Ustam Ocakbaşı 118, **134**
Nature and Peace 118, **134**
Orient Express Restaurant 118, **126**
Pandeli 86, 118, **126**
Poseidon 118, 119, **139**
Pudding Stop 121
Rami 118, **121**
Refik 118, **134**
Rejans 118, **134**
Rumeli Café *119*, 121
Rumeli Iskele 118, **139**
Seasons Restaurant 118, **125**
Secret Garden 190
Sofyalı 9 118, **134**
Sunset Grill & Bar 118, **140**
Tarihi Selim Usta Sultanahmet Köftecisi 125
TGI Fridays 190
Ulus 29 118, **140**
Vogue 118, *135*, **140**, 141
Yakup 2 118, **134**
Zarifi 134
Zencefil 118, 133, **135**

Bars & cafés

Aşşk Cafe 151
Atlas Pasajı 99

Badehane 143
Bebek Bar 141, **152**
Bebek Café 105
Beşincı Kat (5.Kat) 141, **144**
see also Restaurants
Beşincı Peron 144
Beyoğlu Pub 144
Bina 98, 141, *143*, **144**
Büyük Londra 144
Buz 155
Café de Pera 105
Café Fes 80, *145*
Café Marmara 144
Cafein 155
Cheers 143
Çiçek Bar 144
Dulcinea 141, **147**
Ece Bar 152
Enjoyer Café 152
Erenler Çay Bahçesi 152
Eski Kulis 99, 147
Eylülist 153
Gizli Bahçe 147
Havuzlu Lokantasi 81
İç Cebeci Hanı 81
Isis 156
James Joyce 148
Julia's Kitchen 81
Kafe Ara *147*, 148
Kaffeehaus 148
Kaktüs 148
Karga 156
Kethuda 104, **153**
Kino 148
Konyalı **85**, 86
KV Café 98, **148**
Lalezar 84
Leb-i Derya 148
Limonlu Bahçe 148
Madrid 149
Meşale 153
North Shield 149
Nu Teras 141, **149**, *149*
Orient Express bar 141
Palayço 150
Pano 150
Papirüs Cave 151
Pia 151
Pierre Loti Café 94
Pupa 153
Şark Kahvesi 81
Sedir 155, *155*
Sefahathane 99
Smyrna 155
Soho Teras 141, *150*, **151**
Sugar Café 205
Sultan Pub 143
Taps 155
Tophane nargile cafés 141, **152**
Touchdown 156
Yeşil Ev Beer Garden 143

Advertisers' Index

Please refer to the relevant sections for contact details

Turkcell   **IFC**

In Context

Tween   4
Özbi   8, 9
Arena Hotel   12
HotelConnect   12
Carrefour   14
Octopus Travel   18
Herry   22
Global Refund/Tax Free   26
Hotel Valide Sultan Konaği   36

Accommodation

Eresin Hotels   44
Richmond Hotels   48
Hotel Orient Express/Hotel Erboy   50
Bentley Hotel   54
The Madison Hotel   58
Armada Hotel   62

Sightseeing

International Hospital Istanbul   68
Rahmi M. Koç Museum   82

Restaurants

Peymane/Pera Thai   120
Turkoman Hotel   120
Damalis   124
Delight Restaurant   130
Feriye   130
Taps Istanbul   138

Cafés & Bars

The House Café   146
Café Wien   146
Hilton Istanbul/Hilton Park   154

Shops & Services

Metro City   160
ticketturk.com   164
Şişko Osman Carpet & Kilim   164
Mango   168
Kurukahveci Mehmet Efendi   172
Sarar   178

Arts & Entertainment

Biletix   184
PS Clinic   184
Bookinturkey.com   186

Trips Out of Town

Hillside Beach Club   246
Hillside Su Hotel   247

Dentistanbul   **IBC**

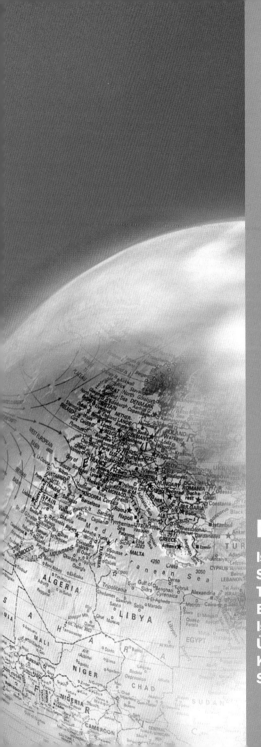

Maps

Istanbul Overview	286
Sultanahmet	288
The Western Districts	290
Beyoğlu	292
Istiklal Caddesi	294
Üsküdar	296
Kadıköy	297
Street Index	298

Istanbul Overview

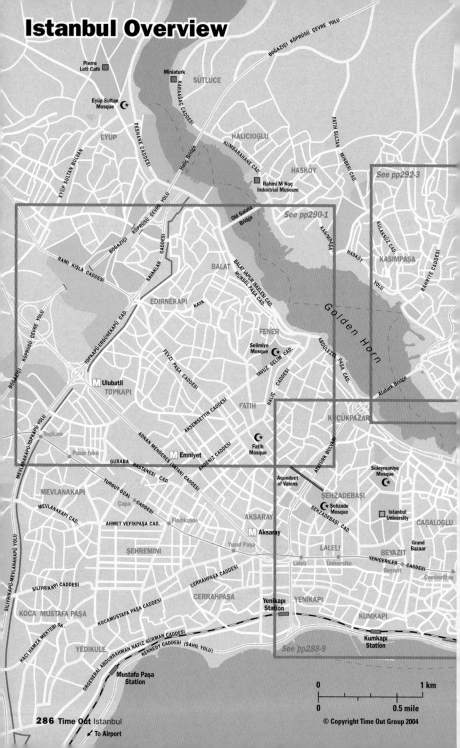

Pierre Loti Café

Miniaturk

SÜTLÜCE

Eyüp Sultan Mosque

EYÜP

FESHANE CADDESI

HALICIOGLU

KUMBARAHANE CAD.

HASKÖY

FATIH SULTAN MINBERI CAD.

BOĞAZİÇİ KÖPRÜSÜ ÇEVRE YOLU

KARAĞAC CADDESI

Rahmi M Koç
Industrial Museum

See pp292-3

Old Galata Bridge

See pp290-1

KILLAKSÜZ CAD.

BAHRIYE CADDESI

KASIMPAŞA

HASKÖY

YOLU

KASIMPAŞA

EYÜP SULTAN BULVARI

BOĞAZİÇİ KÖPRÜSÜ ÇEVRE YOLU

RAMI KIŞLA CADDESI

SAVAKLAR CAD.

CADDESI

BALAT

BALAT VAPUR İSKELESİ CAD.

MÜRSEL PAŞA CAD.

EDIRNEKAPI

KAYA

FENER

Golden Horn

BOĞAZİÇİ KÖPRÜSÜ ÇEVRE YOLU

TOPKAPI-EDIRNEKAPÜ CAD.

FEVZI PAŞA CADDESI

Selimiye Mosque

YAVUZ SELIM CAD.

HALIÇ CADDESI

ABDÜLEZEL PAŞA CAD.

Atatürk Bridge

M Ulubatli

TOPKAPI

AKŞEMSETTIN CADDESI

FATIH

KÜÇÜKPAZAR

MEVLANAKAPI-TOPKAPÜ YOLU

Topkapi

Pazar teke

ADNAN MENDERES (VATAN) CADDESI

M Emniyet

KARADENIZ CADDESI

Fatih Mosque

ATATÜRK BULVARI

Süleymaniye Mosque

GURABA HASTANESI CAD.

Aqueduct of Valens

ŞEHZADEBAŞI

MEVLANAKAPI

TURGUT ÖZAL CADDESI

Çapa

Şehzade Mosque

ŞEHZADEBAŞI CAD.

Istanbul University

ÇAĞALOĞLU

MEVLANAKAPI CAD.

AHMET VEFIKPAŞA CAD.

Findikzade

AKSARAY

Grand Bazaar

ŞEHREMINI

M Aksaray

Yusuf Paşa

LALELI

BEYAZIT

YENIÇERILER CADDESI

SILIVRIKAPI-MEVLANAKAPÜ YOLU

SILIVRIKAPI CADDESI

CERRAHPAŞA CADDESI

Laleli

Üniversite

Beyazıt

Çemberlitaş

KOCA MUSTAFA PAŞA

CERRAHPAŞA

YENIKAPI

Yenikapi Station

YENIKAPI

KUMKAPI

KOCAMUSTAFA PAŞA CADDESI

HACI HAMZA MEKTEBI SK.

YEDIKULE

ORGENERAL ABDURRAHMAN NAFIZ GÜRMAN CADDESI

KENNEDY CADDESI (SAHIL YOLU)

See pp288-9

Kumkapi Station

Mustafa Paşa Station

0   1 km

0   0.5 mile

© Copyright Time Out Group 2004

To Airport

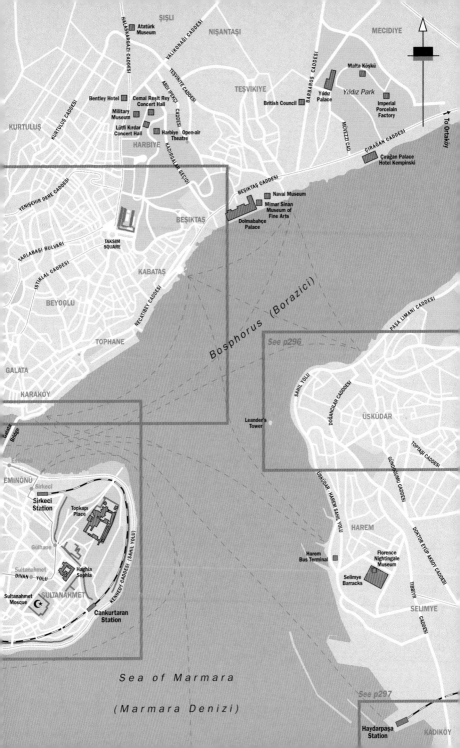

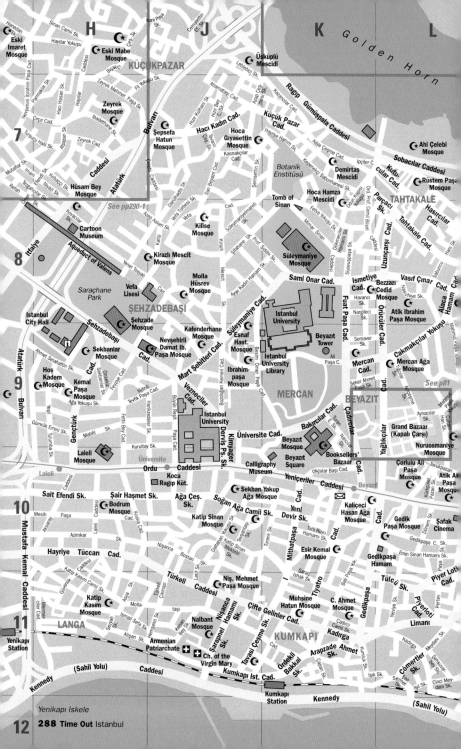

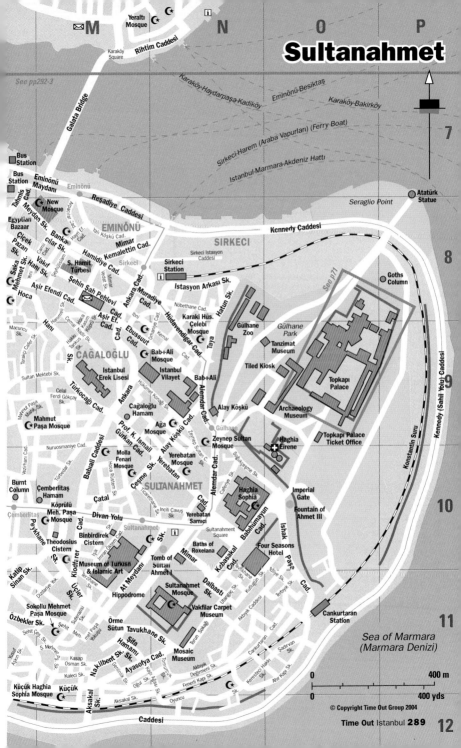

Sultanahmet

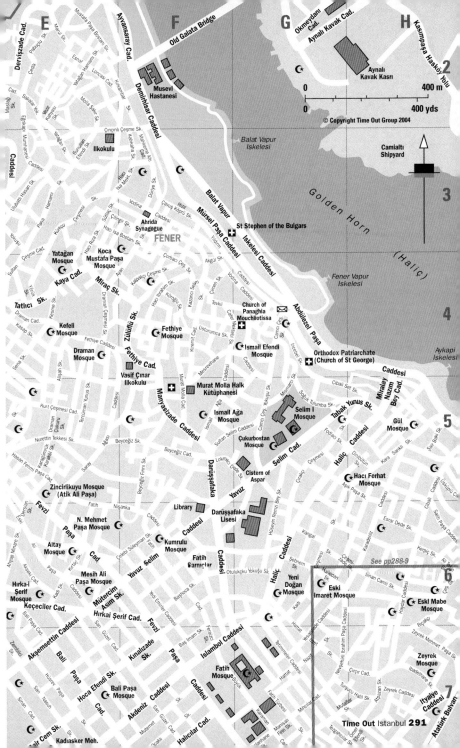

E

F

Okmeydanı Cad.

G

Aynalı Kavak Cad.

H

Kasımpaşa Hasköy Yolu

Dervişzade Cad.

Ayvansaray Cad.

Old Galata Bridge

2

Aynalı Kavak Kasrı

Musevi
Hastanesi

Demirhisar Caddesi

Balat Vapur
Iskelesi

0   400 m

0   400 yds

© Copyright Time Out Group 2004

Caddesi

Ilkokulu

Camialtı
Shipyard

3

Balat Vapur

Mürsel Paşa Caddesi

Golden Horn

Ahrida
Synagogue

St Stephen of the Bulgars

İskelesi Caddesi

FENER

(Haliç)

Yatağan
Mosque

Koca
Mustafa Paşa
Mosque

Fener Vapur
Iskelesi

Kaya Cad.

Miraç Sk.

Abdülezel Paşa

4

Tatlıcı Sk.

Church of
Panaghia
Mouchliotissa

Aykapı
Iskelesi

Kefeli
Mosque

Fethiye
Mosque

Ismail Efendi
Mosque

Orthodox Patriarchate
(Church of St George)

Caddesi

Draman
Mosque

Fethiye Cad.

Zülüflü Sk.

Vasıf Çınar
Ilkokulu

Murat Molla Halk
Kütüphanesi

Miralay
Nazım
Bey Cad.

Manyaszade Caddesi

Ismail Ağa
Mosque

Selim I
Mosque

Tabak Yunus Sk.

Gül
Mosque

5

Çukurbostan
Mosque

Selim Cad.

Haliç

Zincirlikuyu Mosque
(Atik Ali Paşa)

Darüşşafaka

Cistern of
Aspar

Hacı Ferhat
Mosque

Fevzi

Library

Yavuz

Darüşşafaka
Lisesi

Caddesi

N. Mehmet
Paşa Mosque

Paşa

Cad

See pp288-9

6

Altay
Mosque

Kumrulu
Mosque

Caddesi

Haliç Caddesi

Eski
İmaret Mosque

Sinan Camii Sk.

Eski Mabe
Mosque

Mesih Ali
Paşa Mosque

Fatih
Sarnıçlar

Yavuz Selim

Yeni
Doğan
Mosque

Hırka-ı
Şerif
Mosque

Mütercim
Asım Sk.

Haydar Caddesi

Keçeciler Cad.

Hırka-ı Şerif Cad.

Fevzi

Zeyrek
Mosque

Akşemsettin Caddesi

Kınalızade
Sk.

Islambol Caddesi

Paşa

Itfaiye
Caddesi

7

Bali
Paşa

Bali Paşa
Mosque

Fatih
Mosque

Halıcılar Cad.

Atatürk Bulvarı

Hoca Efendi Sk.

Akdeniz

Kadıasker Meh.

Sair Cem Sk.

Time Out Istanbul 291

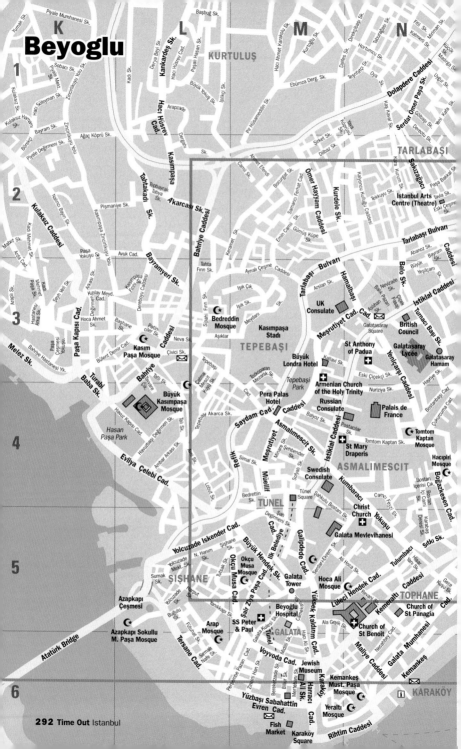

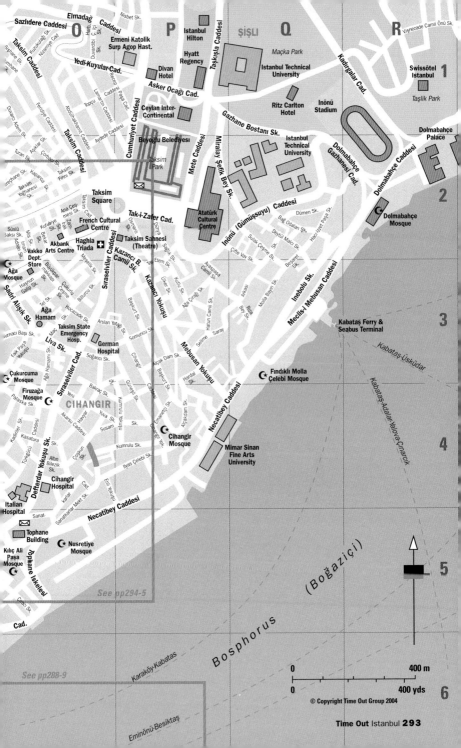

See pp294-5

See pp288-9

© Copyright Time Out Group 2004

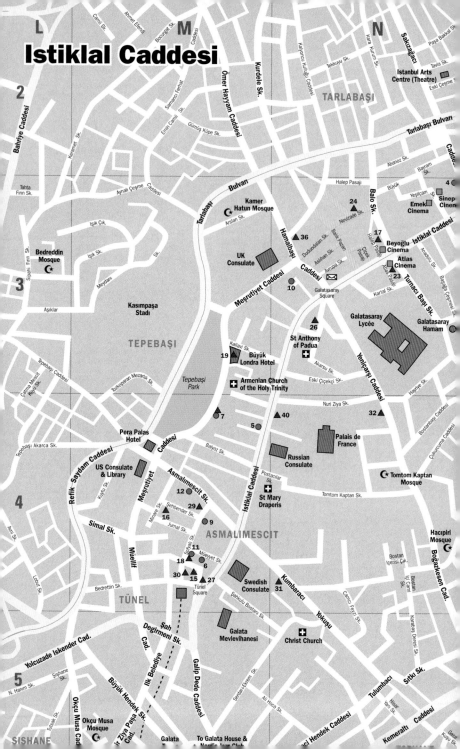

Istiklal Caddesi

L M N

2

Bahriye Caddesi

Cami Sk.
Boçurgat Sk.
Ahmet Efendi
Camii
Kurdele Sk.
Ömer Hayyam Caddesi
Kalyoncu Kulluğu Caddesi
Tekkuyu Sk.
Kara Kurum Sk.
Paşa Bakkal Sk.
Tavla Sk.
Eski Çeşme
Sakızağacı

İstanbul Arts Centre (Theatre)

TARLABAŞI

Tarlabaşı Bulvarı

3

Tahta Fırın Sk.
Keramet Sk.
Işık Çık.
Şamancı Ferhat Sk.
Emin Camii Sk.
Gümüş Küpe Sk.
Aynalı Çeşme Caddesi
Abanoz Sk.
Bayram Sk.
Halep Pasajı
Büyük
Yeşilçam Sk.
4

Sinep Cinema
Emek Cinema

Sıpahi Fırın Sk.
Işık Sk.
Bedreddin Mosque
Meydanı
Aşıklar

Tarlabaşı Bulvarı
Arslan Sk.
Kamer Hatun Mosque
Hamalbaşı
24
Nevizade Sk.
Balık Pazarı
Balo Sk.
17
Beyoğlu Cinema
İstiklal Caddesi

36
UK Consulate
Meşrutiyet Caddesi
Duduodaları Sk.
Asılhan Sk.
Avrupa Pasajı
Çiçek Pasajı
Atlas Cinema
Anadolu Pasajı
Tünaci Başı Sk.
23

Kasımpaşa Stadı
TEPEBAŞI
10
Galatasaray Square
Kartal Sk.
Barağa Çeşmesi Sk.

Galatasaray Lycée
Galatasaray Hamam

Çatma Mescit Müeyt Sk.
Tepebaşı Caddesi
Torkoparan Mezarlık Sk.
Kallavi Sk.
19
Büyük Londra Hotel
26
St Anthony of Padua
Akarsu Sk.
Yeniçarşı Caddesi
Hayriye Sk.

Tepebaşı Park
Armenian Church of the Holy Trinity
Eski Çiçekçi Sk.
Nuri Ziya Sk.
32
Bostanbaşı Caddesi

7
5
40
Çukurcuma Caddesi

Tepebaşı Akarca Sk.
Pera Palas Hotel
Caddesi
Balyoz Sk.
Russian Consulate
Palais de France
Tomtom Kaptan Mosque

Refik Saydam Caddesi
US Consulate & Library
Meşrutiyet
Asmalımescit Sk.
Postacılar Sk.
St Mary Draperis
Tomtom Kaptan Sk.

4

Arnı Sk.
Loknot Sk.
Simal Sk.
Müellif
Minare Sk.
12
Şehbender Sk.
16
29
Jurnal Sk.
9
ASMALIMESCIT
İstiklal Caddesi
Hacıpiri Mosque

Bedrettin Sk.
TÜNEL
Sofyalı Sk.
11
Müeyyet Sk.
18
6
30
15
27
Tünel Square
Swedish Consulate
31
Kumbaracı
Bostan İçerisi Çık.
Boğazkesen Cad.

Şah Değirmeni Sk.
İlk Belediye
Cad.
Galata Mevlevihanesi
Şahkulu Bostanı Sk.
Christ Church
Yokuşu
Camcı Fevzi Sk.
Karadağ Deresi Sk.

Yolcuzade İskender Cad.
Sişhane Sk.
Büyük Hendek Sk.
Galip Dede Caddesi
Serdarı Ekrem Sk.
Ali Hoca Sk.
İç Hendek Caddesi
Tulumbacı Caddesi
Sıttı Sk.

5

N. Hanım Sk.
Okçu Musa Cad.
Okçu Musa Mosque
İr Ziya Paşa Cad.
Galata
To Galata House & Nordic Jazz Club
Kemeraltı Caddesi

SİŞHANE

Restaurants ●

1. Beşinci Kat (5.Kat)
2. Changa
3. Doğa Balik
4. Hacı Abdullah
5. Kösebaşı Pera
6. Lokal
7. Lokanta
8. Musa Ustam Ocakbaşı
9. Refik
10. Rejans
11. Sofyalı 9
12. Yakup 2
13. Zarifi
14. Zencefil

Bars & Cafés ▲

15. Badehane
1. Beşinci Kat (5.Kat)
16. Beşinci Peron
17. Beyoğlu Pub
18. Bina
19. Büyük Londra
20. Café Marmara
21. Çiçek Bar
22. Dulcinea
23. Eski Kulis
24. Gizli Bahçe
25. James Joyce
26. Kafe Ara
27. Kaffeehaus
28. Kaktüs
29. Kino
30. KV Café
31. Leb-i Derya
32. Limonlu Bahçe
33. Madrid
34. North Shield
7. Nu Teras
35. Palyaço
36. Pano
37. Papirüs Cave
38. Pia
39. Smyrna
40. Soho Teras

Üsküdar

© Copyright Time Out Group 2004

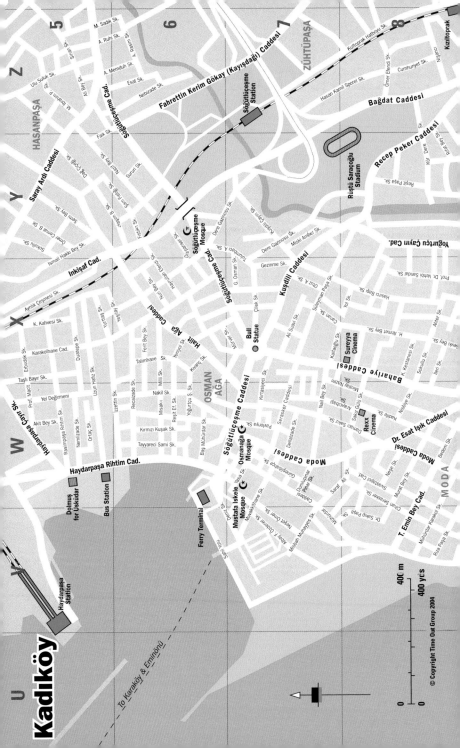

Street Index

Aşık Paşa Sk. - p291 G5/H5
Aşıklar Meydanı Sk. - p292
L3/M3
Aşıklar Sk. - p293 O2
Aşir Efendi Cad. - p289 M8
Abanoz Sk. - p292 N2
Abdülezel Paşa Cad. - p291
G4/H4-5
Abdülhakhamit Cad. - p293
O1-2
Acıçeşme Sk.- p288 L9
Adıvar Sk. - p290 B7
Adliye Sk. - p289 O10-11
Adnan Menderes (Vatan Cad.)
Cad. - p290 B5-6/C6-7/D7
Ağa Çeşmeşi Sk. - p288 J10
Ağa Çırağı Sk. - p293 P3
Ağa Hamamı Sk. - p293 O3
Ağa Yokuşu Sk. - p288 H9
Ağaç Köprü Sk. - p292 K1-2
Ahşap Minare Sk. - p291 E5
Ahır Kapı Sk. - p289 O11
Ahmet Efendi - p292 M2
Ahmet Selahattin Sk.
- p288 H9
Akşemsettin Cad. - p291 E6-7
Akarsu Yokuşu Sk. - p293 O4
Akbilek Sk. - p290 D7
Akbıyık Cad. - p289 N11/O11
Akbıyık Değirmeni Sk. - p289
N11
Akdeniz Cad. - p291 E7/F7
Akgül Sk. - p291 F4
Aksakal Sk. - p289 M12
Aksaray Cad. - p288 H10
Akseki Cad. - p290 D6
- p291 E5
Ala Geyik Sk. - p292 M5/N5
Alaca Hamam Cad. - P288 L8
Alay Köşkü Cad. - p289 N9
Alcaca Tekkesi Sk. - p290 C2
Alçak Dam Sk. - p293 P3
Alçakdam Sk. - p293 P3-4
Alemdar Cad. - p289 N9-10
Ali Hoca Sk. - p292 M5/N5
Ali Kuşçu Sk. - p290 C4/D4
Ali Paşa C. - p288 K9
Ali Tekin Sk. - p291 H6
Alivah Sk. - p291 E4
Alişan Sk. - p288 H11
Altın Bilezik Sk. - p293 O4
Ambar Arkası Sk. - p292 L4
Ana Çeşmesi Sk. - p293 O2
Ankara Cad. - p289 M8-9
Araplı Sk. - p292 K3
Arapzade Ahmet Sk.
- p288 K11
Arapzade Dergahı Sk.
- p292 L1-2
Arda Cad. - p292 K2-3
Armutlu Sk. - p290 D6
Arpa Emini Köprüsü Sk.
- p290 C6-7
Arpa Emini Yokuşu Sk.
- p290 B7
Arpacılar Cad. - p289 M8
Arslan Sk. - p292 M3
Arslan Yatağı Sk.
- p293 O3/P3
Asker Ocağı Cad. - p293 P1
Aslanhane Sk. - p291 G
Aslıhan Sk. - p292 N3
Asmalımescit Sk. - p292 M4
Asya Sk.- p288 H11
At Meydanı Sk. - p289 M10-
11/N10
Atatürk Bridge - p292 K6
Atatürk Bulvarı - p288 G9/
H7-8/J6-7- p291 H7
Atlamataşl Cad. - p288 J7
Atölye Sk. - p290 A2
Atpazarı Sk. - p288 H7
- p291 H7
Avasköyu (Demirkapı Cad.)
Yolu - p290 A2

Avcı Maslağı Sk. - p291 E2
Avni Sk. - p292 L4
Avuk Cad. - p292 K2/L2
Ayşe Kadın Hamam Sk.
- p288 J8
Ayan Sk. - p291 F3-4
Ayaspaşa Camii Sk. - p293 P3
Aydede Cad. - p293 O2/P1
Aynacılar Sk. - p288 L9
Aynalı Çeşme Cad. - p292 M3
Aynalı Kavak Cad. - p291
G2/H2
Ayvansaray Cad. - p291 F2
Ayvansaray Kuyu Sk.
- p291 E2
Azap Çeşmesi Sk.- p288 J7
Azep Askeri Sk. - p288 H8/J8
Azimkar Sk. - p288 H10
Baş Imam Sk. - p291 F7
Başbuğ Sk. - p292 L1
Başhane Sk. - p292 L3
Başhoca Sk. - p291 F6
Başkurt Sk. - p293 P3-4
Babıali Cad. - p289 M9-10
Babıhümayun Cad.
- p289 N10
Bağ Odaları Sk. - p293 Q2
Bahriye Cad. - p292 L2-4
Bahriye Hastanesi Yokuşu -
p292 K3
Bakırcılar Cad. - p288 K9
Bakraç Sk. - p293 O4
Balat Vapur Iskelesi Cad. -
p291 F3/G3-4
Bali Paşa Cad. - p291 E6-7
Bali Paşa Yok. - p288 K10-11
Balık Pazarı- p292 N3
Balo Sk. - p292 N3
Balyoz Sk. - p292 M4
Bankacılar Sk. - p289 M8
Baruthane Cad. - p290 C7
Bayramyeri Sk. - p292 L2-3
Beşaret Sk. - p293 Q2-3
Bedrettin Sk. - p292 M4
Bekar Sk. - p293 O2
Bereketzade Sk. - p292 M6
Besim Ömer Paşa Cad.
- p288 J9/K9
Beyceğiz Cad. - p291 F5
Beyceğiz Fırını Sk. - p291 F5
Beyceğiz Sk. - p291 F5
Beytül Malcı Sk. - p293 Q2
Bıçakçı Çeşmesi Sk. - p288
H6- p291 H6
Bican Bağcıoğlu Sk. - p290 C6
Billur Sk. - p292 M6
Billurcu Sk. - p293 O3
Birol Sk. - p290 B7
Bocurgat Sk. - p292 M2
Boğaziçi Köprüsü Çevre Yolu -
p290 A3-5/ C2/D2
Boğazkesen Cad. - p292 N4-5
Borazan Tevfik Sk. - p290 D4
Börekçi Bayram Sk.
- p292 K1-2
Bostan İçerisi Çık. - p292 N4
Bostan İçi Cami Sk. - p292 N4
Bostanbaşı Cad. - p292 N4
Bozdoğan Kemeri Cad. - p288
J9
Buğulu Sk. - p292 L5
Bülent Demir Cad.
- p292 K3/L3
Büyük Bayram Sk. - p292 N2
Büyük Hendek Sk. - p292 M5
Büyük Karaman Cad.
- p291 F7/G7
Büyük Reşit Paşa Cad.
- p288 J9
Büyük Yokuş Sk. - p292 L1
Büyükparmakkapı Sk.
- p293 O3
Cafer Mektebi Sk. - p291 F4
Caferiye Sk. - p289 N10
Cakmakçılar Yokuşu - p288 L9

Camcı Çeşmesi Yokuşu Sk. -
p291 G4-5
Camcı Feyzi Sk. - p292 N4-5
Camekan Sk. - p292 M5
Camii Sk. - p292 M2
Cankurtaran Cad. - p289
N11/O11
Cebecibaşı Cad.
- p290 C3/D3
Celal Ferdi Gökçay Sk.
- p289 M9
Cemal Nadir Sk. - p289 M8-9
Cemalettin Efendi Sk.
- p288 J6
Cibali Cad. - p291 H5-6
Cibali Set Sk. - p291 G5/H5
Cihangir Cad. - p293 P3-4
Cihangir Yok. - p293 P4
Cinci Meydanı Sk. - p288 L11
Cömertler Sk. - p288 L11
Cuhacı Han Sk.- p288 L9
Cumhuriyet Cad. - p293 P1-2
Çadırcı Camii Sk. - p288 K11
Çadırcılar Cad. - p288 K9-10
Çakırağa Yokuşu - p290 D3
Çaparı Sk. - p288 K11
Çatal Çeşme Sk. - p289 M10
Çatma Mescit Kuyu Sk.
- p292 L3-4
Çayır Meydanı Cad.
- p290 B6/C6
Çeşmizade Sk. - p291 G6
Çedik Pabuçlu Sk. - p291 E2
Çelebi Cad. - p288 J7
Çelebi Süleyman Sk. - p291
F6
Çiçek Pasajı- p292 N3
Çiçek Pazarı Sk. - p289 L8
Çifte Gelinler Cad. - p288
J11/K11
Çifte Vav Sk. - p293 Q2
Çilingir Sk. - p291 E3/F3
Çimen Sk. - p291 F4
Çınarlı Bostan Sk. - p290 C5
Çınçınlı Çeşme Sk.
- p291 E2-3/F2
Çıracı Sk. - p293 O5
Çırakçı Çeşmesi Sk. - p291 G5
Çırçır Cad. - p288 H7
- p291 G7/H7
Çivici Sk. - p292 L3
Çoşkun Sk. - p293 O4
Çömlek Yoğurtçu Sk.
- p290 A7
Çorbacı Çeşmesi Sk.
- p291 F4
Çorbacı Sk. - p293 O2
Çukurcuma Cad. - p292 N4
Çukurlu Çeşme Sk. - p293 O3
Dalfes Sk. - p292 M1
Daltaban Yokuşu Sk.
- p288 J10
Darüşşafaka Cad.- p291 F5-6
Darülhadıs Sk. - p288 J7-8
Davutpaşa Cad. - p290 A6
Değirmen Arkası Sk.
- p292 K3
Değirmen Yolu Sk. - p290
B2/C2
Defterdar Yokuşu Sk.
- p293 O4
Demirhisar Cad. - p291 F2-3
Dereboyu Cad. - p292 L3
Dereotu Sk. - p292 N1-2
Dersian Sk. - p291 E5-6
Dervişzade Cad. - p291 E2
Derya Beyi Sk. - p292 L1
Dilbaz Sk. - p292 M2
Dinibütün Sk. - p291 H5
Direkçibaşı Sk. - p292 N1
Divan Yolu - p289 M10
Dizdariye Yok. - p289 M11
Dökmeciler Hamamı Sk.
- p288 K8
Dolapdere Cad. - p292 N1

Dolmabahçe Cad. - p293 R1-2
Dolmabahçe Gazhanesi Cad.
- p293 Q2/R2
Dönem Sk. - p288 L10
Dr. Nasır Bey Sk. - p290 B7
Draman Cad. - p291 E4
Draman Çeşmesi Sk.
- p291 E4
Draman Çukuru Sk. - p291 E5
Duduodaları Sk. - p308 N3
Dümen Sk. - p293 Q2
Dünya Sağlık Sk. - p293 P2
Düriye Sk. - p291 F3
Duvarcı Adem Sk. - p293 O1-2
Duvardibi Sk. - p293 O1
Ebürriza Dergahi Sk.
- p292 M1
Ebussuut Cad. - p289 M9
Eğrikapı işehane Cad
- p290 D2-3
Eğrikapı Cad. - p290 D2
Eğrikapı Mumhanesi Cad.
- p291 E2/3
Elmadağ Cad. - p293 O1/P1
Emanetçi Sk. - p293 P4
Emek Sk. - p290 B7
Emin Camii Sk. - p292 M2
Emin Molla Sk. - p290 B6
Emin Sinan Hamamı Sk.
- p288 L10
Eminönü Meydanı - p289 M7
Enli Yokuşu - p293 O4
Eski Ali Paşa Cad. - p291 E5
Eski Çeşme Sk. - p292 N2
Eski Çiçekçi Sk. - p292 N3
Esnaf Loncası Cad. - p291 E2
Esrar Dede Sk. - p291 H6
Evliya Çelebi Cad. - p292 L4
Faik Paşa Youşu - p293 O3
Fatih Cad. - p291 F6
Fatih Nişanka Cad.
- p291 E5-6/F6
Fatih Türbesi Sk. - p291 G7
Fatma Sultan C. Sk.
- p290 B6-7
Fenerli Kapı Sk. - p289 N11
Feraizci Sk.- p291 F7
Feridiye Cad. - p293 O1-2
Fethi Bey Cad. - p288 H9-10
Fethi Çelebi Cad. - p290 C3
Fethiye Cad. - p291 E4/F4
Fetva Yokuşu Sk. - p288 K8
Fevzi Paşa Cad.
- p291 D4-5/E6/F6-7
Fevziye Cad. - p288 H9
Fil Yokuşu Sk. - p288 H7/J7
Fitil Sk. - p292 N1
Fodlacı Sk. - p291 G5
Fuat Paşa Cad. - p288 K8-9
Fütuhat Sk. - p292 L5-6
Galata Bridge - p289 M7
Galata Kulesi Sk. - p292 M5
Galata Mumhanesi Cad.
- p292 N5-6
Galatasaray Square - p292 N3
Galipdede Cad. - p292 M5
Gazhane Bostanı Sk.
- p293 P1/Q1
Gece Kuşu Sk. - p292 N2
Gedik Paşa Cad.
- p288 K10-11/L10
Gedikpaşa C. Sk. - p288 L9
Gençtürk Cad. - p288 H9
Genlinlik Sk. - p289 M11
Gölbaşı Sk. - p292 N1
Güldalı Sk. - p290 C2/D3
Gümrük Emini Sk. - p288 H9
Gümüş Küpe Sk. - p292 M2
Güneşli Sk. - p293 P3-4
Guraba Hast. Cad. - p290 C7
Güvenlik Cad. - p288 H10-11
Haşnun Galip Sk. - p293 O3
Hacı Ahmet Karakolu Sk.
- p292 M1
Hacı Ali Sk. - p292 M5-6

Hacı Bilgin Sk. - p290 A2
Hacı Hasan Sk. - p288 H7
Hacı Hüsrev Cad. - p292 L1-2
Hacı Ibrahim Sk. - p291 F4
Hacı Isa Bostanı Sk.
- p291 E3/F3
Hacı Isa Mektebi Sk.
- p291 F3
Hacı Izzet Paşa Sk. - p293 Q2
Hacı Kadın Cad. - p288 J7
Hacı Muhiddin Cammii Sk.
- p290 C4
Hacı Rıza Sk. - p291 E3
Hacı Süleyman Sk. - p292 K1
Hakkı Tarıkus Sk. - p289 M9
Haliç Cad. - p291 G5-6/H5
Halıcılar Cad. - p291 F7
Hallaç Hasan Sk. - p290 B7
Hamalbaşı Cad. - p292 N3
Hamam Odaları Çık.
- p290 B7.
Hamidiye Cad. - p289 M8
Hanedan Sk. - p288 G6
- p291 G6
Hammeli Cit. - p289 M8
Harracı Ali Sk. - p292 M6
Harbiye Çayırı Içi Sk.
- p293 O1
Hardal Sk. - p293 P3
Harikzedeler Sk. - p288 H9/J9
Harput Sk. - p292 L5
Hasan Fehmi Paşa Cad.
- p291 E5
Hasırcılar Cad. - p288 L8
Hastanesi Arka Sk. - p292 K3
Hattat Izzet Sk. - p291 G6-7
Hattat Nazif Sk. - p291 G7
Havancı Sk. - p288 K8
Havuz Kapısı Cad. - p292 L4
Havuzbaşı Değirmen Sk.
- p292 L4
Havyar Sk. - p293 O4
Haydar Cad. - p288 H6-7
- p291 H6
Haydar Yokuşu - p288 H6
Hayriye Hanım Sk. - p288 K7
Hayriye Sk. - p292 N3
Hayriye Tüccarı Cad.
- p288 H10
Hemşehri Sk. - p288 J11
Hırkai Şerif Cad. - p291 E5/F6
Hisar Yanı Sk. - p292 N5
Hızır Bey Camii Sk. - p288 J7
Hızır Çavuş Köprü Sk.
- p291 F3
Hızır Külhanı Sk. - p288 J7
Hoca Ahmet Sk. - p292 K3
Hoca Efendi Sk. - p291 E7
Hoca Hanı Sk. - p289 L8/
M8-9
Hoca Kasım Köprü Sk.
- p289 M8-9
Hoca Rüstem Sk. - p289 M10
Hocaçakır Cad. - p290 D3
Hocaçakır Cad. - p290 C4
Hocazade Sk. - p293 O3
Hortumcu Sk. - p292 N1
Hüdavendigar Cad.
- p289 N8-9
Hükümet Konavı Sk. - p289
M9/N9
Hüseyin Remzi Bey Sk.
- p291 G5-6
Hüsrev Paşa Şk. - p291 E7
Işık Çık. - p292 M3
Işık Sk. - p288 K11/L11
- p289 M10
Işık Sk. - p292 M3
Işıl Sk. - p288 L11
Ibadethane Sk. - p288 H7
- p291 H7
Ibrahim Paşa Yok.
- p288 K10-11
Ilk Belediye - p292 M5
Ilyas Çelebi Sk. - p293 O4/P4
Ilyazde Sk. - p290 A6
Imam Adnan Sk. - p293 O2
Imam Niyazi Sk. - p288 G7
Imran Öktem Cad. - p289 M10
Incebel Sk. - p291 G4
Incili Çavuş Sk. - p289 N10
Inebolu Sk. - p293 Q3
Inönü (Gümüşsuyu) Cad. -

p293 P2/Q2
Ipçiler Cad. - p288 K7
Ipek Sk. - p309 O3
Iplikçi Sk. - p292 L1
Ishak Paşa Cad.
- p289 O10-11
Islambol Cad. - p291 F7/G6
Ismail Ağa Cad. - p291 F4-5
Ismail Sefa Sk. - p288 H11
Ismetiye Cad - p288 K8
Istasyon Arkası Sk. - p289 N8
Istiklal Cad. - p292 M4/N3
Itfaiye Cad. - p288 G8/H7-8
Ityaiye Cad. - p291 H7
Jurnal Sk. - p308 M4
Kaş Kaval Sk. - p292 N1
Kabakulak Sk. - p290 D6
Kabasakal Cad. - p289 N10
Kadı Çeşmesi Sk. - p291 G6
Kadı Mehmet Sk. - p292 K2-3
Kadı Sk. - p291 E6
- p292 L1
Kadırga Limanı Cad.
- p288 K11/L11
Kadırga Meydanı Sk.
- p288 L11
Kadırgalar Cad. - p293 Q1/R1
Kadiriler Sk. - p293 O4
Kahal Bağı Sk. - p290 B6
Kahkaha Sk. - p291 F3
Kaleci Sk. - p289 M11
Kalfa Sk. - p290 D6
Kallavi Sk. - p292 M3
Kalpakçı Çeşme Sk. - p291 F4
Kalyoncu Kulluğu Cad.
- p292 N2
Kalyoncu Kulluğu Cad.
- p308 N3
Kangal Sk. - p291 G6
Kani Paşa Sk. - p288j6
Kankardeş Sk. - p292 L1
Kapanca Sk. - p293 O2
Kapı Ağası Sk.
- p289 M11/N11
Kara Kurum Sk. - p292 N2
Kara Sarıklı Sk. - p291 H5
Karabaş Çık - p290 D6
Karabaş Deresi Sk. - p292 N5
Karadeniz Cad. - p291 H5-6
Karagümrük Karakol Sk. - p291
E5
Karaköy Cad. - p292 M6
Karaköy Square - p289 M6
Kariye Camii Sk. - p290 D4
Kariye Imareti Sk. - p290 D3
Kartal Sk. - p308 N3
Kasap Osman Sk. - p289 M11
Kasap Sk.- p291 E4
Kasatura Sk. - p293 O4
Kasımpaşa Akarcası Sk.
- p292 L2
Kasımpaşa Fırını Sk.
- p292 L3
Kasımpaşa Hasköy Yolu
- p291 H2
Kasımpaşa Zincirlikuyu Yolu
- p292 K2-3
Kasnakçılar Cad. - p288 J7
Katip Kasım Camii Sk.
- p288 H10-11
Katip Sinan Mektebi Sk.
- p288 J10
Katip Sinan Sk. - p289 L11
Katmerli Sk. - p292 N1
Kaya Odd. - p291 F4
Kazancı Başı Camii Sk.
- p293 P2
Kazancı Selim Sk. - p291 F4
Kazancı Yokuşu - p293 P3
Kazancılar Cad. - p288 K7
Keçeci Meydanı Sk.
- p290 C5-6
Keçeciler Sk. - p290 D6
Keçeciler Cad.- p291 E6
Kelebek Sk. - p290 D5/E5
Kemal Cad. - p289 N8-9
Kemankeş Cad. - p292 N6
Kemeraltı Cad. - p292 N5
Kenan Bey Sk. - p288 J11
Kennedy (Sahil Yolu) Cad.
- p288 H11/J11/K11
12/L12
- p290 M12/O11-12/P8-10

Kepenekçi Sabunhanesi Sk.
- p288 K7
Keramet Sk. - p292 L2-3/M2
Keresteci Hakkı Sk.
- p289 N11/O11
Kerpiç Sk. - p291 H6
Kesme Sk. - p291 E4
Kible Çeşme Cad. - p288 K7
Kimyager Derviş Paşa Sk. -
p288 J9-10
Kınalızade Sk. - p291 F7
Kirazlı Mescit Sk. - p288 J8
Kırbaççı Sk. - p288 H7
Kireçhane Sk. - p293 O2
Kiremit Cad. - p291 F4
Kırımı Çeşme Sk. - p290 D2
Kırımı Sk. - p290 C2
Kırkambar Sk. - p291 E2/F2
Kırtay Sk. - p291 E5
Kızılay Meyd. Cad. - p292 K3
Klodfare Cad. - p289 M10
Koca Sinan Cad. - p291 E7
Köroğlu Sk. - p291 F4
Korucu Sk. - p290 D5
Koska Cad. - p289 M10
Kovacılar Sk. - p288 H8
Küçük Ayasofya Cad.
- p289 M11/N11
Küçük Pazar Cad. - p288 K7
Küçük Sk. - p292 N1
Külühli Sk. - p290 D5
Kulaksız Cad. - p292 K2-3
Kulaksız Hamamı Sk.
- p292 K1
Kulaksız Sk. - p292 K1
Kumbaracı Yokuşu- p292 N4-5
Kumkapı Istasyon Cad.
- p288 J11/K11
Kumluk Sk. - p288 K11
Kumrulu Sk. - p293 O4/P4
Kumrulu Yokuşu - p293 P4
Kurabiye Sk. - p293 O2
Kurdele Sk. - p292 M2
Kürçü Bostanı Sk.- p290 B7
Kürkçü Çeşmesi Sk. - p291 E3
Kürkçüler Pazarı Sk.
- p288 L10
Kurt Çeşmesi Cad.
- p290 D4-5
- p291 E5
Kurtoğlu Sk. - p292 M1
Kuru Çınar Sk. - p290 C5
Kurultay Sk. - p288 H9/J9
Kutlu Sk. - p293 P3
Kutlugün Sk. - p289 N11/O10
Kutucular Cad. - p288 L7
Kuytu Sk. - p308 M4
Kuzukulağı Sk. - p293 O1
Küçük Şişhane Sk. - p293 O1
Küçükpamukkapı Sk.
- p309 O3
Laleli Cad. - p288 H10
Lamartin Cad. - p293 O1
Latif Sk. - p288 J10-11
Leblebici Sk. - p288j6
Liva Sk. - p293 O3
Lobut Sk. - p292 L4
Lokal Sk. - p290 B2
Lokmacı Dede Sk. - p291 F5
Lüleci Hendek Cad.
- p292 M5/N5
Mabut Sk. - p292 K2
Maç Sk. - p293 O3
Macuncu Sk. - p289 L9
Madırga Sk. - p292 N1
Mahfil Sk. - p288 H9
Mahkeme Altı Cad. -
p291 F2-3
Mahmut Paşa Mahk. Sk.
- p289 L9
Mahmut Paşa Yokuşu
- p288 L9
Maliye Cad. - p292 N6
Maltepe Cad. - p290 A2-3
Maltepe Çıkmazı - p290 A3
Manisalı Fırın Sk. - p291 G7
Manyasizade Cad. - p291 F5
Marifetname Sk. - p290 B6
Mart Şehitleri Cad. - p288 G9
Marul Sk. - p291 E2
Meşatlık Sk. - p290 D3
Meşelik Sk p293 O2-3
Meşrutiyet Cad.

- p292 M3-4/N3
Mebusan Yokuşu - p293 P3
Meclis-i Mebusan Cad.
- p293 Q3
Mehmet Efendi Çeşmesi Sk.
- p290 A7
Melek Hoca Cad. - p290 D5-6
Melez Sk. - p292 K3
Mercan Cad. - p288 K9
Mermerciler Cad. - p288 H11
Mertebani Sk. - p292 M6
Mesih Paşa Cad. - p288 H10
Mesrevihane Cad. - p291 F4
Mete Cad. - p293 P1-2
Mevlanakapı-Topkapı Yolu
- p290 A7
Meydan Sk. - p289 L8/M8
Midilli Sk. - p292 M6
Mıhcılar Cad. - p291 G7
Millet Cad. - p290 A7/B7
Mimar Dalbasti Sk.
- p289 N10-11
Mimar Kemalettin Cad.
- p289 M8
Mimar Sinan Cad. - p288 K8
Mimar Vedat Sk. - p289 M8
Mihnare Sk. - p292 M4
Miraç Sk. - p291 E4
Miralay Şefik Bey Sk.
- p293 P1-2/Q2
Miralay Nazım Bey Cad.
- p291 H5
Miriman Sk. - p292 N1
Mis Sk. - p293 O2
Mismarcı Sk. - p291 G4-5
Mithatpaşa Cad. - p288 K10
Mobilyacı Sk. - p290 B2
Molla Şakir Sk. - p291 E2
Molla Bayırı Sk. - p293 Q3
Mollataşı Cad.
- p288 H11/J11/K11
Müellif Cad. - p292 M4-5
Müeyyet Sk. - p308 M4
Muhtar Asım Gülyüz Sk.
- p290 D2
Muhtar Muhiddin Sk.
- p290 C4
Mumhane Sk. - p293 O1
Münzevi Cad. - p290 A2/B2
Münzevi Kışla Cad. - p290 B3
Muradiye Cad. - p289 M8/N9
Murat Molla Cad. - p291 F4-5
Mürsel Paşa Cad.
- p291 F3/G3-4
Mustafa Kemal Cad.
- p288 G10-11
Mustafa Paşa Bostanı Sk.
- p291 E2
Mutaflar Sk. - p288 G7
- p291 G7/H7
Mutemet Sk. - p291 F7
Mütercim Asım Sk. - p291 E6
Nakilbent Sk. - p289 M11
Nalıcılar Sk. - p288 K9
Nalıncı Bayırı Sk. - p292 K2
Namazgah Sk. - p290 C3
Nargileci Sk. - p288 K8
Nasuhiye Sk. - p288 L8
Nazlı Hanım Sk. - p292 L5
Neşter Sk. - p290 D4
Necatıbey Cad. - p292 N5-6
- p293 O5/P4
Nevşehirli Ibrahim Paşa Cad.
- p288 G6-7
- p291 G6-7
Neva Sk - p292 L3
Neviye Sk. - p288 L11
Nevizade Sk. - p292 N3
Neyzenler Sk. - p290 C5
Nişanca Bostan Sk.
- p288 J10
Nişanca Hamamı Sk.
- p288 J11
Nisbet Sk. - p293 P1
Niyazi Mısrı Sk. - p290 C5
Nizamiye Cad. - p293 O1
Nöbethane Cad. - p289 N8
Norova Sk. - p290 C7
Nurettin Tekkesi Sk. - p291 E5
Nuriziya Sk. - p292 N4
Nuruosmaniye Cad.
- p289 M9-10
Ocaklı Sk. - p291 F7

Odun Kapısı Yokuşu - p288 K7
Oğul Sk. - p289 M11
Okçu Musa Cad. - p292 M5
Okçular Başi Cad. - p288 K10
Okmeydanı Cad - p291 G2
Old Galata Bridge - p291 F2
Ömer Efendi Sk.
- p288 G7-8/H7
- p291 H7
Ömer Hayyam Cad. - p292 M2
Onsekiz Sekbanlar Sk.
- p288 H9
Ord. Prof. Cemil Bilsel Cad.
- p288 K7-9
Ördekli Bakkal Sk. - p288 K11
Ordu Cad. - p288 H10/J10
Orhaniye Cad. - p289 N8-9
Ortakçılar Mescidi Sk.
- p290 C2/D2
Örücüler Cad. - p288 L8-9
Osmanlı Sk. - p293 P2
Otakçıbaşı Sk. - p290 C3/D3
Otulukçku Yokuşu Sk.
- p291 F6/G6
Oya Sk. - p292 N1
Oyuncu Sk.- p289 N11-12
Özbekler Sk. - p289 L11
Paşa Bakkal Sk. - p292 N2
Paşa Çeşmesi Yokuşu
- p292 K3
Paşa Hamamı Sk. - p291 E3
Paşa Kapısı Cad. - p292 K3
Paşa Odaları Cad.
- p290 A6/7
Paşa Yokuşu Sk. - p292 K2-3
Paşalı Hasan Sk. - p292 L1
Paşmakçı Çayırı Cad.
- p290 B2/C2
Palaska Sk. - p293 O4
Parçacı Sk. - p288 L7-8
Parmaklık Sk. - p288 H7
Pazar Tekkesi Sk.- p290 B7
Perşembe Pazarı Cad.
- p292 M6
Pertev Paşa Sk. - p288 L11
Peykhane Sk. - p289 M10
Pişmaniye Sk. - p292 K2/L2
Pir Hüsameddin Sk.
- p292 M1
Piyale Değirmeni Sk. - p292
K2
Piyale Mekt. Sk. - p292 K1
Piyale Mumhanesi Sk.
- p292 K1
Piyer Loti Cad - p288 L11
Piyerloti Cad. - p288 L11
Postacılar Sk. - p292 N4
Potinciler Sk. - p292 L3
Prof. Kazım Ismail Gürkan
Cad. - p289 M9
Prof. Naci ensoy Cad.
- p290 D5
Prof. Sıddık Sk. - p288 J8/K8
Ragıp Gümüşpala Cad.
- p288 K7
Rami Kışla Cad.
- p290 A2-3/B3/C3
Reşadiye Cad. - p289 M7-8
Recep Paşa Cad. - p293
O1/P1
Refah Sk. - p288 G7/H7-8
Refik Saydam Cad. - p292 M4
Revani Sk. - p292 N5
Rıhtım Cad. - p289 M6/N6
Rıhtım Cad.- p292 M6/N6
Rıza Bey Sk. - p293 Q3
Rıza Uzun Sk. - p290 A2/B2
Sabuncu Hanı Sk. - p288 L8
Sadri Alışık Sk. - p293 O3
Sait Efendi Sk.- p288 H10
Saka Mehmet Sk. - p289 L8
Sakalar Yok. - p291 E2
Sakızağacı Cad. - p292 N2
Salih Paşa Cad. - p291 H6
Samancı Ferhat Cad.
- p292 M2
Sami Onar Cad. - p288 K8
Sanatkarlar Cad - p293 O4-5
Sanatkarlar Mekt Sk.
- p293 O4-5
Saraç Ishak Sk. - p288 K11
Saray Ağası Cad.- p291 E5
Sarı Beyazıt Cad. - p288 J7

Sarı Güzel Cad. - p291 E6-7
- p291 F7
Sarı Nasuh Sk. - p291 E7
Sarmaşık Sk. - p290 C5
Savaklar Cad. - p290 D2-3
Sazlıdere Cad. - p293 O1
Sehzadebaşı Cad. - p288 H8-9
Selime Hatun Camii Sk.
- p293 P3
Selma Tomruk Cad. - p290 D4
Semaver Sk. - p288 K9
Sena Sk.- p291 E4
Serdar Ömer Paşa Sk.
- p292 N1
Serdar-i-Ekrem Sk. - p292 M5
Servi Sk. - p290 B2
Seyyah Sk.- p288 H11
Sifa Hamamı Sk. - p289 M11
Simal Sk. - p292 M4
Sinan Camii Sk. - p288 H6
- p291 H6
Sipahi Fırın Sk. - p292 L3
Sıraselviler Cad. - p293 O2-4
Sirkeci Istasyon Cad.
- p289 N8
Sırmalı Nafe Sk. - p292 L6
Siyavuş Paşa Sk. - p288 K8
Sobacı Sk. - p292 K1
Sobacılar Cad. - p288 L7
Sofalı Çeşme Sk.
- p290 C6/D5
Soğan Ağa Camii Sk.
- p288 J10
Soğancı Sk. - p293 O3
Soğuk Tulumba Sk. - p291 G5
Soğukçeşme Sk. - p289 N10
Sofyalı Sk. - p292 M4
Sofyalı Sk. - p308 M4
Somuncu Sk. - p293 P3
Sıray Arkası Sk. - p293 P3/Q3
Sulak Çeşme Sk. - p293 Q2
Süleymaniye Cad. - p288 J8
Süleymaniyelmareti Sk.
- p288 J8
Sultan Çeşme Cad. - p291 E3
Sultan Mektebi Sk.
- p289 L9/M9
Sultan Selim Cad.
- p291 F5/G5
Sultanahmet Square - p289
N10
Sulukule Cad.
- p290 B5-6/C4-5
Sumak Sk. - p292 L5
Sunullan Efendi Sk. - p291 E3
Susam Sk. - p293 O4/P4
Süslü Saksı Sk. - p293 O2
Suterazisi Sk.- p289 M11
Sütlaç Sk. - p291 E3
Şadırvan Sk.- p289 O11
Şah Değirmeni Sk. - p292 M5
Şahkulu Bostanı Sk.
- p292 M4-5
Şair Baki Sk. - p291 H5
Şair Cem Sk. - p291 E7
Şair Haşmet Sk.
- p288 H10/J10
Şair Mehmet Paşa Sk.- p289
M11
Şair Sermet Sk. - p288 L11
Şair Ziya Paşa Cad. - p292 M5
Şarapnel Sk. - p288 J11
Şebnem Sk. - p291 G6
Şefik Sk. - p290 B7
Şehbender Sk. - p292 M4
- p308 M4
Şehin ah Pehlevi Cad.
- p289 M8
Şehit Çeşmesi Sk.
- p289 L11/M11
Şehit Mehmet Paşa Yokuşu
- p289 M11
Şehsuvarbey Sk. - p288 L11
Şeker Ahmet Paşa Sk. - p288
K9
Şemsettin Sk. - p288 J7
Şeyh Eyüp Sk. - p290 D4
Şeyh Veli Sk. - p292 K3
Şeyhülislam Hayri Efendi Cad.
- p289 M8
Şeyhülislam Sk. - p290 B6
Şişhane Sk. - p292 L5/M5
Şifahane Sk. - p288 J8/K8

Şirket Sk. - p292 M1-2
Taşkışla Cad. - p293 P1
Tabak Yunus Sk.
- p291 G5/H5
Taburağası Sk. - p292 N1
Tahmis Cad. - p289 L7-8
Tahta Fırın Sk. - p292 L3
Tahtakadı Sk. - p292 L2
Tahtakale Cad. - p288 L8
Tak-i-Zafer Cad. - p293 P2
Taksim Cad. - p293 O1-2
Taksim Fırını Sk. - p293 O2
Taksim Square - p293 O2/P2
Taksim Yağhanesi Sk.
- p293 O2
Talı Sk. - p292 L4
Tarakçı Cafer Sk. - p289 L9
Tarlabaşı Bulvarı
- p292 M3/N2
Tatlı Kuyu Hamamı Sk.
- p288 K10
Tatlı Sk. - p292 L3-4
Tatlıcı Sk.- p291 E4
Tatlıpınar Sk. - p290 C7
Tavşantaşı Sk. - p288 J10
Tavanlı Çeşme Sk. - p288 J7
Tavasi Çeşme Sk. - p288 J11
Tavla Sk. - p292 N2
Tavukhane Sk.
- p289 M11/N11
Taya Hatun Sk. - p289 N8-9
Tayyare Çık. - p292 L3-4
Tayyareci Etem Sk. - p293 P3
Teşrifatçı Sk. - p292 N1
Tekkuyu Sk. - p292 N2
Tel Sk. - p293 O3
Tepebaşı Akarca Sk.
- p292 L4/M4
Tepebaşı Cad. - p292 L3/M4
Terbıyık Sk. - p289 O11
Tercüman Yunus Sk.
- p291 E4-5
Tersane Cad. - p292 L5-6
Terzihane Sk. - p289 M11
Tetimmeler Cad. - p291 G7
Tevfikhane Sk. - p289 N10-11
Tezgahcılar Sk.
- p288 G7/H7-8
- p291 G7/H7
Ticarethane Sk.
- p289 M10/N10
Tığcılar Sk.- p288 L9
Tiyatro Cad. - p288 K10-11
Tomtom Kaptan Sk. - p292 N4
Tomurcuk Sk. - p289 N11
Topbayrak Tabya Sk.
- p292 L2
Topçu Cad. - p293 O1/P1
Topçular Cad. - p290 A2
Tophane Iskelesi - p293 O5
Topkapı Bostanı Sk. - p290 A7
Topkapı Cad. - p290 A6/B6-7
Topkapı Erdirnekapı Cad.
- p290 A6-7/B5-7/C4
Torun Sokağı - p289 N11
Tozkoparan Mezarlık Sk.
- p292 M3
Trak Sk. - p290 B2
Tüfekçi Sk. - p290 C2
Tülcü Sk. - p288 L11
Tulumbacı Sıtkı Sk.- p292 N5
Tünel Square - p292 M4
Turşucu Halil Sk.
- p288 G7/H7
- p291 G7/H7
Turabi Baba Sk. - p292 K3-4
Turan Ekmeksiz Sk. - p288 K9
Turan Sk. - p293 O2
Turanlı Sk. - p288 K10
Türbedar Sk. - p289 M10
Türbesi Sk. - p290 D4
Türkeli Cad. - p288 J11
Türkeli Çıkmazı - p288 J11
Türkgücü Cad. - p293 O4
Türkistan Sk. - p290 D5-6
Türkocağı Cad. - p289 M9
Turnacı Başı Sk. - p293 O3
- p292 N3
Tutsak Sk. - p292 L5
Üçler Sk.- p289 M11
Ülker Sk. - p293 P3
Ulubatlı Hasan Sk. - p291 E3
Undeğirmeni Sk. - p290 B6

Üniversite Cad. - p288 J9/K9
Üsküplü Cad. - p291 H5
Usturumca Sk. - p291 F4
Utangaç Sk. - p289 N11
Uygur Sk. - p292 N1
Uzun Yol Sk. - p290 D5
Uzunçarşi Cad. - p288 L8
Vakıf Hanı Sk. - p289 M8
Vasıf Çınar Cad. - p288 L8
Vefa Cad.- p288 J8
Vefa Türbesi Sk. - p288 J7-8
Vezir Kahyası Sk. - p292 L2
Vezirhanı Cad. - p289 L9-10
Vezneciler Cad - p288 J9
Vişnezade Camii Önü Sk.
- p293 R1
Vidinli Tevfik Paşa Cad.
- p288 H9/J9
Viranodalar Sk. - p290 C4/D4
Vodina Cad. - p291 F3-4/G4
Voyvoda Cad. - p292 M6
Yağlıkçılar Cad. - p288 L9-10
Yalı Köşkü Cad. - p289 M8
Yamak Sk. - p290 D6-7
Yanıkkapı Sk. - p292 L5
Yatağan Hamamı Sk.
- p291 E2
Yatağan Sk. - p291 E3
Yavuz Selim Cad.
- p291 F6/G5
Yaya Köprüsü Sk.
- p292 M1/N1
Yeşil Tulumba Sk.
- p288 H9-10
Yeşilçam Sk.- p292 N3
Yedi Emirler Cad. - p291 F6-7
Yedi-Kuyular Cad.
- p293 O1/P1
Yener Tosyalı Cad.
- p288 H8/J8
Yeni Bahçe Deresi Cad.
- p290 C6
Yeni Camii Cad. - p289 L8/M8
Yeni Devir Sk. - p288 K10
Yeni Kafa Sk. - p292 N1
Yeni Yuva Sk. - p293 O4
Yeniçarşı Cad.- p292 N3-4
Yeniçeriler Cad. - p288 K10
Yerebatan Cad. - p289 N10
Yesarizade Cad. - p291 G6-7
Yıldırım Cad. - p291 F3-4/G4
Yolcuzade Iskender Cad.
- p292 L5/M5
Yolcuzade Mektebi Sk.
- p292 L5
Yolcuzade Sk. - p292 L5
Yolgeçen Bostanı Sk.
- p290 D7
Yörük Sk.- p291 E4
Yüksek Kaldırım Cad.
- p292 M5-6
Yumak Sk. - p292 K1
Yusuf Aşkın Sk. - P289 L11
Yüzbaşı Sabahattin Evren Cad.
- p292 M6
Zambak Sk. - p293 O2
Zembilci Sk.- p291 E7
Zeynel Ağa Sk. - p290 C5-6
Zeynep Sultan C. Sk. - P289
N9-10
Zeyrek Cad. - P288 H7
Zeyrek Cad. - p291 H7
Zeyrek Mehmet Paşa Sk.
- p288 H7
Zeyrek Mehmet Paşa Sk.
- p291 H7
Zincirli Han Sk. - p292 M6
Zincirlikuyu Yolu - p292 K1-2
Zülüflü Sk. - p291 F4